FROM SINGLE MARKET TO ECONOMIC UNION

From Single Market to Economic Union

Essays in Memory of John A Usher

Edited by
NIAMH NIC SHUIBHNE
and
LAURENCE W GORMLEY

OXFORD
UNIVERSITY PRESS

OXFORD
UNIVERSITY PRESS

Great Clarendon Street, Oxford, OX2 6DP,
United Kingdom

Oxford University Press is a department of the University of Oxford.
It furthers the University's objective of excellence in research, scholarship,
and education by publishing worldwide. Oxford is a registered trade mark of
Oxford University Press in the UK and in certain other countries

First Edition published in 2012

Published in the United States of America by Oxford University Press
198 Madison Avenue, New York, NY 10016, United States of America

British Library Cataloguing in Publication Data
Data available

Library of Congress Control Number: 2012937856

ISBN 978-0-19-969570-6

Foreword

A Tribute to Professor John Usher

*David Edward**

This book is a tribute to the memory of Professor John Usher, who died in September 2008 at the tragically early age of 63. His death deprived us of one of the outstanding scholars in the field of European Union law. He was a man of truly encyclopaedic learning, always ready to share his knowledge with colleagues and students. 'More than once', said one of them, 'I would ask him if he had heard of a 20-year-old judgment from an obscure court of first instance in an obscure provincial corner of France. Five minutes later he would be at the door with a copy of the judgment—plus an article he had written on it'.

John's outward style was modest and unassuming and, at first, he may have seemed very serious—which he was, about things that mattered. But he had a wry sense of humour and he shared with his wife, Jean, a deep knowledge and love of music. He was an accomplished cellist and was happiest with his family and friends, making music, going to a concert or walking in the country. John was born in Hyde, Cheshire, and never lost the accents of his homeland. After graduating in law at the University of Newcastle in 1966, he won a scholarship to study French private law at the University of Nancy. He then went to the University of Exeter as assistant to Professor Dominic Lasok. At that time, Edinburgh and Exeter were the only universities in the UK that took seriously the study of European law and institutions.

Soon after the UK joined the EEC, John took a research post at the Court of Justice in Luxembourg, and was quickly recruited by the first British Advocate General, Jean Pierre Warner QC, as his Legal Secretary. With the British judge, Lord Mackenzie-Stuart, Warner had the task of introducing our conceptions of law to rather suspicious continental colleagues and of introducing EEC law to an equally suspicious British audience. The Advocate General has the privilege of setting out his own view of the law in his own way. Warner's outstanding contribution was to explain, and embed in European jurisprudence, British conceptions of procedural fairness. John's industry and knowledge of comparative law provided essential support behind the scenes. At that time, most of the work of the European Court concerned technical problems of customs, restrictions on imports and exports, and the minutiae of the Common Agricultural Policy. Few academics found these topics entrancing, but they were meat and drink to John Usher.

* Professor Emeritus, University of Edinburgh; Judge of the European Court of First Instance 1989–92, and of the Court of Justice 1992–2004. The first part of this Tribute is taken from the obituary written for *The Scotsman*. Permission to reproduce it here is gratefully acknowledged.

He said of himself that he was a black-letter lawyer and he made himself a world expert in aspects of European law that call for constant attention to detail and precise knowledge of mind-numbing texts in several languages—agriculture, company law and all aspects of tax and finance.

He brought these skills to Edinburgh in 1978 as Lecturer in the Centre of European Governmental Studies directed by JDB Mitchell, the Salvesen Professor of European Institutions. Mitchell, who had been the pioneer of European studies in the UK, died suddenly in 1980, just when financial constraints had begun to bite. John Usher had the responsibility of maintaining the work and reputation of the Centre (now the Europa Institute), including an annual training course for the Civil Service College. From Edinburgh, John went briefly to University College London until, in 1986, he succeeded Lasok in the Chair of European Law at Exeter. There his national and international reputation became firmly established. He published extensively on his favourite technical topics and also on wider aspects of European law, never forgetting that students need accessible books with clear exposition.

He was constantly in demand as a Visiting Professor, a speaker at conferences and, perhaps especially, as a specialist adviser to parliaments, governments and companies in Britain, Europe and North America. In addition to his teaching in this country, he was a Professor at the College of Europe in Bruges for over 20 years. His scholarly and practical distinction was fittingly recognized when he was called to the English Bar and simultaneously elected an honorary Bencher of Lincoln's Inn in 1993, and elected a Fellow of the Royal Society of Edinburgh in 1998.

Edinburgh was happy to be able to lure him back as Salvesen Professor of European Institutions and Director of the Europa Institute in 1995. He maintained the Institute's 'town and gown' tradition and was unfailingly generous in encouraging the work and ideas of younger colleagues. Almost immediately on his return he served with quiet efficiency a three-year term as Dean of Law, never shirking his teaching load. He had heroically undertaken another term as Dean when Exeter in their turn made him an offer he could not refuse. He returned to Exeter in 2004, and was about to take early retirement when leukaemia struck. John is survived by his wife, Jean, and two sons, one of whom was born in Luxembourg. The bureaucrats said he could not be called Alastair because that was not a saint's name. John won the battle, thereby anticipating by about 25 years the ruling of the European Court of Justice in *Garcia Avello*.[1]

The essays in this book have been written by each contributor as a personal tribute to John, and they reflect the extraordinary range of his interests and knowledge. The focus of the book as a whole is the internal market, its context, its workings and its place in the development towards economic union—the topic with which John was most closely associated.

[1] Case C-148/02 *Garcia Avello v Belgian State* [2003] ECR I-11613.

John's professional career began and ended in times of crisis. By the time he went to the Court in Luxembourg, the brief euphoria that followed British accession had been extinguished by the first oil crisis in October 1973. At the time of his death, the Lisbon Treaty had been signed, but it had been rejected in the first Irish referendum and there was still some doubt as to whether other Member States would refuse to ratify it. Lehman Brothers filed for bankruptcy two days after John's death. That crisis continues.

Between 1973 and 2008, there were many other moments of crisis when the Community and later the Union seemed to stand on the brink of dissolution. The single most important reason for its survival and growth was the internal market. What was then called the common market had been foreseen in the Spaak Report in 1956 as the key to Europe's recovery from economic stagnation. Part Two of the EEC Treaty setting out the Four Freedoms was entitled 'The Foundations of the Community'—a denomination thrown away for no obvious reason in the Maastricht Treaty. In 1973 the common market was, at best, inchoate. The legislative machinery of the EEC had seized up and the end of the transitional period had passed with very few of the measures in place that were envisaged in the Treaty. For almost two decades, until the passing of the Single European Act and the launch of the 1992 Programme, the primary responsibility for maintaining the impetus towards a working internal market fell on the Court, supported by the Commission and teachers and practitioners of Community law. What persuaded the politicians, including Mrs Thatcher, that the legislative machinery must be restarted was 'the cost of non-Europe'—the economic cost of *not* completing the internal market.

Twenty years later, the internal market remains incomplete in consequence of two problems identified by Mario Monti as 'integration fatigue' and 'market fatigue'.[2] No sooner had the Monti Report relaunched the internal market than the crisis of the Eurozone threw the Union into a slough of despond where, at the time of writing, it remains. John would, one suspects, have relished the technical details of the measures that are being taken to deal with the crisis. He would have been caustic about their deficiencies and would certainly have been called upon to help in their improvement.

Meanwhile the internal market must soldier on, fatigued but relaunched (if that is not too gross a mixing of metaphors). Without it, the problems of the Eurozone cannot be resolved and the long-term prospects of the Union itself will not be bright. Indeed, the need to maintain and strengthen the internal market is one of the few things on which all but the most extreme Eurosceptics agree—in principle. What is not agreed is what exactly the expression 'the internal market' means in practice. For some, the essence of the internal market is free trade. By this, they mean the free movement of goods and services, and perhaps also capital, which can be discussed in relatively abstract terms: insofar as they have an effect on the lives of

[2] See Mario Monti, '*A New Strategy for the Single Market: At the service of Europe's Economy and Society*', 9 May 2010, available at <http://ec.europa.eu/bepa/pdf/monti_report_final_10_05_2010_en.pdf>, 6.

ordinary people, the effect is indirect and largely unseen. Free movement of persons is another matter because the effects are visible and unsettling. A spirit of protectionism in labour markets can even be made respectable if it is dressed up in the language of the social market, which is said to make European capitalism virtuous while the American variety, red in tooth and claw, is not. For others, the internal market, as an area without internal frontiers within which goods, persons, services and capital can move freely, must mean all that it says. Protectionism in the market for goods, services or labour has no place in the domestic markets of the Member States and should have no place in the internal market of the Union. It stands in the way of healthy competition, which drives the market economy.

Neither point of view deals adequately with the complexity of life in the twenty-first century. Globalization and technology mean that no market can be purely 'internal'. Services can be provided without physical movement of anything—people or things. Three-dimensional objects (goods), designed in another country, can now be 'printed' as required using the appropriate computer program and raw materials: they do not have to be 'imported'. The protection of intellectual property is increasingly complex and expensive while, at the same time, there are pressures for 'open access' to the fruits of intellectual endeavour. How is copyright to be protected on the World Wide Web? EU law—the product, ultimately, of international law—cannot be insulated from compliance with international law in new forms: investment law and environmental law, to take only two examples. The doctrines of the internal market, which presuppose harmonized, if not uniform, rules of law, are challenged by the equal and opposite pressure of subsidiarity: we want to remain what we are, to do things in our own way, not according to the precepts of 'Brussels' and 'Luxembourg'.

The texts of the Treaties relating to the internal market remain almost unchanged since they were written in 1957–58. They have proved remarkably resilient and adaptable, and one can understand why those responsible for successive Treaty revisions have resisted any temptation to recast them. Do they remain fit for purpose 50 years later? What supplementary legislation is needed to complement them? And in a world of such rapid technological change, is there not a danger—even a probability—that today's legislation will already be out of date by the time it is enacted?

It is hoped that this book will generate discussion of these and other questions, all of which would have fascinated John Usher and stimulated his extraordinary productivity. We remember him as a teacher and scholar, but also as a colleague and friend. As one of us said: 'I think it all boils down to what everyone says of him, that he was a self-effacing and extraordinarily nice bloke. And there are far worse epitaphs.'

Preface

The task of coordinating this collection of essays was undertaken with sadness, given John Usher's untimely death in 2008. But it was also grounded in gratitude for John's contribution to EU legal scholarship, for his collegiality, and for his friendship. David Edward has paid fulsome tribute to John's memory in his foreword and Laurence Gormley wrote an obituary published in (2008) 33 ELRev 775; so the above remarks are brief but the feelings expressed are deep, and John's graciousness and erudition are sorely missed. It has been a privilege to edit this book in his memory.

We are most grateful to all of the contributors to this volume; to the OUP team and, in particular, Elissa Connor, Alex Flach, Natasha Flemming and Zoë Organ; and to Mariola Seeruthun-Kowalczyk and Stephen Thomson at the University of Edinburgh for their research assistance (generously supported by the College of Humanities and Social Sciences at Edinburgh). Special thanks to Jean, Alastair and Richard Usher for supporting the project throughout. The royalties from the sale of this book will go to the Alzheimer's Society, to promote the work of 'Singing for the Brain' in Devon and Cornwall, an activity in which Jean is very involved.

LG and NNS
March 2012

Table of Contents

Table of Cases

COURT OF JUSTICE OF THE EUROPEAN UNION

GENERAL COURT

EUROPEAN COURT OF HUMAN RIGHTS

GERMANY

UNITED KINGDOM

UNITED STATES OF AMERICA

MISCELLANEOUS

Table of Legislation

EUROPEAN UNION

Treaties

Regulations

Directives

Decisions

Resolutions

INTERNATIONAL

NATIONAL LEGISLATION

Austria

New Zealand

List of Abbreviations

AG	Advocate General
AIFMD	Alternative Investment Fund Managers
AKP	Adalet ve Kalkinma Partisi
Art	Article
ASC	Aquaculture Stewardship Certificate
BOI	Binding Origin Information
BTI	Binding Tariff Information
Bull. EC	Bulletin of the European Communities
Cam. YB Eur. L.	Cambridge Yearbook of European Law
CAP	Common Agricultural Policy
CCC	Community Customs Code
CCIP	CCC Implementing Regulation
CDE	Cahiers de Droit Europeen
CEBS	Committee of European Banking Supervisors
CESR	Committee of European Securities Regulators
CFP	Common Fisheries Policy
CFR	Common Frame of Reference
CFSP	Common Foreign and Security Policy
Citizenship Stud.	Citizenship Studies
CJEL	Columbia Journal of European Law
CJEU	Court of Justice of the European Union
CLC	CCH Commercial Law Cases
CMLRev	Common Market Law Review
CN	Combined Nomenclature
CLJ	Cambridge Law Journal
CRA	Credit Rating Agency
CYELS	Cambridge Yearbook of European Legal Studies
DCFR	Draft Common Frame of Reference
Dec	Decision
Dir	Directive
EBA	European Banking Authority
EC	European Community
ECB	European Central Bank
ECHR	European Convention on Human Rights
ECLR	European Competition Law Review
ECJ	European Court of Justice
ECR	European Court Reports
ECOFIN	Economic and Financial Affairs Council
ECSC	European Coal and Steel Community

EDC	Excessive Deficit Criteria
EDP	Excessive Deficit Procedure
EEA	European Economic Area
EEC	European Economic Community
EFSA	European Food Safety Authority
EFSF	European Financial Stability Facility
EFSM	European Financial Stabilisation Mechanism
EHRLR	European Human Rights Law Review
EWHC	England & Wales High Court
EIA	Environmental Impact Assessment
EIOPA	European Insurance Occupational Pensions Authority
Electronic J Comp L	Electronic Journal of Comparative Law
ELJ	European Law Journal
ELRev	European Law Review
EMA	European Monetary Agreement
EMCF	European Monetary Cooperation Funds
EMS	European Monetary System
EMU	Economic and Monetary Union
ENISA	European Network and Information Security Agency
EP	European Parliament
EPC	European Patent Convention
EPO	European Patent Office
EIPR	European Intellectual Property Review
ERM	Exchange Rate Mechanism
ESCB	European System of Central Banks
ESFS	European System of Financial Supervisors
ESM	European Stability Mechanism
ESMA	European Financial Markets Authority
ESRB	European Systemic Risk Board
EU	European Union
EuConst.	European Constitutional Law Review
Eur. J. Migr. & L.	European Journal of Migration and Law
Eur J of Leg Stud	European Journal of Legal Studies
Eur Rev of Contract L	European Review of Contract Law
Eur Rev of Private L	European Review of Private Law
EUTM	European Union Trade Mark
EuZW	Europäische Zeitschrift für Wirtschaftsrecht
EWCA	England and Wales Court of Appeal
EWCA Civ	England and Wales Court of Appeal (Civil Division)
FCTC	Framework Convention on Tobacco Control
FIN	Fishmeal Information Network
Fordham Int'l LJ	Fordham International Law Journal
F Supp	Federal Supplement
GATT	General Agreement on Tariffs and Trade
GDP	Gross Domestic Product
Gen.	Genesis
Harv L Rev	Harvard Law Review

ICES	International Council of Exploration of the Seas
I-CON	International Journal of Constitutional Law
ICLQ	International and Comparative Law Quarterly
ILJ	Industrial Law Journal
I.L.M	International Legal Materials
ILO	International Labour Organization
I.L.Pr	International Litigation Procedure
IMF	International Monetary Fund
Ind J Global Legal Stud	Indiana Journal of Global Legal Studies
Industrial L J	Industrial Law Journal
Int J Popul Geogr	International Journal of Population Geography
Int'l & Comp. L. Q.	International and Comparative Law Quarterly
Int'l Migration Rev	International Migration Review
IRLR	Industrial Relations Law Reports
JCP	Journal of Consumer Policy
JHA	Justice and Home Affairs
J Env L	Journal of Environmental Law
J L Soc Scotland	Journal of the Law Society of Scotland
JMCS	Journal of Common Market Studies
JORF	Journal Officiel de la République Française
J of Consumer Policy	Journal of Consumer Policy
LIEI	Legal Issues of Economic Integration
Lloyds Rep	Lloyd's Law Reports
MCC	Modernised Customs Code
Mich L Rev	Michigan Law Review
Minn. L. Rev	Minnesota Law Review
MJ	Maastricht Journal of European and Comparative Law
MLR	Modern Law Review
Moore's Fed Prac	Moore's Federal Practice
NFFO	English/Welsh/Northern Irish Fishermen's Federation
NGO	Non-Governmental Organisation
NJIL	Nordic Journal of Internation Law
No	Number
NJb	Nederlands Juristenblad
NSRAC	North Sea Regional Advisory Council
OHIM	Office for Harmonisation of the Internal Market
OJ	Official Journal of the European Communities
OMC	Open Method of Coordination
OPEC	Organization of the Petroleum Exporting Countries
Osgoode Hall LJ	Osgoode Hall Law Journal
Para	Paragraph
RAC	Regional Advisory Council
Reg	Regulation

Rev Eur Admin L	Review of European Administrative Law
Romanian J Pol Sci	Romanian Journal of Political Science
RTDE	Revue Trimestrielle de Droit Europeen
SEW	Sociaal-Economische Wetgeving
SFF	Scottish Fishermen's Federation
SGP	Stability and Growth Pact
SMP	Securities Market Programme
TAC	Total Allowable Catch
TEEC	Treaty establishing European Economic Community
TEU	Treaty on the European Union
TFEU	Treaty on the Functioning of the European Union
TQ	Total Allowable Catches and MS Quotas
Tul. Eur. & Civ. L.F.	Tulane European and Civil Law Forum
U Chi L Rev	University of Chicago Law Review
UCITS	Undertakings for collective investment in transferable securities
UN	United Nations
VAT	Value Added Tax
Washburn L.J.	Washburn Law Journal
WCED	World Commission on Environment and Development
WEP	West European Politics
WHO	World Health Organization
WLR	Weekly Law Reports
WTO	World Trade Organization
Yale Hum Rts and Dev L J	Yale Human Rights and Development Law Journal
YB of Consumer L	Yearbook of Consumer Law
YEL	Yearbook of European Law

List of Contributors

Fabian Amtenbrink, Erasmus University Rotterdam

Noreen Burrows, University of Glasgow

Caitríona A Carter, University of Edinburgh

Francesco de Cecco, Newcastle University

Jacqueline Dutheil de la Rochère, Université de Paris II (Panthéon-Assas)

David Edward, University of Edinburgh

Amandine Garde, Durham University

Laurence W Gormley, University of Groningen

Rosa Greaves, University of Glasgow

Thomas Horsley, University of Liverpool

Francis G Jacobs, King's College, London

Jan H Jans, University of Groningen

Dimitry Kochenov, University of Groningen

Marc Maresceau, Ghent University

Joseph A McMahon, University College Dublin

Niamh Nic Shuibhne, University of Edinburgh

Richard Plender, Visiting Professor, University of Groningen; former High Court judge (England and Wales)

Muriel Robison, University of Glasgow

Andrew Scott, University of Edinburgh

Takis Tridimas, Queen Mary, University of London

Stephen Weatherill, University of Oxford

Joseph HH Weiler, New York University

Robin CA White, University of Leicester

1

Introduction

*Niamh Nic Shuibhne**

John Usher approached EU legal scholarship in a comprehensive and also distinct way. I first went to Edinburgh University as a PhD student, as a constitutional lawyer planning to examine how the setting and application of language rules intersected with EU law. John, as my supervisor, facilitated that research through first directing me down the expected channels of EU cultural policy and multilingual programmes, as well as the protection of fundamental rights. The next phase of the thesis, on internal market law, also started with relatively predictable research questions about product labelling rules and employment-linked language tests. Then, things took an unplanned turn into the complex matrices of EU administrative law. John suggested that I should also look at the consequences of different language rules for businesses operating within the single market (or, more typically, the instrumental use of language rules by businesses seeking to have substantively unfavourable decisions annulled). Characteristically, his research instinct led to the uncovering of embryonic general principles in very technical case law that most of us ran a mile from ever reading. Those bare constitutional threads became, much later, properly apparent in landmark language rule decisions of the Court of Justice, such as *Kik* and *Skoma-Lux*.[1] But it took a lot of *BASF* to get there.[2]

John never ignored the detail of the technical, because he saw the constitutional everywhere. He teased out deeper constitutional connections by searching in places that others might never think to look. He mapped the formation and development of EU law in real-time, amassing both breadth and depth through his particular approach to its analysis. He was one of the few to write on the customs union or agriculture; and one of the first to write on the legal implications of monetary union and of flexible integration. The objectives underpinning this collection of essays reflect both the contribution that he made and the way in which he made it.

* School of Law, University of Edinburgh.

[1] Case C-361/01 P *Christina Kik v Office for Harmonisation in the Internal Market (Trade Marks and Designs) (OHIM)* [2003] ECR I-8283; Case C-161/06 *Skoma-Lux* [2007] ECR I-10841.

[2] See, eg, Case C-137/92P *Commission v BASF* [1994] ECR I-2555; Case C-286/95P *Commission v ICI* [2000] ECR I-2341.

In a formal sense, the collection is structured in a way that reflects the core areas of John's work. We have encouraged our contributors to see the trajectory from single market to economic union as a continuing story, emphasizing questions about the purpose, regulation and structures of economic union within the broader objectives of the EU legal and political order. The free movement provisions remain at the core, but the concept of the transnational market must accommodate other, often competing, interests to which the EU is also committed. An important implication of that broad construction is that the protection of these other interests can distort the basic free trade framework (eg intellectual property rights and the promotion of innovation; free movement of workers and the protection of social policy objectives). Which interests should prevail, and who should decide?

The book is structured around five headings that reflect the scale and complexity of these questions. (1) **Economic and monetary law and policy**: chapters in this Part address the legal, fiscal and institutional dimensions of economic and monetary regulation at EU level—a target moving at dizzying speed at the time of writing, but problems for which more stable, longer-term solutions will have to be worked out. (2) **Internal market: evolution and regulation**: contributors to this Part of the collection explore questions about the present and future regulation of the EU's internal market. Some authors adopt a comparative approach. Others explore how underpinning general principles are engaged in the substantive interpretation and application of internal market law, uncovering tensions between the potentially competing dynamics of public law on the one hand and market integration and/or competition policy on the other. (3) **Common policies**: here, both contributors reimagine 'old' regulatory structures in the context of newer, especially environmental, challenges.

The collection also highlights the significance of questions of a structural and administrative nature that flank, uphold and even challenge the core of internal market law. Part (4), on **expanding horizons**, looks at external aspects of the Union's activities but also at issues of competence, testing the parameters and consequences of the EU's economic objectives and their interaction with broader considerations or ambitions. Finally, in Part (5), **judicial protection and access to justice**, both contributions reflect the fact that the realization of EU economic law in practice has been effected in large part through legal challenges at grassroots level. The authors thus explore the extent to which economic actors are catered for in the EU frameworks of access to justice and judicial protection.

The collected essays offer in-depth reflections on different parts of the transnational economic union. But the ideas developed are linked together through cross-cutting concerns about competence and the nature of regulation, and about where and how the economic law of the EU fits in the continuing integration narrative. They take account too of shifting perceptions of space, priorities and potential by considering regional economic integration in a more global context. The following paragraphs introduce particular themes that can be traced across the essays in this manner, focusing especially on themes that link different policy areas together in somewhat unexpected ways.

A. From single market to economic union: development and dependency

In choosing the title for this volume, we have portrayed an evolution: *from* single market, *to* economic union. This depiction is obviously descriptive in temporal terms, but what emerges from many of the essays, not least David Edward's foreword, is a parallel construction of *dependency*. As he points out, '[w]ithout [the internal market], the problems of the Eurozone cannot be resolved and the long-term prospects of the Union itself will not be bright'. The global economic climate remains precarious. Questions about optimal financial and fiscal regulation remain critically significant. The challenge of monetary stability is especially pertinent in the transnational context, given the degree of interdependency generated by EU integration. The tenacity of the single currency is tied inexorably, therefore, to the future shape of the internal market, an argument developed in the contribution by Fabian Amtenbrink. Laurence Gormley uncovers the same path-dependency in his evaluation of the customs union, highlighting how 'the functioning and practice of the customs union and the internal market well demonstrate that in the European Union they are intertwined concepts, forming essential elements of the Union's construction'. Gormley's point also exemplifies the existential dependency question about the relationship between economic union and the persistence of the EU per se. This is a complex dilemma, which can be framed in both positive and negative ways. Reflecting, first, on the positive, Joseph McMahon charts the past and future of the common agriculture policy (CAP), concluding that '[t]he debate on the future of the CAP... should not be limited to the mechanics of the policy but should also extend to its objectives and how they reflect the ultimate basis of the existence of the Union'. Thus he connects both the mechanics and the substance of sectoral policy reform to more general polity conditions within which the policy objectives sit, and which they shape in reciprocal turn.

Perhaps the dominant mood of crisis portrays the negative side of the dependency bond, however, through its persistent fusion of policy stress to polity security. The momentum driving the EU over all of its decades of existence feels, in general terms, to be forward moving. And yet, the fragility of EU integration is exposed (and often exploited) on an almost daily basis. Would less ambitious policy goals that were more strongly and deeply supported by the governments and peoples of (all of) the Member States actually work better? Would they be more legitimate? As Amtenbrink sharply observes, '[i]n the current political climate, it is hardly conceivable that any new equally ambitious European project would stand a realistic chance'. There is an also existential risk, however, attached to any discussion about now turning, in essence, backwards. Amtenbrink is aware of this too, as evidenced by his remark that 'a return to national currencies would have incalculable consequences for the economies of the Member States and the European integration project as a whole'.

If going backwards is not a credible option, for all kinds of reasons, standstill will not work either. In the context of monetary policy, Andrew Scott predicts an inevitable, if staggered, propulsion towards fiscal union. But more intensive integration of the economic union demands an outing of the existential question. Deeper fiscal integration should not occur without proper insulation from democratic norms and constructs. To underline this point, Scott suggests that 'the EU as an international economic and political arrangement stands at a crossroads. Perhaps the most important question is not how or when the current sovereign debt crisis might be resolved, but whether the EU has the capacity—individually and collectively—to exercise the type of leadership that is necessary to navigate its way out of this crisis.' While outlining the choices open to the EU, Scott weaves a legitimacy threshold throughout his chapter. This is also the dominant normative concern in Francis Jacobs's evaluation of both access to and the functioning of the Court of Justice, which he frames against non-negotiable criteria that emanate from the rule of law.

B. The EU as a (co-)regulator

In different ways, many of the contributions are assessing the performance and capacity of the EU as (co-)regulator of the single market and economic union. Three areas of focus in particular are suggested here—regulatory authority; regulatory reach; and regulatory method. Overlap between these concepts will also be flagged where relevant.

First, there is the 'distribution of *regulatory authority*', discussed by Stephen Weatherill through the optic of consumer protection. The Lisbon Treaty's express delimitation of both EU and Member State competence domains brings reassurance in a symbolic way—and we should not underestimate the value of that on its own terms. But Article 4(2) TFEU's listing of the policy areas that constitute the necessarily messy idea of 'shared competences' will not resolve deeper questions about who should do what, and when. As Weatherill reminds (cautions?) us, 'there is no sustainable divide between the Union's interest in market integration and the role of the Member States in matters of market regulation'.

Richard Plender explores the dynamic of Europeanization in his review of applicable law with respect to cross-border transactions. This work demonstrates not only how relevant concepts and principles are applied in complex legal situations, but also how the operation of the EU marketplace has caused us actually to rethink and reconceptualize many of these tools also. Concerns about the distribution of regulatory authority impact on substantive policy development too. We see this most starkly in the chapters addressing the governance of monetary policy against the shadow of the current financial crisis. Bringing an economist's perspective to that debate, Scott's diagnosis is uncompromising: 'the abject failure of the rules that were designed to govern the fiscal policies of Euro area countries has been the major factor that has transformed the financial crisis in Europe to the sovereign debt crisis that is threatening to undermine the EU monetary union'.

Second, we can detect considerable concern about the *reach of regulation*. Weatherill addresses this through his profiling of minimum harmonization as a regulatory method that generates space for the virtue of diversity. The counter-tension is, however, 'a persistingly fragmented regulatory landscape'. In a single market welded together from distinct State pieces, does uniformity or diversity merit greater normative weight? And who should decide? Weatherill's preference is clear: '[i]t is neither politically feasible nor economically desirable to expect all 27 Member States to advance as a single bloc in all the sectors of economic activity now affected by EU policy.' Adjusting the macro template of single market law further away from the sacrificial tenor of uniformity would be an enormous challenge. Moreover there has to be some protected core of sameness, the contours of which would need to be carefully worked out. After all, as Gormley rightly reminds us, '[b]oth the Union legislature and the Court of Justice have sought to develop and maintain the unity of the marketplace and the effectiveness of the economic law which has been established in these areas, and the pursuit of those aims has indeed been very successful.' But if longer-term EU viability is the gain, then a revised appreciation of the *positive* contribution of non-uniformity is not a challenge that can be eschewed. The primary legislative framework for regulating the single market was designed for a union of six States more than fifty years ago. It is naïve to presume that the same framework can be equally effective in the contemporary Union.

Dimitry Kochenov presents a nuanced study of regulatory reach through his discussion of the 'mutation' of Member State nationality laws. Bringing together the technicalities of nationality law and the constitutional impact of EU citizenship, he argues that 'the move from a single market to an economic union has been accompanied by some fundamental mutations at the Member State level which would not necessarily be connected to economic regulation at the first glance, showing how far beyond the objectives stated in the Treaties the deeper consequences of economic integration actually stretch, discovering constitutional questions raised by the internal market on a plane far removed from economic regulation *sensu stricto*.' Interestingly, Kochenov finds both formal and *informal* EU regulatory influence through his case study, both aspects of which 'affect the essence of the State in Europe in ways not necessarily envisaged by the drafters of the Treaties'. This notion of context-integration supports the point expressed above about the limitations of formal competence division in seeking to control the distribution of regulatory authority: 'the indirect influence of the internal market is only likely to grow, presenting the division of competences between the Member States and the Union in a somewhat different light compared with what can be read in the Treaties'. Here, then, we see the impulse of regulatory *reach* displacing formal regulatory *distribution*.

In her contribution on the concept of distinctiveness in EU trade mark case law, Rosa Greaves presents a regulatory picture reflecting partial fragmentation in substantive and also institutional terms. The substantive regulation of trade mark law leads her to critique the ongoing saga of patent regulation. That analysis brings her ideas about the reach of EU intellectual property regulation right up to the boundaries of its institutional design, showing again the unexpected consequences of EU regulatory influence and stressing the value and significance of regulatory *enforcement*. Specifically, Greaves argues that 'it is difficult to refute the need to establish a specialist EU intellectual property law court (or tribunal) as a constituent part of the ECJ'. Moreover, her depiction of an overall 'conservative' approach to copyright regulation jars with the relevance of that rule-book for predominantly 'fast moving industries'—not to mention highly lucrative ones. Jacqueline Dutheil de la Rochère presents a similar picture of the regulation of online gambling. Taken together, these chapters conceive questions about regulatory reach in an especially vital contemporary context: how can regulation best—and effectively—reach into the *virtual* market?

Exploring the reach of EU regulation through substantive market case studies, both Dutheil de la Rochère and Amandine Garde also identify protected spaces for the Member States. These authors explore gambling regulation and advertising restrictions respectively, against varying demands of public interest protection at national level. Dutheil de la Rochère demonstrates how Member States *can* carve space for specific national regulatory preferences, so long as they can show that those policy choices are coherent and genuine and that they respect fundamental principles of EU law such as non-discrimination and proportionality. Importantly, she emphasizes that 'genuine acceptable interests justifying obstacles to the freedoms of the internal market will have to be made out, rather than merely asserted'. This finding links her work even more closely with Garde's contribution, which focuses on precisely these questions at the justification and proportionality stages of the EU free movement paradigm. In the context of regulatory authority, she advocates a limited judicial role in the determination of proportionality, arguing that the Court 'should neither substitute its assessment for that of legislative authorities nor instrumentalize the principle of proportionality to suit its own policy preferences.' But she also argues for a more rigorous approach to questions about the burden of proof, drawing comparative lessons from US Supreme Court case law.

Through his case study on the scope of obstacles to capital movements, however, Thomas Horsley detects a slight but growing preference in the case law of the Court of Justice that requires Member States to justify rules regulating market behaviour *within* State boundaries. More specifically, through the engagement of tests grounded in deterrent or dissuasive effects on free movement, he argues that the Court is '[applying] the Treaty freedoms to review of non-discriminatory national rules that simply define the regulatory environment within a Member State'. This approach is consistent with the increasingly dominant market access philosophy that is evident across the Court's free movement case law. A market access approach undoubtedly dissolves national market protectionism, intended or otherwise. But Horsley flags a point of caution, arguing that the Court is essentially reviewing 'the existence of (certain) non-discriminatory national policies that simply restrict commercial or personal freedom within Member States.' Reflecting the theme of regulatory reach, he characterizes this case law as marking 'a definite shift in the balance of power between the Member States and the Court of Justice. The dangers of judicial overreach into Member State autonomy are well known and the Court has been forced to backtrack already once before', recalling the case law in the 1980s and 1990s which led to the market access clampdown in *Keck*.[3] But for now, at least, no *Keck II* is appearing (yet) on the horizon.

Regulatory reach finds *spatial* reflection in two further chapters in particular. Marc Maresceau looks outwards, reflecting comprehensively on the evolution of EU policy concerning the proposed accession to the Union by Turkey. His analysis deftly exhibits the complex tangling of the legal, political and economic facets of the contemporary EU. The starkness of the following question, for example, illustrates the resulting complexity: 'is Turkey welcome in the EU if it satisfies the Copenhagen criteria in the way other candidates have complied with them and contributes to finding an acceptable solution for the Cyprus question?' Francesco de Cecco, in contrast, engages the TFEU's State aid rules to look inwards—through the glass floor of internal Member State structures. Using the lens of the financial crisis, de Cecco constructs parallels between inter- and intra-State EU constitutionalism: 'EU institutions are often perceived to be at odds with national democracies, as they exert a strong influence over domestic economic policy decisions, particularly in the Eurozone. Moreover, indirect transfers from countries with stronger finances towards countries with weaker finances are a cause of great concern for public opinion in the former countries. Similar tensions are mirrored within individual Member States, as governments attempt to rein in public spending by exercising closer control over financial decisions taken at decentralized level.' While affirming respect for the internal constitutional structures of the Member States in general terms, de Cecco grasps one of the most problematic spatial nettles of the State aid rules, suggesting that 'a more open and explicit articulation of the role played by national constitutional identities in the Court's reasoning would help to justify an otherwise problematic jurisprudential stance'. Arguably, the revised expression of subsidiarity in Article 5(3) TEU opens a constitutional door in this regard that might yet be opened.

Finally, third, there is discussion in several of the chapters about the *method of regulation*. On this theme, Jan Jans's exploration of a common frame of reference for public law provides a useful companion analysis to Kochenov's exposition of indirect regulatory reach. Jans traces the consequences of *non*-harmonization yet notes similarly the reality of less systematic 'piecemeal' harmonization of public and administrative law nonetheless. He also discusses some of the drawbacks generated by this organic approach. Drawing from the ongoing development of a common frame of reference for private law, Jans asks whether comparable work in the field of public law is needed, possible, or even wise. Caitríona Carter's empirical study of the embedding of sustainable development in the regulation of sea fisheries and aquaculture reminds us that a whole range of actors participate in market regulation; her own work outlines the particular contribution of producers, businesses and NGOs. Stakeholder contributions to regulatory methods are one thing; but

[3] Joined Cases C-267 and 268/91 *Criminal Proceedings against Keck and Mithouard* [1993] ECR I-6097.

Carter's preliminary finding that 'there was no immediate evidence of "leadership" by EU public actors over sectoral integration' is another. However, she reaches a less ominous conclusion overall, noting that 'the power of the concept of sustainable development is revealed more as a resource for private actors to bring about change within the economic logic of their industry as part of a competitive strategy, than as a new regulatory device for Commission officials to "govern" industry. This coincides also with a changing regulatory approach to economic union with its current emphasis on self-regulation, voluntary agreements and incentive-based market mechanisms'.

Coupled with this evolution of regulatory method, Carter finds the persistence of another regulatory truism: 'the current character of economic union, with its focus on better regulation tools and impact assessments, serves to further the dominance of experts'. Exploring a policy field in which the expertise of agencies plays a critical part, Takis Tridimas reviews the structure and powers of the European Financial Markets Authority (ESMA) in order to sketch the kind of 'regulatory experimentation of which we need more not less'. He emphasizes in particular the 'heavy hand of soft law' and the often binding-in-fact nature of such instruments. The depiction of ESMA's capacity to generate 'peer pressure to an asphyxiating degree', for example, notwithstanding the limits to its power in a legal sense, brings that analysis strikingly to life. But the pursuit of regulatory effectiveness beyond law will need somehow to reconcile the benefits uncovered by Tridimas with the concerns about legitimacy and competence boundaries identified by, among others, Scott and Weatherill.

McMahon's work on the CAP and Robin White's analysis of EU competence in the field of fundamental rights are thematically discrete but they share two key things. First, they locate the scrutiny of their subject areas in contemporary regulatory methodology and the increasingly complex balancing of interests that regulation, whether legislative or court-led, must hope to achieve. McMahon traces the way in which a burgeoning range of flanking interests and sociological drivers, notably globalization, have bled into the EU regulatory process over time. This finding is mirrored in Carter's conclusions on the 'political usages of sustainable development [which] have brought about a changing logic of economic union in sea fisheries and aquaculture'. White focuses on the way in which the Lisbon reforms sought to entrench a growing set of value criteria in primary EU law. The second shared quality in both chapters is a sense of optimism. McMahon describes the fast-paced changes in the agriculture sector as a 'moving target' while observing that 'at least the thick fog has dissipated'. White presents the expansion of Union competence as a trajectory of regulatory maturity, on which the inherent significance of fundamental rights is now—finally—more aptly reflected through the achievements of the Lisbon Treaty, thinking especially but not exclusively of the legal effect conferred on the EU Charter of Fundamental Rights. It is worth recalling, however, that Dutheil de la Rochère, in her exploration of case law on the regulation of gambling activities, cautioned that even in the established services' sector of free movement law, 'the balancing of factors makes considerable demands of the judiciary, both at European and national levels'. When more law exists, and more requirements are built into it, regulators face even tougher challenges when trying to deal with the complicated balancing of interests that results.

Bringing together the three themes of authority, reach and method, Noreen Burrows and Muriel Robison's analysis of the 'motherhood penalty' and the gender pay gap is perhaps more pessimistic, or at best realistic, but that pessimism is shaped by observation of years of poor progress in this field. Interestingly, from the perspective of regulatory reach, they characterize this policy field as a protected space for Member State regulatory responsibility, remarking that '[t]he absence of a political commitment to renegotiating the Pregnant Workers Directive is also indicative of the continuing wariness of several Member States to having EU level market correcting mechanisms replace domestic welfare policies both on grounds of costs and on grounds of the internal logic of national solidarity principles'.[4] This position is shown empirically to have the support of the Court of Justice, a strategy that has manifested itself through the 'drawing [of] a boundary between equality policies operating at EU level and welfare policies operating at the national level'. In terms of the distribution of regulatory authority, however, Burrows and Robison are highly critical of the outcome, since there are 'wide divergences in benefits available to women and a wide divergence in costs to the Member States and to employers'. Here, then, as we saw also in the contributions on monetary union, we face something of an impasse. We are forced once again to compare the ambition-gap between the objectives of economic union and the structures created for its delivery.

Amtenbrink addresses this conundrum as an inherent design flaw in the EU's polity make-up. He treats the problem as a systemic hangover that still affects the design of EU regulation, in the sense of 'creating a supranational monetary policy authority from scratch in the face of a constitutional system that does not have all the characteristics of a state'. In his exploration of the deepening of EU competence for the protection of fundamental rights, White reminds us, however, that '[t]here is nothing contradictory about an economic constitution that also respects human rights. But it would be wrong to categorize the European Union as offering little more than an economic constitution when it offers much more.'

Whether we go so far as to agree or disagree with the Court of Justice's claim that the EU Treaties constitute an actual constitutional charter, it is difficult to dispel a related claim that constitutional *questions*, at least, underpin both the evolution and interdependency of the single market and the economic union. Moreover, that claim will always be associated with John Usher's remarkable imprint on EU scholarship.

[4] Council Directive 92/85/EEC of 19 October 1992 on the introduction of measures to encourage improvements in the safety and health at work of pregnant workers and workers who have recently given birth or are breastfeeding [1992] OJ L 348/1.

PART I

ECONOMIC AND MONETARY LAW AND POLICY

2

Denationalizing Monetary Policy: Reflections on 60 Years of European Monetary Integration

*Fabian Amtenbrink**

A. Introductory remarks

John Usher was not only part of the post-war generation that witnessed the reconstruction of their war-torn countries and the birth of a European project aimed at the political construction of a peaceful future. He was also a legal scholar who, throughout his remarkable professional career, was a critical commentator on the process of European economic integration. One particular area that attracted Usher's interest was European monetary integration. Indeed he was one of the few internationally recognized scholars that closely followed the developments that would eventually result in the establishment of the European Economic and Monetary Union (EMU). Alongside numerous contributions in leading academic legal journals and edited volumes, he authored one of the leading monographs on the Euro and financial services in the EU, highlighting the close link between the internal market project and European monetary integration.[1]

Commemorating the works of Usher, the present contribution offers a reflection on 60 years of European monetary integration thereby drawing, whenever relevant, on his scholarship. In so doing, the chapter will focus in particular on the normative challenges that arise in the context of shifting public power in the sphere of monetary policy from the national to the European level. As will be highlighted hereafter, monetary integration is deeply rooted in the aims of the European integration project and thus in the pooling of public power in a new supranational organization which, in the course of 60 years, has developed from an advanced form of intergovernmental economic cooperation into a full-blown constitutional legal order, short of constituting a (federal) state.

* Professor of European Union Law at the Erasmus School of Law, Erasmus University Rotterdam, Visiting Professor at the College of Europe (Bruges), and Center for European Financial Integration Studies (ECFIS).

[1] JA Usher, *The Law of Money and Financial Services in the EC*, 2nd edn (Oxford: Oxford University Press, 2000).

As a way of providing background to the institutional developments leading up to the establishment of a European monetary union, the role of monetary policy as an instrument of public policy and its impact on institutional designs will first be briefly recalled. Thereafter the rationale for the allocation of that policy at the European level, as well as the developments leading up to the establishment of a European centre for monetary policy are critically reviewed.[2] In this context, the Maastricht institutional framework will receive special attention. The contribution concludes with a brief assessment of the challenges that the European monetary union faces in the light of the recent global economic and financial crisis and the debt crisis in the Euro area.

B. Monetary policy as a public policy instrument: scope and institutional implications

In a nutshell, the term *monetary policy* refers to the strategies and action to regulate the supply of money. As such, monetary policy is a vital element of the overall economic policy and, more generally, of public policy. By controlling the amount of currency in circulation and as the sole supplier of bank reserves, which financial institutions are by law required to hold with the institution charged with the conduct of monetary policy, a central bank has control over the monetary base of a given economy. Mainly through open market operations (such as refinancing operations), standing (lending and deposit) facilities and the application to credit institutions of minimum reserve requirements, the monetary policy authority is in the unique position to influence money market conditions and money market interest rates.[3] The impact of monetary policy on the real economy takes place through a transmission process that ultimately results in changes in the consumption and investment behaviour of economic actors (private households and companies); and thus, their decision to spend, save or borrow money. Consumption in return influences the demand for domestic and foreign goods and services and thus the development of prices. By generating expectations about future development, monetary policy also has an impact on asset prices and the external value of the currency (exchange rate).[4]

To be sure, while monetary policy influences price developments, its long-term impact on other economic variables is questionable given that 'it is a widely accepted proposition in the economic profession that, in the long run, i.e. after all adjustments in the economy have worked through, a change in the quantity of money in the economy (all other things being equal) will be reflected in a

[2] It should be noted in this context that it is not the aim of this contribution to provide an all-inclusive chronological account of events.

[3] Informative in this context, European Central Bank, *The Implementation of Monetary Policy in the Euro Area*, Frankfurt a.M., November 2008.

[4] Generally on this so-called transition mechanism of monetary policy: ibid 44–9.

change in the general level of prices and will not induce permanent changes in real variables such as real output or unemployment'.[5] This observation coincides with the prevailing view on what monetary policy can and cannot do,[6] and with the conviction that the main contribution of monetary policy to the development of the economy is to ensure low inflation and stable prices. While monetary policy may not, therefore, have a lasting effect on economic growth and employment, inflation has been linked to social justice.[7]

In focusing monetary policy on the battle against inflation, an important institutional design choice has been made in many countries. Democratically elected governments, that is, politicians, are considered to be unsuited to ensure an inflation adverse monetary policy given (partially) conflicting interests and the issue of moral hazard linked to putting elected officials in charge of money supply.[8] Both theoretical and empirical evidence has been offered linking price stability, that is, the level of inflation and inflation variability, to the degree of independence of the monetary policy authority from political influence. Put differently, elected politicians are considered unfit to conduct an important element of public policy effectively. These majority opinions, which are largely derived from political economy thinking, have translated into institutional design. Already prior to the establishment of the European Central Bank (ECB) as the centrepiece of the European System of Central Banks (ESCB), a considerable number of monetary policy authorities around the globe had been *de jure* assigned a price stability objective or have followed such an objective in practice, albeit not in all instances as the sole or even primary monetary policy objective. Indeed, an important example of a monetary policy authority that continues to pursue multiple objectives until the present day is the United States Federal Reserve System which, according to the Federal Reserve Act, 'shall . . . promote effectively the goals of maximum employment, stable prices, and moderate long-term interest rates'.[9] Moreover, independence from government influence has become a characteristic feature of central bank systems and, indeed, for over two decades now, has risen to become

[5] HK Scheller, *The European Central Bank: History, Role and Functions*, 2nd edn (Frankfurt a.M.: ECB, 2006) 77.

[6] See DT Brash, 'Central Banks: What they can and cannot do', speech delivered to the Trans-Tasman Business Circle, Sydney, 30 March 2001. Available at <http://www.rbnz.govt.nz/speeches/0102706.html> (accessed 30 March 2011).

[7] ibid, stating that 'In many ways, keeping the value of money broadly stable makes a bigger contribution to social justice than it does to economic growth.' Generally with regard to the case for price stability, see the several contributions in A Herrero, V Gaspar, L Hoogduin, J Morgan and B Winkler, *Why Price Stability?* (Frankfurt a.M.: ECB, 2001).

[8] F Amtenbrink, *The Democratic Accountability of Central Banks. A Comparative Study of the European Central Bank* (Oxford and Portland, Oregon: Hart Publishing, 1999), with further references to relevant political economy literature.

[9] 12 USC 225a. As added by act of 16 November 1977 (91 Stat. 1387) and amended by acts of 27 October 1978 (92 Stat. 1897); 23 August 1988 (102 Stat. 1375); and 27 December 2000 (114 Stat. 3028).

the global standard, not least due to its promotion by international standard setting bodies, such as the International Monetary Fund.[10]

As will be explained in Section E below, the institutional structure of the ESCB and of the ECB have been greatly influenced by this school of thought, thereby creating legal challenges linked to the position of the ECB as a Union institution in the European constitutional legal order.[11]

C. Rationale for a European monetary union

In the previous section, it has been established that monetary policy forms an important part of economic policy, which represents a core area of (regulatory) activities of any government. Consequently, placing this task outside government or even beyond any one state results in a loss of decision-making power over monetary policy and of the instruments associated therewith. In the state context, this is the case when the task of conducting monetary policy is vested in an independent central bank that is not subject to government instructions and is insulated from political influence.[12] However, even in the case of such independent national central banks' monetary adjustment mechanisms (such as the setting of interest rates), the emission of currency and the lender of last resort function are arguably still available to be geared towards the (creation of a) specific domestic economic environment, albeit within the confines of the law regulating the central bank and the objectives stated therein. Yet where states operate an exchange rate regime, based on which the external value of the national currency is linked (pegged) to another—supposedly stronger—currency, the exercise of an autonomous monetary policy is restricted. In the rather unique case of the abolishing of a national currency in exchange for participation in a joint (supranational) currency, monetary policy functions are fulfilled by a single institution that conducts this task for the whole currency area and thus on behalf of all participating states, as is the case in the Euro area with the ECB.[13]

The rationale for unilaterally curtailing 'monetary sovereignty' in such a way can often be found in the economic advantages that come with parting from an ineffective domestic monetary policy that lacks credibility in the marketplace for the benefit of a more stable exchange rate and, thus, lower exchange rate risk, resulting in an increase in capital mobility and trade. High transaction costs and exchange rate risks may not only form a barrier to trade for individual small

[10] F Amtenbrink, 'The Three Pillars of Central Bank Governance—Towards a Model Central Bank Law or a Code of Good Governance?' in International Monetary Fund, *Current Developments in Monetary and Financial Law*, Vol 4 (Washington DC: IMF, 2005) 101.

[11] It is only since the Treaty of Lisbon that the ECB is considered to be a Union institution, listed in Article 13 TEU.

[12] See Section B above.

[13] Other variations include the adoption of a Currency Interchangeability Agreement (eg Singapore and Brunei) or the informal unilateral adoption of a foreign currency (eg the Turks and Caicos Islands and the British Virgin Islands use the US dollar as their official currency).

and open economies, inducing them unilaterally to peg their currency to another currency, such as the US dollar or the Euro, but also in the case of the removal of barriers to trade between states and the creation of a single market, such as in the case of the EU. As customs duties between the participating Member States are abolished and the free movement of goods, persons, services and capital is promoted, the costs involved with the exchange of currencies and the risks attached to cross-border transactions as a result of the variability of exchange rates aggravate trade between the Member States and, thus, constitute a barrier to trade.[14] As such, the rationale for European monetary integration can be traced back to the very roots of European economic integration, namely in the shape of the 1957 Treaty establishing a European Economic Community (EEC Treaty) that defined the tasks of the Economic Community inter alia as 'establishing a common market and progressively approximating the economic policies of Member States, to promote throughout the Community a harmonious development of economic activities'.[15] History shows, however, that the creation of economic convergence in the EU has proven to be much more difficult than the establishment of a single currency.

D. The path towards European monetary union

Despite the implications of Article 2 EEC, the original EEC Treaty did not foresee a European monetary policy or the establishment of a European common currency. The legal framework provided by Title II of the EEC Treaty on economic policy (and therein chapter 2 on balance of payments) was hardly a sufficient basis for even the coordination of the national policies in this area. With regard to monetary policy, in order to promote coordination of policies, Article 105(2) TEEC provided for a Monetary Committee with the task to keep under review the monetary and financial situation in the Member States and report developments to the Council and to the European Commission, as well as generally to act as an adviser to the Council and Commission. With regard to external monetary policy, Article 107(1) TEEC obliged Member States to treat their policy in this area as a matter of common concern. The very same obligation nowadays applies generally for the economic policies of all Member States[16] and, in particular, for the exchange rate policy of Member States outside the Euro area (so-called Member States with a derogation).[17] Alongside the Monetary Committee, unofficial meetings were held since 1959 under the auspices of the Council with the Ministers of Finance or Economics and the Governors of the central banks. From 1964 onwards, cooperation between the national central banks was institutionalized through the establishment of the Committee of Governors of the Central Banks of the Member States, based on a proposal by the European Commission in the context of the

[14] This includes the costs involved in insuring against such exchange rate risks. As to the economic costs and benefits of a single currency, see, eg, SCW Eijffinger and J de Haan, *European Monetary and Fiscal Policy* (Oxford: Oxford University Press, 2000) 16 et seq.

[15] Article 2 TEEC. [16] Article 121(1) TFEU. [17] Article 142 TFEU.

action programme of the Community for the second stage of the customs union.[18] The initial task of this Committee was 'to hold consultations concerning the general principles and the broad lines of policy of the central banks, in particular as regards credit and the money and foreign exchange markets' and 'to exchange information at regular intervals about the most important measures that fall within the competence of the Central Banks, and to examine those measures'.[19] In the run-up to the establishment of today's EMU the tasks of the Committee were broadened, as it was inter alia 'to promote the coordination of the monetary policies of the Member States with the aim of achieving price stability as a necessary condition for the proper functioning of the European Monetary System and the realization of its objective of monetary stability' and, moreover, to be consulted by national competent authorities in the case of 'decisions on the course of monetary policy, such as the setting of annual money supply and credit targets'.[20] Yet, while Article 104(1) EEC obliged Member States to 'pursue an economic policy needed to ensure the equilibrium of its overall balance of payments and to maintain the confidence in its currency, while taking care to ensure a high level of employment and a stable level of prices', Usher rightly observed that 'those obligations can hardly be said to have been universally observed'. As he points out, in the context of the common agricultural policy (CAP), the Court of Justice of the European Communities (now Court of Justice of the European Union) held in 1978, albeit in an obiter dictum, that contrary to Article 105 EEC the Member States had not achieved the coordination of their divergent monetary policies.[21]

Until the establishment in 1979 of the European Monetary System (EMS), with the Exchange Rate Mechanism (ERM I) at its key component, the European Communities did not feature its own exchange rate system. This is not to say, however, that no coordination took place at all. In fact, the currencies of the Member States of the European Economic Community (later to become the European Community) initially participated in the post-war Bretton Woods System featuring a system of 'adjustable pegged exchange rates', whereby each participating country 'set the par value of its currency in terms of gold or, alternatively, the gold content of the U.S. dollar in 1944'.[22] Yet, the development of the single market, not least due to the rapidly growing case law of the ECJ, increasingly brought to the forefront problems that arose from the autonomous economic and

[18] Council Decision 64/300/EEC of 8 May 1964 on cooperation between the Central Banks of the Member States of the European Economic Community [1964] OJ 77/1206; Memorandum of the Commission on the action programme of the Community for the second stage of 24 October 1962 COM (62) 300 final, para 132.

[19] Council Decision 64/300/EEC, n 18 above, Article 3.

[20] Council Decision 64/300, Article 3, as amended by Council Decision 90/142/EEC of 12 March 1990 amending Council Decision 64/300/EEC on cooperation between the central banks of the Member States of the European Economic Community [1990] OJ L 78/25.

[21] JA Usher, *EC Agricultural Law*, 2nd edn (Oxford: Oxford University Press, 2001) 115, with reference to Joined Cases 80-81/77 *Société Les Commissionnaires Réunis SARL v Receveur des douanes; SARL Les fils de Henri Ramel v Receveur des douanes* [1978] ECR 927, para 37.

[22] See, eg, RJ Carbaugh, *International Economics*, 12th edn (Mason, OH: South-Western Cengage Learning, 2009) 472.

monetary policies conducted by the Member States.[23] Against the background of the gradual deterioration of the Bretton-Woods exchange rate system that saw the devaluation of some European currencies, the European Commission promoted plans to step up coordination of the economic policies of the Member States and monetary cooperation within the Community.[24]

Based on an agreement reached by the Hague European Council in December 1969, the Council of Ministers early in 1970 adopted a decision establishing an expert group charged with drawing up a report on the establishment of economic and monetary union. The result of these efforts took the shape of the so-called Werner Report on the feasibility of economic and monetary union. The Report emphasized that 'general economic disequilibrium in the member countries will have direct and rapid repercussions on the global evolution of the Community' and observed that '[t]he extension of the liberation of movements of capital and the realization of the right of establishment and of the free rendering of services by banking and financial undertakings have not progressed far enough. The delay has been caused by the absence of sufficient coordination of economic and monetary policies and by local peculiarities of law or of fact.'[25] In this context the Report concluded that '[t]he increasing interpenetration of the economies has entailed a weakening of autonomy for national economic policies. The control of economic policy has become all the more difficult because the loss of autonomy at the national level has not been compensated by the inauguration of Community policies. The inadequacies and disequilibrium that have occurred in the process of realization of the Common Market are thus thrown into relief.'[26] The remedy proposed in the Werner Report was the establishment in stages of a European economic and monetary union and the creation of a European centre of economic and monetary decision-making. Yet, despite the endorsement of this plan by the Member States, its implementation did not go beyond initial preparatory measures and it was not only overshadowed by the breakdown of the Bretton Woods exchange rate system, but also by the economic crisis of the 1970s.[27]

The end of the global exchange rate system underlined the need for a European system ensuring stable exchange rates between the currencies of the Member States participating in the internal market. Initiatives from the early 1970s to restrict the

[23] With regard to the establishment in 1950s of the European Payment Union and, thereafter, of the European Monetary Agreement (EMA), as well as the establishment of the ECU as a common denominator to determine and compare values in the Community context, see JA Usher, 'The Legal Regulation of the European Currency Unit' (1988) 37 *Int'l & Comp. L. Q.* 249, 249–67.

[24] See Commission Memorandum to the Council on the co-ordination of economic policies and monetary co-operation within the Community of 12 February 1969, also known as the Barre Memorandum named after the main initiator of the document, then Vice-President of the European Commission, Raymond Barre.

[25] Report to the Council and the Commission on the realization by stages of economic and monetary union in the Community of 8 October 1970 [1970] OJ C 136/1, 8.

[26] ibid 8.

[27] On the failure of the system, see, eg, RP Buckley, *International Financial System: Policy and Regulation* (Alphen aan den Rijn: Kluwer Law International 2009) 9 et seq.

exchange rate of national currencies as part of the preparation for an EMU[28] were translated into a rather more substantive institutional framework with the establishment of the EMS, largely based on the initiative of the European Commission and most prominently supported by France and Germany.[29] The two key elements of this system were a European Exchange Rate Mechanism (ERM I) and a borrowing facility managed by the European Monetary Cooperation Funds (EMCF) that had already been set up in 1973.[30]

While the EMS did not entail a further transfer of national competences in the area of monetary policy to a European authority, ERM I did restrict the participating Member States and namely their monetary policy authorities in the managing of their exchange rates. In fact, the system established fluctuation margins for each currency against a central rate. The central rate was established as a unit of account, referred to as ECU, constituting a basket of the currencies of the participating Member States. Resulting from this was a grid of bilateral exchange rates. A unilateral adjustment of the exchange rate of a national currency (devaluation or revaluation) was excluded as adjustments of central rates were subject to mutual agreement of all participating Member States and the European Commission in a procedure generally referred to as 'realignment'.[31] Fluctuations of the exchange rates vis-à-vis the ECU were initially limited to ±2.25 per cent and in one case to ±6 per cent.[32] Member States' monetary policy authorities were obliged to intervene in the foreign exchange market on behalf of a participating currency if the value of that currency threatened to rise above (ceiling) or drop below (floor) the margin around the central rate determined by the ECU. The EMCF was in charge of borrowing facilities aiding national monetary authorities in case of currency interventions. Overall, the EMS can be viewed as a logical step in an increasingly closer cooperation in the field of monetary policy that had commenced with rather programmatic declarations in the EEC Treaty and that, in due course, would find its tentative crest in the establishment of a European monetary authority and the creation of a single currency. This development did not, however, take place

[28] With regard to these efforts, including the Basle Agreement, the Smithsonian Agreement, the subsequent 'block floating' of European currencies and the establishment of the European Monetary Cooperation Fund (EMCF), see F Amtenbrink, n 8 above, 112 et seq, with further references.

[29] Resolution of the European Council on the establishment of the European Monetary System and related matters from 5 December 1978, Monetary Committee of the European Community, Compendium of Community Monetary Texts, Luxemburg, Office for Official Publications of the European Communities, 1995, 58; Resolution of the European Council of 12/13 March 1979, Bull. EC 7–1979, point 2; Agreement between the central banks of the Member States of the EEC of 13 March 1979 laying down the operating procedures for the European Monetary System, Monetary Committee of the European Communities, Compendium of Community Monetary Texts, Luxemburg, Office for Official Publications of the European Communities, 1995, 62; Council Regulation (EEC) 3180/78 and 3181/78 [1978] OJ L 379/1 and 379/2, as amended thereafter.

[30] Council Regulation (EEC) 907/73 establishing a European Monetary Cooperation Fund [1973] OJ L 89/2.

[31] Realignments have taken place on several occasions.

[32] For the Italian lira, a ±6% margin was observed. See JA Usher, 'Legal Background of the Euro' in P Beaumont and N Walker, *The Legal Framework of the Single European Currency* (Oxford: Hart Publishing, 1999) 13 et seq (also published in *SEW: Tijdschrift voor europees en economisch recht* 1999–2001, 12–23, 14 et seq).

without setbacks, as the crisis of ERM I in the autumn of 1992 highlights.[33] This crisis provided a glimpse of the challenges ahead in the context of the pooling of the monetary policies of Member States with essentially autonomously operating and less than fully convergent national economies, and the effects of increased capital mobility and widespread liberalization of financial markets.[34]

E. The Maastricht institutional framework

By the time ERM I ran into difficulties, new preparations for the establishment of an EMU were already well on the way in the shape of the 1992 Treaty on European Union. While the 1986 Single European Act had provided little more than a reminder of the Member States' obligation to cooperate in monetary matters and a recognition in primary Community law of the EMS,[35] the new Title VI on Economic and Monetary Union of the post-Maastricht EC Treaty would eventually provide for a legal basis in primary Community law to set up a European monetary union in stages.[36] This legal framework was largely based on the blueprint provided by the so-called Delors Report of experts, which had been commissioned by the European Council to study the feasibility of and concrete steps towards an economic and monetary union.[37] What was proposed and thereafter implemented with regard to 'economic union' in reality amounts to a coordination of national economic policies with strong intergovernmental characteristics that prevail until the present day. In fact, the wording of Article 119(1) TFEU underlines the national character of this policy field by referring not only to the adoption of an economic policy by the Union, but also by the Member States. Moreover, Article 120 TFEU obliges Member States to 'conduct their economic policies with a view to contributing to the achievement of the objectives of the Union, as defined in Article 3 [TFEU], and in the context of the broad guidelines referred to in Article 121(2) [TFEU]'. Finally, Article 121(1) TFEU states that 'Member States shall regard their economic policies as a matter of common concern and shall coordinate

[33] The UK pound sterling and the Italian lira had to withdraw from ERM I and a number of currencies had to be devalued. Moreover, the fluctuation margins were widened to ±15% for a majority of participating Member States' currencies, with the exception of the deutschmark and the Dutch guilder, which continued to observe the original margin.

[34] As to the reasons for the ERM crisis, several—not necessarily congruent—explanations have been offered in the literature, highlighting deficiencies of the ERM itself and/or of the domestic policies of the participating countries, see, eg, B Higgins, 'Was the ERM Crisis Inevitable?' (1993) Fourth Quarter *Federal Reserve Bank of Kansas City Economic Review* 27–40; FG Ozkan and A Sutherland, 'A Model of the ERM Crisis', CEPR Discussion Paper No 879, 1994; WH Buiter, GM Corsetti and PA Pesenti, *Interpreting the ERM crisis: country-specific and systemic issues*, Centre for Economic Performance, London School of Economics and Political Science, Discussion Paper No 321, 1997.

[35] See Single European Act, Article 20, [1987] OJ L 169/1, introducing Article 102a EEC.

[36] See Treaty on European Union, Article 25[1992] OJ C 191/1 and the Protocol on the Statute of the European System of Central Banks and of the European Central Bank attached thereto.

[37] Presidency Conclusions, Hannover European Council, Bull. EC 6–1988, point 3.4.1 (para 5); Committee for the Study of Economic and Monetary Union, *Report on Economic and Monetary Union in the European Community*, Luxemburg, Office for Official Publications of the European Communities, 1989.

them within the Council'. In contrast to the Werner Report, which foresaw 'a centre of decision for economic policy' which would have to be 'in a position to influence the national budgets, especially as regards the level and the direction of the balances and the methods for financing the deficits or utilizing the surpluses',[38] the blueprint provided in the Delors Report confined the project of economic 'union' to the coordination of national economic policies based on general European economic objectives and guidelines. This choice is remarkable given that, in the very same Report, it is noted that 'the lack of sufficient convergence of fiscal policies as reflected in large and persistent budget deficits in certain countries has remained a source of tensions and has put a disproportionate burden on monetary policy'.[39] While the drafters of the Delors Report and subsequently the drafters of the provisions on EMU may or may not have believed that the Treaty framework on economic coordination is capable of remedying this situation, they were in any event not willing to transfer extensive powers in the area of economic policy to the European level. The recent Euro area debt crisis highlights in a rather dramatic way the shortcomings of this system.[40] Indeed, as will be argued hereafter, it may be the disparity in the level of economic and monetary integration that is contributing to the fundamental challenges that the European monetary union faces.

Given the limited degree of (macro)economic integration, it has really been the introduction of the institutional framework for the pooling of the monetary policies of the Member States and, linked thereto, the establishment of the ECB that constituted a quantum leap in European integration and namely the development of a single (financial) market. Yet, as Usher has rightly pointed out, it is a 'differentiated integration' for that matter.[41] The differentiation results from two main features of the system. First, participation in the EU (and thus accession to the EU) does not automatically result in *full* participation in EMU. Participation in the Euro area with its single currency is subject to a separate decision subject to the fulfilment of specific economic and legal conditions summarized under the expression 'convergence criteria'. The two most important economic criteria, that is, the government deficit and government debt limits, also form the key benchmarks for surveillance of the Member States in the context of economic coordination in EMU. What is more, apart from Member States that remain outside the Euro area because they actually do not (yet) fulfil these conditions, from the outset two Member States, the United Kingdom and Denmark, managed to negotiate exemptions from the general Treaty regime. Both countries have the express right to remain outside the Euro area regardless of whether they fulfil the convergence

[38] Report to the Council and the Commission on the realization by stages of economic and monetary union in the Community of 8 October 1970 [1970] OJ C 136/1, section III.

[39] Committee for the Study of Economic and Monetary Union, Report on Economic and Monetary Union in the European Community, Luxemburg, Office for Official Publications of the European Communities, 1989, point 5.

[40] For more details on the fiscal dimension of EMU, see the contribution by Andrew Scott in this volume.

[41] JA Usher, n 1 above, 199.

criteria.[42] As to whether—legally speaking—EMU is voluntary for other Member States, as suggested by Usher, is debatable.[43] Neither the former TEC nor today's TFEU foresee a procedure to opt out of the Euro area. What is more, for candidate countries, adherence to the aims of economic and monetary union constitutes one of the prerequisites for accession to the EU.[44] Nevertheless, as the example of Sweden highlights, the formal non-fulfilment of the legal conditions, such as participation in the exchange rate mechanism or a central bank institutional structure in line with that prescribed by primary EU law, can result in the quasi-permanent exclusion from the Euro area regardless of the state of convergence of the economy of a Member State.[45]

The large gap in the level of integration between economic and monetary policy also becomes drastically clear when studying the institutional framework governing the European monetary union.[46] The final objective of a single European currency calls for the integration of the Member States' competences relating to monetary policy in a single European decision-maker for monetary policy. Different from existing central bank systems with a long operational history, in the case of the ESCB and the ECB the drafters of the EU Treaty had the opportunity to design a modern central bank, institutionally, from scratch. In doing so, arguably one of the main challenges was to set up a monetary policy authority capable of operating in the rather unusual supranational legal order of the EU, while at the same time being capable of quickly gaining sufficient credibility in the marketplace to conduct an effective monetary policy for the single currency. As has been pointed out in Section B of this contribution, the institutional legal structure of the ECB has been strongly influenced by the prevailing opinion on institutional design for monetary policy. This can be observed both for the position of the ECB in the European legal order, as well as for its statutory policy objective.[47]

Indeed, from the outset, the ESCB and the ECB have been insulated in a rather rigorous manner from outside influence, both at the European and national level. Neither the ECB nor a national central bank, nor any member of their decision-making bodies, is allowed to seek or take instructions from Union institutions, bodies, offices or agencies, from any government of a Member State or from any other body.[48] Until the coming into effect of the Treaty of Lisbon, the special

[42] Protocol (No 15) on certain provisions relating to the United Kingdom of Great Britain and Northern Ireland [2008] OJ C 115/284; Protocol (No 16) on certain provisions relating to Denmark [2008] OJ C 115/287.

[43] JA Usher, 'The Evolution of Economic and Monetary Union—Some Legal Issues' in A Arnull, P Eeckhout and T Tridimas (eds), *Continuity and Change in EU Law* (Oxford; Oxford University Press, 2008) 297–319, 303.

[44] Based on the accession criteria formulated by the 1993 Copenhagen European Council.

[45] See JA Usher, 'Economic and Monetary Union—A Lawyer's View' in JA Usher, *The State of the European Union* (Harlow: Longman, 2000) 230–52, 233, who emphasizes 'the transitional rather than permanent' character of the status 'Member States with a derogation'.

[46] This contribution will not discuss the three stages towards the single currency and the economic convergence criteria. See, eg, JA Usher, n 32 above; JA Usher, n 45 above.

[47] With regard to the European Monetary Institute, the forerunner of the ECB, see JA Usher, n 1 above.

[48] See currently Article 130 TFEU.

position of the ECB in the European legal order was further highlighted by the absence of this body from the statutory list of Community institutions included in ex Article 7 TEC. With the introduction of Article 13(1) TEU, the ECB is now actually listed as one of the Union's institutions alongside the European Parliament, the European Council, the Council, the European Commission, the Court of Justice of the European Union, and the Court of Auditors. Yet, an analysis of the TFEU does not support the conclusion that the status of the ECB vis-à-vis other Union or national institutions and bodies has been altered as a result of this. The retention of the special position of the ECB becomes clear from the fact that, differently from the other Union institutions, the post-Lisbon TEU does not include any more details on the ECB or the Court of Auditors for that matter. Instead, Article 13(2) TEU simply refers to the TFEU. Articles 130 and 131 TFEU now include the prohibition on Union and national authorities from influencing the ECB,[49] and the new Article 282(3) TFEU not only confirms that the ECB continues to enjoy legal personality, but moreover also reiterates its independence.

The special position of the ECB *within* the Union legal order extends to all relevant institutional, organizational and financial aspects of its operations.[50] The members of the Executive Board, charged with the implementation of Euro area monetary policy, have to fulfil their duties on a full-time basis, may in principle not engage in any other occupation, and are appointed by the European Council, acting by a qualified majority, from among persons of recognized standing and professional experience in monetary or banking matters, for a non-renewable term of eight years.[51] In contrast, both the judges at the ECJ and the members of the European Commission can be reappointed, leading Usher to observe that the independence of the ECB may be even stronger than that imposed on European Commission members.[52] In fact, the independence requirement also extends to the governors of the national central banks, who, together with the members of the Executive Board, make up the Governing Council of the ECB. The Statute of the ESCB and of the ECB provides that national central bank laws must provide that the term of office of a governor of a national central bank is no less than five years.[53] The strict exclusion of government influence from monetary policy in the ESCB has certainly been a paradigm shift in some Member States where government involvement, whether based on institutional arrangements or practice, was a regular feature. However, the loss of monetary policy as an instrument of economic policy results not so much from the insulation of national central banks from government influence, but rather from the transfer of monetary policy tasks onto a supranational monetary policy authority. A study of the current arrangements

[49] Ex Articles 108 and 108 EC.

[50] For more details, see F Amtenbrink, 'Economic, Monetary and Social Policy' in AM McDonnell, PJG Kapteyn, K Mortelmans, CWA Timmermans (eds), *The Law of the European Union and the European Communities*, 4th edn (Alphen aan de Rijn: Kluwer Law International, 2008) 881–989, 951 et seq (sections 1–3), with further references.

[51] Statute ESCB and ECB, Articles 11.1 and 11.2.

[52] JA Usher, n 43 above, 312.

[53] Statute ESCB and ECB, Article 14.2.

applicable to the Bank of England highlights the strictness of these European requirements on the institutional structure of the national central banks. The Chancellor of the Exchequer does not only set the inflation target of the Bank, but also holds a so-called reserve power, allowing the Treasury, after consultation with the Governor of the Bank of England, to issue directions to the Bank with respect to monetary policy if required in the public interest and by extreme economic circumstances.[54] Such an overriding mechanism in the hands of government does not exist for the ECB and, to the extent that it exists for a national central bank participating in the Euro area, has to be considered incompatible with the provisions of the TFEU.

The independence of the ECB is not limited to institutional and organizational aspects, as it also extends to the actual conduct of monetary policy. Primary Union law establishes price stability as a primary objective. In contrast to, for example, the multiple objectives of the Federal Reserve System, Article 127(1) TFEU allows for the support of the general economic policies in the Union only to the extent that this does not conflict with the primary objective of the ECB. The ECB is not only free to decide on the application of the monetary policy instruments at its disposal (instrument independence),[55] but, in the absence of any provisions in the TFEU and the Protocol on the Statute of the ESCB and of the ECB, also to define (quantify) what price stability amounts to (goal independence). Apart from defining and implementing monetary policy for the Euro area, the ECB is also charged with the conduct of foreign-exchange operations, the managing of the official foreign reserves of the Member States and the promoting of the smooth operation of payment systems.[56]

One area where the ECB has explicitly not been given any tasks by primary Union law is the prudential supervision of credit institutions and the stability of the financial system. According to Article 127(5) TFEU, the ESCB is only to contribute to the smooth conduct of policies pursued by the competent national authorities. This abstention from involving the ECB in financial market supervisory tasks may not only be explained by the long-standing reluctance of the Member States to transfer powers in this policy field to the supranational level,[57] but also by the fact that there are good arguments for not placing multiple tasks in the same institution.[58] Yet, as will be explained in Section F, as a consequence of the overall reform of the European system of financial supervision, this separation of tasks has recently been abolished to some degree with the establishment of the European Systemic Risk Board (ESRB).

Given the European legal framework, it is hardly surprising that the ECB is ranked among the most independent central banks in existence, arguably even bypassing the German Bundesbank, on which the ECB has been modelled to a

54 Bank of England Act 1998, s 19.

55 On these instruments see ECB, *The Implementation of the Monetary Policy in the Euro Area* (Frankfurt a.M.: ECB, February 2011).

56 Article 127(2) TFEU.

57 See R Smits, *The European Central Bank: Institutional Aspects* (The Hague: Kluwer Law International, 1997) 334–8.

58 See further Section F below.

considerable extent.[59] The pronounced focus on independence may not only reflect the majority opinion on institutional design of monetary policy authorities at the time of the drafting of the Treaty on European Union, but also reflects the conviction of the drafters of that Treaty to ensure that the institutional design of the new supranational monetary policy authority does not stand in the way of the establishment of a credible monetary policy in the Euro area. Yet, this has also raised concerns about the degree of accountability of the ECB.[60] Indeed, not only has monetary policy in a Member State been placed beyond the influence of government, it has actually been placed outside the constitutional system of any one Member State participating in the Euro area altogether. Any previously existing mechanisms to ensure that the public authority charged with the conduct of monetary policy has to explain its conduct, while at the same time allowing those that have vested these powers in the independent authority to formulate an opinion on the latter's performance and, moreover to sanction bad performance, are no longer available.

At least on paper, the accountability of the ECB is anything but well provided for. The Maastricht legal framework can be criticized for not foreseeing a clear benchmark or yardstick based on which the performance of the supranational monetary policy authority can be evaluated. By providing for both instrument and goal independence, the ECB is effectively free in setting its own benchmark, in stark contrast to, for example, the Bank of England or, outside the European context, the Reserve Bank of New Zealand. Moreover, it can be noted that primary Union law introduces only a minimal legal framework for the transparency of the ECB that primarily focuses on general reporting requirements. In this context, the lack of any requirement or indeed even leeway to publish minutes of the meetings of the Governing Board of the ECB, which takes all monetary policy decisions for the Euro area, can be criticized. This lack of transparency of the decision-making process is at times justified by arguments based on the market sensitivity of the substance of the discussions in this forum and the negative impact that the publication of a detailed account of the bi-monthly meetings would have on the openness of discussions among the governors of the national central banks and the members of the Executive Board assembled in the Governing Council of the ECB. The undesirable consequence of this arrangement is the absence of an important source of information to judge the performance of the Bank, mainly with regard to the adequacy of the assessments made by its main decision-making body. Primary Union law also provides only to a limited extent for institutionalized contacts between the ECB and other Union institutions. As far as the participation of other Union institutions in the Governing Council of the ECB is concerned, this clearly reflects the institutional choice to insulate the ECB from outside influence.

[59] J de Haan, F Amtenbrink and SCW Eijffinger 'Accountability of Central Banks: Aspects and Quantifications' (2009) 52 *Banca Nazionale del Lavoro Quarterly Review*, 167–93, with further references.

[60] For an early assessment see eg RM Lastra, 'The Independence of the European Central Bank' (1992) 33:2 *Harvard International Law Journal*, 475–519; thereafter: LW Gormley and J de Haan, 'The democratic deficit of the European Central Bank' (1996) *ELRev*, 95–112; F Amtenbrink, n 8 above.

Yet, this also includes the extent to which ECB officials and, in particular, members of its Executive Board, including the President of the ECB, are obliged to engage in a regular dialogue with the European Parliament. Article 283(3) TFEU requires the President of the ECB to present an annual report to the Council and to the Parliament, whereby the latter may hold a general debate on that basis. Moreover, the President of the ECB and the other members of the Executive Board *may*, at the request of the Parliament or on their own initiative, be heard by the Parliament standing committee on economic and monetary affairs. Yet, no obligation on the part of ECB officials to appear before the Parliament can be deduced from this provision.

This rather pessimistic evaluation of the scope of legal arrangements on the accountability of the ECB also extends to the actual instruments of accountability that are available in order to act upon an evaluation of the performance of the ECB. Arguably, the biggest safeguard for the ECB in this regard is the inclusion of the institutional framework, and especially its independence, in primary Union law. Prior to the ratification of the Treaty of Lisbon, and thus at the time of the coming into operation of the ECB, the only way to change its institutional structure was by means of the regular treaty amendment procedure pursuant to ex Article 48 EC and thus, essentially, by means of an international treaty.[61] What is more, as has been noted above, primary Union law does not allow for a reserve power on the part of the Council and/or the European Parliament to override or otherwise correct a monetary policy decision of the Governing Council of the ECB. Also, a performance-based dismissal similar to that found, for example, in the Reserve Bank of New Zealand Act 1989 is foreseen neither for the President of the ECB nor for any other members of the Governing Council of the Bank.[62] In fact, the application of such a performance-based dismissal of the President of the ECB would have required the establishment of a centralized structure rather than the principle of collegiality, which currently governs monetary policy decisions of the ECB. The quasi-federal structure of the ESCB, in which national central bank governors of the Member States of the Euro area participate in monetary policy decision-making at the ECB, arguably leaves little room for the accountability of individual central bank governors at the Member State level. This is not only due to the independence requirement in primary Union law, but because individual governors can hardly be held to account for the collective decisions of the Governing Council of the ECB.[63] This side-effect of the transfer of decision-making power onto a supranational body can also be witnessed, for example, for the Council, with the exception of the few remaining areas in which the latter decides by unanimous vote.

All in all, it can be noted, that based on a study of its legal framework, the ECB scores high on independence, but comparatively low on accountability,[64] adding to the general concerns about the existence of a democratic deficit in the Union. This

[61] As to the post-Lisbon situation, see Section F below.

[62] See Reserve Bank of New Zealand Act 1989, s 49(2).

[63] According to Article 10.2 of the Statute of the ESCB and of the ECB, in principle the Governing Council acts by simple majority of the members having a voting right. In the event of a tie, the President has a casting vote.

[64] J de Haan, F Amtenbrink, SCW Eijffinger, n 59 above.

assessment is difficult to reconcile with the ECB's own evaluation that its independent status 'has its counterpart in a well-structured and functioning framework for holding the ECB accountable'.[65] To be fair, this evaluation may, to a large extent, be based on practice at the ECB as it has developed over the last ten years.

F. The coming of age of European monetary union

While it may be premature to determine the final place of European monetary union in the history of European integration, the first ten years of its existence clearly highlight the advantages as well as challenges that derive from the pooling of public power beyond the level of the state. Thus, when examining European monetary policy in isolation, it is safe to state that the Maastricht institutional framework has allowed the ECB successfully to establish itself as a supranational independent policy authority, which conducts monetary policy on behalf of (for now) 17 Member States participating in the Euro area. In the more than ten years of its existence, the ECB has also largely succeeded in what may be the most important objective of any new monetary policy authority, that is, 'to gain credibility and win the confidence of the public and the financial markets that it would maintain price stability.'[66] When observing the track record of the ECB with regard to its primary task, it becomes apparent from Figure 1 that, on average, inflation has remained close to, albeit slightly above, the 2 per cent objective set by the ECB.

Overall, it may thus be argued that as a new supranational monetary policy authority, the ECB has been rather effective in delivering on its primary objective of maintaining price stability in the Euro area. In fact, to counter fears of a bias towards a deflationary monetary policy, the ECB could be seen as somewhat adjusting its definition of price stability over the course of time, no longer aiming at an on-year increase in the Harmonised Index of Consumer Prices for the Euro area of below 2 per cent over the medium term, but rather, below but close to 2 per cent.[67]

The establishment of a single European currency backed by a credible monetary policy has undoubtedly worked in favour of capital mobility and generally reduced transaction costs in intra-Community trade. Moreover, as has been observed elsewhere, benefits have also derived from the Euro having made a successful entrée in the global financial and monetary system.[68] Part of this success story is that the Euro is gradually developing into a real contender as an anchor currency next to the well-established US dollar.

Yet, despite these successes, the single European monetary policy should not be understood as the capstone of the development from a single market to economic union. Indeed, the recent global economic and financial crisis and the subsequent

[65] ECB, 'The accountability of the ECB', Monthly Bulletin, November 2002, 56.

[66] ECB, 10th Anniversary of the ECB, Monthly Bulletin, Frankfurt a.M., 2010, 8.

[67] European Central Bank, *The Monetary Policy of the ECB*, Frankfurt a.M., 2004.

[68] F Amtenbrink, 'EMU and the Overseas' in D Kochenov (ed), *EU Law and the Overseas. Outermost regions, Associated Overseas Countries and territories, territories Sui Generis* (Alphen aan den Rijn: Kluwer Law International, 2011) 271–90.

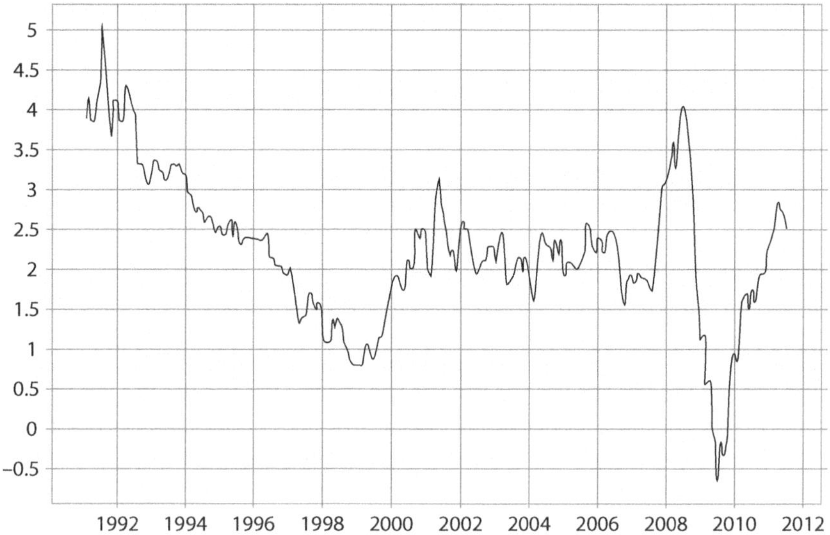

Fig. 1 Inflation in the Euro area (annual percentage changes, non-seasonally adjusted)
Source: <http://www.ecb.int/mopo/html/index.en.html> (accessed 25 August 2011).

debt crisis in the Euro area highlight the vulnerability of a single currency supported by a single monetary policy that is situated in a supranational constitutional environment the main characteristic of which is the lack of a coherent system of economic governance. In the midst of the impending quasi-insolvency of Euro area Member States the ECB finds itself caught up between its primary monetary policy task, that is, to preserve price stability, and demands to come to the financial rescue of failing national economies and, moreover, to play a more substantive institutional role in preventing the next financial market crisis.

The Euro area debt crisis highlights that the challenges which the single monetary policy faces may not primarily lay in the institutional sphere, that is, inter-institutional conflicts and/or encounters with national governments, but rather emerge from the structural deficiencies of the European Economic and Monetary Union as defined in primary Union law. Where the single monetary policy has been geared towards the stability of the common currency, the system of economic coordination in EMU has failed to prevent economic imbalances and the emergence of excessive government deficits in a vast majority of Member States. In order to secure the stability of the single currency as well as their own economic interests, Euro area Member States had little choice but to come to the rescue of the financially failing countries, thereby allowing for a rather questionable interpretation—to say the least—of the Treaty rules on government deficit financing. What started out as bilateral loans for Greece, with the establishment of the European Financial Stability Mechanism and the European Financial Stability Facility, has turned into a structural financial—albeit in the first instance temporary—rescue mechanism for Euro area Member States with excessive government deficits at the (potential) expense of economically better-off Member States. With the signing of the Treaty establishing the European Stability Mechanism in February 2012, this rescue mechanism becomes permanent.[69] The failure of European economic governance moreover has spillover effects on monetary policy in the Euro area.[70] The dramatic deterioration of the financial position of several Euro area Member States to the point of quasi-insolvency has left the ECB with little choice but to substantially support the European rescue attempts inter alia through its interest rate decisions and the buying of government bonds since 2010.[71] The consequences for the single currency of this stepping-in of the ECB in the face of a missing adequate political response are, as yet, incalculable.

What has become clear is that a construction whereby power in the area of monetary policy is pooled in a supranational institution while leaving it up to sovereign national governments to observe government deficit and debt ceilings is politically and financially unsustainable in the medium to long run. Put differently, 10 years of practice have shown that under the legal, economic and political conditions that prevail in the EU, monetary union must go hand-in-hand with a centralization of economic policy that surpasses the type of coordination of national policies foreseen in the Maastricht Treaty and upheld by the Treaty of Lisbon. The recent EU legislative measures to reinforce economic coordination (the so-called Six-Pack) fall short of fully fixing this structural deficiency in European economic governance.[72] Moreover, the signing in March 2012 of the Treaty on Stability, Coordination and Governance in the Economic and Monetary Union outside the EU constitutional framework by 25 of the 27 Member States highlights the—seemingly insurmountable—difficulties involved in amending the legal framework for economic governance in primary Union law.[73]

The global financial and economic crisis has also revealed the extent of the integration of the financial markets in the EU and on a global scale, and the vulnerabilities to global developments that are the consequence thereof. The major reform of the European system of financial market regulation and supervision that has come into effect in 2011 highlights the extent of the regulatory residue in this

[69] This treaty can be found at <http://www.european-council.europa.eu/media/582311/05-tesm2.en12.pdf> (accessed 1 March 2012).

[70] Generally on such spillover effects SCW Eijffinger and J de Haan, n 14 above.

[71] Critically M Seidel, 'Der Ankauf nicht markt- und börsengängiger Staatsanleihen, namentlich Griechenlands, durch die Europäische Zentralbank und durch nationale Zentralbanken—rechtlich nur fragwürdig oder Rechtsverstoß?' (2010) 21:14 *EuZW. Europäische Zeitschrift für Wirtschaftsrecht* 521.

[72] Regulation 1173/2011 on the effective enforcement of budgetary surveillance in the Euro area [2011] OJ L 306/1; Regulation 1174/2011 on enforcement measures to correct excessive macroeconomic imbalances in the euro area [2011] OJ L 306/8; Regulation 1175/2011 amending Council Regulation (EC) No 1466/97 on the strengthening of the surveillance of budgetary positions and the surveillance and coordination of economic policies [2011] OJ L 306/12; Regulation 1176/2011 of the European Parliament and of the Council of 16 November 2011 on the prevention and correction of macroeconomic imbalances [2011] OJ 306 L 306/25; Council Regulation 1177/2011 amending Regulation (EC) No 1467/97 on speeding up and clarifying the implementation of the excessive deficit procedure [2011] OJ l 306/33; Council Directive 2011/85/EU on requirements for budgetary frameworks of the Member States [2011] L 306/41.

[73] The treaty can be found at <http://www.consilium.europa.eu/uedocs/cms_data/docs/pressdata/en/ec/128035.pdf> (accessed 1 March 2012).

area until recently. This deficit has not only been diagnosed in the area of the supervision of individual financial institutions, but also with regard to the monitoring of risks for the financial system as whole, so-called systemic risks. At the time of the establishment of the ESCB, the ECB has been deliberately spared any supervisory tasks in the internal market. Indeed, the latter was dealt with under the so-called Lamfalussy Structure with a strong emphasis on the role of national authorities. However, under the 2011 arrangements the ECB has, for the first time, been assigned a task in this area. As part of the overhaul of the European system of financial supervision, the ESRB has been set up charged with the macro-prudential oversight in order to contribute to the prevention or mitigation of systemic risks to financial stability in the Union that arise from developments within the financial system.[74] While the ESRB has been established separately from the ECB, for the first five years of its existence it is chaired by the President of the ECB, who also represents this body externally, and vice-chaired by an additional members of the General Council of the ECB.[75] Moreover, the ECB facilitates the ESRB by operating its Secretariat, thereby provide analytical, statistical, logistical and administrative support.[76] At least in the short term, therefore, there is a close link between the ECB and the ESRB.

Whether and to what extent this involvement of the ECB in macro-prudential supervision is at odds with its primary monetary policy objective is questionable. Arguments against the placing of financial supervisory tasks with the monetary policy authority are mainly based on the vesting of micro-prudential supervisory tasks with the central bank and the possible conflicts of interests that may arise as a result.[77] An involvement in the monitoring of financial stability and the providing of information and advice may be somewhat less problematic in this regard. Still, the involvement of the ECB does mean that any failure by the ESRB in anticipating systemic risks could also result in a reputational damage for the ECB with consequences for its credibility as the monetary policy authority of the Euro area. What is more, the involvement of the ECB in the ESRB raises new questions about its accountability both with regard to the involvement of the ECB in the ESRB, as well as with regard to the ESRB itself. In this context it is interesting to note that according to the legal basis of the ESRB both the Chair and the Vice-Chairs must inform the European Parliament at a public hearing how they intend to discharge their duties, and the European Parliament can invite the Chair to explain decisions of the ESRB. Regardless of whether in practice these meetings are kept separate from the aforementioned monetary dialogue, the President of the ECB will be effectively perceived in this double capacity. This has the potential to blur the accountability of both of these bodies.

[74] Regulation 1092/2010 on European Union macro-prudential oversight of the financial system and establishing a European Systemic Risk Board [2010] OJ L 331/1, Article 3(1).

[75] ibid Article 5(1)–(2). The Regulation foresees a review of the means of appointing the chair after the initial five-year term.

[76] Council Regulation 1096/2010 conferring specific tasks upon the European Central Bank concerning the functioning of the European Systemic Risk Board [2010] OJ L 331/162, Article 2.

[77] See, eg, C Di Noia and G Di Giorgio, 'Should Banking Supervision and Monetary Policy Tasks be Given to Different Institutions?' (1999) 2:3 *International Finance* 361–78.

G. Concluding remarks

European economic and monetary union undoubtedly still constitutes one of the most ambitious legal and economic integration projects existing today. The unification of the until then separate monetary policies of Member States can be understood as a logical step in an ongoing process that started with the creation of the European Economic Community. More than the oft-cited process of (economic) globalization, it was the inherent logic of European economic integration that provided the rationale for the creation of a common currency and the centralization of monetary policy. At the same time the influence that the more political—and some would say idealistic—ambition of creating a united Europe had on these developments should not be underestimated. In the current political climate it is hardly conceivable that any new equally ambitious European project would stand a realistic chance.

The institutional challenge of creating a supranational monetary policy authority from scratch in the face of a constitutional system that does not have all the characteristics of a state can—to some extent—still be witnessed in today's structure of the ESCB and of the ECB. The latter has been created with a view to providing for a central bank that would not be inferior to the most trusted central banks existing at the time. The track-record of the ECB suggests that the drafters of the Treaties have succeeded in this regard. Some would argue that this has come at a high price, as national governments have lost what may be considered an important tool of economic policy. Yet, such a criticism may at least partially ride on the (economic) assumption that government, that is, elected politicians, should be in charge of monetary policy, whereas empirical evidence of the economic consequences of such legal arrangements suggests differently.

Over the past decade European monetary policy has certainly come of age. It has succeeded in building a reputable European currency backed by a solid institutional design. Yet, in the wake of the global economic and financial crisis and the Euro area debt crisis the Achilles' heel of the system has become blatantly clear. The considerable gradient in the level of economic and monetary integration in the EU constitutes a real threat to the future of the Euro and with it the future prospect of the internal market at a time in which several Euro area Member States have proven to be incapable or unwilling to conduct prudent economic policy. If the single currency is to survive in the medium to long term the only way forward seems to be a further evolutionary step towards an economic union. Maintaining the status quo is financially and politically unsustainable, whereas a return to national currencies would have incalculable consequences for the economies of the Member States and the European integration project as a whole. Yet, for the reasons stated above, it is rather doubtful whether the necessary fundamental reform of the current system of economic governance and the creation of a real economic union can be realized in the foreseeable future.

3

Does Economic Union Require a Fiscal Union?

*Andrew Scott**

A. Introduction

The advent of monetary union in 1999 marked the onset of the boldest stage in the development of the EU as a single economic area. Although the ongoing programme to complete the single market remained the foundational raison d'être of European integration, the introduction of a common currency to replace multiple national currencies appeared to represent an irreversible step towards establishing a comprehensive economic union between the EU Member States. Whilst monetary unions can (and do) break up, this is infrequent as the costs, in terms of the consequential economic and financial disruption, are extremely high. Accordingly, few doubted that creating a currency union within the EU would, if successful, consolidate the process of economic integration as no previous initiative had done. However, if it did not prove successful—at least in political terms—the subsequent unravelling of the currency union could challenge the entire basis of European economic integration.

It was self evident that the main consequence of creating a monetary union would be to remove the possibility of the States involved using domestic monetary policy as an instrument of national economic management. However, the shift to monetary union would also impact on fiscal policies. The Delors Report of 1989 noted explicitly that establishing European monetary union would require that 'binding constraints on the size and the financing of budget deficits' were imposed on the participating States.[1]

It is the fiscal policy dimension to European monetary union that forms the focus of this chapter. The central question explored is the extent to which the shift to European monetary union makes inevitable the emergence of a European fiscal union and, if so, what form this fiscal union might take.[2] Needless to say, this is no longer a matter of idle conjecture. Instead, it an issue about which discussion cannot be—indeed is not being—further delayed. The onset of the global financial

* Professor of European Union Studies, University of Edinburgh.

[1] Report of the Delors Commission on Economic and Monetary Union (1989), point 19.

[2] For a comprehensive analysis of fiscal policies in a monetary union see P De Grauwe, *Economics of Monetary Union*, 6th edn (Oxford: Oxford University Press, 2005) Ch 5.

crisis in 2007 quickly exposed the defects in the fiscal policy arrangements of the EU's monetary union—defects which economic theory predicted were implicit in the design of European monetary union but which had been 'managed' hitherto. However, the rapid and dramatic explosion in levels of sovereign debt[3] across the EU, as Member States responded to the domestic consequences of the global financial crisis, exposed a fundamental fault line in the EU's single currency model which, at the time of writing, threatens the survival of the Eurozone. For many observers, the only lasting solution to this crisis is a decisive shift towards the fiscal unification of the EU, whereupon individual Member States cede substantial sovereignty over taxation and public spending decisions to a central EU fiscal authority in return for which their debts are under-written by the EU as a whole. But whilst this may offer a permanent solution to the underlying financial crisis in the Eurozone, it raises, as discussed below, a wide range of new economic and political challenges for the EU and for individual Member States.

B. Addressing the fiscal dimension to monetary union: towards the Stability and Growth Pact

The ambition to establish a monetary union among the EU Member States can be traced back to 1969 and the conclusions from the Hague Summit. However, this early initiative was frustrated by a combination of the collapse of the Bretton Woods fixed exchange rate regime in 1971 and the worldwide recession that followed the Organization of the Petroleum Exporting Countries (OPEC) oil price rise of 1973. The global shift from fixed to floating exchange rates that occurred in 1973 undermined the initial attempt by EU countries to maintain intra-EU exchange rate stability—known as the snake[4]—this being widely regarded as essential to maintain the integrity of the EU Common Market. In 1978, and against a backdrop of increasingly volatile intra-EU currency movements, an agreement was reached between the Member States to establish the European Monetary System (EMS), at the heart of which was a new fixed exchange rate arrangement known as the Exchange Rate Mechanism (ERM).[5] After a difficult beginning, during which a number of exchange rate realignments took place, by the mid-1980s intra-EU nominal exchange rates had stabilized and the ERM had succeeded in establishing the 'zone of monetary stability' which had underpinned the 1978 initiative. This success not only reflected the strength of the commitment on the part of Member States to support any ERM currency under attack in the

[3] Sovereign debt is debt incurred by governments through the issue of bonds in order to finance public spending. Government bonds are subject to a rating determined by the risk (of default) that investors incur in holding the bonds of any particular country. A fall in the rating attached to a country's bond (ie a rise in the perceived risk) will increase the costs of borrowing for the government concerned.

[4] Initially known as the 'snake in the tunnel', the agreement was to restrict the bilateral movement of any EU currency to ± 2.25% of parity.

[5] The EMS was launched in 1979 following the signing of the Bremen Declaration in July 1978.

global currency markets; more significantly, it is attributed to a convergence of the underlying economic policies of the ERM countries around those of the anchor currency country, namely West Germany.

The launch of the single market programme in 1985 took place, therefore, against a background of increasing intra-EU currency stability. Indeed for advocates of the single EU market, not only was exchange rate stability a necessary pre-condition for further economic integration, achieving a truly unified internal EU market ultimately would require the introduction of a single, common currency.[6] Although the Single European Act made no explicit reference to establishing a single EU currency, it did recognize the need for closer coordination of national monetary policies consistent with the aim of establishing an 'economic and monetary union'. The political commitment to establishing a fully-fledged monetary union took a decisive step forward at the Hanover Summit in June 1988. By then, it was clear that eliminating all restrictions on intra-EU capital flows, consistent with the internal market objective, would make it more difficult for Member States to maintain their fixed exchange rate commitment within the ERM. But any tendency for EU currency values to fluctuate against one another would undermine the single market. The logical solution was to proceed to establishing a single, common currency that would replace the EU national currencies and consolidate the internal market. At the Hanover Council, the EU Heads of Government and State established a Committee chaired by Commission President Jacques Delors to study and propose 'concrete stages leading towards this [economic and monetary] Union'.[7]

The Delors Committee duly reported in June 1989 and provided what was to become the blueprint for the creation of the EU monetary union that was implemented on 1 January 1999. Establishing a monetary union unavoidably required Member States to surrender autonomy over national monetary policy to a new transnational single (or common) monetary authority—the European Central Bank (ECB). As a result, Member States would no longer be able to use either the rate of interest (to be set by the ECB) or the exchange rate as policy levers to achieve domestic economic objectives. However, Delors also noted that monetary union would need to impact on national fiscal policies. The argument is straightforward: 'uncoordinated and divergent national budgetary policies would undermine monetary stability and generate imbalances in the real and financial sectors of the Community'.[8]

Restricting the degree of national autonomy over domestic fiscal policies within a currency union is justified by virtue of spillover effects that characterize this type of regime. These effects arguably provide the opportunity for a country imprudently to spend its way into a fiscal position that is economically *unsustainable*—that is, where the aggregate of successive annual budget deficits creates a total stock of

[6] It is probably fair to say that of the 10 Member States that signed the Single European Act, only the UK subsequently argued there was no such requirement.

[7] European Council in Hanover, Conclusions of the Presidency, June 1988, 7.

[8] Delors Report, 30.

national debt of a scale that necessitates further borrowing simply to service that debt.[9] That an unsustainable fiscal position of one member of a currency union should be a matter of common concern to all members reflects two features of deficit-financed government spending.

The first is that national governments may be unwilling to tackle successive budget deficits when, for instance, these arise as a consequence of a 'local' economic downturn or because doing so would involve introducing politically unpopular reforms to public spending programmes or unacceptable increases in taxation. As membership of a monetary union precludes any government from financing the deficit by increasing the money supply, inevitably it will do so by increasing its borrowing on international capital markets. A failure to address the underlying causes of this imbalance between government revenue and expenditure inevitably will result in a structural deficit and a rising total debt-to-GDP ratio. This will ultimately result in an unsustainable fiscal position emerging, which is a matter of concern for the currency union as a whole for two reasons. The first is that excessive (deficit-financed) public spending in one country can result in inflationary pressures being experienced across the currency union as a whole. The second is that excessive borrowing by one government is likely to raise the cost of borrowing for all other governments in the currency union, thereby pushing up interest rates across the area and—possibly—undermining economic stability for the area as a whole.

This latter problem reveals the second feature of the sovereign debt issue in a monetary union—that the market for the debt instruments of individual governments within a multi-country single currency area may not properly reflect the correct level of 'risk' in its pricing of these debt instruments. The 'risk' here is the risk of default by an individual government when its debt instrument reaches maturity and is to be redeemed. If insolvency risk is *correctly* perceived by markets (ie markets are *efficient* in the economic sense), the capital market will set the marginal cost of acquiring additional debt by any particular government according to that risk, and thereby regulate the extent to which that government can finance successive deficits. If the market perceives that additional debt carried additional risk, then the risk premium attaching to the debt will rise and 'local' interest rates will increase accordingly. By this mechanism, the market regulates (and should restrict) the scope for a government to arrive at an unsustainable fiscal position, by providing a hard budget constraint on government borrowing. No 'centrally' based institutional or legal rules are necessary to regulate decentralized fiscal authorities. However, if the capital market does not work in this way, and—for instance—effectively regards debt instrument from different members of a currency union as perfect substitutes despite differences in the underlying economic conditions, then the market-driven limitation on any individual government's level of indebtedness

[9] The formal condition to ensure a country remains financially solvent is that the budget surplus must be equal or greater than the difference between the nominal interest rate and the nominal rate of economic growth multiplied by the government debt-to-GDP ratio.

is considerably weakened, if not removed entirely. Consequently, the case for imposing fiscal rules on national governments becomes compelling.[10]

One of the main reasons why markets may fail to assign country risk efficiently is if lenders believe that a fiscally profligate government within a larger monetary union will never be permitted to default regardless of the volume of outstanding debt it has acquired—that is, the country will be bailed out.[11] And, of course, should indebted countries inside a monetary union themselves believe that a bail-out mechanism exists, they may be encouraged to be *less* fiscally prudent than otherwise. This scenario describes the problem of *moral hazard*, which occurs where a country that believes it is insulated from financial risk attached to higher borrowing behaves differently than it would if it believed it was fully exposed to that risk. In order to counter moral hazard, the monetary union must combine a binding 'no bail-out' rule with stringent rules preventing any member of a monetary union incurring levels of debt that are not sustainable.

Such considerations clearly informed the monetary union debate in the EU—this being a union in which fiscal policy competence would remain decentralized at the level of the Member State. The fiscal rules deemed to be consistent with monetary union were first elaborated in the EC Treaty, following Maastricht, as preconditions a Member State had to fulfil before being deemed eligible to join the common currency regime. Article 140 TFEU called on aspirant members of the monetary union to ensure: 'the sustainability of the government financial position; this will be apparent from having achieved a government budgetary position without a deficit that is excessive, as determined in accordance with Article 126(6)'.

Under the Treaty an 'excessive deficit' arose:

(i) where the ratio of planned or actual government deficit to GDP exceeded 3 per cent or,

(ii) where the ratio of government debt to GDP exceeded 60 per cent.

However, as the Delors Report had implied, and as the theory of moral hazard demonstrates, it was equally—indeed more—important that Member States continued to observe budgetary discipline as members of the monetary union. At the Amsterdam Council of June 1997, the Member States adopted a resolution establishing a 'Stability and Growth Pact' (SGP), which required governments to adhere to the Excessive Deficit Criteria (EDC) set out in the EC Treaty once they

[10] In the context of the Eurozone sovereign debt crisis, Paul De Grauwe recently wrote: 'Believers in market efficiency have been telling us that this [efficient market] power . . . will act as a disciplining force on bad Governments. I have lost much of my faith in the idea that financial markets are a disciplining force'. See P De Grauwe, *The Governance of a Fragile Eurozone*, Centre for European Policy Studies, Working Document 346, May 2011.

[11] 'Bailing out' means that another government, or the central bank, stands ready to purchase debt instruments issued by a profligate government to ensure it can always finance its debt obligations. The EU Treaties expressly prohibit such interventions. Article 125 TFEU is a general no bail-out clause prohibiting a government from assuming the debt of another Member State, whilst Article 123 TFEU stipulates that the ECB cannot purchase debt from a Member State.

joined the single currency area.[12] Failure to do so would render them subject to a range of financial sanctions and penalties defined by the 'Excessive Deficit Procedure' (EDP). The SGP also required governments of EMU States 'to abide by the medium-term budgetary objective of positions close to balance or in surplus', the view being that this would permit sufficient fiscal scope for Member States to respond to cyclical fluctuations in economic activity without incurring an excessive deficit.

The SGP was thus intended to ensure the potentially damaging features of decentralized national fiscal policies being conducted within a transnational monetary union were avoided by establishing 'preventive' rules restricting annual budget deficits to 3 per cent of GDP and total debt to 60 per cent of GDP *and* by establishing 'corrective' rules to bring into line any government breaching the EDC. The SGP set out the various procedural steps by which national fiscal policies would be appraised against the fiscal reference values. Each year, Eurozone governments would submit a stability programme setting out their medium-term fiscal positions, which would be subject to scrutiny and comment by the European Commission. Where it deemed it to be necessary, the Commission was empowered to adopt an opinion and issue recommendations to a government that it believes is not fulfilling its obligations under the SGP, and to invite the Council to require that Member State to adjust its stability programme accordingly. Ultimately, the Council is empowered to impose sanctions on any EMU member that fails to take the steps necessary to correct an excessive deficit.[13]

The SGP was designed to address concerns, on the part of Germany in particular, that clear and enforceable rules were in place to ensure that the fiscal policies of all members of the European monetary union remained consistent with collective financial and monetary stability over the long term. These rules reflected the view that the main source of instability for the monetary union was the activities of profligate national governments that, unless constrained by such rules, would be incapable of imposing the degree of domestic economic discipline consistent with stability. However, as was to become clear, this view was undone by two factors. First, it soon became apparent that because the SGP rules would not be enforced rigorously, these rules were to become non-credible. Second, and ultimately much more damaging, were the unforeseen consequences that establishing a monetary union within a deregulated single financial area would have on the behaviour of the capital markets. In particular, it seemed that insufficient attention was given—both by EU governments and capital markets—to the total level of a nation's outstanding sovereign debt, indicating, perhaps, that moral hazard had become an endemic feature of the dynamics of European monetary union.

[12] Resolution of the European Council on the Stability and Growth Pact (Amsterdam, 17 June 1997) [1997] OJ C 236/1.

[13] Sanctions take the form of a non-interest-bearing deposit. For a fuller discussion see SCW Eijffinger and J de Haan, *European Monetary and Fiscal Policy* (Oxford: Oxford University Press, 2000) Ch 4.

C. The 'rise and fall' of the SGP

Very soon after monetary union was established, it became clear that some Member States were having difficulty observing both the medium-term objective of a balanced budget and, more significantly, observing the 3 per cent deficit-to-GDP ceiling. Morris et al identify two contributing factors. The first was simply that the degree of fiscal consolidation achieved before 1999, whilst impressive, had been inadequate. In many Member States, the economic reforms necessary for the underlying fiscal dynamics to be consistent with the medium-term objective of a balanced budget had simply not been implemented ahead of monetary union. Further fiscal consolidation was therefore required, although this would be more difficult to achieve as EMU membership was no longer available as an incentive driving forward internal reforms in key States and, in any event, many States were experiencing 'consolidation fatigue'.[14] Second, as it turned out, the early years of EMU were characterized by a period of low economic growth, beginning in 2001 and continuing until the end of 2004, during which government revenues fell whilst expenditures continued to rise as cyclically induced welfare spending increased. Inevitably this pushed budget deficits towards, and for some countries (including Germany, France, Italy and Portugal) beyond, the SGP 3 per cent ceiling during 2002 and 2003. The Commission responded by calling on governments to implement measures to cut their budget deficits as required under the SGP rules, but with no success.[15] France and Germany, in particular, refused to introduce what were in essence deflationary fiscal measures that would serve only to exacerbate the economic downswing, adding further to rising levels of unemployment. Moreover, had they done so, undoubtedly this would have further delayed the economic recovery across the Eurozone as a whole.[16] By mid-2003, the Commission was obliged to initiate SGP non-compliance procedures against both France and, soon after, Germany.[17] In the event, however, sanctions were not imposed on either country because the finance ministers of the Eurozone Member States refused to support the Commission recommendations.

[14] R Morris, H Ongena and L Schuknecht, *The Reform and Implementation of the Stability and Growth Pact*, European Central Bank Occasional Paper 47, June 2006, 15–16. Morris et al report that fiscal consolidation in the Euro area as a whole during the 1990s was attributable to an increase in the revenue-to-GDP ratio from 44% in 1991 to 47% in 1999 rather than expenditure-reducing reforms. The upshot was that as soon as revenues began to decline, budget deficits inevitably began to increase.

[15] In 2003, the European Commission declared both France and Germany to be in breach of the Stability and Growth Pact (European Commission IP/03/640 and IP/03/12).

[16] It is worth noting that budget deficits in excess of 3% are very common in many countries during the recession phase of the economic cycle. These will only become unsustainable if past debt is not repaid from budget surpluses recorded during the growth phase of the cycle.

[17] On 7 May 2003, the Commission recommended the Council began excessive deficit procedures against France (Commission Opinion on the existence of an excessive deficit in France SEC (2003) 514) and on 18 November a similar recommendation was made regarding Germany (Recommendation for a COUNCIL DECISION establishing, in accordance with Article 104(8) of the EC Treaty, that the action taken by Germany in response to the recommendations made by the Council pursuant to Article 104(7) of the Treaty is proving to be inadequate SEC (2003) 1316).

The consequences of the decision not to take action against either France or Germany despite their clear breach of the SGP rules effectively rendered the SGP redundant as a credible framework for disciplining the fiscal policies of EMU Member States, with potentially damaging consequences. The Governing Council of the ECB commented on the Council's failure to back the Commission as follows:

> The failure to go along with the rules and procedures foreseen in the Stability and Growth Pact risks undermining the credibility of the institutional framework and the confidence in sound public finances of Member States across the Euro area.[18]

On 4 December 2003, Jean-Claude Trichet, President of the European Central Bank, made further reference to the 'deeply regrettable developments at the... Council meeting' and continued by drawing a link between those developments and interest rates:

> Let me add that a credible fiscal framework is key not only to stability but also to growth, and is a precondition for low risk premia in financial markets to be preserved.[19]

Elsewhere, reaction was similarly critical. A number of senior politicians from the EU's smaller Member States—who had voted in favour of the Commission recommendation to introduce sanctions against France and Germany—made clear their displeasure that the rules of the SGP were being relaxed in the case of large countries, whilst being rigorously implemented against smaller countries.

In response to the events of 2003, in September 2004 the Commission brought forward proposals to reform the operation of the SGP.[20] In essence, the aim of the reform was twofold: first, to respond to legitimate criticisms that the SGP was too rigid in its present form and that its rules should be tailored to the specific economic circumstances and prospects of the individual Eurozone countries and, second, to restore the badly damaged credibility of the SGP as a framework for regulating the fiscal policies of Eurozone countries. A particular concern was to take into account the impact of the economic cycle on the public finances of a Eurozone Member State, and to assess SGP compliance against the cyclically adjusted budgetary position rather than the unadjusted outturn. This would effectively offer Eurozone countries more latitude in their budgetary policy during the economic downswing—although this did suggest recession-induced deficits would have to be compensated by budget surpluses during the economic upturn.

[18] Statement of the Governing Council on the ECOFIN Council Conclusions regarding the correction of excessive deficits in France and Germany, European Central Bank, 25 November 2003. See <http://www.ecb.int/press/pr/date/2003/html/pr031125.en.html>.

[19] The statement in full can be read at: <http://www.ecb.int/press/pressconf/2003/html/is031204.en.html>.

[20] Communication from the Commission to the Council and the European Parliament, *Strengthening economic governance and clarifying the implementation of the Stability and Growth Pact* COM (2004) 581 final.

The reforms were agreed in 2005 and covered both the preventive and corrective elements of the SGP.[21] Although the deficit and debt thresholds were not modified, the reforms did re-define the circumstances under which a State would be deemed to be in breach of these thresholds. In terms of preventive action, through the requirement that all Member States should have a medium term budget target of 'close to balance or in surplus', the reformed Pact permitted each State to define its own medium-term objective, which would be assessed by the Council on the basis of the circumstances facing that State. Moreover, the 'medium term' was to be treated as over the course of an economic cycle rather than a specific period of time. Finally, in assessing a State's convergence programme, the Council would take into account the degree to which it was pursuing structural reforms in the form of changes to domestic economic and social policies that deliver a more flexible labour market (thus enhancing economic growth) and which secure long-term reductions in the level of public spending. Whilst changes to the preventive arm of the SGP were generally welcomed as an appropriate reaction to an excessively rigid regime, the changes made to the corrective arm of the Pact did nothing to suggest that the compliance mechanism had been improved. Indeed quite the opposite. In essence, these measures amounted to little more than relaxing the criteria according to which the SGP corrective measures would be triggered. Deadlines for compliance were extended, whilst a host of 'other relevant factors' were identified as circumstances under which corrective actions could be delayed or avoided. The proliferation of these 'escape clauses' led critics to claim that far from restoring its credibility, the reforms had further undermined the SGP in this regard.[22] On the other hand, the Commission argued that the reforms increased the likelihood of compliance as Eurozone countries could be expected to conform to a Pact that took into account the specific circumstances of each member, and offered a set of policy prescriptions appropriate to these circumstances.

The principal defect in the SGP reform measures was that they risked increasing rather than diminishing the likelihood that moral hazard would become a more deeply embedded feature of the international capital markets. And if this was the case, these reforms served only to make more not less likely the prospect that some Eurozone members would find themselves in unsustainable fiscal positions thereby jeopardizing the stability of the Eurozone as a whole.

Moral hazard would become more problematic to the extent that lenders took the view that by effectively relaxing the SGP rules, Eurozone countries collectively

[21] See Report from the Council (ECOFIN) to European Council, 22–23 March 2005, Improving the implementation of the Stability and Growth Pact, 7423/05 UEM 97 ECOFIN 104 and Council Regulation (EC) No 1055/2005 of 27 June 2005 amending Regulation (EC) No 1466/97 on the strengthening of the surveillance of budgetary positions and the surveillance and coordination of economic policies [2005] OJ L 174/1, and Council Regulation (EC) No 1056/2005 of 27 June 2005 amending Regulation (EC) No 1467/97 on speeding up and clarifying the implementation of the excessive deficit procedure [2005] OJ L 174/5.

[22] See for instance M Feldstein, *The Euro and the Stability Pact,* National Bureau of Economic Research Working Paper No 11249, 2005; L Diebalek, W Köhler-Töglhofer and D Prammer, *Reform of the Stability and Growth Pact,* Monetary Policy and the Economy Issue 2, Austrian Central Bank, 2006, 78–109.

were signalling their readiness to accept (and implicitly underwrite) higher deficits, even in those members whose economies were in need of significant structural reforms—in the absence of which fiscal policy could quickly become unsustainable. In this situation, lenders took the view that further lending to such countries was implicitly secured by the Eurozone States as a whole, thereby encouraging them to purchase ever higher return debt instruments from those countries with relative impunity. And of course governments in those countries preferred to borrow to finance excessive public spending rather than implement unpopular domestic reforms. In essence, what emerged was a regime in which lenders were seemingly content to purchase successive tranches of sovereign debt from the economically weaker countries of the Eurozone in exchange for high returns, disregarding almost entirely the possibility of default on the part of these increasingly indebted countries.

In and of itself, of course, the 2005 reform of the SGP was unlikely to lead to a situation in which one EMU member found itself subject to a sovereign debt crisis. However, for critics of the SGP, the immediate problem was not temporarily managing breaches of the SGP thresholds. Rather it was the recognition that the SGP regime was simply incapable of requiring governments to implement the structural economic reforms necessary to ensure that they complied with the SGP fiscal conditions over the medium to long term. The evidence supporting the need for reforms in countries such as Greece, Italy, Spain and Portugal was rising unemployment and falling competitiveness, and the non-sustainability of the ever higher public spending required to finance a range of relatively generous social welfare programmes. If comprehensive policy reforms were not forthcoming in those States, to restore their economic competitiveness and to lower public spending obligations, critics argued that either these countries would be forced to leave the single currency zone or the stronger countries would be required to support their increasingly expensive social welfare policies by engaging in direct financial transfers.[23]

D. The onset of crisis

In the event, the threat to the survival of the Eurozone came not through the progressive deterioration in the public finances of a few 'southern' economies, albeit that certainly would have provoked crises ultimately. Instead the proximate cause was the onset of the unprecedented global financial crisis in 2007. Although triggered by the bursting of the US housing bubble, the roots of the financial crisis lay in the credit boom that began in the 1980s with the deregulation of the financial

[23] Critics pointed out that many of the peripheral economies joined the Eurozone at an overvalued exchange rate, which rendered their exports uncompetitive. The increasing competitiveness of Germany since 1999 had exacerbated this, whilst the peripheral countries themselves had made little or no effort to lower real wages or curtail generous welfare policies. For a review of the evidence, see F di Mauro and K Forster, *Globalisation and the Competitiveness of the Euro Area*, European Central Bank, Occasional Paper No 97, 2008. See further P De Grauwe, n 10 above.

services sector worldwide. Deregulation unleashed a wave of innovation in the financial services sector, leading to the introduction of an array of new and increasingly complex financial instruments, which were deemed to carry less risk than traditional financial instruments. This reduction in risk permitted banks and other financial intermediaries to lower their holdings of capital against which an increasing volume of lending was secured. The upshot was that over a period of 20 years, the exposure of the international financial services sector increased dramatically. In the years leading up to the crisis, the vulnerability of the banking sector increased dramatically as a result of the huge increase in the volume of financial assets (such as collateralized debt obligations) whose income streams depended on what turned out to be sub-prime mortgages that underpinned the boom in the US housing market.[24] Once that boom ended, and house prices began to fall dramatically, the market value of these (and related) financial assets collapsed and the banks were overburdened by holdings of 'toxic assets' and facing bankruptcy.[25]

Many of the worst affected financial institutions were headquartered in EU Member States, and by autumn 2008 almost all EU governments were forced to mount substantial rescue operations to save the financial sector from complete collapse. These rescue operations principally involved governments engaging in a combination of massive public borrowing from the capital market to inject funds into their failing domestic banking sector, in order to shore up balance sheets, and nationalizing—in part or whole—those banks where the bail-out costs were simply prohibitive. At the same time, central banks in the United States, United Kingdom and the Eurozone sought to inject liquidity into the financial markets directly through the policy of 'quantitative easing'—that is, increasing the quantity of money in circulation in an attempt to stimulate spending and facilitate bank lending in an attempt to counter the rapidly deepening economic recession triggered by the financial crisis.

It is doubtless the case that the coordinated monetary and fiscal policy response by the world's leading economies (convening in 2008 under the auspices of the newly established G20) to the financial crisis of 2007–08 prevented the global economy from sliding into an unprecedented economic depression. However, it did not prevent the onset of a recession and, in 2009, world output fell by almost 2 per cent, with the fall in output being almost double that in the advanced economies, including the EU.[26] The recession, combined with the financial crisis, which deepened dramatically following the failure of Lehman Brothers in September 2008, resulted in a rapidly deteriorating situation in public finances across the Euro area (and beyond). In the absence of higher revenues from domestic taxation, governments had little alternative but to introduce policy reforms to curtail public

[24] This is a mortgage that is lent to an individual who may have difficulty in repaying the loan. The greater the extent of sub-prime lending the more is the lender exposed to risk.

[25] The most dramatic example was Lehman Brothers, which suffered unprecedented losses as a result of its holdings of sub-prime mortgages and which went bankrupt in September 2008, sparking what became the global financial crisis.

[26] In 2009, output in the Euro area fell by 4.2%. See World Economic Outlook, *Rebalancing Growth*, IMF, April 2010.

spending significantly whilst continuing to borrow from capital markets where this remained a viable option in terms of the interest rate charged by lenders and their capacity to service the higher level of debt. The danger was that by cutting public spending in order to improve public finances, the government was adding to the deflationary pressures, thereby delaying further the onset of a sustained economic recovery. And the longer delayed the economic recovery, the more parlous the position of the country's public finances, as the financial markets demanded ever-higher premiums on successive tranches of debt that increasingly indebted governments were issuing. Inevitably, this viscous circle was most damaging in Euro area economies experiencing the weakest growth, the highest levels of indebtedness and in which there was considerable resistance to implementing the severe fiscal policies needed to curtail public spending. As discussed below, it was this combination of weak growth, high indebtedness and opposition to policy reform that was to result in the onset of the Euro area sovereign debt crisis early in 2010.

Few had predicted the financial and economic crash of 2007–09. Ultimately its causes lie in the utter inadequacy of the regulatory, and self-regulatory, arrangements governing the provision of financial services, including retail and investment banking. And whilst it would be incorrect to suggest that establishing a single currency area across the EU was in any sense a causal factor in this regulatory failure, it is the case that the design and operation of the EU single currency regime contributed greatly to the sovereign debt crisis that was about to engulf the Eurozone. The failure rigorously to implement the SGP rules governing the permitted level of total debt in relation to GDP (of 60 per cent) resulted in a number of the weaker Euro economies entering the financial crisis with debt levels that were already virtually unsustainable in fiscal terms. Accordingly, the governments of these countries were badly placed either to service their existing debt, or to engage in further borrowing once the economic recession took hold. Moreover, the failure of the Euro governance arrangements to ensure that participating States adhered to the SGP rules, even where this would oblige their governments to implement tough domestic policy reforms in order to increase their international competitiveness and reduce public spending obligations, added to the deep-seated sense of social injustice later to be manifest when such reforms simply became unavoidable.

Critics had long argued that the Euro area's failure properly to regulate the fiscal element of EMU had the potential to undermine the stability of the regime as a whole.[27] And whilst none predicted the onset of the financial turmoil in 2007, nor forecast the scale or speed with which it would overwhelm the EMU system, there is little doubt that after a decade in which EU heads of government had failed to enforce the provisions of the SGP, they were ill-prepared to provide the collective

[27] For a review of the literature see P De Grauwe, n 2 above. See further A Fatas and I Mihov, 'On Constraining Fiscal Policy Discretion in EMU' (2002) 19:1 *Oxford Review of Economic Policy* 112; and O Issing, 'On macroeconomic policy coordination in EMU' (2002) 40:2 *Journal of Common Market Studies* 345.

leadership it quickly transpired would be necessary if the sovereign debt crisis which engulfed the EU was to be weathered.

E. Tackling the debt crisis

By early in 2009, it was clear that the Eurozone was experiencing the beginnings of what was to become a fully-fledged sovereign debt crisis. Although initially confined to the traditionally weaker peripheral economies—Ireland, Greece and Portugal—by mid-2011 it had spread to the larger Euro area countries of Spain and Italy, threatening at one stage to involve France. As is the case in all such episodes, the trigger for the crisis was growing concern that the weaker economies—and Greece in particular—would default on outstanding debt due to the slow growth of the economies (and so government revenues) coupled with a failure by the governments to implement reforms that would sufficiently cut public spending thereby restoring some semblance of balance to domestic fiscal policy.[28] A debt default by a Eurozone member would have dramatic implications both for the defaulting member and for the system as a whole. For the defaulting country, such an episode would make it virtually impossible to raise any further loans on the capital market to finance public spending, the only option then being a financial rescue package from the EU and the IMF. At the same time, a default by one country would inevitably increase market expectations that there would be further default by Euro area members and this 'contagion' effect would almost certainly increase the cost of borrowing for all those countries—the impact of which would be to push up domestic interest rates thus adding to the recessionary pressures.[29] It was this threat of contagion that became the principal catalyst in the response made by the Euro area heads of government, and the ECB, to the deepening sovereign debt crisis. The concern was not only the immediate impact of contagion on interest rates. In addition, a debt default on any significant scale would almost certainly necessitate a second wave of bank rescues across the Euro area, as those banks holding bonds of the defaulting government were forced to write down the value of these assets, raising again the possibility of the collapse of the EU banking sector.

[28] The immediate trigger for a default would be the inability of a government to sell further tranches of debt on the capital markets in order to raise funds to redeem outstanding debt and/or finance public spending. The government might then offer to redeem its debt at a discount, leaving the financial institution holding the debt to incur a loss—sometimes described as a 'haircut'—on its investment. An alternative would be for the government to propose extending the date for redeeming (rescheduling) all or part of its outstanding debt rather than repudiating any or all of its debt. However, either approach would be likely to compromise significantly subsequent Greek efforts to raise funds on global capital markets.

[29] Contagion in bond markets describes a process where expectations that one country may default on its debt fuels concerns that the debt of other countries may also be vulnerable to a downgrade or default. Contagion will be particularly severe if the default signifies the failure of a collective commitment by other countries to underwrite the obligations of the prospective defaulting country.

The highly interlinked nature of the post-1999 Euro area financial system provided the rationale for the action undertaken by the Euro area members collectively to support the weaker economies over the course of the sovereign debt crisis. And although the beginning of the acute phase of that crisis can be dated to January 2009, when Standard & Poors cut Greece's credit rating to A– citing the country's failure to stick to budget plans, boost revenue and reduce debt,[30] it was not until early in 2010 that its full scale became apparent. By then, estimates of the Greek budget deficit had increased considerably and Greek bonds were downgraded to 'junk' status. At that stage, it was clear that Greece required external financial support or it would face the prospect of defaulting on its debt and being unable to finance its spending policies. At the same time, concerns about the rising net indebtedness (and poor economic prospects) of both Ireland and Portugal saw a sharp increase in the borrowing costs facing these governments in global markets, as lenders sought higher returns on what were perceived as increasingly risky investments. From April 2010, financial market concerns over the deteriorating fiscal position of these three economies was increasingly manifest in a steady rise in the yields attached to their debt relative to the German (benchmark) rate.

As already noted, the consequences of the gathering sovereign debt crisis would not be confined to the countries directly affected but would inevitably compromise—in part or in whole—stability across the Euro area as a whole. Indeed it was conceivable that the Euro area itself may not survive should the worst affected countries opt to exit the regime and resurrect their pre-1999 currencies, which, by trading at a more competitive rate (than the Euro) in global markets, could be expected to boost exports and stimulate domestic growth. Needless to say, if one country pursued this route it would be very likely that the combination of adverse market expectations and domestic resistance to the imposition of further austerity measures would force other Euro area members down the same route. Should that scenario unfold, there was a real possibility that the entire economic and political foundation of European integration would be compromised.

It was against this highly unstable backdrop that the institutions of the EU—along with the IMF—launched a concerted response to support the Euro area countries at the forefront of the escalating sovereign debt crisis: Greece, Ireland and Portugal. At that time, it was impossible to predict the future path the crisis might take and how long it would last. In responding, the EU collectively—and the Euro area countries in particular—faced two immediate problems. The first was simply that the EU, both institutionally and legally, was ill-equipped to respond speedily or decisively to the deepening debt crisis—a feature of the crisis that was to add to market uncertainty as the crisis unfolded. This is unsurprising given that the fiscal and monetary regulations governing the currency union had been designed to prevent precisely this type of situation from arising. Indeed for the Euro area

[30] Credit Rating Agencies (CRAs) rate government bonds (debt) according lo likelihood of default. The highest rating is AAA ('triple A' status). A rating below BBB– is deemed not to be an 'investment grade' bond. By mid-2011, the rating agencies had downgraded Greek bonds to CC, in effect consigning them to 'junk bond' status, meaning they carried a significant risk of default.

collectively to tackle the debt crisis would require unanimous agreement that some of the existing rules be scrapped and new procedures agreed. Needless to say there were considerable differences of opinion—both between Euro area countries and the EU financial and monetary policy stakeholders—as to how to respond to the debt crisis. The second problem, which was explicitly political, was how to convince citizens in the larger and relatively fiscally strong Euro economies that locally raised tax revenues should be used to finance fiscal bail-outs for countries whose governments had failed properly to manage their own public finances. In the event, the 'domestic politics' of managing the Euro area debt crisis, particularly in Germany, was effectively to become a major source of risk in the determination of yields of sovereign debt instruments in the capital markets. To many observers, it was the Euro area's ongoing inability to resolve these two problems that contributed significantly to both the length of the debt crisis and the contagion which added considerably to its severity.

In May 2010, the framework for the EU response emerged. It comprised two distinct elements. The first was the creation of a European Stabilisation Mechanism—in essence a temporary sovereign debt 'bail-out' facility—comprising the European Financial Stabilisation Mechanism (EFSM)[31] which involved all 27 EU Member States, and the European Financial Stability Facility (EFSF)[32] to be funded only by the (then) 16 Euro area members. Both facilities would be used in conjunction with financial support from the IMF[33] to assist Euro area members in difficulty—that is, unable to raise further funds on capital markets—subject to an agreed package of domestic reforms being implemented by the applicant country.[34] The second element of the package was the establishment of a Securities Market Programme (SMP), which permitted the ECB to purchase—on secondary markets—eligible debt instruments issued by the central governments of the Euro area countries.[35] In essence, this programme enabled the ECB to utilize its own capital resources to purchase the maturing debt of a Euro area country, thereby

[31] Council Regulation (EU) No 407/2010 of 11 May 2010 establishing a European financial stabilisation mechanism [2010] OJ L 118/1. This permits the Commission to contract borrowings with the capital markets or with financial institutions on behalf of the European Union then available as loans to support policies in the debt-ridden countries. The EFSM is not expected to exceed a total of €60bn.

[32] The EFSF was established by an intergovernmental agreement involving the members of the Eurozone. The EFSF is able to issue bonds guaranteed by Eurozone countries for up to €440bn for on-lending to those Eurozone countries in difficulty. The EFSF is intended to cease operations in 2013. For text of the EFSF Framework Agreement see: <http://www.efsf.Europa.eu/attachments/efsf_framework_agreement_en.pdf>.

[33] At that time, the combined financial support available from the EU and IMF totalled approximately €750bn. See *Joint Statement on Greece by EU Commissioner Olli Rehn and IMF Managing Director Dominique Strauss-Kahn* (International Monetary Fund, Press Release No 10/177, 2 May 2010).

[34] Typically this would involve the country cutting public spending, reforming social policies, increasing some taxes, privatizing public undertakings, and other measures to improve public finances.

[35] Decision of the European Central Bank establishing a securities markets programme (ECB/2010/5, 14 May 2010) [2010] OJ L 124/8. Under Article 123 TFEU, the ECB is prohibited from purchasing national debt instruments directly from EU Member States—ie it cannot monetize national debt. However, it is not prohibited from purchasing national debt on secondary markets.

removing the possibility of a default, and—by acting, at least implicitly, as the effective guarantor of outstanding sovereign debt—to encourage a reduction in the cost of borrowing a country faced when placing new debt on the capital market.[36] In launching the SMP, the ECB insisted that it would intervene only where the member government had taken appropriate measures to meet its agreed fiscal targets.

Although the components of the EU response were generally welcomed in principle, almost immediately critics suggested that the resources assigned to the bail-out operations, including the new role of the ECB, were unlikely to be sufficient to resolve permanently the Euro area sovereign debt crisis, especially if that crisis spread beyond the relatively manageable confines of the area's smaller economies (Greece, Ireland, Portugal), as increasingly seemed possible. Ongoing concerns were fuelled by four considerations. The first was the clear indication that, despite the increasing scope of the debt crisis, there was little appetite among the stronger members of the Euro area, particularly Germany, to increase the resources assigned to the EFSF, the principal bail-out fund. The contested 'domestic politics' of supporting the weaker peripheral countries was emerging as the single biggest obstacle to its success, indicating as it did that EU heads of government no longer enjoyed the support of their electorates for their preferred approach. Indeed, calls were growing to end financial support to Greece thereby initiating the debt default that many now regarded as inevitable if the Greek debt crisis is to be resolved. Second, the severity of—and growing domestic resistance to—the austerity programmes required of governments as a condition of EFSF and ECB support was stifling the economic growth these economies needed to escape their debt crisis. Instead, even more funds were required in order to stave off national bankruptcy. Third, in the course of 2011 it became clear that the feared contagion effect had taken hold in the Euro area capital market. Uncertainties that were initially confined to Greece, Ireland and Portugal were now being transferred to Spain and Italy and, given the sheer scale of financial support needed to stave off any debt crisis that may afflict these countries, this had the potential to transform the current sovereign debt crisis into a fundamentally more serious matter.[37] Finally, the continued speculation that any lasting solution to the debt crisis would require a partial default by the most indebted Euro area countries was creating volatility in stock markets across the EU, reflecting anxieties that any default involving the larger economies (Italy or Spain) would trigger a second wave of bank crises across the EU to which very few governments were in a position to respond.

In the course of 2010–11, ongoing market uncertainty was manifest in wildly fluctuating yields on Euro area government bonds and highly volatile stock prices, especially those of the major European banks. Following on the initial support measures extended to Greece, similar packages were agreed with Ireland late in

[36] By July 2011, the ECB held over €70bn of Greek, Irish and Portuguese debt on its balance sheet, and began intervening to buy Spanish and Italian debt.

[37] The trigger for this would be a downgrading of the credit rating assigned to those countries' debt, rumours of which periodically surfaced and caused considerable disruption on global stock markets.

2010 and with Portugal early in 2011. A second Greek bail-out was agreed in July 2011. Aware that the financial markets needed further indication of the Euro area's collective determination to avoid a default by any member country, agreement was reached in October 2010 between the EU heads of government to establish a permanent crisis mechanism under the rubric of the European Stability Mechanism (ESM), to be launched in mid-2013.[38] This required that Article 136 TFEU be amended to include the following paragraph:

> The Member States whose currency is the Euro may establish a stability mechanism to be activated if indispensable to safeguard the stability of the Euro area as a whole. The granting of any required financial assistance under the mechanism will be made subject to strict conditionality.[39]

Although indicative of unanimous political support to do whatever was required to restore confidence in the stability of the Euro area, market reaction would be driven ultimately by the scale of the funds being assigned to this permanent support facility rather than the pronouncements of politicians. After months of debate, which served only to fuel further market uncertainty, the Euro area heads of government finally agreed in July 2011 that the ESM would have an effective lending capacity of €500 billion, of which Germany alone would underwrite some €168 billion.[40] At the same time, it was agreed that the EFSF would be allowed to purchase sovereign debt on secondary markets (that is, not directly from governments) and its resources could be used, if required, to finance the recapitalization of banks. Whilst welcomed, it was generally agreed that these reforms would be adequate to meet any future needs of the smaller countries—especially Greece and Portugal—but it would be utterly inadequate should any of the larger Euro area countries find themselves in a similar situation to Greece, Ireland or Portugal. Moreover, the delay in reaching agreement on the size of this new facility pointed to a lack of firm political leadership within the Euro area, a factor that was to become part of the ongoing dynamic of the debt crisis.[41] This is because markets react to news, rumour and expectations. For governments to be able to respond to market

[38] Decision of the European Council 2011/199/EU of 25 March 2011 amending Article 136 of the Treaty on the Functioning of the European Union with regard to a stability mechanism for Member States whose currency is the euro [2011] OJ L 91/1. For text of the Treaty Establishing the European Stability Mechanism, see <http://www.consilium.Europa.eu/media/1216793/esm%20treaty%20en.pdf>.

[39] The TFEU was subsequently amended by European Council Decision 2011/199/EU, n 38 above, in accordance with Article 48(6) procedure.

[40] See Treaty Establishing the European Stability Mechanism, n 38 above. The ESM did not involve EU Member States outside the Euro area.

[41] Critics, including Belgian Finance Minister Didier Reynders and the influential *Financial Times* columnist Wolfgang Manchau, insist that the ongoing failure of Euro area governments to provide an unconditional guarantee for all Euro area debt—for instance, by agreeing to the issue of a Eurobond—has become a major source of market uncertainty, adding to the upward pressure on the cost of borrowing by the most indebted countries. A Eurobond could be issued by any member of the Eurozone; however, liability for servicing and redeeming the debt falls to the Eurozone membership as a whole. Whilst this would reduce the cost of borrowing for the indebted countries it would essentially transfer the associated debt risk to the Eurozone as a whole. See, eg, P De Grauwe and W Moesen, 'Gains for All: A proposal for a common Eurobond' (2009) 44:3 *Intereconomics*, 132–4.

movements, and prevent these from becoming destabilizing, they have to act speedily and decisively. Events in the course of 2010–11 demonstrated that the governments of the Euro area simply were not capable of exercising this type of collective governance.

At the time of writing, there is no end in sight to the Euro area sovereign debt crisis. The prospect of a permanent debt crisis resolution mechanism (the ESM) being in place by 2013 has had little discernible impact, and contagion continues to be an ongoing feature of the evolving situation. Certainly the absence of a sustained economic recovery in either the EU or the United States along with a belief that no government has the fiscal capacity to inject further stimulus to the domestic economy explain the gloomy economic prognoses which most commentators continue to report with respect to the Euro area's prospects. At the same time, the ECB has come under criticism for continuing to purchase the debt of Euro area countries subject to adverse market movements, particularly by extending this policy to Italian and Spanish debt, indicating the ECB's determination to take whatever action is required to restore stability to the Euro financial system. Not only do many question the wisdom of the underlying policy, instead urging an acceptance of the inevitable debt restructuring with financial institutions absorbing the consequential losses of a debt write-down,[42] but they also point out that the underlying credibility of the ECB is at stake, given that it is no longer operating as an independent monetary authority as intended but as an equal partner with Euro area governments in resolving a fiscal policy crisis. For that reason, if no other, it is inconceivable that further significant reforms to the monetary and fiscal architecture of the Euro system will not be required.

F. Beyond the crisis: is fiscal union inevitable?

Few anticipate a speedy resolution to the sovereign debt crisis that has overtaken the Euro area. Indeed the consensus is that for the Euro area to survive (in part or in whole), and at the time of writing this remains uncertain, significant reforms to the arrangements governing the fiscal dimension of monetary union are essential. Most experts believe that nothing short of a transition to a fully-fledged fiscal union is likely to suffice. In this section, I consider what this might mean in practice, the obstacles that need to be surmounted, and, crucially, the implications of such a radical move for the future development of the EU as single coherent economic order.

The main argument deployed by those currently supporting the development of a fully-fledged fiscal union across the Euro area is the risk to the EU as a whole

[42] The problem with this approach is that no one knows the extent of the debt restructuring needed to end the crisis, or the impact this would have on subsequent market lending to the countries involved. Nor can we predict the impact that this would have on the Euro area banks forced to absorb the lion's share of such losses. Estimates suggest that Euro area banks collectively hold upwards of €2tn in sovereign debt in total from Greece, Portugal, Ireland, Spain and Italy.

associated with any of the alternative courses of action.[43] Unsurprisingly, this analysis incorporates many of the same concerns that were raised in the 1990s by those who insisted then that a shift to European monetary union could not work unless accompanied by a parallel shift to fiscal union. The logic now, as then, is straightforward. As long as the conduct of national fiscal policies remained the exclusive preserve of Member States, and in the context of a failure to design credible (and enforceable) rules limiting the deficit and debt levels of members of the monetary union, there is no mechanism (including capital market discipline) preventing one or more States in the union from continuing to implement fiscal policies that are unsustainable—and destabilizing for the union as a whole—in the longer term. At the stage when a fiscal crisis occurs, adhering to a 'no bail-out' position will jeopardize the integrity of the monetary union and consequently is not a credible option, whilst making a bail-out conditional on austerity measures being implemented through tough domestic reforms is likely to trigger a political and social backlash in the delinquent country and undermine that strategy. Finally, providing ongoing support to finance public spending in the delinquent countries is ruled out by adverse public opinion in the stronger economies.[44]

Advocates of fiscal union see that step as inevitable if the EU monetary union is to survive.[45] By transferring competence for fiscal policy from Member State to the supranational EU level, the tax and spending policies of any member would no longer be determined by national politicians and all borrowing would be undertaken in a new debt instrument—a common Eurobond—to be backed by the combined weight of the Euro area economy. In purely economic terms, establishing a fiscal union would resolve the negative cross-border sovereign debt spillovers lying at the heart of the current crisis, and permit the most indebted members to refinance their existing debt at the much lower Eurobond rate thereby stimulating some measure of economic recovery.[46] Euro area-wide fiscal policy coordination would no longer be voluntary, and regulating national fiscal policies (from deciding the rates at which certain taxes are levied through to deciding entitlement and scale of payment across a range of public spending programmes) would no longer rely on the enforcement of codes of conduct or rules. The central fiscal authority would become responsible for issuing the common Eurobond and for managing the debt

[43] There is a general consensus that closer fiscal integration is required if the Eurozone is to survive, although there is less agreement on how far this would need to go. See, eg, P De Grauwe, n 10 above and J Delpha and J von Weizsacker, *The Blue Bond Proposal,* Bruegel Policy Brief 2010/03, 2010.

[44] eg, on 22 August, Spiegel Online reported that a survey conducted by pollster Emnid for the news channel N24 found that 76% of Germans oppose joint bonds in the Eurozone countries, with only 15% saying they supported the idea of Eurobonds. Instead, tighter restraints on domestic policies by the indebted countries is demanded. On 12 March 2011, EU leaders agreed details of a 'competitiveness pact' designed to strengthen the economic governance of the Euro area. The terms of the pact, which was insisted upon by Germany, require the indebted countries to implement a wide range of domestic economic and social policy reforms in exchange for further financial support.

[45] cf n 43 above.

[46] Of course the introduction of a Eurobond to resolve the crisis in this way does not require the formal establishment of a European fiscal union. It is an option that some wish to see used immediately. But it is unlikely the richer countries would countenance this as long as Member States conduct their own fiscal policies. See J Delpha and I von Weizsacker, n 43 above.

of the area as a whole, almost certainly subject to an overall upper ceiling for the total outstanding stock of debt. As a necessary adjunct to the loss of domestic fiscal policy authority, the poorer members of the union would demand the creation of a significant financial transfer facility in order that tax revenues raised in the richer regions of the union would be applied to support the spending policies in the poorer regions.

Whilst the logic of creating a fiscal union may be compelling for some, self-evidently it involves significant obstacles. In economic terms, the principal difficulty is the loss of fiscal policy as an instrument enabling a government to stabilize the national economy in the event of an unexpected (asymmetric) shock. In that event, the burden of adjustment will fall on local labour and product markets, although it may be partially offset by fiscal transfers from elsewhere in the fiscal union.[47] Moreover, the greater the divergence between the members of the fiscal union in terms of market flexibility and economic structure, the more difficult it will be to agree a common budgetary policy stance between countries with different levels of unemployment.

Even a cursory review of the nature of a fiscal union is sufficient to highlight the profound political challenges any such initiative would have to surmount. There are few matters that challenge the principle of national sovereignty more deeply than those relating to the levels at which domestic taxes should be levied, and on whom, and the scale of social welfare policies that account for the lion's share of public spending. Tax and spending policies thus reflect the underlying principles and ethos that determine the type of society to which the electorate collectively aspires to become.[48] Ceding political authority over these policies to the supranational EU level would represent an unprecedented step towards a single EU state—even though EU fiscal unification would almost certainly be characterized by significant local autonomy over certain taxes. The challenges to establish a pan-EU governance regime which would have the legitimacy to design and implement a common EU fiscal policy are therefore considerable and, arguably, insurmountable; at least over the immediate future. Compelling as the logic might be, however, there is no evidence that any of the EU heads of government have the appetite at this time to launch the political and constitutional debates that would be needed to establish a fully-fledged fiscal union. Nor is there any discernible public support for such an initiative.

Despite this, some of the key elements that would characterize a fiscal union are emerging in the form of significant inter-area financial transfers, an empowered intergovernmental architecture overseeing and shaping fiscal policy developments in the weaker Euro area economies, purchases of government debt instruments by supranational agencies, and the further development of the ESM. At the same time, what is completely absent from the current policy—and what will limit the extent

[47] The extent to which transfers will be used to offset shocks will be a matter for the central fiscal authority.

[48] In this regard, a move to a European fiscal union raises many more complex and controversial issues than did the transition to European monetary union.

to which fiscal union 'by stealth' can develop—is any semblance of democratic accountability over these evolving arrangements.

A final issue surrounding the prospective development of a fiscal union concerns the implications this would have for EU countries outside the arrangement. As noted above, establishing a fiscal union would necessarily create a much deeper form of economic and political (and so policy) integration between the participating countries than presently. The upshot would be the emergence *de facto* of a two-speed EU, characterized by a rapidly integrating 'inner' core group of countries that would effectively operate as a single federal state on the one hand, co-existing with a peripheral 'outer' group that retained domestic sovereignty over their own monetary and fiscal policies on the other hand. It is difficult to predict how this co-existence would be managed, although two sources of tension can readily be identified. First, it is conceivable that an increasing share of EU-wide capital investment would be diverted into the economies of the core group, at the expense of the periphery, attracted by potentially lower average interest rates than those prevailing in the peripheral economies and the more competitive market conditions on average that one would expect to emerge in the aftermath of fiscal union. Should this occur, it could lead to greater divergence in the economic performance of the inner and outer groups. The second source of tension could be the consequences for competitiveness resulting from differences in the fiscal regimes operating in the inner and outer groups of Member States. Should national tax policies be regarded as a source of unfair competition in terms of access to the single EU market, the pressure for tax harmonization that already exists in the EU is likely to intensify considerably, with implications for the coherence of the EU's single internal market.

G. Conclusion

In this chapter, the fiscal dimension to European monetary union was reviewed in the context of the ongoing sovereign debt crisis. Whilst the proximate cause of the current debt crisis was undoubtedly the global financial crash of 2007–08 and the economic recession that followed, it is equally clear that the abject failure of the rules that were designed to govern the fiscal policies of Euro area countries has been the major factor that has transformed the financial crisis in Europe to the sovereign debt crisis that is threatening to undermine the EU monetary union. If that monetary union is to survive, and the indications are that politicians across the Euro area remain committed to ensuring that it does, there will inevitably be fundamental changes in the way in which national fiscal policies are governed. It is inconceivable that the degree of autonomy that Euro area members currently enjoy in setting fiscal policy will survive the crisis. This is already evident under the ambit of the ongoing financial bail-outs to the weakest Euro area economies, where strict conditionality is attached to further tranches of assistance requiring those countries to implement a range of domestic policy reforms aimed at reducing annual budget deficits and the total stock of outstanding debt. The conundrum for the Euro area as a whole is that both the lack of a sustained global economic recovery coupled with resistance to the accompanying austerity packages is jeopardizing the chance of this approach succeeding. Whilst it might be politically acceptable to pursue policies of fiscal consolidation against a backdrop of increasing growth and rising employment, it is quite a different exercise doing so against a backdrop of recession and rising unemployment.

In the final instance, it seems inevitable that the Euro area economies will be forced to choose between a reconfiguration of the single currency area with the weaker (and perhaps the stronger) currencies exiting the regime—and dealing with the considerable financial and economic disruption that would follow—or moving decisively in the direction of fiscal union in which Member States within the Euro area cede a significant element of national sovereignty over tax and spending policies to a common supranational budgetary authority. This need not occur as one 'giant leap'. Indeed, as discussed above, the actions that are being taken to manage the current crisis contain all the institutional and policy building blocks of fiscal union. However, what is lacking, and the issue that could prove to curtail any ambition to establish a fiscal union, is a debate concerning the democratic accountability of any such Euro area 'treasury' and the extent to which inter-union financial transfers would be required.

The question as to whether there is a 'third way' whereby the Euro area can survive the current sovereign debt crisis intact, involving continued bail-out packages for the most indebted countries, depends largely on market sentiment. If those holding the high risk debt instruments are willing to accept voluntarily a debt rescheduling arrangement in exchange for a guarantee this will be the extent of the losses they are required to incur, that is a possibility. However, at the very least, any such change of market sentiment would require as a prerequisite a clear indication both that the most indebted countries were on the road to fiscal sustainability and that any prospect that the larger economies—including Spain and Italy—might default, had receded. At the moment, and indeed for the foreseeable future, neither indication looks to be forthcoming. However, should Germany and France agree to create a new Eurobond debt instrument, this would go far to placate market sentiment. But that would be a major policy change, and one that would inevitably require a significant pooling of authority over the fiscal policies of the participating governments.

It therefore appears that a drift—or discrete move—towards fiscal union across the Euro area is unavoidable if the single currency area is to remain intact. In that sense, the EU as an international economic and political arrangement stands at a crossroads. Perhaps the most important question is not how or when the current sovereign debt crisis might be resolved, but whether the EU has the capacity—individually and collectively—to exercise the type of leadership that is necessary to navigate its way out of this crisis.

4

Financial Supervision and Agency Power: Reflections on ESMA

*Takis Tridimas**

Following a reluctant start in late 1970s, the harmonization programme in financial and capital markets law has developed into one of the most extensive, intense and innovative ventures of EU policy making. Since the Financial Services Action Plan,[1] EU financial law has been the fastest growing area of EU law, its most distinct feature being the trend towards centralization and maximum harmonization.[2] It has also proved a fruitful ground for regulatory experimentation. In earlier years, the Lamfalussy process[3] provided a new paradigm for decision-making. It introduced structures for the interlocking of national and EU interests and elevated the achievement of consistent and equivalent transposition of EU measures to a key objective. More recently, following the 2008 crisis, the EU embarked on a fundamental redesigning of the institutional architecture with the establishment of three independent EU agencies in the fields of securities markets, banking, and insurance and occupational pensions. The purpose of this chapter is to discuss selectively the establishment and powers of the European Financial Markets Authority (ESMA), which is the most powerful of those agencies.

A. Background

In the aftermath of the 2008 financial crisis, the Commission spearheaded a far-reaching programme of law reform. The Commission's response was prompt and

* Sir John Lubbock Professor of Banking Law, Queen Mary, University of London, and Nancy A. Patterson Scholar and Professor, School of Law, Pennsylvania State University.

[1] Commission Communication, *Financial Services: Building a Framework for Action* COM (1998) 625, available at <http://aei.pitt.edu/3353/01/000529_1.pdf>.

[2] For an overview, see T Tridimas, 'EU Financial Regulation: Federalisation, Crisis Management and Law Reform' in P Craig and G De Búrca, *The Evolution of EU Law*, 2nd edn (Oxford: Oxford University Press, 2011) 783–804.

[3] Final Report of the Committee of Wise Men on the Regulation of the European Securities Markets (Lamfalussy Report), 15 February 2001, available at <http://ec.europa.eu/internal_market/securities/docs/lamfalussy/wisemen/final-report-wise-men_en.pdf>.

ambitious. In November 2008, it appointed a High Level Group, chaired by Mr Jacques de Larosière, to make recommendations on how to strengthen financial markets regulation at EU level. The final Report of the de Larosière Group was presented on 25 February 2009.[4] On the basis of this Report, the Commission set out an action plan in its Communication on Driving European Recovery presented on 4 March 2009.[5] This was followed by more detailed policy plans laid down in its Communication on European Financial Supervision of 27 May 2009,[6] and an extensive and fully developed package of reform proposals in September 2009.[7] Those proposals were adopted in late 2010.[8] The post-2008 crisis measures fall essentially into two categories. First, a number of measures sought to introduce or strengthen regulation in substantive areas of law. Secondly, the EU overhauled the financial supervisory architecture by establishing a new pan-European regulatory framework.

The first category includes, among others, regulations on Credit Rating Agencies (CRAs),[9] the Directive on Alternative Investment Fund Managers (AIFMD),[10] the

[4] Final Report of the de Larosière Group, 25 February 2009, available at <http://ec.europa.eu/internal_market/finances/docs/de_larosiere_report_en.pdf>.

[5] Communication from the Spring European Council, *Driving European Recovery* COM (2009) 114 final, available at <http://eurlex.europa.eu/LexUriServ/LexUriServ.do?uri=COM:2009:0114:FIN:EN:PDF>.

[6] See Commission Communication, *European Financial Supervision* COM (2009) 252 final.

[7] The proposals were presented on 24 September 2009, and are available at <http://ec.europa.eu/internal_market/finances/committees/index_en.htm#package>. They included a Proposal for a regulation on Community macro-prudential oversight of the financial system and establishing a European Systemic Risk Board (ESRB); a Proposal for a decision entrusting the European Central Bank (ECB) with specific tasks concerning the functioning of the ESRB; a Proposal for a regulation establishing a European Banking Authority (EBA); a Proposal for a regulation establishing a European Insurance and Occupational Pensions Authority (EIOPA); and a Proposal for a regulation establishing a European Securities and Markets Authority (ESMA).

[8] Note, in particular, the following measures which were adopted on 24 November 2010: Regulation No 1092/2010 on European Union macro-prudential oversight of the financial system and establishing a European Systemic Risk Board [2010] OJ L 331/1; Regulation No 1093/2010 establishing the European Banking Authority [2010] OJ L 331/12; Regulation No 1094/2010 establishing the European Insurance and Occupational Pensions Authority [2010] OJ L 331/48; Regulation No 1095/2010 establishing a European Securities and Markets Authority [2010] OJ L 331/84; Directive 2010/78 of the European Parliament and of the Council of 24 November 2010 amending Directives 98/26/EC, 2002/87/EC, 2003/6/EC, 2003/41/EC, 2003/71/EC, 2004/39/EC, 2004/109/EC, 2005/60/EC, 2006/48/EC, 2006/49/EC and 2009/65/EC in respect of the powers of the European Supervisory Authority (European Banking Authority), the European Supervisory Authority (European Insurance and Occupational Pensions Authority) and the European Supervisory Authority (European Securities and Markets Authority) [2010] OJ L 331/120(Omnibus Directive); and Regulation No 1096/2010 conferring specific tasks upon the European Central Bank concerning the functioning of the European Systemic Risk Board [2010] OJ L 331/162.

[9] Regulation No 1060/2009 on credit rating agencies [2009] OJ L 302/1, as amended by Regulation No 513/2011 [2011] OJ L 145/30.

[10] Directive 2011/61 of the European Parliament and of the Council of 8 June 2011 on Alternative Investment Fund Managers and amending Directives 2003/41/EC and 2009/65/EC and Regulations (EC) No 1060/2009 and (EU) No 1095/2010 [2011] OJ L 174/1.

so-called Omnibus Directive,[11] amendments to the Prospectus and Transparency Directives,[12] amendments to accounting rules,[13] new rules on UCITS,[14] new capital requirements,[15] and initiatives on executive pay.[16] The Commission has also focused its attention on packaged retail investment products which include investment funds, retail structured products and insurance-based investment products.[17] The Commission considers that such products are currently subject to a fragmented regulatory framework that fails to serve investor interests and leads to regulatory arbitrage.[18] It thus intends to propose legislation requiring pre-contractual disclosures and rules on selling practices.[19]

One of the most important post-crisis measures is the Regulation on credit rating agencies.[20] The Regulation is important for a number of reasons. It opts for a hard law, centralized approach in preference to the many soft law options considered and favoured by the Committee of European Securities Regulators (CESR).[21] It is EU-centric in that it requires registration of CRAs by an EU agency despite the fact that most of the leading agencies are based in the United

[11] Directive 2010/78, n 8 above. This Directive makes changes to existing directives in relation to the powers of the new EU supervisory agencies.

[12] Directive 2010/73 of the European Parliament and of the Council of 24 November 2010 amending Directives 2003/71/EC on the prospectus to be published when securities are offered to the public or admitted to trading and 2004/109/EC on the harmonisation of transparency requirements in relation to information about issuers whose securities are admitted to trading on a regulated market [2010] OJ L 327/1.

[13] For an overview, see <http://ec.europa.eu/internal_market/accounting/news/index_en.htm>.

[14] Directive 2009/65/EC of the European Parliament and of the Council of 13 July 2009 on the coordination of laws, regulations and administrative provisions relating to the undertakings for collective investment in transferable securities (UCITS) [2009] OJ L 302/32.

[15] Directive 2010/76/EU of the European Parliament and of the Council of 24 November 2010 amending Directives 2006/48/EC and 2006/49/EC as regards capital requirements for the trading book and for re-securitisations, and the supervisory review of remuneration policies [2010] OJ L 329/3.

[16] Those initiatives are mostly soft law measures in the form of recommendations and communications: see Commission Recommendation on remuneration policies in the financial services sector COM (2009) 211 final, Commission Recommendation complementing Recommendations 2004/913/EC and 2005/162/EC as regards the regime for the remuneration of directors of listed companies C(2009) 3177, and Communication from the Commission accompanying the above Recommendations COM (2009) 211 final; all available at <http://ec.europa.eu/internal_market/company/directors-remun/index_en.htm>. Note also that the amendments to the Capital Adequacy Directive (see previous footnote) require credit institutions to establish remuneration policies that do not reward excessive risk-taking by executives and traders.

[17] <http://ec.europa.eu/internal_market/finservices-retail/investment_products_en.htm>.

[18] See Update on Commission Work on Packaged Retail Investment Products, 16 December 2009, available at <http://ec.europa.eu/internal_market/finservices-retail/docs/investment_products/20091215_prips_en.pdf>, p 2 and the Commission's Working Document, available at <http://ec.europa.eu/internal_market/consultations/docs/2010/prips/consultation_paper_en.pdf>.

[19] Furthermore, the Commission is currently preparing a Directive on legal certainty of securities holding and transactions which will cover, inter alia, rules pertaining to the holding and disposal of securities, the exercise of investor's rights in cross-border situations, the establishment of free, EU-wide choice of issuers regarding the initial entry of their securities in central securities depositories, and safekeeping and administration of securities. See <http://ec.europa.eu/internal_market/financial-markets/securities-law/index_en.htm>.

[20] See n 9 above.

[21] See F Amtenbrink and J de Haan, 'Regulating Credit Rating in the European Union: A Critical First Assessment of Regulation 1060/2009 on Credit Rating Agencies' (2009) 46 *CMLRev* 1915.

States.[22] Furthermore, it departs from the home country control principle introducing for the first time a system of authorization by an EU agency, that is, ESMA, which is exclusively responsible for the registration and supervision of credit rating agencies.[23] Although this applies only to credit rating agencies on the ground that credit ratings are used throughout the EU,[24] it opens the door for an alternative regulatory paradigm which might have wider use. Under this system, a single passport might be granted in the future not by the home national authority but by an EU agency. At the very least, the establishment of centralized agencies will significantly reduce the discretion of national competent authorities.

Whilst the volume of legislation and legislative initiatives has been daunting, one of the main criticisms expressed against the Commission in relation to the post-2008 crisis reform measures has been that it rushed through legislation without conducting proper impact assessments.[25]

The most important reform arguably lies not on the introduction of substantive regulation but on the revamping of the supervisory architecture. The EU has established an enhanced European financial supervisory framework based on two pillars: a European Systemic Risk Board (ESRB) and a European System of Financial Supervisors (ESFS).[26] The ESRB focuses on macro-prudential supervision. Its role is to monitor and assess potential threats to financial stability that arise from macro-economic developments and trends within the financial system as a whole.[27] The ESRB is intended to provide early warning of emerging systemic risks and has power to issue recommendations to deal with such risks. Its tasks include analysing trends, identifying imbalances in the financial system as a whole and detecting systemic risks. The ESFS, by contrast, focuses on micro-prudential supervision and its role is to enhance the day-to-day supervision of the financial industry. It is based on a network of national financial supervisors working together with three newly established EU authorities. This 'network approach' is intended to provide a pragmatic solution. On the one hand, it recognizes that authority for the day-to-day supervision of financial institutions lies with the national authorities since the Member States have ultimate responsibility to fund any necessary rescue plans. On the other hand, the reform package recognizes

[22] Credit rating services are highly concentrated. Standard & Poors and Moody's, both of which are based in the US, have approximately 80% of the market whilst Fitch, which is based in the UK, accounts for 15% of it. See Amtenbrink and De Haan, n 21 above, 1917 where further references are given. Note however that the Regulation has specific provisions on the recognition of credit ratings related to entities established or financial instruments issued in third countries and issued by third country CRAs: see Regulation on credit rating agencies, n 9 above, Article 5. See Amtenbrink and De Haan, n 21 above, 1915.

[23] See Regulation No 1060/2009 as amend by Regulation No 513/2011, n 9 above, Articles 15–21.

[24] See Regulation No 513/2011, n 9 above, preamble, recital 9.

[25] See, eg, in relation to AIFMD, House of Lords European Union Committee, 3rd Report of Session 2009–10, Directive on Alternative Investment Fund Managers, Vol 1, Report, 10 February 2010, HL, Paper 48-I, 54–5, available at <http://www.publications.parliament.uk/pa/ld200910/ldselect/ldeucom/48/48i.pdf>.

[26] See Commission Communication, *European Financial Supervision*, n 6 above and the measures listed in n 7.

[27] See Regulation No 1092/2010, n 8 above and Regulation No 1096/2010, n 8 above.

the need for coordination and for ensuring 'a balanced flow of information between home and host authorities'.[28]

At the heart of the new regulatory architecture is the replacement of the Level 3 committees of supervisors, which had been set up under the Lamfalussy structure[29] with three new fully-fledged European Supervisory Authorities (ESAs), namely, the European Securities and Markets Authority (ESMA),[30] the European Banking Authority (EBA),[31] and the European Insurance and Occupational Pensions Authority (EIOPA).[32] Each of these authorities has legal personality and the status of an EU agency. They are intended to take over the tasks previously performed by the Level 3 committees and, in addition, they have been allocated important decision-making, monitoring and even quasi-regulatory functions. The general objectives of the new committees are to contribute to (a) improving the functioning of the internal market, (b) protecting investors, depositors, and policy-holders and consumers of financial services, (c) ensuring the integrity, efficiency and orderly functioning of financial markets, (d) safeguarding the stability of the financial system, and (e) strengthening international supervisory coordination.[33] The new institutional structure became operational on 1 January 2011. We will focus our analysis on ESMA which is the most powerful of the ESAs.[34] Before doing so, however, it is worth exploring briefly the limitations in agency establishment laid down by the ECJ in *Meroni*.[35]

B. The *Meroni* conundrum

The establishment of independent agencies faces contradictory tensions. On the one hand, the setting up of an agency makes sense only if it can take initiatives and exercise real powers of decision-making. Otherwise, its functionality is much

[28] See Commission Communication, *European Financial Supervision*, n 6 above, 9.

[29] These were the Committee of European Banking Supervisors (CEBS), the Committee of European Insurance and Occupational Pensions Committee (CEIOPS) and the Committee of European Securities Regulators (CESR).

[30] Regulation No 1095/2010, n 8 above.

[31] Regulation No 1093/2010, n 8 above.

[32] Regulation No 1094/2010 n 8 above.

[33] Commission Proposal for a Regulation of the European Parliament and of the Council establishing a European Securities and Markets Authority COM (2009) 503 final, 4 and see further n 70 below and accompanying text.

[34] For a discussion of the ESAs see, among others, E Ferran, *Understanding the New Institutional Architecture of EU Financial Market Supervision*, University of Cambridge Faculty of Law Research Paper No 29/2011, available at <http://ssrn.com/abstract=1701147>; P Schammo, 'The European Securities Markets Authority: Lifting the Veil on the Allocation of Powers' (2011) 48:6 *CMLRev* 1879; N Moloney, 'Reform or Revolution? The Financial Crisis, EU Financial Markets Law and the European Securities and Markets Authority' (2011) 60:2 *International and Comparative Law Quarterly* 521; N Moloney, 'The European Securities and Markets Authority and Institutional Design for the EU Financial Market—a Tale of Two Competences: Part (2) Rules in Action' (2011) 12:2 *European Business Organization Law Review* 177; see further Keynote Speech by Verena Ross, Executive Director of ESMA, at the City of London Brussels Annual Reception, 11 October 2011, ESMA/2011/340, available at <http://www.esma.europa.eu/system/files/2011_340.pdf>.

[35] Case 9/56 *Meroni v High Authority* [1957–58] ECR 133.

restricted and its establishment risks not being cost effective. An agency that enjoys no or little power of decision-making may be useful in carrying out certain limited tasks but is unlikely to reduce substantially the Commission's work burden or provide independent input into decision-making. On the other hand, wholesale delegation of discretionary powers disturbs the institutional balance, runs counter to basic democratic principles of accountability, and risks the development of a 'headless fourth branch of government'.[36] In EU law, the balance between those countervailing forces has traditionally tilted heavily in favour of the latter as a result of the *Meroni* judgment which laid down a number of constraints on the authority of the EU institutions to delegate their power. Despite the fact that *Meroni* is an early case decided even before the establishment of the European Economic Community, it has proved an enduring precedent, and subsequent developments in both case law and policy have been attracted by its constellation.

In *Meroni* the ECJ imposed the following limitations on the authority of EU institutions to set up agencies and delegate their powers to them.

1) *The delegation of powers to an agency must be necessary for the performance of tasks assigned to the delegating institution by the Treaty*.[37] This condition flows from the principle of conferred competences. Since, under Article 13(2) TEU, the institutions may only act within the limits of the powers conferred upon them by the Treaties, an institution may not establish an agency unless this is in furtherance of its constitutionally assigned tasks. This condition does not, however, appear particularly onerous. In fact, *Meroni* does not require an express legal basis as a prerequisite of allowing an institution to delegate its powers. A general power to legislate appears, in principle, to encompass the authority to delegate powers, subject to the conditions of lawful delegation being fulfilled. In fact, the General Court and AG Léger have taken the view that, under EU law, delegation is lawful unless expressly prohibited,[38] although such dicta have been made in the context of staff cases and might not necessarily reflect the general posture of the case law. Implied restrictions on the power to delegate may also exist, and the extent of the power to delegate will depend on the area in question and the nature of the tasks assigned.
2) *The delegating authority cannot confer on the agency powers different from those which it itself possesses*.[39] This condition appears self-evident and serves to avoid abuse since, in its absence, the delegating authority would be able to

[36] The expression was coined by President Franklin Roosevelt's Committee on Administrative Management. For ease of reference, see SG Breyer, RB Stewart, CR Sunstein and ML Spitzer, *Administrative Law and Regulatory Policy* (New York: Aspen Law & Business, 1999) 146.

[37] Case 9/56 *Meroni*, n 35 above, 151.

[38] See Case T-333/99 *X v ECB* [2001] ECR II-3021, para 102 and the Opinion of AG Léger in Case C-301/02 P *Tralli v ECB* [2005] ECR I-4071, para 29.

[39] Case 9/56 *Meroni*, n 35 above, 150 and Opinion of AG Léger in Case C-301/02 P *Tralli v ECB*, n 38 above, para 31.

extend its powers or avoid legal constraints simply by conferring its powers to a delegate.

3) *The exercise of the powers conferred on the agency must be subject to the same conditions as those to which it would be subject if the delegating authority were exercising them directly.*[40] The rationale of this condition is the same as that of the previous one. It applies in particular in relation to process rights and requirements such as the requirement to give reasons, publish administrative acts, and respect the rights of the defence. One of the main concerns of the Court in *Meroni* was that the exercise of the powers conferred to the agencies in issue in that case was not subject to the conditions to which it would have been subject had the High Authority exercised them directly.[41] This condition has particular importance not only as a prerequisite of the validity of delegation but also as a rule of interpretation. Where delegation has been made, it should be accepted that limitations which would constrain the delegating authority are also applicable to the delegate, even in the absence of express provision to that effect, unless such interpretation cannot be borne by the delegating act.
4) *The delegation of powers cannot be presumed but must be expressly provided.*[42] To the extent that an institution can delegate its powers, it must take an express decision to that effect and implied delegation is not valid. This was reiterated in *FMC Chemical SPRL v European Food Safety Authority (EFSA)*,[43] where, in rejecting the argument that the Commission had delegated its powers to adopt binding decisions to EFSA, the General Court stated that powers cannot be presumed to have been delegated and that, even when empowered to delegate its powers, the delegating authority must take an express decision to that effect.
5) *The powers delegated may only involve clearly defined executive powers, the use of which must be entirely subject to the supervision of the delegating institution.*[44] By contrast, discretionary powers involving a wide margin of discretion and a real transfer of responsibility cannot be delegated. This is by far the most important limitation set by *Meroni*. The reason for this restrictive approach is to ensure observance of the principle of institutional balance. Under the EU Treaties, each institution must act within the limits of its powers. If it were possible for an institution to delegate its discretionary powers, that would render the Treaties' guarantees ineffective, since it would

[40] Case 9/56 *Meroni*, n 35 above, 149–50; and Opinion of AG Léger in Case C-301/02 P *Tralli v ECB*, n 38 above, para 31.

[41] Case 9/56 *Meroni*, n 35 above.

[42] Case 9/56 *Meroni*, n 35 above, 150; and Opinion of AG Léger in Case C-301/02 P *Tralli v ECB*, n 38 above, para 31.

[43] Case T-311/06 *FMC Chemical SPRL v European Food Safety Authority (EFSA)* [2008] ECR II-88, para 66.

[44] Case 9/56 *Meroni*, n 35 above.

> replace 'the choices of the delegator by the choices of the delegate and [bring] about an actual transfer of responsibility'.[45]

Since, under *Meroni*, an institution may not delegate discretionary powers entailing a wide margin of discretion, it follows that institutions may not delegate their core functions nor can they delegate rule-making authority. Agencies may be bestowed with decision-making powers but the case law provides little guidance as to the distinction between clearly defined executive powers and powers which entail the exercise of wide discretion. In *Tralli*,[46] AG Léger appeared to suggest that this distinction can benefit by analogy from the distinction drawn in the context of Articles 202 and 211 EC[47] between essential rules which the Council cannot delegate to the Commission and implementing rules which can be so delegated. This analogy is not, however, without problems.[48] It is submitted that *Meroni* should not be interpreted restrictively. It is not to be treated as an unmovable signpost. The case itself related to a situation where the High Authority had delegated tasks falling within its core activities in the field of economic policy. As the Court observed, the ECSC Treaty provided a number of objectives which were generally defined and, to some extent, irreconcilable and thus could not all be pursued at the same time. It was for the institutions to give priority to one or other of them. Delegation of such a fundamental balancing exercise, especially in a novel international organization, appeared to amount to an abrogation of responsibilities.[49] For a case decided before the primacy and direct effect of Community law were established, *Meroni* has shown an unusual degree of endurance. The truth is, however, that, although reiterated several times, the ruling has not been tested. Post-*Meroni* the ECJ has not in fact articulated any standards on the basis of which it can be ascertained whether a given delegation of Community powers may avoid the condemnation of incompatibility. It appears, however, that the ECJ has relaxed the principle in relation to delegation of powers pertaining to the internal organization and management of EU institutions.[50] Also, a condition that must be fulfilled in order for delegation to be lawful is that the agency must be subject to an effective system of supervision and control by the delegating institution.[51] This, if respected properly, is in itself a potent means of protection. In short, on the one

[45] Case 9/56 *Meroni*, n 35 above, 152.

[46] Case C-301/02 P *Tralli*, n 38 above.

[47] These articles have now been repealed. The Lisbon Treaty provides instead for a clearer hierarchy of EU acts and provides expressly for the possibility of delegated and implementing legislation: see Articles 290–1 TFEU.

[48] See T Tridimas, 'Community Agencies, Competition Law and ECB Initiatives on Securities Settlement' (2009) 28 *Oxford Yearbook of European Law*, 216.

[49] It is difficult to see how *Meroni* could have been decided differently. The Court was faced with a new and as yet untested international experiment: the establishment of a supranational institution in the form of the High Authority to which Member States had delegated discretionary powers the exercise of which entailed the making of value judgements in the field of economic policy and compromising conflicting objectives. Allowing such a body to establish another body and delegate to it some of its powers would be not only an abrogation of its responsibilities but also an open-ended challenge to national sovereignty and the rights of individuals.

[50] See eg Case C-301/02 P *Tralli*, n 38 above.

[51] See Case 9/56 *Meroni*, n 35 above, 151.

hand, delegation must not be too restrictive: the Constitution cannot be interpreted 'to demand the impossible'.[52] On the other hand, the delegation of powers must not be 'vagrant' but 'canalized within banks that keep it from overflowing'.[53]

In *Meroni,* the ECJ saw the prohibition of the delegation of discretionary powers as being a fundamental guarantee not only of the rules which govern the powers of the Community institutions vis-à-vis each other but also of the protection of the interests of the citizen vis-à-vis the administration.

Notably, the enduring character of the *Meroni* doctrine is underpinned by political considerations.[54] The Commission, whilst acknowledging the benefits of expertise and specialization that agencies carry, has traditionally favoured a unitary conception of executive function. In the Commission's model of EU governance, delegation of powers to agencies must be seen in the light of, and be limited by, the need to respect 'the unity and integrity of the Community executive function'.[55] This function should continue to be vested to the Commission for reasons of accountability and legitimacy. Under that model, the delegation of true regulatory powers would not be compatible with the Commission's required responsibility vis-à-vis the citizens, the Member States and the other EU institutions.

In this respect, the conservatism of the ECJ, as illustrated in *Meroni,* and the executive's reluctance to let go have been self-reinforcing, leading in effect to a considerable degree of centralization in administrative decision-making and, arguably, being to the benefit of integration. Such centralization has helped the Commission to keep more control of the policy agenda than it would otherwise command, since the expansion and strengthening of independent committees would be likely to change the balance of political powers giving more control to Member States through representation in agency structures.[56]

Still, this model, based on the unity of a broadly conceived executive function, has come under stress for a number of reasons. First, the broader the powers the EU acquires in the field of risk assessment, the more it becomes necessary to rely at least *de facto* on specialist decision-making bodies. Secondly, a number of factors have contributed to greater multi-polarity in decision-making. These include the increase in the number of Member States, the rise in the powers of the Parliament, greater participation of national parliaments, the more vocal representation of industry in certain areas and, in the field of monetary law and finance, the emergence of the ECB as a powerful independent actor. Thirdly, EU agencies may provide in political terms a golden compromise. On the one hand, they meet calls for less centralization at EU level and more representation of State interests and, on the other hand, they ensure through collaborative network action and process-bound decision-making neutralization of individual national interests.

[52] See *Amalgamated Meat Cutters v Connally* 337 F. Supp. 737 (DDD 1971).

[53] Justice Cardozo in *A.L.A. Schechter Poultry Corp. v US* 295 U.S. 495 (1935).

[54] See, for more detail, the analysis of P Craig, *EU Administrative Law* (Oxford: Oxford University Press, 2006) 162–4.

[55] Communication from the Commission, *The Operating Framework for the European Regulatory Agencies* COM (2002) 718, 11 December 2002, 1.

[56] P Craig, n 54 above, 164.

Thus, in a more dispersed decision-making model, agencies may be seen as a source of unity rather than a source of repatriating competences to the Member States.

The perceived advantages of agencies are that they provide the expertise necessary to deal with highly complex assessments in technical and specialized fields, lighten the workload of the Community institutions,[57] reduce transaction costs by streamlining the decision-making process, provide independence from political interests, and even enhance citizens' understanding of the mission and tasks of the EU.[58] By contrast, the main criticisms commonly associated with administrative agencies are that they add a layer of bureaucracy, make the decision-making process less transparent, encourage blame shifting, lead to unaccountable government and detract from democracy. Agencies create problems of accountability and legitimacy. They are not elected by the citizens and may not be subject to the strict requirements of independence that constrain the judiciary. They also pose a threat to personal liberty as they often combine powers of legislating, taking individual decisions, managing and judging, ie powers which under the principle of separation of powers should be entrusted to different organs of government.[59] In the light of such criticisms, the role of the law is to strike a balance facilitating efficient and optimum decision-making in the public interest with respect to fundamental democratic principles. It is pertinent to recall here the principles outlined in the Commission's White Paper on Good Governance, namely independence, accountability, transparency and participation which provide essential yardsticks vis-à-vis which the organization, structure and conduct of EU agencies must be assessed.[60]

In the case of financial regulation and supervision, the establishment of independent EU agencies provides a number of advantages. It provides the optimum mechanism through which the interests of national supervisory authorities can be interlocked. It 'fosters federalism values'[61] whilst enabling representation of national interests to be effected in nuanced ways. The national interests are, at least to some extent, technocratic rather than overtly political since the agency is made up by national regulators. Also, decision by majority voting at agency level enables the neutralization of the interest of any individual Member State. Furthermore, it addresses two of the perceived causes of the financial crisis, namely, lack of cooperation among national regulators and lax enforcement.

[57] This is expressly recognized, eg, in the preamble to Council Regulation No 58/2003 of 19 December 2002 laying down the statute for executive agencies to be entrusted with certain tasks in the management of Community programmes [2003] OJ L 11/1, see recital 4.

[58] The perceived advantages of setting up EU agencies are stated to be the following: (a) they contribute to the decentralization and dispersal of EU activities; (b) they give a higher profile to the tasks that are assigned to them; (c) they develop scientific or technical know-how in certain well-defined fields; and (d) they integrate different interest groups and thus facilitate dialogue at a European or international level (see <http://europa.eu/agencies/community_agencies/>).

[59] For a more detailed analysis, see S G Breyer et al, n 36 above, 146–7.

[60] For a recent critique, see A Renda, 'Advancing the EU better regulation agenda: selected challenges for Europe', *Centre for European Policy Studies,* September 2008, available at <http://ssrn.com/abstract = 1291030>.

[61] CM Sharkey, 'Preemption by Preamble: Federal Agencies and the Federalization of Tort Law' (2007) 56 *DePaul Law Review* 227, 229 and available at <http://ssrn.com/abstract = 900020>.

In its White Paper on Good Governance[62] the Commission stated that, to respect the balance of powers, EU agencies can be set up provided that the following conditions are fulfilled: (a) agencies can be granted the power to take individual decisions in specific areas but cannot adopt general regulatory measures. In particular, they can be granted decision-making power in areas where a single public interest predominates and the tasks to be carried out require particular technical expertise (eg food or air safety); (b) they cannot be given responsibilities for which the Treaty has conferred a direct power of decision-making on the Commission (eg in the area of competition policy); (c) they cannot be granted decision-making power in areas in which they would have to arbitrate between conflicting public interests, exercise political discretion or carry out complex economic assessments; and (d) they must be subject to an effective system of supervision and control.

ESMA, and the ESAs more generally, do not appear to fulfil condition (c): they have power to arbitrate between conflicting interests of national supervisory authorities and exercise at least some discretion in taking individual decisions.[63] The legal framework under which they have been set up can be said to fulfil, in general, conditions (a), (b) and (d) but much will depend on how they will operate in practice. Their *de facto* influence in rule-making may prove particularly strong.

As stated above, ESMA was established as one of the three ESAs as part of the new institutional architecture. We will now examine its status, composition and powers. There is no intention to make a comprehensive analysis of Regulation 1095/2010[64] on the basis of which ESMA was established but to focus selectively on its provisions.

C. ESMA: status, legal basis, objectives and composition

ESMA is an independent EU agency with legal personality[65] established on the basis of Article 114 TFEU. Notably, in *UK v Council and Parliament*[66] the ECJ upheld the use of Article 95 EC (the predecessor to Article 114 TFEU) as the legal basis for the establishment of Community agencies. The case concerned the European Network and Information Security Agency (ENISA), whose mission is to provide supporting action in preventing and resolving network and information security problems. The ECJ held that Article 114 can be used not only for harmonization, that is, to achieve a result which could be attained by the simultaneous enactment of identical legislation in each Member State, but also to establish a new entity provided that the tasks conferred on it are closely linked to the subject matter and the objectives of harmonization legislation.[67] In upholding the use of

62 Commission, European Governance: a White Paper [2001] OJ C 287/1, p 24.
63 This point is discussed and developed in detail below.
64 Regulation 1095/2010, n 8 above.
65 ibid Article 5.
66 Case C-217/04 *UK v Council and Parliament (ENISA case)* [2006] ECR I-3771.
67 ibid para 44.

Article 114, the ECJ pointed out that ENISA was part of a normative context circumscribed by Community directives and was designed to contribute to the harmonized transposition and application of their technical requirements in national laws.[68]

The importance of the *ENISA* ruling lies in the fact that it extended the remit of Article 114 beyond harmonization legislation strictly understood, and also recognized that independent agencies may have a useful role to play in the achievement of core Community objectives. The ECJ provides in effect the green light for a multi-tier institutional model of internal market governance. Notably, AG Kokott took a much more nuanced approach and came to the conclusion that ENISA could not be established on the basis of Article 114. The Advocate General agreed that Article 114 could be used to adopt measures which effect harmonization indirectly, for example by providing for procedures that bring about approximation, but came to the conclusion that the ENISA Regulation could not be considered to be such an intermediate step. ENISA's contribution to the harmonization process remained potential and unpredictable, its establishment being not so much an intermediate step on the way to the approximation of laws as 'a step into the uncertain'.[69]

The Advocate General's view appears unduly narrow. The scope of EU powers under Article 114 should be determined by reference to the substantive content of the measures adopted. The power to harmonize includes the power to experiment with the instrumentalities of harmonization. ENISA does not have any decision-making powers but rather fulfils a coordinating and advisory function. As such, it can legitimately be viewed as an intermediate step in the process of harmonization and the fact that its contribution to that process depends on other actors is simply a reflection of its limited powers. The Opinion of the Advocate General in fact forecloses institutional experimentation of which we need more rather than less. By requiring certainty of result, it leaves, in fact, little room for innovation and hinders the quest for optimum structures of government.

Although the powers of ESMA are more extensive that those of ENISA, it is safe to conclude that its establishment, as that of the other ESAs, can validly be based on Article 114. ESMA's core objectives and tasks are closely linked to the subject matter and the objectives of harmonization legislation, as required by the ECJ in *ENISA*. ESMA's objectives are stated to contribute to the following:[70] (a) improving the functioning of the internal market, including in particular a sound, effective and consistent level of regulation and supervision; (b) ensuring the integrity, transparency, efficiency and orderly functioning of financial markets; (c) strength-

[68] The ECJ also took into account that it was a temporary agency. Under Regulation 460/2004, ENISA was established for a period of five years and the Commission was required to assess its impact in the light of its objectives and its working practices. It thus followed that, before making a decision on the fate of the Agency, the Community considered that it was appropriate to carry out an evaluation of its effectiveness and the contribution to the implementation of Community Directives on electronic communication services.

[69] *ENISA* case, n 66, above, per AG Kokott at para 36 of the Opinion.

[70] See Regulation 1095/2010, n 8 above, Article 1(5).

ening international supervisory coordination; (d) preventing regulatory arbitrage and promoting equal conditions of competition; (e) ensuring that the taking of investment and other risks is appropriately regulated and supervised, and (f) enhancing customer protection. The underlying rationale for setting up the ESAs appears in the Commission's proposal and the preambles to their founding Regulations.[71] The idea is to ensure closer cooperation and exchange of information among national supervisors, facilitate the adoption of EU-wide solutions to inter-state problems, and advance coherent application and interpretation of rules, thus replacing the existing patchwork of disparate national arrangements.

ESMA's organization includes a Board of Supervisors and a Management Board. The Board of Supervisors is composed of voting and non-voting members. Voting members are the heads of the national supervisory authorities in the field of financial services. Non-voting members are the Chairperson, one representative of the Commission, one representative of the ESRB and one representative of each of the other two ESAs.[72] Decisions of the Board are taken by simple majority except for the adoption of draft technical requirements, the budget and certain decisions affecting the Member States, which are taken by qualified majority.[73] The Management Board is made up of the Chairperson and six of the members of the Board of Supervisors who are elected by and from the voting members.[74] The Chairperson is a full-time independent professional who is appointed for a period of five years and has the power to represent ESMA. He is responsible for preparing the work of the Board of Supervisors and chairing the meetings of that Board and of the Management Board.[75] The day-to-day management of ESMA's affairs is entrusted to an Executive Director.[76]

D. Tasks and powers

ESMA combines a number of functions and contributes to law-making, supervision, coordination and enforcement. Its overarching tasks are to contribute to the establishment of common regulatory and supervisory standards and practices and the consistent application of EU measures.[77] Its powers and tasks can be divided into quasi-regulatory, executive, coordinating, advisory and administrative ones. They include the power to develop technical standards;[78] adopt guidelines and recommendations;[79] take action to prevent and terminate breach of EU law;[80] take action in emergency situations;[81] settle disagreements between national supervisors;[82] prohibit or restrict certain financial activities where this is specified by law or by a Council decision declaring an emergency situation;[83] promote and monitor the smooth functioning of colleges of supervisors;[84] take action to monitor

[71] See ibid preamble, recitals 8 and 9. [72] ibid Article 40(1). [73] ibid Article 44.
[74] ibid Article 45. [75] ibid Article 48. [76] ibid Article 51. [77] ibid Article 8(1).
[78] ibid Articles 10–15. [79] ibid Article 16. [80] ibid Article 17.
[81] ibid Article 18. [82] ibid Article 19. [83] ibid Article 9(5) [84] ibid Article 21.

and counter systemic risk;[85] participate in the development of recovery and resolution procedures;[86] contribute to strengthening and enforcing the European system of national Investor Compensation Schemes;[87] contribute to the resolution of failing key financial market participants;[88] facilitate the delegation of tasks from one national competent authority to another;[89] promote a common supervisory culture;[90] fulfil a general coordination role among competent authorities;[91] assess market developments;[92] undertake a supporting role in relations with third states;[93] provide opinions to the European Parliament, the Council or the Commission on all issues related to its areas of competence;[94] cooperate with the ESRB;[95] and strengthen consumer protection.[96] Furthermore, ESMA has been granted exclusive responsibility for the registration and supervision of Credit Rating Agencies in the EU.[97]

As a result of the above, ESMA has more extensive powers than any other agency so far created by the EU.[98] Its powers are circumscribed by EU legislative acts. In particular, it must exercise the tasks and powers assigned to it within the scope of the financial law directives stated in Article 1(2) of Regulation 1095/2010, measures adopted under them, or any future EU measures which may confer tasks upon it.[99] We will here focus selectively on some of ESMA's powers.

(1) Power to develop technical standards

One of ESMA's key functions, which gives it a quasi-regulatory role, is to develop 'technical standards'. In view of the *Meroni* limitations, those standards do not acquire binding force unless they are adopted by the Commission. Thus, to use Justice Scalia's colourful language on agencies, ESMA 'may play the sorcerer's apprentice but not the sorcerer himself'.[100] It may however be able to perform

85 See Regulation 1095/2010, n 8 above, Articles 22–4.

86 ibid Article 25.

87 ibid Article 26.

88 ibid Article 27.

89 ibid Article 28.

90 ibid Articles 29 and 30.

91 ibid Article 31.

92 ibid Article 32.

93 ibid Article 33.

94 ibid Article 34.

95 ibid Article 36.

96 ibid Article 9.

97 See Regulation No 1060/2009 as amended by Regulation No 513/2011, n 9 above.

98 Note that, in exercising its powers and carrying out its tasks, ESMA must reach common positions with the other ESAs, in particular in relation the implementation of Directive 2002/87 on the supervision of financial conglomerates [2003] OJ L 35/1 and also where a financial market participant reaches across different sectors: see Regulation 1095/2010, n 8 above, Articles 56 and 54(3).

99 See Article 1(2). That provision refers to no fewer than 14 directives which make up the core instruments of EU harmonization in financial markets and securities law. They include, among others: Directive 97/9/EC on investor-compensation schemes [1997] OJ L 84/22, Directive 98/26/EC on settlement finality in payment and securities settlement systems [1998] OJ L 166/45, Directive 2001/34/EC on the admission of securities to official stock exchange listing and on information to be published on those securities [2001] OJ L 184/1, Directive 2002/47/EC on financial collateral arrangements [2002] OJ L 168/43, Directive 2003/6/EC on insider dealing and market manipulation (market abuse) [2003] OJ L 96/16, Directive 2003/71/EC on the prospectus to be published when securities are offered to the public or admitted to trading and amending Directive 2001/34/EC [2003] OJ L 345/64, Directive 2004/39/EC on markets in financial instruments [2004] OJ L 145/1, and Directive 2004/109/EC on the harmonisation of transparency requirements in relation to information about issuers whose securities are admitted to trading on a regulated market [2004] OJ L 390/38.

100 See *Alexander v Sandoval* 532 U.S. 275 (2001), 15 of the Opinion of the Court.

legerdemain. Regulation 1095/2010 operates a framework of reverse accountability which brings ESMA's powers close to a regulatory competence: where the Commission decides not to endorse the standards submitted by ESMA or amends them, it must provide reasons for its decision.[101] Also, it can only bring into force rules which are at variance with those recommended by ESMA following a special procedure.[102] The system set up by the Regulation satisfies the *Meroni* standards since the final word rests with the Commission. In *FMC Chemical SPRL*,[103] the General Court held that, where an agency is charged with providing an opinion to the Commission from which the latter can depart, the Commission has not delegated the power to take binding decisions, since only its own final decision has binding effects vis-à-vis third parties.

ESMA may prepare two kinds of technical standards. It may elaborate draft standards to be adopted by the Commission where an EU legislative act has delegated power to the latter under Article 290 TFEU.[104] It may also develop standards to be adopted by means of implementing acts under Article 291 TFEU.[105] The difference between regulatory and implementing acts is drawn in Articles 290 and 291 TFEU but, in fact, it is far from clear. In the case of ESMA, the differences are not significant because, in both cases, the limitations applicable on its powers are equivalent. In both cases, the standards cannot come into force unless they are endorsed by the Commission.[106] Before submitting them to the Commission, ESMA must conduct open public consultations, analyse the potential costs and benefits, and request the opinion of the Securities and Markets Stakeholder Group.[107]

The term 'technical standards' is itself open to interpretation. The Commission's proposal envisaged that the powers of ESAs would be confined to 'issues of a highly technical nature' which did not involve policy decisions and whose content was tightly framed by the Community acts adopted at Level 1 of the Lamfalussy structure.[108] This is reflected in Regulation 1095/2010 which defines them as 'technical' standards, which 'shall not imply strategic decisions or policy choices' and whose 'content shall be limited by the legislative acts on which they are based'.[109] However, drawing the boundaries between technical and policy matters, especially in an area as complex as financial regulation, is notoriously difficult. The intention of the new regulatory framework is to facilitate the adoption by the

[101] See Regulation 1095/2010, n 8 above, Article 10(1), sub-para 6.

[102] See ibid Articles 10 and 15.

[103] Case T-311/06 *FMC Chemical SPRL*, n 43 above.

[104] Regulation 1095/2010, n 8 above, Article 10(1).

[105] ibid Article 15(1).

[106] ibid Article 10(1), sub-para 5; Article 15(1), sub-para 1.

[107] ibid Article 10(1), sub-para 3 and Article 15(1), sub-para 2. Note that consultation and a cost effectiveness analysis need not take place if they would be disproportionate in relation to the scope and impact of the standards proposed or in relation to the urgency of the matter.

[108] See Commission's proposal for a regulation establishing ESMA, n 33 above, 5. Under the Lamfalussy structure, Level 1 measures are legislative acts adopted by the Council and the Parliament.

[109] See Regulation 1095/2010, n 8 above, Article 10(1), sub-para 2 (regulatory standards) and Article 15(1), sub-para 1 (implementing standards). In the case of the latter 'their content shall be to determine the conditions of application of [implementing] acts'.

Commission of a pan-European financial services rulebook: 'To this end, differences in the national transposition of Community law stemming from exceptions, derogations, additions or ambiguities must be identified and removed, so that one harmonised core set of standards can be defined and applied'.[110]

A distinct feature is that, in proposing the standards to be adopted, ESMA acts by qualified majority.[111] The procedure for their approval is complex and involves a delicate balance among several actors. It is essentially the same for both regulatory and implementing standards subject to the exceptions stated below.[112] Where ESMA submits a draft technical standard, the Commission must immediately forward it to the European Parliament and the Council. Within three months of receipt, the Commission must decide whether to endorse it. Where it intends not to endorse it or endorse it in part or with amendments, it must send the draft back to ESMA explaining its objections. Within a period of six weeks, ESMA may amend the standard and resubmit it in the form of a formal opinion to the Commission. ESMA must also send a copy of its formal opinion to the European Parliament and to the Council. If, on the expiry of that six-week period, ESMA has not submitted an amended standard, or has submitted one that is not consistent with the Commission's proposed amendments, the Commission may adopt the standard with the amendments it considers relevant, or reject it.[113]

The initiative for the drafting of standards rests primarily with ESMA. Only where ESMA has failed to submit a standard despite being asked to do so by the Commission, may the latter do so itself without first receiving a draft.[114] Technical standards are adopted by means of regulations or decisions and must be published in the Official Journal.[115]

The essential difference between regulatory and implementing standards is that the adoption of the former by the Commission is subject to a negative resolution procedure by the Parliament or the Council.[116] Also, the delegation to the Commission of power to promulgate regulatory standards is subject to a sunset clause, which can be activated by the European Parliament or the Council.[117] Each of those institutions may also revoke the Commission's power at any time.[118] This is however a draconian rule and it is unlikely to be used. It thus offers limited control over the Commission's powers to adopt delegated legislation.

ESMA has already adopted draft standards in relation to AIFMD (Alternative Investment Fund Managers Directive)[119] and the Prospectus Directive[120] and initiated consultations for the adoption of various regulatory technical standards

[110] See Commission's proposal for a regulation establishing ESMA, n 33 above, 5.

[111] Regulation 1095/2010, n 8 above, Article 44(1), sub-para 2.

[112] ibid Articles 10 and 15. [113] ibid Article 10(1).

[114] ibid Article 10(2) and (3). [115] ibid Articles 10(4) and 15(4).

[116] ibid Article 13. [117] ibid Article 11. [118] ibid Article 12.

[119] Final report—ESMA's technical advice to the European Commission on possible implementing measures of the Alternative Investment Fund Managers Directive, 16 November 2011, ESMA/2011/379, <http://www.esma.europa.eu/system/files/2011_379.pdf>.

[120] See Final report—ESMA's technical advice on possible delegated acts concerning the Prospectus Directive as amended by the Directive 2010/73/EU, 4 October 2011, ESMA 2011/323, <http://www.esma.europa.eu/system/files/2011_323.pdf>.

in relation to the Credit Rating Agencies Regulation.[121] The AIFMD draft standards have been adopted following wide public consultation but not all aspects of them are necessarily welcomed by industry. At a more general level, it remains to be seen to what extent industry interests may lobby effectively either ESMA or the Commission and to what extent the Commission would follow ESMA's advice.

(2) Guidelines and recommendations

ESMA may issue guidelines and recommendations with a view to establishing consistent, efficient and effective supervisory practices. Such guidelines or recommendations may be addressed to competent authorities or even directly to financial market participants.[122] Although *stricto sensu* not binding, those instruments represent the heavy hand of soft law. The competent authorities and financial market participants must make every effort to comply with them.[123] Where a national authority does not intend to comply, it must justify its stance. ESMA must publish the fact that a competent authority does not intend to comply and may publish the reasons for non-compliance.[124] Disclosure here is clearly provided as an enforcement mechanism.

To the extent that failure to comply imposes a duty to give reasons, a guideline or a recommendation may be said to produce binding, albeit procedural, effects. Failure to give reasons might be viewed as a breach of EU law, which may activate ESMA's enforcement powers under Article 17, or lead to a disagreement among national authorities which may activate ESMA's powers under Article 19.[125] If so, it may be said that a guideline or a recommendation produces legal effects but, in any event, the party affected in both cases would be able to challenge the final decision taken against it under the procedures of Articles 17 and 19. Whether there might be any circumstances where a party could challenge the validity of ESMA guidelines remains an open question.[126] Much will depend on the circumstances of the case. The bottom line is that parties whose interests are affected by a *de facto* binding measure should have recourse to legal protection. The powers of ESMA are extensive in this regard and exceed the limited legal force of its rules. The institutional network that has been set up enables the exercise of peer pressure to an asphyxiating degree. Notably, the effect of guidelines and recommendations extends beyond competent authorities to private parties since they may require financial market participants to report in a clear and detailed way whether they

[121] For details, see <http://www.esma.europa.eu/documents/overview/10?page=5>.

[122] Regulation 1095/2010, n 8 above, Article 16(1).

[123] ibid Article 16(3).

[124] ibid Article 16(2) and (3).

[125] See further below.

[126] Note that a non-binding measure may also be important for the interpretation of national law and thus its interpretation may be the subject of a reference for a preliminary ruling: Case C-322/88 *Grimaldi v Fonds des maladies professionnelles* [1989] ECR 4407.

comply.[127] However, this fusion between forms of hard and soft law raises concerns of accountability and legal certainty.

(3) Enforcement powers: breach of EU law

One of the pivotal functions vested in ESMA is to ensure the consistent application of EU rules. To this end, Article 17 of the Regulation provides for an elaborate enforcement procedure that exists alongside the Commission's general enforcement powers under Article 258 TFEU.

The enforcement procedure of Article 17 has a preliminary, albeit formal, investigatory stage, and may involve three enforcement stages. In the first stage, ESMA may investigate on its own motion, or upon request of an institutional actor, whether a national competent authority has failed to apply EU rules correctly.[128] This stage is formal in that the competent authority is under an obligation to provide ESMA with all the information that the latter considers necessary without delay.[129] ESMA's investigation may relate to the possible breach of financial law directives or acts based on them and any further legally binding EU rules which confer tasks on ESMA.[130]

In the second stage, ESMA may, within two months of initiating its investigation, address to the competent authority a recommendation setting out the action necessary to comply with EU law. The authority must, within ten working days of receipt of the recommendation, inform ESMA of the steps it has taken or intends to take to so comply.[131] This stage does not, of course, preclude the possibility of an informal settlement without the issuing of a formal recommendation by ESMA, and one expects that a number of cases will be settled informally by means of a regulatory bargaining process.

The third stage involves the participation of the Commission. Where the competent authority has not complied with EU law within one month from receipt of ESMA's recommendation, the Commission may, after having been informed by ESMA or on its own initiative, issue a formal opinion requiring the authority to take the necessary action.[132] The Commission's act, although labelled 'formal opinion' in the final version of the Regulation, appears to be binding on the national authority, although the Regulation is here awkwardly phrased.[133] If the

[127] Regulation 1095/2010, n 8 above, Article 16(3), sub-para 4.

[128] ibid Article 17(2). The final version of the Regulation has widened the group of actors who may ask for an investigation. An investigation may be requested by the Council, the Parliament, the Commission, the Securities and Markets Stakeholders Group or another competent authority.

[129] Regulation 1095/2010, n 8 above, Article 17(2), sub-para 2.

[130] ibid Article 17(2) in conjunction with Article 1(2).

[131] ibid Article 17(3).

[132] ibid Article 17(4).

[133] Article 17(7) states that when taking action in relation to issues which are subject to a formal opinion, 'competent authorities shall comply with the formal opinion'. This suggests that, where it takes action, the competent authority is bound by the opinion but, strictly interpreted, it does not require the authority to take such action to comply. The true meaning of Article 17(7) appears, however, to be that national authorities must take the action necessary to comply. This derives from the

Commission's formal opinion is indeed binding, it follows that it can be challenged by an interested party before the Board of Appeal.[134]

The relationship between ESMA's recommendation and the Commission's opinion, although clearer than in previous versions of the Regulation, leaves some margin for doubt. Under Article 17(4), the opinion must take into account ESMA's recommendation.[135] This does not make it clear whether the Commission is bound by ESMA's recommendation, that is, whether it may require the national authority to take action other than the action specified in the recommendation. It is submitted that the Commission is in principle so bound and that, in any event, it may not impose on the national authority any additional obligations. This is because the Commission's opinion is the culmination of a process, a necessary step within which is the issuance of ESMA's recommendation. It is ESMA which determines what infringement has been committed by the national authority.

The fourth stage involves the exercise by ESMA of direct supervisory powers over financial market participants. Where a competent authority does not comply with the Commission's formal opinion and it is necessary to remedy in a timely manner the non-compliance in order to maintain or restore neutral conditions of competition or ensure the orderly functioning of the financial system, ESMA may adopt an individual decision addressed to a financial market participant.[136] That decision may require it to take the necessary action to comply with its obligations, including the cessation of any practice. ESMA's decision must be in conformity with the Commission's formal opinion.[137] This is an innovative provision in that it enables an EU agency to exercise direct supervisory powers over market participants bypassing the national supervisory authority.

ESMA may adopt a decision addressed to a market participant only 'where the relevant requirements . . . are directly applicable to financial market participants'.[138] The term 'directly applicable' suggests that ESMA may take such a decision only where the financial institution in question breaches rules contained in EU regulations or decisions and not where it breaches rules contained in directives, since the latter are not directly applicable. This limitation also flows from established principles of EU law, under which the doctrine of direct effect of directives applies only in favour of and not against individuals. Although the case law has developed in relation to national authorities, it should apply by analogy also to EU bodies. This view appears to be the correct one although the opposite might also be supported.[139]

fact that Article 17(7) applies also to ESMA decisions under Article 17(6), which are clearly binding, and from the general tenor and objectives of the enforcement procedure of Article 17.

134 See further below.

135 Regulation 1095/2010, n 8 above, Article 17(4).

136 A market participant is defined by Article 4(1) as any person in relation to whom a requirement in the legislation referred to in Article 1(2) of the Regulation (EU financial law directives) or a national law implementing such legislation applies.

137 Regulation 1095/2010, n 8 above, Article 17(6), sub-para 2.

138 ibid Article 17(6), sub-para 1.

139 It could be argued that where a directive is transposed into national law and the national supervisory authorities fail to enforce it properly, an EU agency should not be prohibited from

The power of ESMA to address a decision against a specific market participant under Article 17(6) operates without prejudice to the Commission's general enforcement power under Article 258 TFEU.[140] In practice, however, it is much easier for ESMA to utilize the procedure of Article 17 than for the Commission to bring enforcement proceedings under Article 258 TFEU.

(4) Action in emergency situations

Under Article 18 of the Regulation, ESMA enjoys extensive powers in emergency situations. In the case of adverse developments that may seriously jeopardize the orderly functioning of financial markets or the stability of the financial system, ESMA must actively facilitate and coordinate any actions undertaken by national supervisory authorities.[141]

Furthermore, it may adopt individual decisions requiring national authorities to take specific action. The text of Regulation 1095/2010 is tortuous in this respect and the scope of ESMA's power is unclear. Article 18(3) states that such power exists (a) where the Council has adopted a decision declaring an emergency situation and (b) in exceptional circumstances where coordinated action by national authorities is necessary to respond to adverse developments which may seriously jeopardize the orderly functioning of financial markets or the stability of the EU financial system. It is not readily clear whether the above conditions are cumulative or alternative. It is submitted that they must both be fulfilled cumulatively. If ESMA had power to take individual decisions even in the absence of a Council declaration of emergency, that would give it wide discretionary powers which would strain the *Meroni* principles. The cumulative application of the conditions appears also to conform to the spirit and the scheme of the Regulation and the statements made in the preamble, although the latter are not unequivocal.[142]

The determination that an emergency situation exists requires the exercise of discretion and thus, under *Meroni*, falls outside agency powers. In the final version of the Regulation, it is a power reserved to the Council and not in the hands of the Commission.[143] The Council may make such a determination by adopting a decision addressed to ESMA on its own initiative or following a request by the

intervening to enforce it. In such a case, the EU agency acts in lieu of the national competent authority and there is no direct effect of a directive since the directive has already been implemented in national law. It is, therefore, a failure of enforcement of correctly implemented EU rules and not of incorrect implementation of those rules. This view is, however, problematic from the point of view of judicial protection and legal certainty and also because it assumes a direct authority on the part of EU bodies to enforce national law norms which does not exist.

[140] Regulation 1095/2010, n 8 above, Article 17(6).

[141] ibid Article 18(1).

[142] This uncertainty did not exist in the Commission's proposal, n 33 above, Article 10 of which only granted power to ESMA to take decisions addressed to the national competent authorities (or directly to market participants) where the Commission had declared by decision the existence of an emergency situation.

[143] Article 10 of the Commission's Proposal, n 33 above, reserved that power to the Commission.

Commission, the ESRB or ESMA itself.[144] The decision to declare an emergency situation is taken after consultation[145] and is subject to a sunset clause.[146] The Council's power is open-ended. The Regulation does not specify in what cases the Council may decide that an emergency situation exists nor does it outline any factors to be taken into account.

In emergency situations and under the conditions stated above, ESMA may adopt individual decisions requiring competent authorities to take the necessary action.[147] It appears that ESMA here enjoys some discretion as to the content of the specific action to be taken but cannot impose requirements other than those already provided for in EU legislation and can only concretize the Council's emergency decision. That decision must itself be based on existing measures and is not a constitutive legal basis for taking action per se other than that found elsewhere in EU law.

For the rest, Article 18 provides for dispositions similar to those of Article 17. Where a national authority fails to comply with ESMA's decision, the latter may directly require a financial market participant to take the necessary action, including the cessation of any practice or the prohibition of a specific activity.[148] Such direct enforcement power may be exercised only where the requirements of EU law are directly applicable and only where justified by urgency. Such decisions prevail over any inconsistent previous decision adopted by the competent authorities and any action by the competent authorities must be compatible with the decisions adopted by ESMA.[149]

(5) Settlement of disagreements between national supervisory authorities

The Regulation also vests ESMA with power to settle disagreements between national competent authorities. Where a competent authority disagrees about the procedure or content of an action or inaction by another competent authority, ESMA may settle the disagreement pursuant to a procedure provided for in Article 19.[150] ESMA may intervene at the request of one or more national authorities or on its own initiative where, on the basis of objective criteria, disagreement between competent authorities from different Member States can be determined.[151]

[144] Regulation 1095/2010, n 8 above, Article 18(1).

[145] The Council consults the Commission and the ESRB and, where appropriate, the ESAs: Article 18(2). Where ESMA or the ESRB considers that an emergency situation may arise, it must issue a confidential recommendation to the Council: ibid Article 18(2), sub-para 2.

[146] The Council must review its decision at least once a month and, if it is not renewed at the end of a one-month period, it lapses: ibid Article 18(2).

[147] ibid Article 18(3).

[148] ibid Articles 18(3) and 9(5).

[149] ibid Article 18(4) and (5).

[150] The power of ESMA in this respect appears wider than that provided by the Commission's proposal, n 33 above, which limited its intervention to settle disagreements in areas where the EU rules require cooperation, coordination or joint decision-making by more than one national authorities: see Article 11(1) of the proposal.

[151] Regulation 1095/2010, n 8 above, Article 19(1), sub-para 2.

The procedure of Article 19 has three phases where ESMA intervenes respectively as a mediator, a decision-maker and a supervisor. Here, in contrast to the situation under Article 17, the gradual transformation of ESMA from a mediator to an enforcer does not require the intervention of the Commission. In the first place, where a disagreement occurs, ESMA sets a time limit for conciliation between the competent authorities, taking into account any relevant time periods specified in EU legislation as well as the complexity and urgency of the matter.[152] If the competent authorities fail to reach agreement by the end of that period, ESMA may take a decision requiring them to take specific action or to refrain from action in order to settle the matter in compliance with EU law.[153] ESMA's decision is binding on the competent authorities. In adopting its decision, ESMA does enjoy some discretionary power.[154]

Finally, if a competent authority does not comply with ESMA's decision, and thereby fails to ensure that a financial market participant complies with requirements directly applicable to it, ESMA may adopt an individual decision addressed to a financial market participant requiring the necessary action.[155] Decisions taken by ESMA pre-empt previous decisions taken by the national competent authority on the same matter.[156] The conciliation procedure operates without prejudice to the special enforcement procedure established by Article 17[157] but it is reasonable to expect that the conciliation rather than the enforcement procedure will be preferred, where possible.[158]

(6) Safeguard clause

ESMA's powers to take action in emergency situations and settle disagreements among national supervisors are subject to a safeguard clause, under which decisions adopted by ESMA may not impinge on the fiscal responsibilities of the Member States.[159] The net effect of the clause is that, where a decision of ESMA has fiscal repercussions for a Member State, its application may be suspended and it is for the Council to settle the matter. The Regulation does not specify when a decision might impinge on the fiscal responsibilities of a Member State. A Member State has to provide reasons, however, and is expressly prohibited from abusing that

[152] Regulation 1095/2010, n 8 above, Article 19(2).

[153] ibid Article 19(3).

[154] ESMA takes its decision in accordance with the procedure set out in Article 44(1), sub-paras 3 and 4; and para 53 of the preamble.

[155] Regulation 1095/2010, n 8 above, Article 19(4). This power is without prejudice to the Commission's enforcement powers under Article 258 TFEU.

[156] ibid Article 19(5).

[157] ibid Article 19(1).

[158] Note that disagreements among national authorities across sectors (ie in banking, financial markets and occupational pensions) are settled by the Joint Committee of European Supervisory Authorities: see ibid Article 20.

[159] ibid Article 38.

clause.[160] Abusive invocation may lead to enforcement proceedings under Article 17 or under Article 258 TFEU.

The procedure is briefly as follows. Where a Member State considers that a decision taken under Article 19(3)[161] impinges on its fiscal responsibilities, it may notify ESMA and the Commission that ESMA's decision will not be implemented by its competent authority. The result of the notification, which must be reasoned, is that ESMA's decision is suspended. Within a month from notification, ESMA must inform the Member State whether it maintains its decision or whether it amends or revokes it. Where ESMA maintains its decision, the decision will stand only if it is approved by the Council.[162] A notification by a Member State that a decision under Article 18(3)[163] impinges on its fiscal responsibilities also has suspensory effect but, in this case, owing to the urgency of the matter, the issue goes directly to the Council. ESMA's decision stands only if it is approved by the Council.[164]

(7) **Credit Rating Agencies**

Regulation 1060/2009, as amended by Regulation 513/2011, has granted ESMA extensive powers in relation to credit rating agencies (CRAs). ESMA is now exclusively responsible for the registration and monitoring of CRAs in the EU. Its supervisory powers are extensive[165] and include the power to request information and the supply of documents, carry out investigations and summon individuals, and carry out on-site inspections and dawn raids. It may also appoint investigators to investigate a possible infringement of Regulation 1060/2009. Failure to comply with ESMA's request for the supply of information may lead to the imposition of a fine as well as a periodic penalty payment. Also, the finding of an infringement may lead to the imposition of a penalty such as a fine, a temporary prohibition on issuing ratings or complete withdrawal of authorization. Regulation 1060/2009 contains detailed guidelines on the types of infringement which may give rise to a fine and its level and method of calculation. Whilst the Regulation seeks to protect the rights of defence and access to the file for those under investigation, the extent of the powers granted to ESMA is formidable and may well give rise to challenges on due process grounds. Judicial protection is provided through recourse to the Board of Appeal and the Court of Justice although the relationship between the two is not made clear.[166] The Regulation also curtails the

[160] ibid Article 38(5).

[161] ie a decision settling a disagreement between competent authorities.

[162] Regulation 1095/2010, n 8 above, Article 38(2).

[163] ie a decision taken in an emergency situation.

[164] Regulation 1095/2010, n 8 above, Article 38(4). If the Council decides not to revoke ESMA's decision, the Member State may ask the Council to reconsider: see the procedure under Article 38(4).

[165] See Regulation 1060/2009, Articles 15–36 as amended by Regulation 513/2011, see n 9 above.

[166] See further below. The Court of Justice has unlimited jurisdiction in relation to fines: see Article 36e of Regulation 1060/2009.

powers of national courts[167] although it must be read subject to the principles of judicial protection derived by the case law directly from the Treaty.[168]

All in all, Regulation 1060/2009 as amended provides for the first time for the granting to an EU agency of powers of supervision and investigation as extensive as those wielded by the Commission in the field of competition law. It remains to be seen whether this governance paradigm will be extended beyond the area of credit rating agencies towards increasing agency supervisory powers in other areas.

E. Good governance

The requirements of good governance include, inter alia, independence, accountability, transparency and participation.[169] The Regulation has gone to great lengths seeking to provide a good balance among those principles. Participation is ensured through the Securities and Markets Stakeholder Group[170] and the requirement to carry out open consultations. Such consultations must be conducted before proposing draft technical standards and, where appropriate, before adopting guidelines and recommendations. ESMA has already conducted consultations in relation to standards pertaining to Credit Rating Agencies, the Alternative Investments Fund Managers Directive and the Prospectus Directive. The extent to which ESMA will be willing to accommodate responses from industry remains to be seen. Transparency is ensured, among other means, through the requirement to give reasons,

[167] Under Articles 23c(6) and 23d(9), where the conduct of investigations or on-site inspections by ESMA requires a judicial warrant, the national court may carry out limited proportionality control but cannot review the necessity for ESMA's inspection or demand for information which can only be reviewed by the Board of Appeal and the General Court.

[168] Article 36d states that ESMA decisions imposing fines or periodic penalty payments can be suspended only by the General Court and not by national courts whose jurisdiction is limited over complaints that enforcement has been carried out in an irregular manner. It is doubtful however whether this provision can take precedence over the general power of national courts to grant interim relief as articulated in the case law of the ECJ which derives from the founding treaties themselves: see Joined Cases 143/88 and C-92/89 *Zuckerfabrik* [1991] ECR I-415; and Case C-465/93 *Atlanta Fruchthandelsgesellschaft I v Bundesamt für Ernährung und Forstwirtschaft* [1995] ECR I-3761.

[169] In its White Paper on Good Governance, the Commission identified five principles, namely openness, participation, accountability, effectiveness and coherence. See Commission, *European Governance: A White Paper* COM (2001) 428 final, 10–11. A principle that is of particular importance in the field of financial law but beyond the scope of this chapter is that of coherence. Much of the post-crisis institutional set-up seeks to ensure coherent cross-sector decision-making. Regulation 1095/2010 provides in this context for the establishment of a Joint Committee of European Supervisory Authorities which serves as a forum for the regular cooperation among the three ESAs and for ensuring cross-sectoral consistency. The Joint Committee is composed of the chairpersons of the three ESAs and also, where applicable, the chairperson of any sub-committee established under Article 57 of the Regulation. Article 57 provides for the establishment of a sub-committee on Financial Conglomerates and allows the Joint Committee to establish further sub-committees. Meetings of the Joint Committee are also attended by representatives of the Commission and the ESRB. The Joint Committee seeks to ensure cross-sector consistency, in particular, with regard to financial conglomerates, accounting and auditing, micro-prudential analyses of cross-sectoral developments, risks and vulnerabilities for financial stability, retail investment products, measures combating money laundering, and relations between the ESAs and the ESRB (see Article 54 of the Regulation).

[170] Regulation 1095/2010, n 8 above, Article 37.

which is incumbent on ESMA where it takes individual decisions—the publication of ESMA's annual report and corresponding obligations imposed on the Commission. The requirements of independence and accountability are examined in further detail below.

(1) Independence

A key principle which underpins the tasks and functions of ESMA is its independence. Article 1(5) of the Regulation states that, when carrying out its tasks, ESMA must 'act independently and objectively and in the interests of the Union alone'.[171] Independence is thus understood, first and foremost, as independence from political interference by the Member States and also the interests of the industry subject to regulation. Specific provisions seek to guarantee the independence of ESMA's Chairperson,[172] Board of Supervisors,[173] Management Board,[174] and its Executive Director.[175] Those provisions make clear that the principle also encompasses independence from the political institutions of the EU. Clearly, independence from national interests is not absolute. ESMA's Supervisory Board includes the heads of the national supervisory authorities who make up its voting members. When they act, they inevitably wear two hats, namely that of a national representative and that of a member of ESMA who must act 'independently and objectively in the sole interest of the Union as a whole'.[176] In that respect, the best guarantee of impartiality is the fact that Supervisory Board decides by simple or qualified majority, depending on the issue, and not by unanimity.[177]

Independence from the EU institutions is understood as functional rather than political independence since ESMA is accountable for its action to the Commission, the Parliament and the Council. Whilst ESMA enjoys functional independence, it does not enjoy much autonomy, its functions being well circumscribed. Nevertheless, it does have the power of initiative in key areas, for example, in adopting recommendations or guidelines, conducting an investigation on whether a national authority has breached EU law, or settling a disagreement among national authorities.[178] How these provisions will operate in practice remains to be seen. A danger is that the work of ESMA might be captured by the interests of the financial institutions that it is intended to regulate, but it is reasonable to suggest that that danger exists less in relation to EU agencies than in relation to national ones. Because of their federal nature and their pan-European composition, the former are further removed from the national commercial sectors and subject to fewer paths of dependency from national political and commercial interests.

[171] ibid Article 1(5), sub-para 4. [172] ibid Articles 42 and 49.
[173] ibid Article 42. [174] ibid Article 46.
[175] ibid Article 52. [176] ibid Article 42.
[177] See the decision-making procedures in Article 44, ibid.
[178] See ibid Articles 16, 17(2), 19(1).

(2) Accountability

The Regulation seeks to strike an appropriate balance between independence and accountability. The latter is understood at three levels: functional, budgetary and judicial. Functional or performance accountability is ensured directly through notification and reporting procedures incumbent on ESMA and also, indirectly, through the Commission's obligations to report to the Parliament and the Council. ESMA must submit an annual report, a multi-annual work programme, and a work plan for each coming year.[179] There are additional reporting requirements in relation to its role on credit rating agencies.[180] Also, the Chairperson of ESMA must report in writing on its main activities to the Parliament and the Council when requested, and may also be invited to make a statement and answer questions before those institutions.[181] The Commission is also subject to various reporting requirements.[182] A comprehensive review evaluating the performance of ESMA must be carried out by the Commission on a triennial basis leading to the publication of a general report on the experience acquired as a result of the operation of ESMA and the procedures laid down in the Regulation.[183] It appears that this is the principal mechanism via which not only a review of the substantive provisions of the Regulation will take place but also a comprehensive assessment of ESMA's performance.

The objective of budgetary accountability is pursued through the mechanisms provided in the detailed financial provisions of the Regulation.[184] ESMA is subject to the general financial provisions applicable to EU bodies and subject to oversight by the Commission, the budgetary authority and the Court of Auditors. Its revenue is made up by obligatory contributions from national financial services authorities, a subsidy from the EU budget, and any fees paid to it in the cases specified by EU measures.[185] Such fees are provided by the credit rating agencies regulation but the rules for the calculation are fixed by the Commission and not by ESMA itself.[186]

Judicial accountability is ensured in two ways. Decisions of ESMA are subject to challenge before a Board of Appeal and the Court of Justice. ESMA can also be subject to an action in damages.

179 See Regulation 1095/2010, n 8 above, Article 43(4), (5), (6).

180 See Regulation on credit rating agencies, n 9 above, Article 21(5) and (6).

181 Regulation 1095/2010, n 8 above, Article 50.

182 Thus, eg, the Commission must notify the Council and the Parliament as soon as it adopts a technical standard and must draw a report in respect of the powers delegated to it to adopt technical standards before the expiry of the four-year period for which the delegation has been conferred upon it: see Regulation 1095/2010, n 8 above, Article 11(1) and (2). It must also draw an annual report on the suitability of entrusting ESMA with further powers of direct supervision of institutions of pan-European reach: Article 81(3).

183 ibid Article 81(1).

184 ibid Articles 62–5.

185 See ibid Article 62(1).

186 See Regulation No 1060/2009, n 9 above, Article 19(2).

The Board of Appeal is a joint body of the ESAs and is best described as an independent administrative review body. It is composed of six members and six alternates, who must be persons of high repute with a proven record of knowledge and experience in financial markets and must include legal expertise.[187] They are appointed for a term of five years which can be renewed once.[188] Although there are several guarantees,[189] independence is somewhat compromised by their method of appointment and the decision-making procedure of the Board. Each ESA appoints two members and two alternates from a shortlist drawn up by the Commission following a public call for expressions of interest.[190] Decisions of the Board are taken by majority of at least four out of its six members but the majority must include at least one of the two members appointed by the ESA to whose decision the challenge relates.[191]

Any natural or legal person, including competent authorities, may appeal against a decision of ESMA that is addressed to that person or against a decision which, although in the form of a decision addressed to another person, is of direct and individual concern to the applicant.[192] It is reasonable to expect that the Board of Appeal will follow the interpretation of direct and individual concern provided by the ECJ but it is arguably not bound to do so and could adopt a more expansive interpretation. Any binding decision of ESMA is subject to challenge. The decisions which appear to be more intrusive and, in practice, are more likely to be challenged are those pertaining to breach of EU law (Article 17), emergency situations (Article 18), disagreements between competent authorities (Article 19), and decisions pertaining to CRAs. The Regulation does not provide for challenge against regulatory acts as ESMA does not have the power to adopt binding acts of general application.[193]

The Board of Appeal decides after an *inter partes* adjudication process. It may confirm the contested decision or remit the case to ESMA which is bound by the Board's decision and must adopt an amended decision.[194] Decisions of the Board of Appeal can be challenged before the Court of Justice.[195] It appears that an action against ESMA can be launched directly before the Court of Justice in the following cases: where there is no right of appeal before the Board of Appeal, where the action

[187] Regulation 1095/2010, n 8 above, Article 58(1) and (2). Since the Board of Appeal is a joint body, the regulations establishing the other ESAs contain similar provisions to those of Regulation 1095/2010. See, in particular, Regulation 1093/2010 establishing the European Banking Authority, n 8 above, Articles 58–61 and Regulation 1094/2010 establishing the European Insurance and Occupational Pensions Authority, n 8 above, Articles 58–61.

[188] Regulation 1095/2010, n 8 above, Article 58(4).

[189] These are prescribed, inter alia, in Articles 58 and 59. Members may not be removed during their term of office except for gross misconduct; in making their decisions, they must act independently in the public interest and not bound by any instructions; and they must not adjudicate in any case where they have a conflict of interests.

[190] ibid Article 58(3).

[191] ibid Article 58(6).

[192] ibid Article 60(1).

[193] cf Article 263(4) TFEU. But see the discussion above on guidelines and recommendations.

[194] Regulation 1095/2010, n 8 above, Article 60(5).

[195] ibid Article 61(1).

is launched by a Member State or an EU institution, and where the applicant brings an action for failure to act.[196] However, where the applicant has the possibility of recourse to the Board of Appeal, it appears that it cannot initiate proceedings before the Court of Justice before exhausting remedies before the Board although the Regulation is silent in this regard.

ESMA may also be liable in damages in accordance with general principles common to the laws of the Member States.[197] Although actions can be expected to be very rare, it is worth recalling that the laws of the Member States view liability of supervisory authorities in the financial sector as exceptional and subject it to stringent conditions.[198] The guiding principle here will remain that of *Bergaderm*.[199] Where an authority enjoys little or no discretion, a breach is easier to establish. In that respect, liability would be easier to establish in the case of violations of specific operational duties than in the case of policy or discretionary decisions.

F. Conclusion

Following the 2008 financial crisis, the Commission pioneered a far-reaching reform of the institutional and regulatory framework governing financial services. The new model is based on four components: the introduction of supervisory agencies at Community level; a higher degree of harmonization through the introduction of a pan-European rulebook; greater consistency in the application of EU rules; and the transfer of direct supervisory powers over market participants to EU agencies although such transfer is limited, hesitant and heavily conditioned. The Commission's response to the financial crisis appears to have set in motion a substantial shift in the balance of powers between national and EU regulators and opened the road for the establishment of a fully-fledged system of EU federal securities regulation.

ESMA and its sister ESAs enjoy more extensive powers than any other agency created at EU level. Their influence and contribution to supervision, enforcement and regulation are likely to exceed their legal powers understood *sticto sensu*. ESMA represents the heavy hand of soft law and heralds an era of direct EU presence in supervision and monitoring of compliance. The new regulatory framework reduces significantly the autonomy of national regulators and, through a network approach, hard-wires national interests into EU-wide structures. It may be that smaller Member States stand to lose more here. Those with developed financial markets and well-resourced experienced regulators are likely to provide leadership and set

[196] Regulation 1095/2010, n 8 above, Article 61.

[197] ibid Article 69.

[198] See P Athanassiou, 'Bank Supervisors' Liability: a European Perspective' (2011) *Oxford Yearbook of European Law*, forthcoming, and see further Case C-222/02 *Paul and Others v Bundesrepublik Deutschland* [2002] ECR I-9425.

[199] Case C-352/98 P *Laboratoires Pharmaceutiques Bergaderm and Goupil v Commission* [2000] ECR I-5291.

the agenda within ESMA. Leaving aside *Meroni* concerns, the key criterion to judge the new entities is not by how much discretion they grant to the ESAs but by how much they constrain the discretion of national supervisors. Whether the new structure will be able to lead to better regulation and enforcement and avert a future financial crisis remains to be seen. Still, in view of the Eurozone crisis, one may be excused the feeling that the Commission stands fighting the last war. The challenge is now not how to achieve a higher level of enforcement by financial institutions but how to improve fiscal discipline by national governments.

PART II

THE INTERNAL MARKET

Evolution and Regulation

5

Some Problems of the Customs Union and the Internal Market

*Laurence W Gormley**

A. Introduction

The original European Economic Community was based upon a customs union which covered all trade in goods and involved the prohibition between Member States of customs duties on imports and exports and of all charges having equivalent effect, and the adoption of a common customs tariff in their relations with third countries.[1] This formula and this basis have survived the Treaty renumbering and renaming exercises,[2] and are now to be found in Article 28(1) TFEU. That provision at once explains the twin aspects of the customs union, its internal and external facets. Article 9(2) EEC proclaimed that the benefits of the elimination of customs duties and charges having equivalent effect[3] and of the elimination of quantitative restrictions and measures having equivalent effect[4] extended not merely to products originating in Member States but also to products coming from third countries which are in free circulation in Member States. This formula too has survived intact as regards the beneficiaries, but while the removal of otiose transitional provisions and renumbering has now made the formula in Article 28(2) TFEU considerably shorter, an unfortunate drafting error has gone unnoticed: Article 28(3) refers to Article 30 TFEU (which is logical) but also to Chapter 2 of Part Three, Title II of the TFEU (which contains only Article 33 TFEU, dealing with customs cooperation between the Member States and between them and the Commission); the correct reference, however, should be to Chapter 3 of Part Three, Title II (which contains Articles 34–7 TFEU) and is the clear successor to Chapter 2 of Part Three, Title I of the EC Treaty (which contained

* Professor of European Law & Jean Monnet Professor, University of Groningen; Professor at the College of Europe, Bruges; Barrister. This contribution seeks to reflect John Usher's interest in the customs union, as expressed through his publications, as well as the author's extensive interest in that subject.

[1] Article 9(1) EEC.

[2] Becoming Article 23(1) EC.

[3] Articles 12–17 EEC (Part Two, Title I, Chapter 1, Section 1 of the EEC Treaty).

[4] Articles 30–7 EEC (Part Two, Title I, Chapter 2 of the EEC Treaty).

Articles 28–31 EC), as is apparent from the Table of Equivalences[5]. For some reason, this has not (yet) been rectified in the corrigenda to the Treaty of Lisbon.[6] However, there is no suggestion that it was the intention of the drafters of the Treaty of Lisbon to change this essential element of the functioning of the customs union.[7]

The customs union formed one of the key elements of the common market established by the EEC Treaty; but, regrettably, that common market concept has now disappeared from the Treaty on the Functioning of the European Union (TFEU). With the development of the internal market concept,[8] the precise relationship between the common market and the internal market had become somewhat unclear, with the Court seeming to make no distinction between them,[9] despite attempts in the literature to keep them separate.[10] The tale of the disappearance of the common market at French insistence in the negotiation of the Treaty of Lisbon has been well recounted by Riley,[11] and the other Member States were determined to retain the importance of the weapons of competition and merger control in the arsenal of the Union's *acquis*.[12] But despite the disappearance of the common market, the role of the customs union as the (economic) foundation stone of the Union's policies and internal actions is unchallenged. The role of the customs union has not, however, stood still. This contribution seeks to examine

[5] Table of Equivalences [2010] OJ L83/361, 368.

[6] Treaty of Lisbon, [2007] OJ L 306/1, corrigenda [2008] OJ C 111/56; [2009] OJ C 290/1.

[7] Indeed, as John Usher recalled in his contribution on 'The consequences of the Customs Union' in N Emiliou and D O'Keeffe (eds), *The European Union and World Trade Law* (Chichester: John Wiley, 1996) 105, 106, the Court interpreted the old Article 95 EEC (now Article 110 TFEU) so as to extend the benefit of the Treaty provisions prohibiting discriminatory taxation of imports and exports to benefit products produced outside the Community but in free circulation in the Member States, see Case 193/85 *Cooperativa Co-Frutta Srl v Amministrazione delle Finanze dello Stato* [1987] ECR 2085, paras 24–9. See too, in relation to what is now Article 34 TFEU, confirming that the free movement of goods benefits products in free circulation, Case 119/78 *SA des Grandes Distilleries Peureux v Directeur des Services Fiscaux de la Haute-Saône et du Territoire de Belfort* [1979] ECR 975, paras 23–6.

[8] With the entry into force in 1987 of the Single European Act; now set out in Article 26(2) TFEU. Generally on the internal market, see R Bieber et al (eds), *1992: One European Market?* (Baden-Baden: Nomos, 1988); C Barnard and J Scott (eds), *The Law of the Single European Market* (Oxford: Hart Publishing, 2002); (1989/1) *LIEI* (whole issue); N Nic Shuibhne (ed), *Regulating the Internal Market* (Cheltenham: Edward Elgar, 2006); GT Davies, *EU Internal Market Law*, 2nd edn (London: Cavendish, 2006); C Barnard, *The Substantive Law of the EU: The Four Freedoms*, 3rd edn (Oxford: Oxford University Press, 2010); N Reich, *Understanding EU Internal Market Law* (Antwerp: Intersentia, 2011), and G Slynn, *Introducing a European Legal Order* (London: Stevens/Sweet & Maxwell, 1992) 41–84.

[9] The Court certainly saw the common market in the Community (now the Union) as analogous to the domestic market of a single state, eg Case 270/80 *Polydor Ltd et al v Harlequin Record Shops Ltd et al* [1980] ECR 329, paras 16–22; Case 15/81 *Gaston Schul Douane-Expediteur BV v Inspecteur der Invoerrechten en Accijnzen, Roosendaal* [1982] ECR 1409, para 33.

[10] eg LW Gormley, 'Competition and Free Movement: Is the Common Market the same as the Internal Market?' (2002) 13:6 *EBLR* 517–22.

[11] A Riley, 'The EU Reform Treaty and the competition protocol: undermining EC competition law' (2007) *ECLR* 703–7.

[12] See Protocol (No 27) on the Internal Market and Competition, annexed to the TEU and TFEU [2010] OJ C 83/309 which makes it clear that the internal market referred to in Article 3(3) TEU includes a system ensuring that competition is not distorted. It should be recalled that both the customs union and the establishment of the competition rules necessary for the functioning of the internal market fall within the Union's exclusive competence, Article 3(1)(a), (b) TFEU.

some of the problem areas in the functioning of the customs union and how they have been and are being addressed: in part these are internal problems, in part external problems, but they are all the subject of not a little controversy and involve both theoretical and practical considerations.

B. Changing instruments of the customs union

Over the years, there has been an ongoing battle to strengthen the customs union by limiting national discretion as far as possible, initially through the move in the mid-1980s from directives to regulations, which are much stronger instruments of coordination; and subsequently through achievement of a long-standing ambition[13] with the introduction of codification through the Community Customs Code (CCC),[14] and now through the Modernised Customs Code (MCC)[15] and improvements designed to take account of risk analysis and the opportunities afforded by information technology developments. The simplification achieved by the CCC and its implementing regulation (the CCIP)[16] was considerable,[17] with the repeal of 105 measures in total, but the CCIP has now been amended 41 times (including twice as a result of accessions) and has expanded so much that its consolidated text covers 416 pages of A4 paper, with the Annexes bringing the total to 1086 pages: simplification is not always for the faint-hearted. The CCC has now been amended seven times (including twice as a result of accessions) and it was felt that the time was ripe for further renewal. Pressure for renewal came—as in the past—from a combination of internal and external developments, as well as from recognition that electronic declarations and processing have become the rule,[18] and

[13] Already in the *General Programme for Harmonization of Customs Legislation*, Commission Document SEC (71) 682 final (28 April 1971).

[14] Council Regulation 2913/92 establishing the Community Customs Code [1992] OJ 1992 L 302/1, as amended: as to the latest consolidation, see <http://eur-lex.europa.eu/LexUriServ/LexUriServ.do?uri=CONSLEG:1992R2913:20070101:EN:PDF>. See LW Gormley, *EU Law of Free Movement of Goods and Customs Union* (Oxford: Oxford University Press, 2009); T Lyons, *EU Customs Law*, 2nd edn (Oxford: Oxford University Press, 2008).

[15] Regulation 450/2008 of the European Parliament and of the Council laying down the Community Customs Code (Modernised Customs Code) [2008] OJ L 145/1. This is as yet only partially in force, see Article 188.

[16] Commission Regulation 2454/93 laying down provisions for the implementation of Council Regulation (EEC) No 2913/92 establishing the Community Customs Code [1993] OJ L 253/1, as amended: as to the latest consolidation, see <http://eur-lex.europa.eu/LexUriServ/LexUriServ.do?uri%20=%20CONSLEG:1993R2454:20110101:EN:PDF>.

[17] See LW Gormley, 'Consolidation, Codification and Improving the Quality of Community Legislation—the Community Customs Code' in N Emiliou and D O'Keeffe (eds), see n 7 above, 124–35.

[18] As to a paperless environment for customs and trade, see Decision 70/2008 of the European Parliament and of the Council on a paperless environment for customs and trade [2008] OJ L 23/21; see too Decision 2004/387 of the European Parliament and of the Council on the interoperable delivery of pan-European e-Government services to public administrations, businesses and citizens, corrigenda [2004] OJ L 181/25. Article 5(1) MCC (when it enters into force) will make express provision for the use of electronic data-processing techniques for exchanges of data, accompanying documents, decisions and notifications between customs authorities and between economic operators

that the paper-based system of the Single Administrative Document (itself in its time revolutionary for the number of forms it replaced) has run its course. Internally, the MCC reflects the expiry of the ECSC Treaty and the developments resulting from the Accessions of 2005 and 2007; externally, it takes account of the Revised Kyoto Convention.[19] The changes in recent years to the CCIP,[20] and the approach now taken in the MCC itself, reflect developments in the changing role of customs authorities, as the importance of customs duties collection has declined over the successive rounds of multilateral liberalization of world trade and with the conclusion of a considerable number of specific multilateral or bilateral trade agreements with third countries. Thus the application of non-tariff measures has become increasingly important.[21] Issues concerning security and safety, the fight against counterfeit goods, money laundering and drugs, and the application of sanitary, health, environmental and consumer protection measures have all increased in importance in recent years as areas of customs activity, meaning that customs officers have become jacks-of-all trades; the collection of VAT and excise duties on importation and the exemption of goods from such taxes on exportation have also increased in importance. The move to electronic declarations and risk-based analysis, with a lighter touch for authorized economic operators, has enabled a streamlining of bureaucracy, with resulting benefits for business, while at the same time permitting more intelligence-based targeting of suspect activity. This culture change, which is also reflected in the working methods of national tax administrations which use risk analysis and confer trusted status on appropriate economic operators to lighten their administrative burden while targeting their activities more effectively, moves customs administrations to the forefront of policy implementation over a wide range of issues. As this occurs, the susceptibility of national customs administrations to challenge and the possibility of reviewing the Commission's activities in relation to various issues of customs law and practice become steadily more important.

C. Challenging customs measures

A particular difficulty has arisen not so much in challenging decisions of national customs administrations (the CCC and the MCC make it clear that a person

and between economic operators and customs authorities required under the customs legislation, and the storage of such data as required under such legislation.

[19] 26 June 1999, in force 3 February 2006, see Council Decision 2003/231 concerning the accession of the European Community to the Protocol of Amendment to the International Convention on the simplification and harmonisation of customs procedures (Kyoto Convention) [2003] OJ L 86/21, as amended by Decision 2004/485 [2004] OJ L162/113. The (now) EU is party to the revised Convention and its Appendices I and II.

[20] Many of these changes reflect and anticipate the approach taken in the MCC.

[21] In particular as regards the administration of import quotas at favourable rates, although this has always been an important task; as to a good example of how sensitive an issue this can be, see Case 175/84 *Krohn & Co Import-Export GmbH & Co KG v Commission* [1987] ECR 97. Other types of trade policy instruments (such as anti-dumping measures and safeguard measures) also remain important. See, further, I van Bael and J-F Bellis, *EU Anti-Dumping and other Trade Defence Instruments*, 5th edn (Alphen aan den Rijn: Wolters Kluwer, 2011).

directly and individually concerned by a decision taken by the customs authorities has the right of appeal),[22] but in mounting a challenge when at EU level the Commission issues a regulation concerning the customs classification of goods in the Combined Nomenclature (CN). In principle, binding tariff information (BTI) is issued by the national customs authorities to whom application is made, and that information is binding on the competent authorities of all the Member States.[23] However, where a regulation is adopted and the BTI is incompatible with the regulation, the BTI ceases to be valid. Attempts to overturn such regulations have almost always met with failure,[24] although Sony scored a spectacular victory in

[22] Article 243(1), 1st sub-para CCC; Article 23(1), 1st sub-para MCC. Appeals may also be lodged by those who have not received a requested decision within the appropriate time limit, Article 243(1), 2nd sub-para CCC; Article 23(1), 2nd sub-para MCC. The appeal procedure may be exercised in two stages: administratively before the customs authorities, and then before an independent body, which may be a judicial authority or an equivalent specialized body, Article 243(2) CCC. Article 23 MCC makes three innovations: first, it alters this to provide that the right of appeal may be exercised in at least two stages; secondly, the first stage may be before the customs authorities or a judicial authority or other body, and the second stage before a higher independent body, or an equivalent specialized body (Article 23(2) MCC); and thirdly, Article 23(4) requires Member States to ensure that the appeals procedure enables the prompt confirmation or correction of decisions taken by the customs authorities. A curious omission in the drafting is the omission of the requirement that at least the second stage of the appeal must be before a court or tribunal capable of making a reference to the Court of Justice under Article 267 TFEU. If the (first or second stage) appeal is to a judicial authority, there is no problem, but if it is to an 'other body' or to 'an equivalent specialised body' as the case may be, the Member State must provide that such a body is to be deemed to be a court or tribunal for the purposes of Article 267 TFEU, otherwise there will be a denial of justice and an infringement of Article 4(3) TEU: cf in relation to remedies in public procurement (admittedly somewhat more specifically regulated), Directive 89/665 on the coordination of the laws, regulations and administrative provisions relating to the application of review procedures to the award of public supply and public works contracts [1989] OJ L 395/33, as amended, Article 2(9) and Directive 92/13 coordinating the laws, regulations and administrative provisions relating to the application of Community rules on the procurement procedures of entities operating in the water, energy, transport and telecommunications sectors [1992] OJ L 76/14, as amended, Article 2(9) which make specific mention of what is now Article 267 TFEU. The two-stage procedure is required under the Revised Kyoto Convention, General Annex, Chapter 10, which refers to an internal stage followed by an independent stage. Both the CCC and the MCC in fact leave it open to Member States to make both the first and second stages of an appeal, judicial or otherwise, independent, bearing in mind the wide diversity of approaches in the national legal systems, and the fact that sometimes the appeals procedure is one-size-fits-all in its approach across the board of national administrative and tax law, and thus introducing specific procedures would fragment rather than improve national legal procedures, as was noted by the Economic and Social Committee in Opinion on the proposal for a Council Regulation (EEC) establishing a Community Customs Code, and the proposal for a Council Regulation (EEC) determining the cases and the special conditions under which the temporary importation arrangements may be used with total relief from import duties [1991] OJ C 60/5, and cited by the Court of Justice in Case C-1/99 *Kofisa Italia Srl v Ministero delle Finanze, Servizio della Riscossione dei Tributi Concessione Provincia di Genova San Paolo Riscossioni Genova SpA* [2001] ECR I-207. In practice, there can be little to criticize in this solution as the spirit of the Revised Kyoto requirement of a two-tier appellate procedure is observed, even if the MCC permits greater flexibility to the Member States. Lyons, n 14 above, 516 observes that the overriding requirement that the appeals procedure be just is assumed.

[23] Article 11 CCIP. As to BTI issued for a third party by the customs authorities of another Member State, see Case C-495/03 *Intermodal Transports BV v Staatssecretaris van Financiën* [2005] ECR I-8151. As to an example of the problems relating to the invocation of BTI, see Case C-153/10 *Staatssecretaris van Financiën v Sony Supply Chain Solutions (Europe) BV* [2011] ECR I-not yet reported (Transcript, 7 April 2011).

[24] eg Case 40/84 *Casteels v Commission* [1985] ECR 667, and the orders in Case T-120/98 *Alce v Commission* [1999] ECR II-1395, Case T-49/00 *Iposea v Commission* [2001] ECR II-163, and Case

relation to its Play Station®2.[25] The regulations on customs classification are now termed Commission implementing regulations[26] and are, it is submitted, classic examples of regulatory acts which are of direct concern to importers and which do not involve implementing measures. Accordingly, it should be easier for those concerned to challenge such implementing regulations, which are adopted after discussion in the Nomenclature Committee, as applicants no longer need to demonstrate individual concern in a challenge before the General Court or on appeal to the Court of Justice. The same approach must apply in respect of any Commission regulations that might be adopted affecting binding origin information (BOI) issued by the national customs authorities. The Commission also issues communications relating to the end of validity of BTI issued by national customs authorities as a result of international tariff measures,[27] but these communications, it is submitted, are not open to review under Article 263 TFEU as they are merely notifications of international action, rather than Commission decisions as such.

D. Treatment of counterfeit goods within the Union

Quite a spectacular body of case law has grown up relating to the treatment of counterfeit and pirated products, which regrettably is of growing economic importance, given a number of circumstances: the top drawer luxury brands do not have seasonal price-reduction sales and succeed in achieving and maintaining very high price levels within the European Union; price differentiation between inside and outside the European Union is rife. The EU legislature and Court of Justice have preferred the (legitimate) interests of the owners of industrial and commercial property rights to the alleged charms of price competition for consumers,[28] who

T-82/06 *Apple Computer International v Commission* [2008] ECR II-279 (which, it is submitted, is just manifestly wrongly decided).

[25] Case T-243/01 *Sony Computer Entertainment Europe Ltd v Commission* [2003] ECR II-4189.

[26] eg Commission Implementing Regulation 447/2011 concerning the classification of certain goods in the Combined Nomenclature [2011] OJ L 122/63; Commission Implementing Regulation 602/2011 concerning the classification of certain goods in the Combined Nomenclature [2011] OJ L 163/8; Commission Implementing Regulation 603/2011 concerning the classification of certain goods in the Combined Nomenclature [2011] OJ L 163/10; Commission Implementing Regulation 604/2011 concerning the classification of certain goods in the Combined Nomenclature [2011] OJ L 163/12. Strangely, earlier regulations of this type adopted since the entry into force of the Treaty of Lisbon (on 1 December 2009) still retained the previous designation of Commission regulation.

[27] See, eg, Communication in accordance with Article 12(5)(a) of Council Regulation (EEC) 2913/92 on the information provided by the customs authorities of the Member States concerning the classification of goods in the customs nomenclature [2011] OJ C 174/3.

[28] As to the legislature, see now Directive 2008/95 to approximate the laws of the Member States relating to trade marks [2008] OJ L 299/25, Article 7 (which reproduces the terms of its predecessor, Directive 89/104 to approximate the laws of the Member States relating to trade marks [1989] OJ L 40/1, Article 7). As to the Court of Justice, see Case C-355/96 *Silhouette International Schmied GmbH & Co KG v Harlauer Handelsgesellschaft mbH* [1998] ECR I-4799; Case C-173/98 *Sebago Incet et al v G-B Unicv SA* [1999] ECR I-4103; Joined Cases C-414–416/99 *Zino Davidoff et al v A & G Imports Ltd et al* [2001] ECR I-8691 (although the Court in effect simply confirmed its approach in the celebrated *EMI v CBS* litigation, see, eg, Case 51/75 *EMI Records Ltd v CBS United Kingdom Ltd* [1976] ECR 811).

might be forgiven for thinking that, as far as concerns those goods which are not counterfeit at all but genuine goods merely not originally destined for sale in the EU, the interest of the consumer in price competition has been sacrificed on the altar of global profiteering through price discrimination. The parallel importer acting solely within the EU is the darling of EU law, but not the parallel importer with an involvement outside. Just as in anti-dumping cases, the Commission has taken a long-term view of consumer interests (consumers are better served by employment being safeguarded by measures to combat unfair trade practices) rather than a short-term view of the (apparent) benefit to the consumer of the availability of goods at low (ie dumped) prices, so too the EU legislature and the Court have regard to myriad other considerations than mere price advantage when balancing the interests of right holders and consumers. Real counterfeiting is indeed a major problem, and in some cases the sale of counterfeit products has serious health and safety risks, not to mention the consumer protection issues that arise through deception as to the nature of the goods being offered.

The regime governing the treatment of counterfeit goods, pirated goods, and, more generally, goods infringing intellectual property rights, is currently laid down in Regulation 1383/2003.[29] It does not apply to the situation of genuine goods not originally destined for the EU or similar situations,[30] nor does it apply where a traveller's personal baggage contains goods of a non-commercial nature within the limits of the duty-free allowance and there are no material indications to suggest the goods are part of commercial traffic.[31] Thus an individual who bought a low-value fake product outside the EU does not suddenly find the full weight of the Regulation being applied against them on entering the EU, but national limitations may apply on the basis of national law.[32] The Regulation permits action to be taken when goods are suspected of infringing an intellectual property right in certain situations, namely when they are entered for release for free circulation, export or re-export, and when they are found during checks on goods entering or leaving the Community customs territory, placed under a suspensive procedure,[33] in the

[29] Council Regulation 1383/2003 concerning customs action against goods suspected of infringing certain intellectual property rights and the measures to be taken against goods found to have infringed such rights [2003] OJ L 196/7. As to these definitions, see Council Regulation 1383/2003, Article 2(1)(a)–(c). The Commission has proposed the repeal and replacement of this Regulation, see Commission Document, Proposal for a Regulation of the European Parliament and of the Council concerning customs enforcement of intellectual property rights COM (2011) 285 final, which is discussed below.

[30] Council Regulation 1383/2003, n 28 above, Article 3(1).

[31] ibid Article 3(2).

[32] This policy may vary from Member State to Member State. The Dutch customs permit an individual to bring in a maximum of three fake watches, 250 ml perfume or eau de toilette, three picture and sound carriers other than master copies (eg DVDs, but if there are three films on one such carrier that counts as three), and three pieces or pairs of other goods; data carriers are not permitted. The items must accompany the passenger, and postal or courier imports will be seized: <http://www.douane.nl/particulier/reizigersbagage/reizigersbagage-12.html>.

[33] ie external transit, customs warehousing, inward processing in the form of suspension, processing under customs control or temporary importation, Article 84(1)(a) CCC. The mere placing of goods under a suspensive customs procedure does not of itself infringe intellectual property rights in the European Union: Case C-23/99 *Commission v France* [2000] ECR I-7653, paras 42–3; Case C-405/03 *Class International BV v Colgate-Palmolive Company et al* [2005] ECR I-8735, para 47; Case C-281/05

process of being re-exported subject to notification or placed in a free zone or free warehouse. The customs authorities may suspend the release of goods or detain them, initially on their own initiative or as a result of an application for measures to be taken; there are also provisions relating to the destruction of goods in appropriate circumstances and allocation of costs. The Regulation does not deal with situations in which the goods have already been placed in free circulation in a Member State, as it is possible for action to be taken domestically against the sale or possession of counterfeit goods; it does, however, cover goods in transit from a third country to another third country through the European Union.[34] The external transit of such non-Union goods is based on a legal fiction that they have not entered the customs territory of the Union, but external transit operations may well have a direct effect on the Union's internal market, because of the risk that the goods may be fraudulently placed on the Union market instead of completing their journey.[35] The Court has refused to let arguments as to the effectiveness of the (predecessor) Regulation justify interference with the free movement of goods within the Union;[36] and the detention of goods from Member State A in transit in Member State B to Member State C could not be justified in the interests of the protection of intellectual property rights.[37] On the other hand, if an act is undertaken which necessarily entails the goods being put on the market in Member State B, the proprietor of the right will be able to act.[38] The Court has also recognized

Montex Holdings Ltd v Diesel SpA [2006] ECR I-10881, para 21; Joined Cases C-446/09 and 495/09 *Koninklijke Philips Electronics NV and Nokia Corporation v Lucheng Meijing Industrial Company Ltd et al and Her Majesty's Commissioners of Revenue and Customs* [2011] ECR I-not yet reported (Transcript, 1 December 2011), para 56.

[34] Case C-383/98 *The Polo/Lauren Company LP v PT Dwidua Langgeng Pratama International Freight Forwarders* [2000] ECR I-2519, paras 26–9 (in relation to the predecessor regime). See further Case C-281/05 *Montex Holdings Ltd v Diesel SpA* [2006] ECR I-10881. It may be that imitations and copies coming from one non-Member State being transported to another may well actually comply with the intellectual property laws in force in each of those countries. In view of the EU's commitment to the progressive abolition of barriers in international trade, now set out in Article 206 TFEU, such goods must be able to pass without hindrance in transit via the EU from one non-Member State to another, in the absence of any indication that they could be fraudulently diverted so as to be sold within the EU. On the basis of TRIPS Agreement [1994] OJ L 336/214, Article 69, appropriate measures to deal with infringement of the intellectual property law of the declared destination non-Member State could be taken in cooperation with the customs authorities of that State.

[35] Case C-383/98 *The Polo/Lauren Company*, n 34 above, para 34.

[36] Case C-23/99 *Commission v France* [2000] ECR I-7653, para 31. See further Case C-115/02 *Administration des douanes et droits indirects v Rioglass SA & Transremar SL* [2003] ECR I-12705.

[37] Case C-23/99 *Commission v France*, n 36 above, para 45. That case involved spare parts for motor vehicles in transit from Spain, where they were lawfully manufactured, to Ireland via France; the detention for up to 10 days was to give the right holder in France the chance to have the goods inspected by an expert to see if they were unauthorized copies of spare parts. The Court found that as the mere transit of unauthorized copies did not form part of the specific subject matter of design rights, the conducting of an inspection by an expert could not justify detention under customs control; any investigation of the origin and destination of the goods in transit could be carried out on the spot if the transporter was in possession of the relevant documents or if he could obtain them immediately.

[38] Case C-405/03 *Class International*, n 33 above, paras 58–61 (a trade mark owner can assert his right of opposition only against a trader who puts or is preparing to put non-Union goods bearing the mark on the market in the EU, or else offers or sells the goods to another trader who is bound to put them on the market in the EU, but the mere fact that the other trader is likely to put the goods on the market in the EU is not on its own a sufficient ground for opposition on the basis of a trade mark

that an infringement of rights may take place if, during the placement of goods under a suspensive procedure in the EU's customs territory, or even before the arrival of the goods in that territory, goods coming from a non-Member State are the subject of a commercial act directed at consumers within the EU, such as a sale, offer for sale, or advertising.[39] Moreover, it has now accepted that other circumstances may also lead to temporary detention by the customs authorities of a Member State where imitations or copies are declared under a suspensive procedure: the destination of such goods is often either unknown or unreliably declared; given the furtive nature of the activities of traffickers of such goods, the detention of such goods cannot be made dependent on proof that the goods have already been sold, offered for sale, or advertised to consumers in the EU. Thus if the customs authorities have indications that one or more of the operators involved in the manufacture, consignment or distribution of goods are about to start directing the goods at consumers in the EU or are disguising their commercial intentions, then action may be legitimately taken.[40] To avoid the risk of random and excessive actions, such a suspicion must naturally be based on factual evidence, which could include the fact that the destination of the goods was not declared, when such a declaration is required, imprecise or unreliable information about the identity or address of the manufacturer or consignor of the goods, lack of cooperation with the customs authorities, or the discovery of documents or correspondence suggesting that the goods might be diverted to consumers based in the EU.[41] Substantive decisions that an intellectual property right under national law has been infringed, however, cannot be based on suspicion: they must be based on whether there is proof of the right relied upon; the sanction—destruction or abandonment of the goods to customs—follows as clearly as night follows day. Similarly, the mere risk of fraud does not justify dispossession or penalties, and in the absence of proof that the goods are intended to be put on sale within the EU a classification of the goods as 'counterfeit goods' or 'pirated goods' or 'goods infringing an intellectual property right' will be impossible. Appropriate evidence may include (but is clearly not limited to) the existence of a sale of goods to a customer within the EU, of an offer for sale or advertising addressed to customers in the EU, or of documents or correspondence concerning the goods involved showing that diversion of those goods to customers in the EU is envisaged.[42]

right); Case C-281/05 *Montex Holdings*, n 33 above, para 24. Internationally registered trade mark holders are assimilated to Community trade mark owners and can also avail themselves of Regulation 1383/2003 in the circumstances permitted by that Regulation, Case C-302/08 *Zino Davidoff SA v Bundesfinanzdirektion Südost* [2009] ECR I-5671.

[39] See Case C-405/03 *Class International*, n 33 above, para 61; Case C-324/09 *L'Oréal SA et al v eBay International AG et al* [2011] ECR I-not yet reported (Transcript, 12 July 2011), para 67.

[40] Joined Cases C-446/09 and 495/09 *Philips and Nokia*, n 33 above, paras 58–60.

[41] ibid paras 61–2.

[42] ibid, paras 68–71. The Court then proceeded to dismiss various arguments relating to the effectiveness of Regulation 1383/2003 and to risks to the health and safety of consumers: the continued status of the goods as being subject to customs supervision and the existence of other provisions of the CCC (Articles 56, 58 and 75) were prayed in aid to this end.

The judgments discussed above show how the Court has become alert to concerns expressed about a relatively restrictive interpretation of Regulation 1383/2003 (and its predecessor regime), but at the same time it is concerned to ensure that the Regulation does not provide a means of right holders or customs authorities simply embarking on fishing expeditions in order to disrupt legitimate traders' activities. While the disruption of the activities of those seeking to flood the EU market with counterfeit, pirated or other goods infringing intellectual property rights is consistent with the purpose of the Regulation, suspicion must be founded on a basis—the logical basis would be a reasonably well-founded suspicion: Advocate General Cruz Villalón has suggested that the customs authorities would need at the very least 'the beginnings of proof'[43] taking account of the danger of the fraudulent entry of the goods into the EU, bearing in mind that even if the external transit procedure were founded on the legal fiction that the goods had not entered the customs territory of the EU, they were very much physically present on that territory. Accordingly, he suggested, without claiming to be exhaustive, that 'circumstances such as the excessive duration of the transit, the kind and number of means of transport used, the greater or lesser difficulty of identifying the consignor of the goods or the lack of information on their physical destination or consignee, could, in particular cases, lend substance to a well founded suspicion that goods appearing in themselves to be "counterfeit" or "pirated" are to be placed on the market of the European Union.'[44] As has been seen above, in *Philips and Nokia*, the Court has also now rightly taken the opportunity to give useful concrete guidance as to the evidence for substantive decisions of infringement of rights. That such guidance and proper respect for the purpose of the EU legislation was necessary is borne out by the following saga which well demonstrates the potential international consequences of alleged misuse of powers.

At the end of 2008, there was a series of detentions by customs authorities of shipments of generic pharmaceutical products in transit through the Netherlands, from one third country to another, which caused a fluttering in the dovecotes of various WTO members, Members of the European Parliament, NGOs and civil society, on the basis that this could hamper legitimate trade in generic medicines, thus contradicting the EU commitment to facilitating access to medicines in the developing world, and possibly infringing WTO rules. As a result, WTO dispute proceedings were lodged against the EU by India and Brazil,[45] as the EU is responsible at that level for the acts of the authorities of its Member States.

In view of these proceedings and in the light of consultations in the course of those proceedings, the Commission has proposed improvements in legal certainty

[43] Opinion of AG Cruz Villalón in Joined Cases C-446/09 and 495/09 *Philips and Nokia*, n 33 above, para 107. The Court (at para 62) followed the learned Advocate General's view (expressed at para 106) that suspicion was inherently bound up with the facts. It did not comment further on his suggestions discussed below.

[44] Opinion of AG Cruz Villalón in Joined Cases C-446/09 and 495/09 *Philips and Nokia*, n 33 above, para 111.

[45] WTO Disputes DS 408 and 409 respectively (India, Brazil *v* EU and Netherlands) in which consultations are still ongoing.

through the adoption of a new instrument to replace Regulation 1383/2003.[46] The proposal would be broader than the present Regulation, also including trade names, topographies of semiconductor products and utility models; infringements resulting from parallel trade and devices to circumvent technological measures would also be covered, as well as other infringements of rights already enforced by customs. The exemption concerning travellers' personal luggage would be simplified, so that the proposed Regulation would not apply to goods of a non-commercial nature contained in such luggage. Customs would maintain the power to control, for the purpose of enforcement of intellectual property rights, in all situations where the goods were under their supervision. The proposal would also emphasize the distinction between the procedural and substantive law on intellectual property, and would greatly simplify the formalities required for the abandonment of goods for destruction without having to resort legal proceedings, which are expensive and formalistic. The new arrangements would be differentiated according to the type of infringement; so for counterfeit and pirated goods, the agreement of the owner to destroy the goods could be presumed if the destruction had not been explicitly opposed, in other cases the owner of the goods would have to agree explicitly to their destruction. Where no agreement could be reached, the right holder would have to initiate legal proceedings to establish the infringement, otherwise the goods would be released.

The proposal also includes a specific procedure for small consignments of suspected counterfeit and pirated goods covered by an application, which would allow for goods to be destroyed without the involvement of the right holder. The proposal further contains additional provisions to ensure the protection of the interests of legitimate traders from possible abuse of the customs enforcement procedures (it should not be thought that right holders are above using bully-boy tactics) and to take full account of the principles of the Charter of Fundamental Rights:[47] to this end, clarification is proposed of the timelines for detaining suspected goods, the conditions under which information about consignments would be passed on to right holders by customs, the conditions for applying the procedure allowing for destruction of the goods under customs control for suspected infringements of intellectual property rights other than for counterfeiting and piracy, and the rights of defence. Finally, as always, issues relating to costs featured clearly in responses to the consultation prior to the finalization of the proposal: while storage and destruction costs directly incurred by customs would continue to be assumed by the right holders requesting customs action (but the latter could take legal action to recover such costs from the primary party liable), an important exception would be introduced for small consignments, so that storage and destruction costs would be assumed by customs. Clearly the Commission has sought to propose a new instrument which would be flexible but also effective as a deterrent to trade in counterfeit or pirated goods, while taking due account of the need to prevent or deter mere posturing and intimidation, and at the same time

[46] Commission Document COM (2011) 285 final, n 29 above.
[47] Charter of Fundamental Rights of the European Union [2010] OJ C83/389.

seeking to facilitate a sensible resolution of the WTO disputes. Attempts to use the present Regulation in situations that it is not meant to cover mean that an instrument which in itself is legitimate is being misused: even if the goods are finally released, the costs occasioned by delays are not insignificant, and feelings that an instrument is being misused do not make for credible and creditable legislation.

The use of Regulation 1383/2003 has expanded dramatically over the years: applications for action to national customs authorities from right holders rose from 981 in 2000, to 5525 in 2005, to 10,260 in 2007 and to 18,330 in 2010. Perhaps unsurprisingly, China continued in 2010 to account for the dragon's share as the source country (85 per cent); but for cases involving foodstuffs, Turkey was the main source country, as was Thailand for non-alcoholic beverages, Hong Kong for memory cards, and—also unsurprisingly in view of the problems in 2008—India for medicines. Cigarettes were the largest category of articles detained, and some 14.5 per cent of the products detained were products for daily use and products that would be potentially dangerous to the health and safety of consumers (food and beverages, body care articles, medicines, electrical household goods, and toys), although as a percentage this was lower than in 2009. The Commission has wryly observed that counterfeiters do not concern themselves with matters such as product development costs, guarantees or advertising; for them, profit is maximized by the theft and copying of an original idea, often with cheaper materials; in many instances, though, infringing goods are increasingly sold at a similar price to the original goods and effectively substitute them on the market, although such effective substitution is less evident for luxury goods such as watches, luxury handbags and other personal accessories.[48] On present form, the fight against counterfeit, pirated and other infringing goods will be with us for some time to come, and the adage used in the financial services sector that if it looks too good to be true, it probably is, applies here too.

E. Does the customs union demand a full internal market?

At first sight, the answer to this question must be obviously positive, and indeed that is the correct answer, but there have been situations in which attempts have been made to promote enclaves of economic activity within Member States in which the free movement of goods rules in particular can be ignored. This observation refers not to the existence of free zones and free warehouses, which are beneficial, promoting a concentration of activities related to external trade and the redistribution of goods both within and outside the European Union,[49] it refers

[48] This information is taken from the Commission's report for 2010 on the application of Regulation 1383/2003, <http://ec.europa.eu/taxation_customs/resources/documents/customs/customs_controls/counterfeit_piracy/statistics/statistics_2010.pdf>.

[49] The list of free zones as of 7 February 2012 can be found at: <http://ec.europa.eu/taxation_customs/resources/documents/customs/procedural_aspects/imports/free_zones/list_freezones.pdf>. At the present time, Austria, Belgium, Hungary, Luxembourg, Slovakia and Sweden have no free zones operating.

rather to attempts to establish or maintain barriers to the free movement of goods *within* a Member State. These are inimical to the unity of the internal market itself, no matter how much it may be argued that they are purely internal matters.[50] Traditionally the Court has required an inter-state element in order to trigger the application of the free movement of goods rules,[51] although this criterion has come under pressure as a result of the French dock dues cases[52] and some other spectacular judgments[53] since; the Court has also felt it appropriate to rule on references for preliminary rulings even when all the facts were confined to one Member State.[54] However, if it is remembered that the Court has traditionally

[50] P Oliver in P Oliver et al, *Oliver on Free Movement of Goods in the European Union*, 5th edn (Oxford: Hart Publishing, 2010) 142–51 is roundly critical of the Court's case law on this basis. See further A Tryfonidou, 'The Overseas Application of the Customs Duties Provisions of the TFEU' in D Kochenov (ed), *EU Law of the Overseas* (Alphen aan den Rijn: Wolters Kluwer, 2011) 221. Much of the discussion has taken place in relation to reverse discrimination, but that aspect is outside the scope of this contribution, although see n 54 below.

[51] See, eg, Joined Cases 314–316/81 and 83/82 *Procureur de la République et al v Waterkeyn et al* [1982] ECR 4337, paras 10–12; Case 286/81 *Oosthoek's Uitgeversmaatschappij BV* [1982] ECR 4575, para 9; Case 355/85 *Driancourt v Cognet* [1986] ECR 3231, para 10.

[52] Case C-163/90 *Administration des Douanes et des droits indirects v Legros et al* [1992] ECR I-4625, paras 16–18: a charge levied at a regional frontier by reason of the introduction of products into a region of a Member State constitutes an obstacle to the free movement of goods which is at least as serious as a charge levied at the national frontier by reason of the introduction of the products into the whole territory of a Member State. The effect of such a regional levy on the unity of the Community customs territory is not altered by the fact that it is also charged on goods from the other parts of the territory of the Member State in question. Thus a charge, proportional to the customs value of goods, levied by a Member State on goods imported from another Member State by reason of their entry into a region of the territory of the first Member State constitutes a charge having an effect equivalent to a customs duty on imports, notwithstanding the fact that the charge is also imposed on goods entering that region from another part of the same State. See too (in particular as to the temporal effect of the judgment in *Legros* and repayment of sums paid but not due) Joined Cases C-363/93, 407–411/93 *René Lancry SA et al v Direction Générale des Douanes et al* [1994] ECR I-3957, ECJ; Case C-126/94 *Société Cadi surgelés et al v Ministre des Finances et al* [1996] ECR I-5647, ECJ (Fifth Chamber); Joined Cases C-192–218/95 *Société Comateb et al v Directeur général des douanes et droits indirects* [1997] ECR I-165, ECJ; Case C-212/96 *Chavassus-Marche v Conseil régional de la Réunion* [1998] ECR I-743, ECJ; Joined Cases C-37 and 38/96 *Sodiprem SARL et al v Direction Générale des Douanes* [1998] ECR I-2039, ECJ. A similar conclusion was reached in relation to charges imposed on movement of goods into and out of the Dodecanese in Joined Cases C-485 and 486/93 *Simitzi v Kos* [1995] ECR I-2655.

[53] See, in relation to municipal dues levied on unworked marble moved out of the municipal boundaries, Case C-72/03 *Carbonati Apuani Srl v Comune di Carrara* [2004] ECR I-8027. The same approach was followed in relation to the export of potatoes from Jersey to the rest of the UK, Case C-293/02 *Jersey Produce Marketing Organisation Ltd v States of Jersey et al* [2005] ECR I-9543. See further, as to compulsory charges to fund a national market organization, Case C-130/93 *Lamaire NV v Nationale Dienst voor Afzet van Land- en Tuinbouwprodukten* [1994] ECR I-3215 and Joined Cases C-441/98 and 442/98 *Kapniki Michaïlidis AE v Idryma Koinonikon Asfaliseon (IKA)* [2000] ECR I-7145.

[54] See Case C-321-324/94 *Pistre et al* [1997] ECR I-2343, 2374–5; Case C-448/98 *Guimot* [2000] ECR I-10663, 10688. In some Member States, national law does not permit reverse discrimination (eg disadvantaging national industry by forcing it to continue to comply with national recipe laws even though similar products from other Member States no longer had to): equality before the law would mean that if a measure could not be enforced against goods imported from another Member State, it could not be enforced in a wholly domestic situation, thus it would be by operation of national law that purely domestic operators benefit from a finding by the Court that a measure infringed Article 34 TFEU; this interest played an important part in the Court's willingness in *Guimot* to answer the questions posed by the national court.

resisted efforts at market partitioning,[55] even where the national rules concerned also disadvantage some national products or services,[56] the Court's approach becomes at once more understandable. By focusing on the rather shrill cries of purely internal situations, sight is lost of the importance of the unity of the market and of the fact that the Court's approach is consistent with its resistance to attempts to create artificial divisions within it: both actual and potential obstacles to trade are caught by the free movement concept (though not merely hypothetical and artificial transactions), and it is right that the Court should take account of the fact that importers may well be affected by legislation which is actually being challenged at that moment only within a domestic context.[57] The Court has made it very plain that no distinction should be drawn between internal frontiers and inter-state frontiers in the definition of the internal market.[58] While it may be that the definition of a customs union in the GATT[59] does not actually require an internal market of the type established in the European Union, and although it is true that the customs union provisions on the one hand and the provisions dealing with the prohibition of quantitative restrictions and measures having equivalent effect and the prohibitions of discriminatory or protective internal taxation on imports or exports on the other are indeed contained in separate parts of the TFEU, the definition of a customs union is, as John Usher observed, 'technically a concept of the EC Treaty'[60] (now of course of the TFEU as required by Article 3(3) TEU).

[55] This has been a long-standing approach, see, eg, in relation to trade between Member States and the use of national industrial and commercial property rights, Case 78/70 *Deutsche Grammophon Gesellschaft mbH v Metro-SB-Großmärkte GmbH & Co KG* [1971] ECR 487, 500 (legitimization of the isolation of national markets would be repugnant to the essential purpose of the Treaty). Admittedly this case concerned an attempt to justify complete territorial protection, but the greater undoubtedly includes the less in relation to threats to the unity of the single market.

[56] Thus in relation to the free movement of goods, as far as EU law itself is concerned, a Member State may make higher demands of its own industry than of imported products, as the domestic retention of the *Reinheitsgebot* for beer demonstrates. Whether this is permitted by national law is entirely another issue (see n 54 above).

[57] See the cases cited in n 54 above. In Case C-212/06 *Government of the French Community and Walloon Government v Flemish Government* [2008] ECR I-1683, at paras 121–57 of her Opinion, AG Sharpston sought to extend the Court's approach from goods to persons, but the Court declined to follow her argument (paras 37–9 of the judgment); it did, however, in para 40 of that judgment follow the approach taken in the cases referred to in n 53: '[I]nterpretation of provisions of Community law might possibly be of use to the national court, having regard too to situations classed as purely internal, in particular if the law of the Member State concerned were to require every national of that State to be allowed to enjoy the same rights as those which a national of another Member State would derive from Community law in a situation considered to be comparable by that court (see, to that effect, Case C-250/03 *Mauri* [2005] ECR I-1267, para 21, and Case C-451/03 *Servizi Ausiliari Dottori Commercialisti* [2006] ECR I-2941, para 29)'.

[58] Case C-293/02 *Jersey Produce Marketing Organisation Ltd v States of Jersey et al* [2005] ECR I-9543, para 64; Case C-30/01 *Commission v United Kingdom* [2003] ECR I-9481, paras 52–3; see further Case C-72/03 *Carbonati Apuani Srl*, n 52 above, para 23.

[59] See GATT, Article XXIV, para 8a. The Court observed in Case 266/81 *Società Italiana per l'Oleodotto Transalpino (SIOT) v Ministero delle Finanze et al* [1983] ECR 731, para 12 that 'the Community must be regarded as a single customs territory because according to Article 9 of the EEC Treaty it is based on the principle of a customs union. It follows that the rules contained in GATT govern only the Community's relations with the other contracting parties and cannot be applied within the Community itself.'

[60] JA Usher in N Emiliou and D O'Keeffe (eds), n 7 above, 105, 106.

The customs union and the internal market form key foundations of the European Union's construction and of its activities, and to permit the re-establishment of artificial barriers to trade within its area is simply incompatible with these concepts. Accordingly, it is respectfully submitted that criticism of the Court's case law on the unity of the market is fundamentally misconceived.

F. Concluding observations

The selected aspects of the functioning and practice of the customs union and the internal market well demonstrate that in the European Union they are intertwined concepts, forming essential elements of the Union's construction. Both the Union legislature and the Court of Justice have sought to develop and maintain the unity of the marketplace and the effectiveness of the economic law which has been established in these areas, and the pursuit of those aims has indeed been very successful.[61] Those aims must not, however, lose sight of the need to apply customs law in a manner which ensures a fair and correct balance between the interests of customs law enforcement and the interests of market participants in their dealings with customs; traditionally that balance has been very much on the administration's side, as the cases dealing with challenges to tariff classifications demonstrate. It is to be hoped that it will now become easier to challenge such acts as a result of the partial relaxation of the standing requirements. The example of the Union's approach to dealing with counterfeit goods has demonstrated just how ready right holders have become to take advantage of the opportunities for enforcing their rights, although also how attempts have sometimes been made to do so in circumstances which are not covered by Union legislation, and how such attempts may lead to international problems.

The Union's vast and frankly complex customs legislation will undergo significant transformation in the coming years, as the implementing provisions are established for the MCC, and it is to be hoped that the result will be simpler, clearer and more user-friendly legislation. One thing is, however, certain: both the customs union and the internal market will remain fertile areas for academic and practical study as long as the Union exists.

John Usher wrote on so many aspects of EU law that he could not be pigeonholed as being interested merely in particular aspects of the subject. Of the UK academics in the field of EU law he was particularly noted for being interested not

[61] However, the Union legislature, now on the basis of Article 349 TFEU (previously on the basis of Article 299(2) EC), still authorizes derogations from the fundamental rules of the Treaties for the *octroi de mer* (dock dues) in the French overseas departments, see December 2004/162 [2004] OJ L52/64, as amended by December 2008/439 [2008] OJ L155/17 and December 448/2011 [2011] OJ L193/1. In Case C-212/96 *Chevasssus-Marche v Conseil regional de la Réunion* [1998] ECR I-743, para 49 (in relation to the predecessor regime), the Court accepted that only necessary, proportionate and precisely determined exceptions could be authorized. See, further, D Kochenov (ed), n 50 above.

only in law as such, but also in its political, social and economic contexts, and he reached out effectively to political scientists and others who were interested in the effects and workings of the European Union. As I wrote in my obituary of him in the *European Law Review*, '[i]n every way, he was a thoroughly decent, gregarious and very learned man, in whose company it was always a pleasure to be.'[62]

[62] LW Gormley, 'Obituary—Professor John Usher (1945–2008)' (2008) 33:6 *ELRev* 775, 776.

6

Betting, Monopolies and the Protection of Public Order

*Jacqueline Dutheil de la Rochère**

A. Introduction

In recent years, the gaming industry has undergone tremendous transformations due essentially to the development of the Internet. Historically, the activity of gambling in European countries has been the subject of regimes intended to protect public order, either through the maintenance of a public monopoly or through systems of licences subject to surveillance. Both systems of control have, incidentally, the added benefit of allowing for a centralized collection of taxes on gaming. Outside Europe, national legislation on online gambling is extremely diversified, from total prohibition (as in the United States), to total freedom (as in Netherlands Antilles or Curaçao).[1] The rise of the Internet makes it possible for gaming industries to offer their services all around the world, without taking account of national legislation; perhaps unsurprisingly, consumers have shown strong interest in these offers. Therefore the problem for targeted countries, among them the Member States of the European Union, has been to decide how to react to these new market developments, which are often in direct competition with existing national arrangements: should the Member States seek to protect their territory for reasons of general interest or open their borders and, potentially, the floodgates? In general, the Member States have not been prompt in opening up their markets and it is unsurprising, therefore, that much litigation has ensued as gaming firms seek to take advantage of the single market within the European Union. As is so often the case, negative integration precedes any possible steps in the direction of positive integration.

In 1992, the European Commission had considered the opportunity to enter into a process of harmonization of national legislation on the offering of games of chance, but had to face a refusal by the Council, which invoked the principle of

* Professeur émérite à l'Université Pantheon-Assas Paris II. I am grateful to Laurence Gormley for his suggestions; the usual disclaimer applies.

[1] A Raiffe, 'A comparative analysis of internet gambling regulations' (2010) 2 *Journal of Regulation* 132–7.

subsidiarity.[2] This reluctance to legislate at European level was confirmed with the express exclusion from the scope of the Services Directive of all activities of gambling, including lotteries and betting.[3] The option of harmonization continues to be excluded. On the other hand, the European Commission has not remained wholly inactive. It launched infringement procedures against certain Member States that did not respect the principles of EU law regarding operators of games established in another country.[4] But whatever the political considerations which lead the Commission and the Council to decide that the time is not yet ripe for legislative action, they cannot control initiatives to enforce the development of EU law by private operators or even individuals concerned to open up the single market and take advantage of its principles. It is in this context that the Court of Justice has had to decide on various preliminary rulings in cases where national courts sought clarification on the compatibility of national legislation with EU law, at a time when contentious situations had developed between the national authorities of the Member States and numerous players in the gaming industry seeking to develop their activities within the single EU market. This case law has seen remarkable twists and turns, in one case even amounting to a round condemnation of the vagaries of bureaucracy in the Italian legal system: an applicant had, contrary to (then) Community law, been unable to obtain a licence; and, because he had no licence, was unable to obtain the necessary police authorization.[5]

While some motives for regulating gambling in a particular way will receive little sympathy from the Court,[6] others receive considerably more respect.[7]

[2] Thus the Commission (clearly rather reluctantly) envisaged in December 1992 not launching any legislative initiatives in the area of gambling, although it noted that it might be necessary to review that position in the light of new and, at that point, still unforeseen trends; CommissionVice-President Martin Bangemann noted that 'Anyone should be able to place a bet anywhere. Controls on operators can remain as effective as ever'; see Commission Press Release IP (92) 1120.

[3] Directive 2006/123 on services in the internal market [2006] OJ L 376/36, Article 2.2(h). Games are also excluded from the scope of Directive 2000/31 on certain legal aspects of information society services, in particular electronic commerce, in the internal market (Directive on electronic commerce) [2000] OJ L 178/1 and from Directive 2010/13 on the coordination of certain provisions laid down by law, regulation or administrative action in Member States concerning the provision of audiovisual media services (Audiovisual Media Services Directive) [2010] OJ L95/1 (which repeals and replaces the 'television without frontiers' directive, Directive 89/552 on the coordination of certain provisions laid down by law, regulation or administrative action in Member States concerning the pursuit of television broadcasting activities [1985] OJ L 298/23, as last amended [2007] OJ L 332/27).

[4] This was the case for France, which received, on 27 June 2007, a reasoned opinion concerning the refusal by French authorities to permit operators legally established in another Member State to offer betting on sport to players in France. The law of 12 May 2010 (JORF no 0110 of 13 May 2010) on the opening to competition and regulation of games of money and hazard online has now modified the French system extensively.

[5] Joined Cases C-338, 359 and 360/04 *Criminal proceedings against Massimiliano Placanica and Others* [2007] ECR I-1891: the Court found that, in these circumstances, the Italian authorities could not impose criminal penalties on the defendants.

[6] eg if the primary motive (as opposed to an incidental beneficial consequence) is the financing of benevolent or public interest activities, see Case C-67/98 *Questore di Verona v Zenatti* [1999] ECR I-7289, para 36; Case C-243/01 *Criminal proceedings against Piergiorgio Gambelli and Others* [2003] ECR I-13031, para 62.

[7] eg a desire to bring about a genuine diminution in gambling activities by confining the desire to gamble and the exploitation of gambling within controlled channels, preventing the risk of fraud or

The requirements of proportionality and suitability for purpose, together with the requirements of consistency and systematic limitation on gambling or betting activities, must always be borne in mind when evaluating alleged justifications.[8] In general, the Court of Justice has recognized the strong specificity of the activity of games, the risks incurred, and the difference of attitudes of the Member States as inspired by different social, cultural and religious values. As so often when faced with 'hot potatoes', the Court has tended to leave the final evaluation of the arguments up to the national court. Yet more recent case law seems perhaps to show that the Court is becoming more willing to accede to national justifications than might have been thought. The *Santa Casa* case,[9] which legitimized Portuguese legislation conferring an historical monopoly on a non-profit organization in charge of social services of general interest, is significant for its acceptance of the national approach. It does not mean that the Court's case law does not impose the primacy of EU law in the activity of gambling, but it does so with special concern for national values. It is quite obvious that John Usher would have been able to offer us a brilliant synthesis of this new domain of confrontation between national legislation and market freedoms, through the prism of EU law. This chapter seeks to illustrate how special consideration is given to national choices concerning games of money and chance, while nevertheless ensuring that the essential principles of EU law are applied, albeit with some specificities.

B. Special consideration given to national choices

The central claim here is that the specificity of games of money and chance, and the cultural dimension of such activities, justify special treatment under EU law, so that Member States may assume their own responsibilities in this regulatory domain.

crime in the context of such exploitation, with the ancillary benefit of using the resulting profits for public interest purposes, see Case C-67/98 *Zenatti*, n 6 above, para 35; on moral, religious and cultural factors, and the morally and financially harmful consequences for the individual associated with gaming and betting see, eg, Case C-243/01 *Gambelli*, n 6 above, para 63.

[8] eg Case C-243/01 *Gambelli*, n 6 above, para 67. However, in his Opinion in Joined Cases C-447 and C-448/08 *Sjöberg & Gerdin* [2010] ECR I-6921, para 66, AG Bot observed that it was apparent from the judgment in Case C-42/07 *Liga Portuguesa de Futebol Profissional, Baw international Ltd v Departemento de Jogas da Santa Casa da Misericordia de Lisboa* [2009] ECR I-7633 that the analysis of a licensing system to prevent consumers from the risks of fraud and crime did not depend on whether the rules at issue are appropriate for the purpose of achieving their other objectives, such as the protection of consumers against excessive incitement to gamble. With respect to the learned Advocate General, the Court did nothing of the sort in *Santa Casa*: it reached a conclusion about appropriateness (see Case C-42/07 *Santa Casa*, paras 66–7) but appropriateness and suitability were expressly maintained as criteria (see Case C-42/07 *Santa Casa*, paras 60–1).

[9] Case C-42/07 *Santa Casa*, n 8 above.

(1) Specificity of games of money and chance

It is not contested that gambling is an economic activity subject to EU law: this was first decided by the Court in *Schindler*,[10] in which it was established that lotteries, although an activity of a very special nature, nevertheless fell within the category of 'economic' activity because a service was offered, and offered for consideration. This was confirmed by a long line of cases concerning either games of pure chance or those that are based only partly on chance (for instance, horse races) and also partly on skill (in some cases of the gambler; in others of a third party, such as a jockey and the horse; or perhaps of all concerned). However, the usual regime of VAT does not apply,[11] not because the activity of gambling is not considered to be an economic activity, but because of its uncertainty, which makes taxation practically impossible to organize. The Court has had the occasion to underline that such an exception does not reflect any intention to favour this activity, as could happen for the social sector.[12]

Successive Advocates General have argued that in view of their specific character, games must receive special treatment under EU law, allowing Member States to assume their own responsibilities, and the Court has followed this approach in its recent and abundant case law.[13] In his opinion in *Santa Casa*[14] and subsequent cases,[15] Advocate General Bot made this point with an exceptional vigour. He recalled that gambling is an economic activity of a special nature for the following reasons. First, moral, religious and cultural considerations lead Member States to limit or even prohibit certain games so that they do not become a source of individual profit. Secondly, the significant amount of money that may be collected through the occasion of gambling implies high risks of fraud and criminal offences. Further, games constitute an incitement to expenses, which may have individual and social prejudicial consequences. The risk of abuse is even stronger with online games, due to the absence of physical contact between the provider and the 'consumer', and the isolation of the players.

(a) Application of EU competition rules

In *Santa Casa*,[16] and in subsequent cases, Advocate General Bot[17] expressed his doubts as to the possibility of applying EU competition rules in the area of

[10] Case C-275/92 *HM Customs & Excise v Gerhart Schindler and Jörg Schindler*[1994] ECR I-1039, para 59.

[11] See now Directive 2006/112 on the common system of value added tax [2006] OJ L 347/1, corrigenda [2007] OJ L 335/60, as most recently amended [2010] OJ L 326/1, Article 135(1)(i).

[12] Case C-58/09 *Leo-Libera GmbH v Finanzamt Buchholz in der Nordheide* [2010] ECR I-5189.

[13] Opinion of AG Fennelly in Case C-67/98 *Zenatti*, n 6 above; Opinion of AG Tizzano in Case C-6/01 *Associação Nacional de Operadores de Máquinas Recreativas (Anomar) and Others v Estado português* [2003] ECR I-8621; Opinion of AG Alber in Case C-243/01 *Gambelli*, n 6 above; Opinion of AG Ruiz-Jarabo Colomer in Joined Cases C-338, 359 and 360/04 *Placanica*, n 5 above.

[14] Opinion of AG Bot in Case C-42/07 *Santa Casa*, n 8 above, para 62 et seq.

[15] eg Joined Cases C-447 and 448/08 *Sjöberg & Gerdin*, n 8 above.

[16] Opinion of AG Bot in Case C-42/07 *Santa Casa*, n 8 above, para 245 et seq.

[17] Joint Opinion of AG Bot in Cases C-203/08 *Sporting Exchange Ltd v Minister van Justitie* [2010] ECR I-4695 and C-258/08 *Ladbrokes Betting & Gambling Ltd et al v Stichting de Nationale Sporttotalisator* [2010] ECR I-4757; see para 57 et seq.

gambling. He considered that one of the reasons enabling States to choose a system of exclusive rights reserved to a unique undertaking is that the activity of gambling does not comply with the objectives of free competition of the common market. According to Advocate General Bot, competition in the EU legal order is not an end in itself but a means of attaining the objectives pursued by the Union: 'Free competition promotes the development of economic activities and employment and thereby raises the standard of living of the citizens of the European Union because, where competition is fair, it ensures technological progress and improves the quality of services or a product, while guaranteeing the reduction of costs.'[18] In his view, however, free competition cannot bring such advantages in the area of gambling:

> Gambling can continue to function only if the very great majority of players lose more than they win. The very principle of that activity, in which the expectation of profit derives from the power of dreams, holds out the illusion of potential enrichment but leads to the impoverishment of those who indulge in it. Competition between services providers for the same type of game, which would be bound to lead them to offer consumers ever more attractive games in order to make the greatest profits, is likely to push households to spend more than their available resources for leisure purposes and even induce a real addiction to gaming.[19]

A first level of conclusion proposed by the learned Advocate General is that the interpretation of the scope of the freedoms of movement in the sphere of gambling should not lead to requiring the Member States to open the market in that field because it is not a source of progress and development.[20] Whatever sympathy may be felt for that analysis, which emphasizes the dangers of addiction to games, this criticism of the rules of competition when applied to the sphere of gambling seems puzzling, to say the least. First, what is in question here, as Advocate General Bot rightly observed in the remainder of his Opinion, is not competition as such but the freedoms of movement and their possible limitation by Member States for reasons of general interest. Secondly, to the extent that gambling is analysed as an economic activity, it is not entirely different from many other activities that engender profit for the providers but imply risks of different nature for consumers. Can it not be said, for instance, that competition in financial services also takes place within a sector 'in which the expectation of profit derives from the power of dreams holds out the illusion of potential enrichment but leads to the impoverishment of those who indulge in it'?[21] The recent financial crisis illustrates the reality of this risk all too well.

The free movement of a number of goods and services implies risks for health or morality; the examples of tobacco, spirits, medical products and services come immediately to mind, and there are certainly many others. The difference with games is more of degree than of nature. Therefore, this pleading against free competition in the sphere of gambling is not really convincing. The scope and approach of EU law have never been to authorize Member States to close up their

[18] ibid para 58. [19] ibid para 59. [20] ibid para 60. [21] ibid para 59.

national markets in cases of risk, but rather to enhance the protection of consumers. Control of the excess and abuse of competition has always been preferred to its abolition.

According to commentators,[22] the approach taken by Advocate General Bot is, in fact, somewhat strategic. When it came to suggesting a line of reasoning for the Court, he reverted back to the essence of the case. He did not call into question the case law which stated that the organization and exploitation of gambling constituted an economic activity; nor did he question the right of operators to take advantage of the freedoms of movement. But having recalled that competition in the area of gambling was not a source of progress and development, he merely observed that 'because of the particular nature of gambling, a Member State should be required to open a specific form of gambling to free competition only if that State chooses to make that form of gambling a normal or ordinary economic activity', for which the primary objective would be the maximizing profit.[23]

(2) Maximum consideration given to national choices

Because of the special risks incurred, however, Member States should be allowed maximum freedom in their determination of the regulatory structure for gambling activity and in their evaluation of the limits to be imposed on the freedoms of movement owing to considerations of general interest. This special consideration given to national choice may be illustrated with various examples in recent case law: for instance, free choice for Member States with respect to the structuring of games of chance, the refusal to apply the mutual recognition principle, and the special treatment of justifications invoked as reasons of general interest for limiting the freedoms of movement. In other words, although gambling does enter the substantive scope of the implementation of EU law, the presumption remains in favour of the competence of the Member States to define their objectives and policies in that domain.

As to the first consideration identified above, the *general organization of the activity of games*, according to current case law it is for each Member State to determine 'in accordance with its own scale of values'[24] the type of organization it considers suitable and to define in detail the level of protection sought. This can range from total prohibition to partial authorization, with either exclusive rights to one public[25] or private operator,[26] or a regime of authorizations conferred on some

[22] J-M Thouvenin, 'Jeux en ligne: les appréciations de l'avocat général Bot' (2010) 536 *RMCUE* 143–7.

[23] Joint Opinion of AG Bot in Cases C-203/08 *Sporting Exchange* and C-258/08 *Ladbrokes*, n 17 above, para 62.

[24] This formula, used in Case C-275/92 *Schindler*, n 10 above, appears also in *Santa Casa*. See Case C-42/07 *Santa Casa*, n 8 above, para 57.

[25] Case C-42/07 *Santa Casa*, n 8 above and Case C-124/97 *Markku Juhani Läärä, Cotswold Microsystems Ltd and Oy Transatlantic Software Ltd v Kihlakunnansyyttäjä (Jyväskylä) and Suomen valtio (Finnish State)* [1999] ECR I-6067.

[26] Case C-258/08 *Ladbrokes*, n 17 above.

entities.[27] *Santa Casa* was the first case in which the Court approved of a public monopoly instituted by Portuguese legislation; and it was followed by two judgments approving Dutch legislation instituting a monopoly[28] and one judgment approving Swedish legislation along the same lines.[29]

In his Opinion in *Santa Casa*, Advocate General Bot considered the hypothesis of a possible approach to the question of structures through the provisions of the Treaties related to competition between undertakings.[30] Considering that the Portuguese legislation conferred exclusive rights to organize gambling on a public monopoly, Advocate General Bot considered that Santa Casa could have availed itself of the provisions of Article 106(2) TFEU (ex Article 86(2) EC) according to which undertakings entrusted with the operations of services of general economic interest are to be subject to the rules on competition contained in the Treaties only insofar as the application of such rules does not obstruct the performance in law or in fact of the particular task assigned to them. He noted that neither the Portuguese Government nor Santa Casa had mentioned these provisions; and concluded that had an argument been based on those grounds, it would not have been different from the approach he suggested on the basis of the provisions applicable to the freedom to provide services and the exceptions allowed to their application. EU competition law has never prohibited the existence of State monopolies in the area of the provision of services, except in the very peculiar and unusual situation where the theory of automatic abuse of dominant position could apply.[31] As clearly repeated by Advocate General Bot in his Joint Opinion in *Sporting Exchange* and *Ladbrokes*, the interpretation of the rules of freedom of movement in the domain of gaming does not tend to impose the opening of the national market on Member States because such opening is not necessarily a source of progress and development. Instead, the Court tends to let them assume their regulatory responsibilities in this field. EU law is not intended to impose one specific type or method of market organization rather than another.

Another illustration of the discretion left to Member States in the domain of gaming lies in the fact that, second, the *principle of mutual recognition does not apply*. There was a time when there was a certain amount of hesitation regarding the extent to which a Member State could be obliged to take into account the conditions imposed on a gaming operator in another Member State as a sufficient guarantee of its integrity.[32] More recently, however, the solution of refusal of mutual recognition has prevailed; it is the only one that is compatible with the wide discretion allowed to Member States in the domain of games. In *Santa Casa*,

27 Case C-67/98 *Zenatti*, n 6 above.

28 Cases C-203/08 *Sporting Exchange* and C-258/08 *Ladbrokes*, n 17 above.

29 Joined Cases C-447 and 448/08 *Sjöberg & Gerdin*, n 8 above.

30 See Opinion of AG Bot in Case C-42/07 *Santa Casa*, n 8 above, para 219.

31 Case C-340/99 *TNT Traco SpA v Poste Italiane SpA* [2001] ECR I-4109.

32 In *Gambelli*, AG Alber considered that mutual recognition should apply as regards the integrity of operators. See Opinion of AG Alber in Case C-243/01 *Gambelli*, n 6 above, para 118. In *Placanica*, AG Ruiz-Jarabo Colomer was of the same view. See Opinion of AG Ruiz-Jarabo Colomer in Joined Cases C-338, 359 and 360/04 *Placanica*, n 5 above, para 130. The Court side-stepped the mutual recognition point in both cases.

the Court, noting that there was no harmonization in the field, considered that the freedom to provide services under EU law does not *oblige* the admission into one Member State of the offer of services by an operator of online games who legally provides the same services in another Member State:

> A Member State is . . . entitled to take the view that the mere fact that an operator . . . lawfully offers services in that sector via the internet in another Member State, in which it is established and where it is in principle already subject to statutory conditions and controls on the part of the competent authorities in that State, cannot be regarded as amounting to a sufficient assurance that national consumers will be protected against the risks of fraud and crime, in the light of the difficulties liable to be encountered in such a context by the authorities of the Member State of establishment in assessing the professional qualities and integrity of operators.[33]

Because of the high level of risks implied by the activity of games of chance, and more especially online games, the principle of mutual recognition does not apply.

Finally, it has been argued that, in the case law on gambling, the Court should refer globally to a *unique regime of exceptions*.[34] More specifically, it would appear that the classical distinction between, on the one hand, derogations expressly provided for by Articles 51 and 52 TFEU (ex Articles 45 and 46 EC), applicable in the area of services by virtue of Article 62 TFEU (ex Article 55 EC) and relevant in the case of restrictive discriminatory measures, and, on the other hand, non-discriminatory measures justified according to overriding reasons in the public interest, as established through case law, has not been made. It seems that, as regards gambling, the Court accepts that it is appropriate to consider a wide spectrum of exceptions which it will examine in turn; and accept the Member State's arguments or not (or leave it to the national court to make the evaluation). For instance, the Court has not accepted the justification of a restrictive measure by the fact that the money collected through games, if not redistributed to players, is used to finance social activities; rather, that is only a subordinate beneficial consequence.[35] Similarly, it will not accept as an overriding reason of general interest the fact that the organization of games on the basis of exclusive rights has a positive effect on public finances; these beneficial financial consequences cannot justify the exclusion of operators established within another Member State. Thus it would appear that there is a tendency towards globalization in the context of derogations and justifications. For instance, in *Santa Casa*, the Court confirmed that it examined the justifications presented by the Portuguese Government both as regards restrictions justified on grounds of public policy, public security and public health but also as regards overriding reasons in the public interest 'such as the objectives of consumer protection and the prevention of fraud and incitement to

[33] Case C-42/07 *Santa Casa*, n 8 above, para 69.

[34] F Peraldi-Leneuf, 'La Cour de Justice et la libéralisation des jeux en ligne: l'exigence de coherence A propos de l'arrêt *Santa Casa*' (2010) 46 *RTDE*:113.

[35] Case C-67/98 *Zenatti*, n 6 above.

squander money on gambling, as well as the general need to preserve public order'.[36]

C. National options and the essential principles of EU law

In the absence of EU harmonization, wide scope is left to the discretion of Member States to choose suitable structures for the offering of games of chance and to determine the objectives of their national legislation. However, restrictive measures will, in any case, have to comply with the principle of proportionality and, to the extent that the adopted structure leaves room for more than one operator, with the principle of non-discrimination. The leading concept is that of coherence between the objectives proclaimed and the solutions adopted in law and in fact. The Court of Justice reviews respect for both the principle of proportionality, with special care for coherence, and the principle of non-discrimination. In the numerous preliminary rulings on which it has had to decide recently, the Court of Justice set out general guidelines in this context, leaving the responsibility to evaluate the precise practical consequences in domestic law to national judges.

(1) Control of proportionality with special care for coherence

The application of the principle of proportionality does not need to be outlined in a general sense here, as the way in which it is applied by the Court to national restrictive measures is well known. However, in the domain of gambling, the Court's case law adds a condition that is worth analysing: restrictive measures are appropriate only if they genuinely reflect a concern to attain the stated objective(s) 'in a consistent and systematic manner'.[37] This approach aims at putting a stop to what one French author[38] qualifies as the '*Gambelli* contradiction'. At the heart of that contradiction lies the fact that the policies of Member States pretend, on one hand, to limit the occasions of games of chance by imposing a structure of monopoly but, on the other hand, support a policy of advertisement and expansion of those games led by the operators invested with exclusive rights. In *Santa Casa*, the Court approved the contested Portuguese legislation because the restrictive policy in the domain of games of chance was considered to be perfectly coherent and systematic.

In its judgments in *Sporting Exchange Ltd*[39] and *Ladbrokes*,[40] the Court of Justice accepted the compatibility with the Treaties of the contested Dutch legislation, considering that the expansionist policy (creation of new games; advertising) was designed to stop illegal offers by confining the operation of gambling within

[36] Case C-42/07 *Santa Casa*, n 8 above, para 56.

[37] Case C-243/01 *Gambelli*, n 6 above, paras 67–9; Case C-42/07 *Santa Casa*, n 8 above, para 61.

[38] D Alland, 'Droit de l'Union européenne et droit français des jeux de hasard et d'argent en ligne Histoire d'une instrumentalisation' (2010) 66 *AJDA* 1970.

[39] Cases C-203/08 *Sporting Exchange*, n 17 above.

[40] Case C-258/08 *Ladbrokes*, n 17 above.

controlled channels. The *Ladbrokes* case is especially clear on this point, with the Court stating that: 'It is possible that a policy of controlled expansion in the betting and gaming sector may be entirely consistent with the objective of drawing players away from clandestine betting and gaming—and, as such, activities which are prohibited—to activities which are authorised and regulated.'[41] Shortly thereafter, the Court of Justice had to examine the objectives underpinning Swedish legislation; it considered that the prohibition of advertising directed at players residing in Sweden for games developed by private operators in other Member States was perfectly consistent with the general objectives of the Swedish legislation: 'it might be considered unacceptable to allow private profit to be drawn from the exploitation of a social evil or the weakness of players and their misfortune.'[42]

The Court adopted the same balanced approach when dealing with the German situation in judgments in a number of cases concerning gaming.[43] With regard to games of chance, regulatory power in Germany is divided between the regional authorities (the *Länder*) and the Federal Government. The Court of Justice did not criticize this sharing of competences, which was of no concern for European Union law, but the fact that the restrictive policy of limiting the activity of gaming was not conducted by the German authorities in a coherent and systematic way and therefore did not comply with the requirements of a proper interpretation of Article 56 TFEU (ex Article 49 EC). More precisely it did not appear coherent on the one hand to establish a monopoly with the objective of reducing the opportunities for gambling, yet on the other hand to allow other types of games of chance to be exploited by private operators and to pursue policies of expanding supply in particular with a view to maximizing revenue derived from games not subject to monopoly.[44]

It is certainly never easy to evaluate the various criteria when applying the principle of proportionality. In the area of games it seems especially difficult to find the right balance for the following reasons: the various justifications either linked to public order or to general interest are examined together; there is a special expectation of coherence while the elements of contradiction between the expansion of the offer and the protection of consumers are of the very nature of that sort of activity.

(2) Full application of the principle of non-discrimination

This principle of EU law is applied in the most traditional, effective way in recent case law concerning games of chance and gambling.

As regards the *selection of authorized operators* the principles of transparency, equality and non-discrimination apply. The national authorities may decide, in the

[41] Case C-258/08 *Ladbrokes*, n 17 above, para 25.

[42] Joined Cases C-447 and 448/08 *Sjöberg & Gerdin*, n 8 above, para 43.

[43] Case C-46/08 *Carmen Media Group Ltd v Land Schleswig-Holstein et al* [2010] OJ C 288/8; Joined Cases C-316, 358–60, 409 and 410/07 *Markus Stroß et al v Wetteraukreis et al* [2010] OJ C 288/7.

[44] Case C-46/08 *Carmen Media*, n 43 above, para 71.

domain of games of chance to allow exclusive rights either to a public operator under direct public control, or to a private operator submitted to strict scrutiny of public authorities; the EU obligations of non- discrimination do not apply as there is no procedure of selection. In any other circumstances, the procedure of selection of operators has to comply with the principles of equality and transparency. In Case C-64/08 *Engelmann*[45] the Court of Justice decided that the Austrian legislation was not in harmony with the EU principles of transparency and non-discrimination as, first, it limited the possibility to obtain an authorization as operator of games only to companies established on the national territory of Austria, and, secondly, as regards the procedure of distribution of those authorizations of exploitation, limited in number and in duration, it did not guarantee any transparency.

The principle of non-discrimination applies equally to *criminal sanctions*. That was made clear by the Court in relation to Swedish legislation in *Sjöberg & Gerdin*.[46] The prohibition of advertisement organized in other Member States aimed at Swedish players could not be sanctioned more severely than the same sort of promotion of games organized illegally on national territory. It was, of course, up to the national court to establish whether such difference of treatment existed; the fact that criminal sanctions were defined in two distinctive texts was not, however, sufficient to establish a difference of treatment.

Further, these principles of equality and non-discrimination apply as general principles of EU law, to the extent that they do not conflict with specific rules of EU law. For instance, the case law in the gambling field concerning Germany shows that if the principle of coherence between the various objectives announced by national legislation has to be complied with in order to justify a regime of exclusivity for certain games, the fact that all games of chance and gambling are not submitted to the same fiscal regime is not incompatible with EU law, because Directive 2006/112[47] on VAT authorizes Member States to decide to grant specific exemption to certain games.[48] The domain of taxes remains an area within which a large amount of discretion is conferred on the national authorities.

D. Concluding observations

This case law of the Court of Justice shows quite clearly that in the domain of games of chance and money EU law does not prohibit monopolies nor restrictions or prohibitions, as long as these constraints are in coherence with the national policy objectives announced (as long, at least, as these can be made out as being genuine objectives). As indicated by the Court in a number of preliminary rulings, it is a matter for the national courts to proceed to an evaluation of the various criteria and to suggest the right balance. This evaluation might prove difficult

[45] Case C-64/08 *Criminal proceedings against Ernst Engelmann* [2010] OJ C 288/9.
[46] Joined Cases C-447 and 448/08 *Sjöberg* & *Gerdin*, n 8 above, para 49 et seq.
[47] See n 11 above. [48] Case C-58/09 *Leo-Libera*, n 12 above.

when, as in the *Gambelli* case, the promotion of the legal availability of gaming is deemed to eradicate illegal gaming; but this apparent contradiction is a national choice and not the result of an EU obligation. It has been emphasized that there is currently no EU harmonization of gaming regulations, and that the Member States have confirmed their hostility as regards any evolution in such direction. Therefore, while a Member State like France had no obligation under EU law to abandon its tradition of exclusive rights, it was certainly difficult not to react to the aggressive policy of certain operators established abroad and multiplying attractive offers directed at players established on the French territory. By the law of 12 May 2010 relating to the opening to competition and regulation the domain of games of money and chance, France has definitely opted for a solution of wide openness of the market whereas it could have maintained more protective, more restrictive solutions. The question of coherence between the objectives announced was duly considered by the legislator. Article 3 of the law enumerates the following objectives: prevention of addiction and protection of young people; reliability and transparency of operations of game; prevention of fraudulent and criminal activities, money laundering and financing of terrorism. The new French law adds a fourth objective: promotion of a balanced development of the various types of games in order to avoid the destabilization of the economic activities concerned. This could be at the origin of a difficult contradiction between protection of morality and traditional values on one side and development of an activity of services on the other. Is the new regime of authorization adequately meeting these contradictory objectives?

Before this law was adopted, the French Conseil d'État posed a question about the coherence of objectives in Case C-212/08 *Zeturf Ltd v Premier Minister*,[49] which the Court answered at the end of June 2011. In this judgment the Court reaffirmed that a Member State which sought to ensure a particularly high level of consumer protection in the gambling sector could be justified in taking the view that only by granting exclusive rights to a single body subject to strict control by the public authorities could it tackle the risks connected with that sector and pursue sufficiently effectively the objective of preventing incitement to squander money on gambling and of combating addiction to gambling. In view of the case law discussed above, this recent judgment is scarcely surprising.

Zeturf is also important for emphasizing matters which the national court had to take into account. The Court emphasized that it was for the national court to decide whether the national authorities genuinely sought, at the material time, to ensure such a high level of protection, and whether, looking at the level sought, the establishment of a monopoly could actually be considered necessary. The national court also had to consider whether the state controls to which the activities of that single body were in principle subject were actually implemented in the consistent and systematic pursuit of the objectives assigned to that body. In order to be consistent with the objectives of combating gambling and reducing criminal

[49] Case C-212/08 *Zeturf Ltd v Premier Minister* [2011] OJ C 252/2. This judgment came too late for inclusion in the discussion above and so is discussed briefly here.

activities, national legislation establishing a gambling monopoly would have to be based on a finding that criminal and fraudulent activities linked to gambling addiction were indeed a problem in the Member State concerned, which could be solved by the expansion of authorized and regulated activities; it could also only allow advertising which was measured and strictly limited to what was necessary to channel consumers towards controlled gaming networks.

Finally, in considering the effects of the French system on the freedom to provide services, the Court observed in *Zenturf* that the national court had to take account of all the substitutable channels for horse-racing betting covered by the exclusive system, unless the result of using the Internet was to increase the risks linked to games of chance beyond those existing in relation to games marketed through traditional channels; if national legislation applied to those channels and to horse-racing betting online, the restriction on the freedom to provide services would have to be assessed from the point of view of the restrictions placed on the whole sector concerned.

As will be apparent, the Court is most concerned to maintain the balance between the competing interests: genuine acceptable interests justifying obstacles to the freedoms of the internal market will have to be made out, rather than merely asserted, and the balancing of factors makes considerable demands of the judiciary, both at European and national levels. The domain of games is an example of the difficulty faced when seeking to find common ground between Member States where moral, religious and cultural questions are at stake together with economic considerations.

This remarkable body of case law well demonstrates that all is not plain sailing in achieving the internal market in all sectors of economic activity. In the absence of the political will for positive integration, the role of the judiciary becomes crucial in finding the balance in negative integration between often deeply felt sensitivities. At the same time, given the cross-border implications of the Internet, the question as to how long a Europe-wide solution will take in coming is ever more timely and pressing. Perhaps as a result of the consultation exercise on the Commission's Green Paper, an initiative may yet come to the table. Whether it will get the same stony reception as past endeavours is something on which it may not be wise to place a bet, unless one has money one can afford to lose.

7

Freedom of Commercial Expression and Public Health Protection: The Principle of Proportionality as a Tool to Strike the Balance

*Amandine Garde**

A. Introduction

John Usher was known for his in-depth knowledge not only of general European Union law, but also of a range of specialist areas. This chapter attempts to draw on two areas on which John wrote extensively: the general principles of EU law and the internal market. More specifically, it focuses on how the European Court of Justice (the Court) applied the principle of proportionality in the *Tobacco Advertising* litigation and compares the Court's approach to advertising restrictions with the approach of the US Supreme Court. While the US Supreme Court has tended to adopt a robust approach to the proportionality assessment of advertising restrictions, the Court has left a particularly broad margin of discretion to the EU legislature and has proven rather reluctant to engage thoroughly with existing evidence supporting (or not) such restrictions, in particular when public health considerations have been at stake. This chapter argues that neither court has struck a suitable balance between, on the one hand, the need to ensure that public authorities adequately discharge the burden of proof resting on them to justify restrictions on the freedom of commercial operators to advertise their goods and services and, on the other hand, the need to ensure that courts do not substitute their assessment for that of the legislature in exercising their powers of judicial review.

B. The proportionality assessment in *Tobacco Advertising II* revisited

As is well known, Germany challenged two Directives (adopted respectively in 1998[1] and in 2003[2]) banning tobacco advertising and sponsorship on a variety of

* Durham Law School.

[1] Directive 98/43/EC on the approximation of the laws, regulations and administrative provisions of the Member States relating to the advertising and sponsorship of tobacco products [1998] OJ L 213/9.

[2] Directive 2003/33/EC on the approximation of the laws, regulations and administrative provisions of the Member States relating to the advertising and sponsorship of tobacco products [2003] OJ L 152/16.

grounds. In particular, the German Government argued that the Directives restricting tobacco advertising and sponsorship violated the freedom of commercial operators to advertise their goods. More specifically, it claimed that, if the objective of the EU legislature was weighted against the prejudice to fundamental rights, the contested provisions contained in Articles 3 and 4 of the Directive were inappropriate and that the EU legislature should not have adopted measures as restrictive as the total prohibition on the advertising and sponsorship of tobacco products in the press.

In the *Tobacco Advertising I* case, the Court did not assess this argument, since it annulled the 1998 Directive in its entirety on the ground that the EU did not have the necessary powers to adopt the measure in question.[3] In the *Tobacco Advertising II* case, however, the Court held that the EU legislature had not infringed the principle of conferral by adopting the 2003 Directive, and then moved on to assess the other arguments invoked by Germany, including whether the measure was too restrictive and, as such, violated the freedom of tobacco manufacturers to promote their goods.[4]

(1) The role of Article 10 ECHR in the Court's decision

Article 10 of the European Convention on Human Rights (ECHR) provides:

> Everyone has the right to freedom of expression. This right shall include freedom to hold opinions and to receive and impart information and ideas without interference by public authority and regardless of frontiers.

Even though the notion of expression has been left undefined, the European Court of Human Rights has extended its scope to cover not only artistic and political but also commercial expression,[5] on the ground that consumers have the right to receive information on the goods and services available to them on a given market: 'For the citizen, advertising is a means of discovering the characteristics of goods and services offered to him'.[6] This echoes the statement of the US Supreme Court in its famous *Virginia Board* decision:

> [T]he free dissemination of commercial information allows businesses to promote their goods and services, while offering the possibility to consumers of being informed about the goods and services in question, which may in turn lead to increased competition between

[3] Case C-376/98 *Germany v Council and the European Parliament* [2000] ECR I-8419 (*Tobacco Advertising I*). John Usher was among the many commentators on this case: J Usher, 'Case C-376/98 *Germany v. European Parliament and Council (Tobacco Advertising)*' (2001) 38:6 *Common Market Law Review* 1520.

[4] Case C-380/03 *Germany v Council and the European Parliament* [2006] ECR I-11573 (*Tobacco Advertising II*).

[5] See, in particular, the decisions in *Markt Intern v Germany* Series A no 165 (1990) 12 EHRR 161; in *Groppera v Switzerland* Series A no 173 (1990) 12 EHRR 321; in *Casado Coca v Spain* Series A no 285 (1994) 18 EHRR 1; and in *Krone Verlag GmbH & Co. KG v Austria* Series A no 9605/03 (14.11.08).

[6] *Casado Coca v Spain* Series A no 285 (1994) 18 EHRR 1, para 51; see further *Krone Verlag GmbH & Co. KG v Austria* Series A no 9605/03 (14.11.08), para 31.

manufacturers and service providers. The underlying assumption is that if a product or a service is lawfully available on the market, consumers should be able to know about it so that they can decide which one to choose among competing products and services.[7]

In other words, to justify the extension of the protection traditionally granted to political and artistic expression to commercial expression, the European Court of Human Rights and the US Supreme Court have invoked not only the right of commercial operators to advertise their goods and services but also the right of the recipients of commercial expression—consumers—to receive the information and rely on it to make informed consumption choices. The role attributed to advertising in a free market economy arguably becomes all the greater in the context of the EU internal market, which rests upon the possibility for traders and consumers alike to engage in cross-border transactions and thus aims to avoid the crystallization of consumer habits along national lines.

Nevertheless, freedom of expression is not absolute and may be restricted for overriding reasons of public interest. As stated in Article 10(2) ECHR:

> The exercise of [the freedoms to hold opinions and to receive and impart information and ideas], since it carries with it duties and responsibilities, may be subject to such formalities, conditions, restrictions or penalties as are prescribed by law and are necessary in a democratic society, in the interests of national security, territorial integrity or public safety, for the prevention of disorder or crime, for the protection of health or morals, for the protection of the reputation or rights of others, for preventing the disclosure of information received in confidence, or for maintaining the authority and impartiality of the judiciary.

The structure of the provision is clear: commercial operators have a right to promote their goods and services, and that right is protected under Article 10 of the ECHR. It may only be restricted if national authorities establish that they have an overriding requirement of public interest for doing so and that the restriction in question is proportionate. The burden of proving that the interference is both justified and proportionate rests on public authorities. Public authorities may invoke public health protection to restrict the advertising and sponsorship of products and services whose consumption is detrimental to public health if they can show that the restrictions in question are 'prescribed by law' and are 'necessary in a democratic society'.

In assessing whether restrictions imposed on commercial speech are proportionate, the European Court of Human Rights has been rather generous, leaving a broad margin of discretion to national authorities when deciding on both the necessity and the scope of the restrictions under review.[8] Nevertheless, it has consistently held that their margin of discretion is subject to European supervision:

> The Court reiterates that under its case law the state parties to the Convention have a certain margin of appreciation in assessing the necessity of an interference, but this margin is subject

[7] *Virginia Pharmacy Board v Virginia Consumer Council* (1976) 425 US 748.

[8] See, in particular, the decisions in *Markt Intern v Germany* Series A no 165 (1990) 12 EHRR 161; *Groppera v Switzerland* Series A no 173 (1990) 12 EHRR 321; *Casado Coca v Spain* Series A no 285 (1994) 18 EHRR 1; and *Krone Verlag GmbH & Co. KG v Austria* Series A no 9605/03 (14.11.08).

to European supervision as regards both the relevant rules and the decisions applying them. Such a margin of appreciation is particularly essential in the complex and fluctuating area of unfair competition. The same applies to advertising. The Court's task is therefore confined to ascertaining whether the measures taken at national level are justifiable in principle and proportionate.[9]

Article 10 of the ECHR as interpreted by the European Court of Human Rights constituted the Court of Justice's starting point in its *Tobacco Advertising II* decision.

In accordance with settled case-law, whilst the principle of freedom of expression is expressly recognized by Article 10 of the ECHR and constitutes one of the fundamental pillars of a democratic society, it nevertheless follows from Article 10(2) that freedom of expression may also be subject to certain limitations justified by objectives in the public interest, in so far as those derogations are in accordance with the law, motivated by one or more of the legitimate aims under that provision and necessary in a democratic society, that is to say justified by a pressing social need and, in particular, proportionate to the legitimate aim pursued.[10]

The Court then recalled its settled case law that the Union's legislature must be allowed a broad margin of discretion in areas which entail political, economic and social choices on its part, and in which it is called upon to undertake complex assessments.

Also, as has been correctly pointed out by the Parliament, the Council and the parties intervening in support of them, the discretion enjoyed by the competent authorities in determining the balance to be struck between freedom of expression and the objectives in the public interest which are referred to in Article 10(2) of the ECHR varies for each of the goals justifying restrictions on that freedom and depends on the nature of the activities in question. When a certain amount of discretion is available, review is limited to an examination of the reasonableness and proportionality of the interference.[11]

(2) The Court's failure to assess the proportionality of the measure under review

On the facts of the case, one may wonder about the extent to which the Court has effectively assessed the proportionality of the measure adopted by the Council and the Parliament as part of the EU Tobacco Control Strategy.[12] Indeed, the Court held that the legality of a measure adopted in that sphere could be affected only if it

[9] *Krone Verlag GmbH & Co. KG v Austria* Series A no 9605/03 (14.11.08), para 30.

[10] Case C-380/03 *Tobacco Advertising II*, n 4 above, para 154. The Court supported its argument by relying on several of its previous cases, including: Cases C-368/95 *Vereinigte Familiapress Zeitungsverlags- und vertriebs GmbH v Heinrich Bauer Verlag* [1997] ECR I-3689; Case C-60/00 *Mary Carpenter v Secretary of State for the Home Department* [2002] ECR I-6279; Case C-112/00 *Eugen Schmidberger, Internationale Transporte und Planzüge v Republik Österreich* [2003] ECR I-5659.

[11] Case C-380/03 *Tobacco Advertising II*, n 4 above, para 155.

[12] Information on the EU Tobacco Control Strategy is available at: <http://ec.europa.eu/health/tobacco/policy/index_en.htm>. See in particular the Green Paper by the Health and Consumer Protection Directorate General of the European Commission, *Towards a Europe Free from Tobacco Smoke: Policy Options at EU Level* COM (2007) 27 final.

was manifestly inappropriate having regard to the objectives which the competent institutions were seeking to pursue.[13] In its earlier ruling in the *Karner* case—a judgment that was explicitly referred to in the *Tobacco Advertising II* judgment—the Court had added that it would be reluctant to intervene with the margin of discretion left to competent authorities in relation to the commercial use of freedom of expression, particularly 'in a field as complex and fluctuating as advertising'.[14] On that basis, in *Tobacco Advertising II*, the Court held:

> In the present case, even assuming that the measures laid down in Articles 3 and 4 of the Directive prohibiting advertising and sponsorship have the effect of weakening freedom of expression indirectly, journalistic freedom of expression, as such, remains unimpaired and the editorial contributions of journalists are therefore not affected. It must therefore be found that the [EU] legislature did not, by adopting such measures, exceed the limits of the discretion which it is expressly accorded. It follows that those measures cannot be regarded as disproportionate.[15]

It is remarkable that the Court did not engage with existing evidence on the role that tobacco advertising and tobacco sponsorship play in increasing smoking rates. In other words, it did not assess either the legitimacy or the proportionality *stricto sensu* of the public health argument put forward by the EU legislature.[16] It is true that, elsewhere in the judgment, the Court made certain statements that may help to determine why the ban on tobacco advertising and tobacco sponsorship was not disproportionate.[17] More specifically, the Court highlighted that the Directive contained exceptions in that it expressly permitted the insertion of advertising for tobacco products in certain publications, in particular in those that are intended exclusively for professionals in the tobacco trade.[18] This suggests that the Directive does not completely ban tobacco advertising, thus allowing tobacco manufacturers to exercise their freedom to promote their goods via certain (though strictly limited) channels. This argument is reinforced by the internal market clause laid down in Article 8 of the Directive, which prevents Member States from restricting the free movement of products or services complying with the Directive's provisions. The adoption of more restrictive national measures is therefore prohibited.

Nevertheless, such statements do not amount to an adequate review of proportionality. There is ample evidence supporting the bans of different forms of marketing for tobacco products. In particular, the Framework Convention on Tobacco Control, which was adopted under the auspices of the World Health

[13] For a discussion of the manifestly appropriate test, see T Tridimas, *The General Principles of EU Law*, 2nd edn (Oxford: Oxford University Press, 2006) 142; see further G de Búrca, 'The Principle of Proportionality and its Application in EC Law' (1993) 13 *Yearbook of European Law* 105.

[14] Case C-71/02 *Herbert Karner Industrie-Auktionen GmbH v Troostwijk GmbH* [2004] ECR I-3025, para 51.

[15] Case C-380/03 *Tobacco Advertising II*, n 4 above, paras 156–8.

[16] In this respect, the Court's reasoning differs markedly from the reasoning of AG Fennelly on exactly the same point in *Tobacco Advertising I*, as well as the reasoning of AG Léger in *Tobacco Advertising II*. See: Opinion of AG Fennelly in Case C-376/98 *Tobacco Advertising I*, n 3 above, paras 152–76; Opinion of AG Léger in Case C-380/03 *Tobacco Advertising II*, n 4 above, paras 209–28.

[17] See in particular Case C-380/03 *Tobacco Advertising II*, n 4 above, paras 72–5.

[18] Article 3(1).

Organization,[19] calls upon Contracting Parties to recognize that a comprehensive ban on advertising, promotion and sponsorship would reduce the consumption of tobacco products and to undertake to adopt, in accordance with their constitutions and constitutional principles, a comprehensive ban on advertising, promotion and sponsorship, including a cross-border ban on advertising, promotion and sponsorship originating in their territories.[20] One would therefore have expected the Court, as the EU's constitutional court, to engage with existing evidence in order to assess the proportionality of the tobacco advertising and sponsorship ban enacted by the EU legislature and, more specifically, the extent to which it could have contributed to a high level of public health protection and whether this warranted the restriction of a competing interest, namely the fundamental freedom of tobacco manufacturers to advertise their products.

If the judgment of the Court in the *Tobacco Advertising II* case may be interpreted as a victory for public health, it is also arguable that the weak proportionality assessment of the measure under review may cut both ways. The Court's lack of guidance on how proportionality should be assessed could indeed have perverse results on the EU legislative process more generally, in that it does not encourage the EU legislature to justify its regulatory choices. The Court is under a duty to ensure that the EU legislature discharges its burden of proof, which the *Tobacco Advertising II* decision fails to acknowledge. If public authorities adequately discharge this burden by adducing relevant evidence, it is arguable that advertising bans would be more persuasive and public health ultimately better protected. If the EU legislature does not attempt to establish the likely impact of marketing practices on public health before adopting legislation restricting such practices, then the risk is that a failure to engage with existing evidence may fuel the arguments put forward by industry operators that the restrictions thus imposed are disproportionate.[21] The more robust the line of reasoning, the more advertising restrictions will withstand criticism and the more legitimate they will be. If the Court does not feel that it has the necessary expertise to assess the evidence on which a given restriction on commercial expression is based, it should nonetheless feel compelled to ensure the quality of the reasoning that has led to its adoption and, in particular, the use that competent authorities have made of such evidence. We will return to the nature of the evidence and how it should impact on the proportionality assessment in the following section of this contribution.

[19] 174 parties to date, including the EU and 26 of its 27 Member States (the odd Member State out being the Czech Republic). For the text of the FCTC, supporting evidence and other relevant information, see <http://www.who.int/fctc/en>. See further the WHO Report on the Global Tobacco Epidemic, the MPOWER Package, Geneva, 2008, 36–8, with references to a range of studies supporting extensive restrictions on tobacco advertising. See <http://whqlibdoc.who.int/publications/2008/9789241596282_eng.pdf>.

[20] Article 13. See further the Guidelines for implementation of Article 13 of the FCTC at <http://www.who.int/fctc/protocol/guidelines/adopted/article_13/en/index.html>.

[21] In the US, eg, the Centre for Consumer Freedom was established in 1996 to promote consumer choice and personal responsibility and, as such, lobbies vigorously against the imposition of advertising restrictions by public authorities: <http://consumerfreedom.com/about.cfm>.

C. The lessons to be learned from the case law of the US Supreme Court

The US Supreme Court has been far more rigorous than the Court in ensuring that public authorities have discharged the burden of proving that the advertising restrictions they have imposed are both legitimate and proportionate under the First Amendment to the US Constitution, which provides that 'Congress shall make no law . . . abridging the freedom of speech, or of the press', even though the outcome of some of its cases involving advertising restrictions appears somewhat surprising.

(1) The US Supreme Court's case law on the burden of proof

The First Amendment does not explicitly provide for derogations (on either public health or any other grounds), as Article 10(2) of the ECHR does. Nevertheless, the US Supreme Court has laid down a test, referred to as the *Central Hudson* test, which resembles the test laid down by Article 10(2) and is intended to determine whether restrictions on commercial expression may be upheld. The *Central Hudson* case involved a New York regulation imposing a complete ban on promotional advertising by electric utilities companies. The regulation rested on the finding that the interconnected utility system in the State of New York did not have sufficient fuel stocks or sources of supply to continue furnishing all customer demands for the winter of 1973–74. Three years later, when the fuel shortage had eased, the New York Public Service Commission requested comments on its proposal to continue the ban on promotional advertising, and decided to extend the prohibition in 1977. Central Hudson Gas & Electric Corporation challenged the New York regulation imposing a complete ban on promotional advertising by electric utilities companies on the ground that it violated the First Amendment. After noting that commercial speech was at stake, the US Supreme Court held:

> If the communication is neither misleading nor related to unlawful activity, the government's power is more circumscribed. The State must assert a substantial interest to be achieved by restrictions on commercial speech. Moreover, the regulatory technique must be in proportion to that interest. The limitation on expression must be designed carefully to achieve the State's goal. Compliance with this requirement may be measured by two criteria. First, the restriction must directly advance the state interest involved; the regulation may not be sustained if it provides only ineffective or remote support for the government's purpose. Second, if the governmental interest could be served as well by a more limited restriction on commercial speech, the excessive restrictions cannot survive.[22]

Four elements must therefore be considered before a ban on advertising is considered to be compatible with the First Amendment. First, the speech in

[22] *Central Hudson Gas & Electric Corporation v Public Service Commission of New York* (1980) 447 US 557, 564.

question must be protected: it must neither be false or misleading nor relate to an unlawful activity. Secondly, the State must assert a substantial interest. The third and fourth parts of the test relate to the need for the public authority to ensure that the measure in question is proportionate: the restriction must not only directly advance the interest pursued (ie whether it is legitimate), but it must also be the least burdensome on competing interests (ie whether it is proportionate *stricto sensu*). Applying this test to the facts of the *Central Hudson* case, the US Supreme Court ruled that even though there was an 'immediate connection' between the advertising ban and the State's interest in energy conservation, 'the energy conservation rationale, as important as it [was] [could not] justify suppressing information about electric devices or services that would cause no net increase in total energy use'. The State could have required instead that adverts should include information about the relative efficiency and expense of the service on offer. Consequently, as the New York Public Service Commission had not demonstrated that its interest in energy conservation could not be protected adequately by more limited regulation of the appellant's commercial expression, the ban was disproportionate.[23]

The *Central Hudson* test has been relied upon in several subsequent rulings involving the compatibility of advertising restrictions with the First Amendment to the US Constitution. Even though it has recognized the protection of public health as a 'substantial interest', the US Supreme Court has tended to apply the third and fourth parts of the *Central Hudson* test much more strictly than the Court applied the proportionality test in its *Tobacco Advertising II* judgment, and it has not hesitated to strike down measures as unconstitutional when public authorities have failed to discharge the high burden of proof resting on them. In particular, the US Supreme Court has insisted that a governmental body seeking to sustain a restriction on commercial speech must demonstrate that the harms it invokes are real and that its restriction will in fact alleviate them to a 'material' degree. Thus, in its seminal *44 Liquormart* decision, it unanimously condemned the State of Rhode Island for its failure to discharge the burden of justifying its complete ban on the advertising of retail liquor prices except at the place of sale. In delivering the Opinion of the Supreme Court, Justice Stevens stated:

> In evaluating the ban's effectiveness in advancing the State's interest [ie the promotion of temperance], we note that a commercial speech regulation 'may not be sustained if it provides only ineffective or remote support for the government's purpose'. For that reason, the State bears the burden of showing not merely that its regulation will advance its interest, but also that it will do so 'to a material degree.' The need for the State to make such a showing is particularly great given the drastic nature of its chosen means—the wholesale suppression of truthful, non misleading information. Accordingly, we must determine

[23] As discussed below, this may give rise to criticism: most notably, Rehnquist J noted in his dissenting opinion in *Central Hudson* that 'a "no more extensive than necessary" analysis will unduly impair a state legislature's ability to adopt legislation reasonably designed to promote interests that have always been rightly thought to be of great importance to the State.'

whether the State has shown that the price advertising ban will significantly reduce consumption.[24]

The US Supreme Court concluded that the State of Rhode Island had failed to demonstrate that the price-advertising ban imposed in this case would significantly reduce consumption, and it therefore held that it was unconstitutional.

The US Supreme Court's reasoning is correct on who should bear the burden of proof: if constitutional courts do not effectively review the evidence presented to them when assessing the proportionality of a given measure, then the risk is that any restriction will be upheld on the ground that public authorities have a broad margin of discretion. If courts hold that the freedom of commercial operators should benefit from constitutional protection under either the First Amendment to the US Constitution or Article 10 of the ECHR (a proposition which is far from straightforward),[25] they must act accordingly and ensure that the burden of proof is discharged by the State authority wishing to restrict the freedom at stake.

One may nonetheless question the assessment that the US Supreme Court has made of the evidence with which it was presented and, consequently, the outcome of some of its rulings. Indeed, it may be argued that it has granted far too great an importance to the right of commercial operators to rely on the First Amendment to the detriment of pressing public health concerns and has, therefore, failed convincingly to assess existing evidence when striking the balance at the proportionality stage of its *Central Hudson* enquiry. Thus, in its *44 Liquormart* ruling,[26] the US Supreme Court somewhat oversimplified the issues at stake by condemning the State of Rhode Island for failing to adopt alternative measures that would not have hindered the freedom of commercial operators to advertise their goods to the same extent as the ban on retail prices (such as the maintenance of higher prices either by direct regulation or by increased taxation, the rationing of per capita purchases, or the use of educational campaigns focused on drinking problems), whilst the evidence unequivocally supports the argument that public authorities must have comprehensive, multi-sectoral strategies in place in order to tackle alcohol-related harm effectively. Notwithstanding the extensive body of evidence supporting the development and implementation of comprehensive strategies on lifestyle determinants such as tobacco and alcohol,[27] the US Supreme Court's case

[24] *44 Liquormart v Rhode Island* (1996) 517 US 484.

[25] This chapter does not purport to lend any support to the extension of the constitutional protection provided under Article 10 ECHR or the First Amendment to the US Constitution to commercial expression. Rather, in light of the fact that this extension has been enshrined in a range of legal systems in Europe, in North America and elsewhere, it merely takes stock of this situation. For a powerful criticism of the rationale for granting constitutional protection to commercial expression, see in particular R Shiner, *Freedom of Commercial Expression* (Oxford: Oxford University Press, 2003).

[26] *44 Liquormart v Rhode Island* (1996) 517 US 484. For another example of a strict approach to the proportionality assessment of restrictions imposed on commercial speech on public health grounds, see *Lorillard Tobacco et al v Reilly, Attorney General of Massachusetts et al* (2001) 533 US 525.

[27] On this point, it is worth noting that, in Resolution WHA63.13, the Sixty-third World Health Assembly affirmed, on 21 May 2010, a global strategy to reduce the harmful use of alcohol in order to give guidance for actions and to set priority areas for global action. In particular, it stressed the importance for State Parties to consider a portfolio of policy options, including marketing, fiscal and

law suggests that other measures should have been preferred to advertising restrictions, thus denoting a misunderstanding of the public health problem at stake: there is no 'magic bullet' and, in light of the complexity of the matter under review, the Supreme Court should not have substituted its own assessment for that of the legislature.[28]

(2) Some reflections on the standard of review

The comments that have been made so far on the Court's decision in the *Tobacco Advertising II* case do not answer the question of how heavy the burden of proof resting on the EU legislature should be when it purports to restrict the freedom of commercial operators to advertise their goods and services in order to ensure a higher level of public health protection. This question on the standard of review is critical. It is arguable that the costs of smoking are so extensive that the relatively small contribution that advertising restrictions may make in curbing smoking rates and thus improving public health suffices to satisfy the test of proportionality. As discussed above, there is ample evidence supporting extensive advertising bans on tobacco products. The EU legislature should therefore be granted a broad margin of discretion in deciding how far tobacco advertising should be banned (subject to the principle of attributed competence, of course).

Assessing the proportionality of advertising restrictions may be more difficult for certain goods or services than for tobacco products. This could result either from a lack of comprehensive evidence on the effects of advertising of a given good or service on transaction decisions and public health, or from the complex nature of the goods and services at stake, or both. Nevetheless, this should not exempt legislative authorities from explaining what has prompted them to prefer a given course of action over an alternative one. When complex choices of economic and social policies are at stake, the Court should not substitute its assessment for that of the legislature; it must nonetheless ensure that the reasoning supporting the rules it has adopted is convincing, that is, that it is based on objective factors amenable to judicial review.[29]

Reliance on *ex ante* impact assessments should help the Court to determine *ex post* whether EU legislative measures are compatible with the general principles of EU law, and with the principle of proportionality more specifically. At present, all major EU policy initiatives with a potential economic, social and/or environmental

other restrictions: '[t]he diversity of alcohol-related problems and measures necessary to reduce alcohol-related harm points to the need for comprehensive action across numerous sectors. Policies to reduce the harmful use of alcohol must reach beyond the health sector, and engage such sectors as development, transport, justice, social welfare, fiscal policy, trade, agriculture, consumer policy, education and employment', WHO, Global Strategy to Reduce the Harmful Use of Alcohol (Geneva, 2010), para. 6(b), available at <http://www.who.int/substance_abuse/activities/globalstrategy/en/index.html>.

28 This being said, however, one may wonder how convincing the evidence presented by the State of Rhode Island to the US Supreme Court was. On this basis, the criticism may have to be tempered.

29 Article 1 of the Protocol on the Application of the Principles of Subsidiarity and Proportionality explicitly requires that 'each institution [including the Court] shall ensure constant respect for the principle of subsidiarity and proportionality, as laid down in Art 5 TEU'.

impact require an integrated impact assessment. This applies in particular to most legislation (proposed directives or regulations) and to White Papers, action plans, expenditure programmes and negotiating guidelines for international agreements.[30] The aim of integrated impact assessments is to ensure, first, that a proposal is sustainable by looking at the broad range of potential economic, social and environmental impacts and, secondly, that it conforms to the key constitutional principles of attributed powers, subsidiarity and proportionality.[31] The Commission has published a series of impact assessment guidelines, which are intended to give general guidance to the Commission services on assessing potential impacts of different policy options.[32] Nevertheless, public health is not singled out: it falls within the broader category of 'social impact'.[33] There is therefore a risk that a proposal with a broad range of social impacts fails to consider specifically potential health impacts.[34] The constitutional obligation on EU institutions to ensure a high level of health in connection with all EU policies,[35] and EU internal market policy in particular,[36] warrants that health should become a separate requirement for consideration.

When discussing the different options available in addressing certain risks to public health, a regulatory authority could rely on different types of evidence in order to restrict certain marketing practices. First, it may be able to invoke 'hard evidence', which is demonstrated scientifically and on which experts are in agreement; for example, that nicotine is addictive and that it is nicotine that creates dependence on smoking. This could lead the authority in question to adopt legislation setting a maximum limit on the nicotine content of tobacco products in order to minimize the dangers smoking entails for public health, as the EU legislature did by adopting Directive 2001/37 on tobacco products.[37] Such evidence would even allow the legislature to go further and ban products containing nicotine altogether from the EU market. In other cases, a regulatory authority may have strong presumptions at its disposal. For example, experiments on a small scale coupled with literature reviews have established that food marketing directly

[30] The list of all impact assessments that the Commission has completed since 2002 (when the impact assessment system was put in place) is available at <http://ec.europa.eu/governance/impact/ia_carried_out/ia_carried_out_en.htm>. On the role that impact assessments can play in judicial review, see A Alemanno, 'A Meeting of Minds on Impact Assessment—When Ex Ante Evaluation Meets Ex Post Judicial Control', (2011) 17:3 *European Public Law* 485.

[31] Article 5 TEU.

[32] The latest guidelines were issued in January 2009. <http://ec.europa.eu/governance/impact/commission_guidelines/commission_guidelines_en.htm>.

[33] Public health is listed as a sub-category of possible social impacts: see the list in Table 2 of the 2009 Impact Assessment Guidelines, at 35.

[34] A study conducted by the National Heart Forum found that in 2005 and 2006, 73 out of the 137 impact assessments carried out by the Commission did not mention the word 'health'. R Salay and P Lincoln, *The European Union and Health Impact Assessments: Are They an Unrecognized Statutory Obligation?* (London: National Heart Forum, September 2008) 13.

[35] Article 9 and Article 168(1) TFEU.

[36] Article 114(3) TFEU.

[37] Directive 2001/37 on the approximation of the laws, regulations and administrative provisions of the Member States concerning the manufacture, presentation and sale of tobacco products [2001] OJ L 194/26. On nicotine content specifically, see Article 3(1).

impacts on children's food choices and, consequently, on their health. Nevertheless, the link between food marketing and childhood obesity rates is not quantified with any degree of precision. Public authorities therefore need to discharge the delicate task of assessing the extent to which food marketing should be restricted to protect children's health. (Should all food marketing be banned? Should unhealthy food marketing only be banned? Which media and settings should be targeted as a priority?)[38] Finally, existing evidence may be such that regulatory authorities will only be able to make reasonable assumptions. For example, there is (to the best of our knowledge) no comprehensive review of the effects of consumer credit advertising on the credit consumption choices of vulnerable consumers. One could reasonably assume, however, that such advertising induces always more consumption notwithstanding the fact that certain categories of consumers are financially vulnerable. It may therefore be legitimate to limit the advertising of consumer credit, not least when it is directed to categories of particularly vulnerable consumers.

A crucial distinction must therefore be drawn between the two different stages of any risk prevention strategy. Experts will have an important role to play in assessing the risk. Subsequently, competent regulatory authorities will manage the risk in light of existing evidence by weighing competing interests, having regard not only to the evidence in question but also taking economic, social and cultural considerations into account. Assessing the risks a particular activity entails is only one of the steps involved in managing such risks. This is what justifies that regulatory authorities should have a broad margin of discretion in deciding how best to strike a suitable balance between the freedom of commercial operators to advertise their goods and services and their responsibility to ensure a high level of public health protection.[39] Nevertheless, a broad margin of discretion is not a *carte blanche*, and the standard of review the Court adopts should nonetheless be sufficiently strict so that public authorities wishing to impose advertising restrictions carefully justify not only why but also how far they intend to interfere with the freedom of commercial operators to advertise their goods and services in order to ensure a high level of public health protection.

D. The coherence of the Court's use of the principle of proportionality

The *Tobacco Advertising II* case is not the only example in which the Court has not fully engaged with existing evidence and in which it has therefore failed to carry out the balancing exercise that the principle of proportionality entails. In the last 10 years, the Court has been called upon to consider a range of cases involving the

[38] For a review of existing evidence supporting the regulation of food marketing to children as part of obesity prevention strategies, see A Garde, *EU Law and Obesity Prevention* (Alphen aan den Rijn: Kluwer Law International, 2010) 171.

[39] In any event, impact assessments should be used to inform policy decisions, rather than justify a preferred policy option determined independently from the impact assessment process: Information Note from the President to the Commission, 'Better Regulation and Enhanced Impact Assessment', 28 June 2007, SEC (2007) 926.

extent to which Member States are entitled to impose advertising restrictions with a view to ensuring a high level of public health protection. In particular, the question of the proportionality of alcohol and gambling advertising restrictions, imposed to limit the harmful consequences of alcohol abuse and gambling addiction respectively, has featured prominently in the Court's case law. These cases contrast sharply with other judgments that the Court has delivered in similarly sensitive areas, thus raising concerns pertaining to the lack coherence of its approach and the uncertainty deriving therefrom.

(1) Advertising for alcoholic beverages and gambling services

In relation to alcohol advertising, we should briefly mention the decision of the Court in *Commission v France*, in which the Commission challenged the *Loi Evin* imposing a near total ban on alcohol advertising in France.[40] In its decision, the Court hardly discussed the proportionality of the measure: as in its *Tobacco Advertising II* ruling, it did not weigh the evidence; rather, it merely observed that the prohibition was appropriate to achieve the objective of public health protection and did not go beyond what was necessary to achieve that objective. As Tridimas has noted, the Court paid lip service to the argument that indirect television advertising was allowed in multinational sporting events, where the French audience was very high, but not in bi-national events, which tended to attract lower audience numbers. The Court confined itself to pointing out that bi-national events targeted specifically a French audience and, therefore, the restriction of the prohibition to such events made it proportionate. The Court was preoccupied not so much with upholding a consistent health policy but with national choice.[41] If the outcome of the case may be defensible, the reasoning certainly is not.[42]

Similarly, in its case law on the advertising of gambling services, the Court has tended to defer to the decisions of national authorities. In particular, the question has arisen whether it is lawful for a Member State to rely on the declared objective of preventing incitement to squander money on gambling and fighting gambling addiction in order to justify a restrictive measure in circumstances where a Member State is not able to prove the existence of a study carried out before the adoption of the measure supporting its proportionality. In the *Lindman* case, the Court held:

[40] Case C-262/02 *Commission v France* [2004] ECR I-6569. See further the judgment delivered on the same day in Case C-429/02 *Bacardi France SAS, formerly Bacardi-Martini SAS v Télévision française 1 SA (TF1), Groupe Jean-Claude Darmon SA and Girosport SARL* [2004] ECR I-6613.

[41] T Tridimas, n 13 above, 222.

[42] Similarly in Case C-405/98 *Konsumentombudsmannen (KO) v Gourmet International Products AB (GIP)* [2001] ECR I-1795, annotated by A Biondi, 'Advertising Alcohol and the Free Movement Principle: the *Gourmet* Decision' (2001) 26 *European Law Review* 616. One should note that in both *Gourmet* and *Commission v France*, the arguments of the parties were not framed in Article 10 ECHR terms. Nevertheless, the structure of both the free movement provisions and Article 10 ECHR requires that the public authority wishing to impose advertising restrictions on public health grounds should bear the burden of establishing that the measure is proportionate. The comparison is therefore warranted.

the reasons which may be invoked by a Member State by way of justification must be accompanied by an analysis of the appropriateness and proportionality of the restrictive measure adopted by that State.[43]

The Court insisted on the fact that the file transmitted by the referring court disclosed no statistical or other evidence that enabled any conclusion as to the gravity of the risks connected to playing games of chance or, *a fortiori*, the existence of a particular causal relationship between such risks and participation by nationals of the Member State concerned in lotteries organized in other Member States.[44] On this basis, the Court concluded that Finnish legislation violated Article 56 TFEU (then Article 49 EC).[45]

Nevertheless, in its more recent ruling in *Stoß*, the Grand Chamber stated:

> [I]f a Member State wishes to rely on an objective capable of justifying an obstacle to the freedom to provide services arising from a national restrictive measure, it is under a duty to supply the court called upon to rule on that question with all the evidence of such a kind as to enable the latter to be satisfied that the said measure does indeed fulfil the requirements arising from the principle of proportionality. It cannot, however, be inferred from that case law that a Member State is deprived of the possibility of establishing that an internal restrictive measure satisfies those requirements solely on the ground that that Member State is not able to produce studies serving as the basis for the adoption of the legislation at issue.[46]

The Court thus adopted a narrow reading of the *Lindman* judgment. It then reaffirmed its previous rulings that national authorities enjoyed 'a broad margin of discretion',[47] and that it was for each Member State to assess whether it was necessary wholly or partially to prohibit activities of that nature or only to restrict them and to lay down more or less strict supervisory rules for that purpose, the need for and proportionality of the measures thus adopted having to be assessed solely in relation to the objectives pursued and the level of protection that the national authorities concerned sought to ensure.[48] This decision does not promote the integration of national markets in the field of gambling services, even though such services have a clear cross-border dimension, not least with the advent of online gambling. Here, again, the Court does not balance conflicting interests. It simply reiterates that it is for Member States to decide how they regulate gambling services, provided that the measures they have adopted are consistent and systematic—the national courts being entrusted to carry out such assessment. The Court seems to focus more on the absence of contradictions in national policies,[49] than on

[43] Case C-42/02 *Diana Elisabeth Lindman* [2003] ECR I-13519, para 25.

[44] ibid para 26.

[45] ibid para 27.

[46] Joined Cases C-316/07, C-358/07, C-359/07, C-360/07, C-409/07 and C-410/07 *Stoß* [2010] OJ C 288/7, paras 71 and 72.

[47] ibid para 92.

[48] ibid para 91, with reference to previous case law.

[49] ibid para 103, the Court highlighted: 'it important, in that respect, that any advertising issued by the holder of a public monopoly remain measured and strictly limited to what is necessary in order thus to channel consumers towards authorized gaming networks. Such advertising cannot, however, in

whether the measures are well-founded. In *Stoß* and other gambling cases, rather little is made of the role of Articles 49 and 56 TFEU in promoting market integration.[50]

It is true that the EU internal market is not, and has never been, unlimited. It is also true, however, that the principle of proportionality is, and has always been, the cornerstone of the Court's free movement case law. It may be right that Member States should not be prevented from acting in the absence of studies establishing that the advertising of gambling increases gambling addiction. As stated above, the detrimental impact of advertising on public health may not be quantified with any precision and, in the absence of scientific evidence, a Member State could prudently infer that the advertising of gambling services may increase their consumption and therefore increase the harm caused by gambling addiction, increasing in turn its individual and societal costs. The Court's decision in *Stoß* implicitly recognizes that evidence may vary in nature, from scientific proof to reasonable assumptions, and that it should ultimately be for competent regulatory authorities (ie Member States in the absence of EU harmonizing legislation) to assess existing evidence, subject to their compliance with general Treaty provisions. Once again, however, the lack of conclusive evidence of impact should not amount to exempting Member States from justifying why they have adopted certain measures restricting the free movement of services, and why they consider these measures to be legitimate and not impinging beyond what is necessary on potentially conflicting interests.

(2) Betting on the Court's approach—rien ne va plus?

In all of these judgments, the Court has left an extremely broad margin of discretion to national authorities. This is all the more surprising as these cases involved the compatibility of national measures with general free movement Treaty provisions, rather than the compatibility of an EU legislative measure with general principles of EU law and the rights protected under Article 10 ECHR more specifically. Traditionally, a distinction has been drawn between the stricter review of the Court when assessing the former restrictions and the lighter review when assessing the latter. Of course, depending on the interests at stake, Member States have always been granted more or less leeway to address national imperatives of public interest, including public health protection.

particular, aim to encourage consumers' natural propensity to gamble by stimulating their active participation in it, such as by trivializing gambling or giving it a positive image due to the fact that revenues derived from it are used for activities in the public interest, or by increasing the attractiveness of gambling by means of enticing advertising messages depicting major winnings in glowing colours.' One is tempted to point out that the line between advertising that encourages consumers to gamble and advertising that does not will be extremely difficult to draw.

[50] On the Court's recent case law in the field of gambling services, see D Doukas, 'In a Bet there is a Fool and a State Monopoly: Are the Odds Staked against Cross-Border Gambling?' (2011) 36 *European Law Review* 243; A Biondi, 'Against the Odds: A Critique of the European Court of Justice *Acquis* on Gambling Regulations' in R Sacco (ed), *Liber Amicorum Professor Frignani* (Turin: Giappichelli, 2011) 901.

Nevertheless, the Court's case law in the last few years does not support the argument that the more sensitive a given area, the less intrusive the Court's proportionality assessment. For example, the cases on patient mobility, in which the Court has proven much more willing to assess whether Member States were justified in refusing prior authorizations to patients requesting treatment in another Member State,[51] or the *Viking* judgment, in which the Court has rather strictly circumscribed the discretion of national courts to assess whether collective action is too restrictive of the freedom of establishment,[52] have shown that the Court does not always shy away from contentious cases. The question therefore arises as to what distinguishes different categories of cases and what explains a stricter rather than a more lenient approach to the proportionality assessment of legislative measures intended to promote public health or other overriding requirements of public interest. The Court's case law has become extremely difficult to systematize.

One may risk the hypothesis that the Court condemns the use of goods such as alcohol or tobacco, and services such as gambling services on the ground that they are 'vice' products or activities.[53] It is therefore willing to allow, in the restriction of the advertising of such products and services, a broad margin of discretion to the EU legislature and to national authorities. If the Court's use of the principle of proportionality is not coherent, however, the suspicion may arise that it solely supports the legislative choices of which it approves on moral grounds. If that is the case, the softer the review, the more the Court makes a value judgement. Such a conclusion would be somewhat ironic, as a soft proportionality review is generally seen as a way for the Court to be neutral. This approach would, in any event, constitute a misuse of the principle of proportionality and a misunderstanding by the Court of its role in the development of EU internal market law.

E. Conclusion

As the impact of advertising on public health is often difficult to quantify, the Court should neither substitute its assessment for that of legislative authorities nor instrumentalize the principle of proportionality to suit its own policy preferences. Rather, the Court should ensure that legislative authorities have discharged the

[51] See in particular Case C-372/04 *The Queen, on the application of Yvonne Watts v Bedford Primary Care Trust and Secretary of State for Health* [2006] ECR I-4325, A Biondi, n 49 above, 910.

[52] Case C-438/05 *International Transport Workers' Federation and Finnish Seamen's Union v Viking Line ABP and OÜ Viking Line Eesti* [2007] ECR I-10779.

[53] Several statements in the Court's case law on gambling services support this analysis. eg, it held in Case C-275/92 *Schindler* [1994] ECR I-1039 that '[e]ven if *the morality of lotteries is at least questionable*, it is not for the Court to substitute its assessment for that of the legislatures of the Member States where that activity is practised legally', para 32 (emphasis added). More recently, in its judgment in *Stoß* (n 46 above), it ruled, referring to its previous judgments, that 'moral, religious or cultural factors, as well as the morally and financially harmful consequences for the individual and for society associated with betting and gaming, may serve to justify a margin of discretion for the national authorities, sufficient to enable them to determine, in accordance with their own scale of values, what is required in order to ensure consumer protection and the preservation of public order' (para 76).

burden of proving that the measures they have adopted are proportionate. In particular, it must verify that they have balanced competing interests on the basis of objective factors amenable to judicial review. If a cautious approach should be favoured in the absence of conclusive evidence, legislative authorities are still required to spell out the reasoning which has led them to adopt certain measures restricting the freedom of commercial operators to advertise their goods and services in order to ensure a high level of public health protection (bearing in mind that competent authorities should monitor and evaluate their policies, should new evidence requiring a different balancing of competing interests come to light). The proceduralization of proportionality should therefore reinforce both the transparency of the legislative process and its long-term credibility. This is particularly important to further the EU's commitment to 'strengthening citizens' confidence in their Internal Market',[54] particularly in 'an area as complex and fluctuating'[55] as advertising.

[54] Commission's Communication, *Single Market Act—Twelve Levers to Boost Growth and Strengthen Confidence 'Working Together to Create New Growth'* COM (2011) 206 final, 3.

[55] Case C-71/02 *Karner*, n 14 above, para 51.

8

A Private Right Conferred Directly by EU Trade Mark Law: An Analysis of the Concept of 'Distinctiveness' under EU Law

*Rosa Greaves**

A. Introduction

A significant obstacle to the establishment of the EU common market[1] (renamed 'the internal market' in the 1980s) was, and remains, the existence of national intellectual property rights conferred by the laws of the Member States, which grant the holders exclusive property rights over the national territory. For example, a trade mark owner, before the establishment of the common market, could register the same trade mark in several Member States, and then rely on the national law of each Member State to prevent parallel imports of its trade marked goods. In this manner, the mark owner was in effect able to divide the European market along national boundaries and benefit from price variations, to the detriment of the European consumer. Thus, the territorial exclusivity of these rights was a major obstacle to the implementation of the EU free movement of goods rules,[2] one of the four fundamental freedoms of the European project. In the context of trade marks, national laws prevented the free movement of the marked goods from one national market to another within the common market.

The solution to the problem set out above is not difficult to find, namely the substitution of national private rights by EU-wide rights, that is, rights conferred over the territory of the EU as a whole.[3] However, given the proprietary nature of these rights, an evolution of the relationship between national law and EU law in this field had to be undertaken before market operators and the Member States

* Universities of Glasgow and Oslo.

[1] The Treaty establishing European Economic Community (1957), Article 2.

[2] The Treaty on the Functioning of the European Union (TFEU) [2010] OJ C 83/47, Articles 34–6. The TFEU (through the mechanism of the Lisbon Treaty) came into force on 1 December 2009. The Treaty replaced and renumbered the 1957 EC Treaty.

[3] The territory over which EU intellectual property law rights are conferred is in fact the European Economic Area, which, in addition to the 27 EU Member States, also includes Iceland, Liechtenstein and Norway.

would accept EU-wide regulation. Initially, the European Court of Justice (ECJ) was the key driver in reconciling the idea of a market within which goods and services placed anywhere in the EU were in free circulation with proprietary rights granted by national intellectual property laws to trade mark owners, conferring on them the right to exclude from the national territory any product bearing their mark which had not been placed on that national market by the trade mark owner himself. However, by the mid-1980s, it became clear that more radical measures needed to be taken to complete the task of establishing an integrated common market. Thus, the more ambitious concept of an internal market was launched by a White Paper[4] setting out approximately 300 legislative measures, which required adoption in order to remove physical, fiscal and technical barriers to trade. As far as trade marks were concerned, two legislative measures were adopted, namely, Council Directive 89/104 (the Trade Mark Directive),[5] which harmonized national trade mark law, and Council Regulation 40/94 (the European Union Trade Mark Regulation or EUTM Regulation),[6] which created an intellectual property right conferred directly by EU law (the EU trade mark).

This chapter will first set out briefly, and by way of background and context, the solutions adopted by the ECJ in order to reconcile the national private law rights of trade mark owners with EU law, up to the adoption of the EUTM Regulation. The chapter will then focus on the requirement of 'distinctiveness' of a mark, which is a crucial element before a mark can be registered as a trade mark under EU law. Thus, in the substantive part of the chapter, the focus will be on some selected but important judgments from the European courts. These cases established the tests to be applied in determining the 'distinctiveness' of combined words and also non-traditional marks such as smells, sounds, colours, shapes and slogans. If these types of marks are devoid of distinctive character, or are exclusively descriptive, then the conditions of Article 7 of the EUTM Regulation are not satisfied and the mark cannot be registered unless distinctiveness has been acquired by use in accordance with the Article 7(3) exception.

This substantive part of the chapter will be structured as follows. First, some general rules on the manner in which 'distinctiveness' can be established will be set out. Secondly, two significant borderline cases, which were appealed to the ECJ, and two preliminary references from national courts will be analysed. Thirdly, a brief reference on 'acquired distinctiveness' under Article 7(3) of the EUTM Regulation will follow. Finally, by way of conclusion, some general observations will be offered on the future of EU regulation of intellectual property rights given

[4] Commission of the European Communities, *Completing the Internal Market: White Paper from the Commission to the European Council*, Milan, 28–29 June 1985 COM (85) 310 final.

[5] First Council Directive of 21 December 1988 to approximate the laws of the Member States relating to trade marks [1989] OJ L 40/1. This Directive has now been replaced by Council Directive 2008/95 of 22 October 2008 to approximate the laws of the Member States relating to trade marks [2008] OJ L 299/25, but the substantive articles and numbering have not been changed.

[6] Council Regulation (EC) No 40/94 of 20 December 1993 on the Community trade mark [1994] OJ L 11/1. The Regulation was replaced by Council Regulation (EC) 207/2009 of 26 February 2009 on the Community trade mark [2009] OJ L 78/1.

that, in May 2011, the European Commission published a Communication setting out a strategy for intellectual property rights in the single European market[7]and outlining the policies that the Commission intends to adopt during its current mandate, which terminates in 2014.

B. The reconciliation of national trade mark law with EU law and the EUTM Regulation

Unlike other areas of economic activity, such as fisheries, the EU does not have exclusive competence in the field of intellectual property law. However, there are two sets of Treaty provisions that have a direct impact on the rights granted by national laws to trade mark owners. First, national intellectual property laws by their very nature are measures having equivalent effect to quantitative restrictions, which are prohibited by Article 34 of the Treaty on the Functioning of the EU (TFEU). These national laws confer rights on individuals, such as trade mark owners, which enable them to prevent parallel imports, and that is incompatible with the concept of an integrated common market. However, recognition of the importance of intellectual property rights is evidenced by Article 36 TFEU, which provides an express derogation from the application of Article 34, if a national measure having equivalent effect to a quantitative measure can be justified on the grounds of protection of industrial and commercial property.

Secondly, trade mark owners may be prohibited from exploiting their proprietary rights by virtue of the EU competition rules. As property rights, trade marks can be sold (assigned) and licensed to other market operators. Such transactions are governed by national laws but must not contain restrictions that are prohibited by the EU competition rules, namely by Article 101 TFEU. Similarly, owners of trade marks must not conduct themselves on the market in a manner which is prohibited by Article 102 TFEU as an abuse of a dominant position.

As stated before, the conflict between these two sets of EU law provisions and the protectionism afforded by national intellectual property laws were resolved, at least in part, by the ECJ. The process may indeed be described as evolutionary. It took a number of judgments before several doctrines were developed not only to accommodate the property rights of trade mark owners conferred by sovereign States, but also to ensure that the primacy of EU law over national law was respected.[8] The ECJ therefore adopted the exhaustion of rights doctrine,[9] invented the existence and exercise dichotomy,[10] and defined the specific subject matter[11] of each intellectual

[7] *A Single Market for Intellectual Property Rights*, COM (2011) 285 final.

[8] Case 6/64 *Costa v ENEL* [1964] ECR 585.

[9] The exhaustion of rights doctrine, in the context of trade marks, provides that once a trade marked good is placed on the market by the owner or with the owner's consent, that trade marked good is free to circulate anywhere within the EU.

[10] The ECJ ruled that whether a right exists is a matter for the national law of the Member States but that the exercise of the right (eg granting a licence) is a matter for EU law.

[11] The specific subject matter relates primarily to the right to place the trade marked goods/services in the market for the first time and the right to commence infringement proceedings.

property right as the core of the existence of the right, which is protected under national law. In the context of trade marks, the relevant judgments are *Consten & Grunding v Commission*[12] (exhaustion doctrine and existence/exercise dichotomy) and *Centrafarm v Winthrop*[13] (specific subject matter of a trade mark).[14]

These doctrines enabled EU law and national laws to co-exist in a relatively harmonious manner and thus ensure that the exercise of national intellectual property rights did not deflect the EU from its primary objective of market integration. However, the political decision to progress from a common market to an internal market in the mid-1980s demanded a more radical approach, which resulted in the harmonization of national trade mark laws (through the EUTM Directive) in 1989 and the creation of an EU trade mark by the adoption of the EUTM Regulation in 1994. Thus, the regulation of intellectual property rights granted by EU law started almost thirty years after the establishment of the common market. A few years later, the EU took the significant step of creating a private property right, the EU trade mark, whose existence and exercise is solely regulated by EU law. In this manner, the EU positioned itself as an integrated market offering a trade mark owner protection under its distinct legal system across a large geographical market with almost 500 million consumers.

The EUTM Regulation provided for the establishment of the Office for the Harmonisation of the Internal Market (OHIM), with powers to take decisions on the registration of European trade marks granting exclusivity to the owner over the whole EU territory. In the Preamble to the EUTM Regulation, it is stated that 'it is necessary to ensure that the parties who are affected by decisions made by [OHIM] are protected by the law in a manner in which is suited to the special character of trade mark law'.[15] That protection is secured by granting exclusive jurisdiction to the General Court, and an appeal on points of law to the ECJ, which may annul or alter a contested OHIM decision.

Article 4 of the Trade Mark Regulation provides that:

> A Community trade mark may consist of any signs capable of being represented geographically, particularly words, including personal names, designs, letters, numerals, the shape of goods or of their packaging, provided that such signs are capable of distinguishing the goods or services of one undertaking from those of other undertakings.

Thus, after the adoption of the EUTM Regulation, expectations were high that non-traditional marks, such as smells and colours, which had failed previously to be registered as a trade mark, might now be so registered. Such expectations were soon quashed, however, with OHIM refusing to register certain marks on the grounds that the marks were not able to satisfy the graphical representation requirement or that they lacked distinctiveness. Several OHIM decisions rejecting applications

[12] Joined Cases 56 and 58/64 *Établissements Consten S.à.R.L. and Grundig-Verkaufs-GmbH v Commission of the European Economic Community* [1966] ECR 299.

[13] Case 16/74 *Centrafarm BV and Adriaan de Peijper v Winthrop BV* [1974] ECR 1183.

[14] For further information on these doctrines, see J Steiner, L Woods and C Twigg-Flesner, *EU Law*, 10th edn (Oxford: Oxford University Press, 2009) 714–20.

[15] EUTM Regulation, n 6 above.

for registration on the grounds that the submitted mark lacks distinctiveness have been appealed to the General Court. Furthermore, preliminary references[16] have been sent from national courts to the ECJ as to the meaning of the concept of 'distinctiveness' under the Trade Mark Directive. Appeals from the General Court to the ECJ began just at the end of the last century, with the first ECJ appeal judgment in *Procter & Gamble (Baby-Dry).*[17]

C. General principles in appraising the 'distinctiveness' of a mark

A large number of appeals against OHIM decisions, including the first appeal to the ECJ from the General Court in this context (*Procter & Gamble*), have concerned the criteria to be applied in order to determine whether a trade mark is 'devoid of any distinctive character', which is an absolute ground for refusal to register under Article 7(1)(b) of the EUTM Regulation. This absolute ground of refusal is linked to another provision, which disqualifies a trade mark from registration if it is exclusively descriptive of the character of the goods or services (Article 7(1)(c)). However, both grounds of refusal can be overcome by evidence that the trade mark has become distinctive through use, under Article 7(3).[18]

In various judgments of the European courts, some principles on the application and scope of these two grounds of refusal have been determined. First, the test to establish distinctiveness is the same for traditional and non-traditional marks. The ECJ has repeatedly confirmed that the assessment test is the same for all types of marks. Secondly, for a mark to possess distinctive character, it must serve to identify the products or services in respect of which registration is applied for as originating from a particular trader or undertaking and thus to distinguish those products or services from those of other traders or undertakings. The distinctive character must be assessed by reference to the products or services and by reference to the perception of them by the relevant public, the consumers. The relevant public consists of the average consumer of the products or services, who is reasonably well informed and reasonably observant and circumspect.[19]

Although each ground of absolute refusal is independent, there is considerable overlap between the assessment of distinctiveness and descriptiveness. A mark that

[16] The ECJ has exclusive competence to interpret and make declarations of validity of EU law. A preliminary reference under Article 267 TFEU enables national courts to refer questions of interpretation and validity of EU law, which have arisen in the national litigation, directly to the ECJ for a definitive ruling. The ruling is binding on the national court which then applies it in the national litigation.

[17] Case C-383/99 P *Procter & Gamble Company v Office for Harmonisation in the Internal Market (Trade Marks and Designs)* [2001] ECR I-6251.

[18] The corresponding provisions in the EU Trade Mark Directive are Articles 3(1)(b), (1)(c) and Article 3(3).

[19] See, inter alia, Case C-342/97 *Lloyd Schuhfabrik Meyer & Co. GmbH v Klijsen Handel BV* [1999] ECR I-3819, para 26; Cases C-53/01 to C-55/01 *Linde AG & Others* [2003] ECR I-3161, para 41; and Case C-363/99 *Koninklijke KPN Nederland NV v Benelux-Merkenbureau* [2004] ECR I-1619, para 34.

is descriptive is, in general, not distinctive. There is indeed a correlation between the degree of descriptiveness of a mark and its lack of distinctiveness.[20] Nevertheless, the fact that a mark is found to be descriptive does not automatically determine the question of distinctiveness. Although a mark cannot be regarded as lacking distinctiveness because it is unimaginative, the presence or absence of any fanciful element is indeed relevant in assessing distinctiveness. If a mark is descriptive to a certain extent, the criterion of imaginativeness could tip the balance of the assessment.[21]

Prior to *Procter & Gamble (Baby-Dry)*, the leading case on descriptiveness was that of *Windsurfing Chiemsee*, in which the ECJ applied a public interest test.[22] The test is based on the premise that descriptive words should be freely available to every trader and not subject to restrictions. The principle behind this test is that it is not in the public interest for one trader or undertaking to register a trade mark and thus gain a monopoly over descriptive terms, as this would prevent other traders or undertakings from using the same words. Whether a public interest test is of a major significance in determining distinctiveness is a matter of opinion. The *Procter & Gamble* judgment, discussed below, seemed to focus on other tests, but *Windsurfing Chiemsee* is still regularly cited in ECJ's judgments[23] and, therefore, it remains a valid test. Nevertheless, in *SAT.1*, the ECJ ruled that it is wrong to consider a public interest criterion when appraising the distinctive character of a mark under Article 7(1)(b).[24] The public interest test is only relevant when considering whether a trade mark is descriptive under Article 7(1)(c).[25] What is important is the guarantee of origin of the trade marked products or services to the consumer or end user.[26]

D. Borderline cases: composite word marks

Establishing 'distinctiveness' for non-traditional marks has proven to be particularly challenging. As to the manner in which the distinctiveness of a composite word mark should be determined, the Court has consistently held that, although it is appropriate to examine each word individually, the mark as a whole must also be considered.[27] It took a series of cases—*Procter & Gamble (Baby-Dry)*,

[20] See Opinion of AG Jacobs in Case C-498/01 P*OHIM v Zapf Creation AG (New Born Baby)* [2004] ECR I-11349, para 48.

[21] OHIM in Case C-498/01 P *Zapf* demonstrated the absence of a fanciful element by stressing the ordinariness of the term 'New Born Baby' in English. See Opinion of AG Jacobs in Case C-498/01 P *Zapf*, n 20 above, para 54.

[22] Joined Cases C-108/97 and C-109/97 *Windsurfing Chiemsee Produktions- und Vertriebs GmbH (WSC) v Boots- und Segelzubehör Walter Huber and Franz Attenberger* [199] ECR I-2779, para 25.

[23] See, eg, Case C-191/01 P *OHIM v Wrigley (Doublemint)* [2003] ECR I-12447.

[24] Case C-329/02 P *SAT.1 SatellitenFernsehen GmbH v OHIM* [2004] ECR I-8317.

[25] ibid para 36.

[26] ibid para 23.

[27] Case C-251/95 *SABEL BV v Puma AG, Rudolf Dassler Sport* [1997] ECR I-6191, para 23. See further Case C-329/02 P *SAT.1*, n 24 above, para 35, where the ECJ allowed an appeal against a judgment of the General Court on the basis that the General Court had based its judgment on an

Doublemint,[28] *Postkantoor*[29] and *Biomild*[30]—before clear guidelines emerged on how to decide whether composite word marks on the borderline of distinctiveness should be registered.

As already stated, the first appeal to the ECJ from the General Court in this context was *Procter & Gamble (Baby-Dry)* in 2001. The trade mark 'Baby-Dry' for nappies was originally refused registration by OHIM on the grounds that the mark consisted exclusively of words that were descriptive of the goods and devoid of any distinctive character and, therefore, the absolute grounds of refusal under Article 7(1)(b) and (1)(c) applied to the mark. OHIM's decision was unsuccessfully challenged before the General Court,[31] which upheld OHIM's refusal to register the mark as it found that the main purpose of the goods was to keep a baby dry; and, therefore, the mark was descriptive and not distinctive. However, the General Court annulled OHIM's decision on the ground that OHIM was wrong not to have considered whether the mark had acquired distinctiveness through use under Article 7(3).

The ECJ took a different approach and closely followed the Opinion of Advocate General Jacobs.[32] Although the Court agreed that the mark undoubtedly referred to the function of the goods, and that each word individually referred to the purpose of the goods, it nevertheless considered that 'their syntactically unusual juxtaposition' was not 'a familiar expression in the English language either for designating babies' nappies or for describing their essential characteristics.'[33] Thus the word 'Baby-Dry' was not, as a whole, descriptive of nappies. It was a 'lexical invention bestowing distinctive power on the mark so formed'.[34] Not surprisingly, several commentators expressed the widely held fear that the floodgates had been opened for the registration of descriptive words provided that they had acquired a second meaning.[35]

However, within two years, the ECJ was given an opportunity to interpret *Procter & Gamble (Baby-Dry)* and reassured the alarmists that the floodgates were firmly on a latch. In *Doublemint*,[36] the full Court ruled that the mark in question

assessment carried out essentially by means of a separate analysis of each element rather than on the examination of the whole. The latter examination, inter alia, was only secondary and no relevance was given to any element of imaginativeness.

[28] Case C-191/01 P *Doublemint*, n 23 above.

[29] Case C-363/99 *Koninklijke KPN (Postkantoor)*, n 19 above.

[30] Case C-265/00 *Campina Melkunie BV v Benelux-Merkenbureau (Biomild)* [2004] ECR I-1699.

[31] Case T-163/98 *Procter & Gamble v OHIM (Baby-Dry)* [1999] ECR II-2383.

[32] The Opinion in *Baby-Dry* was delivered two months after the General Court's judgment in *Doublemint* and AG Jacobs expressly referred to it. See Opinion of AG Jacobs in Case C-383/99 P *Procter & Gamble (Baby-Dry)*, n 17 above, para 95.

[33] Case C-383/99 P *Procter & Gamble (Baby-Dry)*, n 17 above, para 43.

[34] ibid para 44.

[35] eg, I Kilbey, '*Baby-Dry*: A Victory for the Ephemera of Advertising?' (2002) 24:10 *European Intellectual Property Review* 493.

[36] Case C-191/01 P *Doublemint*, n 23 above. The General Court's judgment (Case T-193/99 *Wrigley v OHIM* (Doublemint) [2001] ECR II-417) was delivered before the Opinion and ECJ judgment in *Baby-Dry* and therefore the General Court had, at the time, no interpretative guidance from the ECJ.

was a combination of two words, 'double' and 'mint', and that the words were descriptive of the mint flavoured or mint scented product for which the applicants sought registration, namely chewing gum. The Court found that 'doublemint' was purely descriptive and that the fact that 'double' and 'mint' in combination gave rise to a variety of possible meanings does not automatically mean that the words are *not* descriptive. Thus the absolute ground for refusal set out in Article 7(1)(c) applied to this application for registration.[37]

Advocate General Jacobs directly responded to the criticism that had been expressed after the *Baby-Dry* judgment, and assisted the ECJ towards clarifying and reconciling its case law.[38] He proposed a number of questions to be asked in order to determine whether the mark lacked distinctiveness by being wholly descriptive. His first question determines the relationship between the mark and the product; if the answer was that the mark was a general description in the particular trade, then the registration ought to be denied.[39] The second question relates to the immediacy of the message conveyed by the mark. If the mark conveys the characteristic of the goods or services immediately, then it ought not to be registered.[40] The third and final question centres on the significance of the characteristics of the product in the consumer's mind.[41] So if the characteristics are *intrinsic* to the goods or services, or to the consumer's choice, then the grounds for refusing registration because of the descriptive element are high. Once these questions were applied to the mark in question ('doublemint'), the reference to mint flavour is even stronger by the use of the word 'double', and so immediately recognized; and as the mint flavour is intrinsic to the chewing gum, registration should be denied.

The ECJ followed the Advocate General's reasoning and ruled that registration must be refused where one of the mark's possible meanings is capable of designating a characteristic of the goods concerned.[42] The Court ruled that the test is not based on whether the mark was 'exclusively descriptive' but on whether the mark was capable of being used by a trader to designate a characteristic of their goods or services. The findings of the Court are very brief, but do not overrule *Baby-Dry*. The Court appears simply to conclude that 'doublemint' was less unusual than 'baby-dry'; the only lexical invention was the removal of a space between the two words. Interestingly, in its judgment, the ECJ referred to the public interest test and emphasized it by expressly citing *Windsurfing Chiemsee*.[43] The ECJ stated in *Doublemint* that it is in the public interest that descriptive words are available for

[37] This case contrasts with *Baby-Dry*, given that the General Court found that the mark 'doublemint' was not exclusively descriptive and was 'ambiguous and suggestive' (Case C-191/01 P *Doublemint*, n 23 above, para 30). The judgment was then appealed to the ECJ by OHIM.

[38] On 'the contours of "descriptiveness"' see Opinion of AG Jacobs in Case C-191/01 P *Doublemint*, n 23 above, paras 50–67. On the phrase 'contours of exclusiveness of' in Article 7(1)(c), see paras 68–78 of this Opinion.

[39] ibid para 62.

[40] ibid para 63.

[41] ibid para 64.

[42] Case C-191/01 P *Doublemint*, n 23 above, para 32.

[43] ibid para 25.

free use by every trader.[44] Advocate General Jacobs, in the *Baby-Dry* Opinion, did not approach the question of descriptiveness in terms of public interest.

The judgments in *Baby-Dry* and *Doublemint*, delivered within a short period and seemingly sending two different messages, caused much confusion and appeared to be irreconcilable. In 2004, the ECJ, in two significant judgments delivered on the same day, and which followed the same reasoning, clarified the position further. These two cases, *Postkantoor*[45] and *Biomild*,[46] did not concern refusals to register by OHIM but refusals by a national trade mark office (the Benelux Trade Mark Office), because the mark was descriptive.[47] However, the ECJ's rulings in these two cases apply equally to the corresponding provisions in the Trade Mark Regulation, given that the relevant provisions of the Directive on the absolute and relative grounds for refusal are identical to those of the Trade Mark Regulation.[48] Thus, the ECJ's interpretative rulings in these two cases apply to both legislative measures. The *Biomild* case concerned a mark for dairy products including 'mild flavoured yogurt' products; *Postkantoor* relates to a mark that, in Dutch, means 'post office' for paper, advertising, stamps, telecommunications and education.

As the same question from a similar perspective was raised in both cases, Advocate General Ruiz-Jarabo Colomer delivered a single Opinion. He based his argument on the public interest formula set out in *Windsurfing Chiemsee* and indirectly criticized the ECJ's judgment in *Baby-Dry*[49] for ignoring the public interest that exists in the availability of descriptive words. Although the Advocate General was critical of the ECJ's reasoning in *Baby-Dry*, he did admit that the ECJ was unlikely to reverse that ruling.[50] In its (separate) judgments, the ECJ reiterated that it is in the public interest that a mark which is purely descriptive of the relevant goods or services should be freely available to all traders and that, in the case of composite word marks, where each part is descriptive, then a mere combination does not alter the descriptive nature of the mark. However, the Court stated that a combination of descriptive words may create an 'impression which is sufficiently far removed from that produced by the simple combination of those elements'.[51] One way that such an impression[52] may arise is through an unusual combination of the words such as, for example, 'Baby-Dry'.

[44] ibid para 31.

[45] Case C-363/99 *Koninklijke KPN (Postkantoor)*, n 19 above.

[46] Case C-265/00 *Campina Melkunie (Biomild)*, n 30 above.

[47] National laws are now harmonized as to absolute and relative grounds of refusal, as required by the Trade Mark Directive. Where questions of interpretation of the provisions of the Directive arise in national proceedings, national courts may request a preliminary ruling from the ECJ under Article 267 TFEU on the meaning of the provision, so that they can then apply it to the case before them.

[48] Articles 3(1)(b) and 3(1)(c) of the EUTM Directive are identical to Articles 7(1)(b) and 7(1)(c) of the Trade Mark Regulation.

[49] Opinion of Ruiz-Jarabo Colomer in Case C-363/99 *Koninklijke KPN (Postkantoor)*, n 19 above, para 59.

[50] ibid paras 68–70.

[51] Case C-363/99 *Koninklijke KPN (Postkantoor)*, n 19 above, para 99.

[52] Where the mark is a word that is to be seen and heard, this test applies to both the written and aural impression. See Case C-363/99 *Koninklijke KPN (Postkantoor)*, n 19 above, para 99.

It should be noted that in a preliminary ruling, the ECJ does not rule on whether the trade mark can be registered. The Court merely interprets EU law, that is, the provisions of the Trade Mark Directive. It is for the national courts to apply the interpretation and rule on the facts. The Court therefore stated that it was sufficient for a mark to be refused registration 'if at least one of the possible meanings [of the mark] designates a characteristic of the goods or services concerned'.[53] The Court confirmed, therefore, that EU trade mark law requires that the word itself has not become descriptive of the goods to which the mark is affixed. Thus the tests laid down in *Doublemint* were confirmed.

In these four cases, two appeals from the General Court and two preliminary rulings, the ECJ established and refined the distinctiveness as against the descriptiveness test to be applied under EU law. The rulings in *Postkantoor* and *Biomild* and the judgment in *Doublemint* suggest that the ECJ has slightly shifted the parameters of test by setting a lower threshold for refusal to register a composite word mark. Thus the position seems to be as follows. The *Baby-Dry* judgment is still good law and authority for the proposition that, in order for registration to be denied, a mark must be exclusively descriptive and thus devoid of distinctiveness. So if the words that make up the trade mark are capable of alternative meanings, and in themselves are not descriptive, then registration should not be refused. In *Doublemint,* the Court refined this position by holding that if at least one of the possible meanings of the mark is descriptive, then the mark must be refused registration. *Postkantoor* and *Biomild* expressly follow this refinement, but this does not mean that the reasoning in *Baby-Dry* has been found to be incorrect. The Court stressed that these later cases merely interpreted further the test laid down in *Baby-Dry.* Thus the appropriate conclusion is that, in composite word marks, the test must be applied in a stricter manner than initially envisaged.

Thus distinctiveness of composite descriptive words can be established if (a) the unusual nature of the combination of words making up the mark give the consumer an overall impression of the mark far removed from the descriptive elements of the words themselves; or, (b) the new composite word has established its own meaning independent of its individual elements; or, (c) the mark has become distinctive in relation to the goods or services for which the registration has been sought in consequence of its use.

This last test is laid down in Article 7(3) of the EUTM Regulation and is known as the 'acquired distinctiveness' test. It will be considered further below. However, before considering marks that have acquired distinctiveness through use, the next section of the chapter will consider some difficulties that non-traditional marks, such as smells, colours, shapes and slogans, have faced in meeting the requirements of registration.

[53] Case C-363/99 *Koninklijke KPN (Postkantoor),* n 19 above, para 97.

E. Graphic representation and the distinctiveness of non-traditional marks

One of the key features of EU trade mark law is that it expressly provides for marks that are not perceived visually (ie marks other than words and graphics) nevertheless to be capable of registration.[54] However, the tests to be applied to determine whether marks such as smells, sounds and colours can be registered are no different from those applied to any other sign as required by Article 4 of the EUTM Regulation. First, the mark must be capable of being represented graphically and, secondly, it must capable of distinguishing the products or services of one trader from those of other traders. The public interest issue discussed above is particularly relevant to non-traditional marks, where the overriding interest that prevails is not to allow exclusive rights over smells, sounds and colours to trade mark owners so as to exclude other traders from being able to use them.[55] All the cases considered in this section of the chapter have come before the ECJ through either a refusal of national trade mark offices to register these non-traditional marks or as appeals from the General Court (where appeals from OHIM decisions are heard).[56]

(1) Graphic representation

The requirement of a graphical representation for shapes and slogans has not been difficult to meet, as they are obviously easily capable of being represented graphically. Graphic representation has, however, caused problems, particularly for marks such as smells, sounds and colours.

In the case of *Sieckmann*,[57] which concerned an attempt to register a smell, the ECJ laid down a series of tests that have to be met before non-traditional marks can be registered. The tests require that the graphical representation required to enable the mark to be registered must be precisely identified and self-contained, easily accessible, intelligible, durable, unequivocal and objective.[58] This is a high threshold, which has caused difficulties for the registration of smells as trade marks but not for other kinds of non-traditional marks such as sounds and colour. The standard musical notation on a stave is considered to meet the requirement for sound marks.[59] And there is no problem in accepting that colours are marks that can be graphically represented by the use of widely recognized colour codes, such as

[54] In the landmark ECJ ruling in Case C-299/99 *Koninklijke Philips Electronics NV v Remington Consumer Products Ltd* [2002] ECR I-5475, the Court confirmed in para 39 that 'there is no class of marks having a distinctive character by their nature or by the use made of them which is not capable of distinguishing goods or services' within the meaning of EU trade mark law.

[55] See, eg, Case C-49/02 *Heidelberger Bauchemie GmbH* [2004] ECR I-6129.

[56] For a comprehensive analysis of relevant case law, see P Turner-Kerr, 'Trade Mark Tangles: Recent Twists and Turns in EC Trade Mark Law' (2004) 29:3 *ELRev* 345.

[57] Case C-273/00 *Ralf Sieckmann v Deutsches Patent-Markenamt* [2002] ECR I-11737.

[58] ibid para 55 and Case C-104/01 *Libertel Groep BV v Benelux-Merkenbureau* [2004] ECR I-3793, para 29.

[59] Case C-282/01 *Shield Mark BV v Kist* [2003] ECR I-14313.

Pantone definitions.[60] However, a mark consisting of a combination of colours without contours does not easily satisfy the graphic representation requirement. For example, in *Heidelberger Bauchemie,*[61] the applicant failed to meet the graphical representation test when seeking to register a combination of colours. The ECJ ruled that specific shades of blue and yellow[62] 'used in every conceivable form in particular on packaging and labels' did not satisfy the requirement of graphic representation. The ECJ found that there was a lack of precision in the description of the relationship between the colours. There was very little guidance from the reasoning of the Court, which simply stated that in order to have a combination of colours registered as a trade mark, the colours needed to be 'systematically arranged by associating the colours concerned in a predetermined and uniform way'.[63] Thus the way the colours are to be used must be defined with certainty and in a manner that is not open to different interpretations. The Court failed to provide guidance as to what *degree* of systematic arrangement would suffice and thus left it to the national trade mark offices to apply this requirement.

(2) Distinctiveness

Smell, sound and colour marks have encountered difficulties not only in being represented graphically but also in overcoming the absolute ground of refusal under Article 7(1)(b) of the EUTM Regulation, namely being found to be devoid of distinctive character. These marks are not inherently distinctive and often achieve distinctiveness only through use.[64] Even though colours may express 'feelings', they are unlikely to convey specific information about the origin of the goods or services. Thus a combination of colours may be capable of distinguishing the goods or services of one undertaking from another undertaking only through use. This was confirmed in *Heidelberger,* where the ECJ ruled that colours and colour combinations are signs that are capable of registration, but, nevertheless, concluded that such marks may be capable of distinguishing goods or services only through use. Thus the circumstances in which it would be possible to register a colour combination solely on the basis of inherent distinctiveness are exceptional. By taking this approach, the ECJ has reinforced the public interest aspects of not allowing traders to secure rights over signs that should be left free for other traders to use.

Distinctiveness is, however, easier for three-dimensional shapes[65] and for slogans. Although, as already stated above, the criterion for assessing the distinctive

[60] Case C-104/01 *Libertel,* n 58 above, where the application was for the colour orange in relation to telecommunications services.

[61] Case C-49/02 *Heidelberger Bauchemie GmbH,* n 55 above.

[62] The application was for a rectangular piece of paper with the upper half blue and the lower half yellow.

[63] Case C-49/02 *Heidelberger Bauchemie,* n 55 above, para 33.

[64] eg, OHIM has registered some colour combinations marks such as: yellow and green for BP; blue and silver for Red Bull; and black and yellow for Black & Decker. However, too many have been denied for applicants to be confident that they will secure registration for their particular colour combination mark.

[65] For a detailed discussion, see A Firth, E Gredley and SM Maniatis, 'Shapes as Trade Marks: Public Policy, Functional Considerations and Consumer Protection' (2001) 23:2 *EIPR* 86, and

character of a three-dimensional shape of a product is no different from those applicable to other categories of trade marks,[66] the relevant public's perception is not necessarily the same. There is a difference in the public's perceptions when looking at a three-dimensional mark consisting of shapes and colours drawn from the product itself and perceptions that arise from looking at a word or figuration mark consisting of a sign that is independent from the appearance of the product it denotes. The average consumer does not normally identify the origin of a product on the basis of its shape or packaging in the absence of any graphic or word element, and it could prove more difficult to establish distinctiveness in relation to such three-dimensional marks than for a word or figuration mark.[67] The leading case in respect of shape marks is *Philips v Remington*,[68] which came before the ECJ as a preliminary reference from a national court. The national litigation concerned an infringement action brought by Philips against Remington and the issue of validity of the Philips mark was raised in defence. The mark consisted of the upper half of a shaver with three rotary heads arranged in an equilateral triangle. The ECJ ruled that a mark cannot be registered where the essential functional features of its shape are attributable only to the technical result.[69]

The test for distinctiveness for slogan marks was subject to scrutiny by the ECJ in *Audi*.[70] The case concerned an appeal from the General Court, which had ruled in favour of OHIM's refusal to register a slogan '*Vorsprung durch Technik*'[71] because of the mark's laudatory characteristics. The General Court opined that the consumer perceived the Audi mark primarily as a promotional formula and that this undermined the origin function. In order for a sign, which fulfils an advertising function, to be capable of distinguishing the goods or services of one trader from those of another, it must be immediately perceived by the public as an indication of the origin of those goods or services. Although the ECJ readily accepted the difficulties that advertising slogans may face in the context of establishing distinctiveness, the Court ruled that the same criteria for registration as for all other kinds of marks should be applied to them. The ECJ approach to advertising slogan marks is to determine whether they express an objective message to the consumer that guarantees the origin of goods or services. The ECJ went on to state that where the marks 'are not merely an ordinary advertising message, but possess a certain originality or resonance, requiring at least some interpretation by the relevant public, or setting off a cognitive process in the minds of that public,'[72] they are likely to have a distinctive character. This approach was exactly the opposite of that

A Folliard-Monguiral and D Rogers, 'The Protection of Shapes by the Community Trade Mark' (2003) 25:4 *EIPR* 169.

[66] Case C-299/99 *Philips v Remington*, n 54 above, para 48.

[67] Case C-218/01 *Henkel KGaA v Deutsches Patent- und Markenamt* [2004] ECR I-1725, para 52 citing Cases C-53/01 to C-55/01 *Linde*, n 19 above, para 48, and Case C-104/01 *Libertel*, n 58 above, para 65.

[68] Case C-299/99 *Philips v Remington*, n 54 above.

[69] ibid para 83.

[70] Case C-398/08 P *Audi AG v OHIM* [2010] ECR I-535.

[71] The slogan means advance or advantage through technology.

[72] Case C-398/08 P *Audi*, para 57.

followed by the General Court, which had concluded that these very elements (more than one meaning, a play on words, imaginative, surprising and unexpected, and easily remembered) did not make the mark distinctive.[73]

The ECJ also added that since the slogan had been used for a long time by Audi, the possibility that the relevant public typically linked the slogan to Audi cars could not be ignored, therefore making it easier for the public to identify the origin of the goods or services in respect of which the registration was sought. Thus the ECJ seems to be saying that evidence of acquired distinctiveness, normally only relevant under the exception in Article 7(3) of the EUTM Regulation, may also be utilized in the assessment of inherent distinctiveness under Article 7(1)(b). This is rather surprising, and it blurs the distinction between the rule and the exception. No doubt the ECJ will have an opportunity to resolve this ambiguity in future rulings.

F. Acquired distinctiveness under Article 7(3)

As stated above, the EUTM Regulation provides a significant qualification to the rule that marks lacking distinctiveness, or which are exclusively descriptive, cannot secure registration. Article 7(3) provides that marks may, through use, demonstrate that they have acquired a distinctive character that they initially lacked. Furthermore, non-traditional marks, such as smells, sounds, colour marks, shapes and slogans, are not inherently distinctive and can only be registered by demonstrating that distinctiveness has been acquired through use. This is of course a matter of evidence to be proven to the satisfaction of the court. There are two conditions that need to be met to satisfy Article 7(3). First, the trade mark must be used in a substantial part of the EU and, secondly, a sufficiently large part of the relevant class of consumers must recognize the mark as distinctive at the time when the application is filed.

The problem as far as the first condition is concerned can be illustrated by the case of *Ford*,[74] where the mark 'OPTIONS' was found to be devoid of any distinctive character even though there was evidence of use in the supply of insurance and hire-purchase services in Belgium, Denmark, The Netherlands, Portugal, Sweden and the United Kingdom. However, the mark lacked distinctiveness in the French language and it was acknowledged by Ford that the mark had not acquired distinctiveness through use in France. The question therefore arose whether, in these circumstances, registration should be granted, even though Article 7(2) of the EUTM Regulation provides that a trade mark is not to be registered, given that the ground of non-registrability under Article 7 arises only with respect to a part of the EU. OHIM considered that even if the mark had become distinctive through use in the United Kingdom, it would not be inherently distinctive in France and, therefore, failed under Article 7(2). Ford, on the other hand, argued that Article 7(3) prevails over Article 7(2) where distinctiveness is

[73] Case C-398/08 P *Audi*, paras 46–8 for a criticism of the reasoning of the General Court.
[74] Case T-91/99 *Ford Motor Company v OHIM* [2000] ECR II-1925.

acquired through use that can be demonstrated in a substantial part of the EU, including a major Member State such as the United Kingdom. The Court correctly reaffirmed the unitary character of EU trade marks in relation to absolute grounds of refusal under Article 7,[75] and confirmed that the mark must have a distinctive character throughout a substantial part of the EU. The principle of unitary character of the EU trade mark is expressly codified in Article 7(2), and Article 7(3)—as an exception—must, therefore, be read in the light of that principle.[76]

As far as the second condition is concerned, the ECJ ruled in *Ford* that the distinctiveness acquired through use must be shown in that part of the EU where it was otherwise devoid of such character in the language concerned. Thus, in this case, the mark 'OPTIONS' was devoid of distinctive character both in English and in French and, therefore, distinctiveness through use had to be proven with respect to the English-speaking and French-speaking parts of the EU. In other words, English-speaking and French-speaking consumers must recognize the mark as distinguishing the goods and services of Ford from those of other traders or undertakings.

This is a very high standard that may be justified in the context of word marks devoid of a distinctive character, but it is much more difficult to justify in the case of non-traditional marks which are inherently non-distinctive. It will be interesting to monitor how the Court will develop this aspect of EU trade mark law in the future. It is hoped that the ECJ will be less demanding where, for example, a colour combination can establish distinctiveness through use in a substantial part of the EU, such as Portugal and Spain, but not in any other part of the EU. The kind of evidence that has to be provided includes the market share held by the mark, the amount of investment the trader has undertaken in promoting the mark and statements from professional associations. In this manner, the applicant will demonstrate that the mark has been used in the course of trade in such a manner as to achieve a level of recognition amongst consumers that allows them to associate the mark with the origin of the goods or services.

G. Concluding observations

The EU trade mark 'story' set out above, necessarily focusing on a few highlights, illustrates well the process of ensuring that a national private right with the potential to obstruct the realization of a common market can be regulated at EU level. This has been achieved by a mixture of legislation (namely, partial harmonization of national laws and the creation of an EU-wide private right) and case law from the European courts (on the resolution of conflicts between national and EU law, and judgments and rulings on matters of interpretation of EU legislative provisions). In order to reach this level of uniformity throughout the internal market, it was necessary to regulate the rights of a trade mark owner not only at

[75] ibid para 23. [76] ibid paras 25–6.

EU level but also at national level. Thus the EU adopted legislative measures to secure that the conditions for the grant of a trade mark as well as the rights conferred on the trade mark owner were harmonized at national level and regulated at European level. An important element in the grant of a trade mark is that the mark is not devoid of distinctive character. The case law discussed above focused on the concept of 'distinctiveness' as interpreted by the ECJ in the context of composite word marks and non-traditional marks.

A number of concluding observations in the context of trade marks can be made. First, the ECJ case law confirms clearly that descriptive marks should be freely available to all traders and the grounds for refusal should be considered in light of the public interest that underpins them (*Chemisee*, *Postkantoor*, *Biomild* and *New Born Baby*). In respect of composite word marks, there must be a perceptible difference between the word as a whole and the sum of its individual parts, and the composite word must create an impression that is 'sufficiently far removed' from the simple combination of its parts (*Baby-Dry*). In *Postkantoor*, the ECJ ruled that a composite word may overcome its lack of distinctiveness if it has become part of everyday language and acquired a distinctive meaning that is independent of its parts. But even then, such a word is subject to the test of descriptiveness; and thus a more robust approach to the registration of composite word marks has emerged than previously applied.

Secondly, as far as non-traditional marks are concerned, the ECJ judgments have been conservative in their approach. In *Sieckmann*, the Court set the tone by imposing very strict conditions for meeting the requirement that a sign be graphically represented. Thus, smells have proven difficult in terms of securing registration as a trade mark. Sounds and colour marks have met this requirement more easily but, nevertheless, have often failed to demonstrate they are not devoid of distinctive character. For example, combined colours, as illustrated above, have tended not to overcome this obstacle.

So what has been achieved by the EU regulating the registration of trade mark rights in the internal market? Certainly the general understanding at the time when the European trade mark legislative measures were adopted, that it would be much easier to obtain registration for non-traditional marks, has not materialized. For most of these marks, registration will only be secured if distinctiveness through use is demonstrated. Nevertheless, the early ECJ case law on reconciling national laws on trade mark rights with common market objectives paved the way for the later introduction of an EU trade mark regime operated under EU law. Thus a uniform regulation of these rights at both national and EU levels has been secured.

Nevertheless, there is still much to be done to achieve EU regulation of other intellectual property rights, such as patents and copyright, and to ensure their effective enforcement. As far as patents are concerned, the EU has struggled to adopt an EU patent regulation,[77] which would introduce a similar harmonized and regulated regime for patents. The first proposal for the EU patent was tabled in the

[77] In the context of patents the terms 'EU patent' and 'Community patent' will be used interchangeably.

early 1970s and a Community Patent Convention was negotiated and concluded by the Member States in 1975, but it was never ratified. Since 2000, the Commission's renewed efforts[78] have been focused on building on the successful European Patents regime,[79] established in 1973 when the European Patent Convention (EPC) was concluded. The EPC established a unified procedure for granting a European patent by the European Patent Office (EPO), which was established in Munich. Each European patent becomes a bundle of nationally enforceable patents in the designated States.

Since then, on several occasions, the EU Member States have been close to consensus on the content of a patent regulation, but something always happened to prevent agreement being reached.[80] However, in 2009, the Council revised the 2000 Draft Patent Regulation and the text of a draft agreement on a European and Community Patent Court;[81] it also adopted a recommendation from the Commission seeking authorization to open negotiations for the adoption of an international agreement between the EU Member States and third countries that are parties to the EPC. The objective of the agreement was the creation of a unified patent litigation system at European and EU level, which would be enforceable by the creation of a European and Community Patent Court[82] with jurisdiction to hear actions related to European and Community patents.[83]

Given the controversial nature of the proposed agreement, the Council asked the ECJ for an Opinion on the compatibility of the proposed international agreement with the TFEU.[84] The full Court of 27 Judges held in March 2011 that the proposed combined system of European Patent Convention courts (including non-EU Member States) and EU courts would be incompatible with EU law.[85] The ECJ reasoned that by conferring on an international court, which is outside the institutional and judicial framework of the EU, an exclusive jurisdiction to hear a significant number of actions brought by individuals in the field of the Community patent, and to interpret and apply EU law in that field, would deprive courts of Member States of their powers in relation to the interpretation and application of EU law. The proposed agreement would also affect the powers of the ECJ to reply,

78 *Proposal for a Council Regulation on the Community patent*, COM (2000) 412 final, providing for the accession of the EU to the EPC, the creation of a unitary industrial property right valid throughout the EU and the granting of that right by the EPO.

79 The term 'EU Patent' must not be confused with 'European Patents'. European Patents are granted under the European Patent Convention (EPC), which operates amongst a large number of States in Europe.

80 eg in March 2003, the Council reached political agreement on a Community patent regulation but, at the very last stages, the regulation was not adopted as the problematic issues that had arisen throughout the discussions proved insoluble. These problems concerned mainly the time delays for translating the claims and the authentic text of the claims in case of an infringement.

81 The European and Community Patent Court created a hierarchy of specialized patents courts.

82 The proposed court would comprise a central division and local and regional divisions, as well as a court of appeal and a joint registry.

83 The proposed court would have exclusive jurisdiction to hear disputes relating to the EU patent, and the exclusive power to make a preliminary reference to the ECJ in respect of such disputes.

84 Article 218(11) provides a procedure for obtaining an Opinion from the ECJ as to the compatibility of an international agreement with the provisions of the EU Treaties.

85 Opinion 1/09 of 8 March 2011, para 89 [2011] OJ C 211/2.

by preliminary ruling, to questions referred by those national courts. Accordingly, the ECJ concluded the agreement would alter the essential character of the powers conferred on the EU institutions and on the Member States, which are indispensable to the preservation of the very nature of EU law.

There is also a need to regulate copyright and neighbouring rights at EU level, but a radical approach to these intellectual property rights is not likely to be pursued in the near future. To date, there has been a degree of harmonization of national copyright laws (such as in respect of databases,[86] lending rights[87] and software)[88] but nothing more comprehensive has been attempted. The concept of copyright has been extended beyond recognition to accommodate new technologies. However, the Internet and the digital revolution have posed challenges to copyright that seem impossible to overcome. It is tempting to propose that the EU should take a radical and innovative approach to new technologies and remove them from the protection of copyright. Where there has been an inventive step, they could be protected either under patent law or through the creation of a distinct property right at EU level. The inventor/creator would be rewarded when the product is launched on the EU market, by charging a higher price and marketing the product well. If this proposal is *too* radical, however, then a limited property right protection with a limited period of validity, for example, ten years, should be sufficient for these fast-moving industries.

The reality is, however, that no such radical approach to copyright regulation is likely to happen. Indeed, the Commission, in its 2011 Communication,[89] sets out a strategy for the future of intellectual property rights in the single European market[90] but, as far as copyright is concerned, the approach remains rather conservative.[91]

As far as effective enforcement is concerned, it is difficult to refute the need to establish a specialist EU intellectual property law court (or tribunal) as a constituent part of the ECJ. This proposal is not new[92] but it is submitted that it needs to be

[86] Commision Directive 96/6/EC of 16 February 1996 amending Council Directive 74/63/EEC on undesirable substances and products in animal nutrition (Text with EEA relevance) [1996] OJ L 77/20.

[87] Council Directive 92/100/EEC of 19 November 1992 on rental right and lending right and on certain rights related to copyright in the field of intellectual property [1992] OJ L 346/61.

[88] Council Directive 2009/24/EC of 23 April 2009 on the legal protection of computer programs [2009] OJ L 111/16.

[89] *A Single Market for Intellectual Property Rights*, n 7 above.

[90] ibid.

[91] The proposals for copyright include a proposal to simplify the collective management of copyright in the EU, which will aim to enhance the governance and transparency of collecting societies, as well as to create a legal framework for multi-territorial licensing of musical works for online services; a proposal to facilitate the digitization of works still protected by copyright but whose copyright owners are unknown or untraceable ('orphan works'); a proposed feasibility study to determine whether a European Copyright Code can be created codifying the existing EU copyright directives. The possibility of an optional unitary copyright title, enabling right holders to choose whether to license and enforce their copyrights nationally or on a multi-territory basis, will also be considered.

[92] See fn 7 of the draft proposing amendments to the Statute of the ECJ sent by the President of the ECJ to the Presidents of the European Parliament and the EU Council at <http://curia.europa.eu/jcms/upload/docs/application/pdf/2011-04/projet_en.pdf> stating that the establishment of such a

pursued more vigorously, given the ECJ's Opinion on the establishment of a European and Community Patent Court. It is true that this intellectual property court would initially be occupied mainly with the enforcement of EU trade mark law, but its competence should be broader and include the enforcement of all intellectual property rights conferred by EU law. The significant number of trade mark cases and the technical intellectual property law issues that the European courts have had to consider and rule upon demonstrate the need for such a specialist court, with specialist judges, to be established at EU level. Such a court would speed up appeals against OHIM decisions and deal with preliminary rulings on the interpretation of relevant EU trade mark law. As an intellectual property law court, its competence could be extended, when desirable, also to cover preliminary references on the interpretation and validity of copyright and copyright-related secondary legislation, as well as the EU patent regulation once it is finally adopted.

Given the recent ECJ Opinion on the proposed establishment of a Community and European Court, noted above, it seems likely that any proposal for conferring competence on a court other than the ECJ over EU intellectual property law will be found to be incompatible with the EU Treaties. The Opinion therefore reinforces the submission that the establishment of a specialist EU intellectual property law court *within* the current hierarchy of European courts is the way forward in terms of establishing an effective enforcement regime for EU intellectual property rights.

Alas, there is still some time to go before any of these developments are likely to become a reality.[93] Nevertheless, in almost fifty years, much has been achieved towards regulating the grant and use of trade marks, including, in particular, the grounds under which a mark may be refused registration at national or EU levels.

court is the option proposed by the General Court, which adopted that position at its plenary meetings on 8 April 2008 and 22 April 2009, and confirmed its choice to the President of the Court of Justice on 22 December 2009.

[93] However, although the General Court favours a specialized court this is not the view of the ECJ itself. Soon after Opinion 1/09 was delivered, the ECJ rejected the idea of a specialist court and proposed instead an increase in the number of judges of the General Court by at least 12: ibid 6–10.

9

The Concept of an Obstacle to Intra-EU Capital Movement in EU Law

*Thomas Horsley**

A. Introduction

The free movement of capital is an essential component of an integrated market.[1] In particular, a liberalized capital market ensures that economic operators are able to satisfy their requirements for investment to support transnational growth.[2] Equally, the free movement of capital provides investors with the opportunity to direct their funds to those States where the regulatory and fiscal conditions are most favourable to them.[3] In the context of European integration, liberalizing intra-EU capital movements has always formed one of the Treaty's core economic objectives. Alongside provisions on the free movement of goods, services and persons, the original EEC Treaty included a series of provisions designed to facilitate the abolition of obstacles to capital movements within the internal market.[4] However, in contrast to the other economic freedoms, the liberalization of intra-EU capital movements has followed a very different evolutionary trajectory.[5]

For many years, the fourth economic freedom remained firmly in the shadows of its relations in the Treaty. In *Casati*, the European Court of Justice (ECJ) famously ruled that Article 67(1) EEC—the central provision on the abolition of obstacles to

* PhD graduand, School of Law, Edinburgh University; Lecturer in Law, University of Liverpool. My sincere thanks, with the usual proviso, go to Professor Nic Shuibhne for her invaluable comments.

[1] On the economics of capital market liberalization see, eg, W Molle, *The Economics of European Integration: Theory, Practice, Policy*, 5th edn (Aldershot: Ashgate, 2006).

[2] ibid 218.

[3] ibid.

[4] In particular, Title III Ch 4 Articles 67–73 EEC.

[5] For reflections on the evolution of the Treaty rules on capital see, eg, J Snell, 'Free Movement of Capital: Evolution as a Non-Linear Process' in P Craig and G de Búrca (eds), *The Evolution of EU Law*, 2nd edn (Oxford: Oxford University Press, 2010); JA Usher, 'The Evolution of the Free Movement of Capital' (2008) 31:5 *Fordham Int'l LJ* 1533; L Flynn, 'Coming of Age: The Free Movement of Capital Case Law 1993–2002' (2002) 39:4 *CMLRev* 773 and S Peers, 'Free Movement of Capital: Learning Lessons or Slipping on Spilt Milk?' in C Barnard and J Scott (eds), *The Law of the Single European Market: Unpacking the Premises* (Oxford: Oxford University Press, 2002).

capital movements in the original EEC Treaty—was not directly effective.[6] This finding left the pace and depth of capital market integration squarely with the Member States as a matter of policy.[7] Acting through the Council, the Member States then took a series of steps to liberalize intra-EU capital movements through secondary legislation.[8] This process culminated in the adoption of Directive 88/361, which required, in Article 1(1), the full liberalization of capital movements in the EU.[9] The Maastricht Treaty then amended the original Treaty rules on capital movements to reflect the substance of Directive 88/361.[10] The revised Treaty provisions on the free movement of capital (Articles 63–6 TFEU) now characterize an important dimension of the second stage of Economic and Monetary Union (EMU) that applies throughout the Union and not only to those operating within the Eurozone.

In response to a gradual, but significant, increase in the number of decisions on capital movements, this chapter surveys the Court's evolving interpretation of Article 63(1) TFEU. In a volume celebrating Professor John Usher's contribution to legal scholarship on European economic and monetary integration, this seems an entirely appropriate subject for review. Throughout his career, Professor Usher maintained a keen interest in the development of Treaty rules governing the liberalization of capital movements. Indeed, at a time when most commentators overlooked the fourth Treaty freedom, Usher presented several illuminating accounts of their ongoing evolution.[11] The primary focus of this chapter is the Court's approach to defining what constitutes an 'obstacle to intra-EU movement'[12] for Article 63(1) TFEU. As is true across the Treaty freedoms, the scope attributed to this term by the Court of Justice has a direct impact on the distribution of competence between the Member States and Union for the regulation of

[6] Case 203/80 *Casati* [1981] ECR 2595, para 8. This finding was based on the fact that Article 67(1) was drafted in non-absolute terms. See JA Usher, n 5 above, 1534.

[7] JA Usher, n 5 above, 1535. See further J Snell, n 5 above, section B.

[8] First Council Directive for the implementation of Article 67 of the Treaty [1959–62] OJ Spec Ed, 49; Second Council 63/21/EEC Directive of 18 December 1962 adding to and amending the First Directive for the implementation of Article 67 of the Treaty [1963–4] OJ Spec Ed, 5; Council Directive of 20 December 1985 amending the Directive of 11 May 1960 on the implementation of Article 67 of the Treaty (85/583/EEC) [1985] OJ L 372/39; and Council Directive of 17 November 1986 amending the First Directive of 11 May 1960 for the implementation of Article 67 of the Treaty 86/566/EEC [1986] OJ L 332/22. For discussion, JA Usher, n 5 above, 1535–9.

[9] Council Directive 88/361/EEC of 24 June 1988 for the implementation of Article 67 of the Treaty [1988] OJ L 178/5.

[10] The entry into full force of the revised Treaty rules on capital movements (Article 73b EC) was set to coincide with the transition to the second stage of economic and monetary integration. See Article 73h EC and Article 109e EC. On this point, see further J Snell, n 5 above, section B.

[11] From a substantial list of contributions see, eg, JA Usher, n 5 above; JA Usher, 'Monetary Movements and the Internal Market' in N Nic Shuibhne (ed), *Regulating the Internal Market* (Cheltenham/Northampton, Mass.: Edward Elgar, 2006), JA Usher, *The Law of Money and Financial Services in the European Community*, 1st edn 1994, 2nd edn 2000 (Oxford: Oxford University Press) and JA Usher, 'Capital Movements and the Treaty on European Union' (1992) 12 *YEL* 35.

[12] Throughout this chapter, the term 'obstacle to intra-EU movement' is taken to refer to a measure falling within the scope of the Treaty freedoms and thus requiring justification in EU law.

the internal market.[13] At a time when attention is being re-focused on this core substantive area, the chapter asks: is the Court's interpretation of the scope of Article 63(1) TFEU evolving differently from the approach developing for the other Treaty freedoms?

To answer this question, the chapter begins, in Section B, with a brief overview of the Treaty framework on intra-EU capital movements, together with an examination of the Court's interpretation of the term 'capital movement'. Section C assesses the ECJ's approach to defining the scope of Article 63(1) TFEU against the background of its case law on the other Treaty freedoms. Section D then focuses on the decisions currently marking the 'outer limits' of Article 63(1) TFEU.[14] The concern here is with the identification of limits to the use of Article 63(1) TFEU to scrutinize genuinely non-discriminatory national rules. Related to this, Section E examines the market access concept in more depth. The chapter concludes with some broader reflections on the evolving trajectory of the Court's case law on obstacles to intra-EU movement.

In short, this chapter argues that, post-Maastricht, the case law on capital movements within the Union is remarkable largely only for its similarity with the other Treaty freedoms.[15] The ECJ has rapidly integrated Article 63(1) TFEU into its established and essentially coherent free movement framework. However, this finding does not mean that the Court's interpretation of Article 63(1) TFEU is problem-free. On the contrary, it is argued that aspects of the Court's case law on intra-EU capital movements can be located within a broader, more controversial trend that is now emerging across the Treaty freedoms. This refers to the Court's use of the Treaty freedoms as tools to scrutinize non-discriminatory national legislation that simply characterizes the conditions for economic activity *within* individual Member States. The application of the Treaty freedoms in this manner presents a direct challenge to national regulatory autonomy and has steered the Court into difficulties before. As we enter a new phase in the evolution of the internal market, it remains as yet unclear just how far the Court is prepared to go.

B. Intra-EU capital movements

(1) The Treaty framework

The Treaty rules on intra-EU capital movements are now found in Chapter 4 of Title IV of the Treaty on the Functioning of the European Union (TFEU).[16] Article 63(1) TFEU (ex Article 56(1) EC) provides that 'within the framework of the provisions set

[13] M Dougan,'Legal Developments' (2010) 48 Issue Supplement s1 *JCMS* 163, 165, and M Poiares Maduro, *We the Court: The European Court of Justice & the European Economic Constitution* (Oxford: Hart Publishing, 1999).

[14] The phrase 'outer limits' is borrowed from C Barnard and O Odudu (eds), *The Outer Limits of European Union Law* (Oxford/Portland, Oregon: Hart Publishing, 2009).

[15] This was the conclusion of L Flynn, n 5 above, 804.

[16] Consolidated version of the Treaty on the Functioning of the European Union [2010] OJ C 83/47.

out in this Chapter, all restrictions on the movement of capital between Member States . . . shall be prohibited'. This prohibition follows that set out in Directive 88/361 and, in contrast to the Treaty provision that it replaced, makes no reference to the prohibition of discrimination. Article 63(1) TFEU is also unique amongst the freedoms in that it applies to both intra-EU capital movements and those between the Member States and third countries. However, this external aspect of the provision will not be discussed further.[17] In common with the other freedoms, the prohibition on obstacles to intra-EU capital movements is not absolute. Article 65 TFEU (ex Article 58 EC) sets out two grounds for derogation. As we are concerned here primarily with the scope of Article 63(1) TFEU, the justification framework will not be examined in any detail.[18]

(2) The definition of capital movements

The term 'capital movement' is not defined in the Treaty. In itself, this is not unusual. The Treaty also leaves, for example, the meaning of goods and workers undefined, although it does offer some guidance on the interpretation of services in Article 57 TFEU. However, in contrast to the other Treaty provisions,[19] the Court is yet to exploit this gap and adopt a general definition of a capital movement along the lines of the movement of 'resources used for, or capable of investment intended to generate revenue'.[20] So far, the ECJ's only broad statements have arisen in connection with its attempts to delimit the scope of Article 63(1) TFEU from that of other provisions of the Treaty. On several occasions, the Court has stated what the term is *not*, namely: (1) a movement of capital in connection with a payment for goods or services (Article 63(2) TFEU on payments)[21] or (2) the acquisition of shares granting the investor 'definite influence' in the management of the undertaking concerned (Article 49 TFEU on establishment).[22] In other words, rather than formulate a general, *positive* definition of a capital movement, the ECJ has instead adhered to a more cautious, incremental approach. It continues to follow the list of transactions detailed in the nomenclature annexed to Directive 88/361. For the Court, this instrument continues to have 'indicative value' for the purpose

[17] For analysis of the external dimension of Article 63(1) TFEU see J Snell, n 5 above, section D; S Hindelang, *The Free Movement of Capital and Foreign Direct Investment* (Oxford: Oxford University Press, 2009) 162–200 and JA Usher, n 5 above, 1562–9.

[18] As with the other freedoms, the express derogations in Article 65 TFEU have been extended by the judicial creation of additional justifications based the protection of non-discriminatory 'overriding interests'. See Case C-319/02 *Manninen* [2004] ECR I-7477, para 29. For discussion of the derogation framework see, eg, C Barnard, *The Substantive Law of the EU: The Four Freedoms*, 3rd edn (Oxford: Oxford University Press, 2010) 581–91.

[19] See for Article 34 TFEU, Case 7/68 *Commission v Italy* [1968] ECR 617, 626; for Article 45 TFEU, see Case 66/85 *Lawrie-Blum* [1986] ECR 2121, para 17; and for Article 49 TFEU, see Case 197/84 *Steinhauser* [1985] ECR 1819, para 16.

[20] This possible broad definition is taken from L Flynn, n 5 above, 776.

[21] Joined Cases 286/82 and 26/83 *Luisi and Carbone* [1984] ECR 377, para 21 and Case 308/86 *Lambert* [1988] ECR 4369, para 10.

[22] Case C-436/00 *X and Y v Riksskatteverket* [2002] ECR I-10829, para 68.

of defining capital movements.[23] Following the nomenclature closely, the ECJ has to date ruled that the following transactions constitute capital movements under Article 63(1) TFEU: the acquisition and transfer of shares,[24] the acquisition of property,[25] the transfer of immoveable and moveable property by inheritance[26] or gift,[27] currency movements not associated with payments for goods or services,[28] the receipt of share dividends[29] and income from property investments,[30] credit guarantees,[31] and the provision of loans.[32]

C. Obstacles to intra-EU movement under Article 63(1) TFEU

The term 'obstacle to intra-EU movement' is of central importance in EU free movement law. The scope attributed to this term by the Court of Justice has a direct impact on the balance of power between the Member States and the Union in connection with the regulation of the internal market.[33] If the ECJ opts to define the scope of the Treaty freedoms broadly, it thereby increases its own power of review over the substantive policy preferences of the Member States in this area of shared competence.[34] By contrast, a narrower approach operates to immunize a greater body of national law from scrutiny against the Treaty framework. There is as yet no consensus on how to strike the appropriate balance between Union and Member State competence in this context and the issue remains hotly contested.[35]

23 See Case C-222/97 *Trummer and Mayer* [1999] ECR I-1661, para 21. For some, this determination confirms the Court's continued and rather unique deference to the Union legislature—and ultimately, the Member States—in the area of capital market integration. For discussion of this issue, see R Murphy, 'Changing Treaty and Changing Economic Context: The Dynamic Relationship of the Legislature and the Judiciary in the Pursuit of Capital Liberalisation' in P Syrpis (ed), *The Legislature, the Judiciary and the Completion of the Internal Market* (Cambridge: Cambridge University Press, 2012 forthcoming).

24 Case C-200/98 *X AB and Y AB v Riksskatteverket* [1999] ECR I-8261, para 66. For further discussion of the relationship between Article 63(1) TFEU and the other Treaty freedoms see, eg, C Barnard, n 18 above, 567–8.

25 Case C-302/97 *Klaus Konle v Republik Österreich* [1999] ECR I-3099, para 22.

26 Case C-364/01 *The heirs of H. Barbier* [2003] ECR I-15013, para 58.

27 Case C-318/07 *Hein Persche* [2009] ECR I-359, paras 24 and 30.

28 Joined Cases C-163/94, C-165/94 and C-250/94 *Sanz de Lera and Others* [1995] I-ECR 4821. See too earlier, Joined Cases C-358/93 and C-416/93 *Aldo Bordessa and Others* [1995] ECR I-361 (interpreting Article 1 of Directive 88/361/EEC). On the distinction between capital movements and payments, see n 22.

29 Case C-35/98 *Verkooijen* [2000] ECR I-4071, paras 25–9.

30 Case C-386/04 *Centro di Musicologia Walter Stauffer* [2006] ECR I-8203, paras 23–4.

31 Case C-279/00 *Commission v Italy* [2002] ECR I-1425, para 36.

32 Case C-452/04 *Fidum Finanz AG* [2006] ECR I-9521, para 42.

33 See M Dougan, n 13 above, and M Poiares Maduro, n 13 above.

34 See Article 4(2)(a) TFEU.

35 Some commentators favour a discrimination or mutual recognition-based approach. Others advocate broader tests, typically based on a measure's effect on access to the market or its impact on the commercial and/or personal freedom of Member State nationals as Union citizens. Contrast, eg, the views of N Bernard, 'Discrimination and Free Movement in EC Law' (1996) 45:1 *ICLQ* 82; G Davies, *Nationality Discrimination in the European Internal Market* (The Hague/London: Kluwer, 2003); or S Enchelmaier, 'Always at Your Service (Within Limits): The ECJ's Case Law on Article 56 TFEU (2006/11)' (2011) 36:5 *ELRev* 615 with those of S Weatherill, 'After *Keck*: Some Thoughts on

It is therefore particularly interesting to see what, if any, insights can be gleaned from the Court's interpretation of Article 63(1) TFEU—the most recent addition to the Treaty's free movement framework.[36]

(1) Measures liable to 'deter' or 'dissuade' intra-EU movement

The ECJ has historically favoured an expansive approach to the interpretation of obstacles to intra-EU movement. The first move in this respect came in the field of goods. In *Dassonville*, the Court famously adopted a broad, effects-based definition of a measure having equivalent effect to a quantitative restriction.[37] After a slight delay, the Court adopted comparable effects-based definitions for establishment (eg *Kraus*),[38] services (eg *Säger*, *Alpine Investments*)[39] and the free movement of workers (eg *Bosman*).[40] Generally speaking, we have now reached a position in the case law where the Court prefers to rule in terms of a prohibition of national rules that are either 'liable to deter, hinder or render less attractive' the exercise of the Treaty freedoms or affect 'access to the market' for imported products or non-nationals (in terms of both natural and legal persons).[41]

Post-Maastricht, the Court's interpretation of the scope of Article 63(1) TFEU has followed the same trajectory. After confirming that this provision was directly effective,[42] the Court moved quickly to define the concept of an obstacle to intra-EU capital movement in similarly broad terms. In *Trummer and Mayer*, the ECJ found that a national rule permitting only the registration of mortgage debts denominated in the currency of the relevant Member State infringed Article 63(1) TFEU.[43] For the Court, this requirement was 'liable to dissuade' persons from securing a mortgage in the currency of another Member State.[44] In short, the language of 'deterrent' or 'dissuasive' effects now finds expression across the case law

How to Clarify the Clarification' (1996) 33:5 *CMLRev* 885; E Spaventa, *Free Movement of Persons in the European Union: Barriers to Movement in the Constitutional Context* (AH Alphen aan den Rijn: Kluwer, 2007); or A Tryfonidou, 'Further Steps on the Road to Convergence among the Market Freedoms' (2010) 35 *ELRev* 36.

[36] Article 63(1) TFEU is the most recent of the Treaty's *economic* rights of movement to be confirmed as directly effective.

[37] Case 8/74 *Dassonville* [1974] ECR 837, para 5, and Case 120/78 *Rewe-Zentral AG v Bundesmonopolverwaltung für Branntwein (Cassis de Dijon)* [1979] ECR 649, para 8.

[38] Case C-19/92 *Kraus* [1993] ECR I-1663.

[39] Case C-76/90 *Säger* [1991] ECR I-4221, para 12, Case C-384/93 *Alpine Investments* [1995] ECR I-1141, paras 35 and 38. However, it should be noted that in its case law on services, the ECJ referred early on to the elimination of non-discriminatory 'obstacles' to movement in Case 33/74 *Van Binsbergen* [1974] ECR 1299, para 10.

[40] Case C-415/93 *Bosman* [1995] ECR I-4921, para 103.

[41] See further C Barnard, n 18 above, 574. For legal persons, Member State nationality is determined by the location of the registered office. See Article 54 TFEU as interpreted by the Court in eg Case C-212/97 *Centros* [1999] ECR I-1459, para 19 and Case C-167/01 *Inspire Art* [2003] ECR I-10155, para 97.

[42] The direct effect of Article 63(1) TFEU was confirmed in Joined Cases C-163/94, C-165/94 and C-250/94 *Sanz de Lera*, n 28 above, para 41.

[43] Case C-222/97 *Trummer and Mayer* n 23 above, para 26.

[44] ibid.

on Article 63(1) TFEU. This has been supplemented by familiar references to the effects of national rules on 'access to the market'.[45] Finally, as with the other freedoms, the Court now tends to avoid express references to the prohibition of discrimination in its judgments.[46]

(2) Obstacles to intra-EU movement—language versus substance

The Court's expansive, effects-based reading of the scope of the Treaty freedoms is actually rather misleading. In a great many cases, the language of deterrent or dissuasive effects is applied to the review of national measures that are simply discriminatory.[47] Take, for example, the decisions in *Cassis* (Article 34 TFEU) and *Säger* (Article 56 TFEU).[48] In both cases, the Court set out expansive definitions of an obstacle to intra-EU movement. However, the prohibition of discrimination would have been sufficient in both cases to bring the contested measures within the scope of the Court's review. In *Cassis*, the German rules prescribing minimum alcohol content for certain products discriminated against imported products that had been lawfully produced in other Member States according to different requirements.[49] Similarly, the indistinctly applicable rules in *Säger* discriminated against out-of-state service providers. The discriminatory effect in this case arose through the equal treatment of objectively distinct situations.[50] Importantly, the same gap between language and substance can be seen in the Court's case law on Article 63(1) TFEU. The decisions on national tax rules provide the clearest illustration of this point.[51] Moreover, this body of case law now makes up a significant proportion of the jurisprudence on Article 63(1) TFEU. For these reasons, this area is selected for more detailed analysis.

(a) National tax rules

The decision in *Verkooijen* marks the starting point in the case law on taxation and intra-EU capital movements.[52] In this case, the ECJ (Full Court) condemned as an

[45] eg Case C-463/00 *Commission v Spain* [2003] ECR I-4581, para 61.

[46] The exceptions to this rule include several early examples of national rules discriminating directly on the grounds of the nationality of natural persons, eg Case C-302/97 *Konle*, n 25 above, para 23; and a number of direct tax cases, eg Case C-376/03 *D v Inspecteur van de Belastingdienst Heerlen* [2005] ECR I-5821, para 38.

[47] See further, eg, G Davies, n 35 above, 87.

[48] Case 120/78 *Cassis* n 37 above, and Case C-76/90 *Säger*, n 39 above.

[49] Following N Nic Shuibhne, 'The Free Movement of Goods and Article 28 EC: An Evolving Framework' (2002) 27 *ELRev* 408, esp 410, who also interprets the ruling in *Cassis* through the lens of (indirect) discrimination.

[50] The contested German rules imposed a requirement of (permanent) establishment on a service provider who was already lawfully established in another Member State as a provider of the services at issue and was seeking only to provide services in Germany *temporarily*.

[51] Adopting this view, eg K Banks, 'The Application of the Fundamental Freedoms to Member State Tax Measures: Guarding against Protectionism or Second-Guessing National Policy Choices?' (2008) 33 *ELRev* 482 and J Snell, 'Non-discriminatory Tax Obstacles in Community Law' (2007) 56:2 *ICLQ* 339, esp 349.

[52] Case C-35/98 *Verkooijen*, n 29 above. See further thereafter, for natural persons, eg Case C-315/02 *Lenz* [2004] ECR I-7063 and Case C-242/03 *Weidert and Paulus* [2004] ECR I-7379. For legal

obstacle to Article 63(1) TFEU a national rule making the grant of a tax advantage for share dividends subject to a condition that the dividends were paid by companies established in that Member State. The ECJ ruled that this requirement had the effect of, inter alia, 'dissuading nationals of a Member State residing [in that State] from investing their capital in companies which have their seat in another Member State'.[53] However, the broad, effects-based language of the Court does not alter the fact that the contested rule was discriminatory. The Belgian measure introduced, for resident taxpayers, a difference in treatment based on the place of establishment of the undertaking paying the taxable income. This is a classic statement of (indirect) discrimination.[54]

The true scope of Article 63(1) TFEU as a prohibition of (only) discriminatory national tax rules is exposed most clearly in the subsequent ruling in *Kerckhaert and Morres*.[55] In this case, the applicants contested a refusal by the Belgian tax authorities to offset, from the income tax due in that State, the sum of tax already paid in another Member State. The tax in question had been imposed on shares held by the applicants in an undertaking established in the second State. The applicants maintained that this refusal was contrary to Article 63(1) TFEU. Indeed, on the strength of the Court's language in *Verkooijen*, it could be argued convincingly that the contested measure operated to deter or dissuade the applicants from investing in undertakings established in other Member States. This finding would follow from the simple fact that any income from their investment could be subject to double taxation (ie by both the source State and State of destination).

However, in *Kerckhaert and Morres*, the Court concluded that the national measure did *not* constitute an obstacle to intra-EU movement.[56] Specifically, the ECJ ruled that the contested Belgian rule '[did] not make any distinction between dividends from companies established [on the national territory] and dividends from companies established in another Member State'.[57] Both categories of dividend were taxed in Belgium at an identical rate. In the absence of any evidence of an objective difference between the situations of the applicants and other resident

persons see, eg, Case C-377/07 *STEKO Industriemontage GmbH* [2009] ECR I-299. Discrimination analysis is also at the core of the Court's case law on inheritance tax. In this context, the Court's effects-based language has been even broader. eg, in Case C-364/01 *Barbier*, n 26 above, para 62 the ECJ noted the contested measure's effect on the decision to purchase property that might *then* one day by transferred by inheritance.

[53] Case C-35/98 *Verkooijen*, n 29 above, para 34.

[54] See, eg, Case C-175/88 *Biehl* [1990] ECR I-1779, para 14.

[55] Case C-513/04 *Kerckhaert and Morres* [2006] ECR I-10967 as confirmed thereafter in Case C-298/05 *Columbus Container Services* [2007] ECR I-10451.

[56] For criticism, see J Snell, n 5 above, section C. For Snell, the ECJ's approach to international double taxation in *Kerckhaert and Morres* represents a departure from it established case law on double *regulation* (eg *Cassis*). However, it is respectfully suggested that this view is premised on too broad an interpretation of the case law on double regulation. In particular, it is argued here that the principle of mutual recognition in *Cassis* deals only with the allocation of competence between the Member States for the regulation of 'product characteristics' and not, by contrast, with other post-production trading rules (including national rules on taxation) that define only the regulatory environment *within* individual national markets. See Sections D and E below for further discussion of the ECJ's review of the latter category of measures as obstacles to intra-EU movement.

[57] Case C-513/04 *Kerckhaert and Morres*, n 55 above, para 17.

taxpayers receiving share income from undertakings established in Belgium, this did not amount to discrimination.[58] On this point, the Court noted that the situation of the applicants was no different from that of other resident taxpayers receiving income from a domestic shareholding.[59] For that reason, it concluded that the contested rule escaped the prohibition in Article 63(1) TFEU.

In summary, the Court's discrimination-based approach to tax measures in Article 63(1) TFEU is broadly in line with that applied to the other freedoms.[60] Across the freedoms, the Court generally respects the autonomy of Member States to determine, in principle, the rules of taxation applicable within their national territories. Accordingly, Member States are free to tax, as they see appropriate, both the worldwide income of their residents and the income of non-resident taxpayers generated within their jurisdiction. The ECJ imposes only a (strict)[61] requirement of equal treatment in the application of these autonomous tax choices as between Member State nationals and situations involving intra-EU movement. For example, a Member State may not discriminate between resident taxpayers on the basis of the source or destination of their taxable income.[62] By contrast, there is no obligation on Member States to manage the (negative) effects arising from the continued co-existence of different but non-discriminatory national tax regimes.[63]

(3) Non-discriminatory obstacles to intra-EU capital movements

Although discrimination better explains much of the evolving jurisprudence on intra-EU capital movements (including virtually all of the case law on taxation),[64] the Court's interpretation of Article 63(1) TFEU is not limited to discrimination analysis. On the contrary, in a number of cases, the Court has gone further and applied the substance of its broad, effects-based definition in order to capture genuinely non-discriminatory rules as obstacles to intra-EU movement. This includes, in particular, national rules making the actual *conclusion* of capital movements subject to prior or *ex post* authorization. For example, in *Konle*, the ECJ condemned as an obstacle to Article 63(1) TFEU an Austrian rule requiring all persons—without distinction on nationality grounds—to obtain prior authorization

[58] ibid para 18. The Member State carries the burden of demonstrating the situations at issue are not objectively comparable.

[59] ibid para 19.

[60] See, eg, K Banks, n 51 above; J Snell, n 51 above; and JA Usher, n 5 above.

[61] The ECJ scrutinizes the objective comparability of the situations of resident and non-resident taxpayers very closely. See, eg, Case C-234/01 *Gerritse* [2003] ECR I-5933, esp para 43 and paras 50–3, and Case C-290/04 *Scorpio* [2006] ECR I-9461, para 43.

[62] Case C-279/93 *Schumacker* [1995] ECR I-225 (Article 45 TFEU); Case C-80/94 *Wielockx* [1995] ECR I-2493 (Article 49 TFEU); Case C-234/01 *Gerritse*, n 61 above (Article 56 TFEU) and Case C-446/04 *FII* [2006] ECR I-11753 (Articles 49 and 63(1) TFEU).

[63] See here especially, the arguments of Opinion of AG Geelhoed in Case C-374/04 *ACT Group Litigation* [2007] ECR I-11673, paras 37–40. For detailed discussion of discrimination analysis in the review of national tax law see, see S Kingston, 'A Light in the Darkness: Recent Developments in the ECJ's Direct Tax Jurisprudence' (2007) 44:5 *CMLRev* 1321.

[64] The exception is discussed in Section D(1) below.

for the acquisition of land in specific parts of the national territory.[65] Without detailed explanation, the ECJ stated that this requirement 'entail[ed], by its very purpose, a restriction on the free movement of capital'.[66]

The application of Article 63(1) TFEU to genuinely non-discriminatory measures was confirmed in *Commission v Portugal (Golden Shares)*.[67] In this case, the Court was requested to review national rules governing, inter alia, the acquisition of shares in certain strategic and previously nationalized undertakings. In its reply, the ECJ stated that the prohibition in Article 63(1) TFEU 'went beyond the mere elimination of unequal treatment, on grounds of nationality, as between operators on . . . financial markets'.[68] According to the Court, that provision also captured national measures that, although not giving rise to unequal treatment, were liable simply to 'impede' capital movements or 'dissuade' investors from other Member States from concluding the same.[69] This covered, in the instant case, national rules making the acquisition of shares above a certain threshold in specific strategic undertakings by all persons—irrespective of their nationality—subject to prior authorization by the competent authority.

The ruling in *Commission v Portugal (Golden Shares)* brought the case law on capital movements in line with the other freedoms. In terms of language, the decision echoes the Court's ruling in *Säger* on services.[70] In the latter case, the ECJ also noted that Article 56 TFEU 'requires *not only the elimination of all discrimination* against a person providing services on the grounds of his nationality, *but also* the abolition of any restriction . . . when it is liable to prohibit or otherwise impede the activities of a provider of services established in another Member State where he lawfully provides similar services'.[71] In substance, the decision in *Commission v Portugal* confirmed that Article 63(1) TFEU also extends to cover genuinely non-discriminatory rules. This follows the Court's judgments in *Alpine Investments, Bosman* and (thereafter) *Commission v Italy (Motorcycle Trailers)*—all of which bring genuinely non-discriminatory rules within the scope of the Treaty freedoms.[72]

[65] Case C-302/97 *Konle*, n 25 above. See further, eg, Case C-300/01 *Doris Salzmann (No 2)* [2003] ECR I-4899 and Case C-213/04 *Burscher* [2005] ECR I-10309. In the latter case, the validity of legal title was conditional on the completion of a declaration concerning the intended use of the property acquired.

[66] Case C-302/97 *Konle*, n 25 above, para 39. In support of its finding, the Court referred to its earlier decisions on (discriminatory) authorization requirements, eg Joined Cases C-163/94, C-165/94 and C-250/94 *Sanz de Lera*, n 28 above. See further, eg, Case C-478/98 *Commission v Belgium (Eurobonds)* [2000] ECR I-7587 and Case C-54/99 *Association Eglise de scientologie de Paris* [2000] ECR I-1335.

[67] Case C-367/98 *Commission v Portugal* [2002] ECR I-4731. The case law on 'golden shares' is discussed in Section D(2) below.

[68] ibid para 44.

[69] ibid para 45.

[70] Supporting this view, eg C Barnard, n 18 above, 572.

[71] Case C-76/90 *Säger*, n 39 above, para 12 (emphasis added). This followed the interpretation of AG Jacobs in para 27 of his Opinion in that decision. However, as noted in Section C(2) above, this decision can in fact be squared with the prohibition of discrimination.

[72] Case C-384/93 *Alpine Investments*, n 39 above; Case C-415/93 *Bosman*, n 40 above and Case C-110/05 *Commission v Italy (Motorcycle Trailers)* [2009] ECR I-519.

D. Locating the outer limits of Article 63(1) TFEU

In the previous section, it was argued that the Court's interpretation of Article 63(1) TFEU is now very much in line with its approach to the other Treaty freedoms. In reviewing national rules on taxation, the Court has followed its interpretation of the other freedoms by adhering closely to the discrimination model. By contrast, in other areas, including the review of authorization requirements for intra-EU capital movements, the Court has gone further and extended the scope of Article 63(1) TFEU to scrutinize genuinely non-discriminatory national rules. In this section, we turn now to examine the decisions marking the outer limits of Article 63(1) TFEU. The focus here is on identifying limits to the prohibition of *non-discriminatory* national measures as obstacles to intra-EU capital movements. To date, this issue has arisen in two distinct contexts.

(1) Early case law

The tension over the limits of the prohibition of non-discriminatory obstacles in Article 63(1) TFEU surfaced early on, in *Sandoz*.[73] This case addressed an Austrian law imposing stamp duty on certain types of loan. The duty was imposed on loans secured from domestic providers *and* those obtained from institutions established in other Member States. However, although applicable without distinction according to the nationality of the contracting parties *or* the place where the loan was secured, the ECJ ruled that this measure infringed Article 63(1) TFEU. For the Court, it was sufficient that the contested measure was 'likely to deter' residents from obtaining loans from providers in other Member States.[74] In this connection, the ECJ pointed directly to the fact that the Austrian law 'deprived residents [of that State] of *the possibility of benefiting from the absence of taxation* which may be associated with loans obtained outside the national territory'.[75]

The ruling in *Sandoz* represents, in the area of direct taxation, the high-water mark in the Court's review of non-discriminatory national rules as obstacles to intra-EU movement. In contrast to the jurisprudence on tax law discussed in Section C(2)(a) (eg *Verkooijen*), the Court in *Sandoz* actually relied on the substance of its deterrent, effects-based test to bring the contested rules within the scope of its review. As a result, the Court's decision obliged the Austrian State to justify, under EU law, its decision not to adjust its non-discriminatory tax rules to preserve, for resident taxpayers, an advantage arising through 'disparities' between different tax regimes within the Union. Admittedly, the Court ruled, in the final analysis, that the Austrian rules could be justified.[76] However, this conclusion does not detract from its finding of an obstacle to intra-EU movement in the first instance.

[73] Case C-439/97 *Sandoz* [1999] ECR I-7041.
[74] ibid para 19.
[75] ibid emphasis added.
[76] ibid paras 24–7.

(2) Golden shares

Post-*Sandoz*, case law on the outer limits of the obstacles to intra-EU movement that fall within Article 63(1) TFEU centres on the Court's golden shares jurisprudence.[77] As noted above, this line of case law addresses national measures designed to manage the transition to private ownership of certain previously nationalized undertakings.[78] The creation of special classifications of shareholdings—labelled 'golden shares'—is intended to enable the Member State in question to maintain a degree of influence in the structure and management of the company concerned. This attempt to retain some degree of political influence post-privatization is often justified by the perceived need on the part of the Member States to ensure security of supply in the delivery of certain core services.[79] Broadly speaking, golden shares can be divided into two distinct categories.[80] First, they may grant the relevant Member State the right, as shareholder, to control the *acquisition/disposal* of shares in the undertaking concerned. In most cases, this amounts to a requirement for prior approval from the competent minister for investments above a certain threshold. Secondly, golden share provisions may go further and reserve to the Member State special rights over the company's continued *management*. For example, they may confer on that Member State the right to approve or veto certain corporate resolutions or to appoint members of the board.[81]

In a series of decisions, the Commission requested the Court to rule on compatibility of both categories of golden share provisions with Article 63(1) TFEU. In so doing, it charged the ECJ with the important task of adjudicating further on the limits imposed by EU law on the activities of Member States as market actors.[82] The Court's response in all its decisions has made it absolutely clear that *both* forms of golden share provisions (ie rules on share acquisition/disposal and management rights) infringe Article 63(1) TFEU. This finding applies irrespective of whether or not the golden share provisions are discriminatory. For the Court, the very introduction by Member States of special shareholdings operates to 'limit the acquisition of shares' by investors.[83] Accordingly, the ECJ requires that such provisions are justified in EU law. In effect, this approach has

[77] For Article 63(1) TFEU starting with Case C-367/98 *Commission v Portugal*, n 67 above. See thereafter, inter alia, Case C-463/00 *Commission v Spain*, n 45 above; Case C-98/01 *Commission v United Kingdom* [2003] ECR I-4641; Joined Cases C-282/04 and C-283/04 *Commission v Netherlands* [2006] ECR I-9141; Case C-112/05 *Commission v Germany* [2007] ECR I-8995 and Case C-171/08 *Commission v Portugal* ECR I-6817.

[78] For discussion see, eg, H Fleischer, 'Case Note on the Golden Share Cases' (2003) 40:2 *CMLRev* 493 and E Szyszczak, 'Golden Shares and Market Governance' (2002) 29:3 *ILEI* 255.

[79] E Szyszczak, n 78 above, 262.

[80] This distinction follows that adopted by the Commission in its Communication on 'Certain Legal Aspects Concerning Intra-EU Investment' [1997] OJ C 222/15. See further the Opinion of AG Colomer in Case C-367/98 *Commission v Portugal*, n 67 above, para 30. The AG juxtaposes the terms 'access' and 'management' to the same effect.

[81] eg Case C-112/05 *Commission v Germany*, n 77 above.

[82] As noted by AG Poiares Maduro in his Opinion in Joined Cases C-282/04 and C-283/04 *Commission v Netherlands*, n 77 above, para 26.

[83] eg Case C-367/98 *Commission v Portugal*, n 67 above, para 45.

significantly limited the scope for Member States to deviate from the normal rules governing corporate activity within that State. This encroachment on national regulatory autonomy has been repeatedly attacked by both the defendant Member States and others. However, that criticism has fallen on deaf ears.

(a) Advocate General Colomer's critique

Advocate General Colomer strongly criticized the Court's 'catch-all' approach to the review of golden shares against Article 63(1) TFEU. In several Opinions, he sought repeatedly to convince the Court to reconsider its analysis in light of the demands of Article 345 TFEU.[84] That provision provides that 'the Treaties shall in no way prejudice the rules in Member States governing the system of property ownership'. For the Advocate General, this obligation did not simply refer to civilian rules on property ownership in the narrow sense.[85] Instead, he argued that it reserves to the Member States the right to intervene in the organization and management of undertakings established on the national territory where those undertakings contribute to certain strategic (national) economic policy objectives, that is, objectives *other* than profit maximization.[86]

Formulating his conclusions into a substantive test, Advocate General Colomer maintained that the ECJ should acknowledge a key distinction between the *existence* and *exercise* of golden share rights. He argued that, by virtue of Article 345 TFEU, national measures granting Member States powers in strategic undertakings for the purposes of securing economic policy objectives must be *presumed* not to fall within the scope[87] of Article 63(1) TFEU.[88] That said, the Advocate General accepted that, whilst the existence of such reserved rights was not per se contrary to Article 63(1) TFEU, their discriminatory or anti-competitive exercise by the Member States concerned could infringe that provision.[89] However, this remained, in his view, a distinct issue to be assessed on a case-by-case basis.

(b) Golden shares and Keck?

Although insightful, Advocate General Colomer's criticism distracts attention from the more obvious basis for 'judicial restraint' to be found *within* the EU free

[84] Starting with his Opinion in Case C-367/98 *Commission v Portugal*, n 67 above.

[85] ibid para 54. See further his Opinion in eg Case C-112/05 *Commission v Germany*, n 77 above, para 48 and Case C-326/07 *Commission v Italy* [2009] ECR I-2291, para 36.

[86] To reach this point, the AG adopted an historical and teleological approach to the interpretation of Article 345 TFEU. See his Opinion in Case C-367/98 *Commission v Portugal*, n 67 above, paras 49–56.

[87] See Opinion of AG Colomer in Case C-98/01 *Commission v United Kingdom*, n 77 above, esp para 37.

[88] Opinion of AG Colomer in Case C-367/98 *Commission v Portugal*, n 67 above, para 67. See further thereafter eg Case C-98/01 *Commission v United Kingdom*, n 77 above, para 57, and Case C-326/07 *Commission v Italy*, n 77 above, paras 40–1.

[89] Opinion of AG Colomer in Case C-367/98 *Commission v Portugal*, n 67 above, para 68.

movement framework: the decision in *Keck*.[90] In that case, the Court responded directly to criticism over its application of Article 34 TFEU (goods) to non-discriminatory trading rules.[91] In order to curtail the tentacles of its broad, effects-based definition of a measure having equivalent effect to a quantitative restriction, the ECJ famously introduced a distinction between two distinct categories of national measure. It concluded that national rules prescribing 'product characteristics' are presumed to infringe Article 34 TFEU.[92] By contrast, rules regulating 'selling arrangements' fall outside the scope of that provision *provided* that two cumulative conditions were met.[93] Of the two conditions, the second has emerged as the key substantive test. It requires that the contested rule is genuinely non-discriminatory, applying without distinction to both domestic and imported products.

The potential transposition of the decision in *Keck* to the review of golden shares was first mooted by the United Kingdom Government in its submissions to the Court in *Commission v Spain*.[94] In that case, the United Kingdom Government argued that the ECJ should distinguish between the two categories of golden shares noted in Section D(2) above. Specifically, the United Kingdom Government maintained that the Court should distinguish between the reservation of statutory powers that (1) authorize the acquisition (and disposal) of shares and those (2) granting Member States rights in the ongoing management of undertakings.[95] According to the United Kingdom Government, Article 63(1) TFEU should be interpreted as precluding *only* the first category measure. It maintained that the per se review of the second category of non-discriminatory rules (management rights) was tantamount to an overextension of that provision—comparable to that giving rise to the decision in *Keck*.[96]

There is much to commend the arguments of the United Kingdom Government. In common with the rules on non-discriminatory selling arrangements at issue in *Keck*, the non-discriminatory golden share management rights do not actually block intra-EU movement.[97] The *existence* of the power for Member States to approve or veto certain corporate decisions (other than those governing the

[90] Joined Cases C-267/91 and C-268/91 *Keck and Mithouard* [1993] ECR I-6097.

[91] For discussion see, eg, E White, 'In Search of Limits to Art 30 of the EEC Treaty' (1989) 26 *CMLRev* 235 and, more recently, L Gormley, 'Silver Threads among the Gold... 50 Years of the Free Movement of Goods' (2008) 31:6 *Fordham Int'l LJ* 1637, 1648–60.

[92] Joined Cases C-267/91 and C-268/91 *Keck and Mithouard*, n 90 above, para 15.

[93] ibid para 16.

[94] Case C-463/00 *Commission v Spain*, n 45 above, paras 49–50. See further thereafter, eg, the arguments of the Portuguese Government in Case C-171/08 *Commission v Portugal*, n 77 above, para 43.

[95] Case C-463/00 *Commission v Spain*, n 45 above, para 49.

[96] This assertion was added in its submission to the Court in Case C-98/01 *Commission v United Kingdom*, n 77 above, para 28.

[97] Contrast here the prohibition of the non-discriminatory rules in eg Case 34/74 *Henn and Darby* [1979] ECR 3795 (Article 34 TFEU); Case C-415/93 *Bosman*, n 40 above (Article 45 TFEU) and Case C-384/93 *Alpine Investments*, n 40 above (Article 56 TFEU) as obstacles to intra-EU movement. In all of these cases, the contested measures blocked movement *between* Member States.

acquisition/disposal of shares)[98] does not prevent, in any way, the right of non-resident investors to purchase shares in the undertaking concerned. As with genuinely non-discriminatory rules on trading hours (excluded from the scope of Article 34 TFEU using the selling arrangement test in *Keck*), non-discriminatory golden shares (management rights) only affect the commercial freedom of investors within that Member State.[99] In practical terms, this is likely to translate into a reduction in share value. However, is judicial scrutiny on this basis even necessary? Is it the function of the Treaty freedoms to maximize share value? Indeed, any detrimental effect on share value will *already* have been priced into the value of the shares at the time of acquisition. In sum, there is a good argument that such rules should enjoy the same presumption of legality as selling arrangements and similarly escape the Court's review in the absence of any discrimination.

Admittedly, there is perhaps little practical value in defending a rigid distinction between the existence and (discriminatory) exercise of non-discriminatory management rights. In the majority of cases before the Court, the contested golden share rights were clearly conceived with discriminatory action in mind.[100] As such, the Court's preferred effects-based approach might simply be thought of as bringing forward future conflicts. Moreover, there is arguably real value associated with this pre-emptive move. The Court's interventionist stance has made it clear to investors in advance the terms under which the exercise of special rights by the State will be tolerated under EU law. Following the decision in *Commission v Belgium*, it is clear that Member States may only retain powers to object to corporate resolutions *ex post* and on very specific non-economic grounds, which must be clearly defined in advance.[101] Finally, the exercise of such retained rights is also subject to strict procedural safeguards and, ultimately, judicial review.[102] This further enhances legal certainty for investors.

However, none of the above weakens the argument that a *Keck*-inspired reading of non-discriminatory management rights would have achieved the same end result, albeit in a manner that better respected Member State autonomy in principle. In any case, the Court has repeatedly rejected arguments in favour of the transposition of the decision in *Keck* to the interpretation of Article 63(1) TFEU.[103] In *Commission v Spain*, the ECJ stated that the provisions on golden shares do not have

[98] See further here, eg, Case C-302/97 *Konle*, n 25 above; Case C-300/01 *Doris Salzmann (No 2)*, n 65 above, and Case C-213/04 *Burscher*, n 65 above.

[99] On this point, see Joined Cases C-282/04 and C-283/04 *Commission v Netherlands*, n 77 above, para 27. The Court's comments that management rights are capable of depressing the (stock market) value of the shares of that company carry distinct echoes of the Court's pre-*Keck* (and now also, in part, post-*Keck*) arguments based on the *volume* of intra-EU trade.

[100] For a clear example, see Case C-174/04 *Commission v Italy* [2005] ECR I-4933 and, in particular, the Opinion of AG Kokott in that decision, which notes that the Italian Government's creation of special rights was designed specifically to prevent takeovers by *French* public undertakings. See para 2.

[101] Case C-503/99 *Commission v Belgium* [2002] ECR I-4809, paras 49–55.

[102] ibid.

[103] eg Case C-463/00 *Commission v Spain*, n 45 above, para 59 and Case C-171/08 *Commission v Portugal*, n 77 above, paras 65–7.

'comparable effects' to the measures at issue in *Keck*.[104] In support of its conclusion, the ECJ pointed to the fact that the existence of such shareholdings 'affect[s] the position of a person acquiring a shareholding as such and [is] thus liable to deter investors from other Member States from making such investments and, consequently, *affect access to the market*'.[105]

E. The outer limits of Article 63(1) TFEU: market access

As the previous section has shown, the case law marking the outer limits of the prohibition on non-discriminatory national rules as obstacles to intra-EU movement in Article 63(1) TFEU now centres on the Court's golden shares jurisprudence. The application of that provision to review of genuinely non-discriminatory tax rules (as in *Sandoz*) has not been repeated elsewhere in the case law on capital.[106] In addition, we also noted the Court's refusal to explore parallels between aspects of its golden shares case law and the 'selling arrangement' proviso in *Keck*.

In this section, we turn now to examine (briefly) the concept of market access. As the golden shares case law illustrates, this term now defines the outer limits of Article 63(1) TFEU. The Court's use of market access to manage the scope of the obstacle concept is not new. However, the ECJ's application of the term in its golden shares case law differs markedly from earlier interpretations. In its case law on golden shares, the Court uses the term, for the first time, as more than just a synonym for discrimination analysis or a device to capture national rules that *block* movement between the markets of different Member States. Instead, market access is used to guide the Court's review of non-discriminatory legislation that simply characterizes the conditions *within* individual Member States. Significantly, this new, expanded view of market access has also taken hold in the Court's interpretation of the other Treaty freedoms with a detrimental effect on Member State autonomy.

(1) Market access: evolution and implications

Prior to the Court's case law on golden shares, the market access concept was used to review two distinct categories of national measure: (1) discriminatory national measures and (2) non-discriminatory national rules that *block* intra-EU movement. In the case law on goods, market access simply 're-badged' discrimination analysis (category 1). For example, in *Gourmet International Products*, the ECJ invoked

[104] eg Case C-463/00 *Commission v Spain*, n 45 above, para 59.

[105] ibid para 61 (emphasis added). See further Case C-98/01 *Commission v United Kingdom*, n 77 above, para 47 and Case C-171/08 *Commission v Portugal*, n 77 above, para 67.

[106] However, the very same issue has arisen in subsequent cases in other areas. See, eg, Joined Cases C-430/99 and C-431/99 *Sea-Land Service* [2002] ECR I-5235 and Case C-464/02 *Commission v Denmark (Vehicle Registrations)* [2005] ECR I-7929.

market access to capture indirectly discriminatory rules on advertising.[107] In the case law on persons and services, market access was used to bring genuinely non-discriminatory rules within the scope of the Court's review. However, in each case, the non-discriminatory rules in question operated to *block* intra-EU movement (category 2). For example, in *Alpine Investments* (Article 56 TFEU), the contested prohibition on cold-calling prevented the applicant from leaving the market of that State in order to provide services in another State where this technique was legal. Similarly, in *Bosman* (Article 45 TFEU), the non-discriminatory transfer rules under review *blocked* the applicant's right to move *between* football clubs established in *different* Member States. By contrast, non-discriminatory national measures that did *not* block intra-EU movement escaped the Court's review.[108]

The Court's Article 63(1) TFEU case law on non-discriminatory golden shares (management rights) challenged the above framework. In *Commission v Spain (Golden Shares)*, the Court invoked, for the first time, the market access concept in connection with the review of genuinely non-discriminatory national rules that simply defined the market within that particular Member State.[109] Significantly, this broader reading of the market access has since taken hold in the Court's case law across the other Treaty freedoms. For example, and perhaps most famously, the Court has relied on market access in connection with its review of non-discriminatory national rules regulating the use of products. In *Commission v Italy (Motorcycle Trailers)*, the Grand Chamber of the Court was requested to rule on the compatibility with Article 34 TFEU of Italian legislation that prohibited the use of motorcycle trailers within that State.[110] As Advocate General Bot rightly noted in his Opinion, this required the Court to rule—once again—on the scope of its 'selling arrangement' formula in *Keck*.[111] Should non-discriminatory national rules on the use of products within a State benefit from the same presumption of legality as non-discriminatory 'selling arrangements'?

Following its approach *Commission v Spain (Golden Shares)*, the Court in *Commission v Italy (Motorcycle Trailers)* stubbornly refused to explore the existence of any parallels between product use rules and non-discriminatory selling arrangements. The Grand Chamber concluded that the contested Italian legislation prohibiting the use of motorcycle trailers on the national territory fell within the scope of Article 34 TFEU. In the subsequent case of *Mickelsson and Roos*, the Court (Second Chamber) reached the same conclusion with respect to Swedish legislation restricting the use of personal watercraft (specifically, jet-skis) within that State.[112]

[107] Case C-405/98 *Gourmet International Products* [2001] ECR I-1795. The same is true for Case C-254/98 *TK-Heimdienst Sass* [2000] ECR I-151 and Case C-322/01 *DocMorris* [2003] ECR I-14887.

[108] eg Case C-190/98 *Graf* [2000] ECR I-493 (Article 45 TFEU).

[109] Case C-463/00 *Commission v Spain*, n 45 above, para 61.

[110] Case C-110/05 *Commission v Italy (Motorcycle Trailers)*, n 72 above; Case C-142/05 *Mickelsson and Roos* [2009] ECR I-4271. See too earlier, Case C-265/06 *Commission v Portugal* [2008] ECR I-2245 and Case C-473/98 *Toolex Alpha* [2000] ECR I-5681. For persons see Case C-325/08 *Olympique Lyonnais SASP v Olivier Bernard and Newcastle UFC* [2010] ECR I-2177, para 36.

[111] Opinion of AG Bot in Case C-110/05 *Commission v Italy (Motorcycle Trailers)*, n 72 above, para 1.

[112] Case C-142/05 *Mickelsson and Roos*, n 110 above.

In both cases, the Court concluded that the contested national rules affected market access for the products concerned. According to the Court, 'a prohibition on the use of a product on the territory of a Member State has a considerable influence on the behaviour of consumers, which, in its turn, affects the access of that product to the market of that Member State'.[113] However, in respect of the non-discriminatory Member State legislation in point, this reference to market access can only mean one thing: the right to maximize commercial/personal freedom within that State. After all, the contested legislation did not block the free importation of the products concerned into the respective Member States (eg *Alpine Investments* or *Bosman*). Equally, the same legislation was not shown to discriminate in favour of competing products on the national market (as in *Gourmet International Products*).

The Court's expansion of the obstacle concept in this manner is nothing new. As noted in Section D(2)(b) above, in its pre-*Keck* case law on Article 34 TFEU, the Court lost sight of the scope of that provision and ended up reviewing against the Treaty justification framework a variety of genuinely non-discriminatory trading rules that affected only the *volume* of intra-EU trade in goods.[114] Even in the post-*Keck* period, it is possible to point to the Court's (exceptional) application of the other Treaty freedoms to the same effect without any reference to the market access concept. For example, in several cases, the Court has concluded that Article 56 TFEU extends to capture non-discriminatory national tax rules on the basis that the existence of such measures was 'liable to impede or render less attractive' the provision of intra-EU services.[115] However, whether relying on the language of deterrent effects or—more recently—market access, the Court's progressive broadening of the scope of the obstacle concept is controversial. In effect, it amounts to using the freedoms as tools to scrutinize the existence—or better, *quality*—of Member State regulation. This represents a definite shift in the balance of power for the regulation of the internal market. It requires Member States to subsume and defend a far broader range of policy preferences within the Union justification framework.

Of course, it does not necessarily follow that the ECJ will, in the final analysis, conclude that contested non-discriminatory legislation is contrary to the Treaty. This finding depends entirely on the outcome of the Court's second-stage justification analysis. Significantly, in most cases, the Court ultimately concludes that non-discriminatory rules that simply define the conditions within individual Member States can be justified under EU law. This includes, for example, the Court's (exceptional) review of the non-discriminatory tax rules in *Sandoz* discussed above. Similarly, in respect of product use rules, the Court is also yet to conclude

[113] Case C-110/05 *Commission v Italy (Motorcycle Trailers)*, n 72 above, para 56 and Case 142/05 *Mickelsson and Roos*, n 110 above, para 26.

[114] eg Case 286/81 *Oosthoek's Uitgeversmaatschappij BV* [1982] ECR 4575; Joined Cases 60 and 61/84 *Cinéthèque* [1985] ECR 2605 and Case 145/88 *Torfaen* [1989] ECR 3851.

[115] Joined Cases C-430/99 and C-431/99 *Sea-Land Service*, n 106 above, para 38, and Case C-464/02 *Commission v Denmark (Vehicle Registrations)*, n 106 above, para 50. See further, outside of the case law on taxation, eg Case C-108/96 *Mac Quen and Others* [2001] ECR I-837 (Article 49 TFEU) and Case C-294/00 *Gräbner* [2002] ECR I-6515 (Articles 45 and 56 TFEU).

that the relevant Member State policy cannot be squared with the Union justification framework. Interestingly, the position does seem to be rather different in the case law on Article 63(1) TFEU. In its judgments on non-discriminatory golden shares (management rights), the ECJ nearly always concludes that the contested Member State legislation cannot be justified under EU law.[116] Through adopting this firm stance on golden shares, the Court has, in result, effectively implemented the Commission's policy objective in this area. In its 1997 Communication on intra-EU capital movements, the Commission took the clear view that the retention by the Member States of management rights, in derogation from ordinary company law, should be prohibited by Article 63(1) TFEU.[117]

F. Concluding remarks

In a relatively short space of time, the Court's case law on capital movements within the Union has come a long way. In terms of the definition of an obstacle to intra-EU movement—the primary focus of analysis here—the Court's case law is evolving very much along established lines. As with the other freedoms, this term is now defined broadly by reference to the deterrent or dissuasive effects of national rules on intra-EU movement. Equally, in line with the provisions on goods, services and persons, this expansive approach to defining the scope of Article 63(1) TFEU masks a more sober reality. In the majority of decisions, it is old-fashioned discrimination analysis that operates behind the more dynamic language of deterrent and dissuasive effects.

However, by following the established trajectory, the case law on intra-EU capital movements has not escaped controversy. On the contrary, in its development of Article 63(1) TFEU, the Court has taken us back to an enduring controversy in EU free movement law: the application of the Treaty freedoms to review non-discriminatory national rules that simply define the regulatory environment within a Member State.[118] In the case law on Article 63(1) TFEU, this point of tension in EU free movement law appears—for now—to have settled on golden share provisions. The Court rules consistently that the retention by Member States of any special rights in the management of previously nationalized undertakings requires justification under EU law. On one view, it is possible to argue that this line of case law is simply exceptional. We could suggest, for example, that the Court's decision to extend the scope of Article 63(1) TFEU to capture the aforementioned rights flows directly from the wording of Directive 88/361, according to which the term 'direct investment' (defining a specific 'capital movement') denotes the right of shareholders 'to participate effectively in the management of

[116] For an exception, see Case C-503/99 *Commission v Belgium*, n 101 above.

[117] See Communication on 'Certain Legal Aspects Concerning Intra-EU Investment', n 80 above.

[118] On this point see, eg, Maduro, n 13 above, 40; J Snell, 'The Notion of Market Access: a Concept or a Slogan' (2010) 47:2 *CMLRev* 437, 470, and the Opinion of AG Bot in Case C-110/05 *Commission v Italy (Motorcycle Trailers)*, n 72 above, para 75.

the undertaking concerned'.[119] However, it is suggested that the evidence in the case law points—at the time of writing—firmly in favour of an alternative argument.

The case law on Article 63(1) TFEU appears to mark the beginning of a new development in EU free movement law. Once again, the Court appears to be extending the scope of the Treaty freedoms to review the existence of (certain) non-discriminatory national policies that simply restrict commercial or personal freedom within Member States. This represents a definite shift in the balance of power between the Member States and the Court of Justice. The dangers of judicial overreach into Member State autonomy are well known and the Court has been forced to backtrack already once before (*Keck*). However, through its preferred conceptual device, the market access test, the Court has arguably found its own solution to the problem. As Snell notes, market access opens up a 'third way', allowing the Court to steer an intuitive course between two competing visions of the internal market.[120] The concept's ambiguity enables the Court to navigate a path between a decentralized approach to market integration, based on the principles of non-discrimination and mutual recognition, and a more centralized position, which advocates the use of the Treaty freedoms to scrutinize the efficiency or reasonableness of Member State regulation per se. At a time when the internal market is being pushed back into the spotlight, the Court appears increasingly to be tilting towards the latter of the two alternatives. But how far dare the Court go?

[119] Directive 88/361, n 9 above (emphasis added).
[120] J Snell, n 118 above, 470–1.

10

Maximum versus Minimum Harmonization: Choosing between Unity and Diversity in the Search for the Soul of the Internal Market

*Stephen Weatherill**

A. Introduction

In *Buet v Ministère Public* the European Court of Justice (ECJ) ruled that a French decision to ban doorstep selling of certain educational materials was not incompatible with Directive 85/577 which governs exactly that marketing practice and which requires only that the consumer be given a seven-day cooling-off period after concluding such a contract.[1] The Court took the view that because the Directive, though adopted under what was then Article 100 EEC (now Article 115 TFEU), provides explicitly in Article 8 that the Directive 'shall not prevent Member States from adopting or maintaining more favourable provisions to protect consumers in the field which it covers', stricter rules were allowed even where they obstructed imported goods, provided only that they were justified according to the familiar principles which are rooted in Article 36 TFEU and have been (re-)shaped imaginatively over time by the Court. And it concluded, in terms obviously favourable to the French regulatory choice, that the prohibition of doorstep selling was designed to protect consumers against the risk of ill-considered purchases, which was a particular concern where, as in the case, the potential sale was of educational material to vulnerable consumers.

By contrast, in *VTB-VAB NV* the Court found that a presumption of unlawfulness attached by Belgian law to a particular marketing strategy which was stricter than the requirements laid down by Directive 2005/29 on business-to-consumer commercial practices in the internal market could no longer be applied.[2] In *Plus*

* Faculty of Law and Somerville College, University of Oxford. This chapter was completed at the beginning of November 2010 and states the law at that time.

[1] Case 382/87 *Buet v Ministère Public* [1989] ECR 1235; Council Directive 85/577/EEC of 20 December 1985 to protect the consumer in respect of contracts negotiated away from business premises [1985] OJ L 372/31.

[2] Case C-261/07 *VTB-VAB NV* [2009] ECR I-2949; Council Directive 2005/29/EC of 11 May 2005 concerning unfair business-to-consumer commercial practices in the internal market and

Warenhandelsgesellschaft the same fate befell a German rule against combining participation in a prize competition with the purchase of goods which took no account of the specific circumstances of individual cases.[3] There was no scope to test the national rules against the standards familiar in the law governing the free movement of goods in the European Union. They were stricter than the standards set by the Directive—and that, without more, condemned them as incompatible with the demands of EU law. Directive 2005/29 was based on Article 95 EC (now Article 114 TFEU), so it was, like Directive 85/377 which was at stake in *Buet*, a measure of legislative harmonization designed to promote the integration of markets in the EU according to common rules adopted at EU level. But whereas in *Buet* the national regulator was found to have room to set stricter rules than those set at EU level, in *VTB-VAB NV* and in *Plus Warenhandelsgesellschaft* such leeway was emphatically ruled out.

The explanation for the difference in treatment of the national rules in these cases lies in the model of harmonization chosen in the relevant Directives. *Buet* concerns the so-called 'Doorstep Selling' Directive, Directive 85/377, and it is a measure of *minimum harmonization*. This means that it sets a common floor of regulation, which all Member States must respect, but it does not set a ceiling. The ceiling is set only by the broader legal rules of the internal market, such as those governing non-discrimination and free movement, which is why in *Buet* the French rule, stricter than the Directive, fell to be assessed against the requirements of (what is now) Article 34 TFEU on the free movement of goods. By contrast, Directive 2005/29 on unfair commercial practices is a measure of *maximum harmonization*. This means that it serves as both floor and ceiling. Member States must implement the rules that have been chosen as the EU regime—and they must apply *only* those rules. They are not permitted to apply stricter rules at all—the maximum model, in contrast to the minimum model, has robbed them of any space to argue that they are justified in choosing a higher ceiling of protection.

A minimum model allows more space for diversity and local autonomy; a maximum model seems to promise greater uniformity in the pattern of regulatory intervention chosen for the internal market. A minimum model preserves to a degree the independence of relevant institutions at State level; the maximum model transfers regulatory responsibility to the EU's legislative institutions—and to its Court too. There are fierce debates about the appropriateness of these competing models for the structure of the internal market, and there are varying legislative preferences too, as this Introduction's glance at the case law has made plain. At the heart of the debate, however, is a profound choice—one that concerns the distribution of regulatory authority in the European Union. The purpose of this contribution is to show how, in the consumer law field, the first decade of the

amending Council Directive 84/450/EEC, Directives 97/7/EC, 98/27/EC and 2002/65/EC of the European Parliament and of the Council and Regulation (EC) No 2006/2004 of the European Parliament and of the Council [2005] OJ L 149/22.

[3] Case C-304/08 *Zentrale zur Bekämpfung unlauteren Wettbewerbs eV v Plus Warenhandelsgesellschaft mbH* [2010] ECR I-217.

current millennium has witnessed a vivid and as yet incomplete debate about which model of harmonization to select. It is a battle for the soul of the internal market—even for the soul of the European Union itself. 'United in diversity' would have been the Union's motto under the ill-fated Treaty establishing a Constitution:[4] but how much unity? And how much diversity? The choice between minimum and maximum harmonization puts these tensions to the test.

B. The EU's legislative *acquis* affecting consumer protection

Consumer protection was largely left unmentioned in the original Treaty of Rome. It was inserted into the Treaty as an explicit, albeit textually limited, legislative competence only as late as 1993, on the entry into force of the Maastricht Treaty. The relevant (and amended) provision after the entry into force of the Lisbon Treaty in 2009 is Article 169 TFEU.

The constitutional purist would fasten on 1993 as the key date. The principle of conferral contained in Article 5 TEU dictates that the Union shall act only within the limits of the competences conferred upon it by the Member States. In the consumer field, therefore, as in all fields, the answer to the question 'what may the EU do?' is 'as much as, but no more than, the Treaties permit'. And, as far as legislative action was concerned, only after 1993 was there any such permission.

However, this understanding would be deeply misleading. In fact, the EEC (as was) had already made politically significant rhetorical incursions into the area of consumer protection as early as 1972. The 'Paris Summit' famously initiated an attempt to broaden the appeal of the EC beyond economic affairs. A programme of consumer protection formed part of this agenda. The first Council Resolution on a preliminary programme for a consumer protection and information policy was issued in 1975[5] and it has been followed over time by a long series of Commission and Council policy statements and programmes which have given shape to a distinctively European understanding of the function of consumer protection—in particular concerning the intended place of the consumer as beneficiary of the project to complete the internal market.[6] Lately the Commission's Strategy to cover 2007–13, entitled 'Empowering consumers, enhancing their welfare, effectively protecting them',[7] emphasizes the benefits to the consumer of a successful internal market, whilst identifying three main objectives—empowering consumers, enhancing welfare, and protection from risks that consumers cannot cope

[4] Treaty establishing a Constitution [2004] OJ C 310, Article I-8.

[5] Council Resolution of 14 April 1975 on a preliminary programme of the European Economic Community for a consumer protection and information policy [1975] OJ C 92/1.

[6] Especially Council Resolution of 23 June 1986 concerning the future orientation of the policy of the European Economic Community for the protection and promotion of consumer interests [1986] OJ C167/1; and the Commission's second three-year action plan, covering 1993–1995 COM (93) 378 final.

[7] Communication from the Commission to the Council, the European Parliament and the European Economic and Social Committee, *EU Consumer Policy Strategy 2007–2013: Empowering Consumers, Enhancing Their Welfare, Effectively Protecting Them* COM (2007) 99 final.

with individually. And the 'empowering' motif pops up again in the 'Monti report' on the future of the single market, submitted to the President of the Commission in the spring of 2010.[8]

But there have been significant legislative initiatives too. A batch of directives has an impact on the formation of particular *consumer* contracts: those concluded away from business premises ('on the doorstep'),[9] package travel,[10] timeshare,[11] consumer credit,[12] distance contracts,[13] payment services in the internal market,[14] electronic commerce,[15] and distance marketing of consumer financial services.[16] The marketing practice subject to regulation is typically *not* prohibited. Instead the chosen technique involves requirements that the consumer be provided in advance with specified information about a contemplated transaction. Information disclosure has frequently been combined with protection in the post-contractual phase, most strikingly through the prescription of a 'cooling-off' period within which the consumer is entitled to exercise a right to withdraw from an agreed deal.

Mandatory pre-contractual disclosure supplemented by the 'cooling-off' period suggests an emphasis on transparency and the perfecting effect on the competitive market of the attentive consumer. But the legislative *acquis* is not confined to an informational model. A pair of more ambitious directives go beyond contract formation and information disclosure and instead assert control over the *content* of the bargain. Directive 93/13 prohibits unfair terms in consumer contracts.[17] Directive 99/44 on certain aspects of the sale of consumer goods and associated

[8] *A New Strategy for the Single Market: at the service of Europe's Economy and Society* (9 May 2010) available at <http://ec.europa.eu/internal_market/strategy/docs/monti_report_final_10_05_2010_en.pdf>, 41.

[9] Directive 85/577/EEC, n 1 above.

[10] Council Directive 90/314/EEC of 13 June 1990 on package travel, package holidays and package tours [1990] OJ L 158/59.

[11] Council Directive 2008/112/EC of 16 December 2008 amending Council Directives 76/768/EEC, 88/378/EEC, 1999/13/EC and Directives 2000/53/EC, 2002/96/EC and 2004/42/EC of the European Parliament and of the Council in order to adapt them to Regulation (EC) No 1272/2008 on classification, labelling and packaging of substances and mixtures [2009] OJ L33/10, replacing with effect from February 2011 Council Directive 94/47/EC of 26 October 1994 on the protection of purchasers in respect of certain aspects of contracts relating to the purchase of the right to use immovable properties on a timeshare basis [1994] OJ L 280/83.

[12] Council Directive 2008/48/EC of 23 April 2008 on credit agreements for consumers and repealing Council Directive 87/102/EEC [2008] OJ L 133/66.

[13] Council Directive 97/7/EC of 20 May 1997 on the protection of consumers in respect of distance contracts [1997] OJ L144/19, as amended by Council Directive 2007/64/EC of 13 November 2007 on payment services in the internal market amending Directives 97/7/EC, 2002/65/EC, 2005/60/EC and 2006/48/EC and repealing Directive 97/5/EC [2007] OJ L 319/1.

[14] Directive 2007/64/EC, n 13 above.

[15] Council Directive 2000/31/EC of 8 June 2000 on certain legal aspects of information society services, in particular electronic commerce, in the Internal Market (Directive on electronic commerce) [2000] OJ L 178/1.

[16] Council Directive 2002/65/EC of 23 September 2002 concerning the distance marketing of consumer financial services and amending Council Directive 90/619/EEC and Directives 97/7/EC and 98/27/EC [2002] OJ L 271/16.

[17] Council Directive 93/13/EEC of 5 April 1993 on unfair terms in consumer contracts [1993] OJ L 95/29.

guarantees imports standards of required quality into consumer contracts.[18] And there is tort law too: Directive 85/374, commonly labelled the 'Product Liability Directive', harmonizes laws concerning liability for defective products.[19] The producer shall be liable for damage caused by a defect in his product, and a product is defective 'where it does not provide the safety which a person is entitled to expect'.

C. The impetus provided by legislative harmonization in the consumer field

Some of these legislative measures pre-date 1993, others are more recent. But how could such an impressive, if rather jumbled, body of consumer protection laws have been enacted at EU level when, as explained above, it was only with effect from 1993 that consumer protection became a legislative competence explicitly conferred on the EC (now in Article 169 TFEU)? The truth is that although Maastricht was formally important as the birthplace of what are now Articles 4(2)(f), 12 and 169 TFEU, which embed consumer protection in the Treaty, the bulk of what is conventionally labelled 'EU consumer policy' was and remains shaped by activities underpinned by Treaty provisions which are not explicitly presented as instruments of consumer protection. It is principally the programme of harmonization that is relevant.

Harmonization secures the realization of the objectives that underpin permitted national measures through the medium of common rules. The fact that the legislation applies across the entire territory of the Union removes the inhibition to trade consequent on national diversity. On the most simple model, 27 national laws become one *Union* law. Where the laws subject to harmonization are consumer laws, then the fruits of the process are harmonized Union consumer laws. So the *effect* of harmonization is *not only* to accelerate integration, achieve deregulation and serve the consumer interest in a better functioning economy *but also* to assert a process of re-regulation at EU level.

And this is the background to the package of legislative measures briefly surveyed above. From package travel to consumer credit, unfair terms to consumer sales—the EU has adopted legislation which sets harmonized standards governing the relevant fields of consumer law as part of a stated commitment to promote an integrated market. 1993—the entry into force of the Maastricht Treaty—was of little significance because harmonization in the service of market-making has *always* been a competence conferred on the EU by its Treaty, ever since the 1950s. The

[18] Directive 1999/44/EC of the European Parliament and of the Council of 25 May 1999 on certain aspects of the sale of consumer goods and associated guarantees [1999] OJ L 171/12.

[19] Council Directive 85/374/EEC of 25 July 1985 on the approximation of the laws, regulations and administrative provisions of the Member States concerning liability for defective products [1985] OJ L 210/29 amended by Council Directive 1999/34/EC of 10 May 1999 amending Council Directive 85/374/EEC on the approximation of the laws, regulations and administrative provisions of the Member States concerning liability for defective products [1999] OJ L 141/20.

original Treaty focused on use of what is now Article 115 TFEU as a legal base, but this has been superseded in practice by a provision inserted by the Single European Act. This is Article 114 TFEU which, prior to the entry into force of the Lisbon Treaty, was Article 95 EC. This empowers the adoption of measures to approximate national provisions 'which have as their object the establishing and functioning of the internal market'. Not least because it envisages nothing more ambitious than EU measures which 'support, supplement and monitor' Member State initiatives of consumer protection, Article 169 TFEU (and its predecessors) has been of negligible significance in expanding the *acquis*.[20] By contrast, harmonization—driven powerfully most of all today by Article 114 TFEU, to which Article 169 cross-refers—has long been a vigorous source of EU activity.

Harmonization has an unavoidable *dual function*: it involves the setting of common rules for the European market but it also inevitably involves a choice of the appropriate common standard and technique of re-regulatory protection. The Treaty makes plain this association between harmonization as a tool of market integration and harmonization as an exercise in selecting the appropriate technique for (re-)regulating the European market. Articles 12, 114(3) and 169 TFEU all provide examples, different in detail, of the general truth that the *quality* of a harmonized regime is constitutionally relevant. So the Court accepts that, provided that the conditions for recourse to Article 114 TFEU are fulfilled, the legislature 'cannot be prevented from relying on that legal basis on the ground that public health protection is a decisive factor in the choices to be made'.[21] The same principle applies where other non-market values are subjected to the discipline of legislative harmonization. This is how harmonization policy also becomes an exercise in selecting a pattern of regulatory protection for the EU. True, the legislative consumer *acquis* is far from systematic. It is an odd mix of measures, delivered by periodic bursts of political opportunism: 'a stone from Brussels here and there inserted into the edifices of national private law'.[22] But even so, it is not devoid of principles and themes. Harmonization develops its own momentum, as commentators on the package of European (consumer) contract law debate the weight and merits of (potentially competing) principles and techniques within the *acquis* such as information disclosure, respect for party autonomy, protection of the weaker party and inquiry into substantive unfairness. Here is not the place to explore this rich vein of scholarship further—save only to note that not only is the nature of the principles to be extracted and the techniques employed contested,[23]

[20] See, eg, the hardly groundbreaking Decision 3092/94 of the European Parliament and of the Council OJ 1994 L 331/1, amended by Council Decision 95/184 OJ 1995 L 120/36, on the establishment of a system of information on home and leisure accidents; Council Directive 98/6 of 16 February 1998 on consumer protection in the indication of the prices of products offered to consumers OJ 1998 L 80/27 on indication of prices offered to consumers.

[21] eg Cases C-154/04 and C-155/04 *Alliance for Natural Health* [2005] ECR I-6451, paras 30–1.

[22] O Remien, 'Uber den Stil des Europäischen Privatrechts' (1996) 60 *RabelsZ* 2, 8 (this author's translation).

[23] See, eg (and in diverse veins), F Rischkowsky and T Döring, 'Consumer Policy in a Market Economy: Considerations from the Perspective of the Economics of Information, the New Institutional Economics as well as Behavioural Economics' (2008) 31:3 *J of Consumer Policy* 285; H Rösler,

but moreover the very advisability and feasibility of making a 'system' out of this incrementally, even eccentrically, nurtured material remains methodologically controversial.[24]

D. Constitutional insincerity

This is a classic story of 'spillover' in the EU. There is no sustainable divide between the Union's interest in market integration and the role of the Member States in matters of market regulation. The fact that national public authorities have asserted a (principally) post-war commitment to legislative consumer protection has the consequence that the Union too, in pursuit of its goals of market integration and market (re-)regulation, must take consumer policy seriously. These rhythms are typical of the pathways along which the search for an 'EU policy' is conducted in many areas in which Treaty-conferred competence is or has been ambiguous, limited or even non-existent.

Nonetheless, it is undeniable that there is a strand of constitutional insincerity lurking beneath this tale. Article 114 TFEU is functionally broad. But it is not unlimited. Article 5 TEU declares that the Union shall act only within the limits of the competences conferred upon it by the Member States, and this statement of principle finds particular expression in relation to Article 114 TFEU in the case law of the Court. A 'mere finding of disparities between national rules' is inadequate to justify harmonization pursuant to Article 114 TFEU.[25] A connection with the achievement of the internal market foreseen by Article 26 TFEU is required. In *Tobacco Advertising* the Court famously ruled that Article 95 EC, the predecessor to Article 114 TFEU, had been stretched too far by the legislative institutions: it ruled Directive 98/43 invalid for want of a valid legal base.[26] Prohibitions against tobacco advertising on posters, parasols, ashtrays and other articles used in hotels,

Europäisches Konsumentenvertragsrecht (München: CH Beck, 2004); H-W Micklitz, 'The Relationship between national and European consumer policy' (2008) *YB of Consumer L* Ch 3; J Basedow, 'Freedom of Contract in the European Union' (2008) 16 *Eur Rev of Private L* 901; J Davies, 'Entrenchment of New Governance in Consumer Policy Formulation: a Platform for European Consumer Citizenship Practice?' (2009) 32:3 *J of Consumer Policy* 245.

24 eg contrast the enthusiastic approach of O Lando, 'Is Good Faith an Over-arching General Clause in the Principles of European Contract Law?' (2007) 15 *Eur Rev of Private L* 841 with (the more cautious but still basically positive) J Basedow, 'The Court of Justice and Private Law: Vacillations, General Principles and the Architecture of the European Judiciary' (2010) 18 *Eur Rev of Private L* 443 and (the still more cautious, even sceptical) T Wilhelmsson and C Twigg-Flesner, 'Pre-contractual information duties in the *acquis communautaire*' (2006) 2 *Eur Rev of Contract L* 441. For a still more sweeping critique see L Niglia, 'Beyond Enchantment—The Possibility of a New European Private Law' (2009) 28 *YB of Eur L* 60.

25 Cases C-154/04 and C-155/04 *Alliance for Natural Health*, n 21 above, para 28.

26 Directive 98/43/EC of 6 July 1998 on the approximation of the laws, regulations and administrative provisions of the Member States relating to the advertising and sponsorship of tobacco products [1998] OJ L 213/9; Case C-376/98 *Germany v Parliament and Council* [2000] ECR I-8419.

restaurants, cafes and cinemas 'in no way help facilitate trade in the products concerned'.[27]

This was public health policy improperly dressed up as legislative harmonization in a manner reaching beyond the mandate granted by the Treaty. It is not inconceivable that some of the legislative *acquis* on consumer protection might, if challenged, meet a similar fate. Is harmonization of laws governing doorstep selling,[28] or even unfair terms,[29] *really* sufficiently closely connected to the market-making project to fall within the legitimate scope of (what is now) Article 114 TFEU? Even though the Court's case law subsequent to *Tobacco Advertising* discloses a generous attitude to legislative ambition, in particular in allowing wide scope for 'preventive harmonization' designed to addresses obstacles that are likely to emerge,[30] it is at least arguable that some of the consumer *acquis* is sailing close to the constitutional wind. The political reality was (and to some extent still is) that if there is sufficient support among the Member States for the adoption of a particular initiative then constitutional disquiet may readily be suppressed.[31]

E. Minimum harmonization as part of the political bargain

The political bargain underpinning this legislative programme had two elements. The Member States were, as observed above, prepared to take a broad approach to the scope of legislative competence to harmonize laws in the field of consumer protection—but, as part of the deal, they were also anxious to embed in the relevant legislative measures the minimum formula which ensured that EC intervention did not deprive them of scope to maintain or develop more ambitious forms of protection.

Some Treaty provisions make plain that EU legislative measures adopted pursuant to them permit stricter national rules, provided only that they comply with the Treaty. This is minimum rule-making and, of direct relevance to consumer protection, it appears in Article 169(4) TFEU—as well in Article 153(4) (social matters) and Article 193 (environmental protection). Article 114, by contrast, contains no such *general* concession, but rather only the derogations supervised by the Commission contained in Article 114(4) et seq TFEU. And although Article 4 TFEU lists both the internal market and consumer protection as areas of competence shared between the EU and the Member States, this does not solve

[27] Case C-376/98 *Germany v Parliament and Council*, n 26 above, para 99.

[28] Directive 85/577/EEC, n 1 above.

[29] Directive 93/13/EEC, n 17 above.

[30] Case C-380/03 *Germany v Parliament and Council* [2006] ECR I-11573, para 41. See too Cases C-154/04 and C-155/04 *Alliance for Natural Health*, n 21 above; Case C-66/04 *UK v Parliament and Council* [2005] ECR I-10553; Case C-58/08 *Vodafone Ltd et al* [2010] ECR I-4999. cf M Seidel, 'Präventive Rechtsangleichung im Bereich des gemeinsamen Marktes' (2006) 41:1 *Europarecht* 25.

[31] See S Weatherill, 'European Private Law and the Constitutional Dimension' in F Cafaggi (ed), *The Institutional Framework of European Private Law*, Collected Courses of the Academy of European Law, Vol XV/2 (Oxford: Oxford University Press, 2006).

the particular question of the extent to which legislative action pursuant to Article 114 TFEU excludes residual Member State competence.

However, legislative practice reveals that much of the harmonized *acquis* pertaining to the protection of the economic interests of consumers is built on an assumption that minimum harmonization shall be the norm.[32] Minimum directives do not set a single rule as both floor and ceiling, but rather only a floor. Member States may maintain stricter rules, up to the ceiling set by primary law. This reconnects the analysis with *Buet*, encountered in the Introduction to this chapter.[33] The Court ruled that although Directive 85/577 on 'doorstep selling' merely requires that a consumer be allowed a right to cancel the contract concluded on the doorstep within a defined period, a total ban imposed by France on doorstep selling was compatible with the Directive (in view of the minimum standards clause) and, given its contribution to consumer protection, also with what is now Article 34 TFEU. Like Article 114(4) et seq, this model reflects the notion that harmonization need not involve the automatic subordination of national choices about market regulation to the dictates of trade liberalization, but minimum harmonization is more flexible in the leeway offered to Member States than the relatively tightly defined provisions of Article 114(4) et seq.

This, then, was the political bargain. The pressure exerted on the very constitutional foundations of conferred competence under the Treaty by this broad approach to legislative harmonization was released by the 'safety valve' of minimum harmonization which shielded Member States from the brutal consequence that applies under the orthodoxy of classic legislative 'pre-emption'. Minimum harmonization promotes the integration of markets whilst also preserving regulatory diversity and it ensures space for expression for cultural particularity. Article 169(4) TFEU, of course, makes plain that minimum rule-making is envisaged as far as supportive rules adopted under Article 169(2)(b) are concerned, but legislative practice has aligned Article 114 TFEU (and its predecessors) with this model too. In this way, both the EU and the Member States retain competence to protect consumers even after the EU has intervened by way of secondary legislation.

F. The Commission's attack on 'minimum harmonization'

The political bargain which has long embraced minimum harmonization in this field is now under attack. Beginning in 2001, the Commission has initiated a wide-ranging debate about the proper role of the EC, now the EU, in the field of contract law. The Commission's July 2001 Communication on European Contract Law

[32] See S Weatherill, *EU Consumer Law and Policy* (Cheltenham: Elgar European Law, 2005) Ch 3; J Stuyck, 'Patterns of Justice in the European Constitutional Charter: Minimum Harmonisation in the field of Consumer Law' in L Krämer, H-W Micklitz and K Tonner (eds), *Law and Diffuse Interests in the European Legal Order* (Baden-Baden: Nomos, 1997).

[33] Case 382/87 *Buet*, n 1 above.

initiated the current inquiry.[34] This was followed up by the February 2003 Action Plan on a more coherent European Contract Law.[35] In October 2004, the Commission released 'European Contract Law and the revision of the acquis: the way forward'.[36] Its concern has not been confined to *consumer* contract law, but, as noted above, that is the area in which the EU has been most active. There are several themes and tensions evident in the progress of the debate, but one of the more prominent is an increasing distaste for the long-established model of minimum harmonization.

The legislative *acquis* sketched above is a patchwork. As a matter of substance, the most potent concern in the Commission's review process has been the search for 'a significantly higher degree of coherence in European contract law', to borrow the words of one of the principal architects of the review in the Commission.[37] Although the priorities chosen, the scale of ambition and the way(s) forward appear to have fluctuated periodically, this quest for enhanced 'coherence', an element in the broader project of 'better regulation' designed to secure improved economic performance, runs like a golden thread through the Commission's review. 'Coherence' is to be improved by ironing out detailed internal inconsistencies within the sector-specific measures, thereby to improve the quality of the *acquis*; and by devising a 'Common Frame of Reference' (CFR) which would set out common fundamental principles of contract law (and which has itself spawned a cascade of comment, part bemused, part intrigued, part critical).[38]

But 'coherence' is also to be promoted by abandoning the minimum model of harmonization.

The Commission's Consumer Policy Programme for 2002–06 revealed a growing preference for full or maximum harmonization.[39] It advocated a 'move away

[34] Communication from the Commission to the Council and the European Parliament on European Contract Law COM (2001) 398 final.

[35] Communication from the Commission to the European Parliament and the Council, *A More Coherent European Contract Law: An Action Plan* COM (2003) 68 final.

[36] Communication from the Commission to the European Parliament and the Council, *European Contract Law and the Revision of the Acquis: the Way Forward* COM (2004) 651 final.

[37] D Staudenmayer, 'The Place of Consumer Contract Law within the Process on European Contract Law' (2004) 27:3 *J of Consumer Policy* 269, 277.

[38] eg M Hesselink, 'European Contract Law: a Matter of Consumer Protection, Citizenship, or Justice?' (2007) 15 *Eur Rev of Private L* 323; J Smits, 'Democracy and (European) Private Law: a Functional Approach' (2009) 2:2 *Eur J of Leg Stud* 26; N Jansen and R Zimmermann, '"A European Civil Code in all but name": discussing the nature and purposes of the draft common frame of reference' (2010) 69 *CLJ* 98. The final 'academic' text is available as C von Bar et al (eds), *Principles, Definitions and Model Rules of European Private Law: Draft Common Frame of Reference* (Munich: Sellier, 2009) and for rich inquiry see H-W Micklitz and F Cafaggi (eds), *European Private Law after the Common Frame of Reference* (Cheltenham/Northampton, Mass.: Edward Elgar, 2010). In 2010, the Commission established an Expert Group on a Common Frame of Reference in the area of European Contract Law, mandated to use the draft CFR as a 'starting point' and to help the Commission select those parts of the draft CFR 'which are of direct or indirect relevance for contract law, and restructure, revise and supplement the selected contents': Commission Decision 2010/233 of 26 April 2010 setting up the Expert Group on a Common Frame of Reference in the area of European contract law [2010] OJ L 105/109.

[39] Communication from the Commission to the European Parliament, the Council, the Economic and Social Committee and the Committee of the Regions, *Consumer Policy Strategy 2002–2006* COM (2002) 208 final.

from the present situation of different sets of rules in each Member State towards a more consistent environment for consumer protection across the EU'. As far as protection of consumers' economic interests is concerned, it stated that there is a need 'to review and reform existing EU consumer protection directives, to bring them up-to-date and progressively adapt them from minimum harmonisation to full harmonisation measures'. The Commission's October 2004 document on contract law referred critically to perceived failings of a minimum model of rule-making—most of all that minimum EU rules create unevenness in the legal regulation of the internal market insofar as Member States choose to apply stricter rules.[40] In February 2007, the Green Paper on the *Review of the Consumer Acquis* concluded the 'diagnostic phase' of the Commission's review, setting out the main options for reform.[41] The orthodox model of minimum harmonization was not even allowed as a possible option for the future.

Ruling out space for stricter national rules has become the Commission's driving concern in consumer policy-making. Just as it asserts a dominant concern for the 'unity of the internal market' in its supervision of the derogations envisaged by Article 114(4) et seq TFEU,[42] so too, in seeking to suppress the even greater flexibility for national variation inherent in the minimum model of harmonization, it is intent on an agenda that would sanctify the level playing field built on maximum harmonization as apt to serve both the business interest and the consumer interest.[43]

G. Minimum versus maximum—costs versus benefits

The Commission is correct to connect the technique of minimum harmonization with a persistingly fragmented regulatory landscape. That is the very nature of minimum harmonization and, for its adherents, this is its very appeal—it leaves space for diversity. The Commission has assembled compelling evidence that the model of minimum harmonization leads to a fragmented pattern of laws, because Member States regularly and in very different ways take advantage of their preserved competence to apply stricter rules.[44] Academic investigations

[40] *European Contract Law and the Revision of the Acquis: the Way Forward*, n 36 above, 3.

[41] *Green Paper on the Review of the Consumer Acquis* COM (2006) 744 final.

[42] See, eg, Commission from the Commission concerning Article 95 (paragraphs 4, 5 and 6) of the Treaty Establishing the European Community COM (2002) 760 final, para 4.

[43] In the background is also a constitutional argument that minimum harmonization is not even valid under Article 114 TFEU insofar as it does not perfect the internal market. I think and hope that *Tobacco Advertising* is not to be read in such brutal fashion, see S Weatherill, 'Minimum Harmonisation as Oxymoron? The Case of Consumer Law' in H-W Micklitz (ed), *Verbraucherrecht in Deutschland—Stand und Perspektiven: Tagungsband der 1. Bamberger Verbraucherrechtstage* (Baden-Baden: Nomos Verlagsgesellschaft, 2005).

[44] eg Communication from the Commission to the European Parliament and the European Economic and Social Committee on the implementation of Directive 1997/7/EC of the European Parliament and of the Council of 20 May 1997 on the Protection of Consumers in respect of Distance Contracts COM (2006) 514 final; Communication from the Commission to the Council and the European Parliament on the implementation of Directive 1999/44/EC of the European

confirm this.[45] The question is, however, whether the *benefits* of moving instead to a maximum model of harmonization outweigh the *costs*. This is the calculation which the Commission is reticent to pursue as it energetically aims to break decisively with past practice in the matter of harmonization of consumer law—as it places greater weight on unity in the EU than on diversity.

The Commission is openly pursuing a change of balance. The pursuit of market integration is to be driven harder, under a model of common rules—more common than is the case under the model of minimum harmonization. More emphasis is to be placed on integrated European product and service markets regulated according to common standards, whilst less emphasis is placed on varying local choices about how to protect consumers from malfunctioning or unfair markets. That means the EU must build not only the floor but also the ceiling of regulatory protection. It is this perspective which has dominated the Commission's review of contract law. This is not intended to be in any sense 'anti-consumer'. The consumer benefits from a better functioning internal market; and the Commission commits itself to providing a high level of consumer protection in the adopted rules (as Article 12 TFEU foresees). The risk from the consumer perspective is that common rules will—at least for some groups of consumers, in some Member States—result in a depreciation in standards of protection from market failure and/or market inequities. Equally, the shift to maximum harmonization involves a significant choice in favour of a priority for market-making to the exclusion of local regulatory autonomy. It asserts a single notion of consumer protection when in fact consumer preferences, tastes and capabilities differ in Europe.[46]

So the Commission, in advocating a shift to maximum harmonization, does not neglect a policy commitment to levelling that field at a high standard of consumer protection—but what this means, and how/whether it can be guaranteed through the EU political process, evidently becomes a great deal more important to the advocate of effective consumer protection. There is a profoundly significant *constitutional* dimension. Under previous practice, minimum rule-making left space for upgrading consumer protection via the adoption of stricter local rules. The game changes dramatically under the Commission's proposed new model. A maximum directive sets a floor and also a ceiling: it effects a *complete* transfer of regulatory responsibility from Member States to the EU. This reinforces appreciation that fixing the standard of protection under the directive has to be carefully negotiated, well understood and effectively applied. For if a Member State considers the

Parliament and of the Council of 25 May 1999 on certain aspects of the sale of consumer goods and associated guarantees including analysis of the case for introducing direct producers' liability COM (2007) 210 final.

[45] See, eg, L Miller, 'After the Unfair Contract Terms Directive: Recent European Directives and English Law' (2007) 3:1 *Eur Rev Contract L* 88.

[46] cf T Wilhelmsson, 'The abuse of the confident consumer as a justification for EC consumer law' (2004) 27:3 *J of Consumer Policy* 317; S Weatherill, 'Maximum or Minimum Harmonisation—What kind of "Europe" do we want?' in K Boele-Woelki and W Grosheide (eds), *The Future of European Contract Law* (Alphen aan den Rijn: Wolters Kluwer, 2007); V Mak, 'Review of the Consumer Acquis: Towards Maximum Harmonisation?' (2009) 17:1 *Eur Rev Private L* 55.

directive sets too low a standard, it has nowhere to go (other than to seek to induce legislative reform at EU level). And it changes the nature of the implementation process at national level. If the minimum model is abandoned in favour of the maximum model, then *even if there is no alteration in the substantive content of the harmonized regime at EU level*, there is nonetheless a very significant change in the nature of the obligation imposed on the Member States. For they must eliminate any provisions of national law that fall within the material scope of the harmonized regime insofar as those national rules impose stricter obligations than those mandated by the directive. This is plainly a much more arduous task than that which is imposed in the case of implementation of a minimum EU measure, which tolerates the retention or introduction of stricter national rules. If the substantive content of the EU regime *is* altered, then the job at national level is bigger still.

The heavy demands placed on the implementation process are increased further where the maximum EU measure is drafted in ambiguous fashion. If it is unclear what precisely is the material scope of and/or the nature of the substantive control envisaged, then it is incumbent on the Member States to implement it, and in doing so to set aside any stricter national measures falling within its material scope—but they must do so without a secure grasp of precisely what is required as a matter of EU law. And for reasons of (inter alia) linguistic variation, legal cultural differences and old-fashioned political compromises that contaminate the precision sought by legal texts, it is far from uncommon to run across EU legislative measures which are less than obvious in their precise intent. The less precise the material scope and/or substantive content, the heavier the burden, the higher the costs—and, as will be discussed below, the more influential the role allocated to the Court of Justice.

Moreover, the more 'coherent' the EU regime, the less coherent national systems may become. Maximum harmonization may make the EU rules look much 'cleaner' but, at national level, significant dismantling of established rules that are found to fall within the material scope of the EU measure may be required, to the detriment of accumulated local preferences. Member States may be forced to decide whether also to alter existing national laws which are close to, but just outside, the area occupied by the directive or to leave them unchanged, with the consequence that existing national patterns and linkages are shattered along the faultline located at the EU directive's outer limits. Under a maximum model, unlike a minimum model, Member States cannot simply implement the EU rules alongside domestic rules and allow the system(s) to evolve: they must scrutinize the existing pattern of national law which falls within the material scope of the EU measure and ruthlessly exterminate any provisions that are stricter. To claim that this process is liable to lead to the 'demolition of national legal systems' may still count as exaggeration[47]—but it highlights the depth of the concern, and it has particular resonance in the context of the cherished but imperilled 'integrity' of domestic legal systems. EU law has not initiated, but has

[47] Study Group on Social Justice in European Private Law, 'Social Justice in European Contract Law: a Manifesto' (2004) 10:6 *ELJ* 653, 656.

certainly accelerated, the separation of consumer contract law from general contract law, and this is but one area of anxiety about its destabilizing effect.

The shift from minimum to maximum harmonization goes to the very heart of deciding which institution(s) are responsible for delivering regulation of the European market which, as recent events in the banking sector in particular have so vividly reminded us, is vulnerable to appalling malpractice if left inadequately supervised. A maximum model radically shifts the pattern of European law-making away from a cooperative model towards a more hierarchical pattern. Maximum harmonization is a centralizing, homogenizing approach. Moreover, it cleaves open national systems along lines of demarcation that may make some sort of sense at EU level, but frequently will not at national level. From this perspective there is a respectable case to be made *against* coherence at EU level—at least, one must appreciate that pursuit of coherence at EU level cannot possibly be cost-free.

H. The legislative turn to maximum harmonization

The Commission's preferences require alignment with a sufficient majority in the Council and Parliament for the shift to maximum harmonization to take legislative effect. This is happening.

Directive 2002/65 on distant selling of financial services was the first measure in the heartland of EU consumer policy to reflect this new policy preference.[48] It renounces the minimum formula and applies a model of maximum harmonization to the field in question, though a small concession was made to national deviation in Article 4 governing pre-contractual information.

The same approach dominated the debate about a directive on unfair commercial practices. In 2001, the Commission published a Green Paper on Consumer Protection.[49] It described the heap of diverse national laws that are relevant to the regulation of marketing practices as 'off-putting' to 'nearly all businesses but those who can afford to establish in all Member States', and, in addition, as a brake on consumer confidence. This was plainly intended to establish competence to harmonize, as well as to make the substantive case in favour of intervention. The model is a classic instance of the 'dual function' of harmonization—harmonization would lead to integration, by virtue of the adoption of common rules, but it would also involve choices made at EU level about the style and technique of (common) regulation. And it was proposed that the rules should exclude the possibility for Member States to apply a stricter notion of what is 'unfair'.

In May 2004, the Council reached a political agreement on the Directive.[50] But Denmark and Sweden voted against the proposal in Council. They took the

[48] Directive 2002/65/EC, n 16 above.
[49] *Green Paper on European Union Consumer Protection* COM (2001) 531 final.
[50] Outcome of proceedings of Council, 2003/0134 (COD), 25 May 2004.

view that the chosen model of maximum harmonization would be likely to exert a negative impact on the level of consumer protection in specific areas where Member States already possessed stricter rules than those provided for in existing (minimum) measures. Here, then, was the political bite: this is a debate which transcends technical market-making. But the Danish and Swedish protests were in vain. The final version of Directive 2005/29 concerning unfair commercial practices[51] adopts a maximum model of harmonization.

The Directive requires the suppression of unfair business-to-consumer practices in the internal market. It prohibits practices which, contrary to 'professional diligence', 'materially distort the economic behaviour' of an average consumer. Even in advance of the adoption of this Directive it was possible to deduce a European-level understanding of fair trading from analysis of the Court's treatment of national measures that obstructed cross-border commerce in the name of (often varying notions of) fair trading.[52] Directive 2005/29 takes the search for common standards further, for it establishes through legislative act a European standard of permissible market behaviour.[53] The notions of forbidden 'misleading' and 'aggressive' practice are elaborated in the body of the Directive, and its Annex contains a 'Black List' of practices considered unfair in all circumstances. But there is no scope for Member States to choose to establish stricter standards within the field occupied by the Directive. If a practice falling within the Directive's material scope is not 'unfair' within the meaning of the Directive, a Member State may not treat it as unfair. This is the stern message of the two decisions of the Court of Justice mentioned in the Introduction to this chapter.

The maximum model is based on a significant transfer of regulatory competence from the Member States to the EU.[54] What counts as 'unfair' is determined according to the standards set out in the Directive. In 2009, the Commission published guidance on its own understanding of the proper interpretation and application of Directive 2005/29,[55] but ultimately the authoritative source of interpretation is the Court of Justice. Its powerful position is considered further below.

[51] Directive 2005/29/EC, n 2 above.

[52] For fuller investigation see M Radeideh, *Fair Trading in EC Law: Information and Consumer Choice in the Internal Market* (Groningen: Europa Law Publishing, 2005), which also anticipates Directive 2005/29, n 2 above.

[53] For discussion see S Weatherill and U Bernitz (eds), *The Regulation of Unfair Commercial Practices under EC Directive 2005/29* (Oxford: Hart Publishing, 2007); G Anagnostaras, 'The Unfair Commercial Practices Directive in Context: from Legal Disparity to Legal Complexity?' (2010) 47:1 *CMLRev* 147; C Willett, 'Fairness and Consumer Decision Making under the Unfair Commercial Practices Directive' (2010) 33 *JCP* 247.

[54] See further Directive 2007/64/EC, n 14 above; Directive 2008/48/EC, n 12 above.

[55] Commission Staff Working Document: Guidance on the implementation of Directive 2005/29/EC on unfair commercial practices SEC (2009) 1666, 3 December 2009, available via <http://ec.europa.eu/consumers/rights/docs/Guidance_UCP_Directive_en.pdf>.

I. The proposed Directive on consumer rights

In October 2008, as a result of its review of the consumer *acquis*, the Commission adopted a proposal for a directive on Consumer Rights which would replace Directives 85/577, 97/7, 93/13 and 99/44 with a 'horizontal instrument'.[56] This would pursue what the Commission describes as *targeted full harmonization*. This, it is argued, would provide a simplified and more consistent regulatory framework apt to realize the advantages of the internal market whilst also achieving a high level of consumer protection. It is constitutionally consistent and entirely unsurprising that the chosen legal base for this proposed measure was Article 95 EC, the predecessor of Article 114 TFEU. In this vein, it would also move away from minimum harmonization to full or maximum harmonization, in order to reduce inter-State fragmentation in the application of consumer law.

So here is the next battlefield. Were the Commission's proposal to be accepted, it would mean, inter alia, that all matters falling within the material scope of the Directive would be subject to the rules set by the Directive—and scope for stricter rules at national level would be excluded. Matters pertaining to doorstep selling, distance selling, unfair terms and consumer sales would, insofar as they fell within the regime, be regulated at the standard dictated by the EU, and national variation would be ruthlessly suppressed.

The coupling of the notion of 'targeting' to the maximum harmonization model is presumably designed to counter anxieties that the EU is intent on occupying wide expanses of national contract law.[57] There is admittedly nothing new in the idea that harmonization operates only within a defined area—one must always identify what a measure's material scope is: what its 'target' is. Moreover, targeting the problems that amount to the most serious blockages to the functioning of the internal market reminds us that Article 95 EC, now Article 114 TFEU, does not have an unlimited scope. The Commission's documentation on contract law has been marked throughout by a low hum of 'competence sensitivity', motivated by fear of falling foul of the strictures of *Tobacco Advertising*,[58] even if it has generally preferred to avoid active engagement with this constitutional conundrum.[59] However, for all the rhetorical agility displayed by the Commission, the basic facts of EU constitutional law remain inescapable. The measure's material scope must be identified in order to determine the precise scope of the task of implementation cast on Member States; and, within that material scope, the level of regulatory protection must be identified. Any uncertainty at either level is costly—more costly

[56] Proposal for a Directive of the European Parliament and of the Council on consumer rights COM (2008) 614 final.

[57] See esp ibid 7 on why (the Commission believes) the model of full harmonization complies with the subsidiarity principle.

[58] Case C-376/98 *Germany v Parliament and Council*, n 26 above.

[59] See S Weatherill, 'Constitutional Issues—How much is best left unsaid?' in S Vogenauer and S Weatherill (eds), *The Harmonisation of European Contract Law: Implications for European Private Laws, Business and Legal Practice* (Oxford: Hart Publishing, 2006).

than under a regime of minimum harmonization that tolerates stricter rules. Any diminution in the standard of protection enjoyed in at least some Member States exposes the initiative to criticism from those who champion high levels of consumer protection—again, criticism that would not be feasibly directed at a measure of minimum harmonization.

The Commission's 2008 proposal for a Directive on Consumer Rights has attracted criticism on both counts—that its material scope lacks precision and that its standard of protection will drive down existing levels of protection in some areas in some Member States. The accusation is that the drive for maximum harmonization is not accompanied by realistic assessment of the costs to be imposed on the national implementing process nor, more generally, of costs measured in damage inflicted upon the integrity of national legal orders.

The purpose of this chapter is not to pursue an exhaustive testing of these criticisms but only to note them, in order to underline the point that choosing maximum harmonization over minimum harmonization is not a technical matter, but rather one that engages potentially high costs whilst also confronting deeply sensitive questions about the proper location of regulatory responsibility in Europe. So, for example, Jules Stuyck has tracked Directive 93/13 on unfair terms and its associated case law before assessing the changes intended by the Commission. He finds that the uncertain location of the outer edges of the proposed Directive is deeply troubling in the light of the preference for maximum harmonization.[60] Christian Twigg-Flesner has provided a comparable investigation of Directive 99/44 on consumer sales. He finds obscurities in the Commission's proposed changes, and he also finds instances where the proposed measure will diminish existing levels of consumer protection.[61] Marco Loos agrees: aspects of sales law in some Member States would have to be set aside insofar as they assert a stronger level of protection than that mandated by the proposed Directive, to the benefit of sellers.[62] Examination by Annette Nordhausen Scholes of information requirements at the level of both policy and detail generates her finding that the Commission's proposal suffers from definitional ambiguities in this respect.[63]

Plenty of other insightful commentators have expressed anxiety about imprecisions in the material scope of the Commission's proposed regime and/or its depressive effect on existing levels of consumer protection in some Member States.[64] There are, of course, connections between the two types of anxiety: a

[60] J Stuyck, 'Unfair Terms' in G Howells and R Schulze (eds), *Modernising and Harmonising Consumer Contract Law* (München: Sellier European Law Publishers, 2009).

[61] C Twigg-Flesner, 'Fit for Purpose? The Proposals on Sales' in Howells and Schulze, n 60 above.

[62] M Loos, 'Consumer Sales Law in the Proposal for a Consumer Rights Directive' (2010) 18 *Eur Rev Private L* 15.

[63] A Nordhausen Scholes, 'Information Requirements' in Howells and Schulze, n 60 above.

[64] See, eg, S Whittaker, 'Unfair Contract Terms and Consumer Guarantees: the proposal for a Directive on Consumer Rights and the significance of Full Harmonisation' (2009) 5:3 *Eur Rev Contract L* 223; H-W Micklitz and N Reich, 'Crónica de una Muerte Anunciada: the Commission Proposal for a Directive on Consumer Rights' (2009) 46:2 *CMLRev* 471; V Mak, n 46 above. For a more favourably disposed judgement see E Hondius, 'The Proposal for a European Directive on Consumer Rights: a Step Forward' (2010) 18:1 *Eur Rev Private L* 103.

lack of precision may mean that one does not even know for sure how far, if at all, protection is diminished. One obvious possible source of clarification would be the draft CFR. However, oddly enough, the Commission chose to exclude any linkage to the CFR in its proposed draft Directive. This suggests a certain lack of 'coherence' in the Commission's own review process, although in any event it has been observed that attempting to examine the draft Directive in the light of the CFR creates its own frictions.[65]

The preference for the maximum model plainly generates real anxieties. This is not merely resistance from those who instinctively prefer national-level solutions or even simply a plea to respect difference within the EU. The key insight is that once one shifts from minimum to maximum rule-making the costs of implementation at national level are increased. Under a minimum regime, one may tolerate rough edges where the EU-sourced rules touch the established domestic rules, because the latter, even if falling within the material scope of the EU measure, may be applied even if stricter than those mandated by the EU. By contrast, under a maximum regime one must agonize over determining the precise boundaries of the measure's material scope, for within it—but *only* within it—it is incumbent on national authorities to remove national laws which go beyond the intervention chosen by the EU. This may in some circumstances cause a depreciation in standards of consumer protection. Furthermore it may deepen the fragmentation of general contract law principles, in particular by promoting the separation of consumer contract law from other areas.

A preference for minimum harmonization over maximum harmonization is the most prominent way to avoid these alarming consequences. It is not the only alternative route, however. Another model available instead of embracing maximum harmonization is to leave in place the existing legislative *acquis* but to create in addition an extra optional instrument, defined by EU law. The most recent Commission intervention in this debate, the Green Paper on policy options for progress towards a European Contract Law for consumers and businesses published in July 2010,[66] opens a fresh round of public consultation. At page five, the Green Paper refers to 'intense negotiations' in Council and Parliament about its proposed full harmonization model, which might more candidly be described as growing political resistance.[67] The Commission, whilst seeking to present the invitation to further consultation in a neutral manner, gently conveys an impression of a re-directed preference for an EU regulation creating an optional instrument. This would be a second regime for each Member State—an overall twenty-eighth

[65] eg E-M Kieninger, 'Die Vollharmonisierung des Rechts der allgemeinen Geschäfstbedingungen—eine Utopie?' (2009) 73 *RabelsZ* 793. For an attempt to make smoother the relationship, see T de Booys, M Hesselink and C Mak, 'How the CFR can improve the Consumer Rights Directive', CSECL Working Paper 2009/09 (Amsterdam), available via <http://papers.ssrn.com/sol3/JELJOUR_Results.cfm?form_name=Pip_jrl&journal_id=956327>.

[66] *Green Paper on policy options for progress towards a European Contract Law for consumers and businesses* COM (2010) 348 final.

[67] For a snapshot see M Schmidt-Kessel, 'Zum Stand der Beratungen der Horizontalrichtlinie Verbraucherschutz—Meilensteine auf dem Weg zum legistischen Desaster' (2010) 7:3 *Zeitschrift für Gemeinschaftsprivatrecht* 129.

regime.[68] It would serve as an alternative to, not a replacement for, national regimes. It will thrive if there is demand for its use. It is not orthodox harmonization though it might feasibly encourage convergence in national practice. However, the main thematic point is that both the preference for minimum harmonization and the appeal of an optional instrument, a twenty-eighth regime, are rooted in the greater flexibility allowed to the shaping of appropriate solutions for the national context in conjunction with evasion of the ruthless (yet potentially imprecisely shaped) demands to curtail stricter national law that is inherent in the maximum model.

However the Commission chooses to proceed, it is right to seek to calculate benefits in making EU rules more coherent but it needs to be more consistently attentive to costs in robbing national systems of certainty and choice, as well as the costs involved in the potential disintegrative effect on national legal systems.

J. And the Court, too

An emphasis is commonly placed on the re-distribution of *legislative* competence in favour of the EU that follows harmonization. But the empowering of the Court of Justice is also significant. And just as maximum, rather than minimum, harmonization is the most radical possible re-distribution of competence in favour of the EU's political institutions, so too a choice in favour of maximum harmonization is the most significant means to empower the Court.

Sometimes the Court's role is trivial. Do inter-State educational exchanges during which the student stays with a host family free of charge for several months fall within the scope of the Package Travel Directive? No, they do not.[69] Such a ruling defines the material scope of the Directive but is hardly a threat to the integrity of national private law. Similarly, a ruling that under the 'e-Commerce' Directive a supplier must provide a means for the recipient to make contact rapidly other than by e-mail but that this does not have to be by telephone is important in fixing the content of the harmonized regime,[70] but reveals little about broader questions of regulatory technique.

But the Court's role readily extends beyond the technical. It frequently falls to the Court to determine important issues concerning the content or material scope of a measure—in circumstances where its ruling has potential to strike at long-established practices at national level. This will be especially sensitive where maximum, rather than minimum, measures are involved. A maximum measure

[68] See *Green Paper on policy options for progress towards a European Contract Law*, n 66 above, 9; and the Monti Report, n 8 above also makes some play of the 28th regime. In fact, such a tally is neglectful of the presence of more than one legal order already in at least one Member State: the importance of Scots law should not allow English law to be ignored.

[69] Case C-237/97 *AFS Intercultural Programs Finland* [1999] ECR I-825; Directive 90/314/EEC, n 10 above.

[70] Case C-298/07 *Bundesverband der Verbraucherzentralen v deutsche internet versicherung* AG [2008] ECR I-7841; Directive 2000/31/EC, n 15 above.

places a heavier burden on national implementation practice than does a minimum measure: its level of protection *and no more* must be secured at national level.

One dimension of the anxiety relates simply to workload—both before national courts and before the Court of Justice. Consider a national court faced with this situation: a national measure is stricter than the standard required by an EU directive, but it is not clear whether the national measure actually falls within the material scope of that directive. If the directive is minimum in nature, the question is not in practice important—the national measure may be applied whether or not it falls within the directive's scope. But if the directive is maximum in nature, the question is vital. The national measure survives *only* if it escapes the material scope of the directive. And consider this alternative. A national measure certainly falls within the scope of the directive, but it is not clear whether it merely replicates the directive's standard of protection or instead envisages something stronger. Again, under a minimum regime there is no need to decide, because the national measure, even if stricter, may be applied, whilst by contrast under a maximum regime resolution of the point is essential, for the national measure may not make sterner demands than does the directive. National courts will accordingly have to work harder. And the Court of Justice can expect to receive an increased number of preliminary references. Consequently it is no surprise that the Court is already receiving a lusty stream of preliminary references concerning Directive 2005/29 on unfair commercial practices, both with regard to its content (most obviously the nature of the unfairness test) and to its material scope.[71] Hard work for the Court in Luxembourg—potentially disruptive for national legal orders.

The greater the textual ambiguity or imprecision in material scope of a measure—whether by accident or by legislative design—the more painful the headache. Once again, Directive 2005/29 on unfair commercial practices provides a good example. The radical implications of the vertical transfer of regulatory competence from national to EU level which is at stake under the chosen maximum model is here betrayed by exclusions (of sorts) in the text of the Directive and its Recitals. Treatment of matters of 'taste and decency', which varies widely among the Member States, is left outwith the Directive's scope of application, according to Recital 7. Member States remain free to make their own, diverse choices about what types of commercial practice to tolerate in the name of taste and decency (subject to compliance with Treaty rules such as those governing nationality discrimination and free movement of goods and services). But when is a measure directed at 'taste' or 'decency' and when is it associated with 'ordinary' commercial

[71] Two rulings were mentioned in this chapter's Introduction, Case C-261/07 *VTB-VAB NV*, n 2 above; C-304/08 *Zentrale zur Bekämpfung unlauteren Wettbewerbs*, n 3 above; Case C-540/08 *Mediaprint Zeitungs- und Zeitschriftenverlag GmbH & Co KG v 'Österreich'-Zeitungsverlag GmbH* [2011] OJ C 13/3 was decided on 9 November 2010 and the finding that a general rule suppressing assessment of the particular circumstances pertaining to a commercial practice was incompatible with the Directive has much in common with Case C-304/08; whilst currently pending before the Court are Case C-122/10 *Ving Sverige AB* [2010] OJ C 113/35, Case C-288/10 *Wamo BVBA* [2010] OJ C 246/20.

objectives?[72] Here is another likely source of preliminary references to the Court, and its task in making some sort of sense of such calculatedly fuzzy distinctions is not to be envied. For present purposes I simply use this as an example to demonstrate that Member States are prepared to include ambiguous provisions in directives in order to reflect, if not fully to allay, fears about the destabilizing effect of EU measures on national policy choices. In any circumstances this delegates power to the Court, but where the EU measure in question is maximum in character—which is true of Directive 2005/29—such legislative imprecision entails an especially significant delegation of power to the Court.

One should also appreciate that the Court's approach is inconsistent.[73] If EU law generally is a jack-in-the-box,[74] then the Court itself can pack an unexpected punch. *Simone Leitner* offers a vivid illustration.[75] Article 5 of the Package Travel Directive does not provide any detailed account of the damage for which the consumer is entitled to claim compensation. Article 5(2) provides that Member States may allow compensation for damage other than personal injury to be limited under the contract provided that such limitation is not unreasonable. In *Simone Leitner* the Court ruled that this meant that the Directive implicitly recognizes the existence of a right to compensation for not only personal injury but also non-material damage. So a concession to State autonomy was interpreted to extend the reach of the measure. The Court added that the Directive's purpose of eliminating disparities between national laws pushed in favour of bringing rules governing compensation for non-material damage within its scope, for otherwise distortion caused by legal diversity would persist. Moreover, compensation for non-material damage arising from the loss of enjoyment of a holiday is of particular importance to consumers.

The Court's broad approach in *Simone Leitner*, stepping beyond the explicit terms of the Package Travel Directive, is driven by an emphasis on the 'dual function' of the measure, as a means of integrating markets and protecting the consumer. The difficulty with this reasoning is—where to stop? Such an expansive approach to the material scope of harmonization curtails the autonomy of national law and adjusts the balance between courts and legislatures in favour of the former (at national and at EU levels).[76] Simply to rely on the strengthening of harmonized consumer protection as a sufficient reason for stepping beyond the explicit limits of

[72] cf H-W Micklitz, 'Das Konzept der Lauterkeit in der Richtlinie 2005/29/EG' in L Thevenoz and N Reich (eds), *Liber Amicorum Bernd Stauder* (Zürich: Schulthess, 2006); T Wilhelmsson, 'Harmonizing Unfair Commercial Practices Law: the Cultural and Social Dimensions' (2006) 44:3 *Osgoode Hall LJ* 462.

[73] See, eg, O Gerstenberg, 'Private Law and the New European Constitutional Settlement' (2004) 10:6 *ELJ* 766; H Unberath and A Johnston, 'The Double-Headed Approach of the ECJ concerning Consumer Protection' (2007) 44:5 *CMLRev* 1237; S Weatherill, 'Interpretation of the Directives: the role of the Court' in A Hartkamp et al (eds), *Towards a European Civil Code*, 4th edn (Alphen aan den Rijn: Kluwer Law International, 2011).

[74] T Wilhemsson, 'Jack-in-the-Box theory of European Community Law' in Krämer, Micklitz and Tonner (eds), n 32 above, 177–94.

[75] Case C-168/00 *Simone Leitner v TUI Deutschland GmbH & Co. KG* [2002] ECR I-2631.

[76] cf W-H Roth, 'Annotation' (2003) 40:4 *CMLRev* 937.

a directive leaves out of account other concerns, including those of a constitutional nature.

In three recent cases, the Court has seen fit to rely on general principles of civil law as a source of interpretation even though the relevant legislative texts make no such reference. *Hamilton*[77] concerned the question of whether it was compatible with the 'Doorstep Selling' Directive to provide that the consumer's right of withdrawal expired one month after both parties had performed in full their obligations under the contract. This was not covered by the explicit terms of the Directive, but the Court did not simply consider that the matter fell to be resolved under national law. It relied on 'one of the general principles of civil law, namely that full performance of a contract results, as a general rule, from discharge of the mutual obligations under the contract or from termination of that contract'.[78] The German law was therefore compatible with the Directive. *Messner*[79] concerned the right to withdraw from a contract, which is provided for by Directive 97/7 on contracts concluded at a distance: specifically, the Court was asked whether a consumer could be required to pay compensation for the use made of a product after receiving it and before sending it back. The Directive refers only to charging the consumer for the direct cost of returning the goods. The Court held that national law may require a consumer 'to pay fair compensation in the case where he has made use of the goods acquired under a distance contract in a manner incompatible with the principles of civil law, such as those of good faith or unjust enrichment'.[80] Then, in *E Friz GmbH*, the Court referred to the national rule in question being 'intended to ensure, in accordance with the general principles of civil law, a satisfactory balance and a fair division of the risks among the various interested parties'.[81] It relied on these principles to limit the level of consumer protection provided by Directive 85/577 on doorstep selling in the event that a consumer withdraws from a contract, admittedly in an atypical set of circumstances. Plainly, the truly intriguing element of these three rulings is the Court's reliance on the principles of civil law. Where do they come from? How many more of them are there? The Court's identification of general principles is breathtakingly thinly explained.[82] The constitutional dimension is sorely neglected: legislative solutions at EU level stop short, so what is so wrong with deferring to the autonomy of national private law solutions? Especially when it is far from clear that general principles of *civil law*, even if here correctly identified as such by the Court, are apt to inform the elaboration of general principles of *EU law*, a system doubtless associated with, but in its methodology not identical to, civil law.

[77] Case C-412/06 *Annelore Hamilton* v *Volksbank Filder* eG [2008] ECR I-2383.

[78] ibid para 42.

[79] Case C-489/07 *Pia Messner v Firma Stefan Krüger* [2009] ECR I-7315.

[80] ibid para 26.

[81] Case C-215/08 *E Friz GmbH v Carsten von der Heyden* [2010] ECR I-2947, para 48.

[82] This chapter is confined to the consumer *acquis* but similar anxieties are caused by other instances of judicial 'discovery' of general principles of EU law—see in particular Case C-144/04 *Mangold v Helm* [2005] ECR I-9981.

This confirms and highlights the point made earlier: the more assiduous the attempt to make more systematic and coherent the *EU*'s legislative *acquis*, the greater the threat to the systematic and coherent character of *national* law—and the judicial, not merely the political, institutions of the EU are involved in this trend. And, once again to repeat an argument made above, these developments are especially significant where they occur in an environment of maximum harmonization. Neither the Package Travel Directive, which was at stake in *Simone Leitner*, nor the measures which have lately prompted the Court to resort to 'general principles' were of this type, but if the Commission's drive to convert some or all of the harmonized *acquis* from minimum to maximum is successful, then the Court's role in interpreting the texts, and determining what is required of and forbidden to Member States, will become correspondingly more important. Were one to embrace an approach driven by eager judicial discovery of 'general principles' and to attach that to a rather wide-ranging measure of maximum harmonization, such as that envisaged in the Commission's 2008 draft Directive on Consumer Rights, then the anxiety is that, first, national autonomy is set aside within the material scope of the measure of maximum harmonization and, moreover, that depth and breadth of that preclusion might be extended unexpectedly by adventurous rulings of the Court.

The Court is influential not only as a source of interpretation of a measure's material scope or of its content. Whether or not a measure is maximum or minimum in character may itself form the basis of intervention by the Court—and here too it may spring surprises. This has not commonly been a feature of the interpretation of the harmonized rules affecting the economic interests of consumers. Most are drawn with precision by the legislature—usually by asserting explicitly that the rules apply only as a minimum or, more recently, by making plain the choice of the maximum model. In such circumstances the Court's creativity is excluded. But the Product Liability Directive, Directive 85/374,[83] is instructive of what happens if the matter is not nailed down.

The only provision in Directive 85/374 that addresses its relationship with national law in the relevant field is Article 13. It stipulates that the Directive 'shall not affect any rights which an injured person may have according to the rules of the law of contractual or non-contractual liability or a special liability system existing at the moment when this Directive is notified'. In *María Victoria González Sánchez v Medicina Asturiana SA*, the Court, faced with rights afforded to consumers under pre-existing Spanish law which were more extensive than those available under the rules introduced to transpose Directive 85/374, identified the purpose of the Directive as 'to ensure undistorted competition between traders, to facilitate the free movement of goods and to avoid differences in levels of consumer protection'.[84] It determined that accordingly Article 13 did not permit the Member States the possibility of maintaining a general system of product liability different

[83] Directive 85/374, n 19 above.

[84] Case C-183/00 *María Victoria González Sánchez v Medicina Asturiana SA* [2002] ECR I-3901 para 26.

from that provided for in the Directive. The Court's ruling heavily emphasizes the function of the Directive in levelling the commercial playing field and provides a vigorous reminder that identifying the allocation of regulatory responsibility post-harmonization—of which the minimum/maximum debate is one prominent manifestation—is highly significant in ascertaining the permissible protective scope of national consumer law.

The autonomy of the Court was vividly highlighted by a subsequent intervention on the part of the Council. It adopted a resolution a few months after the judgment.[85] This states a need to assess whether the Directive should be modified in such a way as to allow for national rules on liability of suppliers based on the same ground as the liability system in the Directive concerning liability of producers. This is all very well—but it is too late. The Council can do more than regret it participated in the adoption of a measure that neglected to permit such a possibility. Power has passed to the Court, in interpreting the measure, and to the Commission, in considering whether to propose amendment to it. When the Court next addressed the matter it did not change its position;[86] whilst the Commission's third report on the Product Liability Directive, published in 2006, simply stated that if the Council Resolution were given effect, 'this would mark a departure from the objective of harmonization of product liability laws under the Directive'.[87] The Commission is visibly protective of the existing model—which easily conforms to its recent preference for maximum harmonization in the field of contract law as a vehicle to drive forward market integration more vigorously.

K. Conclusion

Consumer protection offers a vivid insight into the battle for the soul of harmonization, the soul of the internal market, even the soul of the European Union. Under the 'top-down' maximum model, the EU always leads the way, to the exclusion of dialogue and learning: and the EU's lead is driven by its legislature and, perhaps unexpectedly, by its Court too. It is deeply questionable whether the Commission's general policy preference in favour of maximum harmonization applied to the consumer *acquis* is well suited to a Union of 27 culturally, socially, legally and economically diverse Member States. Maximum harmonization involves a sufficiently radical vertical re-distribution of regulatory competence to call into question the very legitimacy of the EU's law-making pretensions. At the very least, there is a strong case to be made for regarding maximum harmonization as applicable only in

[85] Council Resolution of 19 December 2002 on amendment of the liability for defective products Directive [2003] OJ C26/02.

[86] Case C-402/03 *Skov and Bilka* [2006] ECR I-199.

[87] Report from the Commission to the Council, the European Parliament and the European Economic and Social Committee: Third report on the application of Council Directive on the approximation of laws, regulations and administrative provisions of the Member States concerning liability for defective products (85/374/EEC of 25 July 1985, amended by Directive 1999/34/EC of the European Parliament and of the Council of 10 May 1999) COM (2006) 496 final, 11.

particular sectors and only where its use has been carefully justified in the prevailing sector-specific conditions.

There are legal principles that support an interpretation in favour of the constitutional vitality of minimum harmonization, although it is freely conceded that they are of an ambiguous nature. Article 38 of the Charter on Fundamental Rights provides that 'Union policies shall ensure a high level of consumer protection'. Article 12 TFEU provides that 'Consumer protection requirements shall be taken into account in defining and implementing other Union policies and activities'. An argument may be constructed that these identified objectives are most effectively achieved by retaining a model of consumer protection built *not only* on EU rule-making *but also* on national level contributions above the EU minimum. Maximum harmonization suppresses one important—national—source of consumer protection. That prescription is directed at the EU legislature but one could plausibly add that there should be a supplementary *judicial* presumption against finding that EU legislative acts pre-empt national competence in the field which they cover.[88]

Recognition that the adoption of a rigid, uniform and immutable EU norm is not the necessary and inevitable consequence of EU intervention in a particular field is highly significant. It is neither politically feasible nor economically desirable to expect all 27 Member States to advance as a single bloc in all the sectors of economic activity now affected by EU policy. Any trend away from the single rule carries the potential to cause the fragmentation of the internal market, yet it may be seen as a realistic attempt to accommodate diverse national tradition and consumer expectation within the process of integration. This breeds scepticism about the value or even the sheer feasibility of securing uniformity in the wider sweep of EU activity. That should not alarm us. Uniformity is not an end in itself. To return to the motto in Article I-8 of the (lost) Treaty establishing a Constitution—this holds that the EU is *united in diversity*. Why not also in *diverse* patterns of consumer protection, underpinned by a *unified* minimum standard?

[88] cf R Schütze, 'Subsidiarity after Lisbon: Reinforcing the Safeguards of Federalism' (2009) 68:3 *CLJ* 525. And see much more broadly in this vein the same author's *From Dual to Cooperative Federalism: the Changing Structure of European Law* (Oxford: Oxford University Press, 2009).

11

The Motherhood Penalty: The Contribution of Europe

Noreen Burrows and Muriel Robison•*

A. Introduction

We have argued elsewhere that:

> The failure . . . to incorporate the relevant provisions of the Pregnant Workers Directive [into the Recast Directive] is a missed opportunity to revise the difficulties arising from the lack of clarity in relation to the interplay between the provisions of Article 157 TFEU (then Article 141 TEC), the Equal Pay Directive, the Equal Treatment Directive, and the treatment of pregnant workers and those on maternity leave, particularly in relation to illness and sick pay . . . [1]

Having set out the challenge in this field, in this chapter we examine the interface between these measures and offer a critique of the approach taken by the European Court of Justice in order to suggest a way forward.

In this chapter, we argue that the interpretation of the provisions of the Pregnant Workers Directive by the European Court of Justice relating to the level of 'a payment' in Article 11 is a contributory factor to the ongoing gender pay gap.[2] We argue that the Member States, in framing the Pregnant Workers Directive in restrictive terms, and the Court, in prioritizing the provisions of the Pregnant Workers Directive over concepts of equal pay inherent in Article 157 TFEU, have undermined the potential of the equal pay provisions of European Union law to address aspects of the 'motherhood penalty'. Furthermore, there is still a lack of clarity arising from the case law of the Court as to the level of pay a woman might

* Noreen Burrows is Jean Monnet Professor of European Law at the University of Glasgow.

• Muriel Robison is former Head of Legal at EHRC Scotland and part-time lecturer at the University of Glasgow.

[1] N Burrows and M Robison, 'An Assessment of the Recast of Equality Laws' (2007) 13:2 *ELJ* 186–203, 194. Directive 2006/54/EC of the European Parliament and of the Council of 5 July 2006 on the implementation of the principle of equal opportunities and equal treatment of men and women in matters of employment and occupation (recast) [2006]OJ L 204/23.

[2] Council Directive 92/85 of 19 October 1992 on the introduction of measures to encourage improvements in the safety and health at work of pregnant workers and workers who have recently given birth or are breastfeeding [1992] OJ L 348/1, hereafter the Pregnant Workers Directive.

expect under different scenarios during and after pregnancy. A proposal to amend the Pregnant Workers Directive is currently under discussion in the European Parliament and the Council. Given the approach taken by the Court, we argue that, without legislative intervention, the motherhood penalty will continue to exist; however, the proposed amendments fall short of what is required to reduce those elements of the gender pay gap which can be traced to the negative influences of pregnancy and maternity leave.

According to Smith, 'The gender pay gap captures the enduring gendered inequalities that exist in the labour market... [M]easures to eradicate male and female wage gaps require more significant changes in labour market behaviour... [I]nequalities multiply over the life course and so reinforce gender disadvantages from a single point to accumulate over the life course.'[3] Such single points might arise in the employment history of a woman at several crucial junctures: becoming pregnant, we argue, is one such point.

There is a substantial body of research which shows that motherhood impacts negatively on women's pay both in the short run and over lifetime earnings, which then impacts on a woman's pension into old age. In her review of the research on the gender pay gap, Metcalfe concludes that 'the main additional influence on the gender pay gap in lifetime earnings is motherhood, with motherhood affecting labour market participation, hours of work and work patterns' although the gap is influenced by both the number of children and the level of education and qualifications.[4] What Metcalfe calls the 'motherhood penalty' is traced to changes in work patterns, including moving to part-time working and taking career breaks, but also in attitudes to working women and women's own views of their careers since 'the gender pay gap is apparent well before women become mothers... gender differences in career expectations explained 18 per cent of the gender pay gap.'[5] The Equality and Human Rights Commission in the United Kingdom has concluded that '60,000 women experience some form of financial loss due to their pregnancy and maternity leave, in the form of lost promotions, reduced salary or benefits and losing out on pay rises.'[6] Furthermore, it has found that 'the gender pay gap more than trebles when women reach 30 years of age which is thought to result largely from the financial penalties associated with motherhood'.[7] Summing up her review of existing research on gender pay gaps, Metcalfe argues that further labour market research is not required but what is important is research by which we might understand 'the processes by which the gender pay gap develops over an

[3] M Smith, 'Analysis Note: The Gender Pay Gap in the EU—What Policy Responses?' (2010) February *European Network of Experts on Employment and Gender Equality Issues* 2. A copy of this report can be found at <http:ec.europa.eu/justice/gender-equality/document/index_en.htm>.

[4] H Metcalfe, *Pay Gaps Across the Equality Strands: a Review*, EHRC, Research Report: 14, 2009, 14. A copy of this report can be found at <http://www.equalityhumanrights.com/uploaded_files/research/14_pay_gaps_across_equalities_review.pdf>.

[5] ibid.

[6] *Equality and Human Rights Commission: Policy Briefing: EU Pregnant Workers Directive*, July 2010, 6. A copy of this briefing can be found at <http://www.equalityhumanrights.com/legal-and-policy/european-policy/eu-pregnancy-directive/>.

[7] ibid 7.

individual's career'.[8] We argue that at certain crucial junctures in the working lives of women who become pregnant and take maternity leave, the European legal framework and its interpretation by the Court of Justice disadvantages women by consciously reducing their earnings when they can least afford it.

B. The current legal framework

The confusion that we have identified essentially arises from the interplay between the equal pay provisions, particularly Article 157 TFEU, Article 11 of the Pregnant Workers Directive and, in one instance, the Equal Treatment Directive (now recast). Article 157 TFEU in paragraph 1 requires that 'each Member State shall ensure that the principle of equal pay for male and female workers for equal work or work of equal value is applied'. Pay is defined in paragraph 2 as being 'the ordinary basic or minimum wage or salary and any other consideration, whether in cash or in kind, which the worker receives directly or indirectly, in respect of his employment, from his employer'. The Court of Justice has held that maternity pay paid to an employee by an employer is pay within the meaning of Article 157 TFEU, as are payments made to women who are absent due to pregnancy related illness prior to maternity leave and payments made to women transferred to alternative duties as a result of health and safety assessments.[9] Article 157 provides a legal base for legislation in the area of equal pay[10] and also for positive action measures to make it easier for a member of an underrepresented sex 'to pursue a vocational activity or to prevent or compensate for disadvantages in professional careers'.[11]

The Pregnant Workers Directive makes no reference to the definition of pay as it appears in Article 157 TFEU. This is a Directive that aims to protect pregnant workers and those who have recently given birth and does so in two ways. The first is to ensure that a pregnant woman works in a safe working environment. An employer is required to undertake a risk assessment and to take action on the basis of that assessment. The employer must adjust the working conditions or the hours worked to avoid the risk. If this is not possible, the employer should move the worker to another post; and if this is not possible she must be granted leave.[12] The Directive categorically prohibits an employer from exposing pregnant women to agents or working conditions listed in the Directive itself and which are known to risk the health and safety of the woman or her child.[13] Pregnant women cannot be required to perform night work but must be transferred to daytime work or, if this is not possible, granted leave.[14] In all of these cases, Article 11(1) provides that the employment rights of such workers be maintained, 'including the maintenance of a payment to, and/or entitlement to an adequate allowance... in accordance with national legislation and/or national practice'. The second way in which women are

[8] H Metcalfe, n 4 above, 29.
[9] This case law is discussed below.
[10] Article 157(3) TFEU.
[11] Article 157(4) TFEU.
[12] Pregnant Workers Directive, n 2 above, Articles 4 and 5.
[13] ibid Article 6.
[14] ibid Article 7.

to be protected is to provide for a period of maternity leave of 14 continuous weeks.[15] During this period women are entitled to 'a payment . . . and/or entitlement to an adequate allowance'.[16] The allowance is deemed adequate if it 'guarantees income at least equivalent to that which the worker concerned would receive in the event of a break in her activities on grounds connected with her state of health, subject to any ceiling laid down under national legislation.'[17] In both situations, Member States may lay down conditions of eligibility for pay or allowances although these conditions may not provide for periods of employment to be in excess of 12 months prior to confinement.

The case law of the Court of Justice analysed below illustrates some of the crucial junctures at which the motherhood penalty begins to bite. The first issue raised before the Court was the appropriate level of pay for a woman taking maternity leave and any appropriate comparator. The second is the level of pay for women absent from work due to pregnancy related illness. The Court was asked whether European law governed this second situation—it is clearly not covered by the Pregnant Workers Directive. The third problem was that of the level of pay for women who are unable to perform their jobs during their pregnancy because of health and safety reasons. The Pregnant Workers Directive provides guidance on this question. The fourth issue was whether an additional payment given to women about to take maternity leave is compatible with Article 157 TFEU.

In these cases, the Court of Justice has struggled to enunciate clear principles in matters related to pregnancy and pay. This contrasts sharply with its approach to matters of equal treatment in working conditions where the Court has taken the view that discriminatory treatment of pregnant women is direct discrimination that cannot be justified since only women can become pregnant.[18] In *Gillespie* (discussed below),[19] Advocate General Léger recommended to the Court that a similar line of argument should be followed in cases relating to the level of pay for women absent for pregnancy related illness. He argued that:

> Article 1 of Directive 75/117 does not refer to pregnant women, but in so far as only women can give birth, the biological difference between women and men must not be used to discriminate as regards pay. Consequently, the fact that a woman is pregnant cannot be relied on to reduce her pay on the grounds that she has become less productive or that her

[15] Pregnant Workers Directive, n 2 above, Article 8.

[16] ibid Article 11(2)(b).

[17] ibid Article 11(3).

[18] Cases C-177/88 *Dekker* [1990] ECR I-3941; C-179/88 *Handels- og Kontorfunktionaerernes Forbund i Danmark v Dansk Arbejdsgiverforening* [1990] ECR I-3979; C-32/93 *Webb* [1994] ECR I-3567; C-421/92 *Habermann-Bettermann* [1994] ECR I-1657; C-394/96 *Brown* [1998] ECR I-4185; Case C-207/98 *Mahlburg* [2000] ECR I-549, C-438/99 *Jimenez Melgar* [2000] ECR I-6915; C-320/01 *Busche* [2003] ECR I-2041; C-460/06 *Paquay* [2007] ECR I-8511; C-506/06 *May*r [2008] ECR I-1017. For commentary on this case law see M Wynn, 'Pregnancy Discrimination: Equality, Protection or Reconciliation?' (1999) 62:3 *MLR* 435; E Szyszczak, 'Pregancy Discrimination' (1996) 59:4 *MLR* 589; I Hare, 'Pregnancy and Sex Discrimination' (1991) 20:2 *Industrial L J* 124, S Honeyball, 'Pregnancy and Sex Discrimination' (2000) 29:1 *Industrial L J* 43.

[19] Case C-342/93 *Gillespie and others v Northern Health and Social Services Board* [1996] ECR I-475.

pregnancy entails special arrangements justifying a pay cut. Therefore in accordance with Article [157 TFEU] of the Treaty and Article 1 of Directive 75/117, a woman's pregnancy has no bearing on her pay while she is working, that is to say before her maternity leave. To hold otherwise would beyond any doubt constitute direct discrimination on grounds of sex.[20]

The Court did not follow this line of reasoning and has not done so in other pay related cases. In effect, the Court, whilst repeating that the payments received in the four scenarios outlined above constitute pay within the meaning of Article 157 TFEU, does not apply an equality analysis but treats 'motherhood related' pay issues outwith an equality framework. In writing about the recast Directive, our hope had been that the Court might bring these pay cases into an equality framework, but it has not done so. Motherhood related pay issues are now clearly governed with reference to, although not wholly governed by, the Pregnant Workers Directive. The United Kingdom, in implementing its European obligations, takes this same approach. However, in United Kingdom law there is now an explicit decoupling of equal pay and pregnancy related and maternity pay issues, so much so that judges can use the term 'a separate code' in applying UK legislation in specific cases.[21] The Court of Justice does not use language comparable to the term 'separate code' but, in effect, it has decoupled Article 157 TFEU from pay issues around pregnancy and maternity.

C. Maternity pay before the Court

Gillespie is the first case in which the Court of Justice interpreted provisions of European Union law on pay and their connection with maternity pay. The case turned on how the Court would interpret Article 157 TFEU and Directive 75/117/EEC.[22] The Pregnant Workers Directive had been agreed in the Council but the date of its transposition had not yet passed. It did not, therefore, apply *ratione temporis* to the facts in *Gillespie*; nonetheless, it had a major influence on the approach taken by the Court in this case.

The Court was asked whether European Union law required women on maternity leave to receive full pay or whether it provided the criteria determining the amount of pay. The Court reasoned, based on settled case law, that 'since the benefit paid by an employer under legislation or collective agreements to a woman on maternity leave is based on the employment relationship, it constitutes pay within the meaning of Article [157 TFEU]'.[23] However, the Court held that

[20] Opinion of AG Léger, ibid para 26; Directive 75/117/EEC on the approximation of laws of the Member States relating to the application of the principle of equal pay for men and women (subsequently repealed by the recast directive) [1976] OJ L 39/40. One writer has suggested that the Court, by failing to apply a single analysis, has created 'chaos'. S Simon, 'Discrimination on the Ground of Pregnancy: Chaos or Consistency from the ECJ?' (1999) 3 *ELRev* 217–28.

[21] Clark [1996] *IRLR* 578, 582.

[22] Directive 75/117/EEC, n 20 above.

[23] Case C-342/93 *Gillespie*, n 19 above, para 14.

women taking maternity leave 'are in a special position which requires them to be afforded special protection, but which is not comparable either with that of a man or with that of a woman actually at work'.[24] The absence of a comparator means there is no equal pay claim and failure to provide for full pay is not direct discrimination. Instead the Court referred to the Pregnant Workers Directive, which requires the maintenance of a payment to and/or entitlement to an adequate allowance for women taking maternity leave. The Court stated that 'it follows' from the Directive that neither Article 157 TFEU nor Directive 75/117 requires that women should continue to receive full pay during maternity leave. Neither do these provisions lay down any means for determining the specific rate of payment. However, the Court stated that payment could not be so low as to undermine the purpose of maternity leave.

Had the Court brought maternity pay fully within the ambit of Article 157 TFEU, which would have been an entirely plausible interpretation of it, the Court would have come into conflict with the Member States. Article 11 of the Pregnant Workers Directive relating to pay would be incompatible with Article 157 TFEU. This would not have been the first time that the Court had been faced with a directive governing aspects of pay which it subsequently held to be incompatible with Article 157 TFEU. The Court's case law on occupational pension schemes in the 1980s 'scalped the Community legislator' and resulted in the radical amendment of Directive 86/378/EEC to make it compliant with Article 157 TFEU. The Member States had stepped into the dispute with the Barber Protocol attached to the Maastricht Treaty bringing that episode to a close.[25]

The 1990s were not a good time for the Court to engage in a stand-off with the Member States since this was the time when social policy was most acutely contested.[26] The United Kingdom opt-out from the social policy provisions of the Maastricht Treaty and its challenge to the validity of the Working Time Directive were highly visible signs that at least some of the Member States intended to retain strict control over the boundaries between European Union and Member State competence.[27] In *Gillespie*, therefore, the Court deferred to the Member States. This is the beginning of the Court's retreat from equality principles in this area and the beginnings of a separate code approach; where separate does not envisage 'separate but equal', rather separate but disadvantaged.

[24] Case C-342/93 *Gillespie*, n 19 above, para 17.

[25] See N Burrows and J Mair, *European Social Law* (Chichester: Wiley, 1996) Ch 5. Directive 86/378/EEC had sought to regulate occupational pension schemes. In its case law, the Court brought occupational pensions schemes into the ambit of (then) Article 119 making several aspects of Directive 86/378/EEC incompatible with the Treaty. D Curtin, 'Scalping the Community Legislator: Occupational Pensions and *Barber*' (1990) 27:3 *CMLRev* 475. Council Directive 86/378/EEC of 24 July 1986 on the implementation of the principle of equal treatment for men and women in occupational social security schemes [1986] OJ L 225/40. This Directive is now repealed and occupational social security matters are governed by the provisions of the Recast Directive. Case C-262/88 *Douglas Hervey Barber v Guardian Royal Exchange Assurance Group* [1990] ECR I-1889.

[26] A point made by McGlynn in her commentary on *Gillespie*. See C McGlynn, 'Equality, Maternity and Questions of Pay' (1996) 21 *ELRev* 327–32.

[27] Case C-84/94 *UK v Council* [1996] ECR I-5755.

Whilst this approach had merits politically, it raises analytical problems: in particular, how to reconcile a difference in approach to the principle of equality between conditions of employment and questions of pay. McGlynn argues that the equal pay provisions are not framed to prevent unfair pay but to achieve equal pay and there must, therefore, be a comparative approach. By contrast, the equal treatment provisions are designed to redress disadvantages, including those brought about by pregnancy.[28]

The Court's ruling that women who are on maternity leave are in a special position and not comparable to anyone who is actually at work begs the question as to the actual level of pay which European Union law requires. The Court's reasoning that the level of pay must not be such as to undermine the purpose of maternity leave is not helpful since it is entirely subjective. The Commission's Impact Assessment for the proposals to amend the Pregnant Workers Directive points out that 'there are marked differences between the Member States in terms of policy in facilitating reconciliation. Maternity leave provisions range roughly from 14 to 52 weeks, with payments ranging from 55 per cent (subject to a ceiling) to 100 per cent (subject to no ceiling)'.[29] The Pregnant Workers Directive requires that the level of the payment or allowance must not fall below the level of sickness pay. Whether 55 per cent of pay meets the Court's test that the level must not undermine the purpose of maternity leave is a moot point given the additional costs faced by women on maternity leave. However, if 55 per cent of pay is the level paid to workers on sick pay, then it is apparently permissible under EU law. The point has not been tested before the Court.

Boyle concerned a requirement on women to pay back maternity pay if they failed to return to work when other workers, such as those on sick leave, were not similarly obliged to repay.[30] The Court held that this requirement was not contrary to European Union equal pay provisions. A pregnant woman is essentially differently situated from other workers, including those on sick leave. The fact that she is adversely differently situated is an irony lost on the Court, particularly in view of its acknowledgement that 'pregnant workers and workers who have recently given birth are in an especially vulnerable situation which makes it necessary for the right to maternity leave to be granted to them'.[31]

In *Alabaster*, a pay rise had been awarded outwith the reference period for calculating maternity pay.[32] The Court held that Article 157 TFEU must be interpreted as requiring that, 'insofar as the pay received by the worker during her maternity leave is determined, at least in part, on the basis of the pay she earned

[28] C McGlynn, n 26 above, 5, 6.

[29] Commission Staff Working Document accompanying the Proposal for a Directive of the European Parliament and of the Council amending Council Directive 92/85/EEC on the introduction of measures to encourage improvements in the safety and health at work of pregnant workers and workers who have recently given birth or are breastfeeding: Summary of the Impact Assessment Report SEC (2008) 2595, 3.

[30] Case C-411/96 *Boyle v Equal Opportunities Commission* [1998] ECR I-6401.

[31] ibid para 40.

[32] Case C-147/02 *Alabaster* [2004] ECR I-3101.

before maternity leave began, any pay rise awarded before the beginning of the period covered by the reference pay and the end of the maternity leave must be included in the elements of pay taken into account in calculating the amount of such pay. This requirement is not limited to cases where the pay rise is backdated to the period covered by the reference pay.'[33] Here, the Court appeared to base its decision on Article 157 TFEU despite the absence of a comparator: in both *Gillespie* and *Boyle*, the Court relied upon the absence of a comparator to exclude reliance on Article 157 TFEU. What these cases show is that women who take maternity leave cannot rely on European Union law to argue that their maternity pay must be equal to their pay prior to that leave. Whereas the Recast Directive, as interpreted by the Court, guarantees the maintenance of their employment rights in relation to working conditions, Article 157 TFEU does not guarantee their employment rights in relation to pay. *Gillespie* therefore marks a retreat on the part of the Court from its very strong defence of women's employment rights during pregnancy and maternity leave; the so-called protected period.

D. Pregnancy related illness prior to maternity leave

Høj Pederson concerned applicants who were declared unfit for work due to pregnancy related illnesses prior to their maternity leave.[34] Their employer informed them that they had ceased to be employed and they were advised to claim maternity benefits. Another applicant in this case was declared partially unfit. She suggested she might work part-time but her employer refused and she was replaced by a full-time employee. Again she was advised to apply for maternity benefits.

The Court held that 'the fact that a woman is deprived, before the beginning of her maternity leave, of her full pay when her incapacity for work is the result of a pathological condition connected with the pregnancy must be regarded as treatment based essentially on the pregnancy and thus as discriminatory'.[35] In this respect, it followed its line of cases under the Equal Treatment Directive relating to dismissals on the grounds of pregnancy related illness, citing *Webb* and *Brown*. It also follows the logic of Advocate General Léger in *Gillespie*. The Court appears to say that European Union law entitles a woman absent from work because of pregnancy related illness to full pay and, on this point, it is applying an equality analysis.

Maternity pay or allowances are not always paid by the employer. In many Member States, there is an attempt to mutualize the costs of maternity and pregnancy across employers and the state. This is the case too with the costs of sick pay or other benefits. The Court examined the question of mutualization of payments made to women absent from work due to pregnancy related illness and held that where the state, rather than the employer, pays the equivalent of a

[33] Case C-147/02 *Alabaster* [2004] ECR I-3101, para 50.

[34] Case C-66/96 *Høj Pederson* [1989] ECR I-7327.

[35] ibid para 35.

woman's full salary, it is for the national court to determine if this gives rise to discrimination. However the Court held that the same rules must apply to women who are absent from work because of a pregnancy related illness and other workers who are absent from work due to sickness. In other words, there cannot be different rules in sickness and maternity pay schemes in this regard. But where the woman exercises a choice not to work without any medically certified reason, she forefeits some or all of her salary.

Finally the Court was required to rule on the question of the legitimacy of national legislation which allows an employer to send a woman who is pregnant, but not unfit for work, home, without paying her salary in full, when he considers that he cannot provide work for her. This situation is, of course, governed by the Pregnant Workers Directive but, at the relevant time, the date for implementation of that Directive had not expired. Curiously, the Court did not treat this situation as a breach of the equal pay provisions, despite the fact that the question at issue related to pay, but turned to the Equal Treatment Directive. The Court treated this situation as tantamount to dismissal and therefore governed by Article 5 of the Equal Treatment Directive, which provides that men and women should enjoy the same working conditions, including the conditions governing dismissal. The Court dismissed any idea that the Equal Treatment Directive, which allowed Member States to introduce provisions to protect women in connection with maternity and pregnancy, could govern the situation provided for in Danish law. On the contrary, the Court held, these provisions were intended to protect the employer and could not, therefore, fall within the ambit of Article 2(3) of the Equal Treatment Directive. The Court went on to warn Denmark that the provisions in question were also in breach of the Pregnant Workers Directive.

McKenna related to the applicable rules in the case of a woman who was on sick leave for almost the entire duration of her pregnancy with a pathological condition connected to pregnancy.[36] In this case, Advocate General Léger pointed to the confusion developing in the case law of the Court depending on which provisions the Court was required to interpret. He stated that the Court had given no general definition of the concepts of 'aspects and conditions of remuneration' found in Directive 75/117 and 'working conditions' in Directive 76/207. Instead, he argued that the Court worked on a 'case by case basis' as to what relevant provisions of European Union law are to be applied in a particular context.[37]

Mrs McKenna argued that she was subject to discrimination in that her pregnancy related illness had been treated as a normal illness and her period of absence had been offset against her sick leave entitlement. The Court held that the payment of wages to a person in the event of illness is pay and quoted *Rinner-Kűhn* and *Høj Pederson* to this effect. It then went on to state it had not yet been asked to rule specifically 'whether a female worker is entitled, in any event, to continue to receive full pay in the event of a pregnancy-related illness arising prior to her maternity leave, even if the contested national rule provides for the application of a reduction

[36] Case C-191/03 *North Western Health Board v Margaret McKenna* [2005] ECR I-7631.

[37] Opinion of AG Léger, ibid para 41.

in the same measure to the remuneration paid to a worker in the event of an illness unrelated to a condition of pregnancy'.[38] In setting the question this way, the Court distinguished the facts of *McKenna* from those in *Høj Pederson*. In the latter case, the national rules provided for full pay in the event of sickness.

The Court argued that 'it does not necessarily follow from the finding that pregnancy-related illnesses are *sui generis* that a female worker who is absent by reason of a pregnancy related illness is entitled to maintenance of full pay, whereas a worker absent because of a reason unrelated to pregnancy does not have such a right'.[39] In relation to dismissals because of a pregnancy related illness, the Court argued that the only way to protect the woman in this situation was to prohibit the dismissal. In relation to pay, the special nature of pregnancy could be recognized by a scheme that provides for a reduction in pay. The Court then restated that European Union law does not require full pay during maternity leave and quoted *Gillespie*. Arguing by analogy, the Court went on to hold that 'if a rule providing, within certain limits, for a reduction in pay to a female worker during her maternity leave does not constitute discrimination based on sex, a rule providing, within the same limits, for a reduction in pay to that female worker who is absent during her pregnancy by reason of an illness related to that pregnancy also cannot be regarded as discrimination of that kind'.[40] Therefore European Union law does not require full pay for a woman absent because of a pregnancy related illness. The Court then went on to introduce the sick worker as a comparator and held that, provided that the pregnant woman is treated in the same way as the sick man and that the level of pay is not so low as to undermine the objective of protecting pregnant workers, such a scheme would not violate European Union law.

The Court also examined the scheme whereby absence on the grounds of illness was to be offset against the total number of days of paid sick leave to which a worker is entitled over a specified period—in this case, four years. The Court stated that such a scheme treats all workers in an identical manner and does not take into account the special nature of pregnancy. However it did not hold such a scheme to be contrary to EU law except if such a scheme had the effect that, during the absence affected by that offsetting, after maternity leave, the female worker receives lower pay than the minimum amount to which she was entitled over the course of the illness that arose during her pregnancy. Member States must enact special provisions to ensure that this does not occur.

Høj Pederson and *McKenna* are clearly contradictory judgments. The former case appeared to be a clear statement that a woman could rely on Article 157 TFEU and equality arguments to ensure that her level of pay was not reduced if she is ill for pregnancy related reasons prior to her maternity leave. The latter case appears to consolidate the approach of the Court to treating reductions in pay as permissible since, in the absence of a comparator, it is not discrimination to reduce the level of pay. The Court relies on *Gillespie* to come to this conclusion. As noted above, the situation in *Gillespie* is governed by the Pregnant Workers Directive, but issues

[38] Case C-191/03 *McKenna*, n 36 above, para 55.
[39] ibid para 57. [40] ibid para 60.

stemming from pregnancy related illness are not so covered. Arguing by analogy with maternity pay, the Court brings absences due to pregnancy related illness into that separate framework and, once more, out of an equality discourse. The Court therefore appears to be moving in the direction of a separate code on these issues.

E. Women who continue working—assignment to different duties

Parviainen v Finnair Oyj illustrates the difficulties in interpreting the concept of pay in the context of the rights of pregnant women to receive 'a payment' under the Pregnant Workers Directive.[41] The applicant had been a purser since October 2005. In that position, she was paid a range of additional allowances. She became pregnant at the beginning of 2007 with a due date of October 2007. As from April 2007, she was transferred to office work and she remained a member of ground staff until September 2007 when she commenced maternity leave. During this period she lost her additional allowances. The referring Helsinki Court wished to know whether Article 11 of the Pregnant Workers Directive requires that a person moved to alternative duties be paid 'as much as she received on average before her transfer' and whether the fact that her previous pay was made up of both basic pay and supplementary pay was relevant (paragraph 28).

The Court examined the interplay between Article 157 TFEU and Article 11 of the Pregnant Workers Directive. Accepting that the money received by Mrs Parviainen from Finnair was pay within the meaning of Article 157 TFEU, the Court turned to Article 11, which requires the maintenance of 'a payment' and not 'the payment' to the worker concerned.

If 'the' payment was not required, the Court then had to turn to what level of payment a worker who had been transferred to other activities should be entitled to under European Union law. It turned to its own case law on equal pay for work of equal value. In *JämO*, the Court had held that 'the facts relating to the nature of the work done and the conditions in which it is carried out may, if appropriate, be considered factors unrelated to any discrimination on grounds of sex such as to justify any differences in pay between different groups of workers'.[42] Applying the logic of *JämO* but without exploring the conceptual relationship, if any, between equal pay for work of equal value and the levels of payment required by Article 11, the Court pointed out that some of the allowances earned by Mrs Parviainen were dependent on specific functions which she no longer performed and this was a factor that the Court took into consideration.

The Court then pointed to Article 11 of the Pregnant Workers Directive; this time to paragraph 1, which stated that a payment for workers who had been transferred to different duties 'must be ensured in accordance with national legislation and/or national practice.' The Court interpreted this to mean that Member States, and, where relevant, management and labour, have 'a certain

[41] Case C-471/08 *Sanna Maria Parviainen v Finnair Oyj* [2010] ECR I-6533.
[42] Case C-236/98 *JämO* [2000] ECR I-2189, para 52.

amount of discretion' in defining the 'conditions for the implementation of the entitlement' of pregnant workers. That discretion is tempered, however, and Member States (and/or management and labour) must not undermine the health and safety of pregnant workers or ignore the fact that such workers are still working.

The Court then went on to set out some criteria to determine the pay that must be protected: the level of pay cannot be lower than the pay accorded to workers occupying the job to which the pregnant worker is temporarily assigned; during the temporary transfer, the pregnant worker is entitled to the pay components and supplementary allowances relating to that job provided she fulfils the eligibility requirements for them. Member States and, where relevant, management and labour, must also honour those pay components and supplementary allowances 'which relate to her professional status such as, in particular, her seniority, her length of service and her professional qualifications'.[43] However they are not bound to honour pay components or supplementary allowances which are dependent on performance of specific functions that are designed to compensate for disadvantages related to that performance. In the case of a purser, these would include overtime allowances and allowances for long-haul flights. Thus the Court held that the Pregnant Workers Directive does not require that a woman be paid the equivalent of her average pay before transfer to other duties.

The Court held that, in principle, the Finnair scheme was not incompatible with European Union law. However, insofar as it failed to take into account the supplementary allowances that relate to the professional status of the worker in question such a scheme was incompatible with Article 11(1) of the Pregnant Workers Directive. It is for the national court to investigate whether the application of the scheme did deprive her of those supplementary allowances.

On the same day as the Court gave its decision in *Parviainen*, it handed down its judgment in *Gassmayr*.[44] This case related to additional payments for on-call services for hospital doctors. It was medically certified that Dr Gassmayr could not continue with on-call duties during her pregnancy and that she would be unable to perform such duties during an extended period of maternity leave. She argued that she should be paid, in addition to her basic salary, an average of her on-call allowances.

In giving its judgment, the Court distinguished two periods of time: the period when Dr Gassmayr was unable to work prior to her maternity leave and the extended period of her maternity leave. Dr Gassmayr did not continue working during the first period—unlike Mrs Parviainen who continued working but in alternative employment. The Court held that Dr Gassmayr was not entitled to receive the on-call duty allowance for that period. Whilst holding that these allowances were indeed pay within the meaning of Article 157 TFEU, the Court pointed to Article 11(1) of the Pregnant Workers Directive, which provides that a

[43] Case C-471/08 *Parviainen*, n 41 above, para 60.

[44] Case C-194/08 *Susanne Gassmayr v Bundesministerin fur Wissenschaft und Forschung* [2010] ECR I-6281.

woman in this situation is entitled to 'a' payment and not 'the' pay which she had hitherto received. The Court pointed to Article 11(4), which entitles Member States 'to make entitlement to pay or the allowance referred to in Article 11(1) conditional upon the worker fulfilling the eligibility criteria for such benefits laid down under national legislation'. It referred again to the decision in *JämO*, as it had done in *Parviainen*, to the effect that the nature of the work done and the conditions in which it is carried out may under certain circumstances provide objective facts unrelated to sex discrimination which may justify differences in pay between different groups of workers. Then, applying its logic in *Parviainen* to the effect that employers are not required to maintain pay supplements that depend on the performance of certain duties by employees, which are intended to compensate for disadvantages relating to that performance during a temporary transfer, the Court held that this was also the case where a woman was granted leave under Article 5(3). As in *Parviainen*, the Court referred to the degree of latitude open to Member States, and to management and labour where relevant, in defining the conditions for the exercise and implementation of the entitlement to an income of pregnant workers who are required to take leave from their employment on health and safety grounds. That discretion cannot undermine the objective of protecting women in these circumstances and, therefore, the allowance or payment must be sufficient to guarantee the effectiveness of the protection and cannot be used as a mere cost saving exercise for employers.

As in *Parvianenen*, the Court laid down the minimum criteria for the level of payment; it must include the worker's basic monthly salary; and the pay and components or supplements relating to her occupational status, including seniority, length of service and professional qualifications payments. In the case of Dr Gassmayr, her pay was calculated taking her average salary in the 13 weeks prior to her leave into account and excluding the on-call supplements. The Court held that this was not contrary to Article 11 (1) of the Pregnant Workers Directive.

In respect of pay received during the extended maternity leave which was required under Austrian law, the Court relied on its earlier case law to the effect that despite the fact that maternity payments were pay for the purposes of Article 157 TFEU, women on maternity leave could not rely on that Article or on the Pregnant Workers Directive to claim that they should receive any particular level of pay whilst on maternity leave. All that European Union law requires in terms of the level of pay is that it must be at least equivalent to the sickness allowance provided by national social security legislation, irrespective of how this is paid. This minimum protection does not require the person concerned to receive full pay or the payment of on-call duty allowances. At the same time, the Court repeated that EU law does not prevent the Member States from adopting more stringent protective measures, including that the level of maternity pay be above the minimum required by the Pregnant Workers Directive.

Once again in these cases, the Court refers to Article 157 TFEU but does not then apply an equality discourse to it. The reference to *JämO* in both judgments might suggest that there should be an equal value assessment of the work performed by the woman who is moved from her duties for health and safety reasons, given that *JämO* is a case about equal value. However, the Court does not suggest such an evaluation and the criteria that it sets down in relation to determining the level of pay relate to both the work performed and the existing status and qualifications of the worker. *JämO* must be a red herring in this context and merely serves to undermine the lack of clarity in the legal argumentation of the Court. These cases further underline the fact that the Court has developed a type of 'separate code' approach in relation to motherhood pay issues.

F. Additional payments to women taking maternity leave

A rather different scenario was presented in *Abdoulaye*.[45] Here women taking maternity leave were granted a lump sum payment in addition to their maternity pay. The employer argued that this payment was to compensate employees for the disadvantages arising from the woman taking maternity leave. Male employees argued that this payment was pay within the meaning of Article 157 TFEU and it was discrimination to pay it only to female workers as the birth of a child affected the family as a whole and that, therefore, male workers whose wives gave birth should also be entitled to an allowance. The Court held that such a payment was pay within the meaning of Article 157 TFEU, relying on *Gillespie* to the effect that the compatibility of such a payment with Article 157 TFEU depended 'on whether, with regard to that payment, female workers are in a situation comparable to that of male workers'.[46] The employer, Renault, had listed a number of disadvantages faced by women who take maternity leave and argued that the payment was designed to compensate for some of those disadvantages. In this argument, Renault was supported by the Commission and the United Kingdom Government.

The Court held that such a payment was not incompatible with Article 157 TFEU provided that it was indeed designed to offset occupational disadvantages faced by women taking maternity leave and it was for the national court to decide if this was indeed the case. This case turned solely on the interpretation of Article 157 TFEU. The Court appears to reject an argument that women on maternity leave and men whose wives take maternity leave can be relevant comparators since it is the former who suffer disadvantages rather than the latter. Where payments are intended to compensate for such disadvantages then they are not contrary to Article 157 TFEU. It could be argued that this case is an acceptance by the Court that positive action measures can be taken in the area of equal pay. If that is so, then this case is the only case relating to motherhood payments where the Court does engage with equality arguments.

[45] Case C-218/98 *Oumar Dabo Abdoulaye and others v Régie Nationale des Usines Renault SA* [1999] ECR I-5723.

[46] ibid para 17.

G. Is there a separate code?

The United Kingdom Court of Appeal applied the *Gillespie* ruling in *Clark*.[47] Neill LJ observed that:

> In my judgment it is now clear that Community law entitles Member States to make special provisions for women who are absent from work because of pregnancy or confinement. *The provisions that are made then become a separate code.* The code provides pregnant women with special protection but when in receipt of payments under the code their protection cannot be 'compared' with that of a man or with that of a woman at work.[48]

Whilst this chapter is not the place for a discussion of the United Kingdom provisions, it is interesting to note that the right to maternity leave and pay is set out in the Employment Rights Act, with the right not to be discriminated against because of pregnancy and maternity in the Equality Act. In the United Kingdom, where an adequate allowance is provided for under national legislation, a woman cannot make an equal pay claim.[49] In other words, the provisions are mutually exclusive.

In its interpretation of the interplay between Article 157 TFEU and the Pregnant Workers Directive, the European Court has, in effect, treated these provisions as mutually exclusive. Whilst maintaining always that the payment made is a payment within the meaning of Article 157 TFEU, the Court has effectively rejected the argument that an equal pay claim can be made. The equal pay provisions of EU Law are a separate code from those relating to maternity and pregnancy pay. We argue that taking maternity and pregnancy pay out of the equal pay discourse reinforces the motherhood penalty, which is major contributor to the gender pay gap.

H. Proposed amendments to the Pregnant Workers Directive

In 2008, the Commission proposed amendments to the Pregnant Workers Directive.[50] The Commission's impact assessment states that 'there are marked differences between the Member States in terms of policy on facilitating reconciliation. Maternity leave provisions range roughly from 14 to 52 weeks, with payments

[47] Clark, n 21 above.

[48] ibid para 34 (authors' emphasis).

[49] *British Airways v Moore and Botterill* [2000] IRLR 296. This case relates to the level of pay for an air stewardess moved to different duties following a health and safety assessment. Section 67(s) of the Employment Rights Act requires the level of payment not to be 'substantially less favourable' than her previous terms and conditions. In this respect UK law appears to be more generous than the Pregnant Workers Directive as interpreted by the European Court.

[50] Proposal for a Directive of the European Parliament and of the Council amending Council Directive 92/85/EEC on the introduction of measures to encourage improvements in the safety and health at work of pregnant workers and workers who have recently given birth or are breastfeeding COM (2008) 637 final.

ranging from 55 per cent (subject to a ceiling) to 100 per cent (subject to no ceiling).'[51] Clearly, the margin of discretion referred to by the Court in its case law is being interpreted very widely by the Member States.

The Commission proposed an extension of paid maternity leave from 14 to 18 weeks. This would bring the European Union into line with the ILO Maternity Protection Recommendation (2000). Two further amendments in respect of pay were proposed. First, where an employer excludes an employee because he considers that she is not fit for work and where the employee herself has not supplied medical evidence, she is entitled to a payment equivalent to her full salary. This is a codification of one aspect of the judgment of the Court in *Høj Pederson*, discussed above.

The second amendment relates to the allowance to be paid to women on maternity leave. In its proposal, the Commission states that the proposed Directive 'provides for the principle of the payment of the full monthly salary received prior to the maternity leave'.[52] However national legislation may provide for a ceiling on this allowance. The precise wording of the proposal is as follows: 'the allowance referred to in point 2(b) shall be deemed adequate if it guarantees income equivalent to the last monthly salary or an average monthly salary, subject to any ceiling laid down under national legislation. Such a ceiling may not be lower than the allowance received by workers within the meaning of Article 2 in the event of a break in activity on grounds connected with the worker's state of health. The Member States may lay down the period over which this average monthly salary is calculated.'[53]

These proposed amendments have proved controversial both in terms of the extension of the length of the maternity leave period and in the reference to the full monthly salary. Several key issues have emerged in the discussions. The European Parliament's Committee on Women's Rights and Gender Equality commented on the draft proposal in November 2009.[54] The Committee recommended that the period of maternity leave should be extended to 20 weeks rather than the 18 proposed by the Commission. The rationale for this extension is that 'it is important that Member States which already have provision for longer periods of parental leave for both parents can keep their generous provisions, without this affecting other Member States or diminishing the effect of this proposal for a directive prolonging the maternity leave across the EU'.[55] The Committee also stressed that 20 weeks was sufficient 'to enable women to breastfeed in comfort' as well as giving a sufficient period of recovery for the mother and to enable her to forge a strong bond with her baby. The Committee added that 'a longer period might diminish women's prospects of returning to the labour market'.[56]

[51] SEC (2008) 2595, n 29 above.

[52] ibid 8.

[53] Proposed Article 1 amending Article 11 of the Pregnant Workers Directive. COM (2008) 637 final, 15.

[54] EP 2008/0193 (COD) of 12.11.2009. The report can be accessed at <http://www.europarl.europa.eu/sides/getDoc.do?type=COMPARL&mode=XML&language=EN&reference=PE430.593>.

[55] ibid 10. [56] ibid 17.

The Committee also proposed that the pay provisions be amended. It recommended that the compulsory period of six weeks after childbirth be fully paid on the grounds that women should not lose out financially because they are mothers.[57] Full pay was defined as 100 per cent of the last monthly salary or the average monthly salary. For the remainder of the period of leave, the payment should not be lower than 85 per cent of the last monthly salary or the average monthly salary.[58] In order to provide protection for low paid women and to protect families from the risk of poverty and social exclusion, the Committee also proposed that the payment received should not be lower than sick pay.

In October 2010, Parliament narrowly approved these changes with 327 votes in favour of the extended 20-week period of leave, with 320 votes against; and 354 MEPs voting in favour of the full pay proposal, with 308 against.[59] Arguments in favour of the enhanced proposals were that women should not lose out financially when giving birth, that the proposal would improve reconciliation of work and family life, that the health of working mothers and that of their babies would be improved, that equal opportunities between men and women would be better fostered, and that women would have less recourse to parental leave if they returned to work when their babies were slightly older. For employers, they would have more certainty about the length of leave and the payments required. However the Commission's approach, rejected by the Parliament, would have allowed Member States to cap the level of pay, thereby providing a common minimum standard in contrast to the Parliament's view that women should not be disadvantaged by virtue of having children.

Arguments against the proposal have sometimes been based on the costs to employers as well as on ideological issues. For example, it is reported that the Federation of Small Businesses and other employer organizations in the United Kingdom are opposed to the measures on grounds of cost to employers.[60] The United Kingdom Government has estimated that the proposal would double the costs of providing paid maternity leave and therefore price women of child bearing age out of the market.[61] The United Kingdom Employment Relations Minister is also on record as stating that the proposals are regressive in the sense that higher paid women will benefit more than lower paid women.[62]

Aside from issues of cost, the proposals also raise ideological issues. Extending the period of paid maternity leave underlines the gender divide in child rearing roles. Whilst it is true that women after childbirth need time both to recover physically and to bond with their babies as well as to establish routines of breastfeeding, the emphasis on child care in the proposals does nothing to support men who wish, for whatever reason, to become involved in the care of their babies.

[57] ibid 38. [58] ibid 41. [59] EP A6-0267/2009.

[60] <http://www.bbc.co.uk/news/business-11560112>. This is reflected in the responses to the UK Government consultations on the Commission's proposals see <http://www.bis.gov.uk/search?keywords=pregnant+workers+directive&type=all>.

[61] On the UK position see <http://nds.coi.gov.uk/content/Detail.aspx?ReleaseID=416884&NewsAreaID=2>.

[62] ibid.

It can be argued that the more extended the period of paid maternity leave, the less likely that men will become involved, meaning that child care and family matters become reinforced as the prerogative of the woman. These arguments have been rehearsed in the Employment, Social Policy, Health and Consumer Affairs formation of the Council on four occasions. During the first policy debate in March 2009, there appeared to be majority support for the initial Commission proposal to extend leave from a 14-week to an 18-week period.[63] However, by June 2009, concerns were raised in the Council about the length of maternity leave and its impact on national paternity and parental leave policies.[64] Opposition to the proposals, was compounded by the European Parliament's proposals for amendments so that, by December 2010, there was a very large majority of States that did not think that the Parliament's amendments constituted an appropriate basis for negotiation.[65] By June 2011, several ministers were expressing concern and opposition to the proposal, with some ministers, in light of the differing views of the Member States, advocating that the Council should not continue its work on the proposal.[66] It has been decided to defer the issue further until the December 2011 Council, although it hardly seems likely that given the strength of opposition, the proposed Directive will be approved by the Council.[67]

The Equality and Human Rights Commission, by contrast to the position of the current coalition government in the United Kingdom, supports the extension of paid maternity leave. Arguing that 'maternity leave affects differentials in both basic pay and in performance based pay', the EHRC advocates a policy of full pay both to offset the negative effects of maternity leave and to secure women's income in the long run as well as to encourage women of lower incomes to take up their entitlements to leave.[68] However, the EHRC classifies full pay as being 90 per cent of the pay received by the mother prior to her leave, since it calculates full pay according to a complex formula which subtracts the 'costs' of working, for example travel to and from work, from the overall salary.[69]

It is clear that there is no agreement on issues of pregnancy, maternity leave and pay. From the point of view of working mothers, this confusion leads to a substantial motherhood penalty. Despite the rhetoric of the Court in relation to Article 157 TFEU, EU law treats these issues of pay as a separate code from matters

[63] <http://www.europarl.europa.eu/oeil/resume.jsp?id=5697042&eventId=1070372&backToCaller=NO&language=en>.

[64] <http://www.europarl.europa.eu/oeil/resume.jsp?id=5697042&eventId=1077748&backToCaller=NO&language=en>.

[65] <http://www.europarl.europa.eu/oeil/resume.jsp?id=5697042&eventId=1133718&backToCaller=NO&language=en>.

[66] Council Press Release 11574/11 PRESSE 176 PR CO 40. <http://www.europarl.europa.eu/oeil/resume.jsp?id=5697042&eventId=1156950&backToCaller=NO&language=en>.

[67] Both the UK and Germany are opposed to the measure on the grounds that the proposal will disturb the ability of the Member States to find a solution in the best interests of parents. See <http://nds.coi.gov.uk/content/Detail.aspx?ReleaseID=419979&NewsAreaID=2>.

[68] Equality and Human Rights Commission, Policy Briefing: EU Pregnant Workers Directive, July 2010, 7.

[69] The EHRC briefing can be found at <http://www.equalityhumanrights.com/legal-and-policy/european-policy/eu-pregnancy-directive/>.

of equal pay. However, that code is absolutely lacking in clarity and leaves substantial discretion to Member States as to how they deal with the motherhood penalty. One solution might be to provide for a shorter period of maternity leave where, following the United Kingdom Employment Rights Act, the level of pay is not 'substantially less generous' than the woman's previous pay with a more extended period of leave to be taken by either parent on a similarly paid basis.[70] This solution avoids the ideological issue of who has responsibility for child rearing between parents and it offers them choice. It also avoids pricing women of child-bearing age out of the market.[71] The problem still is to determine the length of that leave, raising issues of costs. A similar approach could be taken to levels of pay during maternity related illness or to situations where a woman is moved to an alternative post for reasons of health and safety. A 'substantially less generous' test has the merit of at least maintaining her level of wages during this most difficult of periods in the working life of women.

I. A mothers' union?

The Council Conclusions on priorities for re-launching the single market were published in July 2011.[72] Based on the Monti Report on a new strategy for the single market[73] and the Commission's communication on a renewed social market economy, no mention is made in the Conclusions of priorities for equality issues or for reconciliation policies.[74] Tensions between the social and labour market priorities highlighted in the Monti Report are limited to tensions created by the Member States' failure to implement free movement policies fully and by the interpretation by the Court of the Posted Workers Directive.

This absence of discussion of, or commitment to, social policy objectives in such recent strategy documents underlines the position of writers such as Syrpis that the political commitment within the EU to social objectives remains thin and that there is a continuing 'constitutional asymmetry' between the EU's market and welfare policies.[75] The absence of a political commitment to renegotiating the Pregnant Workers Directive is also indicative of the continuing wariness of several

[70] The coalition government in the UK has recently published proposals to cut back maternity leave reserved exclusively for mothers from 52 weeks to 18 weeks, with the remainder reclassified as parental leave. The proposal is for existing pay arrangements to be retained (see BIS, Modern Workplaces Consultation, <http://discuss.bis.gov.uk/modernworkplaces>).

[71] See 'The Pregnant Workers Directive: European social policy between protection and employability' in G Falkner, O Treib, M Hartlapp, S Leiber, *Complying with Europe: EU Harmonisation and Soft Law in the Member States* (Cambridge: Cambridge University Press, 2005).

[72] <http://www.consilium.europa.eu/uedocs/cms_data/docs/pressdata/en/ecofin/123628.pdf>.

[73] <http://ec.europa.eu/bepa/pdf/monti_report_final_10_05_2010_en.pdf>.

[74] Communication from the Commission to the European Parliament, the Council, the European Economic and Social Committee and the Committee of the Regions, *Commission Work Programme 2010: Time to Act* COM (2010) 135 final.

[75] P Syrpis, *EU Intervention in Domestic Labour Law* (Oxford: Oxford University Press, 2009) on the thinness of the commitment, and F Scharpf, 'The European Social Model: Coping with the Challenges of Diversity' (2002) 40:4 *JCMS* 645.

Member States to having EU-level market correcting mechanisms replace domestic welfare policies both on grounds of costs and on grounds of the internal logic of national solidarity principles.

Meanwhile the Court, by effectively removing motherhood pay issues from the ambit of equal pay and into social welfare, has deferred to the Member States on these issues by drawing a boundary between equality policies operating at EU level and welfare policies operating at the national level. This means that without a national commitment to tackling the motherhood penalty, there will continue to be wide divergences in benefits available to women and a wide divergence in costs to the Member States and to employers. For the foreseeable future, therefore, labour market and welfare policies in this area remain in the hands of the Member States despite the rhetoric of the EU social market. We are no further forward than in the 1990s in this respect.

12

State Aid and Self-Government: Regional Taxation and the Shifting Spaces of Constitutional Autonomy

*Francesco de Cecco**

A. Introduction

The power to tax is an essential feature of political autonomy, and claims to self-government that revolve around it are a recurring theme in history. A number of reasons explain why political communities should wish to set, impose and collect taxes from their own members. Not only are such communities attracted by the outcome of the exercise of fiscal power, the revenue that allows them to shape their own collective destinies; they are also drawn to the power to distribute the tax burden and redistribute wealth as they desire; and, crucially, they aspire to control the power to restrict the enjoyment of their own property rights, for, as the term suggests, this is the mark of autonomy.[1]

In Europe, self-government and fiscal decentralization feature prominently in a number of constitutional systems and in national political discourses. Until recently, however, these matters were believed to lie outside the domain of EU law. A recent development in the State aid case law has prompted a reversal of this belief. The upshot of this case law is that an autonomous region should be able, under certain conditions, to introduce separate corporate tax measures without, in doing so, triggering the prohibition of State aid. However, this chapter argues that the internal logic of State aid law is, taken in isolation, unable to capture the full significance of this development, and that the normative justification for the CJEU's approach lies outside the domain of State aid law. Moreover, the chapter argues that the new emphasis on regional autonomy may cause a shift in the space where tax competition occurs from the inter-State to the infra-State level, and that

* Lecturer, Newcastle Law School. This chapter is based in part on the forthcoming monograph, F de Cecco, *State Aid and the European Economic Constitution* (Oxford: Hart Publishing, forthcoming).

[1] Autonomy, as the etymology (from the Greek *autós*, self, and *nómos*, law) suggests, implies the power by a community to make its own laws, which includes tax laws—hence the motto 'no taxation without representation'.

the Court's approach frames the scope of the Commission's action in relation to harmful tax competition.

The chapter begins by introducing some concepts that are central to the definition of State aid in relation to regulatory and fiscal measures; it then moves on to evaluate the recent case law on regional tax autonomy and to explore alternative normative justifications. The final part evaluates the significance of this case law in relation to tax competition.

B. State aid and fiscal decentralization

The fact that State aid should concern itself with fiscal measures is by no means novel. The existence of State aid constraints on fiscal policy emerged at an early stage in the evolution of the case law in this area, when the Court made clear that the purview of Articles 107 to 109 TFEU did not exhaust itself in the notion of subsidy, but encompassed 'interventions which, in various forms, mitigate the charges which are normally included in the budget of an undertaking and which, without, therefore, being subsidies in the strict meaning of the word, are similar in character and have the same effect'.[2] Attempts by domestic governments to fence off their fiscal or social policies have since been rebuffed with the remark that 'Article [107] does not distinguish between the measures of State intervention concerned by reference to their causes or aims but defines them in relation to their effects', and, as a consequence, 'the alleged fiscal or social aim of the measure in issue cannot suffice to shield it from the application of Article [107]'.[3]

Cases concerning fiscal measures often turn on the fundamental question as to whether the scope of a measure is general or selective: a measure falls, other things being equal, within the definition of State aid if it is selective.[4] The distinction, whilst controversial among international economic lawyers and economists,[5] seems all but natural under EU law, as far as its textual foundations are concerned. The focus of State aid on selective measures derives not only from the wording of Article 107(1) TFEU, which requires aid to favour '*certain* undertakings or the production

[2] Case 30/59 *Steenkolenmijnen v High Authority* [1961] ECR 1, para 1.

[3] Case 173/73 *Italy v Commission* [1974] ECR 709, para 13. See further Case C-241/94 *France v Commission (Kimberly Clark)* [1996] ECR I-4551.

[4] Other things being equal means: if the other cumulative conditions for a measure to constitute aid are present. See Case C-280/00 *Altmark Trans GmbH, Regierungspräsidium Magdeburg v Nahverkergesellschaft Altmark GmbH* [2003] ECR I-7747, para 75. This language may mislead us into thinking that the case law on the definition of State aid exhibits the hard-edged clarity associated with logical inference. In reality, the case law on the definition of State aid contains a number of inconsistencies and grey areas. R Plender, 'Definition of Aid' in A Biondi, P Eeckhout and J Flynn (eds), *The Law of State Aid in the European Union* (Oxford: Oxford University Press, 2003); M Schütte, 'The Definition of State Aid' in M Sánchez Rydelski (ed), *The EC State Aid Régime: Distortive Effects of State Aid on Competition and Trade* (London: Cameron May, 2006); L Rubini, *The Definition of Subsidy and State Aid* (Oxford: Oxford University Press, 2009).

[5] On which, see L Rubini, n 4 above, 359–77.

of *certain* goods', but also from the fact that the other provisions in the Treaty that address distortions of competition stemming from legislative or regulatory measures have as their object distortions arising from differences in the legislation and regulations of *different* Member States (Articles 116 and 117 TFEU, in particular), rather than regulatory and legislative differences within Member States.[6] The Treaty points to a clear division of roles between Article 107 and the provisions on approximation and harmonization.[7]

The clear logic behind this distinction, however, is overshadowed by its practical application. Many of the complexities that arise here stem from the tension, from which the case law on the definition of State aid generally suffers, between the competing commitments to a functional approach, on the one hand, and to legal certainty, on the other. A functional approach requires a wide net to be cast in order to safeguard the Commission's control over potentially distortive public intervention, and to underpin its monopoly over the evaluation of the costs and benefits of individual State measures. At the same time, however, the commitment by public authorities across borders to play by the same rules across time, which is essential to the effectiveness of State aid, requires stability in the definition of State aid.

This tension is also seen when considering the desirability or otherwise of a rule of reason in State aid law.[8] The Court insists that the definition of State aid is an *objective* exercise.[9] A measure may not escape the prohibition of State aid on the basis of policy considerations, as these come into play once the question as to the existence of a State aid is answered affirmatively. It is then for the Commission, and for the Commission alone, to evaluate a State measure in light of the policy that it pursues. There is, in the Court's view, no room for a rule of reason, no open mechanism to attenuate the expansive force of the prohibition by recognizing legitimate policy concerns. Yet this approach runs into difficulty as soon as it is realized that its application would lead to questioning, as one Advocate General put it, 'the entire social and economic life of a member state'.[10] The Court, as result, is cornered by its own commitments: it is forced to open up new pathways to prevent crossing the State aid threshold, but, at the same time, is compelled to dress up its constructs in objective garb, so as to maintain the distinction between prohibition and justification. The outcome of this exercise is not neutral: it shifts the boundaries of State, national and, as we shall see, regional autonomy.

[6] The exclusive reference in Article 107(1) TFEU to manufacturing is an anachronism. Undertakings carrying out services are regularly treated as aid recipients.

[7] Chapter 3 (entitled 'Approximation of Laws') of Title VII, which comprises Articles 114–18 TFEU.

[8] eg K Bacon, 'The Concept of State Aid: The Developing Jurisprudence in the European and UK Courts' (2003) 24:2 *ECLR* 54; A Bartosch, 'Is there a Need for a Rule of Reason In European State Aid Law?' (2010) 47:3 *CMLRev* 729.

[9] Case C-241/94 *France v Commission* [1996] ECR I-4551, paras 19 and 20; Case T-52/94 *Ladbroke Racing Ltd v Commission* [1998] ECR II-1, para 52.

[10] Opinion of AG Jacobs in Cases C-52-54/97 *Viscido and others v Ente Poste Italiane* [1998] ECR I-2629, para 16; on similar lines, S Weatherill, *Law and Integration in the European Union* (Oxford: Oxford University Press, 1995) 272.

(1) Material selectivity

The distinction between general and selective measures revolves around the idea that a measure is selective if it singles out, either in law or in fact, its beneficiaries.[11] The focus on the economic impact of State aid requires the Court to consider as selective those measures that appear to be general in scope but, in their application, may favour certain undertakings or sectors.[12] *De facto* selectivity may also arise where *discretion* is involved in the application of a prima facie general measure.[13]

Surprisingly, perhaps, given the emphasis on promoting undistorted competition, the Court does not actually require discrimination to be understood as unequal treatment of *competing* undertakings, but, instead, as different treatment of undertakings that fall within a *common reference framework*. Selectivity includes, in fact, not only measures that favour certain undertakings, but also measures that favour certain sectors over others, regardless of the competitive relationship between them.[14] For instance, in *Adria-Wien Pipeline*, the Court found that a rebate on energy taxes in favour of undertakings in the manufacturing sector to the exclusion of undertakings in the services sector was a selective measure.[15] The reason for this is that the presence of a competitor at *national* level is not a necessary condition for establishing a competitive imbalance between the beneficiary of aid and its EU competitors. In other words, favouring one sector over another may not translate into relative competitive advantage at a domestic level, but it may translate into a cross-border distortion of competition.[16] What matters is that, as a result of a measure of State intervention, certain undertakings are favoured over 'other undertakings which are in a legal and factual situation that is comparable in the light of the objective pursued by the measure in question'.[17] Undertakings operate in a given context and on the basis of a set of assumptions which form the backdrop of their decisions; among these are assumptions regarding the regulatory framework and the costs associated with it. Any intervention that alters an undertaking's regulatory and economic environment therefore alters its competitive position. Thus, a reduction in social security charges creates an advantage in favour of the undertakings that benefit from it, even if there are no direct competitors in the same Member State. What matters is that the alteration of those undertakings' costs enables them to exploit the artificially induced change in their competitive

[11] Some authors associate selectivity with the concept of discrimination. See K Bacon, 'State Aids and General Measures' (1997) 17 *YEL* 269; P Werner, 'Fiscal State Aid' [2006–07] 9 *CYELS* 481. The Court avoids the term discrimination in relation to State aid. See, however, the Opinion of AG Trstenjak in Case C-428/07 *Horvath* [2009] ECR I-6355, paras 103–7.

[12] Case T-55/99 *CETM v Commission* [2000] ECR II-3207, para 40.

[13] Case C-241/94 *Kimberley Clark*, n 3 above, paras 23–4; Case C-295/97 *Piaggio* [1999] ECR I-3735, para 39.

[14] Case 173/73 *Italy v Commission* [1974] ECR 709, para 33; Case 248/84 *Germany v Commission* [1987] ECR 4013, para 18; Case C-75/97 *Belgium v Commission* [1999] ECR I-3671, para 32.

[15] Case C-43/99 *Adria-Wien Pipeline* [2001] ECR I-8365.

[16] B Kurcz and D Vallindas, 'Can General Measures be... Selective? Some Thoughts on The Interpretation of a State Aid Definition' (2008) 45:1 *CMLRev* 158.

[17] Case C-43/99 *Adria-Wien Pipeline*, n 15 above, para 41.

position. If selectivity covered only situations in which Member States discriminate among competitors, State aid law would fail to take account of this distortion.

For similar reasons, selectivity is also unconcerned with the position of the aid beneficiaries' competitors in other Member States. In *Italian Textiles*,[18] the Italian Government tried to argue that, by reducing the social charges for the Italian textile industry, which were higher than those occurring elsewhere in the EU, its intervention sought to realign the competitive position of the domestic textile industry with that of its European competitors. In rejecting this view, the Court held that the competitive position of an undertaking or an economic sector was determined by *various factors*, including social charges, which affected production costs differently in different Member States.[19] Whilst cross-border differences stemming from legislative and regulatory measures could be targeted by relying on (the precursors to) Articles 114 to 117 TFEU, Article 107 prevents Member States from attempting to reduce specific costs affecting a particular economic sector, as this type of intervention would have the effect of 'disturbing the existing equilibrium'.[20]

(2) Geographic selectivity

The concept of selectivity also includes those measures that favour undertakings in a certain geographic area. Until recently, however, the full meaning of geographic selectivity was not readily determined: it was plain that the concept captured a Member State's decision to limit certain advantages to part of its territory; but what if those measures were, instead, an emanation of a regional authority—would they count as selective? This was the central question in the *Azores* case.[21] Under the Portuguese Constitution, the Azores islands are an autonomous region with their own government, and with fiscal competence and the power to adapt national fiscal provisions to regional specificities. The Azores introduced a scheme aimed at adapting the Portuguese tax system to the special needs and characteristics of those islands, by calibrating the corporate tax rate to a level that was markedly lower than the one in force in mainland Portugal. The Commission was in no doubt that the lower tax rate amounted to State aid. On its view, since undertakings established in the Azores operated in the same political and economic environment as those established in mainland Portugal, selectivity arose from the comparison between the former and the latter. Portugal challenged that decision. Among its pleas was the contention that the decision to lower the tax rate resulted from the exercise of the regional legislature's competences and was addressed to all undertakings established in the region. Moreover, the tax reduction stemmed from the exercise of constitutional sovereignty as it was intended to rectify the inequalities in

[18] Case 173/73 *Italy v Commission* [1974] ECR 709.
[19] ibid para 17.
[20] ibid.
[21] Case C-88/03 *Portugal v Commission* [2006] ECR I-7115. See R Greaves, 'Autonomous Regions, Taxation and EC State Aids Rules' (2009) 34:5 *ELRev* 779.

economic development from which the islands suffered, in line with the constitutional principle of solidarity.

In what was to be one of his most influential opinions on State aid, Advocate General Geelhoed argued that the issue of selectivity in relation to fiscal measures introduced by devolved authorities turned on the degree of autonomy that the taxing authority enjoyed from central government. In cases involving *genuine* autonomy, he submitted, it was appropriate to locate the benchmark at the devolved rather than at the national level. That would certainly be the case where symmetrical devolution was involved.[22] Asymmetrical devolution required, instead, a more complex analysis to determine whether the decision was taken by a truly autonomous entity; and true autonomy, according to the Advocate General, was to be found where, in taking the specific decision regarding its tax rates, the region enjoyed *institutional*, *procedural* and *economic autonomy*. By which, he meant that the region had a 'constitutional, political and administrative status separate from that of the central government' (institutional autonomy);[23] that the central government did not have any power to intervene directly in the devolved authority's procedure in setting the tax rate, and that the local authority was not obliged to take the interest of the central State into account in setting the tax rate (procedural autonomy); and, finally, that the economic consequences of setting a lower tax rate would be borne by the devolved entity without there being a cross-subsidization or other form of funding from central government (economic autonomy). In the case at issue, the Azores were undoubtedly autonomous from an institutional point of view, but their decision on corporate taxation lacked both procedural and economic autonomy, as it was taken on the basis of the principle of national solidarity, which entailed cooperation between the autonomous region and central government, and also entailed a direct transfer from the Portuguese State to the autonomous region so as to compensate for the reduction in the corporate tax rate.

The Grand Chamber followed the Advocate General. The starting point for a selectivity analysis was, it held, to find the 'reference framework' upon which the question as to whether certain undertakings received more favourable treatment than others would have to hinge. That reference framework did not necessarily have to coincide with the national territory of a Member State—it could be made up by part of it. An 'infra-State body' could in fact enjoy a legal and factual status that would make it 'sufficiently autonomous in relation to the central government of a Member State' and, as a result, that body and not the central government would 'play a fundamental role in the definition of the political and economic environment in which undertakings operate'.[24] The Court then went on to apply the three criteria that the Advocate General had outlined. It found that whilst the Azores region could be regarded as institutionally *and* procedurally autonomous from the

[22] Where symmetrical devolution occurs, each region enjoys the same powers; conversely, devolution is asymmetrical where autonomy is not equally distributed among regions.

[23] Opinion of AG Geelhoed in Case C-88/03 *Portugal v Commission*, n 21 above, para 54.

[24] ibid para 34.

Portuguese State, it did not enjoy the same degree of autonomy in the economic and financial sense. The existence of budgetary transfers from the central government, which compensated for the reduced revenue resulting from the reductions in tax rates, meant that the region could not be regarded as being sufficiently autonomous to constitute the reference framework for the selectivity test.

Later, the question of regional tax autonomy resurfaced in *UGT-Rioja*,[25] and in the General Court's ruling in *Gibraltar v Commission*.[26] The *UGT-Rioja* case displayed some important analogies with the *Azores* case. The context was crucially different though. As Advocate General Kokott pointed out,[27] whilst, in *Azores*, the Court itself had to decide on whether the Commission had demonstrated the existence of State aid, in the latter case, the Court's task was to interpret Article 107(1) TFEU, leaving the referring court to decide on the selective or general nature of the measure. The questions referred concerned measures adopted by the three independent provincial authorities (the 'Diputaciones Forales' of Vizcaya, Álava and Guipúzcoa) that form the Autonomous Community of the Basque Country, which have the power to introduce tax legislation, such as the legislation at issue, that set the corporation tax rate at 32.5 per cent, below the 35 per cent rate generally applicable in Spain.

Regional autonomy is at the heart of the constitutional arrangements in contemporary Spain, and Advocate General Kokott identified the heightened constitutional sensitivity of the issues at stake. Article 4(2) TEU, she pointed out, requires the EU to respect the 'national identities of its Member States', a duty reinforced in the Lisbon Treaty, which expressly mentions respect for the 'constitutional structures' of the Member States.[28] On the other hand, the Advocate General recalled that the Court has consistently held that internal situations resulting from constitutional provisions are not immune from the application of EU law. On her view, the Court in *Azores* 'struck a reasonable balance between these two principles': '[o]n the one hand, it respects the autonomy which the Constitution of the Member State in question grants to its local and regional authorities', whilst, on the other hand, 'the requirements relating to the autonomy of the local legislator ensure that the Member States cannot hide behind their constitutional order and circumvent the prohibition on aid under Article 107 TFEU through a purely formal transfer of legislative powers'.[29]

The Advocate General rejected the Commission's suggestion that the assessment of the degree of autonomy enjoyed by a sub-national authority was to be based on its *general* freedom to determine its economic policy. She focused instead on its

[25] Joined Cases C-428/06 to C-434/06 *Unión General de Trabajadores de La Rioja (UGT-Rioja) v Juntas Generales del Territorio Histórico de Vizcaya* [2008] ECR I-6747.

[26] Cases T-211/04 and T-215/04 *Gibraltar v Commission* [2008] ECR II-3745.

[27] Opinion of AG Kokott in Joined Cases C-428/06 to C-434/06 *UGT-Rioja*, n 25 above, paras 59–60.

[28] The first sentence of Article 4 TEU as amended by the Treaty of Lisbon states: 'The Union shall respect the equality of Member States before the Treaties as well as their national identities, inherent in their fundamental structures, political and constitutional, inclusive of regional and local self-government.'

[29] Opinion of AG Kokott in Joined Cases C-428/06 to C-434/06 *UGT-Rioja*, n 25 above, para 57.

autonomy in adopting the *specific* measures in question. The Court's response was along similar lines: the fact that an authority played a fundamental role in the definition of the political and economic environment in which undertakings operated was not a precondition for autonomy, but a consequence of the autonomy that the region enjoyed from the institutional, procedural and economic point of view. The Court went on to offer some additional guidance on the second and third criteria. Procedural autonomy occurred, on the Court's view, even where a process of consultation and conciliation between the national and sub-national levels was in place, and where national authorities were required to take the State interest into account in order to respect the limits of their powers.[30]

On the economic and financial autonomy front, the Court considered whether the existence of transfers from the centre to the regions was an indication of their lack of autonomy. The Court, along with the Advocate General, held that the existence of financial transfers was not sufficient to demonstrate the absence of sufficient autonomy for the regions, given that those transfers could take place for 'reasons unconnected with the tax measures'.[31] Whether the correct reference framework was the Spanish State or, instead, the Historical Territories, it added, was a question that had to be determined not only on the basis of the three criteria outlined in *Azores*, but also, as a preliminary matter, given that financial transfers had been drawn up on the basis of a precise division of competences and on the basis of limits to the exercise of devolved powers, by examining whether the regions had overstepped their competences.

The General Court's *Gibraltar* ruling has added a further piece to this mosaic.[32] Gibraltar, an independent overseas territory of the United Kingdom, had planned to introduce a reform of its tax system consisting of a general abolition of taxation of company profits, with the exception of top-up taxes on utilities and financial services activities. The general tax system introduced would consist of a payroll tax, a business property occupation tax (BPOT) and an annual company registration fee. Liability for payroll tax together with BPOT would be capped at a maximum of 15 per cent of profits—the maximum UK corporate tax rate in place at the time was 30 per cent. The Commission found, therefore, that the reform was regionally selective since it provided for a system under which companies established in Gibraltar would be taxed, in general, at a lower rate than those in the United Kingdom.

That decision was challenged, but the General Court held that the three *Azores* criteria were satisfied. The competent Gibraltar authorities that had devised the tax reform enjoyed, from a constitutional point of view, a political and administrative status separate from that of the central government of the United Kingdom. The United Kingdom's residual power to legislate for Gibraltar and the various powers

[30] Cases C-428/06 to C-434/06 *UGT-Rioja*, n 25 above, paras 102–8.

[31] ibid para 135.

[32] Joined Cases T-211/04 and T-215/04 *Government of Gibraltar and United Kingdom v Commission* [2008] ECR II-3745; on appeal, the CJEU did not deal with regional selectivity, as it found the measures to be materially selective: Joined Cases C-106/09 P and C-107/09 P *Commission and Spain v Government of Gibraltar and United Kingdom*, judgment of 15 November 2011, not yet reported.

granted to the Governor of Gibraltar were to be interpreted as means of enabling the United Kingdom to assume its responsibilities towards the population of Gibraltar and to perform its obligations under international law, and not as allowing the United Kingdom to intervene directly on the content of individual tax measures adopted by the Gibraltar authorities, in particular since those residual powers had never been exercised in matters of taxation.

As to financial autonomy, the General Court found that none of the financing measures referred to by the Commission served to offset any financial consequences that the tax reform would entail for Gibraltar. As the Court of Justice had done in *Rioja*, the General Court made clear that the absence of offsetting mechanisms should be interpreted narrowly. The verb 'offset' used by the *Azores* ruling implied a causal link between the tax measure adopted by the infra-State body and the financial support from other regions or the central government.[33]

(3) The relevant economic space

The *Azores* jurisprudence is not without its critics, who claim that the Court may have sacrificed the objectivity of the definition of State aid and the effectiveness of State aid control on the altar of regional autonomy.[34] The focus, they argue, should be on the effects of the measure, not on the constitutional status of the authority from which it originates. Moreover, critics point out that the State aid rules are addressed to States and that the Treaty does not contemplate the existence of regional authorities.[35] Whilst it may be the case that many important powers have shifted from the national to the sub-national level, this state of affairs should find recognition in a Treaty amendment rather than through a novel approach which, in attempting to accommodate a pressing political need, may result in exonerating measures that have a potentially damaging impact on competition.

In order to evaluate this criticism, it is necessary to consider whether the presence of autonomy really does make a difference in terms of anti-competitive effects; whether, in other words, genuine autonomy rules out the existence of an impact on competition equivalent to the impact that would potentially arise from a measure enacted by a region that lacks such autonomy, or from a regionally circumscribed measure enacted by a central government. Consider the hypothetical example of a region of a Member State where nearly all the country's financial services industry is clustered. Suppose that the central government decided to confer on that region autonomous status and to provide it with tax and spend powers, and that such powers were exercised autonomously, without interference from central government. Suppose, moreover, that the region set its tax rate at a significantly lower level than the national equivalent. Imagine, also, that the region was able to rely on its

33 ibid para 106. For criticism of the General Court's *Gibraltar* ruling, see P Rossi-Maccanico, 'Gibraltar and the Unsettled Limits of Selectivity in Fiscal Aids' (2009) 1 *European State Aid Law Quarterly* 63.

34 B Kurcz, 'How Selective is Selectivity? A Few Thoughts on Regional Selectivity' (2007) 66:2 *CLJ* 313; J Winter, 'Case C-88/03, *Portuguese Republic v. Commission*' (2008) 45:1 *CMLRev* 183.

35 eg Winter, ibid.

low tax rate to draw to its jurisdiction undertakings operating in the financial sector from other countries. On the strength of this effect, the region would be able to afford the decision to set the tax rate without any transfers from central government. On the *Azores* approach, this region would be regarded as sufficiently autonomous and its corporate tax rate would not constitute State aid.

What, then, is the difference between this scenario, where the region enjoys full autonomy, and cases where such autonomy is missing? The Court's answer is that the key lies in the fact that, in the autonomy scenario, undertakings operate under a political and economic environment that is separate from the national framework. If a region exercises its fiscal powers under institutional and procedural autonomy, and does not receive cross-subsidies or transfers from the state, its decisions in the fiscal sphere only affect the infrastructure and business environment in which undertakings operate. That is because, under autonomy, a region must take political responsibility for *individual* decisions and accept the financial consequences of reductions in fiscal revenue.[36] In doing so, the region needs to devise means of absorbing the budget effects of its fiscal policy decisions. It might, for instance, reduce spending on infrastructure, or on public services. In a region that lacks autonomy, the responsibility for such decisions and/or their financial consequences may be shouldered by other regions and/or by the central government. Thus, undertakings that are subject to taxation in an autonomous region operate in a different economic environment from undertakings that live in the rest of the country: they may have lower corporate taxation but, as a result, may not benefit from the same level of public spending as occurs in other parts of the country.

The crucial assumption in *Azores* seems, therefore, to be that genuine autonomy creates a distinct *economic space*, such that the relationship in terms of economic space between an autonomous region and the Member State of which it is part is equivalent, *mutatis mutandis*, to the relationship between *different* Member States.[37] Just as the comparison between undertakings operating in different national regulatory regimes is deemed irrelevant,[38] the comparison between undertakings operating under an autonomous region and undertakings operating in other parts of the country becomes devoid of relevance. The fundamental reason behind this assumption is that a genuinely autonomous tax regime creates separate cost structures for undertakings. Moreover, the absence of cross-subsidies means that undertakings in other parts of the country are not affected by the fiscal decisions taken by the authorities in the autonomous region. Conversely, in the absence of financial autonomy, a decision taken by the regional authorities may have

[36] The point was made by the UK Government in *Azores* and referred to by the Court in Case C-88/03 *Portugal v Commission*, n 21 above, para 68.

[37] The term 'economic space' is borrowed from Andrew H Hallett and D Scott, *Scotland: A New Fiscal Settlement*, Centre for Dynamic Macroeconomic Analysis Working Paper Series, 10/09, 2010, available at <http://www.st-andrews.ac.uk/economics/CDMA/papers/wp1009.pdf> (accessed 10 February 2011). The Court uses the term 'reference framework'.

[38] Given that undertakings operating in different national regulatory regimes have to bear different regulatory costs. See Section B(1) above.

implications for undertakings located in other parts of the country (as the transfer is funded by central government).

The argument based on economic space and autonomy runs into several problems, however. The economic space in which undertakings operate does not necessarily coincide with the jurisdiction of the tax authority. Undertakings that are subject to corporation tax in one Member State are likely to operate beyond regional borders and may in fact conduct most of their business outside those borders. In the absence of adequate mechanisms to allocate profits among different corporation tax jurisdictions, it may well be that undertakings that effectively operate within the same economic space gain a competitive edge because of the autonomous status of the regions in which they are domiciled for tax purposes. Secondly, whilst the absence of financial transfers is an essential requirement for a region to be regarded as genuinely autonomous, the *UGT-Rioja* ruling makes plain that the requirement applies exclusively to the specific tax measure under consideration. Since the financial autonomy test focuses on the individual decision and on direct links between a transfer and the decision, any type of indirect compensation will fall through the net. Given that the Court does not go as far as to require comprehensive economic and financial autonomy, its test does not rule out indirect compensation mechanisms. For instance, the test does not rule out the possibility that lower taxation may in the long term lead to a budget deficit and, eventually, to a bail-out by the central government.[39] Of course, Member States may be able to eliminate *ex ante* indirect transfers or compensation mechanisms, and to introduce safeguards designed to reduce the likelihood of bail-outs.[40] But the *Azores* approach does not compel them to do so.

(4) The constitutional dimension

To this point, close analysis of the *Azores* jurisprudence has concluded that the test advanced by the Court is not as far-reaching as to exclude the risk of distortions of competition caused by regional tax measures. However, this analysis has so far neglected the constitutional dimension of this case law. The fundamental question that needs to be considered here is whether the constitutional status of regional autonomy is only relevant as an element in the selectivity test, or whether the existence of a constitutional dimension also colours the Court's approach to the problem in a more general sense.

As seen above, in *UGT-Rioja*, Advocate General Kokott expressed the view that the *Azores* ruling struck the right balance between, on the one hand, the obligation, under Article 4(2) TEU, to respect national constitutional identities and, on the

[39] Sub-national governments often act as if under a 'soft budget constraint': they are inclined to spend and/or borrow excessively and disinclined to tax at the appropriate level. See generally J Rodden, G Eskeland and J Litvack (eds), *Fiscal Decentralization and the Challenge of Hard Budget Constraints* (Cambridge, Mass./London: MIT Press, 2003). For a recent example of this phenomenon, see V Mallet and J Ford, 'Zapatero warns on regional spending' *Financial Times* (16 January 2011).

[40] For instance, by adopting similar solutions to those proposed in H Hallett and D Scott, n 37 above.

other, the principle that Member States are barred from pleading internal constitutional reasons to escape the application of EU law. The Court, whilst following the Advocate General's advice in large part, did not mention Article 4(2) TEU. This is not the first instance in which the Court has not shared an Advocate General's enthusiasm for this provision.[41] Yet, it may be wondered whether, in this particular area of EU law, the omission may actually inhibit an exhaustive justification from being provided for the significant leap away from EU law orthodoxy taken in *Azores*. In effect, the adoption of a Member State's jurisdiction as the natural reference framework for the selectivity test flows naturally from the structure of the Treaty, which assumes that regulatory or tax jurisdictions are drawn along national lines and that the relevant economic space in which undertakings operate is the national territory. In the absence of a compelling economic argument to overcome the fact that regions, as far as the definition of State aid is concerned, are irrelevant, and in the absence of reasons inherent to State aid law that justify such a move, the constitutional argument offered by Advocate General Kokott may provide the basis for a normative justification.

Arguably, only once it is accepted that EU law should be interpreted in such a way as to avoid encroaching upon national constitutional identities, does the *Azores* test acquire a coherent shape. The starting point is the tension between Article 4(2) TEU and Article 107 TFEU. A strict interpretation of the definition of State aid would prevent asymmetrically devolved regions from exercising the power to tax, or would prescribe that Member States introduce precise and detailed arrangements in order to exclude the possibility of indirect transfers or future bail-outs. The latter solution appears to be disproportionate, however—it would be extremely difficult to police, and would severely constrain the choices open to Member States in pursuing tax decentralization. The opposite solution, to give regional authorities *carte blanche* in matters of taxation, would be equally undesirable as it would present a high risk of abuse and would leave the door open to potential distortions of competition. Instead, the balance struck by the Court in *Azores* constrains Member States in order to minimize distortions and, at the same time accepts, to a certain extent, the risk that some distortions may occur. But these side effects are necessary in order to maintain the effectiveness of State aid policy, whilst showing deference towards a core feature of national constitutional identity.[42]

[41] See Opinion of AG Poiares Maduro in Case C-213/07 *Michaniki* [2008] ECR I-9999, paras 31–3. See further the Opinion of AG Ruiz-Jarabo Colomer in Case C-205/08 *Umweltanwalt von Kärnten v Kärntner Landesregierung* [2009] ECR I-11525, para 47. There are, nonetheless, a couple of instances in which the Court has referred to the provision. In Case C-473/93 *Commission v Luxembourg* [1996] ECR I-3207, the Court recognized that respect for national identity (which was, at the time, acknowledged in Article F(1) TEU) could, in principle, justify a derogation from the free movement provisions, but rejected that justification in the case at hand. And see, more recently, in relation to Article 21 TFEU, Case C-208/09 *Sayn-Wittgenstein* [2011] OJ C 63/4. The *Omega* judgment is often cited as an example of sensitivity towards domestic constitutional identity, although, interestingly, it contains no mention of Article 4(2) TEU: Case C-36/02 *Omega* [2004] ECR I-9609. For discussion, see LFM Besselink, 'National and constitutional identity before and after Lisbon' (2010) 6:3 *Utrecht Law Review* 36.

[42] LFM Besselink, ibid, believes that the obligation stemming from Article 4(2) TEU may concern the core of national constitutional identity rather than any constitutional provision.

This interpretation may appear to resonate with the arguments of a certain strand of constitutional pluralism, which holds that, in the presence of competing claims to normative authority, which are equally valid from the perspective of the legal orders from which they each emanate, the Court should explore new means of avoiding conflicts between constitutional orders.[43] Yet, whilst a loose association with the broad ideas of constitutional pluralism may be legitimate in respect of Advocate General Kokott's reasoning, the language of the Court does not lend itself to such an interpretation. Granted, the Court cannot be expected to adopt the academic vernacular of constitutional pluralism; but it can reasonably be expected to make use of existing normative tools, namely Article 4(2) TEU, in order to provide its reasoning with greater openness and coherence. There is little doubt that the avoidance of conflict with national constitutional identities ranks high among the Court's priorities. After all, the Court created, over the years and well before the explosion of interest in constitutional pluralism, a number of juridical devices designed to compose potentially conflicting EU and national claims: one need only think of the doctrine of mandatory requirements, or the creation of an EU doctrine of fundamental rights as general principles drawn from national constitutional traditions and from the ECHR. And whilst much of the constitutional pluralist's attention has been directed towards the resolution of hypothetical conflicts arising from major ruptures in constitutional dialogue between the EU and its Member States, as Davies has argued, there is much to commend to the idea that the legal reasoning employed in avoiding conflicts between constitutional systems in those day-to-day situations in which they are more likely to arise should be articulated more openly. Perhaps, as far as the *Azores* jurisprudence is concerned, Article 4(2) TEU holds the key to such openness.

C. Shifting the scope of tax competition

The shift in the definition of the relevant reference framework is predicated, as seen before, on the recognition of the autonomous region as the relevant economic space. There are important implications that turn on this new relevance of autonomous regions. For, whilst the system of State aid law prescribes a rigid separation between the prohibition of State aid and the compatibility of its justifications, such that policy considerations are expected to feature only in the latter stage, the very prohibition of State aid has nonetheless served as a powerful policy tool in the Commission's efforts to curb harmful tax competition. A redefinition of the boundaries of the concept of selectivity along regional lines carries with it, therefore, a redefinition of the space in which tax competition may take place. This section examines, first, the background to the Commission's policy on tax

[43] See in particular G Davies, *Constitutional Disagreement in Europe and the Search for Pluralism*, Eric Stein Working Paper 1/2010, 2010, available at <http://papers.ssrn.com/sol3/papers.cfm?abstract_id=1559323> (accessed 28 July 2011).

competition and the role of State aid in this connection, and then goes on to consider, second, the significance of the *Azores* case law for this policy.

The starting point in the debate on tax competition is the idea that, when economic factors are able to move across jurisdictions, decisions regarding the allocation or the level of the tax burden influence businesses' choice of location; governments therefore deliberately engage in a process of mutual rivalry aimed at attracting or retaining the establishment of business activities within their respective jurisdictions. In this light, businesses are seen as consumers to whom governments offer a choice of different combinations of tax and public goods' provision. Much as in competition among undertakings, rivalry focuses on price or on the quality of the product offered (respectively the tax system and the public goods): certain States may opt for a low-tax competitive strategy; others may decide to compete on the quality of the provision of public goods.

Different schools of thought have emerged in relation to the assessment of the impact of tax competition. One view holds that tax competition acts as a powerful and positive constraint on politicians' tendency to pursue their own self-interest by exerting a downward pressure on taxation and public spending—competition, on this view, represents a means of disciplining governments whose fiscal appetite is at odds with the general welfare of society.[44] On this view, governments' recourse to taxation is an expression of their desire to increase their own powers (the Leviathan argument) and/or of pressures from particular interest groups. Competition among governments may reduce the influence of these interests and yield outcomes that better match the preferences of those who choose a jurisdiction on the basis of the combination of the level of taxation and level of public service provision that it has to offer. Tax competition is, according to such a view, 'an objective to be sought in its own right'.[45]

Opponents of this view argue that the use of fiscal measures to influence the choice of business location creates negative cross-border externalities. Not only are governments severely limited in their powers to deploy fiscal policy to stimulate domestic growth and to pursue redistributive goals, but national electorates are also prevented from being able to exercise effective influence over their governments' fiscal policies.[46] When governments compete on corporate taxation, the argument goes, the outcome is a generalized downward pressure on corporate taxation levels (a 'race to the bottom'), even in States that would not necessarily share the same preference on the relative allocation of the tax burden as those States that initiated the 'race to the bottom'. In other words, lowering the tax burden for undertakings may not always be linked to a clear strategy aimed at attracting relocation; it may—rather—be a move dictated by necessity rather than by choice. The move may be a response to aggressive competitive strategies on the part of other States. Yet,

[44] G Brennan and JM Buchanan, *The Power to Tax: Analytical Foundations of a Fiscal Constitution* (Cambridge: Cambridge University Press, 1980) Ch 9.

[45] ibid 186.

[46] H-W Sinn, *The New Systems Competition* (Oxford: Wiley-Blackwell, 2003); F Scharpf, *Governing in Europe: Effective and Democratic?* (Oxford: Oxford University Press, 1999).

a generalized reduction in tax rates may only be sustainable if accompanied by a reallocation of the fiscal burden from mobile to less mobile economic factors.

Both of these views agree on the proposition that competition among jurisdictions leads to a 'race to the bottom'. The so-called 'new economic geography' literature questions, however, the extent and inexorability of such an effect.[47] The level of taxation, according to this literature, may not necessarily be a decisive factor in influencing location. An exodus of corporations towards a low tax jurisdiction may not be inevitable. Other factors that may be more powerful than tax rates in determining location choices ('agglomeration forces', in the language of new economic geography) may in effect have a defining impact on such decisions, as industrial activity tends to agglomerate in countries that have a widespread presence of advanced economic activity.[48] The design of corporate taxation differs accordingly: larger States with more advanced economies tend to have higher tax rates, whereas smaller States with less developed economies are more likely to gain from aggressive tax competition.[49]

There is a significant European dimension to the debate on tax competition, which raises issues that lie at the heart of European integration. A crucial feature of this debate is the link between taxation and national democratic sovereignty. The delicate nature of such a link is reflected in the unanimity requirement for legislation to be introduced in the fiscal area.[50] Although attempts to introduce harmonizing legislation in the field of direct taxation have emerged periodically, all such attempts have floundered in the absence of unanimous agreement among the Member States. In the 1990s, however, partly as a result of the growing salience of subsidiarity, the Commission changed its stance on the matter. Plans to harmonize corporate taxation were put on ice, leaving the Member States fully in control of their tax systems,[51] whilst the focus of Community intervention was placed on major distortions of competition. This proved more attractive to the Member States, given the difference in views among them as to the appropriate level and scope of intervention in the field. The increase in interdependence, amplified in the European context by the removal of obstacles to the free flow of economic factors and, in particular, by the liberalization of capital movements, coupled with the adoption of the European single currency, which eliminated monetary policy as a

[47] eg R Baldwin and P Krugman, 'Agglomeration, Integration and Tax Harmonisation' (2004) 48:1 *European Economic Review* 1.

[48] This may explain why a country such as Germany, which has one of the highest levels of corporate taxation among industrialized countries, is also very successful in attracting foreign direct investment.

[49] The examples of Ireland, the Baltic states and Cyprus appear to confirm this. However, some point out that tax is not the only factor in attracting businesses to these jurisdictions. Among the 'agglomeration factors' that have facilitated foreign direct investment in Ireland, Krugman emphasizes the high level of education of its workforce. P Krugman, 'Good News from Ireland: A Geographical Perspective' in A Gray (ed), *International Perspectives on the Irish Economy* (Dublin: Indecon, 1998).

[50] Articles 114(2) and 115 TFEU.

[51] There is, however, an important (ongoing) project to establish a Common Consolidated Corporate Tax Base (CCCTB). In 2004, the Commission set up a working group made up of national experts to formulate technical solutions to be elaborated in a directive based on Article 115 TFEU. See <http://ec.europa.eu/taxation_customs/taxation/company_tax/common_tax_base/index_en.htm>.

means of achieving comparative advantage,[52] increased the tendency of Member States to acquire or consolidate their competitive edge through taxation and exacerbated the distortions caused by these strategies.[53] In this environment, whilst some Member States (plainly, those that stood to gain from tax competition) opposed any move towards coordination in the tax area, others (those that perceived tax competition as a threat) called for decisive intervention at supranational level.[54]

The Commission's new approach, which focused on 'harmful tax competition', was therefore an attempt to mediate between apparently irreconcilable positions. In December 1997, agreement was reached in the ECOFIN Council on the three areas that the Commission had highlighted as deserving greater coordination: business taxation; withholding taxes on cross-border interest and royalty payments between companies; and taxes on savings. In the first area, the finance ministers passed a resolution in respect of a Code of Conduct on business taxation and the Commission undertook to publish guidelines on the application of State aid to business taxation.[55] In the other two areas, the Commission was asked to issue proposals for directives. The Code of Conduct on business taxation, a soft law instrument, provided for a roll-back of existing measures and a 'stand-still' commitment (a commitment, that is, to refrain from introducing any such measures in the future). Both were, of course, voluntary commitments. Subsequently, a Code of Conduct Group was established in order to identify the tax measures that may fall within the scope of the Code of Conduct for business taxation. In a report of November 1999, the Group identified 66 tax measures with harmful features.[56] Finally, in June 2003, the Council reached an agreement on adopting the Code of Conduct.[57] Alongside the adoption of the Code, the Commission undertook to publish guidelines on the application of Articles 107 to 109 TFEU to measures relating to direct business taxation and expressed commitment to 'the strict application' of the State aid rules.[58]

Interestingly, State aid became an effective means of achieving clout against the Member States in negotiations leading to the adoption of the Code of Conduct. In fact, because of the (partial) overlap between the Code and the State aid rules, the latter could be said to have achieved through legal obligation part of what was to be achieved, according to the Code of Conduct, through voluntary cooperation.[59] Moreover, the pressure exerted through the State aid investigations is widely acknowledged to have acted as a 'hard law stick' in inducing Member States to

[52] Within the 'Eurozone'.

[53] Though the constraints associated with the Stability and Growth Pact, which requires Member States to converge around criteria aimed to achieve price stability and to contain their budget deficit, also act as a brake on Member States' ambitions to pursue competitiveness through fiscal means.

[54] CM Radaelli and US Kraemer, 'Governance Areas in EU Direct Tax Policy' (2008) 46:2 *JCMS* 315.

[55] Conclusion of the ECOFIN Council Meeting Concerning Taxation Policy [1998] OJ C 2/1.

[56] 40 in EU Member States, 3 in Gibraltar and 23 in dependent or associated territories.

[57] The Code remains a soft law instrument.

[58] Code of Conduct, para J.

[59] CM Radaelli and US Kraemer, n 54 above.

reach agreement on the Code of Conduct.[60] As the Commission itself recognized in its 2004 report on State aid relating to business taxation, the application of the State aid rules in parallel with the work on the Code of Conduct had 'facilitated the conclusion of an agreement on the Code of Conduct'.[61] This relationship may be seen at play in the Commission's decision-making practice in the field of corporate taxation, which became particularly intense between 2001 and 2003, during which time investigations were launched against 15 different aid measures across 12 Member States, all of which were found to fall within Article 107(1) TFEU.[62]

Whilst some commentators have encouraged the use of State aid as a 'majoritarian' means of dealing with the lack of the necessary unanimous consensus for harmonization, others have stigmatized this practice as a form of tax harmonization by stealth.[63] A third group has questioned the effectiveness of the use of State aid as a means of dealing with harmful tax competition. The application of State aid in such a function may, they argue, turn out to be counterproductive, as it may encourage Member States to replace preferential regimes with generally applicable low tax regimes thus creating a more serious distortion than the original one.[64]

[60] The expression is used by WW Bratton and JA McCahery, 'Tax Coordination and Tax Competition in the European Union: Evaluating the Code of Conduct on Business Taxation' (2001) 38:3 *CMLRev* 677. According to Radaelli and Kraemer, 'different modes of governance have been used strategically to reinforce each other in the same governance arena. Some Member States have not liked it and argued that the Commission could not demand agreement on a soft learning process within the code and at the same time dangle the Damocles' sword of the Treaty-based State aid procedure on the recalcitrant governments. But this is precisely what the Commission's political strategy was trying to achieve.' CM Radaelli and US Kraemer, n 54 above, 328.

[61] European Commision, 'Report on the implementation of the Commission notice on the application of the state aid rules to measures relating to direct business taxation' (C(2004) 434, 9 February 2004), available at <http://ec.europa.eu/competition/state_aid/studies_reports/rapportaidesfiscales_en.pdf>.

[62] ibid.

[63] From the former camp, Scharpf argues that 'if there are good reasons to use legal, rather than political, processes for the control of State aids, these would also support the use of the same kinds of procedures for controlling the temptations of unfair regulatory competition'. FW Scharpf, 'Democratic Legitimacy under Conditions of Regulatory Competition: Why Europe Differs from the United States' in K Nicolaidis and R Howse (eds), *The Federal Vision* (Oxford: Oxford University Press, 2000) 355. From the latter camp, F Nanetti and G Mameli, 'The Creeping Normative Role of the EC Commission in the Twin-Track Struggle Against State Aids and Harmful Tax Competition' (2002) 11:4 *EC Tax Review* 185; A Fantozzi, 'The Applicability of State Aid Rules to Tax Competition Measures: A Process of *de Facto* Harmonization in the Tax Field?' in W Schön (ed), *Tax Competition in Europe* (Amsterdam: IBFD, 2003).

[64] M Keen, 'Preferential Regimes Can Make Tax Competition Less Harmful' (2001) 54:4 *National Tax Journal* 757; a similar argument is made by G Meussen, 'Fiscal Support Measures and Harmful Tax Competition' (2000) 9:3 *EC Tax Review* 152. The Irish 'manufacturing relief' scheme could be described as an example of this phenomenon. The scheme provided for a preferential corporate tax rate of 10% in favour of undertakings in the manufacturing industry in Ireland. In its infancy, the scheme was considered to be lawful: the Commission initially raised no objections to it, as it considered the measure to have a general scope and, hence, to fall outside the scope of Article 107(1) TFEU; nor did it raise any objections when, in 1990, the Irish Government notified its intention to extend this rate until 2010. It was only in 1998, in light of the events that set the Code of Conduct process in motion, that the Commission decided that the Irish manufacturing relief scheme was to be regarded as aid (albeit existing rather than new aid). Subsequently, the Commission negotiated with Ireland the phasing out of the existing scheme and its replacement with a general corporate tax with a 12.5% rate on trading

If State aid is an effective tool in the pursuit of the Commission's policy against harmful tax competition, that tool may have been blunted by the *Azores* jurisprudence. The potential effect of the *Azores* test is to shift the space for tax competition from the inter-State to the infra-State level. One may see this as a natural consequence of tax decentralization, and some may even regard this as a positive development: proponents of tax competition will argue that it leads to a more efficient allocation of business across regions; its detractors may argue, instead, that such tax competition may lead to an unequal distribution of wealth across regions and may ultimately threaten the bond of solidarity among regions. Yet, given the well-known agglomeration effects that arise where certain industries are clustered around a circumscribed geographic area, there is a real danger that regional autonomy could be used to replicate similar states of affairs to those that the Commission's application of the State aid rules had attempted to bring to an end. Instead of singling out certain economic sectors for competitive tax measures, Member States may well choose to go down the regional autonomy route to achieve the same effect. Nonetheless, the *Azores* test contains some form of safeguard against the excesses of strategic decision-making, as the requirement for regions to bear the financial consequences of their decisions in tax matters could act as a disincentive for regions to engage in aggressive competitive tactics, and should, to an extent, prevent Member States from providing regions with the funds that would allow such tactics to be exploited.

D. Conclusion

At a time when, as a consequence of the banking and/or the Eurozone crises, public finances are, in a number of Member States, under severe strain, and fiscal retrenchment is the order of the day, the debate on self-government and fiscal autonomy is necessarily coloured by the prevailing economic climate. In this state of affairs, tensions between different levels of governance are exacerbated. EU institutions are often perceived to be at odds with national democracies, as they exert a strong influence over domestic economic policy decisions, particularly in the Eurozone.[65] Moreover, indirect transfers from countries with stronger finances towards countries with weaker finances are a cause of great concern for public opinion in the former countries. Similar tensions are mirrored within individual Member States, as governments attempt to rein in public spending by exercising closer control over financial decisions taken at decentralized level.

These tensions are the result of the direct and indirect connections between different economic and political spaces. Thus, fiscal profligacy in, say, Catalonia is

income and a 25% rate on other income. See European Commission, *Proposal for appropriate measures under Article 93(1) of the EC Treaty concerning Irish corporation tax* [1998] OJ C 395/09.

[65] On which see FW Scharpf, *Monetary Union, Fiscal Crisis and the Preemption of Democracy*, LSE 'Europe in Question' Discussion Paper Series No 36/2011, 2011, available at <http://www2.lse.ac.uk/europeanInstitute/LEQS/LEQSPaper36.pdf>.

no longer exclusively a Spanish problem but, as a result of economic and monetary union, becomes a European issue. Similarly, Northern Ireland's plan to introduce a corporate tax rate to match the Republic of Ireland's rate, if it will ever materialize, is not simply a matter that concerns the United Kingdom alone, but raises issues of comparative advantage within the EU. To complicate matters further, since fiscal autonomy is often enshrined in national constitutional structures, interactions between different economic and political spaces may also be regarded as interactions between different constitutional spaces.

State aid is part of this picture. The significance of the line of case law developed since the *Azores* ruling is that it brings about a fundamental shift in the definition of the relevant economic space in State aid law from the exclusively national to the sub-national level. Yet, as this chapter has shown, that case law takes on a distinctly constitutional flavour as the internal constitutional structures of the Member States, their constitutional spaces, become integral to the State aid test where fiscal autonomy is concerned. There is no doubt that, as a matter of EU constitutional law, the internal constitutional structures of the Member States should be given due weight; yet, as this chapter has argued, a more open and explicit articulation of the role played by national constitutional identities in the Court's reasoning would help to justify an otherwise problematic jurisprudential stance.

Finally, even if the legal definition of the scope of Article 107(1) TFEU cannot explicitly take account of the Commission's commitment to preventing harmful tax competition, the effect of the case law on this issue is to frame the scope of tax competition within the EU and within the Member States. Plainly, if the scope of Article 107(1) TFEU permits different corporate tax regimes to co-exist within individual Member States, the potential for arbitrage increases. The *Azores* test, the rationale of which is to ensure that decentralized corporate tax regimes are grounded in local economic realities and are not merely a means of circumventing the State aid provisions, is—arguably—not watertight. It is not unthinkable that Member States, in their efforts to operate aggressive tax competition strategies, effect, without falling foul of the State aid provisions, indirect transfers in the direction of decentralized governments so as to compensate for lower tax rates. Perhaps this is the price to be paid for the recognition of the fact that even this segment of the EU's economic law does not exist in a constitutional vacuum.

13

Member State Nationalities and the Internal Market: Illusions and Reality

*Dimitry Kochenov**

A. Introduction

The breadth of Professor Usher's scholarship is overwhelming, dealing with virtually all the key issues of internal market regulation, including the profound constitutional questions arising in the course of the development of the European integration project. He conceived of the internal market in the broadest possible sense, addressing economic regulation in the context of other, at times competing, objectives of the Treaties, as well as highlighting some unexpected consequences of the economic project's development. Such an approach, marked by not shying away from complexity and viewing economic integration in its broader socio-constitutional context, is increasingly being adopted by the leading scholars of European integration. Building on this tradition, this chapter aims to look behind the façade of the internal market and even the Treaties themselves in an attempt to discover important unforeseen consequences that the articulation of the internal market had for the Member States on the constitutional scale. Relying on the mutation of Member States' laws on nationality as an example, it is demonstrated that the move from a single market to an economic union has been accompanied by some fundamental mutations at the Member State level which would not necessarily be connected to economic regulation at first glance, showing how far beyond the objectives stated in the Treaties the deeper consequences of economic integration actually stretch, and discovering constitutional questions raised by the internal market on a plane far removed from economic regulation *sensu stricto*.

That the European integration project would affect all spheres of the law of the Member States could be anticipated from the very beginning. All the history of

* University of Groningen. A draft of the argument presented in this chapter first appeared as part of a longer Working Paper of the European University Institute in Florence, *Rounding up the Circle*, RSCAS 2010/23, available at <http://eudo-citizenship.eu/docs/RSCAS_2010_23.pdf>. The final draft was presented in its present form at the W.G. Hart Workshop of the Institute of Advanced Legal Studies, School of Advanced Study, University of London in June 2011. I am grateful to Niamh Nic Shuibhne and Rainer Bauböck for helpful suggestions. The assistance of Martijn van den Brink is kindly acknowledged.

European integration can in fact be read as a constant restatement by the Court of Justice of the European Union (ECJ) of a simple fact that domains exclusively reserved for the Member States to regulate are unknown to EU law: any situation is potentially covered by EU rules.[1] Although this finding is certainly not surprising, it has a consequence that might seem unexpected to some.[2] Namely that those fields of national law which are not in any way covered by the *acquis* and lie outside the scope of EU competences are nonetheless bound to be adapted to the realities of the internal market.[3] In the context of such adaptation, it is of no relevance whether the Union has competence in the related fields or not: required by the basic considerations of mere coherence and functionality of the law, if the EU is powerless, such adaptation will stem from the Member States' own initiative.

This contribution focuses on the analysis of an adaptation that is taking place in the field of nationality law in the Member States[4] under the influence of the internal market in unison with the maturing of EU citizenship.[5] Analysis of the law of the Member States demonstrates that it is already possible to decipher a trend in the accommodation of Member States' nationalities to the new reality, which is likely to have far-reaching consequences for the very essence of the concept of nationality itself, as well as, potentially, having the ability to affect the core relationship between statehood, sovereignty and nationality through a profound reinterpretation of the notion of the 'people' of each Member State.

Such adaptation, this chapter argues, takes place on two levels: formal and informal. The formal level represents amendments of nationality laws which can

[1] A von Bogdandy and J Bast, 'The European Union's Vertical Order of Competences: The Current Law and Proposals for Reform' (2002) 39:2 *CMLRev* 227. See further E Spaventa, 'Seeing the Wood despite the Trees? On the Scope of Union Citizenship and its Constitutional Effects' (2008) 45:1 *CMLRev* 13; D Kochenov, 'Citizenship without Respect: The EU's Troubled Equality Ideal' (2010) Jean Monnet Working Paper No 08/10, NYU Law School, available at <http://centers.law.nyu.edu/jeanmonnet/papers/10/100801.pdf>.

[2] See, eg, HU Jessurun d'Oliveira, 'Ontkoppeling van nationaliteit en Unieburgerschap?' (2010) 85:16 *NJb* 1028; HU Jessurun d'Oliveira, 'Nationaliteit en de Europese Unie' in JDM Steenbergen (ed), *Ongebogen recht: Opstellen aangeboden aan Prof. Dr. H. Meijers* (The Hague: Jongbloed, 1998) 80–1, arguing for reserved domains shielded from the effects of EU law.

[3] Article 26(2) TFEU.

[4] It is surprising that this important topic has never enjoyed sufficient scholarly attention. For one of the best early contributions, see A Evans, 'Nationality Law and European Integration' (1991) 16 *ELRev* 190. See further G-R de Groot, 'The Relationship between Nationality Legislation of the Member States of the European Union and European Citizenship' in M la Torre (ed), *European Citizenship: An Institutional Challenge* (The Hague: Kluwer Law International, 1998) 115; G-R de Groot, 'Towards a European Nationality Law' (2004) 8:3 *Electronic J Comp L* (pagination not available); K Rostek and G Davies, 'The Impact of Union Citizenship on National Citizenship Policies' (2007) 22 *Tul. Eur. & Civ L.F.* 89.

[5] In fact, it seems somewhat half-hearted to divide the two: EU citizenship has been profoundly affected by the internal market since its inception and still remains, to a large extent, a market citizenship: N Nic Shuibhne, 'The Resilience of EU Market Citizenship' (2010) 47:6 *CMLRev* 1597. In fact, successful EU integration clearly presupposes, to agree with Poiares Maduro, the need 'to reconcile the principle of respect for state competences and the safeguarding of the objective of establishing an internal market in which the rights of citizens are protected': Opinion of AG Poiares Maduro in Case C-446/03 *Marks & Spenser plc v Halsley (Her Majesty's Inspector of Taxes)* [2005] ECR I-10837, para 37. In this context, EU citizenship and the internal market are two sides of the same coin.

be clearly linked to the European integration project, while the informal reflects the *de facto* influence of European integration on the essence of nationality of the Member States, which does not necessarily find direct reflection in nationality laws.[6] This chapter argues that the nationalities of EU Member States are affected beyond adaptation to the technicalities of the European integration project, as their very essence necessarily undergoes a profound transformation, shaping a distinct legal reality which is different from that of non EU countries. This is thus just one more in an array of examples of how the European integration project, mostly through its citizenship and the internal market, affects the essence of the State in Europe in ways not necessarily envisaged by those who drafted the Treaties.[7]

This contribution is structured as follows. After a brief overview of the trend in the development of Member States' nationality laws under the influence of the internal market, which this chapter deciphers (Section B), the meaning of Member State nationalities is analysed in terms of shaping the legal environment in which the lives of those in possession of this status are lived, comparing Member State nationalities with EU citizenship: two different legal statuses conferred simultaneously on the same people (Section C). The argument then proceeds towards a brief assessment of the formal and informal levels of adaptation, outlined through the influence of EU citizenship and the internal market on the nationality laws of the Member States. The gradual revision of the legal essence of nationalities, which is a natural immediate consequence of the process of maturation of the economic union in Europe as well as EU citizenship, provides a new context for the assessment of the viability of the current rules making the enjoyment of the status of EU citizenship derivative from the nationalities of the Member States (Section D). The last section focuses on the positive and negative sides of this arrangement for the citizens themselves, as well as the likely impact of EU integration on Member State nationalities in the near- to mid-term future (Section E). The conclusion sketches some wider implications of the new trend in the regulation of nationalities by the Member States in the context of EU integration for the essence of statehood and sovereignty in Europe. The profound nature of the indirect effects of the internal market is highlighted, opening up a possibility to approach the EU from a new angle: that of necessary adaptation of national law to the new reality shaped by a maturing project of European integration in all fields of

[6] The realization of the profound influence of the internal market on the nationalities of the Member States considerably pre-dates the introduction of EU citizenship: G Cansacchi, 'La cittadinanza comunitaria e i diritti fondamentali dell'uomo' in AM Calamia (ed), *Studi in onore di G. Sperduti*, (Milano: Gioffrè, 1984) 435; AC Evans, 'European Citizenship' (1982) 45:5 *MLR* 497; G van den Berghe and CH Huber, 'European Citizenship' in R Bieber and D Nickel (eds), *Das Europa der zweiten Generation: Gedächtnisschrift für Christoph Sasse*, Vol II (Kehl am Rhein: N.P. Engel Verlag, 1981) 755; M Sica, *Verso la cittadinanza europea* (Florence: Le Monnier, 1979); R Plender, 'An Incipient Form of European Citizenship' in FG Jacobs (ed), *European Law and the Individual* (Amsterdam: North Holland Publishing, 1979) 39; Lord Mackenzie Stuart, 'Recent Trends in the Decisions of the European Court: Towards the Creation of a Community Citizenship' (1976) 21 *J L Soc Scotland* 40.

[7] See, for different aspects of this relationship, G Davies, 'The Humiliation of the State as a Constitutional Tactic' in F Amtenbrink and P van den Berg (eds), *The Constitutional Integrity of the European Union* (The Hague: T.M.C. Asser Press, 2010) 147.

national law, with no regard to the formal division of competences between the EU and the Member States and the presence or absence of the legal pressure from the EU side. Rather, the internal market shapes its own environment.

B. Member State nationalities and the internal market: the trend

The successful development of the internal market was bound to diminish the legal effects of particular Member States' nationalities due to four key factors, all striking at the core of the essence of nationality: EU law prohibits the Member States from favouring their own nationals in a growing array of situations; it seriously limits any discretion enjoyed by the Member States not to admit foreigners who are EU citizens or to deport them; it severely restricts the Member States' ability to impose specific duties of nationality by providing for a simple escape route for evading such duties through free movement; and it makes it impossible for the Member States to claim that equality among their citizens is safeguarded, since the situation of some, but not all, of them is covered by EU law.[8] Member States are thus severely limited in what they can and cannot do: their nationality now comes with virtually no 'bonus' and is just as good as any other EU nationality. This is an important part of what Davies characterized as 'humiliation of the State',[9] when describing the constitutional essence of the Union. Importantly, such 'humiliation' is not a specific consequence of the introduction of EU citizenship or any other particular development of the *acquis*: it flows directly from the very essence of the Union rooted in the internal market, where internal borders are abolished and discrimination on the basis of nationality is outlawed.

Humiliating the State is not necessarily a bad thing, as it can simultaneously empower individuals in their quest for better lives.[10] So, on the positive side of the same coin, European citizens residing in a Member State other than their Member State of nationality are not simply 'foreigners'.[11] The ECJ, acting together with other institutions of the Union, shaped a legal reality where citizenship of the EU

[8] See Section C below.

[9] G Davies, n 7 above.

[10] But see JHH Weiler, 'Europa: "Nous coalisons des Etats nous n'unissons pas des hommes"' in M Cartabia and A Simoncini (eds), *La Sostenibilità della democrazia nel XXI secolo* (Bologna: Il Mulino, 2009) 51.

[11] EU law thus questions the foreigner–citizen dichotomy: the lines between 'us' and 'them' are necessarily blurred in the borderless internal market. This blurring of the lines of belonging is not unique to the EU, however, and is a general trend, observable in a number of jurisdictions around the world: T Brøndsted Sejersen, '"I Vow to Thee My Countries"—The Expansion of Dual Citizenship in the 21st Century' (2008) 42:3 *Int'l Migration Rev* 523, 524. The signs of this erosion are not only seen in the equality of legally resident foreigners with citizens in the majority of spheres ranging from non-discrimination at work to social security. Recent decisions of international tribunals have also demonstrated that the international human rights protection regime can stand in the way of the use by states of the previously unconditional right to deport an alien. See, eg, *Beldjoudi v France* (App no 12083/86) ECHR 26 March 1992; *Stewart v Canada*, UN Doc CCPR/C/58D/538/1993. See further D Kochenov, '*Ius Tractum* of Many Faces: European Citizenship and the Difficult Relation Between Status and Rights' (2009) 15:2 *CJEL* 169, 175–81; L Bosniak, 'Citizenship Denationalized' (2000) 7 *Ind J Global Legal Stud* 447.

acquired clear and identifiable scope and a direct ability to influence the rights of those in possession of this status, enlarging their horizon of opportunities.[12] To pretend that EU citizens are not, potentially at least, quasi-nationals of any of the Member States where they choose to reside[13] would amount to closing one's eyes to the current level of development of EU law.

Consequently, although acquisition and loss of nationality are not among the issues which the Union is empowered to regulate,[14] the very functioning of the internal market amplified by the notion of EU citizenship makes the retention of the pre-existing modes of regulation of such *de jure* extra-*acquis* issues by the Member States unsustainable. The internal market and EU citizenship work together to transform the nationality policies of the Member States, not by empowering the Union to act in the field of the conferral of nationalities by the Member States[15]—even though there are some limitations here, too, on what the Member States can do[16]—but simply by bringing a profound change to the whole meaning of Member States' nationalities in contemporary Europe through the four avenues outlined above.

It has taken the Member States a long time to wake up to the realization of this state of affairs. However, their reaction to recent developments, which put their nationalities into the broader context of the internal market, EU citizenship and the territory of the Union,[17] is already clearly decipherable, forming a trend to treat EU citizens and third country nationals differently also in the context of acquisition and loss of nationality, thus providing for a *de jure* recognition of the reality affecting Member States' nationalities *de facto* for quite a while.

[12] For a very informative analysis of this process, see D Kostakopoulou, 'Ideas, Norms and European Citizenship: Explaining Institutional Change' (2005) 68:i *MLR* 233, 244–61. See further F Wollenschläger, 'A New Fundamental Freedom beyond Market Integration' (2011) 17 *ELJ* 1; MJ Elsmore and P Starup, 'Union Citizenship—Background, Jurisprudence, and Perspective: The Past, Present, and Future of Law and Policy' (2007) 26:1 *YEL* 57; FG Jacobs, 'Citizenship of the European Union—A Legal Analysis' (2007) 13 *ELJ* 591; W Maas, *Creating European Citizens* (Lanham and Plymouth: Rowman and Littlefield, 2007).

[13] This notwithstanding the limitations in secondary law, discussed briefly in Section C below.

[14] eg Opinion of AG Poiares Maduro in Case C-135/08 *Janko Rottmann v Freistaat Bayern* [2010] ECR I-1449, para 17: 'the determination of conditions for the acquisition and loss of nationality,—and therefore of Union citizenship—, falls within the exclusive competence of the Member States' (see too the references cited therein). This notwithstanding the famous obiter dictum in *Micheletti* that decisions on nationality should be taken by the Member States with 'due regard of Community law'. Case C-369/90 *Mario Vicente Micheletti et al v Delegación del Gobierno en Cantabria* [1992] ECR I-4239, para 10.

[15] In practice, the Union took part in the framing of state nationality laws on several occasions, all during the pre-accession process, when dealing with the Member States-to-be. For analysis, see D Kochenov, 'Pre-accession, Naturalization, and "Due Regard to Community Law": The European Union's "Steering" of Citizenship Policies in Candidate Countries during the Fifth Enlargement' (2004) 4:2 *Romanian J Pol Sci* 71.

[16] As expressed by the ECJ in *Rottmann* and *Micheletti*, for instance: Case C-369/90 *Micheletti*, n 14 above; Case C-135/08 *Rottmann*, n 14 above. See further D Kochenov, 'Annotation of Case C-135/08 *Rottmann*' (2010) 47:6 *CMLRev* 1831; S Hall, 'Loss of Union Citizenship in Breach of Fundamental Rights' (1996) 21 *ELRev* 129.

[17] Case C-34/09 *Gerardo Ruiz Zambrano v Office national de l'emploi* [2011] OJ C 130/2, para 44. For analysis, see D Kochenov, 'A Real European Citizenship: A New Jurisdiction Test: A Novel Chapter in the Development of the Union in Europe' (2011) 18 *CJEL* 56.

Already, six Member States—Austria, Germany, Hungary, Italy, Romania and Slovenia—formally differentiate between EU citizens and third country nationals in their naturalization procedures and these differences are certainly not minor. In Italy, to take one example, the length of minimal legal residence in order to qualify for naturalization is drastically different for the two categories in question: while EU citizens become naturalized in four years, third country nationals have to wait six (!) years longer.[18] In the near future, the number of Member States introducing such differences, as well as the reach of the differences themselves, is likely to proliferate. This prediction simply reflects the existing reality on the ground and amplifies the importance of EU citizenship, which is now capable of providing the holder with easy access to the nationalities of other EU Member States even at the formal level of the naturalization procedure: not only by providing virtually unlimited access to residence,[19] thus infinitely simplifying the meeting of any standard naturalization requirements too.

Ultimately, the establishment of diverging naturalization requirements for EU citizens in the new Member States of residence, compared with third country nationals, means that a distinction is made between the acquisition of EU citizenship (necessarily coupled with a Member State's nationality) and merely the acquisition of another Member State nationality. This is a fundamental development. It is bound to have far-reaching consequences for the legal essence of both legal statuses. In other words: although the Treaties do not empower the Union to regulate the nationality law of the Member States, the influence of the European integration project is such that the Member States are bound to adapt their nationality legislation to the changing reality. That this process is not formally initiated by the EU changes little: the internal market, which removed borders and outlawed nationality discrimination, having also supplied the general context where EU law takes precedence vis-à-vis national rules, is responsible for a tectonic shift in the understanding of the whole context in which nationalities operate, as well as of the whole context of what they do (and do not do). Responding to this change is not a luxury, but a pure necessity; and all the Member States are expected to follow the six front-runners sooner rather than later.

The situation of EU citizens and third country nationals in any Member State is categorically different,[20] permitting us to speak of an 'unfulfilled promise of

[18] Legge N. 91/1992; G Zincone and M Basili, *Country Report: Italy*, 2010, EUDO EUI RSCAS Paper, available at <http://eudo-citizenship.eu/docs/CountryReports/Italy.pdf>, 13.

[19] To say nothing about access to the majority of rights which were previously exclusively associated with nationality.

[20] The EU and the Member States announced on a number of occasions that this difference is bound to be reduced, with third country nationals gradually coming to be treated as EU citizens. However, as Directive 2003/109/EC of 25 November 2003 concerning the status of third-country nationals who are long-term residents [2004] OJ L 16/44 overwhelmingly demonstrates, the differences are there to stay. For an assessment of the legal position of third country nationals in the EU see, eg, D Kochenov, n 11 above, 225–9; M Hedemann-Robinson, 'An Overview of Recent Legal Developments at Community Level in Relation to Third country Nationals Resident within the European Union, with Particular Reference to the Case-law of the European Court of Justice' (2001) 38:3 *CMLRev* 525; H Staples, *The Legal Status of Third-country Nationals Resident in the European Union* (The Hague: Kluwer Law International, 1999); I Ward, 'Law and the Other Europeans' (1997)

European citizenship'.[21] Naturalization in the Member State of residence is already far less important for EU citizens than for third country nationals. This is so since a number of key rights formerly associated with state nationality are granted to EU citizens directly by the EU legal order and do not depend per se on the law of the new Member State of residence. Among these are virtually unconditional rights of entry, residence, taking up of employment and, crucially, non-discrimination on the basis of nationality.[22] It is evidently so that less is left for Member States' nationalities in terms of the ability to generate unique legal consequences that would not be matched by those attached to any other legal status for their bearers. An oft-cited phrase coined by Davies attributes to Article 18 TFEU the abolition of the nationalities of the Member States.[23] In the context of the completion of the internal market, it seems that it is not a Member State nationality, but EU citizenship, which provides Europeans with the most considerable array of rights, as long as, by virtue of this status, rights in 27 States instead of only onc arc guaranteed and any discrimination on the basis of nationality is prohibited.

These developments, which are supported by the ECJ case law on the free movement of persons and EU citizenship, are bound to have two main consequences. The first is the further widening of the gap between EU citizens and third country nationals in the EU. The second is the obvious need to adapt the Member States' nationalities to the new reality, constructing legal statuses more aware of their limitations. The diminishing in importance of the nationalities of the Member States as legally meaningful statuses naturally reaffirms the rise of EU citizenship to the most prominent regulatory source for the rights of EU citizens.

C. Member States' nationalities: the legal essence in the EU context

At present, European citizenship in the context of the internal market grants individuals in possession of this status a constantly growing number of rights, the majority of which were previously associated with state nationalities only. These rights touch upon the core understanding of nationality, moving a number of areas of regulation previously considered as belonging to vital components of national sovereignty away from the jurisdiction of the Member States, handing them over to the EU.

35:1 *JCMS* 79; S Peers, 'Towards Equality: Actual and Potential Rights of Third-Country Nationals in the European Union' (1996) 33:1 *CMLRev* 8.

[21] W Maas, 'Migrants, States, and EU Citizenship's Unfulfilled Promise' (2008) 12:6 *Citizenship Stud* 583.

[22] For critical analysis, see D Kochenov, n 11 above, 206 (and the literature cited therein). See further N Nic Shuibhne, 'Derogating from the Free Movement of Persons: When Can EU Citizens Be Deported?' (2006) 8 *Cam. YB Eur. L.* 187.

[23] G Davies, '"Any Place I Hang My Hat?" or: Residence is the New Nationality' (2005) 11:1 *ELJ* 43, 55. A Evans, n 4 above, 195 put it slightly differently: 'possession of the nationality of one Member State rather than that of another loses all real significance'.

These rights include, first, the right to enter state territory and the right to remain, accompanied by the right to work, open a business, and bring your family, of any nationality, with you.[24] Another, equally important, right concerns non-discrimination on the basis of nationality within the material scope of application of EU law, established by *lex generalis* Article 18 TFEU and a number of *lex specialis* provisions.[25] Just as in the previous example, a classical understanding of nationality would make these rights available uniquely to the home state nationals.[26] Article 22 TFEU establishes the application of the logic of non-discrimination on the basis of nationality also within the sphere of political participation rights, providing for rights to vote and run for office for all EU citizens legally resident in the Member States other than their own on an equal basis with locals.[27] Two levels of political representation are covered: local elections[28] and European Parliament elections.[29] The national, most important, level of political representation is a glaring omission in this context.[30]

[24] Case C-127/08 *Metock v Minister for Justice, Equality and Law Reform* [2008] ECR I-6241. For a very concise overview, see D Kochenov, n 11 above, 194–7 (and the literature cited therein). For a recent important development, see Case C-34/09 *Ruiz Zambrano*, n 17 above (on the right of third country nationals to stay in the country of EU nationality of their minor children under EU law). For analysis, see D Kochenov, n 17 above; P Van Elsuwege, 'Shifting Boundaries? European Union Citizenship and the Scope of Application of EU Law' (2011) 38:3 *LIEI* 263; P Van Elsuwege and D Kochenov, 'On the Limits of Judicial Intervention: EU Citizenship and Family Reunification Rights' (2011) 13 *Eur. J. Migr. & L.* 443.

[25] eg Article 45 TFEU, Article 49 TFEU. For assessment, see, eg, G Davies, *Nationality Discrimination in the European Internal Market* (The Hague: Kluwer Law International, 2003).

[26] In line with the traditionalist reading of the scope of EU law entitlements, the ECJ refuses to apply Article 18 TFEU to third country nationals notwithstanding the non-restrictive wording of the provision. For criticism, see D Kochenov, n 11 above, 206–9; P Boeles, 'Europese burgers en derdelanders: Wat betekent het verbod van discriminatie naar nationaliteit sinds Amsterdam?' (2005) 53 *SEW* 502; A Epiney, 'The Scope of Article 12 EC: Some Remarks on the Influence of European Citizenship' (2007) 13:5 *ELJ* 611, esp n 4, 612, listing the recent case law of the ECJ most relevant for the interpretation of Article 18 TFEU. See further C Hublet, 'The Scope of Article 12 of the Treaty of the European Communities *vis-à-vis* Third-Country Nationals: Evolution at Last?' (2009) 15:6 *ELJ* 757.

[27] J Shaw, *The Transformation of Citizenship in the European Union* (Cambridge: Cambridge University Press, 2007). See further D Kochenov, n 11 above, 197–205; G Zincone and S Ardovino, 'I diritti elettorali dei migranti nello spazio politico e giuridico europeo' (2004) 5 *Le istituzioni del federalismo* 741; S Day and J Shaw, 'European Union Electoral Rights and the Political Participation of Migrants in Host Policies' (2002) 8:2 *Int J Popul Geogr* 183.

[28] Article 22(1) TFEU; Council Directive (EC) 94/80 of 19 December 1994 laying down detailed arrangements for the exercise of the right to vote and to stand as a candidate in municipal elections by citizens of the Union residing in a Member State of which they are not nationals [1994] OJ L 368/38, as amended. Analysed by J Shaw, n 27 above, 142–53.

[29] Council Directive (EC) 93/109 of 6 December 1993 laying down detailed arrangements for the exercise of the right to vote and stand as a candidate in elections to the European Parliament for citizens of the Union residing in a Member State of which they are not nationals [1993] OJ L 329/34.

[30] For analysis, see D Kochenov, 'Free Movement and Participation in the Parliamentary Elections in the Member State of Nationality: An Ignored Link?' (2009) 16 *MJ* 197. A Evans, n 4 above, 194 has rightly underlined that this state of affairs is not entirely logical, as the national-level elections are the most consequential also for the EU legal order, affecting the formation of the Council.

The possible limitations of the rights mentioned above are interpreted by the ECJ very narrowly.[31] Practically speaking, the Member States are not given any possibility to abuse the grounds for derogations provided for in the Treaty.[32] Moreover, even in the situations where the Member States do not rely on derogations, the possibility to undermine the rights of EU citizens is minimized by the ECJ.[33] The Court made it clear that Article 21 TFEU, granting EU citizens a general free movement right, although allowing for derogations,[34] cannot give rise to secondary legislation which would, if applied strictly, undermine the provision itself.[35] In practice, it means that the Court is bound to interpret the relevant secondary law[36] constantly keeping in mind the principles established by Part II TFEU dealing with European citizenship. This approach has resulted in the substantial growth in importance of the status of EU citizenship[37] and limited the Member States' ability to act in cases where they seemingly just 'enforce the law'.[38] Consequently, EU citizens cannot be automatically deported from their new Member State of residence on failing to demonstrate compliance with the provisions of secondary law;[39] the requirement to have sufficient resources is interpreted in such a way that the Member States are not permitted actually to check how much money EU citizens have;[40] and permanent banishment of an EU citizen from a particular Member State is prohibited.[41] What is even more important, once residence in a new Member State is established,[42] is that non-discrimination on the

[31] eg Joined Cases C-482 and 493/01 *Georgios Orfanopoulos et al and Raffaele Oliveri v Land Baden-Württemberg* [2004] ECR I-5257; Case 149/79 *Commission v Belgium* [1981] ECR 3881.

[32] Articles 45(3) and (4), 52(1) and 62 TFEU, and the relevant secondary law. Among the grounds are public policy, security, health and employment in the public sphere.

[33] For a detailed analysis of the recent case law see, eg, D Kochenov, n 17 above.

[34] Article 20(1) TFEU. For an assessment of the clause of Article 20 TFEU that allows for the limitations of the right, see G Davies, n 25 above, 188.

[35] eg Case C-456/02 *Michel Trojani v Centre publique de l'aide sociale de Bruxelles (CPAS)* [2004] ECR I-7573; Case C-209/03 *R. (on the application of Danny Bidar) v London Borough of Ealing, Secretary of State for Education and Skills* [2005] ECR I-2119; Case C-413/99 *Baumbast and R.* [2002] ECR I-7091; Case C-184/99 *Rudy Grzelczyk v le Centre public d'aide sociale d'Ottignies-Louvain-la-Neuve* [2001] ECR I-6193. See further inter alia S Gastaldi, 'L'égalité de traitement au service de la citoyenneté européenne' in C Chappuis, B Foëx and T Kadner Graziano (eds), *L'harmonisation internationale du droit* (Zürich: Schulthess, 2007) 326, 342–4.

[36] Especially Council Directive (EC) 2004/38 of 29 April 2004 on the right of citizens of the Union and their family members to move and reside freely within the territory of the Member States [2004] OJ L 158/77.

[37] FG Jacobs, n 12 above; MJ Elsmore and P Starup, n 12 above; J Kokott, 'EU Citizenship—*citoyens sans frontières*?' Durham European Law Lecture 2005, available at <http://www.dur.ac.uk/resources/deli/annuallecture/2005 _DELI_Lecture.pdf>.

[38] As happened in *Bidar*, for instance: Case C-209/03 *Bidar*, n 35 above. This consideration also holds when no discrimination on the basis of nationality can be observed: eg Case C-353/06 *Stefan Grunkin and Dorothee Regina Paul* [2009] ECR I-7639.

[39] Case 149/79 *Commission v Belgium*, n 31 above, para 72; N Nic Shuibhne, n 22 above.

[40] Directive 2004/38, n 36 above, Article 8(4); Case 149/79 *Commission v Belgium*, n 31 above.

[41] Case C-348/96 *Criminal proceedings against Donatella Calfa* [1999] ECR I-11. Obviously, it would have been a clear violation of Article 18 TFEU to allow the banishment, as States are not free to banish their own citizens from their territory.

[42] To which end a residence permit is issued, which is not strictly necessary as the right emerges from the Treaties directly: Case 157/79 *R. v Stanislaus Pieck [1980] ECR 2171*; Joined Cases 389 and 390/87 *G.B.C. Echternach and A. Moritz v Minister van Onderwijs en Wetenschappen* [1990] ECR 723.

basis of nationality applies to EU citizens even in cases where they objectively fail to meet the minimum requirements of secondary law necessary to establish residence at the moment of the dispute.[43]

The pro-citizenship position embraced by the Court ensures that the Member States are not able, legally,[44] to deprive EU citizens of their rights using either Treaty derogations or 'strict application' of secondary EU law as a pretext. The EU citizenship status can also be used against one's own Member State of nationality as the introduction of obstacles to the free movement of persons, even non-discriminatory ones, is prohibited in EU law.[45] A similar prohibition also extends to national regulation capable of making the use of EU citizenship rights difficult or impossible.[46] This recent development has profound implications for the scope of EU law,[47] as the array of situations where EU law potentially applies thereby grows exponentially.

All of this has deprived the Member States of the ability to decide who will reside and work in their territory, who needs to be sent away, and—probably harder to swallow for some—means that they find themselves in a situation where privileging their own nationals vis-à-vis other EU citizens is illegal.

Moreover, as far as 'duties of nationality' are concerned, Member States are powerless in front of the EU, as virtually any duties they might wish to attach to their nationalities are by definition unable to undermine EU citizens' ability to make use of the fundamental freedoms associated with the internal market: EU law prevails, in its sphere of competence, above national law. Since Member States cannot attach duties to their nationalities by way of applying EU law, whatever citizenship duties they invent, the application of such duties is not absolute any more. This diminishes the States' grip on their own nationals even further. Practically speaking, it means that any Greek not willing to serve in the army (which is one of the duties of male Greek nationals) should simply move to a different Member State, using EU citizenship rights.[48] The same applies to a Belgian not willing to vote (voting is a citizenship duty in that State). EU citizens

[43] eg Case C-456/02 *Trojani*, n 35 above. The Court underlined that to rely on Article 12 EC [18 TFEU], a residence permit is enough (para 43).

[44] The Member States sometimes deviate from the norms of the law. See, eg, European Roma Rights Centre, *Security a la Italiana: Fingerprinting, Extreme Violence and Harassment of Roma in Italy*, ERRC, Budapest 2008), available at <http://www.errc.org/db/03/4D/m0000034D.pdf>.

[45] Case C-192/05 *K. Tas-Hagen en R.A. Tas v Raadskamer WUBO van de Pensioen- en Uitkeringsraad* [2006] ECR I-10451. Besides, turning EU citizenship against your Member State of nationality is also possible for EU citizens falling within the scope of EU law: Case C-224/98 *Marie-Nathalie D'Hoop v Office national d'emploi* [2002] ECR I-1691; Case C-353/06 *Grunkin and Paul*, n 38 above.

[46] Case C-34/09 *Ruiz Zambrano*, n 17 above. P Van Elsuwege, n 24 above; D Kochenov, n 17 above. See further in this context, Ankersmit and Geursen, who draw an interesting parallel between the recent citizenship case law and the principles of equivalence and effectiveness governing the Member States' procedural autonomy: L Ankersmit and W Geursen, '*Ruiz Zambrano*: De interne situatie voobij' (2011) 4 *Asiel en migrantenrecht* 156.

[47] P Van Elsuwege, n 24 above; D Kochenov, n 17 above; K Hailbronner and D Thym, 'Annotation of Case C-34/09 *Ruiz Zambrano*' (2011) 48:4 *CMLRev* 1253.

[48] For indirect confirmation, see Case C-376/89 *Panagiotis Giagounidis v Stadt Reutlingen* [1991] ECR I-1069.

falling within the scope of EU law are thus protected by the EU from the irrational demands of their Member States, sold by the official propaganda as sacred attributes of nationality.[49] Consequently, an answer to the question 'what will happen if allegiance to the Union comes into conflict with allegiance to our country?', once raised in the House of Lords,[50] is clear.

All of these developments notwithstanding, to pretend that Member State nationalities are legally meaningless would be unwise. Besides opening the way to the status of EU citizenship in the first place, the possession of a particular Member State's nationality has positive legal consequences for European citizens in three main cases. First, and most importantly, it brings an entitlement to vote and stand for election at the national level of political representation. Secondly, it enables qualification for certain jobs in public service[51] in derogation from the non-discrimination principle of Article 45 TFEU.[52] Thirdly, the nationality of a particular Member State theoretically provides the owner of this status with unconditional access to the territory of the Member State in question.[53] Note moreover that this list only concerns the legal attributes of nationality and does not touch upon the sociologically important factors, such as 'the feeling of belonging',[54] which can have implications for the functioning of democracy.[55]

There is also a possible negative side to possessing a particular Member State's nationality. This paradoxical situation is a direct consequence of one of the main functions of Member State nationality in EU law: Member State nationality has a potential to activate reverse discrimination.[56] Only those in possession of the

[49] D Kochenov, n 11 above, 215.

[50] As reported by W Maas, n 12 above, 58.

[51] Article 45 (4) TFEU. The ECJ interprets this derogation narrowly, meaning that the majority of jobs in the state administration at different levels are not reserved to EU citizens possessing particular nationalities. See, eg, Case 149/79 *Commission v Belgium* [1980] ECR 3881 (interim judgment) and [1982] ECR 1845; Case C-473/93 *Commission v Luxembourg* [1996] ECR I-3207; Case C-173/94 *Commission v Belgium* [1996] ECR I-3265; Case C-290/94 *Commission v Greece* [1996] ECR I-3285; Case 307/84 *Commission v France* [1986] ECR 1725; Case 225/85 *Commission v Italy* [1987] ECR 2625. For analysis, see N Beenen, *Citizenship, Nationality and Access to Public Service Employment* (Groningen: Europa Law, 2001).

[52] Article 45(2) TFEU.

[53] This is so since the Member States cannot apply TFEU derogations referring to public health, security and policy to their own citizens exercising free movement rights. The ECJ clarified that own nationals have an absolute right to enter and to stay under international law: Case C-434/09 *McCarthy* [2011] OJ C 186/5, para 29.

[54] For discussion of the broad implications of this notion for the legitimacy of the Union, see G Palombella, 'Whose Europe? After the Constitution: A Goal-Based Citizenship' (2005) 3 *I-CON* 357, 367.

[55] JHH Weiler, 'Fundamental Rights and Fundamental Boundaries: Common Standards and Conflicting Values in the Protection of Human Rights in the European Legal Space' in R Kastoryano and S Emmanuel (eds), *An Identity for Europe: The Relevance of Multiculturalism in EU Constitution* (New York: Palgrave Macmillan, 2009) 73.

[56] P Van Elsuwege and S Adam, 'Situtations purement internes, discriminations à rebours et collectivités autonomes après l'arrêt sur l'Assurances soins flamande' (2008) 44 *CDE* 655; A Tryfonidou, 'Reverse Discrimination in Purely Internal Situations: An Incongruity in a Citizens' Europe' (2008) 35:1 *LIEI* 43; N Nic Shuibhne, 'Free Movement of Persons and the Wholly Internal Rule: Time to Move on?' (2002) 39:4 *CMLRev* 731; M Poiares Maduro, 'The Scope of European Remedies: The Case of Purely Internal Situations and Reverse Discrimination' in C Kilpatrick, T Novitz and

nationality of the Member State of residence can legally be discriminated against in the EU, as possession of the status of EU citizen alone is not enough, according to the ECJ, in order to fall within the scope *ratione materiae* of EU law,[57] unless the very status of EU citizenship is in jeopardy[58] or the ability to exercise EU citizenship rights is made *de facto* impossible by Member State rules.[59] Consequently, while discrimination on the basis of nationality is outlawed in the situations covered by the Treaty,[60] it is legal outside the Treaty's scope even when EU citizens suffer because of it.[61]

The Court has done a lot to remedy this drawback inherent in the law in force.[62] At present, it is not necessary to cross borders any more, for instance, in order to fall within the scope of EU law and thus benefit from the non-discrimination principle.[63] Possession of a second Member State's nationality helps,[64] but not always, as *McCarthy* has demonstrated.[65] It seems that the very logic of market integration in the EU contradicts the ideal of equality inherent in the notion of citizenship,[66] as the non-discrimination principle of Article 18 TFEU does not have a self-standing value in connection with the status of EU citizenship and has to be 'activated' separately from it.[67] Davies made a compelling demonstration of the clash between equality and market freedoms using the Services Directive[68] as a case

P Skidmore (eds), *The Future of Remedies in Europe* (Oxford: Hart Publishing, 2000) 117; G Gaja, 'Les discriminations à rebours: Un revirement souhaitable' in *Mélanges en Hommage de Michel Waelbroeck* (Brussels: Bruylant, 1999) 993, 997–8. For an impressive overview, see A Tryfonidou, *Reverse Discrimination in EC Law* (The Hague: Kluwer Law International, 2009).

[57] Joined Cases C-64/96 and C-65/96 *Uecker and Jacquet* [1997] ECR I-3171, para 23; Case C-148/02 *Garcia Avello* [2003] ECR I-11613: 'citizenship of the Union, established by Article 17 EC [20 TFEU], is not intended to extend the material scope of the Treaty to internal situations which have no link with Community law' (para 26).

[58] Case C-135/08 *Rottmann*, n 14 above; J Shaw (ed), *Has the European Court of Justice Challenged the Member State Sovereignty in Nationality Law?*, 2011, EUI RSCAS Paper (forthcoming); D Kochenov, n 16 above.

[59] Case C-34/09 *Ruiz Zambrano*, n 17 above; P Van Elsuwege, n 24 above; D Kochenov, n 17 above; K Hailbronner and D Thym, n 47 above.

[60] Article 18 TFEU.

[61] eg Case C-212/06 *Government of the French Community and Walloon Government* [2008] ECR I-1683. See further the Opinion of AG Sharpston in this case, esp paras 117–18.

[62] It has not done enough, however, as the problem seems only to be growing: D Kochenov, n 1 above, 34–58 (and the literature cited therein).

[63] eg Case C-403/03 *Egon Schempp v Finanzamt München V* [2005] ECR I-6421, para 22: 'the situation of a national of a Member State who . . . has not made use of the right to freedom of movement cannot, for that reason alone, be assimilated to a purely internal situation'; Case C-60/00 *Carpenter* [2002] ECR I-6279.

[64] Case C-148/02 *Garcia Avello*, n 57 above.

[65] Case C-434/09 *McCarthy*, n 53 above, para 41.

[66] See D Kochenov, n 1 above. In general on equality, see E Chemerinsky, 'In Defence of Equality: A Reply to Professor Westen' (1983) 81:3 *Mich L Rev* 575 (and the literature cited therein). For a US perspective: KL Karst, 'The Supreme Court 1976 Term Foreword: Equal Citizenship under the Fourteenth Amendment' (1977) 91:1 *Harv L Rev* 1; Sir Isaiah Berlin, 'Equality' (1955–1956) 56 *Proceedings of the Aristotelian Society* 301.

[67] D Kochenov, n 11 above, 234.

[68] Council Directive (EC) 2006/123 of the European Parliament and of the Council of 12 December 2006 on services in the internal market [2006] OJ L 376/36. For analysis, see C Barnard, 'Unravelling the Services Directive' (2008) 45:2 *CMLRev* 323.

study.[69] Regrettably, this clash covers a wide array of other issues too.[70] Moreover, it necessarily extends also to the application of the principle of equality to Member State nationals at the level of their Member States, thus eliminating the essential starting point of national citizenship, which is constituted by the presumption of equality before the law. This in turn produces a 'citizenship without respect'[71] and reflects the impoverished understanding of justice[72] and political participation[73] adopted in the context of the European integration project.

Agreeing with Tryfonidou, it is indeed so that the reverse discrimination concept, pre-citizenship in nature, simply does not take the EU citizenship status as a legally meaningful construct into account.[74] So while serving well in the context of purely economic integration, in the Union of citizens it is entirely out of place. In fact, the application of the concept effectively comes down to punishing those who do not contribute to the internal market—as they and they alone are worse off as a result of its application.[75] At the same time, a 'properly functioning Internal Market'[76] does not seem, per se, to be conducive to reverse discrimination either: if the borders between the Member States do not exist any more within such a market, how can it logically be argued that some situations within it are 'internal' while others are not?[77] The ECJ has accepted this argument in a number of cases,[78] making Tryfonidou argue that 'one thing is certain: reverse discrimination is, indeed, a problem that falls within the scope of EC law'.[79] The ECJ's important recent departure from the reverse discrimination logic in the *Ruiz Zambrano* case, where the Court ruled that measures 'which have the effect of depriving citizens of the Union of the *genuine enjoyment of the substance of the rights* conferred by virtue of their status as citizens of the Union'[80] are within the scope of EU law, does not solve the problem entirely, as has already been demonstrated by later case law.[81] It can, however, provide a first step in the right direction.

[69] G Davies, 'Services, Citizenship and the Country of Origin Principle', 2007, Mitchell Working Paper 2/2007, Edinburgh, 7 available at <http://www.law.ed.ac.uk/file_download/series/29_servicescitizenshipandthecountryoforiginprinciple.pdf>: 'an individual who is present in the jurisdiction but not subject to its regulation, and operating under a more beneficial regime, is a direct challenge to the content of citizenship—national or European—and its associated guarantees of equality and privilege'.

[70] D Kochenov, n 11 above, 234.

[71] D Kochenov, n 1 above.

[72] Williams, *The Ethos of Europe* (Cambridge: Cambridge University Press, 2010).

[73] JHH Weiler, n 10 above.

[74] A Tryfonidou (2009), n 56 above, 129–66.

[75] A Tryfonidou (2008), n 56 above, 54.

[76] A Tryfonidou (2009), n 56 above, 199.

[77] ibid 178. Tryfonidou's argument echoes that of Kamiel Mortelmans, 'The Common Market, the Internal Market and the Single Market, What's in a Market?' (1998) 35:1 *CMLRev* 101, 136.

[78] See, eg, Case C-293/02 *Jersey Potatoes Marketing Organisation Ltd v States of Jersey and Jersey Potato Export Marketing Board* [2005] ECR I-9543; Joined Cases C-363/93, C-407/93, C-409/93 and C-411/93 *Lancry SA v Direction générale des douanes* [1994] ECR I-3957. For thought-provoking analyses of the new approach to reverse discrimination in the recent case law of the Court, see A Tryfonidou (2009), n 56 above, 64–126; P Van Elsuwege and S Adam, n 56 above, 655.

[79] A Tryfonidou (2009), n 56 above, 232.

[80] Case C-34/09 *Ruiz Zambrano*, n 17 above, para 42 (emphasis added).

[81] Case C-434/09 *McCarthy*, n 53 above. For analysis see D Kochenov, n 17 above.

Comparing the number of EU citizens who fall within the scope *ratione materiae* of EU law with the number of those who do not, the main function of Member State nationalities in EU law becomes clear (statistically at least). The majority of EU citizens stay in their own Member States, caught by reverse discrimination by virtue of possessing the nationality of that, not some other, Member State. This is not what your MP would tell you about your nationality.

D. European integration shaping nationalities of the Member States: elaboration

The internal market, coupled with EU citizenship, thus affects the very essence of Member States' nationalities in a fundamental way. This is particularly evident in the most vital aspect of nationality regulation, that is, the rules on the acquisition and loss of nationality, which determine the borderline between EU citizens and third country nationals. The EU gradually came to affect the legal determination of who is an EU citizen and who is a 'real' foreigner in the Union.[82] As this section will demonstrate, nationality acquisition rules applicable in the Member States depend to a great extent on whether the applicant has EU citizenship status already, which theoretically amounts to claiming that Member States enforce separate rules for the conferral of a duo of EU citizenship *and* the local nationality, compared with the acquisition of the local nationality alone.

The internal market and EU citizenship both ensure that the possibility for one Member State to have a 'better nationality' within the EU, as far as the scope of rights enjoyed in connection with it is concerned, is non-existent, legally speaking at least.[83] This is especially evident once one takes into account the importance of residence, to which the majority of practically usable rights are connected in any Member State, as well as the fact that such residence can be established through the use of EU citizenship status,[84] or, often easier, through migrant worker status within the internal market.[85]

[82] D Kochenov, n 11 above, 182–6.

[83] This statement should be qualified with regard to the legal effects of possession of particular Member States' nationalities *outside* the EU, EEA and Switzerland. When EU citizens travel in third countries, their Member State nationality, not EU citizenship, is the main status affecting the rights they enjoy. Consequently, differences exist between the attractiveness of different Member States' nationalities, as different visa regimes apply to different EU passports: travelling with a Slovenian passport to the US is much easier, for instance, than with a Polish one. The Commission is doing its best in order to ensure that the same visa regimes apply to all EU citizens: eg L Kubosova, 'Brussels to press for US visa free entry to EU newcomers', EU Observer, 24 February 2006, available at <http://euobserver.com/?aid=20982>.

[84] G Davies, n 23 above; S Maillard, *L'émergence de la citoyenneté sociale européenne* (Presses Universitaires d'Aix-Marseille, 2008) 353.

[85] Workers, able to travel around the EU and stay in any of the Member States as long as it pleases them, enjoy much better protection than European citizens experiencing health problems and economic hardship, since all persons not falling within the EU definition of a 'worker' should, according to the general rule, be covered by sickness insurance and have sufficient resources in order to benefit from the right 'of residence on the territory of another Member-State for a period of longer

In this situation, the lack of any coordination between the Member States in terms of access to their nationality was bound to result in the mutation of access to the status of nationality even without any formal intervention by the EU, which is prohibited from acting in this domain in any event.[86] Such mutations happen at two different levels. At an informal level, the change occurred without any amendments of the Member States' nationality laws in order to accommodate the special position of EU citizens; while at the formal level, the nationality laws were changed in order to reflect the reality of European integration.

As to the *informal* level: even when there are no formal provisions facilitating EU citizens' access to nationality of the Member State of residence, it is clear that the virtually complete transfer of the core regulation of residence of EU citizens from the level of the Member States to the EU shaped a reality where naturalization of EU citizens in the Member State of residence became simplified. This development, observable already in the pre-citizenship context,[87] has only been intensified through the introduction of EU citizenship, as the preceding section has demonstrated. The main hurdle that third country nationals face—which is connected with acquiring rights of entry, work and residence, as well as constantly prolonging the former for a required period of time in order to qualify for naturalization—does not exist in the case of EU citizens. Consequently, at the informal level, naturalization of EU citizens and of third country nationals has parted ways in *all* the Member States of the Union.

The sharp distinction between EU citizens and third country nationals is also reflected in the way in which culture and language testing of newcomers is conducted in the Member States. Two points are important in this regard. First, while more and more Member States introduce such testing for those willing to apply for permanent residence[88] and naturalization,[89] EU citizens are exempt from

than three months': Directive 2004/38/EC, n 36 above, Article 7(1). However, the Member States are not entitled to conduct strict checks of the sufficiency of resources: Case C-408/03 *Commission v Belgium* [2006] ECR I-2647. See, in general, P Minderhoud and N Trimikliniotis (eds), *Rethinking the Free Movement of Workers: The European Challenges Ahead* (Nijmegen: Wolf, 2009). There is a certain competition between workers' rights and EU citizens' rights under the current regime. For discussion see, eg, A Tryfonidou, 'In Search of the Aim of the EC Free Movement of Persons Provisions: Has the Court of Justice Missed the Point?' (2009) 46:5 *CMLRev* 1591, 1592–5; O Golynker, 'European Union as a Single Working-Living Space: EU Law and New Forms of Intra-Community Migration' in A Halpin and V Roeben (eds), *Theorising the Global Legal Order* (Oxford: Hart Publishing, 2009) 145, 151 (embracing opposing points of view on how the scope of the two blocs of rights is to be constructed). See further D Kochenov, n 1 above, 52–4; D Kochenov, n 17 above.

86 The status quo is not as categorical any more after *Rottmann*, in which the ECJ obliged the Member States to take EU law into account and apply the principle of proportionality when ruling on nationality issues in cases where the EU citizenship status of a person can be affected: Case C-135/08 *Rottmann*, n 14 above, para 55.

87 A Evans, n 4 above, 193.

88 Such tests are also allowed by Directive 2003/109/EC, n 20 above, Article 5(2).

89 For an overview and analysis, see R Bauböck and C Joppke (eds), 'How Liberal Are Citizenship Tests?' 2010, EUI RSCAS Working Paper 2010/41, available at <http://eudo-citizenship.eu/docs/RSCAS_2010_41.pdf>; R van Oers, E Ersbøll and D Kostakopoulou, 'Mapping the Redefinition of Belonging in Europe' in R van Oers, E Ersbøll and D Kostakopoulou (eds), *A Re-definition of Belonging?* (The Hague: Koninklijke Brill, 2010) 307; C Joppke, 'Beyond National Models: Civic Integration Policies for Immigrants in Western Europe' (2007) 30:1 *WEP* 1.

these tests for the acquisition of permanent residence status—which is a natural application of the principle of non-discrimination on the basis of nationality within the internal market.[90] Naturally, this exemption undermines the legitimacy of the dubious practice of such testing espoused by the Member States: if an EU citizen, say a Dutchman from the island of Curaçao, can permanently reside in Denmark without any officially certified knowledge of the local language and culture, an argument that a Moldovan cannot do the same becomes far less convincing.[91] It is clear that Romanian written in Cyrillic script is at least as 'dangerous' for Danish culture as Papiamento and salsa.

Secondly, and more importantly, given that naturalization of a third county national in a Member State also makes such a person an EU citizen, the contents of the tests are bound to reflect this reality. An important tension arises in this context: while the tests generally aim at ensuring that all new citizens know the local realities of the Member State of naturalization well, this is unlikely to be of much help to them should they opt for benefiting from the main right of EU citizenship—that is, to move to another Member State of the Union, where many of the local realities and, in the majority of cases, the language will be different. Consequently, besides exposing the illogical thinking behind such culture tests, the European integration project is also bound to affect the tests' contents, whether the Member States want this or not. Advocate General Poiares Maduro highlighted this point well in his Opinion in *Nerkowska*:

> Citizenship of the Union *must* encourage Member States to no longer conceive of the legitimate link of integration only within the narrow bonds of the national community, but also within the wider context of the *society of peoples of the Union*.[92]

As to the *formal* level, six Member States introduced formal distinctions into their legislation on the acquisition (and loss) of nationality in order to reflect the gap *de facto* separating EU citizens and third country nationals even in situations when both are branded as 'foreigners'[93] in a particular Member State. The formal distinction

[90] AG Jacobs explained the mechanics of this with admirable clarity in his Opinion in Case C-148/02 Garcia Avello, n 57 above, para 63 (citations omitted):

> The concept of 'moving and residing freely in the territory of the Member States' is not based on the hypothesis of a single move from one Member State to another, to be followed by integration into the latter. The intention is rather to allow free, and possibly related or even continuous, movement within a single 'area of freedom, security and justice', in which both cultural diversity and freedom from discrimination [are] ensured.

It is impossible to agree with Weiler in this context, who seems to disapprove of this vision, speaking of the 'ghettoisation' of migrants. In Weiler's view, 'la Corte dissuade dall'integrazione dei migranti nelle loro comunità ospiti': JHH Weiler, n 10 above, 82. His presumption of the usefulness of integration tests seems too optimistic in the light of their contents. For an explanation see, eg, D Kochenov, '*Mevrouw de Jong Gaat Eten*: EU Citizenship and the Culture of Prejudice', 2011, EUI RSCAS Working Paper 2011/06, available at <http://eudo-citizenship.eu/docs/RSCAS_2011_06.pdf>.

[91] D Kochenov, n 90 above, 12–15.

[92] Opinion of AG Poiares Maduro in Case C-499/06 *Halina Nerkowska v Zakład Ubezpieczeń Społecznych Oddział w Koszalinie* [2008] ECR 3993, para 23 (emphasis added).

[93] EU law as it stands does not prohibit Member States from including EU citizens in foreigners' registers: Case C-524/06 *Huber v Germany* [2008] ECR I-9705. Analysed by K Hailbronner, 'Are

between EU citizens and third country nationals for the purposes of naturalization is made in two interrelated respects. The first concerns providing EU citizens with a possibility to become naturalized faster by applying a shorter naturalization term to them. The second consists of applying different renunciation requirements to EU citizens, thus not requiring them to get rid of their initial Member State nationality and facilitating their naturalization.[94] The first approach is adopted in Austria, Hungary, Italy and Romania; the second, in Germany and Slovenia.

The approach to the naturalization of EU citizens adopted in Austria, Hungary, Italy and Romania goes to the core of the most important naturalization requirement, that is, the time one is required to spend in the country before becoming naturalized. A clear distinction is made here between the naturalization requirements concerned with the minimum length of residence required before an application for naturalization can be filed that are applicable to EU citizens and to third country nationals. So to become Austrian through the discretionary naturalization procedure, EU citizens (and EEA nationals) need to reside in Austria for two years less than third country nationals do.[95] Moreover, unlike third country nationals, EU citizens and EEA nationals enjoy 'a legal entitlement to naturalisation'.[96] A preference being extended to EU citizens in procedures of naturalization can also be observed in Hungary, where they may become naturalized faster.[97] To become Italians, EU citizens need to reside in Italy six years less than third country nationals do.[98] In Romania, the difference between the naturalization requirements for EU citizens and third country nationals is equally considerable. EU citizens become naturalized after 'half the period of regular naturalisation',[99] that is, in less than four years.[100] The inclusion of EEA nationals among those becoming naturalized more quickly is very telling in this regard, as it points to the key importance of the internal market rationale behind the introduction of the simplified rules, as opposed to EU citizenship considerations alone: EEA citizens are not EU citizens.

All of the differences between the naturalization requirements for EU citizens and for third country nationals are relatively new: Italy was the first EU Member State to give priority to EU citizens in the process of naturalization. The relevant legislation entered into force in 1992,[101] in Austria in 1998,[102] in Hungary in 2003,[103] and in 2008 in Romania.[104]

Union Citizens Still Foreigners?' in P Minderhoud and N Trimikliniotis (eds), *Rethinking the Free Movement of Workers: The European Challenges Ahead* (Nijmegen: Wolf Legal Publishers, 2009).

94 See D Kochenov, 'Double Nationality in the EU: An Argument for Tolerance' (2011) 17:3 *ELJ* 323.

95 D Çinar, *Country Report: Austria*, 2010, EUDO EUI RSCAS Paper, available at <http://eudo-citizenship.eu/docs/CountryReports/Austria.pdf>, 8.

96 ibid 15.

97 M Kovács and J Tóth, *Country Report: Hungary*, 2010, EUDO EUI RSCAS Paper, available at <http://eudo-citizenship.eu/docs/CountryReports/Hungary.pdf>, 1, 3.

98 G Zincone and M Basili, n 18 above, 1.

99 C Iordachi, *Country Report: Romania*, 2010, EUDO EUI RSCAS Paper, <http://eudo-citizenship.eu/docs/CountryReports/Romania.pdf>, 8.

100 The regular residence period for naturalization in Romania amounts to seven years: ibid.

101 G Zincone and M Basili, n 18 above, 1, 2.

102 D Çinar, n 95 above, 8.

103 M Kovács and J Tóth, n 97 above, 1.

104 C Iordachi, n 99 above, 8.

Germany is among 11 Member States of the EU where the general renunciation requirement is enforced.[105] This means that naturalization is subject to the renunciation of one's previous citizenship. Germany does not require EU citizens to meet this requirement,[106] which leads to their becoming naturalized more easily. Slovenia, applying similar law, is more restrictive: 'The condition of a release from current citizenship is waived for citizens of those EU Member States where reciprocity exists.'[107] In the eight countries where no exceptions from the renunciation requirement for EU citizens are made, the naturalization rates of EU citizens are extremely low, which is easily explainable; given that there is no 'better nationality' in the EU, renouncing one for acquiring another predictably makes no sense and people realize this perfectly well.[108]

Without any doubt, more countries will follow the six examples provided in differentiating between EU citizens and third country nationals for the purposes of nationality regulation, reflecting the change in the status quo between EU citizenship and Member States' nationalities marked by the growing mutual interpenetration of the two statuses.[109] Relevant proposals are being discussed at the time of writing, for example, in Lithuania[110] and Spain.[111]

Differentiating between EU citizens and third country nationals in the nationality legislation of the Member States *de facto* leads to the establishment of a separate procedure for the acquisition of EU citizenship. Those not in possession of this status are asked to meet more stringent formal requirements in order to become naturalized in the Member State of residence compared with EU citizens who are not in possession of the local nationality. This state of affairs reflects a reality that is absolutely different from the promise of a merely derivative EU citizenship status in the Treaties and demonstrates, once again, that a clear distinction needs to be made between the acquisition of EU citizenship (which is purely derivative as it follows the nationalities of the Member States) and the essence of this status, which is not. The analysis of some distinguished commentators, such as Tesauro, claiming the non-existence of a 'real' European citizenship based on the fact that access to it is derivative is logically unsound: if *ius soli* citizenship is no better or worse that *ius*

[105] These Member States are the Czech Republic, Denmark, Estonia, Germany, Hungary, Latvia, Lithuania, the Netherlands, Poland, Slovakia, Slovenia (numerous exceptions apply). See G-R de Groot and M Vink, *Meervoudige nationaliteit in Europees perspectief: Een landenvergelijkend overzicht* (The Hague: Adviescommissie voor Vreemdelingenzaken, 2008). On the general context of dual nationality in the EU, see M Morjé Howard, 'Variation in Dual Citizenship Policies in the Countries of the EU' (2005) 39:3 *Int'l Migration Rev* 697, esp Table 4, 713; D Kochenov, n 94 above.

[106] G-R de Groot and M Vink, n 105 above, 73–5.

[107] F Medved, *Country Report: Slovenia*, 2010, EUDO EUI RSCAS Paper, available at <http://eudo-citizenship.eu/docs/CountryReports/Slovenia.pdf>, 12.

[108] D Kochenov, n 94 above, 337–40.

[109] In the Member States where the law is silent on this matter, scholars argue for amending the law. See, eg, C Sawyer, *Country Report: United Kingdom*, 2010, EUDO EUI RSCAS Paper, available at <http://eudo-citizenship.eu/docs/CountryReports/United%20Kingdom.pdf>, 28.

[110] E Kūris, *Country Report: Lithuania*, 2010, EUDO EUI RSCAS Paper, available at <http://eudo-citizenship.eu/docs/CountryReports/Lithuania.pdf>, 40–1 (the law was vetoed by the President).

[111] R Rubio Marín and I Sobrino, *Country Report: Spain*, 2010, EUDO EUI RSCAS Paper, available at <http://eudo-citizenship.eu/docs/CountryReports/Spain.pdf>, 17.

sanguinis citizenship, then there is no reason to claim that the same should not be valid for *ius tractum* (that is, derivative) citizenship;[112] certain rules of access to the status have nothing to do with the existence of the status as such, let alone the rights associated therewith.[113] It is impermissible to ignore the fact that, as outlined by Poiares Maduro, 'Union citizenship assumes nationality of a Member State but it is also a legal and political concept *independent* of that of nationality. Nationality of a Member State not only provides access to enjoyment of the rights conferred by Community law; it also makes us citizens of the Union.'[114]

Application of different naturalization procedures to EU citizens and third country nationals at the national level is a sign of the maturing of EU citizenship. The prospects for the acquisition of nationalities of specific Member States directly depend on the possession (or not) of the status of EU citizenship in EU law. Even in the Member States where this connection is not formally adopted as part of nationality legislation, the internal market coupled with EU citizenship provides an easier access to nationality in practice through the lifting of residence and immigration controls for EU citizens.

E. Member States' nationalities: the illusion of control

Precisely because the acquisition of EU citizenship is derivative in nature,[115] the power of the Member States is severely weakened, since while each one of them taken separately can maintain an illusion that it controls access to EU citizenship, taken together they do not, as long as naturalization regimes are not harmonized at least to some extent. Huge disparities between the citizenship laws of all the Member States[116] lead to the multiplication of the ways of acquisition of the same status of European citizenship which, as has been demonstrated above, has the potential to affect an important number of the main attributes of Member State nationalities. In failing to regulate the issue of access to EU citizenship effectively, the Member States have opted for the illusion of control rather than the resolution of outstanding problems, which include, most importantly, the need to design an

112 For an analysis of EU citizenship as a *ius tractum* citizenship, see D Kochenov, n 11 above.

113 Tesauro submits that: 'non esiste, né potrebbe allo stato ippotizzarsi, una nozione communitaria di cittadinanza, sì che le norme che ne prescrivono il possesso come presupposto soggettivo per la loro applicazione in realtà rinviano alla legge nazionale dello Stato la cui cittadinanza viene posta a fondamento del diritto invocato.' G Tesauro, *Diritto comunitario*, 5th edn (Padova: CEDAM, Wolters Kluwer Italia, 2008) 480 [At the moment the Community notion of citizenship does not exist, not even hypothetically, given that the norms requiring its possession as a subjective condition for their application in reality refer to the national law of the State whose nationality turns into the basis of the invoked right]. See further L Besselink and JH Reestman, 'Editorial: Dynamics of European and National Citizenship: Inclusive or Exclusive?' (2007) 3:1 *EuConst.* 1, 2.

114 Opinion of AG Poiares Maduro in Case C-135/08 *Rottmann*, n 14 above, para 23 (emphasis added).

115 Article 20 TFEU.

116 For detailed country-by-country information, see the documents available on the web-page of the EUDO project: <http://eudo-citizenship.eu/>.

effective immigration policy for the Union, while ensuring that the rights of EU citizens and third country nationals are respected.

In a borderless Union, the current approach means that more than 27 highly heterogeneous sets of legal rules regulating the acquisition of the same status applicable in all the Member States are in existence.[117] In the light of federalism's potential to enhance freedom,[118] the discrepancy between nationality legislation in different Member States is highly beneficial for those willing to acquire EU citizenship. Informed third country nationals are free to choose the Member State where access to nationality is framed in the most permissive terms,[119] in order to move to their 'dream Member State' later, in their capacity as EU citizens. The Member States are thus unable to make a coherent claim to be able to control the access of non-nationals to their territory.[120] No matter how they frame their citizenship laws, the mere existence of the internal market has already eliminated any direct logical connection between the territory of a particular Member State and the 'people' of that Member State. Any backlash, like the abolition of pure *ius soli* approach in Ireland following *Chen*, is merely a reminder that the Member States are powerless to maintain a coherent control claim. Such backlashes do not thus affect the core of the problem: it is not the perceived 'softness' of Irish law but the principled discrepancy between countless modes of EU citizenship acquisition which is of importance here.

This discrepancy is fuelled by the conceptual contradiction between the nationality policies of the Member States and EU citizenship rights which the Member States have so far failed to grasp. While the Member States grant nationality to those connected with their territory or populace assuming that the nationals would keep such connections, EU citizenship follows an opposing rationale, aiming at encouraging people to move, to benefit from the opportunities that the internal market has to offer and to think beyond their Member States.

Consequently, third country nationals becoming naturalized in a particular Member State can do so for two reasons: either to stay in the new motherland, or to leave immediately, benefiting from the main right of EU citizenship. Both are equally natural and legitimate. Currently, the Member States seem to pretend that the latter choice is not an option, since all the naturalization policies are built on the

117 D Kochenov, n 11 above, 182–6.

118 eg SF Kreimer, 'Federalism and Freedom' (2001) 574 *Annals AAPSS* 66; M McConnell, 'Review: Federalism: Evaluating the Founders' Design' (1987) 54:4 *U Chi L Rev* 1484, 1494. Applied to the context of the EU, see D Kochenov, 'On Options of Citizens and Moral Choices of States: Gays and European Federalism' (2009) 33:1 *Fordham Int'l LJ* 156.

119 This is exactly what happened in the *Chen* case, where a Chinese mother came to Belfast in order to give birth to her daughter in defiance of the Chinese one child policy. The girl acquired Irish nationality by birth and immediately fell within the scope of EU law as an EU citizen, since the birth actually took place in the UK: Case C-200/02 *Kunqian Catherine Zhu & Man Lavette Chen v Secretary of State for the Home Department* [2004] ECR I-9925. As one could guess, '[t]he choice of Ireland as Catherine's place of birth had not been accidental but rather influenced by the peculiarities of Irish Nationality laws in force at that time, which had been brought to the Chens' attention by their lawyers'. B Hofstotter, 'A Cascade of Rights, or Who Shall Care for Little Catherine? Some Reflections on the *Chen* Case' (2005) 30 *ELRev* 548.

120 See further W Maas, n 9 above, 8.

assumption that a new citizen will *stay* in the Member State (which provides, as noted above, justification for linguistic, cultural and other tests that newcomers are asked to pass before national (and thereby) EU citizenship is conferred on them). Once the EU dimension is taken into account, however, the illusory world in which the Member States are still living crumbles in a second. In the words of Advoate General Poiares Maduro, as he then was,

> That is the miracle of Union citizenship: it strengthens the ties between us and our States (in so far as we are European citizens precisely because we are nationals of our States) and, at the same time, it emancipates us from them (in so far as we are now citizens beyond our States).[121]

Naturalization statistics coming from different Member States prove that, unlike States, ordinary people are less prone to living in dream worlds and understand the current *status quo* pretty well. In one example, the number of applications for recognition of Polish citizenship increased almost five-fold upon Poland's accession to the EU,[122] indicating that 'Polish accession to the EU had an effect on the interest in the Polish citizenship among diaspora members',[123] or, to put it differently, the interest of the diaspora members in the EU citizenship status—since this is the only fundamental addition to Polish nationality which made it overwhelmingly attractive on 1 May 2004 when the country joined the Union. Similarly, in Italy, the number of marriages involving Romanian citizens decreased substantially after Romania's accession to the EU, demonstrating that it was not Italian nationality as such, but the status of EU citizenship that Romanians were seeking.[124] Speaking of marriages is particularly relevant in this context, since this is by far the most important mode of acquisition of Italian nationality. Naturalization by residence in the country only accounts for 1 per cent of naturalizations.[125]

The Member States are happy to pretend that they regulate access to EU citizenship and state territory, while they do not,[126] and the candidates for inclusion benefit from the differences in regulation existing between the Member

[121] Opinion of AG Poiares Maduro in Case C-135/08 *Rottmann*, n 14 above, para 23.

[122] A Górny and D Pudzianowska, *Country Report: Poland*, 2010, EUDO EUI RSCAS Paper, available at <http://eudo-citizenship.eu/docs/CountryReports/Poland.pdf>, 8: the number of applications for Polish nationality in 2000 was 765. In 2004, it reached 3805.

[123] ibid.

[124] G Zincone and M Basili, n 18 above, 13.

[125] ibid.

[126] It is evident that even if the EU does not step in, a certain coordination among the Member States will arise. As early as in 1983, Evans acknowledged that 'harmonisation of the nationality laws of the Member States may ultimately prove necessary.' AC Evans, 'Nationality Law and the Free Movement of Persons in the EEC: With Special Reference to the British Nationality Act 1981' (1982) 2 *YEL* 173, 189; similarly see C Blumann, 'La citoyenneté de l'Union européenne (bientôt dix ans): Espoir et désillusion' in V Epping, H Fischer and W Heintschel von Heinegg (eds), *Brücken Bauen und Begehen: Festschrift für Knut Ipsen zum 65 Geburtstag* (München: Verlag C.H. Beck, 2000) 3, 16. Becker suggested 'harmonisation—or even standardization of national citizenship across the European Union.' MA Becker, 'Managing Diversity in the European Union: Inclusive European Citizenship and Third-Country Nationals' (2004) 7 *Yale Hum Rts and Dev L J* 132, 159. See further the European Parliament's view on this issue: Resolution on the British Nationality Bill [1981] OJ C 260/100.

States. Apart from notions of common sense, almost nothing seems to suffer from this arrangement with the exception of the third country nationals who frequently change their Member State of residence, or those who ended up living in a Member State where naturalization possibilities are particularly restricted.

It seems that the proposals for full harmonization of EU citizenship law that would lead to the effective loss by the Member States of the capacity to regulate access to their nationalities fall short of being convincing: besides being highly unrealistic in the current political climate, they are also not desirable, as they are likely to lead to stricter regulation on average in EU-27 compared with that in place in the most liberal Member States, thus undermining the vulnerable position of third country nationals in the EU even further.[127] As opposed to full harmonization, mid-way solutions incorporating access to EU citizenship via Member States' nationalities alongside direct conferral of EU citizenship by the Union might provide a better option. The fact that this does not seem feasible at the moment, politically speaking, is a very bad example of national politics affecting common sense, as plenty of acute problems are bound to remain unsolved before the Member States finally manage to cope with their distorted self-vision, which severely lags behind reality.

There is no reason to believe that the process of increasing interdependency between EU citizenship and the nationalities of the Member States as providers of rights in the context of the EU's internal market will stop or be reversed. The contrary seems more likely—its dynamics will only intensify in the near future, as it will be clearer to Member States' authorities and EU citizens alike that the status provided by the EU is likely to become ever more important for all the individuals in possession of it, than any Member State nationality.

Whether or not Member State nationality will survive as a legal status connecting individuals and the EU, it will certainly mutate to a considerable extent under the EU pressures of the internal market and non-discrimination on the basis of nationality, to say nothing of EU citizenship. The result of this mutation will necessarily be a legal status that is substantially different from the nationalities of the Member States today. Most likely, it will eventually move away from providing its bearers with practical rights, remaining merely the main legal reference for the emotional connection existing between nationals and their Member States, thus reinforcing the EU's legitimation via the multiplicity of peoples—*dēmoi*—of Europe.[128] This reinvention of nationality will necessarily result in critical scrutiny of all its attributes, which are taken for granted in the law of the Member States today. Irrelevant and antiquarian requirements of naturalization, for instance, or nationality-related duties peculiar to some Member States, will be under pressure

[127] To take one example, it is unlikely that being appointed a full professor at an institution of higher education would be enough to allow one to become a European citizen (which is the case in Austria) once the laws of the 27 Member States are harmonized: Article 25(1) of the Austrian Nationality Act, *FLG* No 311/1985.

[128] G Palombella, n 54 above, 365; JHH Weiler, 'In Defence of the *Status Quo*: Europe's Constitutional *Sonderweg*' in JHH Weiler and M Wind (eds), *European Constitutionalism beyond the State* (Cambridge: Cambridge University Press, 2003) 7.

to go no matter which scenario of future development of nationalities in the Union becomes operational.

F. Conclusion

The European integration process, having gained momentum, has a profound ability to affect the Member States in seemingly unexpected ways, even in the areas that national politicians do their best to shelter from European influence. The indirect effects of the internal market and EU citizenship are far-reaching, stretching beyond the areas potentially covered by the Treaties. Regarding nationalities of the Member States, we are witnessing an ongoing process of constitutional change at the Member State level, which—although obviously triggered by the internal market and EU citizenship—is not directly mandated by the Union. In other words, the internal market is shaping its own environment not only through the functioning of EU law, but also indirectly, through the Member States' adaptation to the new reality, shaped by European integration.

This chapter has demonstrated in detail how far-reaching the consequences of this process are in a fundamental area of constitutional law of the Member States—the way in which they determine who their nationals are. A number of other key aspects of national law, going to the very essence of the Member States, are equally affected. In the context of a constant rise in the importance of the EU, and unavoidable growth in economic interdependence in Europe, the array of fields of law which come to be subjected to the indirect influence of the internal market is only likely to grow, presenting the division of competences between the Member States and the Union in a somewhat different light than that projected in the Treaties. In a way, as long as the importance of European integration is growing, it becomes much less important whether the Union actually has competence in regulating a certain area, since the national regulation by the Member States will necessarily take the changing reality into account, adapting national law to the internal market. There is no choice left to the Member States about whether to do it or not. EU demands in such a context are absolutely unnecessary, as the example of Member State nationalities demonstrates.

PART III

COMMON POLICIES

14

Chasing a Moving Target through a Thick Fog: Questioning the Objectives of the Common Agricultural Policy

*Joseph A McMahon**

A. Introduction

The original Treaty of Rome has been amended on several occasions since 1957, most recently by the Treaty of Lisbon, and what is notable about these amendments is that they have not involved any alteration to the objectives of the Common Agricultural Policy (CAP). Indeed by remarkable coincidence the Treaty on the Functioning of the European Union (TFEU) restores the numbering of the provisions of the Treaty establishing the European Economic Community. So, the objectives of the CAP are once again found in Article 39, common organizations and the principle of non-discrimination in Article 40, the application of competition law in Article 42 and the legislative procedure in Article 43.[1] There have, of course, been changes to the Chapter of the Treaty on Agriculture. Whilst Article 3 of the original Treaty provided that 'the activities of the Community shall include . . . a common policy in the sphere of agriculture and fisheries', the TFEU provides in Article 4 that agriculture shall be an area of shared competence between the Union and the Member States. By virtue of Article 2(2) TFEU, this means that both the Union and the Member States may legislate and adopt legally binding acts in this area, with the latter having legislative competence if the Union has not exercised or has ceased to exercise its competence. This should not result in significant changes in the legislative competence of either the Union or the Member States given the jurisprudence of the European Court of Justice (the Court) which has clearly articulated the scope of the shared competence of the Union and the Member States in agriculture.[2]

* Professor of Commercial Law, School of Law, University College Dublin.

[1] Unless otherwise indicated, all references are to the new numbering of the provisions on agriculture.

[2] Case 31/74 *Galli* [1975] ECR 47, Case 111/76 *Van den Hazel* [1977] ECR 901 and Joined Cases 141/81 and 143/81 *Holdijk* [1982] ECR 1299.

A provision of the original Treaty that has since been deleted, Article 43(1), provided that 'In order to evolve the broad lines of a common agricultural policy, the Commission shall . . . convene a conference of the Member States with a view to making a comparison of their agricultural policies, in particular by producing a statement of their resources and needs'. The conference was duly convened and the CAP has evolved considerably since then. It has two pillars—producer support and rural development—and, despite a long period of legislative complexity, the CAP is now governed by four main instruments. Regulation 73/2009 is the latest iteration of the parameters of the Single Farm Payment, various direct support schemes and the cross-compliance criteria.[3] Regulation 1698/2005 lays down the strategic objectives for a single programme for rural development, with various axes, funded by the Community through the European Agricultural Fund for Rural Development.[4] This Fund, together with the European Agricultural Guarantee Fund, which finances the Single Payment Scheme, was created by Regulation 1290/2005 establishing a single legal framework for the financing of the CAP.[5] The final instrument of note is Regulation 1234/2007, which replaced the myriad of common organizations with a single common organization of the market, thus contributing significantly to the simplification of the policy.[6]

These four measures have dissipated the 'thick fog' which characterized the CAP until fairly recently. It is against this backdrop, and the fact that by 2013 a new framework for European agriculture will have to be agreed, that this contribution seeks to explore a number of questions: how have the original objectives of the CAP been interpreted? How have new policy areas been accommodated within the objectives of the CAP as the policy has evolved? And should the 2013 reform include a debate on the objectives of the policy? The following sections will examine each of these questions after a brief discussion of the evolution and reform of the CAP.

[3] Council Regulation No 73/2009 of 19 January 2009 establishing common rules for direct support schemes for farmers under the common agricultural policy and establishing certain support schemes for farmers, amending Regulations (EC) No 1290/2005, (EC) No 247/2006, (EC) No 378/2007 and repealing Regulation (EC) No 1782/2003 [2009] OJ L 30/16. The Regulation has been subject to frequent amendment, a recent example being Commission Regulation (EU) No 360/2010 of 27 April 2010 amending Annex IV and Annex VIII to Council Regulation (EC) No 73/2009 establishing common rules for direct support schemes for farmers under the common agricultural policy [2010] OJ L 106/1.

[4] Council Regulation No 1698/2005 of 20 September 2005 on support for rural development by the European Agricultural Fund for Rural Development (EAFRD) [2005] OJ L 277/1. This act has also been subject to amendment; eg, Council Regulation (EC) 473/2009 of 25 May 2009 amending Regulation (EC) No 1698/2005 on support for rural development by the European Agricultural Fund for Rural Development (EAFRD) and Regulation (EC) No 1290/2005 on the financing of the common agricultural policy [2009] OJ L 144/3.

[5] Council Regulation No 1290/2005 of 21 June 2005 on the financing of the common agricultural policy [2005] OJ L 209/1.

[6] Council Regulation No 1234/2007 of 22 October 2007 establishing a common organization of agricultural markets and on specific provisions for certain agricultural products (Single CMO Regulation) [2007] OJ L 299/1.

B. Evolution and reform of the CAP

The original Treaty of Rome singled out agriculture for special treatment. The conference anticipated by the original Article 43(1) was convened at Stresa in July 1958 and it concluded that the structure of European agriculture needed to be reformed; such reform would have to respect the family character of agricultural holdings. It was also agreed that Community-wide prices would be set at a level slightly above world prices; this would lead to the adequate remuneration of farmers without encouraging surplus production. Finally, the Community would not aim to achieve total self-sufficiency in agricultural production and thus would remain open to international trade, although measures were anticipated which would prevent distortions of competition of external origin.[7]

In December 1960, the Council made its first substantive decision on the CAP, paving the way for its introduction. The significance of this decision rests with its establishment of the three basic principles of the original CAP.[8] First, common prices, to be achieved through the elimination of barriers to trade and distortions of competition between Member States. Secondly, common financing, under which all Member States would contribute to the financing of the common organizations of the market to be established over the transitional period. To ensure that the Member States enjoyed the advantages of integration foreshadowed by the Treaty, Community preference became the third principle of the CAP. The original decisions taken on the policy were to have a profound effect on its future development, since the resulting policy was more protectionist than the various national polices that preceded it.[9]

According to Article 40, in order to implement the objectives in Article 39, common organizations of agricultural markets were to be established and Article 40 afforded a menu of choices on the nature of the common organizations: (a) common rules on competition; (b) compulsory coordination of the various national market organizations; or (c) a European market organization. The choice of form would depend on the particular product concerned. The special position of agriculture demanded a choice between options (b) and (c) and the reference to a 'market organization' in both of these options also dictated that some form of interference with the market would be required. As for the contents of the 'organization', some indication is given in Article 40 with the list of measures that can be adopted to regulate the market, the endorsement of the general principles of proportionality and non-discrimination, provision for the financing of the measures adopted and the choice of the applicable competition regime under Article 42.

[7] For the resolution of the Stresa Conference see *Recueil des documents de la Conférence agricole des Etats membres de la Communauté économique européenne à Stresa du 3 au 12 juillet 1958* (Luxembourg, Service des publications des Communautés européennes, 1958).

[8] EC Bull, No 1/61, 83.

[9] See, eg, T Heidhues et al, *Common Prices and Europe's Farm Policy*, Thames Essay no 14, Trade Policy Research Centre, London, 1978, 7.

In making the choice demanded by Article 40, the Community opted for the establishment of a European market organization, with the objective of establishing a single market for that product. Each of the regulations establishing common organizations shared a similar structure. After outlining the scope of the common organization, the market regime was established before the external regime was dealt with and the concluding provisions dealt with such matters as State aids and financing. The core element of all common organizations was the price structure. Commenting on this price structure, Usher noted:[10]

> This price structure rests to a very large degree on the premise that the product is one in which the Community is largely self-sufficient and of which Community production is to be encouraged, and that imports will be the exception and must not be allowed to disturb Community prices. It also assumes, in the system of import levies and export refunds, that world prices will be lower than Community prices.

The original principles of the CAP were designed to meet the situation in which the Community was still a net importer of agricultural products. The support of farm incomes through internal price arrangements, and the partial or total exclusion of imports for certain products as a result of increased border protection, ensured that the policy met the problems with which it was initially designed to deal. Once the situation had been reached, the instruments of policy were not changed. As a result, surpluses appeared in a number of areas. This led to increased budgetary expenditure, and trade relations with third countries deteriorated as the Community subsidized exports and continued to impose import restrictions. Initially prompted by internal concerns but ultimately required by external demands, reform of the CAP would be evolutionary rather than revolutionary. Although various reforms had been made to a number of common organizations throughout the 1980s, the first major set of reforms occurred in 1992, the so-called MacSharry reforms.[11]

These reforms were necessary to cope with the demands that would be imposed by the Uruguay Round Agreement on Agriculture. Just as agriculture had been treated as an exceptional area in the process of European integration, the treatment of agriculture in the General Agreement on Tariffs and Trade (GATT) was equally exceptional. From the granting of a waiver to the United States from certain GATT obligations in 1953, agriculture had somehow been exempted from its rules and disciplines.[12] During the Kennedy Round in the 1960s and the Tokyo Round in the 1970s, the Community had argued strongly for the continuation of this exceptional treatment. However, during the Uruguay Round it was agreed that agriculture would be gradually re-integrated into the rules and disciplines of the international trading system. The Agreement on Agriculture represents the first step in this re-integration as it establishes new rules on market access, domestic

[10] JA Usher, *Legal Aspects of Agriculture in the European Community*, 1st edn (Oxford: Oxford University Press, 1988) 56.

[11] For a fuller discussion, see JA McMahon, *EU Agricultural Law* (Oxford: Oxford University Press, 2007) 90–7.

[12] GATT, *Basic Instruments and Selected Documents*, 3rd Supp 141 (1953).

support and export competition.[13] Although the Agreement represents a considerable improvement on the discipline that prevailed during the GATT era, its provisions are not beyond reproach. Whilst import protection is now limited to tariffs and tariff quotas, tariffs remain high and quotas are restrictive. The discipline on domestic support may be viewed as relatively weak with control being imposed on policies that distort trade except those exempted, for example, those under the notorious Blue Box which was introduced to accommodate the MacSharry reforms. There is no doubt that the provisions on export competition are the most successful pillar of the Agreement, but no agreement was possible on the use of export credits. Article 20 of the Agreement provides for the continuation of the reform process and negotiations for a new Agreement have been folded into those initiated in 2001 by the Doha Declaration.

In preparation for these negotiations, the CAP underwent further reform as part of the Agenda 2000 reform package. Neither this set of reforms nor the earlier MacSharry reforms fundamentally altered the nature of the policy.[14] It was the 2003 Mid-Term Review of the Agenda 2000 reforms that signalled a new direction for the CAP with the introduction of a single decoupled income payment per farm.[15] Under the Review, the overall market orientation of agriculture would be improved as farmers would benefit directly from supplying products demanded by consumers and greater environmental protection could be expected by the removal of production-specific incentives. Such payments would also benefit from inclusion within the Green Box (Annex II of the Agreement on Agriculture) which imposes no ceilings on such payments. These reforms were carried through into other sectors in the years after the Mid-Term Review and have recently been confirmed by the 2008 Health Check.[16] The overall impact of the reforms has been to reduce the exceptional nature of agriculture and agricultural products within the Community as the role of the market has increased.

The ideational change of the CAP continued in its 2008 Health Check; as the process of decoupling payments from production continued, provision was made for additional modulation of payments, changes were made to the cross-compliance criteria and greater flexibility was given to the Member States.[17] The market orientation of the policy will be further accentuated if agreement is reached on a

[13] For a fuller discussion, see, eg, JA McMahon, *The Agreement on Agriculture: a Commentary* (Oxford: Oxford University Press, 2006).

[14] See European Commission, *Agenda 2000* (Brussels, 1997) Ch 3.3 for an assessment of the MacSharry reforms.

[15] See Communication from the Commission to the Council and the European Parliament, *Mid-Term Review of the Common Agricultural Policy* COM (2002) 394 final.

[16] For a summary of the Commission proposals and the Council Decisions see 'Health Check of the Common Agricultural Policy' available at <http://ec.europa.eu/agriculture/healthcheck/index_en.htm> (accessed June 2011).

[17] See Council Regulation (EC) No 72/2009 of 19 January 2009 on modifications to the Common Agricultural Policy by amending Regulations (EC) No 247/2006, (EC) No 320/2006, (EC) No 1405/2006, (EC) No 1234/2007, (EC) No 3/2008 and (EC) No 479/2008 and repealing Regulations (EEC) No 1883/78, (EEC) No 1254/89, (EEC) No 2247/89, (EEC) No 2055/93, (EC) No 1868/94, (EC) No 2596/97, (EC) No 1182/2005 and (EC) No 315/2007 [2009] OJ L 30/1; Regulation 73/2009, n 3 above; and Council Regulation (EC) No 74/2009 of 19 January 2009 amending Regulation

new Agreement on Agriculture. Current proposals would suggest a further liberalization in the area of market access, considerable reductions in the amount of domestic support that can be offered to agriculture, and the elimination of all export subsidies. The question that must be asked now is: what does the future hold for the CAP?

A recent European Parliament report on the future of the Single Payment argues that 'direct CAP payments should be reallocated towards the provision of public goods, which is the only uncontested reason why society should provide money to farmers in the long run'.[18] It continues:

> With the public goods component becoming the key element in the future CAP, it is increasingly important to have an harmonized legislative baseline with respect to what farmers are required to do. Beyond that, a high degree of subsidiarity should be given to Member States in order to better address demands for services, better known at the local level, and to tailor measures so as to match the increasingly heterogeneous structures and situations within EU agriculture.[19]

Given the current budgetary situation of various Member States, it is likely that the CAP will come under particular pressure. This pressure will be accentuated as the TFEU has ended the distinction between compulsory EU expenditure (under which CAP funding fell) and non-compulsory expenditure, thus subjecting agriculture to the same discipline as other expenditure as part of the multi-annual financial framework, thereby increasing the role of the European Parliament in decisions on the CAP's budget.

In April 2010, the Commission initiated a widespread public consultation on the future of the CAP, centred around four questions: Why do we need a CAP? What do citizens expect from agriculture? Why reform the CAP? And, what tools do we need for the CAP of tomorrow? The resulting contributions were brought together and presented at a conference in July 2010.[20] In response to the four questions, there was support for a CAP at European level as opposed to a series of national policies. The policy would promote equality of competition, maintain the diversity of farming systems and ensure the delivery of important public goods. Such goods included environmental protection and biodiversity support, and these goods would be realized whilst offering consumers high quality food at affordable/reasonable prices. As for how this would be achieved, the responses suggested continuing the current method of support or refocusing the policy to link agricultural support more closely with the delivery of specific public goods. Among the many conclusions offered from the consultations was the suggestion that the EU should 'take a

(EC) No 1698/2005 on support for rural development by the European Agricultural Fund for Rural Development (EAFRD) [2009] OJ L 30/100.

[18] *The Single Payment Scheme after 2013: New Approach New Targets*, available at <http://www.europarl.europa.eu/activities/committees/studies/download.do?language=en&file=31208>, 11 (accessed June 2011).

[19] ibid 13.

[20] See <http://ec.europa.eu/agriculture/cap-post-2013/conference/index_en.htm> (accessed June 2011).

strategic approach to CAP reform [and] go for total, not partial, solutions taking account of CAP challenges on the one hand and the interplay between the CAP and other internal and external EU policies on the other hand'.[21] A Commission paper on the options for reform, using the consultation exercise, was published in November 2010; before it is considered, a discussion of the objectives of the CAP and their expansion is undertaken.

C. The objectives of the CAP

The objectives for the CAP are laid down in Article 39(1), which provides:

1. The objectives of the common agricultural policy shall be:
   (a) to increase agricultural productivity by promoting technical progress and by ensuring the rational development of agricultural production and the optimum utilisation of the factors of production, in particular labour;
   (b) thus to ensure a fair standard of living for the agricultural community, in particular by increasing the individual earnings of persons engaged in agriculture;
   (c) to stabilise markets;
   (d) to assure the availability of supplies;
   (e) to ensure that supplies reach consumers at reasonable prices.

These objectives reflect the need for agriculture to contribute to overall economic growth in the Member States, a concern with the welfare of the rural population, and a concern with adequate food supplies for consumers.

The objective of an increase in agricultural productivity in Article 39(1)(a) is to be pursued by promoting technical progress and a rational development and optimum use of agricultural production factors, implying a type of regional structural policy. The use of the word 'thus' in paragraph (b) connects the first two objectives, leading to an argument that the regional structural policy must lead to an achievement of a fair standard of living for the agricultural community. However, the second part of paragraph (b) may suggest that it constitutes a type of income guarantee that would have to be achieved over the longer term. Paragraph (c) is more interested in the short-term effects of fluctuations in prices, demand and supply. The policy must include mechanisms designed to smooth out these fluctuations, thereby connecting paragraph (c) with paragraph (d) although no reference is made to techniques that would ensure such availability of supplies or to the scope of Community activity in this area. Finally, paragraph (e) confirms that the scope of the policy is not to be limited to producers and processors but is to extend to consumers. Prices for them are to be 'reasonable' as opposed to the standard of living of farmers, which is to be 'fair'.

[21] See <http://ec.europa.eu/agriculture/cap-post-2013/debate/report/summary-report_en.pdf> for a summary of the submissions. An executive summary is available at <http://ec.europa.eu/agriculture/cap-post-2013/debate/report/executive-summary_en.pdf> (accessed June 2011).

Turning from the literal approach to Article 39(1) to the jurisprudence of the Court, a range of possible approaches to the future development of the policy may be identified. For example, in *Danske Landboforeninger*, the Court pointed out that: 'the very wording of Article [39](1) shows that the increase in the individual earnings of persons engaged in agriculture is envisaged by being primarily the result of the structural measures described in sub-paragraph (a)'.[22] The Court has also declared that Article 39(1)(b) does not constitute an income guarantee for farmers.[23] Indeed, measures that reduced the prices payable to producers have been upheld as measures to stabilize markets.[24] Measures to achieve such stability that impact adversely on individuals do not give those individuals the right to complain.[25] In relation to the safeguarding of supplies, there are no fixed mechanisms to achieve this. As for paragraph (e), the Court made it clear in *Germany v Commission* that reasonable prices did not mean the lowest possible prices but had to be considered in the light of the CAP overall.[26] In a later case, the Court would rule that Article 39 would only be breached if a measure led to consumer prices that were obviously unreasonable.[27]

No hierarchy of objectives is indicated in Article 39(1). As early as 1968, the Court recognized that the Community institutions would have to balance the competing demands of Article 39(1) as they could not 'all be realised simultaneously and in full'.[28] The classic formulation of this balancing act occurred in *Balkan*, where the Court stated:

> In pursuing these objectives the Community institutions must secure the permanent harmonisation made necessary by any conflict between these aims taken individually and, where necessary, allow one of them temporary priority in order to satisfy the demands of the economic factors or conditions in view of which their decisions are made.[29]

This formulation (usually referred to as the *Balkan* formula) has been repeated on several occasions, with the Court limiting itself to an examination of whether the measure in question contains a manifest error, constitutes a misuse of power

[22] Case 297/82 *De Samvirkende Danske Landboforeninger v Ministry of Fiscal Affairs* [1983] ECR 3299, 3317. See further Joined Cases 36/80 and 71/80 *ICMSA* [1981] ECR 735.

[23] See, eg, Case 2/75 *Mackprang* [1975] ECR 607 and Case 281/84 *Bedburg* [1987] ECR 49.

[24] See, eg, Case 138/78 *Stölting* [1979] ECR 713, Case 250/84 *Eridania* [1986] ECR 117, and Case 46/86 *Romkes* [1987] ECR 2687.

[25] Joined Cases 63/72 and 69/72 *Wehrhahn* [1973] ECR 1229. See further Case C-353/92 *Greece v Council* [1994] ECR I-3411 involving a challenge to Council Regulation (EEC) No 1765/92 of 30 June 1992 establishing a support system for producers of certain arable crops [1992] OJ L 181/12, where the Court accepted that stabilizing markets can take precedence over a fair income for farmers in certain circumstances.

[26] Case 34/62 *Federal Republic of Germany v Commission of the European Economic Community* [1963] ECR 131.

[27] Case 5/73 *Balkan* [1973] ECR 1091.

[28] Case 5/67 *Beus* [1968] ECR 83, where the Court stated that: 'As those objectives are for the protection of agricultural producers as well as of consumers, they cannot all be realised simultaneously and in full'.

[29] Case 5/73 *Balkan*, n 27 above, 1112.

or whether the discretion enjoyed by the Community institutions has been exceeded.[30]

The *Balkan* formula conflicts with the approach adopted by the Court to the interpretation of Article 2 of Regulation 26/62 whereby an agreement hoping for exemption from the competition provisions must satisfy all the objectives of the CAP, as demonstrated by the decision in *FRUBO*.[31] The *Balkan* formula also suggests that, at some stage, the Court may overrule a measure of the institutions if the situation of 'temporary priority' is continued for a substantial period of time, thus jeopardizing the achievement of the other CAP objectives. The possibility that the Court could adopt such an approach was highlighted in its decision in *Behla-Mühle,* in which the Court used the objectives in Article 39(1), the rule on non-discrimination contained in Article 40(2) and the general principle of proportionality to rule that the obligations imposed by the contested Regulation were not necessary to attain the objectives of the CAP.[32] Considerable latitude has been given to the institutions by the *Balkan* formula but, as *Behla-Mühle* indicated, there are limits to that latitude. The limits were hinted at in *Crispoltoni II* where, after repeating the *Balkan* formula, the Court continued: 'That harmonisation must preclude the isolation of any one of those objectives in such a way as to render impossible the realisation of other objectives.'[33]

It is only to be expected that the objectives set for the CAP in the original Treaty would be very economically oriented—securing a fair standard of living for the agricultural community, stabilizing markets and ensuring reasonable prices for consumers. The Chapter on Agriculture does make reference to other objectives—rational development of agricultural production, the gradual structural reform of the sector, vocational training of the agricultural workforce and economic development of rural areas. With the transformation of the European Economic Community into the European Union, the demands placed on the CAP would become less focused on the economic welfare of the individual farmer and more focused on the contribution that agriculture could make to a wider variety of economic, social and cultural objectives.

[30] See, eg, Case 29/77 *Roquette Frères* [1977] ECR 1835; Case 203/86 *Spain v Council* [1988] ECR 4563, Case C-311/90 *Hierl* [1992] ECR I-2061 and Case C-280/93 *Germany v Commission* [1994] ECR I-4973. See further the repetition of the *Balkan* formula by the then Court of First Instance (now the General Court) in Case T-489/93 *Unifruit Hellas* [1994] ECR II-1201.

[31] Case 71/74 *Nederlandse Vereniging voor de fruit- en groentenimporthandel, Nederlandse Bond van grossiers in zuidvruchten en ander geimporteerd fruit 'Frubo' v Commission of the European Communities and Vereniging de Fruitunie* [1975] ECR 563.

[32] Case 114/76 *Bela-Mühle Josef Bergmann KG v Grows-Farm GmbH & Co. KG* [1977] ECR 1211, para 6. See further Case 116/76 *Granaria* [1977] ECR 1247.

[33] Joined Cases C-133/93, C-300/93 and C-362/93 *Antonio Crispoltoni v Fattoria Autonoma Tabacchi and Giuseppe Natale and Antonio Pontillo v Donatab Srl.* [1994] ECR I-4863, 4903. See further Joined Cases 197–200, 243, 245 and 247/80 *Ludwigshafner Walzmühle* [1981] ECR 3211 for a similar statement.

D. Expanding the scope of the CAP

Article 40 makes it clear that 'the common organisation shall be limited to pursuit of the objectives set out in Article 39'. The ordinary legislative procedure, as set out in Article 43, was to be used to establish the common organizations of the market but this procedure has also been used as a legal base, either singly or with another provision of the Treaty, for legislation covering measures with objectives not found in Article 39. An early example cited by Usher is Community health legislation, more particularly Directive 69/464 on the control of potato wart disease and Directive 69/465 on the control of the potato cyst eelworm.[34] Although these measures had joint legal bases, subsequent legislation would be adopted on the basis of Article 43 alone and this would be challenged before the Court, for example, in a challenge by the United Kingdom to the legal base used for Directive 85/649 on the use of hormones in beef.[35]

The United Kingdom, supported by Denmark, argued that Article 43 did not constitute a sufficient legal basis for the Directive as although it had agricultural policy objectives, it was also directed at harmonizing the laws of the Member States safeguarding the interests and health of consumers, which is not one of the objectives of the CAP. In response, the Court noted that Article 43 has to be interpreted in the light of both Articles 39 and 40, and that it follows from the second paragraph of Article 39 that 'agricultural policy objectives must be conceived in such a manner as to enable the Community institutions to carry out their duties in the light of developments in agriculture and in the economy as a whole'.[36] It continued:

> Efforts to achieve objectives of the common agricultural policy, in particular under common organizations of the markets, cannot disregard requirements relating to the public interest such as the protection of consumers or the protection of the health and life of humans and animals, requirements which the Community institutions must take into account in exercising their powers.[37]

For the Court, there was thus no need to have recourse to another provision of the Treaty as a joint legal basis as this particular measure contributed to the achievement of one or more of the objectives listed in Article 39.

The Court went on to point out that, by virtue of Article 38(2), which accords precedence to the specific provisions on agriculture over the more general provisions on the establishment of the internal market, in the absence of specific provisions outlining other objectives, the general provision on harmonization

[34] JA Usher, *EC Agricultural Law*, 2nd edn (Oxford: Oxford University Press, 2001). The Directives were published in [1969] OJ L 323/1 and 3.

[35] Council Directive 85/649/EEC of 31 December 1985 prohibiting the use in livestock farming of certain substances having hormonal action [1985] OJ L 382/228.

[36] Case 68/86 *United Kingdom v Council* [1988] ECR 855, para 10.

[37] ibid para 12.

cannot restrict the scope of Article 43.[38] This approach has been followed in subsequent cases but the judgment suggests that in those instances in which there is a specific legal base elsewhere in the Treaty, that provision should be joined to Article 43.[39] Although the Court chose to ignore the introduction of Article 152 (now Article 168 TFEU), which required that health protection measures should form a constituent part of other Community policies, in the challenge to Regulation 820/97 introducing a new system for the identification and registration of bovine animals and the labelling of beef and beef products, the immediate successor to this Regulation was based on Article 152(4)(b) (now Article 168(4)(b) TFEU).[40]

As specific legal bases for Community action, whether joint or shared, have been added to the Treaty and as the scope of Community activities has enlarged, so too have the demands placed on the CAP. At the 2001 Göteborg European Council, it was agreed that:

> the Common Agricultural Policy and its future development should, among its objectives, contribute to achieving sustainable development by increasing its emphasis on encouraging healthy, high quality products, environmentally sustainable production methods, including organic production, renewable raw materials and the protection of biodiversity.[41]

These demands would have represented a considerable challenge for the future direction of the CAP had it not been for the fact that the policy had already been active in these areas. Alongside the development of a prices and markets policy, the Community had also been active in developing the second pillar of the CAP, a structural policy which was anticipated in Article 39, especially in paragraph 2.

In comparison with the prices and markets policy, structural policy was slow to develop, with the first legislative measures not emerging until 1972.[42] A further Directive on mountain and hill farming emerged in 1975.[43] A higher profile began to emerge as these measures were replaced by Regulation 797/85 and strengthened further by Regulation 1760/87 as part of the move from a structural policy to a

[38] ibid para 16. The Court cited here both Case 83/78 *Pigs Marketing Board v Redmond* [1978] ECR 2347 and Case 177/78 Case 177/78 *Pigs and Bacon Commission v McCarren* [1979] ECR 2161.

[39] See, eg, Case 131/86 *United Kingdom v Council* [1988] ECR 905.

[40] Council Regulation No 820/97 of 21 April 1997 establishing a system for the identification and registration of bovine animals and regarding the labelling of beef and beef products [1997] OJ L 117/1. See Case C-269/97 *Commission and European Parliament v Council* [2000] ECR I-2257 and Council Regulation (EC) 999/2001 of 22 May 2001 laying down rules for the prevention, control and eradication of certain transmissible spongiform encephalopathies [2001] OJ L 147/1. According to the third recital of the Preamble to this Regulation, it 'directly concerns public health and is relevant to the functioning of the internal market. It covers products which are included in Annex I to the Treaty as well as products which are not. Consequently, it is appropriate to choose Art 152(4)(b) of the Treaty as the legal basis'.

[41] Bulletin of the EU, 6-2001, I 15.

[42] Council Directive 72/159/EEC of 17 April 1972 on the modernization of farms [1972] OJ L 96/1; Council Directive 72/160/EEC (2) of 17 April 1972 on measures to encourage the cessation of farming and the reallocation of utilized agricultural areas for the purposes of structural improvement [1972] OJ L 96/9; Council Directive 72/161/EEC of 17 April 1972 concerning the provision of socio-economic guidance for and the acquisition of occupational skills by persons engaged in agriculture [1972] OJ L 96/15.

[43] Council Directive 75/268 on mountain and hill farming and farming in certain less favoured areas [1975] OJ L 128/1.

rural development policy.[44] With the reform of the policy in the 1990s, rural development policy would become even more significant, notably with the introduction of various accompanying measures as part of the 1992 reform package and the confirmation of the move to a true rural development policy through Regulation 1257/99, which was part of the Agenda 2000 reforms.[45] Further reforms followed in 2005 with Regulation 1698/2005 on support for rural development by the European Agricultural Fund for Rural Development, which had the goal of supporting sustainable rural development through focusing on three key areas; the agri-food economy, the environment, and the broader rural economy and population.[46] As reform progressed, support under this Regulation would increasingly be tied to supporting the cross-compliance criteria introduced as part of the Single Farm Payment introduced in the 2003 Mid-Term Review.[47] These criteria would include environmental protection, public health (including animal and plant health) and animal welfare.

The animal welfare cross-compliance criteria include the Directives on the protection of animals kept for farming purposes and those laying down minimum standards for the protection of calves and pigs.[48] The first of these may be seen as Community recognition of the Council of Europe's Convention for the Protection of Animals kept for Farming Purposes, which all Member States have ratified. The emphasis on animal welfare is also evidence of the growing importance of promoting animal welfare, which was recognized in the Protocol on the Protection and Welfare of Animals attached to the Treaty of Amsterdam. The Community has argued for the inclusion of animal welfare in the negotiations for a new Agreement on Agriculture and, in the absence of an international consensus on standards in this area, has adopted an Action Plan on the Protection and Welfare of Animals.[49]

[44] Council Regulation (EEC) No 797/85 of 12 March 1985 on improving the efficiency of agricultural structures [1985] OJ L 93/1 and Council Regulation (EEC) No 1760/87 of 15 June 1987 amending Regulations (EEC) No 797/85, (EEC) No 270/79, (EEC) No 1360/78 and (EEC) No 355/77 as regards agricultural structures, the adjustment of agriculture to the new market situation and the preservation of the countryside [1987] OJ L 167/1.

[45] See Council Regulation (EEC) 2079/92 of 30 June 1992 instituting a Community aid scheme for early retirement from farming [1992] OJ L 215/91, and Council Regulation (EC) No 1257/99 of 17 May 1999 on support for rural development from the European Agricultural Guidance and Guarantee Fund (EAGGF) and amending and repealing certain Regulations [1999] OJ L 160/80.

[46] Regulation 1698/2005, n 4 above.

[47] Council Regulation (EC) 1782/2003 of 29 September 2003 establishing common rules for direct support schemes under the common agricultural policy and establishing certain support schemes for farmers and amending Regulations (EEC) No 2019/93, (EC) No 1452/2001, (EC) No 1453/2001, (EC) No 1454/2001, (EC) 1868/94, (EC) No 1251/1999, (EC) No 1254/1999, (EC) No 1673/2000, (EEC) No 2358/71 and (EC) No 2529/2001 [2003] OJ L 270/1. See further Regulation 73/2009, n 3 above, Article 6 and Annex II which lays down the current Community framework for standards of good agricultural and environmental condition.

[48] Respectively, Council Directive 98/58/EC of 20 July 1998 concerning the protection of animals kept for farming purposes [1998] OJ L 221/23; Council Directive 91/629/EEC of 19 November 1991 laying down minimum standards for the protection of calves [1991] OJ L 340/28, and Council Directive 91/630/EEC of 19 November 1991 laying down minimum standards for the protection of pigs [1991] OJ L 340/33.

[49] See Press Release *Improving Animal Welfare: EU Action Plan Adopted*, IP/06/64, 23 January 2006.

The importance of animal welfare has been further accentuated by Article 13 TFEU which, like the Protocol, requires the Union and the Member States to 'pay full regard to the welfare requirements of animals, while respecting the legislative or administrative provisions and customs of the Member States relating in particular to religious rites, cultural traditions and regional heritage'. As for the impact of this objective of promoting animal welfare, reference can be made to the interpretation of the Treaty of Amsterdam's Protocol in *Jippes*, in which the Court pointed out that 'it is apparent from its very wording that it does not lay down any well defined general principle of Community law which is binding on the Community institutions'.[50]

Animal health also features in the cross-compliance criteria requiring recipients of the Single Farm Payment to respect various provisions of Union law on the notification of various diseases.[51] Further measures in this area include those dealing with the identification and registration of animals.[52] Moving into the more general area of public health, cross-compliance criteria include compliance with the Directive on the prohibition on the use of certain substances having a hormonal effect,[53] and compliance with various provisions of Regulation 178/2002 laying down the general principles and requirements of food law. The relevant provisions of the latter Regulation provide that food and feed business operators should not place either food or feed on the market if it is unsafe (ie injurious to health or unfit for human consumption) and establishes the responsibilities of these operators with

[50] Case C-189/01 *H. Jippes, Afdeling Groningen van de Nederlandse Vereniging tot Bescherming van Dieren and Afdeling Assen en omstreken van de Nederlandse Vereniging tot Bescherming van Dieren v Minister van Landbouw, Natuurbeheer en Visserij* [2001] ECR I-5689, 5718.

[51] The diseases are foot and mouth disease, see Council Directive 85/511/EEC of 18 November 1985 introducing community measures for the control of foot-and-mouth disease [1985] OJ L 315/11, Article 3 (now Council Directive 2003/85/EC of 29 September 2003 on Community measures for the control of foot-and-mouth disease repealing Directive 85/511/EEC and Decisions 89/531/EEC and 91/665/EEC and amending Directive 92/46/EEC [2003] OJ L 306/1); swine vesicular disease, see Council Directive 92/119/EEC of 17 December 1992 introducing general Community measures for the control of certain animal diseases and specific measures relating to swine vesicular disease [1992] OJ L 62/29, Article 3; and bluetongue, see Council Directive 2000/75/EC of 20 November 2000 laying down specific provisions for the control and eradication of bluetongue [2000] OJ L 327/74, Article 3. A further cross-compliance criterion relates to the prevention, control and eradication of transmissible spongiform encephalopathies, Regulation 999/2001, n 40 above.

[52] See Council Directive 2008/71/EC of 15 July 2008 on the identification and registration of pigs [2008] OJ L 213/31; Council Regulation (EC) No 1760/2000 of 17 July 2000 establishing a system for the identification and registration of bovine animals and regarding the labelling of beef and beef products and repealing Council Regulation (EC) No 820/97 [2000] OJ L 204/1; and Council Regulation (EC) No 21/2004 of 17 December 2003 establishing a system for the identification and registration of ovine and caprine animals and amending Regulation (EC) No 1782/2003 and Directives 92/102/EEC and 64/432/EEC [2004] OJ L 5/8.

[53] Council Directive 96/22/EC of 29 April 1996 concerning the prohibition on the use in stockfarming of certain substances having a hormonal or thyrostatic action and of beta-agonists, and repealing Directives 81/602/EEC, 88/146/EEC and 88/299/EEC [1996] OJ L 125/3. See, for another example of cross-compliance criteria, Council Directive 91/414/EEC of 15 July 1991 concerning the placing of plant protection products on the market [1991] OJ L 230/1.

respect of the traceability of their products.[54] The Regulation is the centrepiece of the new EU Food Strategy promoting the safety of food from farm to fork and has a legislative basis encompassing agriculture, harmonization, international trade and public health.[55]

Other elements of the Food Strategy have a more specific agricultural legislative base. Regulation 510/2006 offers Union protection to Protected Designations of Origin, that is, products whose qualities and characteristics are essentially or exclusively a result of the particular geographical environment in which they originate, and Protected Geographical Indications, that is, products having a link with a specific geographical area in at least one of the stages of production, processing or preparation.[56] Also based on Article 43 is Regulation 834/2007 laying down a legal framework for organic products setting out the basic objectives and general principles for organic farming.[57] Whilst the former mechanisms focus on sustainable agriculture and production quality, the latter includes specific production methods and restrictions on the use of chemicals. As from July 2010, the use of the EU Logo on organic food products has been mandatory. An EU Ecolabel may be awarded to products that have a lower environmental impact than other products that have a similar purpose, use or properties, and are similar in terms of consumer perception. The label is to be awarded taking into account a number of European environmental objectives, for example, the impact of goods on climate change, nature and biodiversity.[58] No reference is made to Article 43 as the legal base of this Regulation, which is actually based on Article 175 (now Article 192 TFEU), from the environmental chapter of the Treaty.

The final set of cross-compliance criteria, of which there are five, relate to environmental protection. Two of these concern water pollution caused by the use of nitrates and certain dangerous substances.[59] Pollution is defined in the Nitrates Directive as the direct or indirect discharge of nitrates from agricultural sources 'into the aquatic environment, the results of which are such as to cause hazards to human health, harm to living resources and to aquatic ecosystems,

[54] Articles 14, 15, 17(1) and 18–20 of Council Regulation (EC) No 178/2002 of 28 January 2002 laying down the general principles and requirements of food law, establishing the European Food Safety Authority and laying down procedures in matters of food safety [2002] OJ L 31/1.

[55] See *White Paper on Food Safety* COM (1999) 719 final for an early discussion of the scope of the Food Strategy.

[56] Council Regulation (EC) No 510/2006 of 20 March 2006 on the protection of geographical indications and designations of origin for agricultural products and foodstuffs [2006] OJ L 93/12. See further Council Regulation (EC) No 509/2006 of 20 March 2006 on agricultural products and foodstuffs as traditional specialities guaranteed [2006] OJ L 93/1, setting out the requirements for the registration of agricultural products and foodstuffs as traditional specialities guaranteed, provided that they comply with certain specifications concerning their composition or method of production.

[57] Council Regulation (EC) No 834/2007 of 28 June 2007 on organic production and labelling of organic products and repealing Regulation (EEC) No 2092/91 [2007] OJ L 189/1.

[58] Council Regulation (EC) No 66/2010 of 25 November 2009 on the EU Ecolabel [2010] OJ L 27/1.

[59] Council Directive 91/676/EEC of 12 December 1991 concerning the protection of waters against pollution caused by nitrates from agricultural sources [1992] OJ L 375/1, Articles 4 and 5; and Council Directive 80/68/EEC of 17 December 1979 on the protection of groundwater against pollution caused by certain dangerous substances [1980] OJ L 20/43.

damage to amenities or interference with other legitimate uses of water'.[60] Waters with a nitrate content above a certain threshold are regarded as being polluted and an obligation is imposed on the Member States to designate all lands draining into those waters as being 'Nitrate Vulnerable Zones'.[61] Within such zones, an action programme must be implemented to reduce the level of nitrate pollution, irrespective of the source of such pollution. These two Directives are part of a wider Union programme with respect to water which includes the Urban Waste Water Treatment Directive and the Water Framework Directive; Article 22 of the latter provides for the repeal of Directive 80/68 by 22 December 2013.[62]

A further two Directives in the cross-compliance criteria category deal with the contribution of agriculture to nature conservation, namely Directive 79/409 on the conservation of Wild Birds and Directive 92/43 on the conservation of Natural Habitats and of Wild Fauna and Flora.[63] The Wild Birds Directive imposes an obligation on the Member States to take action to preserve, maintain or re-establish a sufficient diversity and area of habitats of all, naturally occurring, species of wild birds that occur within their territory. Special conservation measures are also required to protect the habitats of a number of particularly vulnerable species of wild birds listed in Annex I of the Directive, through the designation of Special Protection Areas and measures to avoid the pollution or deterioration of habitats. The Habitats Directive, which can be viewed as an extension of the Wild Birds Directive, seeks to protect wild animals and plants, and it is 'to contribute towards ensuring biodiversity through the creation of natural habitats and of wild fauna and flora in the European territory of the Members States'.[64] In both cases, measures taken by the Member States are required to take into account economic, social and cultural requirements, and regional and local characteristics. Under the Directive, there is a four-step process designed to create what is referred to as *Natura 2000*. Member States were required to propose a list of potential sites of Union interest to the Commission, which was required to establish a draft list of sites of Union importance that would be approved at European level and then Member States would be placed under an obligation to designate each site of Union importance as being a Special Area of Conservation. An obligation is imposed on the Member States to prevent the deterioration of such areas, specifically requiring

[60] Directive 91/676, ibid Article 2(j).

[61] ibid Article 3(2). The threshold is 50mg/l is based on standards recommended by the World Health Organization. Under Article 3(5), Member States may alternatively declare their whole national territory to be a Nitrate Vulnerable Zone.

[62] Respectively, Council Directive 91/271/EEC of 21 May 1991 concerning urban waste-water treatment [1991] OJ L 135/40 (as amended by Commission Directive 98/15/EC [1998] OJ L67/29), and Council Directive 2000/60/EC of 23 October 2000 establishing a framework for Community action in the field of water policy [2000] OJ L 327/1. Pending the repeal and replacement of Directive 80/68, n 59 above, its provisions are supplemented by Council Directive 2006/118/EC of 12 December 2006 on the protection of groundwater against pollution and deterioration [2006] OJ L 372/19.

[63] Respectively, Council Directive 79/409/EEC of 2 April 1979 on the conservation of wild birds [1979] OJ L 103/1 and Council Directive 92/43/EEC of 21 May 1992 on the conservation of natural habitats and of wild fauna and flora [1992] OJ L 206/7.

[64] ibid, Council Directive 92/43 Article 2(1).

the conducting of an environmental impact assessment of any plan or project that may have a significant effect on the area.[65] A negative assessment can be ignored where imperative reasons of overriding public interest would justify overruling the plan or project and no alternative exists.[66]

Although the two Directives establish a comprehensive legal framework to protect biodiversity within the Community, it has been noted that: 'in reality, Member States' implementation record in relation to each Directive has been less than impressive'.[67] The Commission has emphasized that the CAP must do more to protect biodiversity through the support of environmentally friendly farming practices.[68] The Member States also have an important role to play in this area as sitting alongside the cross-compliance criteria is a requirement for the Member States to develop codes of practice on maintaining land in good agricultural and environmental condition as a further eligibility requirement for the Single Payment. The 2008 CAP Health Check acknowledged the central role played by agriculture in protecting and enhancing biodiversity, managing and protecting water resources, and in tackling climate change. However, considerable effort will be needed to reverse the negative effects of agriculture in each of these areas.

Reflecting on the aspirations of the Göteborg European Council for the future development of the CAP, the emphasis in the cross-compliance criteria is on the promotion of an environmentally friendly policy that promotes high levels of food quality, through the operation of the European Food Safety Authority, which seeks to assure a high level of consumer protection. Other policies promote high quality products through the extension of the Community's intellectual property regime to geographical indications and the encouragement given to organic production. Should all of these areas be incorporated, as suggested by the Göteborg Council, into the objectives of the CAP?

E. New objectives for the CAP?

The CAP has evolved considerably since its introduction and it no longer is as heavily reliant on market management tools. In addition to the objectives listed in Article 39, the policy also seeks to realize a number of other objectives. These include the protection of the environment and biodiversity, animal health and welfare, and a contribution to consumer health and welfare through the production of safe food. These objectives can be found elsewhere in the Treaty and the

[65] See Council Directive of 27 June 1985 on the assessment of the effects of certain public and private projects on the environment [1985] OJ L 175/1, as amended by Council Directive 97/11/EC of 3 March 1997 amending Directive 85/337/EEC on the assessment of the effects of certain public and private projects on the environment [1997] OJ L 73/1.

[66] ibid Article 6(4).

[67] B Jack, *Agriculture and EU Environmental Law* (Farnham/Burlington, Vt.: Ashgate Publishing, 2009) 157.

[68] See European Commission, *Preparing for the 'Health Check' of the CAP Reform* COM (2007) 722 final, 9. See further *Biodiversity Plan for Agriculture: Implementation Report* COM (2001) 162 final.

question arises as to whether the objectives of the CAP should be reframed to take into account the demands that are placed upon it. One obvious answer to this question is 'no'. As the scope of the Treaty has expanded into new areas, objectives have been formulated which are attuned to the demands of that area and the legal base for the realization of these objectives can be added to Article 43, if there is a particular agricultural dimension to the realization of those objectives.

However, such a negative answer ignores the reality that the CAP has changed considerably from the policy introduced during the 1960s and maintained without major reform until the 2003 Mid-Term Review. The idea behind that policy was that agriculture was special and that specific support was needed to realize a fair standard of living for the farming community, to promote agricultural productivity, realize security of supply and secure reasonable prices for consumers. Agricultural productivity has increased and security of supply has been achieved—the Community is now a major exporter of some agricultural products. It could be argued that as Treaty bases exist for legislative activity in areas covered by the existing CAP, the CAP itself should be abandoned and agriculture should be treated like any other sector of the economy. However, this conclusion ignores the fact that there remains something special about agriculture which necessitates the existence of a common policy. It has been noted that: 'Farming created the countryside as it is today. Without farmers cultivating the soil and tending livestock, the countryside would gradually become a wilderness'.[69] This statement confirms that farming is special and support, if it is to be offered, should be offered in recognition of the public goods realizable though the continuation of farming.

Such public goods include the protection of the environment, the preservation of biodiversity, the promotion of animal health and welfare, rural and regional development and, more recently, the contribution that agriculture can make to addressing climate change. The 2003 Mid-Term Review, the 2005 Rural Development Regulation and the 2008 Health Check confirm a new orientation for agriculture within the Union in the form of support for the contribution that agriculture can make to the realization of these public goods. These changes to the very idea of the CAP have been made against the backdrop of the existing objectives of the policy. However, realization of these objectives has, for example, led to significant damage to the environment.[70] The problems caused by the CAP to the environment arise as a result of agricultural intensification through, for example, increasing specialization and increased livestock numbers. Improved use of technology, in particular fertilizers and pesticides, has had a major impact on biodiversity, has significantly increased water pollution and caused soil erosion. In its 2007 Report on the State of the Environment, the European Environmental Agency commented that the CAP 'can no longer be regarded as a major driver of

[69] House of Lords Select Committee on the European Communities, *20th Report: Agriculture and the Environment* (HMSO, 1984) para 127.

[70] For fuller discussion, see European Environmental Agency, *Fourth State of the Environment Report* (2007) at <http://www.eea.europa.eu/publications/state_of_environment_report_2007_1/chapter7.pdf> (accessed June 2011).

agricultural intensification. The main challenge appears to be to secure enough funding for the rural development pillar of the CAP and to ensure the successful implementation of agri-environment measures at Member State level'.[71] Mechanisms already exist to secure both of these requirements and proposals have been made to amend those mechanisms to secure these objectives.[72] The debate to be had reflects the need to promote legitimacy for continued support of farming by framing objectives for the policy that promote the 'interplay' between the CAP and other EU policies.

The Commission, in the *Agenda 2000* document, suggested that the objectives of the policy should be reframed, in particular by seeking to improve the competitiveness of Union agriculture, whilst guaranteeing the safety of food to consumers and ensuring a fair standard of living for the agricultural community.[73] Beyond these objectives, which are closely tied with the existing objectives, the Commission proposed that the policy should promote the stability of farm incomes, preserve sustainable farming through the integration of environmental goals, and create complementary or alternative income and employment opportunities for farmers and their families. Overall, the policy, which would have a more rural than agricultural focus, would also contribute to economic cohesion within the Union. Member States did not avail of the opportunity to reconsider the objectives of the policy during the Agenda 2000 discussions. With the change to the nature of the CAP, from market management to fully decoupled income support and a more active rural development policy, is the 2013 reform an opportunity for changes to be made to the objectives of the CAP?

The options for the 2013 reform were canvassed in a November 2010 Commission communication—*The CAP towards 2020: Meeting the Food, Natural Resources and Territorial Challenges of the Future*.[74] The Commission offered a choice between three broad policy options. Under the first option, there would be a harmonization of the Single Farm Payment across all the Member States and the focus of the policy would remain income support for 'active' farmers. There would also be some changes to the market management measures, especially in the area of risk management, and this would allow the EU to cope more efficiently with exceptional situations such as those that arose in the dairy sector in 2009.[75] As

[71] European Environmental Agency, *Fourth State of the Environment Report* (2007), 303.

[72] See, eg, *The Single Payment Scheme after 2013: New Approach New Targets*, available at <http://www.europarl.europa.eu/activities/committees/studies/download.do?language=en&file=31208>, Ch 2 (accessed June 2011) for a discussion of proposals from the various stakeholders.

[73] *Agenda 2000*, n 14 above, Ch 3.4.

[74] Communication from the Commission to the European Parliament, the Council, the European Economic and Social Committee and the Committee of the Regions, *The CAP towards 2020: Meeting the Food, Natural Resources and Territorial Challenges of the Future* COM (2010) 672 final.

[75] The recent milk market crisis was dealt with by allowing farmers to benefit from temporary State aids under the Temporary Crisis Framework, a measure available to all sectors across the Union. See [2009] OJ C 83/1 Temporary Community framework for State aid measures to support access to finance in the current financial and economic crisis. For details of other dairy support measures, see <http://europa.eu/rapid/pressReleasesAction.do?reference=IP/09/1599&format=HTML&aged=0&language=EN&guiLanguage=en>. The High Level Group appointed in the aftermath of the crisis recommended a series of market measures to ensure that farmers were much more prepared for future

for the second pillar, there would be strengthening of measures in accordance with the 2008 Health Check (climate change, water, biodiversity and renewable energy) but the increase in funds for these measures would be limited. Overall, the extent to which this reform scenario would refocus the policy in the way that was noted in the public consultations that preceded the Commission's communication may be doubted.

Under the second option, there would be a (substantial) re-design of direct payments, with the basic rate serving as income support and a compulsory additional aid for those extra costs associated with realizing the public goods demanded from agriculture.[76] Further additional payments would be available to compensate for specific natural restraints and a new scheme would be introduced for small farms. In the second pillar, the Commission would propose measures to ensure that existing instruments would be better aligned with priorities in the areas of the environment, climate change and/or restructuring and innovation at national/local levels. Whereas the first option envisaged risk management measures under the first pillar, this option would see the introduction of such measures as part of second pillar measures.[77]

It is implicit in the Commission document that it is this option which will lead to 'green growth in the agricultural sector and the rural economy as a way to enhance well-being by pursuing economic growth while preventing environmental degradation'.[78] The sense that this is the favoured option can also be gleaned from what the Commission suggests should be the three strategic aims of the policy in the period up to 2020, that is, to guarantee long-term food security, to provide European citizens with high quality food that is produced in a sustainable manner and to maintain the viability of rural communities. It suggested that:

> Reform of the CAP must also continue, to promote the greater competitiveness, efficient use of taxpayer resources and effective public policy returns European citizens expect, with regard to food security, the environment, climate change and social and territorial balance. The objective should be to build more sustainable, smarter and more inclusive growth for rural Europe.[79]

The third option presented by the Commission would be a much more far-reaching reform which would involve the gradual move away from income support and most market measures with a stronger focus on environmental and climate change, which would be addressed through the Rural Development Framework.[80] It

instances of instability, through measures such as forward contracting and the possible use of a futures market. See <http://ec.europa.eu/agriculture/markets/milk/hlg/report_150610_en.pdf> (accessed June 2011).

[76] *The CAP towards 2020*, n 74 above, 12 and Annex.

[77] As a result of being moved from Pillar 1 under the limited adjustment option to Pillar 2 under the integration option, implementation of risk management options would be a matter of discretion for the Member States.

[78] *The CAP towards 2020*, n 74 above, 6.

[79] ibid 3.

[80] ibid 12.

seems unlikely that this option would be in accordance with the prior public consultation exercise; however, others have suggested that it does represent the best way forward. For example, a proposal from five non-governmental organizations for a new CAP sets out a system of public payments rewarding farmers for the provision of public goods whilst maintaining that the 'polluter pays principle' should apply to all farming activity.[81] Discussion within the Council ahead of the publication of the Commission communication suggested that such a radical reform of the existing policy would be unacceptable.[82]

A Franco-German position paper maintained that the original objectives of the policy 'are still valid today' although it recognized the need for a wider vision of the CAP to allow the policy to adapt to the new global environment and to the needs and demands of European citizens.[83] The paper argued for the continuation of the reform path already set out through successive reforms and confirmed by the 2008 Health Check. Although greater market orientation in the CAP is endorsed, the position paper suggested that countervailing measures are needed 'to buffer the devastating effects of growing price volatility and market crises' but that risk assessment measures to stabilize farm incomes over time, such as insurance and mutual funds, would be investigated by Member States on a voluntary basis. The two-pillar structure would be maintained, and once the budget for each pillar had been decided there would be no modulation between pillars. The paper rejects national co-financing of expenditure under the first pillar and an EU-wide flat rate for direct payments, arguing that the rate should be set with regard to the net budgetary positions of Member States. Greater flexibility is supported on the distribution of direct payments and in rural development policies and measures to address new challenges (eg further streamlining of the cross-compliance criteria) would 'take very carefully into account the financial implications for each Member State'. Decisions on the future CAP budget would be made 'when decisions are made on all policies and the entire EU financial framework'.

Debate within the Council was crystallized by an informal meeting of the Agriculture Council held under the Belgian Presidency in September 2010.[84] The results of the meeting indicated that there was no questioning of the two-pillar structure, but it was noted that they should be complementary with tasks divided between pillars. As for the first pillar, a balance would have to be struck

[81] The proposal from the five NGOs (Birdlife International, European Environmental Bureau, European Forum on Nature Conservation and Pastoralism, International Federation of Organic Agriculture Movements and World Wide Fund for Nature) is available at <http://www.birdlife.org/eu/pdfs/Proposal_for_a_new_common_agricultural_policy_FINAL_100302.pdf> (accessed June 2011).

[82] See, eg, *Future of the CAP: Market management measures in the years after 2013* (15 February 2010) available at <http://register.consilium.europa.eu/pdf/en/10/st06/st06063.en10.pdf> and <http://www.consilium.europa.eu/uedocs/cms_data/docs/pressdata/en/agricult/113353.pdf> for the reaction of other Member States to the paper from the Spanish Presidency (accessed June 2011).

[83] See <http://capreform.eu/franco-german-position-on-future-of-the-cap/> for further details of the paper titled *Franco-German position for a strong CAP beyond 2013—new challenges and expectations for food biomass and the environment* (accessed June 2011).

[84] See <http://register.consilium.europa.eu/pdf/en/10/st15/st15339.en10.pdf> (accessed June 2011).

between income support and rewarding of farming's contributions to public goods. A safety net would also be necessary for cases of extreme price volatility and crises. Ministers recognized that the future CAP would have to address issues of competitiveness, climate change and biodiversity whilst also contributing to food security in a sustainable way. They concluded that the budget for agriculture should allow agriculture to fulfil its objectives. Debates within the Council since the publication of the Commission communication suggest that only minor changes to the policy are contemplated.[85] However, the decision on reform is no longer solely for the Council because, as a result of the Lisbon Treaty, the European Parliament is now a co-legislator in agricultural matters.

For the European Parliament's Committee on Agriculture and Rural Development, its June 2010 report suggested that the main challenge after 2013 would be ensuring food security at a European and global level, but increased food production will have to deal with the challenge of climate change.[86] A more competitive European agriculture sector would be needed to tackle climate change and promote innovation through green growth whilst ensuring balanced territorial development. The differences between the views of the Parliament and the Council would suggest a possible conflict between the two institutions. However, the extent of the conflict may not be significant as both institutions are in agreement on the fundamentals (greater integration of environmental concerns and the promotion of rural development) but are likely to disagree on the budgetary settlement.

F. Conclusion

Legislative proposals are due from the Commission later in 2011, which will undoubtedly reflect the discussions within the Council and the Parliament since the publication of the November 2010 communication. Discussion of these proposals provides an ideal opportunity to question and reframe the objectives of the policy in order to reflect its new and emerging ideational underpinnings. The recent reform path would suggest that these relate primarily to rewarding farmers for the provision of public goods, but the failure of the policy as reformed to have a positive impact on these public goods, such as the environment, has been widely noted. Part of the reason for this is that reform has been reactive and these public goods have never been treated as a central feature of agricultural policy.[87] This is

[85] See, eg, the meeting of the Agriculture Council on 13 and 14 December available at <http://www.consilium.europa.eu/uedocs/cms_data/docs/pressdata/en/agricult/118455.pdf>, and the meeting of 24 January 2011, available at <http://www.consilium.europa.eu/uedocs/cms_data/docs/pressdata/en/agricult/118939.pdf> (accessed June 2011).

[86] See *Report on the future of the Common Agricultural Policy after 2013* (2009/2236(INI)) Committee on Agriculture and Rural Development (Rapporteur: George Lyon) available at <http://www.europarl.europa.eu/sides/getDoc.do?pubRef=-//EP//NONSGML+REPORT+A7-2010-0204+0+DOC+PDF+V0//EN&language=EN> (accessed June 2011).

[87] See, eg, J Ockenden and M Franklin, *European Agriculture: Making the CAP Fit the Future* (London: Pinter, 1995) who noted at 44 the symbolic importance of the absence of an environmental aim from Article 39.

despite the wording of Article 11 TFEU (formerly Article 6 EC) which requires that 'environmental protection requirements must be integrated into the definition and implementation' of all Union policies and activities to promote sustainable development.[88]

Looking at the section of the Treaty in which Article 11 is located, other provisions call for consistency between the Union's policies and activities (Article 7), the promotion of a high level of employment (Article 9), the need for consumer protection requirements to be taken into account in defining and implementing Union policies and activities, and for specific policies, which include agriculture, and the need to have regard to animal welfare requirements (Article 13). These are provisions which have general application and are characterized as 'principles'. The latter are defined in the *Oxford English Dictionary* as 'a fundamental source, a primary element, force or law which produces or determine particular results; the ultimate basis of the existence of something'. This contribution began by noting the absence of Treaty amendments with respect to the objectives of the CAP but has shown that the policy has evolved to incorporate new objectives that have changed the idea of the CAP. Over that period, the idea of the Community also evolved and perhaps it is now time to interpret the objectives of the CAP in line with the principles that lie at the heart of the European Union. The debate on the future of the CAP in the run-up to the 2013 reform should not be limited to the mechanics of the policy but should also extend to its objectives and how they reflect the ultimate basis of the existence of the Union. Whilst this may be a moving target, at least the thick fog has dissipated.

[88] See Decision 2179/98 [1998] OJ L 275/1 which was the Agriculture Council's response to the 1998 Cardiff European Council's invitation to all relevant Councils to establish a strategy for environmental integration and sustainable development within their respective policy areas (EU Bull 6-1998, I.11.34). See, further, reaffirmation of this by the 1999 Helsinki European Council (EU Bull 12-1999, I.14.46–50) and the Biodiversity Action Plan for Agriculture and Regulation 870/2004 [2004] OJ L 162/18, launching a Community programme on the conservation, characterization, collection and utilization of genetic resources in agriculture.

15

Integrating 'Sustainable Development' in the European Government of Industry: Sea Fisheries and Aquaculture Compared

*Caitríona A Carter**

> It is in the sphere of agriculture that many of the fundamental institutional, financial and legal developments in the history of the Community have occurred.[1]

A. Introduction

Since the 1990s, European Union (EU) actors have sought to renew the transnational economic union with an ambitious political project of 'sustainable development'. Currently, this project's core policy goals are to combat global poverty; bring about climate change, clean energy, sustainable transport, sustainable consumption and production practices; conserve and manage natural resources, public health, social inclusion, demography and migration.

To meet these goals, actors across the EU are under a current duty to 'integrate' sustainable development into EU policies and industrial practices. This sectoral integration is considered crucial to the success of the EU's economic union: 'DG Environment has been at the forefront of efforts to push *integration* as a key (perhaps *the* key) substantive principle of sustainable-development'.[2] The extent to which these actors—and hence the 'EU'—have been effective in so doing has received mixed reviews in the literature. For example, Lightfoot and Burchell cite the World Development Movement's observation that whereas 'the US is undoubtedly the rogue state threatening the very concept of [sustainable development] . . . it

* Europa Institute, University of Edinburgh.

[1] J Usher, *Legal Aspects of Agriculture in the European Community* (Oxford: Clarendon Press 1998) 1.

[2] E Bomberg, 'Adapting Form to Function: From Economic to Sustainable Development Governance in the EU' in W Lafferty (ed), *Governance for Sustainable Development: The Challenge of Adapting Form to Function* (Cheltenham: Edward Elgar Publishing Ltd, 2004) 61–94, 71–2.

is the EU that has the potential to save the day'.[3] Some are more critical: 'The EU is both commended as a leading advocate of sustainable development and condemned for its failure to deliver on its commitments and promises.'[4] Others view the EU's commitment to sustainable development as an important symbolic strategy of action, which nonetheless remains at the level of symbolism.[5]

This chapter engages with these debates, arguing that a focus on industry is central for any critical assessment of sectoral integration to be made. This is because industries (or sectors) are viewed as significant spaces in which EU reality is co-produced by groups of actors on a daily basis.[6] Conceptualizing sustainable development as a contested social construction of development, I identify the challenges that actors face when seeking to integrate it within their industry—here, in European sea fisheries and aquaculture. In particular, I focus on problems identified (and solutions found) in giving meaning to sustainable development in both these industries and the processes through which this comes about.

European sea fisheries and aquaculture are interesting cases in which to explore sectoral integration for three main reasons. First, integration within these industries links to EU stated policy objectives to conserve and manage natural resources and to encourage sustainable production and consumption practices. Choices made in both industries also connect to public health. Scientific research has demonstrated that eating fish is not only good for you but also essential for mental health development. Sustainable development of both industries is consequently viewed as being in the (global) public interest.

Second, whereas European sea fisheries has, since 1983, been governed through the rules of a Common Fisheries Policy (CFP), European aquaculture has been regulated through EU general rules. Consequently, we can compare sectoral integration in an industry governed by a common policy with one that is not. What different challenges does this pose for integration, if any?

Third, internal market regulation of both industries has recently been subject to review and critically, for both, at a time when discussions of sectoral integration were high on the EU's agenda. Examining actor debates around reform processes is therefore a useful starting point for identifying arguments for change in the name of sustainable development. This is particularly so because there are contradictory statements about the trajectories of these two industries concerning their respective sustainable development. Collapsing EU fish stocks were evoked by actors in 2002 arguing for reform of the CFP away from 'command and control' management and

[3] Press Release, World Development Movement, *The Zero Sum Summit*, 30 August 2002; S Lightfoot and J Burchell, 'The European Union and the World Summit on Sustainable Development: Normative Power Europe in Action?' (2005) 43:1 *Journal of Common Market Studies* 75–95, 81.

[4] E Bomberg, n 2 above, 61.

[5] S Baker, 'Sustainable development as symbolic commitment: Declaratory politics and the seductive appeal of ecological modernization in the European Union' (2007) 16:2 *Environmental Politics* 297–317.

[6] C Carter and A Smith, 'Revitalizing Public Policy Approaches to the EU: "Territorial Institutionalism," Fisheries and Wine' (2008) 15:2 *Journal of European Public Policy* 263–81; C Carter and A Smith, 'What has Scottish Devolution Changed? Sectors, Territory and Polity-building' (2009) 4:3 *British Politics* 315–40; J Usher, n 1 above.

towards 'sustainable fisheries production'. Organizational changes made in response to these arguments have not only facilitated a rescuing of some stocks but also enhanced eligibility for international sustainable development accreditation. This stands in contrast with aquaculture, whose industrial development initially symbolized sustainable development of fisheries; indeed, it was seen as *the* sustainable solution to the decline in capture fisheries. More recently, however, sustainable development of industry practice must be constantly demonstrated across the food chain from feed-to-farm-to-fork.

To pursue these points further, the chapter is organized as follows. Section B reviews the stabilization of official EU formulations of sustainable development. Section C draws on empirical material from two funded-research projects to present and compare our two cases of sectoral integration. Detailed illustrations of the kinds of challenges that this has produced are drawn from Scottish-EU industry practice.[7]

B. Interpreting sustainable development: official EU formulations

As Haughton and Counsell have argued, there is no 'definitive meaning of sustainable development', rather 'it is necessary to recognise the multiplicity of sustainabilities and to analyse the ways in which these are shaped and mobilized in political discourse'.[8] Before examining these in our two industry cases, this section first reviews official EU formulations.

The EU's strategy has been shaped over the years through the interactions of a wide range of actors (both public and private) to become institutionalized as 'the overarching policy framework for all Union policies and strategies'.[9] It is not possible to do justice to the complexity of this process here, nor offer a detailed critique thereof.[10] Rather, I briefly illustrate how three core problematizations first

[7] The chapter draws on research findings from a British Academy funded project on 'Better Regulation and the Transformation of UK-EU Fisheries: A Re-defining of Regional Governance' (2005–07) and an Agence Nationale de La Recherche funded project on 'Le Gouvernement Europeén des Industries' (2009–13). During these projects, as well as documentary analysis and observation, the author has conducted semi-structured elite interviews with a range of EU, English and Scottish public and private actors, including European Commission and European Parliament officials, fishers, scientists, feed companies, salmon producers, e-NGOs amongst others.

[8] G Haughton and D Counsell, *Regions, Spatial Strategies and Sustainable Development* (London: Routledge, 2004) 72–3.

[9] European Council, European Council Conclusions, Euco 6/09, 11 December 2009, Brussels, 21.

[10] But see, eg, C Opoku and A Jordan, 'The European Union and the External Dimension of Sustainable Development: Ambitious Promises but Uncertain Outcomes?', paper presented at the Berlin Conference on the Human Dimension of Global Environmental Change, Potsdam, 2–3 December 2005; M Fergusson, C Coffey, D Wilkinson and D Baldock, *The Effectiveness of EU Council Integration Strategies and Options for Carrying Forward the Cardiff Process* (London: Institute for European Environmental Policy, 2001); D Wilkinson, M Fergusson, C Bowyer, J Brown, A Ladefoged, C Monkhouse and A Zdanowicz, *Sustainable Development in the European Commission Integrated Impact Assessment for 2003* (London: Institute for European Environmental Policy, 2004); U Collier,'Sustainability, Subsidiarity and Deregulation: New Directions in EU Environmental Policy' (1997) 6:2 *Environmental Politics* 1–23.

discussed in the 1987 United Nations' World Commission on Environment and Development (WCED) 'Brundtland Report'[11] were subsequently taken up and shaped by EU public actors to become institutionalized as core principles of the EU strategy. These are (a) sectoral integration; (b) the making of informed sustainable development choices; and (c) the consideration of the international dimension of sustainable development. Clearly, for each there exists a strong literature questioning the extent to which these notions are merely declaratory in nature, as distinct from actualized in practice. I do not address this question in this section, however. Rather, my aim is to describe and trace these formulations, leaving my analysis of their implementation for Section 2.

(1) Sectoral integration

'Sectoral integration' has been advanced by both EU actors and commentators as a key element of EU policy and has its roots in the Brundtland Report, widely accepted as the first formalized problematization of sustainable development on a global scale.[12] Brundtland argued that economic development had incurred 'environmental stress', whereby thresholds for eco-system integrity were being reached, potentially causing irreversible ecological damage and placing limits on future economic development.[13] A reproblematization of development was necessary to 'meet the needs of the present without compromising the ability of future generations to meet their own needs'.[14]

The organization of government business—with a separation of sectoral departments from environmental ministries—was a consistent explanation given for development-caused environmental degradation:

> Society has failed to give responsibility for preventing environmental damage to the 'sectoral' ministries and agencies whose policies cause it.[15]

Handling business in this way neither acknowledged nor reflected the reality of the interconnectedness of economic and ecological systems and reduced environmental departments' role to redressing environmental effects caused by others.[16] The authors therefore called for a '[n]ew approach.... [one] that *integrates* production with resource conservation and enhancement'.[17] The case for integration of the 'economic' with the 'environment' was argued at length and consistently throughout, whereby mandates of sectoral departments had to be expanded to include environmental responsibilities.[18]

[11] World Commission on Environment and Development (WCED), *Our Common Future* (Oxford: Oxford University Press, 1987).

[12] W Lafferty,'Introduction: Form and Function in Governance of Sustainable Development' in W Lafferty (ed), *Governance for Sustainable Development: The Challenge of Adapting Form to Function* (Cheltenham: Edward Elgar Publishing, 2004) 1–31.

[13] WCED, n 11 above, 44, 47.

[14] ibid 54. [15] ibid 50. [16] ibid 25.

[17] ibid 50 (emphasis added). [18] ibid 26, 50–1, 71.

That sectoral integration be the *a priori* starting point for the implementation of a strategy of sustainable development is an argument that was taken up and ultimately accepted by all EU public bodies. This was facilitated because 'environmental integration' was already a concept that had been developed and mobilized by DG Environment to enhance the effectiveness of EU environmental policy.[19] Whereas environmental integration had remained a tool predominantly used by DG Environment, instigating 'sectoral integration' was soon taken up by the Commission as a whole, for example, in the Commission's Communication 'Partnership for Integration',[20] which formed the basis of the 'Cardiff Process' agreed by the European Council in 1998. There, Member States established 'sectoral integration' and sectoral councils of ministers were tasked with identifying challenges for achieving sustainable development in their respective sector. Critically,

> [t]his pushed [environmental integration] from merely a principle being championed by DG Environment in successive Environmental Actions Plans to a concept which entailed action from all sectors within the EU.[21]

Whereas sectoral integration was initially stabilized in this way, the question of 'what' required to be integrated was still being posed by the end of the 1990s. For example, did sustainable development in fact demand more than the integration of the 'environment' into the 'economic'? Asking this question was particularly significant because although the Brundtland Report made links between environmental problems, economic development and political and social factors, their collective connection to the concept of 'integration' was less well articulated.[22] Opoku and Jordan argue that at the beginning of 2000s, EU documentation was being published which suggested that its 'use of the concept of [sustainable development was beginning] to merge with the trends in the common understanding of the concept post-Brundtland'[23] and, in particular, as discussed at the UN conference in Rio. They cite a reformulation by the Commission that

> sustainable development must strike a balance between the economic, social and environmental objectives of society, in order to maximise well-being in the present, without compromising the ability of future generations to meet their needs.[24]

This evolution in the concept of sustainable development can be traced in successive EU documentation since the early 2000s. More substantively, this reformulation was codified in Commission integrated impact assessment tools, whereby Commission officials were expressly requested to illustrate potential economic, environmental *and social* impacts of a proposed regulatory instrument or policy reform.

[19] U Collier, n 10 above, 2.
[20] Commission of the European Communities, *Partnership For Integration: A strategy for Integrating Environment into EU Policies* COM (1998) 333 final.
[21] C Opoku and A Jordan, n 10 above, 5.
[22] WCED, n 11 above, 49.
[23] C Opoku and A Jordan, n 10 above, 6.
[24] ibid.

Additionally, the Commission was to review inter-sectoral strategies, action plans and Member States' meeting of EU targets from this perspective.[25]

These reformulations have ultimately resulted in stabilizing within EU discourse two slightly different meanings of integration. First, sectoral integration means that those responsible, for example, for regulating sea fisheries must take responsibility for sustainable development of their sector. Second, the principle of integration subsequently requires that, once mainstreamed, 'some balance of economic, environmental and social priorities' must thenceforth be sought by actors when developing regulatory instruments.[26]

(2) The making of informed choices

The second EU official formulation discussed here is the making of 'informed' sustainable development choices. Again, this notion can be traced back to Brundtland.[27] To render sustainable development choices legitimate, it was necessary to include a range of actors in decisional processes:

> Making the difficult choices in achieving sustainable development will depend on the widespread support and involvement of an informed public and of NGOs, the scientific community, and industry.[28]

As Brundtland made clear, there was no single way to implement sustainable development within sectors. Different interpretations were possible and change could be brought about through direct interventionist regulation or through market mechanisms. The key principle in all of this was one of social justice. For any choice made would entail winners and losers. Therefore, even if in parts of this Report the relation of the 'social' to integration was underspecified, nonetheless the authors made clear that, for them, social justice 'within and amongst nations' must be a core guiding principle of sustainable development regulatory practice.[29]

The 'making of informed choices' was also taken up and adapted as a core notion of EU sustainable development, for example, the 2005 EU policy guiding principles include solidarity within and between generations; involvement of citizens, businesses and social partners; and the use of best available knowledge.[30] Additionally, impact assessments must include evidence of consultation of 'relevant stakeholders' in the development of policy options. This is also the case for policy reform, whereby the Commission is under the obligation to conduct open external consultation exercises before setting out reform strategies. As with sectoral

[25] Commission of the European Communities, *On the Review of the Sustainable Development Strategy: a Platform for Action* COM (2005) 658 final; Commission of the European Communities, *Mainstreaming Sustainable Development into EU Policies: 2009 Review of the European Union Strategy for Sustainable Development* COM (2009) 400 final.

[26] S Connelly, 'Mapping Sustainable Development as a Contested Concept' (2007) 12:3 *Local Environment* 259–78, 269.

[27] WCED, n 11 above, 25.

[28] ibid 36.

[29] ibid 59.

[30] *On the Review of the Sustainable Development Strategy: a Platform for Action*, n 25 above, 23–4.

integration, scholars have argued that the adoption of this notion was facilitated by the fact that the EU had already institutionalized stakeholder participatory norms following the 2000 good governance agenda.[31] The making of informed sustainable development choices seemed to 'fit', therefore, with already stabilizing consultation practices, and built upon and extended these.

(3) The international dimension of sustainable development

A final EU formulation discussed here is the requirement to consider the global impact of internal market choices. And, like the other two, this also had its origins in the Brundtland Report, which made a strong connection between the internal and external dimensions of sustainable development.[32] At its most fundamental, the global goal for sustainable development was to meet the needs of the world's poor and encourage growth in developing countries. For this to happen, radical lifestyle changes, including changes in consumption patterns, values and constructions of needs are required to take place for those living in rich countries.[33] This was linked to the idea of the global reach and interdependence of markets and lifestyles and the understanding that consumption and regulatory choices made in one trading bloc affected the content of development and growth in another. Therefore, although Brundtland did not argue against continued growth per se, it did call for a radical change in the content of that growth.[34]

Scholars have argued that that the external dimension of sustainable development has taken time to stabilize as part of the EU strategy, with actors such as the World Wide Fund for Nature exerting pressure on EU organizations to bring this about.[35] Nonetheless the commitment to reconcile internal sectoral integration with the external operation of a single market does now form part of this strategy:

> This link between the external and the internal dimensions of sustainability is a hugely ambitious policy objective, which sets the EU apart from other broadly comparable political entities such as the US.[36]

Once again, many policy documents and political statements issued by EU organizations and actors make statements to this effect and the EU has been active in the international arena.[37] Additionally, impact assessments conducted by Commission officials are required to take into account external impacts of applying sectoral integration and the European Commission, European Parliament and Council have begun to explore how to affect change in consumers' lifestyle choices

[31] E Bomberg, n 2 above.
[32] C Opoku and A Jordan, n 10 above.
[33] WCED, n 11 above, 25.
[34] ibid 62.
[35] B Dalal-Clayton, *The EU Strategy for Sustainable Development: Process and Prospects* (London: International Institute for Environment and Development, 2004).
[36] C Opoku and A Jordan, n 10 above, 3.
[37] S Lightfoot and J Burchell, n 3 above.

and eco-innovation.[38] In short, as with integration and the making of informed choices, the taking into account of the international dimension of sustainable development has, officially at least, been endorsed as a core element of the EU's overall policy.

In summary, EU declarations of sustainable development can be conceptualized as procedural, in that they anticipate the taking of action by regulators of sectors. Yet, they are also value-laden in that they anticipate the asking and answering of specific questions: What balance of economic, social and environmental goals? Who should decide and why? What is the potential international impact?

Conceptualizing EU sustainable development as in Table 1 therefore leads us to hypothesize that the implementation of EU formulations through sectoral integration is likely to give rise to multiplicities of sustainable development, whereby one might find many answers to the questions posed and/or not all questions asked and answered. Empirical research of sectoral integration is therefore critical in order to understand why and how actors mobilize around EU declarations and settle upon certain interpretations of sustainable development within their industry. It is to this we now turn.

Table 1 Conceptualizing EU sustainable development as value-laden procedures

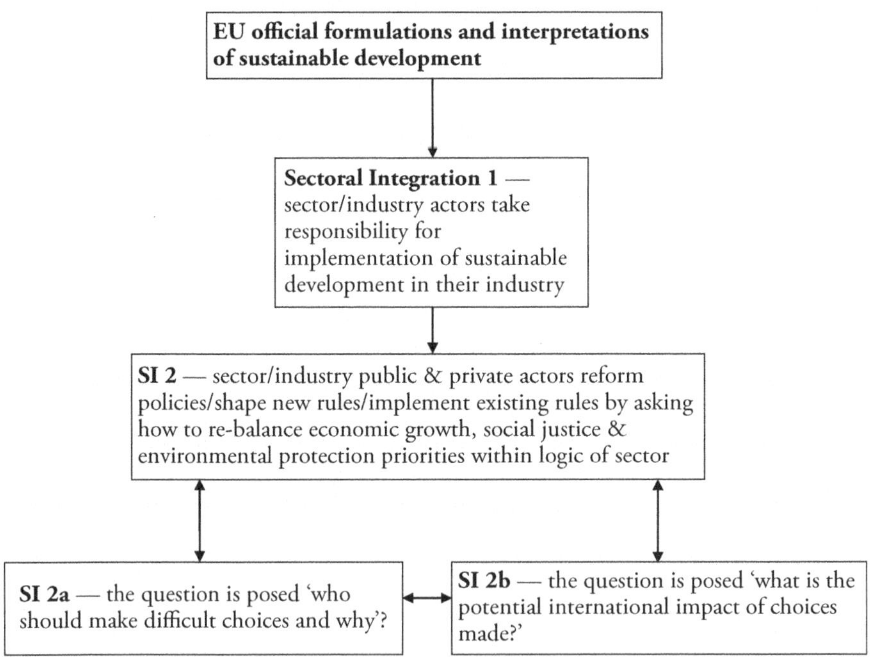

[38] *Mainstreaming Sustainable Development into EU Policies: 2009 Review of the European Union Strategy for Sustainable Development*, n 25 above, 7.

C. From interpretation to implementation: EU sea fisheries and aquaculture

Before presenting my cases, I briefly explain my analytical approach. This is important not least because scholars have cautioned against normative approaches within sustainable development studies. Connelly argues that many texts assessing sustainable development practices assume definitive understandings of either what sustainable development *should* be—or what *strong* sustainable development *is*—against which actor practices are measured.[39] Here, I understand sustainable development to be a social construction of development that is essentially contested. This notwithstanding, I also understand that certain interrogatory interpretations of sustainable development have become stabilized as representative of the EU's approach. These anticipate change, and to capture their effects therefore requires holding a theory of change.

Here, I study change using tools developed within interpretivist institutionalism.[40] Put simply, this theory gives prominence to 'beliefs' as sources of change, and hence of power and conflict. Yet, it also holds that these beliefs require to be mobilized within institutionalized environments. By 'institutionalized environments', I mean that industries will be governed by actors who tend to be ordered in power hierarchies (which may be stable or unstable) and that these actors will tend to act within a common logic of economic action (routines, techniques, procedures, tools, skills), relevant to the industry and developed over time. The mobilization of 'new beliefs' by actors within these environments potentially puts pressure on these hierarchies of power and/or logics of action. Actors seeking to institutionalize their interpretations of sustainable development might already be in positions of power and mobilize around these in order to protect their authority. Alternatively, sustainable development might be mobilized by actors who hitherto have been weak and who propose policy innovation to seek to influence.[41] For, 'if sustainable development is indeed emerging as a dominant discourse, astute actors recognise that the terms of this discourse should be cast in terms favourable to them'.[42] Studying sectoral integration within an institutionalized industry, therefore, will always require that pre-existing hierarchies of actors and substantive logics of action are taken into account in order to evaluate change in these which can be linked to actor deliberations over sustainable development.

Groups of actors seeking to impose *their* definition of sustainable development on others within an industry will have to develop persuasive arguments and

[39] S Connelly, n 26 above.

[40] C Hay, 'Interpreting Interpretivism, Interpreting Interpretations: the New Hermeneutics of Public Administration' (2011) 8:1 *Public Administration* 167–82; C Carter, 'Making Politics Through Regulation: How Interpretivist Institutionalism Can De-centre Sustainability Policymaking' paper presented at 6th International Conference in Interpretive Policy Analysis, Cardiff, 23–25 June, 2011.

[41] W Genieys, and M Smyrl (eds), *Elites, Ideas and the Evolution of Public Policy* (Basingstoke: Palgrave MacMillan, 2008).

[42] J Dryzek, *The Politics of the Earth* (Oxford: Oxford University Press, 1997) 124.

knowledge and build alliances. As Connelly states, 'arguments over the meaning of sustainable development are to be expected'.[43] Critically in this process, pre-existing framings or problematizations of production and commercial practices might require to be reframed or reproblematized. These activities—(re)problematization, making of arguments, alliance-building—can collectively be analysed as 'political work'.[44] In political work, the social construction of actors' interests is critical. This is because, as new institutionalist accounts have convincingly argued, institutions tend not to change and this because of heavily invested beliefs of dominant groups of actors. Research must capture therefore 'the social and political processes in and through which [sustainable development] interests are identified, constructed and rendered.... "actionable"'.[45]

Finally, we stress that of course EU policies do not operate in a vacuum. This might seem obvious, yet it is surprising how many writers look for evidence of implementation of sustainable development by only examining EU official documentation.[46] We have argued that finding evidence of sustainable development practice requires that research look within industries, where EU formulations of sustainable development will be translated within pre-existing sectoral logics. Given the extent of interdependence of economic action, it is likely that dominant representations and routines of these logics will have been established through struggles over the intersections of EU with global, state, regional and local public policies and action. Additionally, in industry practice, choices over production methods are interconnected with commercial ones. This means that one must also take into account private rules and other devices constructing markets and sales. Any translation of sustainable development will therefore be incorporated within other rules and norms, potentially reshaping them or being reshaped by them, and research must capture this process. To show this here, for both European sea fisheries and aquaculture, I will illustrate the challenges of sectoral integration of sustainable development with examples from these two industries in Scotland.

(1) Sectoral integration and sea fisheries: from 'command and control' to 'sustainable fisheries production'?

Sustainable development is not a term generally associated with EU capture fisheries. Yet, organizational changes made to EU regulation-setting following the 2002 reform provide a first illustration of actor mobilizations around the 'making of informed decisions' to bring about sustainable development of their industry. In EU fisheries, the main regulatory goal is to set fishing effort—how much (or little) you can fish without either depleting resources or collapsing an industry which

[43] S Connelly, n 26 above, 262.

[44] B Jullien and A Smith (eds), *Industries and Globalization: the Political Causality of Difference* (Basingstoke: Palgrave Macmillan, 2008).

[45] C Hay, 'Ideas and the Construction of Interests' in D Beland and RH Cox (eds), *Ideas and Politics in Social Science Research* (Oxford: Oxford University Press, 2011) 136.

[46] S Baker, n 5 above.

provides economic and social structures in coastal areas of Europe. Part of this calculation, that is, the impact of fishing on fish stocks, is modelled by marine biologists, and fishermen have had little say in these calculations. The case study reveals how fishers (and e-NGOs) sought to legitimize their right to have greater influence in the making of these calculations through evoking sustainable development arguments. In particular, it reveals the role of 'knowledge' in sectoral integration, as actors sought to demonstrate their worth through claiming 'legitimate knowledge' of the seas.

(a) Pre-existing actor hierarchies and logics of action (1983–2001)

Since 1983, resource management of EU fisheries has been one of 'command and control' governed through the rules of the CFP. Annual quantitative instruments of Total Allowable Catches and MS Quotas (TQs) have determined fishing effort as well as power hierarchies between actors. The Commission holds exclusive authority to propose fishing effort for the EU as a whole, yet due to its limited resources, it depends upon scientific advice on the status of EU fish stocks provided by the International Council of Exploration of the Seas (ICES), composed of marine biologists.[47] Once the Commission has issued its proposals in any given year, it has then been up to Member States, negotiating with each other and Commission representatives within the December Council of Ministers, to agree catch limitations.

'Command and control' management has given power to the Commission, the scientific community and national governments in setting fishing effort. Fishers for the most part have been 'outside' key decision-making arenas. Whereas scientists were constructed as legitimate holders of knowledge of fish stocks, fishers were not. 'Command and control' management was rather premised upon constructions of fishers' role in industry, derived from neoclassical economics as 'exploiters' of the common resource. Accordingly, fishers' perceived 'natural' behaviour—to fish without care for future generations—had to be controlled through regulation. The fishing industry was thereby given a limited consultative role:

> Scientists did the analysis, gave the results to the Commission, Commission discussed it with Member States and Norway and a decision was made. Industry was outside that.[48]

This organizational separation of fishers from scientists and managers gave rise to strong competitions between these groups of actors and ultimately led to regulatory failure to control fishing activities. Different problems emerged in the 1990s. In a context where TQs were consistently being reduced to conserve fish stocks, competitions between fishers versus managers and scientists became increasingly hostile as fishers began to mobilize collectively to contest the validity of ICES advice and the final choices made by Member States. Although at times these

[47] C Lequesne, 'The Common Fisheries Policy' in H Wallace and W Wallace (eds), *Policy-Making in the European Union* (Oxford: Oxford University Press, 2000).

[48] Interview material, n 7 above.

mobilizations took the form of organized protest, such as blockading ports, mostly they consisted of non-compliance with quotas set.

This behaviour in turn was evoked by others to justify continued representation of catchers as 'rogues', strengthening arguments for more 'command and control' of production practices. It also caused problems for the science. Stock assessment derived from modelling, whereby 'commercial catch and effort data' as well as scientific 'research vessel data' were fed into a model and used to construct stock histories and predict their futures.[49] However, scientists' assumptions about commercial catch and effort data were increasingly at odds with actual catchers' practices, where black landings were frequent. This created bias in the modelling and even greater uncertainty on the health of the stock. But acquiring accurate data was not possible, given the by then deeply institutionalized hostilities between fishers and scientists. Consultation within Commission advisory committees did not even extend to exchange between groups of actors on modelling assumptions. Rather 'people come with their set speeches . . . fishermen sit on one side, scientists on the other, and lob bricks at one another'.[50]

For all these reasons, therefore, even though levels of effort were being decreased in line with precautionary principles, for some stocks they required to be much lower and were, in any case, being ignored by some catchers. In the case of North Sea cod, this came to a head in 2000–01, when stocks were identified as being on the verge of collapse and the fishery was closed for weeks at a time. Of course, much more can be said about the causes and responsibilities of policy failure. The point to stress is that a certain logic of action had become institutionalized, which was itself causing consistent unsustainable development and it was hard to see how this could change.

(b) Reform processes: actor mobilizations and arguments (2001–2004)

Up until 2002, one cannot talk about sustainable development within EU sea fisheries. Yet, by 2004, actors were setting up new organizational structures to meet this objective. How did this come about? In 2001, the Commission launched a reform of the CFP. From the Commission's point of view (and the European Parliament), reform would enable discussion on sectoral integration in fisheries.[51] But sustainable development depends not only on the political will of public organizations, but critically on attitudes of private sector enterprises.[52] Was change possible given the conflictual logic of action already institutionalized in EU sea fisheries? Findings from our research reveal that, during this period, key political work was carried out by fishers' organizations to reconstruct fishers' interests and, importantly, to seek to change how others perceived their professionalism. Not all

[49] A Karagiannakos, 'Total Allowable Catch (TAC) and quota management system in the European Union' (1996) 20:3 *Marine Policy* 235–48, 237.

[50] Interview material, n 7 above.

[51] Commission of the European Communities, *Reform of the Common Fisheries Policy ('Roadmap')* COM (2002)181 final, 4–5.

[52] WCED, n 11 above, 73.

fishers had been breaking the rules, and indeed lack of compliance had caused conflict within both the industry and local communities.[53] In Scotland, key actors within the Scottish Fishermen's Federation (SFF) began to talk about lack of compliance as a 'thing of the past' and to reframe professional identities of catchers from 'exploiters' to 'custodians' of natural resources.

A core element of this political work was the rebuilding of relations with scientists. This would depend upon the extent to which each community came to accept and value each other's claim to hold legitimate knowledge of the seas. Within ICES, groups of scientists were increasingly recognizing that both fishers' commercial data *and* qualitative knowledge of fish behaviour were valuable resources for risk assessment: 'if you know that last year there were more discards, or that the fish moved to a different area... this is extremely important data'.[54] Similarly, some fishers shifted their approach, no longer 'condemning the science' but 'seeking to refute it' through evidence/experience-based argumentation.[55]

Political work was not only aimed at building relations with scientists. Indeed, the SFF found common cause with the English/Welsh/Northern Irish Fishermen's Federation, NFFO, whose members were also working to politicize the worth of fishers' knowledge for sustainable development.[56] Leaders within the SFF also made concerted efforts to persuade others (eg public authorities within Scotland, the United Kingdom and Spain) of the sustainable development value of setting up new organizational structures that would give the catching sector a voice in risk assessment of stocks. Moreover, arguments evoked made connections between engagement of 'responsible' fishers in instrument-setting, on the one hand, and conserving stocks and protecting jobs and local communities, on the other. In short, allowing catchers a greater role informing risk management decisions was presented as a prerequisite to achieving sustainable development.

During this reform period, other actors too mobilized around notions of sustainable development to bring about change in the regulation of sea fisheries—although this for different reasons. E-NGOs such as the WWF argued that 'command and control' management did not achieve sustainable development: what was required was ecosystem management. For these actors, ecosystem management was predicated upon stakeholder engagement.

Within DG MARE too, officials supported stakeholder engagement to give expression to sustainable development—even if achieving sustainability was framed differently by different units. Finally, we must also mention political work of MEPs, who commissioned a report into regional management and worked to support stakeholder engagement from a sustainable development perspective.

In short, although different groups of actors advanced sustainable development arguments for different reasons, they came to hold in common an interpretation of

[53] M Nuttall, 'Crisis, Risk and Deskilment in North-East Scotland's Fishing Industry' in D Symes (ed), *Fisheries Dependent Regions* (Oxford: Fishing News Books, 2000) 106–15.

[54] Interview material, n 7 above.

[55] ibid.

[56] B Deas, 'Regional Advisory Councils and the Future of Fisheries Policy', unpublished Buckland lecture, 2006.

sustainable development in sea fisheries as including *a minima* the setting up of a sea regional organization of stakeholders which would enable 'informed decisions' to be made on fishing effort. Following a Commission proposal supported by the European Parliament, consensus was reached within the Council in 2004 to create Regional Advisory Councils (RACs) of stakeholders. It is important to stress that this reconstruction of different interests around a single idea meant that RACs were not brought about by some grand sustainable development design that was Commission-led. Rather, agreeing on RACs as an expression of sustainable development resulted from independent co-adaptation of interests towards this idea during the reform process—interests, which nonetheless continued to be framed by different constructions of sustainability. This would be important for how the RACs would subsequently work.

(c) RACs and sustainable development

Through including stakeholders in the making of the 'difficult decisions' necessary to recover fish stocks, stabilize economic activity and protect local communities simultaneously, RACs created opportunities for a changed logic of action towards sustainable fisheries production. But, what challenges have actors faced in realizing sustainable development?

The first RACs set themselves up in 2004–05. According to EU rules, membership should represent economic, environmental and social interests. Producers were entitled to two-thirds membership of RACs (in practice, representation from each of the Member States' federations whose vessels fish in the region), and NGOs and other interested actors, one-third. On the North Sea RAC (NSRAC), the WWF is represented, as are local community networks and the European processing industry.

RACs have powers to provide advice to the Commission to inform risk management decisions in setting instruments. Yet, providing advice first entails generating that advice and this has been a considerable challenge for a number of reasons. RAC members could generate their advice based upon political compromise of their various associations' interests. But the Commission has stated that for DG MARE to even consider advice, it must be based on consensus. Finding consensus is particularly hard when members simply repeat static organizational positions of 'we want higher TQs' (fishers) versus 'we want lower TQs' (e-NGOs). Importantly, RAC advice is provided in addition to ICES advice, itself predicated upon scientific modelling of stocks. RACs have therefore had to find ways of accessing regulatory science in order to be persuasive. For some RACs, routines have developed whereby ICES scientists are invited to RAC meetings to explain their modelling assumptions, followed by discussion. In these instances, fishers have drawn upon their knowledge acquired through fishing and have presented data, for example, from skippers' diaries, which has enabled modelling results to be more accurately interpreted. In doing so, actors have sought to direct dialogue towards assessments of whether there is a 'scientific case' for reconsidering the percentage reduction in fishing effort. In this work, the ICES has made changes too, providing the RAC with a range of options, specifying assumptions underlying each option and clarifying consequences of choices for rebuilding of fish stocks. Critically, winning arguments have to be premised upon presenting a knowledge of the fishery in question, for example, actors reported deliberations on flat fish as 'working' when those involved (catchers, scientists and e-NGO representative) had expertise of the stock and when members were able to move the discussion on through proposing different options: 'if data is not on the table, the discussion collapses'.[57]

Achieving consensus therefore forces discussion over sustainable development trade-offs. Yet, whereas the rule of consensus creates the potential for a changed approach to fisheries management, it reveals too the challenge of meeting sustainable development compromises in practice. On the one hand, when actors have been able to generate consensus-based advice, through confronting different interpretations of the 'correct' balance of economic, environmental and social goals, they have had considerable successes. Members believe that 'many of most of the innovative ideas in fisheries management in recent years have come from [RACs]', that 'RACs are uniquely equipped to contribute to the debate on the integrated and sustainable use of the oceans' and that RACs have built 'trust through dialogue'.[58] For some fisheries, for example, West of Scotland herring, the work of the Pelagic RAC to produce a long-term management plan has been a key driver in their application for Marine Stewardship Council (MSC) accreditation, widely understood to be the global gold standard for ecosystem management.[59]

On the other hand, RACs are limited in their ability to bring about sustainable development when working only on production practices, with commercial choices largely left for federations to address separately and within their own markets. In Scotland, where there has been considerable recent success in achieving MSC accreditation for several species, for example North Sea haddock, the key explanation for this success given in interview was not so much the political work of the RAC, but the political work of a range of actors within Scotland. Public and private actors developed responsible fishing and conservation credits schemes, the former being market-driven and the latter stemming from the way in which the implementation of the cod recovery plan was carried out in Scotland. Referred to as the 'carrot rather than the stick' approach, these schemes not only reward fishers financially for changed practices, but, importantly, seek to reconstruct markets and encourage consumers to buy responsibly sourced fish. The experience in Scotland thus highlights the limits of RACs in bringing about sustainable development in ecosystem management terms. First, not all members agree on the necessity of ecosystem management accreditation to demonstrate sustainable

[57] Interview material, n 7 above.

[58] Inter-RAC Conference Report, 'Decision-Making in the Reform of the Common Fisheries Policy', Conference hosted by the Scottish Government and jointly funded by Marine Scotland and DEFRA, Edinburgh, 3–4 November 2009, 5, 7, 37.

[59] Interview material, n 7 above.

development of fisheries and, second, bringing about ecosystem management requires investment in producers' market activities as well as production practices, at the moment outside the scope of the CFP.

(d) Summary

The case of sea fisheries provides us with our first illustration of how industry actors have sought to interpret and integrate sustainable development within industry practices and, in particular, around the setting of regulatory instruments. In this case, sustainable development was not so much an idea 'handed over' to industry actors by EU officials/politicians; rather, for different reasons, groups of actors across the industry invested in political work and mobilized around EU declarations of sustainable development as cognitive resources to bring about this change. In this work, hierarchies of actors have been reordered. Actors who either held weak powers or who were absent from risk management decisions have gained access to advisory arenas. This has helped them to transform a conflictual regulatory logic of action into one formally coordinated within RACs, leading to successes, for example long-term management plans.

(2) Sectoral integration and aquaculture: sustainable development from 'feed to farm to fork'?

Unlike in sea fisheries, sustainable development *is* a term initially associated with aquaculture, whereby the growth of this industry symbolized one sustainable development solution to collapsing wild fish stocks.[60] And where the main challenge in fisheries has been how to conserve fish sustainably, the main problem in European aquaculture has been how to *grow* fish sustainably.[61] As in fisheries, this problem is managed through knowledge-based calculations, whereby impacts of fish farms are modelled. One such impact is that of fish feeds, which are subject to scientific risk assessment by the European Food Safety Authority (EFSA). Yet, although Commission risk management decisions consider inter alia impacts of feeds on the EU environment once digested by fish, they do not take into account the sustainable development of raw materials at source, that is, when produced or harvested outside the EU. The case study shows how, this notwithstanding, actors across the industry have politicized the global dimension of feeds and argued that sustainable development at source of imported feed materials should nonetheless be demonstrated. Once again, the case study highlights actor competitions over 'knowledge' in sectoral integration.

[60] WCED, n 11 above, 67.

[61] C Carter and C Cazals, 'The European Union Government of Aquaculture: Spatial Issues, Fish Feeds and Competition with non-EU Products', paper presented at the GEDI workshop, Sciences-Po Bordeaux, June 2010.

(a) Pre-existing actor hierarchies and logics of action (1990–2007)

European aquaculture is governed through EU general rules. These include rules on conservation, environmental impacts, animal health, animal transportation, medicines and vaccines, feed materials and food safety. Horizontal government has affected the organization of industry public and private actors, which has been fragmented and lacking in consistent leadership. Formally DG MARE has the lead on aquaculture under the CFP, but in practice other DGs, especially DG ENVI and DG SANCO, have been the regulators of aquacultural production through general legislation. Hierarchies of actors across this industry are thus unstable—certain actors dominate over some policy issues but not others. Additionally, alliance-building between EU-wide associations has been rare, with individualistic lobbying strategies over specific rules being the norm.

Because the development of aquaculture was frequently upheld against sea fisheries as being sustainable fisheries production, and because many aquacultural practices were governed by EU environmental rules, the connection between sustainable development and aquaculture seemed natural. This notwithstanding, towards the end of the 1990s, aquaculture's association with sustainable development became destabilized as the negative environmental impacts of increasingly intensive production came to light, for example fish escapees, diseases and eutrophication. In 2002, in response to these and other concerns, the Commission published its first EU-wide strategy for the sustainable development of aquaculture, in which it sought to address these challenges and restate aquaculture's relationship with sustainable development of fish production.

These attempts to present anew a positive image of aquaculture were, however, soon undermined by the fall-out from the 1999 dioxin feed/food safety crisis, following which e-NGOs, in particular, would question aquaculture's relationship with sustainability on the subject of fish feeds. The discovery of harmful levels of dioxins in poultry feeds in Belgium prompted a review by the Commission of EU feed regulation and the enactment of new rules on contaminants. Whereas the latter would have a positive impact on fish feed ingredients (in the past, feeds sometimes contained slaughterhouse trash and/or antibiotics),[62] they would also focus attention more generally on feed ingredients. Conflicts between US/Canadian scientists versus aquaculturers and the Commission took place in 2004, following publication of research findings claiming unsafe levels of dioxins in Scottish salmon.[63] These were rebutted by EU and Scottish actors, who argued that levels were below EU/WHO thresholds. Yet, even if arguments on food safety were ultimately won by aquaculture producers, political work of e-NGOs continued on feed ingredients, this time not on safety but on sustainability grounds. This was because fish feeds include within them fish meal (FM) and fish oil (FO) sourced from feed capture fisheries mostly outside the EU (as well as cereal sources,

[62] Interview material, n 7 above.

[63] R Hites, J Foran, D Carpenter, M Hamilton, B Knuth and S Schwager, 'Global Assessment of Organic Contaminants in Farmed Salmon' (2004) 303: 9 January *Science* 226–9.

vegetable proteins, eg soya, vitamins, minerals and feed additives). Feed fish stocks in the NE Atlantic, Peru and Chile were claimed either to be stable yet fished to their limits, thereby mitigating against growth, or were overfished and in danger of collapse—and, consequently, unsustainable. In other words, rather than being separate from capture fisheries, aquaculture was dependent on capture fisheries for feeds.

This was a critical debate, as aquacultural development was now represented as being connected with sea fisheries and all its problems, whereas in the past it had been seen as a solution to all these problems.

(b) Strategy renewal: actor arguments on feeds (2007–2010)

In 2007, DG MARE reviewed its European strategy, publishing a renewed strategy in 2009. In 2010, the EP PECH committee additionally published a self-initiative report, the Milana Report. Both these processes created many opportunities for actors across the industry to discuss on an EU-wide basis aquaculture's connection with sustainable development including, amongst other critical issues, on fish feeds.[64] Actors agreed that sustainable development of European finfish and crustacean aquaculture required that action be taken on feeds. However, what form that action should take and whether it should be a common EU action was not agreed by all.

Some of the tensions stemmed from disagreements over trade-off calculations. Although many accepted that the percentage of FMFO in feed recipes must be reduced, and this has already happened for some species (eg Scottish salmon feeds have reduced FMFO from *c*.75 per cent to *c*.25 per cent since the 1980s), certain quality labels like the French certificate '*label rouge*' require that high levels of FMFO be retained to legitimize quality products. Tensions also existed over trade-offs between FO reduction versus protecting mental health. FO is a critical source of DHA, EPA and other nutrients that render the fish 'healthy' to eat and provide essential and irreplaceable components for mental health development. Reducing FO below certain thresholds, scientists argued, both threatens mental health and potentially incurs heavy costs for health services.[65] Other tensions stemmed from lack of expertise. Uncertainties held by MEPs on the PECH committee were revealed in a long and unsettled discussion on feeds:

> [W]e want sustainable aquaculture. . . . it's been very controversial and the question is still about, What is sustainable? How do you define sustainability? What is technically feasible? What makes sense? What doesn't make sense?[66]

[64] C Carter and C Cazals, n 59 above.

[65] M Crawford, 'The importance of long chain omega-3 fatty acids for human health', paper presentation at conference, Can a growing aquaculture industry continue to use fishmeal and fish oil in feeds and remain sustainable?, European Parliament, Brussels, 3 March 2010.

[66] Interview material, n 7 above.

However, a key tension that we focus on here emerged over the international dimension of sectoral integration in feeds and the challenge of how to address global impacts of internal market choices. The international dimension of feeds was evoked as critical for addressing sustainable development. This was because although EFSA risk assessment procedures assess EU environmental impacts of feeds, the broader issue of sustainable development (which goes beyond the environmental question) was rather posed at source and outside the EU, where fish are harvested to be processed into feed. Moreoever, EU-funded research projects, for example, AQUAMAX, prioritized vegetables/cereals as FMFO replacement, a vast majority of which are also imported from outside the EU. Actors argued that it was not acceptable to replace one non-sustainable resource with another non-sustainable resource, so any alternatives to FMFO must also be accompanied by a demonstration of their sustainable development. Therefore, even if EU rules on cereal imports do not assess sustainable development at source, nonetheless this should be taken into consideration by feed companies and producers when choosing their replacements.

But what action could be taken on an EU-wide scale to address this? The Milana Report made a very general call to the Commission 'to ensure that the sourcing of raw materials used for fish feed follows an environmentally acceptable practice and does not have negative impacts on the ecosystems from which these ingredients are harvested', leaving the details of how this could be operationalized underspecified. Additionally, this Report urged 'the Commission to issue specific technical guidelines on the certification of sustainable fish feed'. Yet, it was ambiguous whether these were intended as guidelines for EU imports of feeds or on sustainable impacts of feeds once inside the EU. The Commission, for its part argued, that 'we cannot govern extra-territorially'.[67] From this perspective, although EU sustainable development standards could be set, there was concern that the WTO would perceive any EU rules on sustainable development criteria for imports as technical barriers to trade. Rather than acting through direct intervention of sustainable development at source, therefore, the Commission is currently acting to ease internal market entry of possible replacement sustainable ingredients, both by amending current EU rules on use of animal by-products in feeds and by funding research on feed innovation.

Yet, even though debates remained unsettled about public EU action on this question, nonetheless and in the meantime, private actors have already engaged in political work to integrate EU/global norms of sustainable development into private commercial practices in feeds, stabilizing (contested) answers to questions raised.

(c) Market devices and sustainable development in feeds

Political work on private market standards for sectoral integration of sustainable development in fish feeds began in the mid-2000s. In the case of the Scottish salmon industry, a critical moment was the publication of a joint e-NGO

[67] ibid.

commissioned report which politicized methods used by feed companies and producers to judge the sustainability of salmon feeds.[68] The report's argument was that it was common UK practice to base sourcing choices on assessments made by the Fishmeal Information Network (FIN) Sustainability Dossier, which did not evaluate feed fisheries according to eco-system management criteria. The FIN SD based its assessment on scientific stock reports (eg by ICES) and the presence of regulatory frameworks, for example, TQs. E-NGOs argued that this approach missed wider ecosystem impacts that would be captured through applying MSC methods instead, for example, biodiversity impacts, usage of local knowledge, compliance. A key problem was that no feed fishery at that time had MSC certification: therefore, according to this logic, industry practice was necessarily unsustainable. Indeed, the mediatization of this report was articulated in these terms.

The making of arguments to place companies' sourcing policies in the public domain continued into 2005, with Greenpeace's campaign to mediatize first UK then other European supermarkets' seafood sourcing policies. Ranking UK supermarkets' seafood sourcing policies inter alia against MSC criteria, Greenpeace named and shamed retailers.[69] A year later, Greenpeace published a follow-up report on action taken, which revealed that all retailers had acted to improve their sourcing policies.[70] Yet, critically, whereas for some supermarkets (eg Iceland) only minimal policies had been introduced, for others (eg Marks and Spencer, Waitrose and Sainsbury's), sustainable development was being clearly articulated as part of a changing competitive strategy.

However, tensions still remained over how to judge sustainable development of feed fisheries. Finding solutions that satisfied business relations (and a wider consumer audience), retailers established partnerships with producers, feed companies and e-NGOs to agree sourcing policies. To justify choices of supplies, some companies developed 'traffic light' systems to categorize sourcing choices, whereby through negotiation, they graded different stocks on grounds of sustainable development (green/amber/red) and set up private audits.[71] Evoking EU rules on traceability, companies further claimed transparency of purchase choices along the supply chain. This political work has resulted today in a situation whereby feed companies, producers and supermarkets all assert an ownership of knowledge of sustainable development of feed fisheries. They claim knowledge of origins of raw materials as well as knowledge of their harvesting practices. Moreover, they have developed tools to demonstrate sustainable development: 'we have a means of *expressing* sustainability'.[72] By codifying sustainable development through the

[68] TC Huntington, 'Feeding the Fish: Sustainable Fish Feed and Scottish Aquaculture', Report to the Joint Marine Programme Scottish Wildlife Trust and WWF Scotland and RSPB Scotland, 2004.

[69] Greenpeace, *A Recipe for Disaster: Supermarkets' Insatiable Appetite For Seafood* (London: Greenpeace, 2005).

[70] Greenpeace, *A Recipe for Change: Supermarkets Respond to the Challenge of Sourcing Responsible Seafood* (London: Greenpeace, 2006).

[71] Interview material, n 7 above.

[72] ibid (emphasis added).

acquisition of data around private instruments, actors have thus worked to depoliticize and technicize purchase choices and induce a sense of certainty over an ultimately contested concept in order to continue commercial transactions.

These market initiatives have moreover recently been joined up with political work conducted on a global scale to coordinate conflictual interpretations of sustainable development of feed fisheries. In October 2010, draft standards were agreed for an Aquaculture Stewardship Certificate (ASC) in salmon. In agreeing these standards, compromises were reached between e-NGOs and private enterprises across the international feed and food chain. Although the WWF's ultimate goal for all feed fisheries is that they receive MSC accreditation, in the meantime scoring systems which are not evaluating fisheries according to ecosystem management criteria are nonetheless accepted. One such score is the FishSource score, developed by the Sustainable Fisheries Partnership. This draws upon scientific assessments, such as by ICES, and looks at regulatory systems, including compliance. Indeed, it is this score that currently underpins the UK's FIN SD, rejected by e-NGOs in 2004. In accepting FishSource scores, it is noted that they 'are not a firm guide to how a fishery will perform overall [but] [n]onetheless..... do capture the main outcome-based measures of sustainability': however, 'the SC is faced with the challenge that this FishSource score does not represent ecological sustainability'.[73] Political work has thus produced compromises, even if underlying tensions between ecosystem scoring versus individual stock assessment scoring persist. Indicators emerge from (temporary) trade-offs over economic, environmental and social priorities. Moreover, it is these trade-offs which will guide market choices in the future, for example, in the United Kingdom, the WWF has already begun discussions with leading retailers on policies to stock only ASC accredited farmed fish.[74]

Finally, political work has not been limited to the international impact of marine ingredients. The argument advanced in EU-wide debates that it is inappropriate to replace one unsustainable product with another one has also been operationalized in companies' practices. For some feed companies, usage of palm oil as a replacement for FO is not deemed appropriate due to sustainable development concerns over its acquisition. Regarding the sourcing of soya, some companies will only source soya from others who are part of the Roundtable for Responsible Soya Production and exclude soya bought on the market without any prior knowledge. In short, demonstrating the sustainability of replacement raw materials has also been regularized according to particular values. And, having a sustainable sourcing policy for replacements has also been written into ASC draft standards.

[73] Steering Committee for the Salmon Aquaculture Dialogue (SAD), 'Draft Salmon Dialogue Standards for Public Comment', 3 August 2010, 72, 33.

[74] Interview material, n 7 above.

(d) Summary

This second case study illustrates actor attempts to address the international dimension of sectoral integration and, in the absence of common EU instruments, take responsibility within their sector to calculate economic, environmental and social trade-offs and institutionalize these through private market instruments. Once again, EU formulations provide useful cognitive resources for actors leading political work. In the case of feeds, however, it is either actors seeking greater influence, for example e-NGOs, or already dominant actors seeking to retain their market positions who are leading on political sustainable development work. Because political work described here is taking place in some European markets and not others, the fragmented organization of industry continues. Nonetheless, supermarkets are consolidating their strong position over value choices from feed-to-farm-to-fork.[75] This work has therefore brought about change in the economic logic of action of fishfeeds. New routines, techniques, tools and procedures have been put in place and for some feed companies and producers, demonstrating sustainable development of raw materials used in feeds is part and parcel of everyday practice. Of course, this is not the case for all firms and in all markets. Consequently, further research is required on this point.

D. Conclusions and discussion points

This chapter has examined how political usages of sustainable development have brought about a changing logic of economic union in sea fisheries and aquaculture. Arguing that a focus on industrial production and commercial practices is critical for assessing EU sectoral integration, our findings suggest that actors *are* engaging over sustainable development calculations in their daily work. They have re-problematized industry conditions, generated knowledge and expertise, and worked on inter-stakeholder dialogue to produce compromises, even if temporary, to dilemmas posed. From this perspective, sustainable development is being operationalized, in the sense that industry actors continue to struggle to give it meaning. Indeed, in these two cases, it is the primary struggle within sectoral public and private regulation.

For both industries, EU politicization of sectoral integration as a question-oriented procedure has provided an official framework and ideational resources on which private actors can draw and mobilize to bring about change. In this sense, EU official action on sustainable development has not been unimportant. However, in both cases, there was no immediate evidence of 'leadership' by EU public actors over sectoral integration. Rather, in sea fisheries, producers and e-NGOs

[75] See further G Rayner, D Barling and T Lang, 'Sustainable Food Systems in Europe: Policies, Realities and Futures' (2008) 3:2 *Journal of Hunger & Environmental Nutrition* 145–68.

appear as leaders, whilst in aquaculture, e-NGOs, supermarkets and feed companies do so. This initial conclusion is, however, based on a first review of empirical material and therefore requires further investigation. Yet, leaving to one side e-NGOs' interests, our hypothesis is that the power of the concept of sustainable development is revealed more as a resource for private actors to bring about change within the economic logic of their industry as part of a competitive strategy, than as a new regulatory device for Commission officials to 'govern' industry. This coincides also with a changing regulatory approach to economic union with its current emphasis on self-regulation, voluntary agreements and incentive-based market mechanisms.

The cases also revealed challenges for achieving economic/environmental/social sustainable development trade-offs. Common to both was the importance of generating and possessing knowledge and expertise to legitimate one's eligibility to negotiate them and furthermore to persuade others of the legitimacy of compromises reached. In both our examples, trade-offs appeared to be being negotiated more along the economic-environmental axis of sustainable development, with social justice less well articulated or represented. This does not necessarily render these forms of sustainable development weak; rather, to avoid normativity, one requires to analyse them as political choices that only empirical research can explain.[76] In both cases, the 'social' is not entirely absent, but is more represented by proxy, than by public or civil society participation in decision-making. In RACs, somewhat abstract 'local communities' are evoked in actor calculations over sustainability, and social scientists are from time to time invited to engage in impact assessment modelling.[77] In feeds, supermarkets claim to represent the 'consumer' and e-NGOs do invite public responses to private standards being set, for example the salmon ASC standards are currently on the web for public reactions. Yet, the very technical and knowledge-based nature of inter-stakeholder dialogue is hard to access and, in these two cases at least, sectoral integration calculations appear dominated by experts and professional elites. Once again, the current character of economic union, with its focus on better regulatory tools and impact assessments, serves to further the dominance of experts in regulation.

Finally, our case on feeds reveals a challenge for the EU in operationalizing the external aspects of sectoral integration. In a context where the European Commission does not seek to politicize sustainable development as a legitimate barrier to global trade (like food safety), this necessarily limits its scope of internal market regulatory action. In the absence of EU public action on standards for feed imports, private actors have, however, determined their own. Of course, these could be constructed as indirect barriers to trade, protecting and promoting those products that have been produced sustainably over those which have not. Yet, e-NGOs represent them rather as market opportunities and incentives for companies within developing countries, thereby enhancing sustainable development on a global scale.

[76] S Connelly, n 26 above, 266–7.
[77] Interview material, n 7 above.

However constructed, the political and ethical values which underpin these private standards are nonetheless being decided in the absence of EU public actors' input. Once again, examining sectoral integration enables a deeper understanding of the form of economic union currently being institutionalized and questions the role of public authorities therein.

PART IV

EXPANDING HORIZONS

16

Turkey: A Candidate State Destined to Join the Union

*Marc Maresceau**

The first time I met John Usher was when Professor John Mitchell, Director of the Centre of European Governmental Studies[1] at the University of Edinburgh, introduced him to me. John was then a freshly appointed lecturer at the Centre in charge of an impressive series of tutorials while I, I must confess, had the more relaxed status of Leverhulme Fellow. In the initial phase of my Edinburgh period, Professor Mitchell suggested that I share an office with John for a few weeks while a small office was being refurbished for me. John, who was a bit more senior than I, also seemed in so many ways that bit more professional as well. As a very friendly colleague, he was kind enough to help me become more acquainted with what seemed to me, at first sight, strange meanders of British academic life. So much seemed different to me, with my Continental experience. However, gradually but surely, I became a great fan of the sometimes hidden but exquisite pleasures of British academia.

During my stay at the Centre, I often had discussions with John and I greatly appreciated his vast knowledge, but I cannot recall us ever having addressed the topic of the place of Turkey in Europe. At the time, so many other themes took greater priority for us both. Also, in John's writings afterwards, insofar as I have been able to retrace them, I have not found any reference to Turkey. The nearest I got was a volume on Malta,[2] but after the Sultan's failed siege of 1565, Malta remained a Christian stronghold in a largely Ottoman environment. My choice of Turkey for this contribution, although not directly linked to John, has, strangely enough, nevertheless very much to do with Edinburgh, since it was in a dusty cellar of a very tiny Edinburgh second-hand bookshop near The Meadows on Marchmont Road (at the time, you had dozens of these true popular palaces of culture in that great city) that I acquired my first three volumes on the history of the Ottoman Empire. They were all extremely interesting but, as often happens on

* Professor of EU law, European Institute—Faculty of Laws, Ghent University, Jean Monnet Chair *ad personam*, Jean Monnet Centre of Excellence.

[1] Now the Europa Institute.

[2] See John A Usher, *Malta and the EU: three issues* (Msida: Malta University Press, 1995).

these expeditions, of unequal bibliophilic quality.[3] What I did not realize then was that this humble acquisition would become the cornerstone of an almost uncontrollable book-collecting passion on Turkey and the Ottoman Empire.

For those readers unfamiliar with EU-Turkey relations, it may come as a surprise that the same wording as the title of my contribution was first used in the Conclusions of the 1999 Helsinki European Council. Almost ten years later, in 2008, the European Commission, in its *Enlargement Strategy and Main Challenges 2008–2009* Communication, noted the following with regard to Turkey as a candidate State:

> Turkey's strategic importance to the EU has further increased in key areas such as energy security, conflict prevention and resolution and regional security in the Southern Caucasus and the Middle East. The country's engagement with the EU, through the negotiations and related reforms which are underway, makes it a stronger force for stability in a region facing many challenges . . . The pace of accession negotiations with Turkey reflects the pace of reform as well as the country's fulfilment of the relevant conditions. Turkey now needs to renew its political reform effort.[4]

The subsequent annual *Enlargement Strategy Communications* from the Commission continue to reiterate the strategic importance of Turkey's geo-political position and it is recognized that 'Turkey plays a key role in regional security and the promotion of dialogue between civilisations'.[5] In the *Enlargement Strategy 2010–2011* Communication, it is noted that Turkey 'has become more active in its neighbourhood'. Certainly, this is considered to be an asset for the EU provided, however, '[that] it is developed as a complement to Turkey's accession process and in coordination with the EU'.[6] In all the *Enlargement Strategy* Communications, including the latest one for 2011–12, the Commission stresses that ultimately it is the pace of reforms in Turkey that is the key consideration in taking forward the accession process and this process provides 'a strong incentive for Turkey to pursue reforms, strengthen democracy and human rights and further modernise the country'.[7]

[3] The 'lot' comprised E Bradford, *The Great Siege: Malta 1565* (London: Reprint Society, 1962); E Hamley, *The War in the Crimea*, 7th edn (London: Seeley, 1896); and a first edition of J Stoye's invaluable *The Siege of Vienna* (London: Collins, 1964), still one of the best books on that crucial turning-point of European history and an absolute must for any student of EU-Turkey relations. It also included a fourth and rare (but unfortunately odd) volume on Russia ('Russie: Tôme deuxième contenant la fin de la Russie d'Europe . . . et les provinces russes en Asie', *L'Univers: Histoire et description de tous les peuples* (Firmin Didot Frères, 1838) (with numerous engravings). This old volume is still fascinating reading for the study of the Ottoman Empire—Russia relations, in particular the chapters 'La Crimée' and 'Circassie et Géorgie' by César Famin and above all the contribution 'Arménie' by the orientalist Eugène Boré.

[4] Communication from the Commission to the Council and the European Parliament, *Enlargement Strategy and Main Challenges 2008–2009* COM (2008) 674 final, 2, 3.

[5] Communication from the Commission to the European Parliament and the Council, *Enlargement Strategy and Main Challenges 2009–2010* COM (2009) 533 final, 17.

[6] Communication from the Commission to the European Parliament and the Council, *Enlargement Strategy and Main Challenges 2010–2011* COM (2010) 660 final, 19.

[7] See n 5; also Communication from the Commission to the European Parliament and the Council, *Enlargement Strategy and Main Challenges 2011–2012* COM (2011) 666 final, 3. The Commission reiterates that in Turkey the accession process 'remains the most effective framework for promoting EU-related reforms'.

The Commission's annual progress reports on the state of the enlargement process with candidate States usually concentrate on the reforms that need to be undertaken by the candidates. Thus, the reports on Turkey provide a comprehensive picture of the number, content and size of the various legislative and administrative reforms and adaptations needed in order for it to comply with the EU *acquis*. Turkey has embarked on a huge process of reforms and this process, with its ups and downs, is ongoing. What is striking in these reports is that the Commission remains largely silent on the domestic difficulties within the EU that need to be overcome in order to move forward. It might, therefore, be useful to try to shed some light on certain aspects of these difficulties that the possible accession of Turkey to the EU is facing.

Of course, the limits imposed on a contribution in this *liber memorialis* are such that by no means may an exhaustive analysis be provided and only a few ingredients for further in-depth reflection are given. In the first part of this chapter, some comments are made on the fundamental political objective of the 1963 Association Agreement with Turkey, which was—and one should not forget this—progressively to prepare that country for EEC membership. For that purpose, the wording and spirit of the 1963 Agreement need to be revisited and the gradual alignment of Turkey to common market (now internal market) principles highlighted. An interesting question in this regard is whether the interpretation of that Agreement, which is, today, one of the oldest bilateral agreements concluded by the EEC still in force, has been affected by the changing political climate over the years within and outside the EU. In the second part of the chapter, the position of the Court of Justice of the European Union towards the 1963 Agreement is examined. Finally, a short account of how Turkey evolved from an applicant State to a candidate State negotiating accession is given. The question of whether 'privileged partnership', something strongly promoted by the current French and German political leadership, is a valid alternative for accession is also briefly addressed.

A. The pre-accession nature and the 'integration dimension' of the 1963 Association Agreement

Turkey occupies a special place as a candidate State for EU accession. More than 95 per cent of its territory is located in Asia and also its capital, Ankara, is plainly in Asian central Turkey. But however small the European part of Turkey may be today, it is difficult to ignore Turkey's very strong bonds with Europe and with European history.[8] It is this European dimension, based on geography and history,

[8] Cyprus, although geographically belonging to Western Asia, is Europe; see, eg, the interesting publication of the Government of Cyprus, *Cyprus Has Always Been Europe* (Nicosia: Press and Information Office, 2006). The 'European-ness' of Cyprus was never an issue in its application for EU membership. In the 1993 Opinion on Cyprus's application for EU membership, the European Commission confirmed, without any need for further explanation, the European character and European vocation of Cyprus, see JS Joseph, 'Cyprus and the European Union' in *Cyprus Has Always Been Europe*, 239.

which probably explains why, in 1963, the EEC was able to sign an Association Agreement with Turkey stating in the Preamble that the Agreement aimed to improve the standard of living of the Turkish people and 'facilitate the accession of Turkey to the Community at a later date'. In addition, Article 28 of the Agreement held that 'as soon as the operation of this Agreement has advanced far enough to justify envisaging full acceptance by Turkey of the obligations arising out of the Treaty establishing the Community, the Contracting Parties shall examine the possibility of the accession of Turkey to the Community'. The references to accession in the Ankara Agreement were word for word identical to those made in the Association Agreement with Greece signed in 1961. In other words, the Agreement with Turkey, together with that of Greece, was a *genuine pre-accession agreement*, aiming at preparing Turkey to become a member of the European Community. It is worthwhile to note, and this may sound strange today, that at the moment of signature and conclusion of the Ankara Agreement, its unequivocal pre-accession nature was not considered to be a political or legal issue. It was simply taken for granted that the enlargement objective could be pursued with Turkey and that 'Turkey belonged to Europe', as was so eloquently recalled by Walter Hallstein, then President of the Commission, on the occasion of the signature of the Agreement in Ankara.[9]

One of the compelling conditions for becoming a member of the Community, and now the Union, was and continues to be that the application for membership has to be made by a 'European State'. When the 1963 Agreement with Turkey was signed, the then Article 237 EEC, now Article 49 TEU, already stipulated that 'any European State' may apply to become a member of the European Community, now European Union. That Article has never clarified what precisely was meant by the expression 'European State' but the explicit references to a possible later accession of Turkey in the Preamble and in Article 28 of the Association Agreement can only be understood in the sense of assuming Turkey to be at least 'eligible' for membership and thus satisfying the 'European State' condition of Article 237 EEC at the time. Another interpretation would have meant that the Agreement of 1963, with the wording it contains, could and should simply not have been signed by the EEC and its Member States. With the conclusion of the Association Agreement, perhaps the strongest possible obstacle to a later Turkish application for membership—that Turkey was not a 'European State'—had been taken away. A comparable situation had already arisen regarding Turkey's membership of the Council of Europe. In fact, here also, there seems to have been no doubt about Turkey's 'European-ness'. In 1949, Turkey became a Member State of the Council of Europe: that is, only a few months after the signature of the Statute of the Council.[10] When, at the first session of the Committee of Ministers of the Council of Europe, the Committee invited Greece, Iceland *and Turkey* to become members

[9] For the text of Hallstein's speech, see T Opperman (ed), *Walter Hallstein: Europäische Reden* (Stuttgart: Deutsche Verlags-Anstalt, 1979) 438–40.

[10] See AH Robertson, *The Council of Europe: Its Structure, Functions and Achievements* (London: Stevens, 1956) 20.

of the Council, nobody raised any question as to whether Turkey was sufficiently European to be a 'European State', while, as the name of the organization indicates, the purpose of the Council of Europe was to bring 'European States' into closer association.

The 1963 Ankara Agreement not only referred to the general political objective of preparing Turkey for accession to the European Community but also included substantive law provisions with an evident 'integration dimension'. Provisions in the Agreement with such a dimension incorporate principles, substantive rules and methods used in the intra-Community context. Certainly, an integration dimension does not always mean pre-accession or preparing for accession, as demonstrated by the European Economic Area Agreement or the Agreement on free movement of persons with Switzerland which was part of the package of the 1999 *Bilateral I* Agreements. Integration-oriented approaches can, in some instances, be used as an alternative to pre-accession or accession. However, the situation is fundamentally different in EU-Turkey relations. Integration-oriented provisions in the Ankara Agreement cannot and should not be disconnected from its pre-accession nature. In the Ankara Agreement, the integration dimension is not a value in its own right but serves the purpose of a higher objective, which is that of the gradual preparation for the accession of Turkey to the European Community.

This idea of gradual preparation for accession was reflected in the various stages for the implementation of the objectives of the Association Agreement. The association, as established by the Agreement, comprised three stages: a preparatory, a transitional and a final stage. The preparatory stage was supposed to last for five years (Article 3(2)) and was to evolve towards a transitional stage, which was not to last more than twelve years, subject to possible exceptions by mutual agreement (Article 4(2)). What exactly the 'final phase' implied and how this was to be achieved was not further addressed in the Agreement itself, but a key role for the implementation of the objectives of the Agreement was attributed to the Association Council, consisting of representatives of the Member States, the Council, the Commission and of the Turkish Government. The Association Council was given the power to take binding decisions in this respect, acting by unanimity.

Among the provisions of the substantive part of the Ankara Agreement having an integration dimension, Article 9 must first be mentioned. This provision, formulated in general terms, holds that any discrimination on grounds of nationality 'shall be prohibited *in accordance with the principle laid down in Article 7 of the Treaty establishing the Community*'[11] (now Article 18 TFEU). The following provision, Article 10, provides for the establishment of a customs union. Of course, a customs union is a very exceptional, almost unattainable, objective in trade relations with a third country[12] and the ultimate purpose of this objective in the Ankara Agreement was to prepare Turkey for membership of the Community. In practical terms, this meant the integration and acceptance of the EEC customs union *acquis* by Turkey:

[11] Emphasis added.

[12] For the moment, the EU—which is, of course, itself a customs union—has customs union agreements only with, besides Turkey, Andorra and San Marino.

nothing more, nothing less. The concrete and progressive establishment of that union, which had been further worked out in the 1970 Additional Protocol (see further below), was for a long time afterwards, subject to opposition by Greece, but in 1995 a political compromise, whereby Cyprus was to be included in the negotiations for EU accession, led to the lifting of the Greek objection. Consequently, on 1 January 1996, more than thirty years after the signature of the Ankara Agreement, the customs union with Turkey became a reality.[13] In this context it is worth recalling that the 1963 Association Agreement also assigned an important role to the Association Council to lay down conditions and rules for the application of the EC competition rules (Article 16). This would only be achieved in Decision 1/95 establishing the customs union through the inclusion of a specific chapter on competition, incorporating the then Articles 85, 86 and 92 of the EC Treaty (Articles 32–34 of Decision 1/95). Article 35 of that Decision explicitly stipulated that any practice contrary to Articles 32, 33 and 34 'had to be assessed on the basis of criteria arising from the application of the rules of Articles 85, 86 and 92 of the Treaty establishing the European Community and its secondary legislation.'

Besides the customs union objective and the inclusion of references to the EC competition rules, the 1963 Agreement also included 'other economic provisions' with an integration dimension. Articles 12, 13, and 14 stipulated that for the purpose of progressively securing freedom of movement of workers, abolishing restrictions on freedom of establishment and the provision of services, the Parties agreed 'to be guided' by the relevant provisions of the EEC Treaty. However, for the achievement of these free movement objectives, further implementation measures by the Association Council were necessary.

In 1970, an Additional Protocol with Turkey was signed, laying down provisions relating to conditions, arrangements and timetables for the implementation of the transitional stage.[14] This Protocol, while in many respects incomplete in view of the ambitious objectives set out in the 1963 Agreement, nevertheless provided a number of useful clarifications and formed an integral part of the Association Agreement itself (Article 62). Regarding the phase-oriented implementation of the Ankara Agreement, the Parties agreed to move from the 'preparatory' to the 'transitional stage'. The Protocol contained provisions on workers, establishment and services. Article 36 provided that freedom of movement of workers between the EC and Turkey was to be secured by progressive stages in accordance with the principles set out in Article 12 of the Association Agreement 'between the end of

[13] Legally, this was achieved by means of a decision of the Association Council, see Decision No 1/95 of the EC-Turkey Association Council of 22 December 1995 on implementing the final phase of the Customs Union [1996] OJ L 35/1. For a detailed legal analysis of the EU-Turkey customs union, see HA Kabaalioğlu, 'The Turkish Model of Association: Customs Union before Accession' in P Demaret, J-F Bellis and G Garcia Jimenez (eds), *Regionalism and Multilateralism after the Uruguay Round* (Brussels: European University Press, 1997) 115–60, and J Lebullenger and C Rapoport, 'Les contraintes générées par l'union douanière' in E Lannon and J Lebullenger (eds), *Les défis d'une adhésion de la Turquie à l'Union européenne* (Brussels: Bruylant, 2006) 243–66.

[14] Additional Protocol and Financial Protocol signed on 23 November 1970, annexed to the Agreement establishing the Association between the European Economic Community and Turkey and on measures to be taken for their entry into force [1972] OJ L 293/4.

the twelfth and the twenty-second year after the entry into force of that Agreement'. It was for the Association Council to take the necessary implementing decisions, including in the field of social security (Articles 38 and 39). Article 37 laid down a general prohibition of discrimination based on nationality as regards salary and other working conditions, in respect of workers holding the nationality of the Contracting Parties. With regard to establishment and services, the most relevant provision was Article 41(1), which stipulates that the Parties 'shall refrain from introducing between themselves any new restrictions on the freedom of establishment and the freedom to provide services'. For the removal of existing obstacles it was again the task of the Association Council to take the measures required. These measures have never, however, been taken, although the standstill clause of Article 41(1) has on various occasions been subject to interpretation by the Court of Justice, which has considerably contributed to the effectiveness of certain aspects of the progression towards free movement (see further below).

It should now be clear that a pivotal role for the implementation of the Association Agreement had been assigned to the Association Council. While, on the whole, the number of decisions taken by the Association Council has been limited, some of them, such as that already mentioned on the establishment of the customs union (Decision No 1/95)[15] and those on Turkish workers (Decisions Nos 2/76,[16] 1/80,[17] 3/80)[18] are nevertheless particularly important. The decisions on workers, although not providing for full free movement between the EU and Turkey, do improve the status of Turkish workers legally working in a Member State of the EU considerably. In particular, Articles 6(1) and 7 of Decision No 1/80 have proved to be of crucial importance as a consequence of the recognition of their direct effect potential by the Court of Justice. Article 6(1) provides for a far-reaching integration-oriented treatment of Turkish workers duly registered as belonging to the labour force of a Member State. Such a worker is entitled in that Member State, after one year's legal employment, to the renewal of his permit to work for the same employer, if a job is available; and, after three years of legal employment and subject to the priority given to workers of Member States of the Union, to respond to another offer of employment, with an employer of his choice, made under normal conditions and registered with the employment services of that State, for the same occupation. Such a worker also enjoys free access in that Member State to any paid employment of his choice, after four years of legal employment. Furthermore, Article 7 of Decision No 1/80 provides that members of the family of a Turkish worker duly registered to the labour force of a Member State and who have been authorized to join him 'shall be entitled—subject to the priority given to be given to workers of Member States of the Community—to

[15] Decision No 1/95, n 13 above.

[16] Not published in OJ.

[17] Decision No 1/80 of the Association Council of 19 September 1980 on the development of the association, not published in OJ.

[18] Decision No 3/80 of the Association Council of 19 September 1980 on the application of the social security schemes of the Member States of the European Communities to Turkish workers and members of their families [1980] OJ C 110/60.

respond to any offer of employment after they have been legally resident for at least three years in that Member State'. In addition, they 'shall enjoy free access to any paid employment of their choice provided they have been legally resident there for at least five years'. Some of the salient aspects of the Court's case law in this respect are briefly examined in Section B of this contribution.

Finally, it might be worthwhile to add a few comments on the place of the free movement principles in EU-Turkey relations in the light of the internal market 'screening' to which any candidate State negotiating EU accession is submitted. Certainly, the 1963 Association Agreement, by aiming at establishing a customs union, clearly went far beyond the creation of a classical free trade area. Even existing models of internal markets between EU and non-EU Member States, such as the EEA or the partial and incomplete bilateral internal market with Switzerland, do not establish a customs union. But if a customs union is established, as is the case with Turkey, additional regulatory measures regarding standardization, conformity assessment, accreditation and so on may still be required. This explains why, with regard to the chapter on free movement of goods, the Commission's Screening Report stated that Turkish legislation was 'partially in line with the *acquis*'. While alignment was complete in certain sectors, there was nevertheless a need for further upgrading in others, 'especially as regards the horizontal measures and removal of non-tariff barriers to trade'.[19] In the *Enlargement Strategy 2010–2011* Communication, the Commission refines this statement and reiterates that legislative alignment is 'quite advanced' but various technical barriers to trade continue to hinder the free movement of goods. Consequently, and this notwithstanding the customs union, additional efforts are still needed to meet the standards of the EU *acquis* regarding the free movement of goods and 'it is crucial that Turkey improves its administrative capacity to cope with the *acquis*'.[20]

As far as the free movement of persons, services and capital is concerned, the Association Agreement did not provide much more than a legal basis for moving in that direction but, as the formulation of Articles 12, 13 and 14 of the Agreement also implied, the strong political will of the Contracting Parties was indispensable in order to move forward. There is, for the moment, no Screening Report from the Commission for the chapter on free movement of persons and this aspect of the internal market remains, no doubt, one if not the most sensitive aspect of future negotiations for accession. In the *Enlargement Strategy 2010–2011* Communication, the Commission largely avoids addressing the issue and only observes that in the area of freedom of movement of workers, 'little progress has been made' and 'alignment is at an early stage'.[21] Paradoxically, there is a considerable amount of case law of the European Court of Justice not exactly on free movement of persons in EU-Turkey relations but on non-discrimination with respect to Turkish nationals in the EU (see further below).

[19] *Screening Report Turkey: Ch 1—Free Movement of Goods*, 18 June 2007; see further *Enlargement Strategy and Main Challenges 2011–2012*, n 7 above, 76.
[20] *Enlargement Strategy and Main Challenges 2010–2011*, n 6 above, 65.
[21] ibid 65; also *Enlargement Strategy and Main Challenges 2011–2012*, n 7 above, 76.

Regarding the right of establishment and freedom to provide services, Turkey's autonomous alignment is, so far, only 'at an early stage'. With regard to the free movement of capital, progress is reported in the fight against money laundering[22] but here also there is still a long way to go. Finally, as far as adaptation to the EU's anti-trust and merger policy is concerned, Turkey has reached 'a high level' of alignment and, according to the Commission, demonstrates the capacity to implement the *acquis* and 'enforces the *acquis* competition rules effectively'.[23] A weaker point was compliance with the EU State aid rules. In the Screening Report, the Commission observed that administrative capacity was still lacking and there was not yet a solid legislative framework with the necessary mechanisms to enforce it.[24] However, recently, a State aid monitoring authority has been established and this is undoubtedly a step in the right direction, but it is probably too early to assess the full impact of this initiative on the compliance of Turkey with the EU State aid *acquis*.[25]

B. The integration-oriented interpretation of the European Court of Justice

Of course, it cannot be the task of the Court of Justice to intervene in the political debate on the desirability or not of the accession of Turkey to the EU. Thus, it is not for the Court to interpret the political statement that Turkey is 'a candidate State destined to join the European Union'. Having said that, there is abundant case law indicating that the Court of Justice is certainly not blind to the references to accession in the Association Agreement. When a case is brought before the Court concerning the interpretation of the Association Agreement, the Court usually starts its examination by recalling the reference to accession as formulated in the Agreement. But there is more. There is, as has already been made clear, a solid bilateral legal framework established through the Association Agreement, its Additional Protocol, which forms part of the Association Agreement, and the binding decisions of the Association Council. These various legal instruments have all, on multiple occasions, been the subject of interpretation by the Court of Justice and it might be helpful to examine whether and to what extent the political objective of the Ankara Agreement, of progressively preparing Turkey for accession, has been taken into consideration by the Court in interpreting these instruments.

As a preliminary remark, it must be observed that the Association Agreement with Turkey is the bilateral agreement concluded by the EC/EU with a third State that has been invoked most frequently before the Court of Justice. More than sixty cases directly concern the interpretation of the 1963 Agreement and/or Decisions

[22] *Enlargement Strategy and Main Challenges 2010–2011*, n 6 above, 65.

[23] ibid, 66; and also *Enlargement Strategy and Main Challenges 2011–2012*, n 7 above, 77.

[24] *Screening Report Turkey: Ch 8—Competition Policy*, 3 May 2006, 10.

[25] See Law no 6015 on the monitoring and control of state aids (2010). In the *Enlargement Strategy and Main Challenges 2011–2012*, n 7 above, 77, the Commission acknowledges that 'good progress' in this field has been made.

of the Association Council. Most of these cases are preliminary rulings concerning Turkish nationals before national courts of the EU Member States in dispute with authorities of those States but, exceptionally, a case may also be brought against a Member State by the Commission. A considerable number of cases explicitly or implicitly concern the question of direct effect and/or the substantive scope of the invoked provision. As regards the examination of direct effect, it does not appear that the accession objective of the Association Agreement has played a decisive role as such. This is not astonishing. Certainly, the fact that the 1963 Agreement has a pre-accession objective is not an obstacle to the examination of its direct effect, but many agreements with third States having no pre-accession objective also contain provisions having direct effect. While it is standard practice that when examining the direct effect of a provision of an agreement concluded by the EU—besides answering the question of whether the provision is clear and precise—the Court observes that regard must be had to the purpose and nature of the agreement itself, it is also true that, except for the treatment of provisions of some multilateral agreements, in particular GATT/WTO, this particular point does not seem to have had any concrete bearing on the examination of a provision's direct effect or otherwise. This has even led former Advocate General Francis Jacobs to speak of this reference as 'a ritual refrain in which an agreement of almost any nature could be said nevertheless to be capable of having direct effect'. In his view such emphasis on the object and purpose of the agreement, and on the relationship between the parties, might be open to question and '[i]f the substantive provisions of the agreement purport to impose clear obligations, why should they not be enforceable in the courts of the Community and the Member States?'[26]

The *Demirel*[27] ruling was the first case on the possible direct effect of a provision of the 1963 Association Agreement and the Court of Justice rightly refused to recognize direct effect of Article 12 of that Agreement. The Court concluded that the expression 'agree to be guided', referring to the EEC Treaty provisions on free movement of workers, needed further implementation, and that Articles 12 and 36 combined 'essentially serve to set out a programme and are not sufficiently precise and unconditional' to have direct effect.[28] No decisions of the Association Council implementing Article 12 and establishing free movement of workers within EU-Turkey relations had been taken. However, the effect of the *Demirel* judgment seemed limited to the interpretation of Article 12 and the judgment was not, as such, a ruling on the direct effect of the Agreement as a whole. Hence, after the

[26] FG Jacobs, 'Direct Effect and Interpretation of International Agreements in the Recent Case Law of the European Court of Justice' in A Dashwood and M Maresceau (eds), *Law and Practice of EU External Relations: Salient Features of a Changing Landscape* (Cambridge: Cambridge University Press, 2008) 32–3. The former Advocate General considers that this reference 'is perhaps a relic of an earlier period in which the Court was more cautious, and placed more emphasis on the category of agreement in question'; see further FG Jacobs, 'The Internal Legal Effects of the EU's International Agreements and the Protection of Individual Rights' in A Arnull, C Barnard, M Dougan and E Spaventa (eds), *A Constitutional Order of States? Essays in EU Law in Honour of Alan Dashwood* (Oxford: Hart Publishing, 2011) 536.

[27] Case 12/86 *Meryem Demirel v Stadt Schwäbisch Gmünd* [1987] ECR 3719.

[28] ibid para 23.

Demirel case, it was not excluded that other substantive provisions in the Agreement or in the Additional Protocol did perhaps satisfy the conditions for direct effect. More than a decade later, the *Savas* case would provide an opportunity for the Court to refine its thoughts on the matter. In that ruling, the Court qualified Article 41(1) of the Additional Protocol as 'an unequivocal *standstill* clause' which was, according to the Court, clearly, precisely and unconditionally formulated and thus capable of having direct effect.[29]

If the nature and scope of the Ankara Agreement, and thus also its pre-accession character, seem to have had no determinant effect on the examination of the direct effect question and consequently need not be addressed further, the same cannot be said regarding the substantive interpretation of its provisions. Especially revealing in this regard is the *El-Yassini* ruling,[30] in which the Court compared the 1963 Association Agreement with Turkey with the Co-operation Agreement with Morocco.[31] According to the Court, the principle of non-discrimination as formulated in the two Agreements could not have an identical meaning. In the Court's view, the Agreement with Morocco was very different from the Ankara Agreement precisely because it did not go so far as to provide for the possibility of the accession of Morocco to the Community. Furthermore, the EEC-Morocco Agreement, unlike the Agreement with Turkey, did not intend to secure the freedom of movement of workers progressively. Finally, the EEC-Morocco Co-operation Council had not taken a decision comparable to Decision No 1/80 of the EEC-Turkey Association Council. Therefore, it was impossible to transpose the Court's case law on the EEC-Turkey Agreement to the EEC-Morocco Agreement. The Court thus concluded that Member States were entitled to refuse to renew a residence permit for a Moroccan national in respect of whom they had previously authorized entry to their territory and to take up employment there, when the initial reason for the grant of his leave to stay no longer existed by the time that this residence permit had expired,[32] something which would have been impossible with respect to a Turkish worker coming within the scope of Article 6(1) of Decision No 1/80.

The potential for the direct effect of standstill provisions contained in the Protocol subsequently led to intensive judicial activity concerning the delimitation of the substantive scope of this potential. Clear illustrations of such a dynamic interaction between direct effect and substantive interpretation are, for example, the *Abatay*[33] and *Soysal*[34] judgments. In *Abatay*, the Court extended the *Savas* interpretation of the standstill clause related to establishment to the freedom to provide services. In the Court's view:

[29] Case C-37/98 *The Queen v Secretary of State for the Home Department, ex parte Abdulnasir Savas* [2000] ECR I-2927, paras 46–54 and 71.

[30] Case C-416/96 *Nour Eddline El-Yassini v Secretary of State for Home Department* [1999] ECR I-1209.

[31] ibid para 61.

[32] ibid para 62.

[33] Case C-317/01 *Eran Abatay and Others* [2003] ECR I-12301.

[34] Case C-228/06 *Mehmet Soysal and Ibrahim Savatli v Bundesrepublik Deutschland* [2009] ECR I-1031.

Article 41(1) of the Additional Protocol thus appears to be the necessary corollary to Articles 13 and 14 of the Association Agreement, and constitutes the indispensable means of achieving the gradual abolition of national obstacles to the freedom of establishment and the freedom to provide services.[35]

Later in the judgment, the Court drew attention to the fact that:

from the wording of Article 14 of the Association Agreement, as well as from the objective of the EEC-Turkey Association, . . . the principles enshrined in Article 55 of the EC Treaty (now Article 45 EC[36]) and 56 of the EC Treaty (now, after amendment, Article 46 EC[37]), and in the provisions of the Treaty relating to the freedom to provide services, must be extended, *so far as possible,* to Turkish nationals to eliminate restrictions on the freedom to provide services between the contracting parties.[38]

The 'so far as possible' reasoning is perhaps the clearest signal of the integration-oriented interpretation, and more of these examples can be given regarding the interpretation of decisions of the Association Council (see further below). The Court also held that national legislation of Member States which did not exist at the moment of entry into force of the Additional Protocol, and which had the effect of rendering the economic freedoms guaranteed by the Association Agreement more strict, constituted a 'new restriction' within the meaning of Article 41(1). Consequently, new visa requirements for admission to the territory of a Member State are incompatible with Article 41(1).[39] In the *Tum and Dari* judgment,[40] the Court had already made clear that the objective of Article 41(1) was to create conditions for the progressive achievement of freedom of establishment. There was, according to the Court, an absolute prohibition on national authorities in terms of creating any new obstacle to the exercise of that freedom by making more stringent the conditions which exist at a given time, so as not to render more difficult the gradual securing of that freedom between the Member States and the Republic of Turkey.[41] In addition, on 29 April 2010, the Court interpreted the scope of the standstill provision of Article 41(1) in the light of pecuniary charges that the Dutch Law on Foreign Nationals had introduced for applications for a residence permit or renewal of such a permit. The

[35] Case C-317/01 *Abatay*, n 33 above, para 68. For more details on the direct effect analysis in EU-Turkey relations, see M Maresceau, 'Bilateral agreements concluded by the European Community' in *Collected Courses Academy of International Law*, Vol 309 (Leiden/Boston: Martinus Nijhoff, 2006) 268–80.

[36] In the post-Lisbon numbering, Article 51 TFEU.

[37] In the post-Lisbon numbering, Article 52 TFEU.

[38] Case C-317/01 *Abatay*, n 33 above, para 112, emphasis added.

[39] For more details on the case law regarding Article 41(1) of the Additional Protocol, see P Mavridis, *Les Turcs dans l'Union européenne: Réflexions sur la pré-eminence du droit* (Brussels: Bruylant, 2009) 198–228; more in particular on visa policy, see K Groenendijk and E Guild, *Visa policy of Member States and the EU towards Turkish nationals after Soysal*, Economic Development Foundation Publications, no 232, 2010. So far, the Court has not yet ruled on the relevance of the standstill clause of Article 41(1) of the Additional Protocol for Turkish receivers of services. This may not last for long, since a case on this question is now pending, see Case C-221/11 *Demirkan* [2011] OJ C 232/15.

[40] Case C-16/05 *The Queen, Veli Tum and Mehmet Dari v Secretary of State for the Home Department* [2007] ECR I-7415.

[41] ibid para 61.

Court concluded that the prohibition of discrimination applied to all the charges imposed on Turkish nationals which are disproportionate when compared with those applied to citizens of the Union for the issue of similar documents.[42] Seen from this perspective, Turkish nationals are a privileged category of third country nationals in EU law.[43] Of course, the Court's ruling on direct effect and on the substantive scope of Article 41(1) should not be misunderstood. It does not, as such, confer on Turkish nationals a right of entry into the territory of a Member State 'since no such a positive right can be inferred from Community rules currently applicable, but, on the contrary, remains national law'. Consequently, the standstill clause of Article 41(1) 'does not operate in the same way as a substantive rule by rendering inapplicable the relevant substantive law it replaces, but as a quasi-procedural rule which stipulates, *ratione temporis*, which are the provisions of a Member State's legislation that must referred to for the purposes of assessing the position of a Turkish national who wishes to exercise freedom of establishment in a Member State'[44] or who wishes to provide services in a Member State.

It is thus evident from the case law cited that the scope of the standstill obligation as contained in Article 41(1) of the Additional Protocol has received an integration-oriented interpretation.[45] An additional but substantial opening towards increased potential for direct effect was created when the Court of Justice admitted decisions of the EC-Turkey Association Council to be capable of direct effect even if the provisions of the Agreement on which they were based were lacking such effect. The leading case on this point is the *Sevince* ruling,[46] confirmed two years later by the *Kus* judgment.[47] A subsequent abundance of case law again demonstrates the intense interaction between confirmation of direct effect and refining the substantive scope of provisions of the Decisions of the Association Council. In particular, Decision No 1/80 has often been subject to interpretation by the Court of Justice. This is not surprising in light of the large number of Turkish workers fulfilling the criteria laid down in Article 6(1) of that Decision. In addition, that provision is particularly relevant for sensitive questions such as the renewal of work permits and access to employment. A crucial question for the interpretation of the scope of

[42] Case C-92/07 *European Commission v Kingdom of the Netherlands* [2010] ECR I-3683; see further Case C-242/06 *Sahin* [2009] ECR I-8465.

[43] For another illustration, see Case C-256/11 *Murat Dereci*, judgment of 15 November 2011, not yet reported; on this point, see S Adam and P Van Elsuwege, 'Citizenship Rights and the Federal Balance between the European Union and its Member States: Comment on *Dereci*' (2012) 37 *ELRev*, 186–7.

[44] See Case C-16/05 *Tum and Dari*, n 40 above, paras 54–5; also Case C-256/11 *Murat Dereci*, n 43 above, para 89.

[45] It is worth noting that the Court also achieves the integration-oriented approach by applying the interpretation of the standstill provision of Article 41(1) of the Additional Protocol regarding freedom of establishment to the standstill provision of Article 13 of Decision No 1/80 regarding access to employment applicable to workers and their family which satisfy the conditions laid down in the decision. In the *Toprak* and *Oguz* cases, the Court refers to 'the need of convergence in the interpretation of both Article 41 of the Additional Protocol and Article 13 of Decision No 1/80 as regards the objectives pursued'. See Judgment of 9 December 2010, Joined Cases C-300/09 and C-301/09 *Staatssecretaris van Justitie v F. Toprak and I. Oguz*, not yet reported, para 54.

[46] Case C-192/89 *S. Z. Sevince v Staatssecretaris van Justitie* [1990] ECR I-3461.

[47] Case C-237/91 *Kazim Kus v Landeshauptstadt Wiesbaden* [1992] ECR I-6781.

Article 6(1) was whether the principles laid down in the context of free movement of workers in the EC Treaty could and should be applied. A milestone judgment in this respect was the *Ahmet Bozkurt* ruling,[48] in which the Court examined whether the reasoning in the *Lopes da Veiga* judgment[49] on free movement for workers in an intra-EC context could also be applied to Turkish workers falling within the scope of Decision No 1/80. The Court concluded that the EEC-Turkey Association Council had adopted social provisions in Decision No 1/80 aiming to go one stage further, guided by Articles 48, 49 and 50 of the EC Treaty, towards securing freedom of movement for workers. It then held, against the submissions of the German, Greek and Dutch Governments and also that of the United Kingdom, '[that] in order to ensure compliance with the objective, it would seem to be essential to transpose, *so far as possible*, the principles enshrined in those articles to Turkish workers who enjoy the rights conferred by Decision No 1/80'.[50] Later case law confirms the following three points reasoning: first, the terms of Article 12 of the Association Agreement are recalled, in which provisions the Contracting parties agree 'to be guided by Articles 48, 49 and 50 of the Treaty establishing the Community for the purpose of progressively securing freedom of movement of workers between them'; second, Article 36 of the Additional Protocol specifies the stages by which free movement of workers is to be secured progressively and provides that the Association Council shall decide on the rules necessary to that end; finally, Decision 1/80, taken on the basis of these provisions, seeks 'to improve, in the social field, the treatment accorded to workers and members of their family'.[51] The 'so far as possible' mode of interpretation has been applied to clarify various concepts in the context of EC-Turkey relations, inter alia those of 'worker',[52] 'member of the family of the worker',[53] 'being duly registered as belonging to the labour force',[54] 'legal employment',[55] 'prohibition of discrimination as regarding conditions of work'[56] and 'the scope of the public policy, public security or public health exception'.[57] What is striking is that the Court's 'integration approach' continues to be based on the initial objective laid down in the 1963 Association Agreement. Moreover, this approach does not seem to have been

[48] Case C-434/93 *Ahmet Bozkurt v Staatssecretaris van Justitie* [1995] ECR I-1475.

[49] Case 9/88 *Mário Lopes da Veiga v Staatssecretaris van Justitie* [1989] ECR 2989.

[50] Case C-434/93 *Ahmet Bozkurt*, n 48 above, paras 19–20, emphasis added; see further Case C-171/95 *Tetik* [1997] ECR I-329, paras 20, 28; Case C-36/96 *Günaydin* [1997] ECR I-5143, para 21.

[51] For other examples in the case law, see Case C-1/97 *Birden* [1998] ECR I-7747, para 23; Case C-351/95 *Kadiman* [1997] ECR I-2133, para 30; Case C-317/01 and C-369/01 *Abatay*, n 33 above, para 112.

[52] Case C-1/97 *Birden*, n 51 above, paras 23–32; Case C-188/00 *Kurz* [2002] ECR I-10691, paras 30–6; Case C-14/09 *Genc* [2010] ECR I-931, paras 18–33.

[53] Case C-275/02 *Ayaz* [2004] ECR I-8765, paras 38–48; Case C-351/95 *Kadiman*, n 51 above, para 30.

[54] Case C-188/00 *Kurz*, n 52 above, paras 37–47; Case C-1/97 *Birden*, n 51 above, paras 33–54.

[55] Case C-188/00 *Kurz*, n 52 above, paras 48–61; Case C-1/97 *Birden*, n 51 above, paras 55–69; Case C-98/96 *Ertanir* [1997] ECR I-5179, para 21.

[56] Case C-171/01 *Wählergruppe* [2003] ECR I-4301, paras 72–94.

[57] Case C-340/97 *Nazli* [2002] ECR I-957, paras 55–64; Case C-467/02 *Cetinkaya* [2004] ECR I-10895, paras 43–8; Case C-136/03 *Dörr* [2005] ECR I-4759, paras 62–9; Case C-349/06 *Polat* [2007] ECR I-8167, paras 29–39.

affected or hurt by the political reorientation of EU-Turkey relations and growing opposition in a number of Member States towards further integration of Turkey in the EU, an objective that has acquired almost mythical proportions today. The Court has, within the limits of the terms of the Association Agreement, continued to rely heavily on the 'integration philosophy' of that Agreement notwithstanding strong resistance by some Member States.

Of course, these limits are for the Court also the limits to what it can do under the mentioned 'so far as possible' reasoning. The *Ahmet Bozkurt* ruling gives us an illustration of such a limit. Neither the Association Agreement nor the Additional Protocol or Decisions of the Association Council deal with the free movement of workers from Turkey to the EU. Applied to the contents of Decision No 1/80, this means that Article 6 of that Decision is only applicable to Turkish workers who are working or are temporarily incapacitated: however, '[i]t does not, on the other hand, cover the situation of a Turkish worker who has definitively ceased to belong to the labour force of a Member State because he has, for example, reached retirement age or . . . become totally or permanently incapacitated for work'.[58] Another, even more explicit, example of a limitation on the 'so far as possible' reasoning is the recent *Ziebell* judgment of 8 December 2011[59] where the Court rightly refused to apply a provision of Directive 2004/38 on the right of citizens of the Union and their family members to move and reside freely within the territory of the Member States[60] to a Turkish national who enjoyed rights under the EEC-Turkey Association. This Directive, as its preamble and its provisions clearly demonstrate, is based on the concept of 'Union citizenship'. In the *Ziebell* case, it had been argued that the provisions providing for protection against expulsion laid down in Article 28(3)(a) of the Directive should also be applied to members of the family of a Turkish worker who had been authorized to join the worker. However, in this case, the Court refused to apply the 'by analogy' approach and held that '[i]t thus follows from the substantial differences to be found not only in their wording but also in their object and purpose between the rules relating to the EEC-Turkey Association and European Union law concerning citizenship that the two legal schemes in question cannot be considered equivalent.' Consequently, the protection against expulsion enjoyed by Union citizens on the basis of the Directive 'cannot be applied mutatis mutandis for the purpose of determining the meaning and scope of Article 14(1) of Decision No 1/80'.[61] The end result of the Court's interpretation is correct: Directive 2004/38 applies 'to all Union citizens who move or reside in a Member State other than that of which they are a national, and to their family members' (Article 3) and, consequently, cannot, by simple analogy, be relied upon by a family member of a Turkish worker. However, in order to reach this rather evident result, the Court felt the need to examine the purpose of the

[58] Case C-434/93 *Ahmet Bozkurt*, n 48 above, para 39.

[59] Case C-371/08 *Ziebell* [2012] OJ C 32/2.

[60] Directive 2004/38 of the European Parliament and of the Council of 29 April 2004 on the right of citizens of the Union and their family members to move and reside freely within the territory of the Member States [2004] OJ L 158/77.

[61] Case C-371/08 *Ziebell*, para 74.

EEC-Turkey Association Agreement and came to the conclusion, hereby following the opinion of Advocate General Bot, that 'the EEC-Turkey Association pursues a solely economic purpose'.[62] Such statements by the Court, however, do not provide additional clarity. Did the Court refer to the fact that the EEC was in 1963 merely an economic community? Did the Court want to stress that the 1963 Association Agreement had no political significance at all? Together with the 1961 Association Agreement with Greece, the 1963 Association Agreement with Turkey was a genuine pre-accession agreement, that is, an agreement which aimed at preparing the associated State for later accession to the EEC. Certainly, this is more than a 'solely economic' purpose as the Court pretends in *Ziebell*. The strange thing about this statement is that the qualification of the purpose of the 1963 Association Agreement, as the Court has given, was totally unnecessary to reach the result it has reached.

C. Turkey: 'a candidate State' negotiating accession

When, in 1989, the European Commission gave a negative opinion on Turkey's application for EC membership, the following arguments were used: inappropriate timing, since the Community was so heavily involved in its project on the completion of the internal market; the difficult economic situation in Turkey; at the political level, considerable efforts had still to be made to bring parliamentary democracy in Turkey closer to the Community model; the human rights situation and protection of minorities had to be improved; the pending dispute between Turkey and Greece as well as the Cyprus problem also constituted serious obstacles. The Commission therefore concluded that accession negotiations could not be opened, and it recommended that the Community propose that Turkey make efforts to increase interdependence and to move forward on the road of integration 'in accordance with the political will shown at the time of the signing of the Ankara Treaty'. The Commission suggested a deepening of the bilateral relationship by concentrating on completion of the customs union, resumption and intensification of financial cooperation, promotion of industrial and technical cooperation, and the strengthening of political and cultural links. The Commission was also keen to emphasize that its opinion did not intend to '[cast] doubt on [Turkey's] eligibility for membership of the Community' but in practice it did mean, at least for a number of years, a freeze on Turkey's accession ambitions. Shortly after this opinion, Cyprus and Malta applied for membership and both received a positive opinion from the Commission in 1993. The positive opinion on Cyprus's application was, of course, a very sensitive matter for Turkey and brought the question of its own accession request again to the political forefront. However, it was also in 1993 that the EU, for the first time, through the Copenhagen European Council, was able to proclaim that it was willing to enlarge towards the countries of Central

[62] Case C-434/93 *Ahmet Bozkurt*, n 48 above, para 64. Elsewhere the Court even holds that the 1963 Association Agreement 'pursues solely a *purely* economic objective' (para 72, emphasis added).

and Eastern Europe. To this end, political and economic conditions for EU membership were formulated, afterwards known as the Copenhagen criteria for EU membership. They implied that a candidate State had to achieve stability of institutions guaranteeing democracy, the rule of law, respect for and protection of minorities; and to have a functioning market economy. Membership presupposed 'the candidate's ability to take on the obligations of membership including adherence to the aims of political, economic and monetary union'. The 1993 Copenhagen European Council also drew attention to the Union's absorption capacity and observed that 'maintaining the momentum of European integration' was an important consideration in the general interest of both the Union and the candidate countries.

In the following years, this orientation of the Union towards enlargement would lead to ten applications for EU membership from countries in Central and Eastern Europe and the EU's new approach created a very strong focus on pre-accession strategies towards these countries. EU-Turkey relations were rapidly overshadowed by this new orientation. However, even in this new context, Turkey could not be completely ignored, all the more since Greece was eager to include Cyprus in the EU's pre-accession policies. When, in December 1995, Decision No 1/95 of the EC-Turkey Association Council on implementing the final phase of the customs union with Turkey was taken,[63] reference was made in the preamble to that Decision to the objectives of the Ankara Agreement and, in particular, to Article 28. These objectives, it was recalled, 'maintained their significance at this time of great political and economic transformation on the European scene'. When, later, the true pre-accession process was initiated for the countries of Central and Eastern Europe, the EU also incorporated Cyprus, as mentioned, in the group of countries with which accession negotiations could be opened. However, *Agenda 2000*, the Commission's strategic document on enlargement published on 15 July 1997[64] together with the individual opinions on each application for EU membership from the countries of Central and Eastern Europe, was particularly disconcerting for Turkey. Indeed, in this crucial phase of the EU's enlargement process, Turkey had been largely ignored and channelled into a separate *Communication on the Further Development of Relations with Turkey*,[65] which only made some general and vague references to the deepening of certain aspects of bilateral relations without offering any perspective on possible EU accession. Certainly, the Commission still proclaimed '[that] the EU has a particularly close relationship with Turkey whose eligibility for EU membership [had] been recently reaffirmed'[66] but one thing was unmistakably clear: Turkey would have to satisfy increasingly more precise

[63] Decision No 1/95, n 13 above.

[64] *Agenda 2000* COM (97) 2000 final.

[65] Communication from the Commission to the Council and the European Parliament on the Further Development of Relations with Turkey COM (97) 394 final.

[66] The Commission probably referred to a statement by the President of the EC-Turkey Association Council who at its meeting of 29 April 1997 reconfirmed 'Turkey's eligibility' for EU membership: see Bulletin of the European Union, 4-1997, 1.4.74.

preconditions before accession negotiations could be opened[67] and was definitively left out of the EU's ongoing enlargement strategy.

The reaction of Turkey to this turn of events was, as could be expected, one of great disappointment and frustration, and initiated a period of gloom in EU-Turkey bilateral relations. A totally failed attempt by the EU to improve the relationship after the publication of *Agenda 2000*, which in the end only served to exacerbate the tension rather than soften it, was the proposal to set up a *European Conference* in which Turkey was to have had a prominent place. This was an idea that had been strongly supported by the then new British Government, which, moreover, in the first half of 1998 was to hold the EU Presidency. The December 1997 Luxembourg European Council, the first European Council after *Agenda 2000*, proposed formally to set up such a conference bringing together the EU Member States and those States aspiring to accede to the EU and sharing its values as well as internal and external objectives. Initially, the EU offer was 'addressed to Cyprus, the applicant States of Central and Eastern Europe *and Turkey*'.[68] The main objective of the Conference was to provide 'a multilateral forum for political consultation, intended to address questions of general concern to the participants and to broaden and deepen their cooperation on foreign and security policy, justice and home affairs, and other areas of common concern, particularly economic matters and regional cooperation'. However, the European Conference appeared totally disconnected from the *accession process*, the second but main theme of the Luxembourg European Summit. The European Council indeed decided in Luxembourg to launch 'the process of accession and negotiation', which was to become the leading vehicle for EU enlargement and, moreover, laid down the various components of the *enhanced pre-accession strategy*, such as accession partnerships, increased pre-accession aid and a specific procedure regularly reviewing the progress made by each candidate for accession. While the idea to set up a European Conference was clearly aiming—as a matter of fact was the sole *raison d'être*—to provide Turkey with a European 'anchor', it was also quickly becoming clear that this forum meant that Turkey was to remain sidelined while the real enlargement process with the other applicants for accession was elsewhere firmly put into motion. Seen in this context, the European Council's references to 'a European strategy for Turkey' concentrating on the Ankara Agreement, the customs union, financial cooperation, approximation of laws and the participation of Turkey in certain Community programmes sounded hollow and were a far cry from the enhanced pre-accession strategy applied to the countries of Central and Eastern Europe and to Cyprus. This explains easily the negative and also very sharp Turkish response to the type of treatment the EU intended to offer. When finally, on 31 March 1998, the EU accession negotiations officially started with the '1 + 5', that is with Cyprus and the five countries of Central and Eastern Europe which had received a positive opinion from the European Commission (Poland, Hungary, the Czech Republic, Estonia and Slovenia), this had the effect in Turkey of waving a red rag to a bull and brought the

[67] On this specific point, see K Inglis, *Evolving Practice in EU Enlargement: With Case Studies in Agri-Food and Environment Law* (Leiden/Boston: Martinus Nijhoff, 2010) 75–7.

[68] Emphasis added.

general atmosphere of EU-Turkey bilateral relations to an absolute low. This situation was to last until the Helsinki European Council of December 1999. In Helsinki, Turkey achieved an impressive upgrade and, for the first time, was defined as '*a candidate State destined to join the Union* on the basis of the same criteria as applied to other candidate States'.[69] While, on the one hand, qualifying Turkey as a country 'destined to join the Union' gave a particularly strong and at first sight surprising[70] political signal, on the other hand, the European Council also made clear that no accession negotiations could be opened until additional efforts were made by Turkey to comply with the Copenhagen political criteria for accession. Turkey was to be treated as any other candidate State and, from then onwards, was included in the EU's pre-accession strategy. But the Helsinki Summit Conclusions also had adverse implications for Turkey. First, it was agreed in Helsinki that Cyprus would be able to join the EU once accession negotiations had been completed, even in the event that no settlement of the Cyprus Question could be secured. Second, there was no commitment to a date for the opening of accession negotiations with Turkey. The 1999 Helsinki European Council made clear that Turkey did not yet sufficiently comply with the Copenhagen criteria for accession and important efforts for reform were needed before negotiations could be opened.

In 2001, the *Accession Partnership for Turkey* was formally established to implement what was agreed at the Helsinki Summit, namely including Turkey in the EU's pre-accession strategy and extending support for its reforms. The Decision laid down the principles, priorities, intermediate objectives and conditions for such assistance,[71] and was subsequently adjusted and refined.[72] Turkey was required, like all the other candidate States, to prepare a national programme for the adoption of the *acquis,* setting out a timetable for achieving the priorities and intermediate objectives established by the Accession Partnership.[73] 2002 was a turning point from two different perspectives. First, after general elections in Turkey, it brought to power the AKP. This created a totally new but paradoxical situation. While, on the one hand, the Erdogan Government committed itself to substantial political

[69] Emphasis added.

[70] Before the meeting in Helsinki, there had been signs of improved bilateral relations between Greece and Turkey; eg, the psychological impact of Greek assistance after the terrible earthquake in Turkey in August 1999 helped to improve those relations. For a more in-depth analysis of Greek approaches to EU-Turkey relations, see A Kazamias, 'The Greek Variable in EU-Turkey Relations' in JS Joseph (ed), *Turkey and the European Union: Internal Dynamics and External Challenges* (Basingstoke:Palgrave, 2006) 138–60. Also the Commission's Progress Reports on Turkey of 1998 and 1999 had provided a more positive global assessment.

[71] See Council Decision 2001/235/EC of 8 March 2001 on the principles, priorities, intermediate objectives and conditions contained in the Accession Partnership with the Republic of Turkey [2001] OJ L 85/13.

[72] Most recently in 2008, see Council Decision 2008/157/EC of 18 February 2008 on the principles, priorities and conditions contained in the Accession Partnership with the Republic of Turkey and repealing Decision 2006/35/EC [2008] OJ L 51/4; also Council Decision 2003/398/EC of 19 May 2003 on the principles, priorities, intermediate objectives and conditions contained in the Accession Partnership with Turkey [2003] OJ L 145/40; and Council Decision 2006/35/EC of 23 January 2006 on the principles, priorities and conditions contained in the Accession Partnership with Turkey [2006] OJ L 22/34.

[73] In 2001 the National Programme was adopted and reviewed, and updated in 2003 and 2008.

and legislative reforms in the light of Turkey's EU membership preparations, something which the EU would of course follow closely and also appreciate, on the other hand, the domestic political reorientation of the new Turkish Government towards a less secular Turkey and a greater impact of Islam in politics, was not necessarily conducive to creating an ideal pre-accession climate. It was against this new political background that, in December 2002, from the perspective of EU enlargement, the very important Copenhagen European Council took place, where it was decided that accession negotiations with eight countries of Central and Eastern Europe as well as Cyprus and Malta could be concluded. Regarding Turkey, the European Council strongly welcomed 'the important steps taken by Turkey towards meeting the Copenhagen criteria, in particular through the recent legislative packages and the subsequent implementation measures which cover a large number of key priorities specified in the Accession Partnership'. The European Council also explicitly acknowledged the firm determination of the new Turkish Government to take further steps and urged the Government to address the path of reform 'not only with regard to legislation but also in particular with regard to implementation'. Most importantly, the Union agreed that if the European Council in December 2004, on the basis of a report and a recommendation from the Commission, decided that Turkey fulfilled the Copenhagen political criteria, then it would open accession negotiations 'without delay'. Moreover, to assist Turkey towards EU membership, the pre-accession strategy was considerably strengthened through a revised Accession Partnership and an intensification of the process of legislative scrutiny; the EC-Turkey customs union was to be extended and deepened; and pre-accession financial assistance significantly increased.

In October 2004, the Commission, as requested, published a new assessment of the reforms undertaken and recommended the opening of accession negotiations. Consequently, the 2004 December Brussels European Council reiterated its magic formula that Turkey 'was a candidate country destined to join the Union' and decided that Turkey sufficiently fulfilled the Copenhagen political criteria to go ahead with the opening of accession negotiations, provided that the proposed legislative reforms were brought into force. The European Council welcomed 'the decisive progress made by Turkey in its far-reaching reform process' and expressed confidence that Turkey would sustain the process of reform on which it had embarked. The European Council also invited the Commission to present to the Council (of Ministers) a proposal for a framework for negotiations with Turkey and requested the Council to agree on that framework with a view to opening accession negotiations on 3 October 2005. For the first time in the more than forty years of bilateral relations between the EU and Turkey, there was now a precise date for the opening of accession negotiations.

However, rather unexpectedly, 2005 was to bring increasingly dark clouds over Turkey's accession bid. The first had to do with the controversy surrounding the ratification of the Treaty on the European Constitution. The effects of this outcome were amplified by the lack of enthusiasm of some Member States towards the prospect of a possible accession of Turkey. The negative result of the referendums in France and the Netherlands seriously affected the envisaged opening of accession negotiations. As a matter of fact, the controversy on the ratification of the

Constitutional Treaty and the effects of that controversy indirectly affected the EU enlargement process as a whole and that with Turkey in particular. How could the EU further enlarge if it was not even able to put order in its own house? In addition, the outspoken positions of French and German political leaders, in particular of President Sarkozy and Chancellor Merkel, on the non-European identity of Turkey introduced very heavy obstacles of principle into the enlargement debate. Both political leaders seemed to share the same position: Turkey could never become a member of the EU since it was not a 'European State', one of the few but essential conditions for EU membership explicitly mentioned in Article 49 TEU.

Of course, nobody, including the French and German political leadership, wanted to alienate Turkey from Europe or to cut off ties with this strategic EU partner. Therefore, the French President and the German Chancellor have suggested a 'privileged partnership' with the EU instead of full accession. However, this approach also faces formidable hurdles. First, it is not clear what the concept of a 'privileged partnership' really means and none of those advocating this alternative have so far been able to define it properly. And the most difficult obstacle to that alternative is undoubtedly the categorical refusal by Turkey to accept it. One can understand the Turkish lack of enthusiasm for 'privileged partnership', which resembles the traumatic European Conference approach that so exercised the Turkish authorities in the second half of the 1990s. 'Privileged partnership' could probably be not much more than a kind of upgraded status quo but, above all, the 'privileged partnership' option is not in line with the political commitments of the 1963 Association Agreement. If 'privileged partnership' becomes an alternative for accession as a result of Turkey's insufficiently European character, then the 1963 Agreement itself needs to be renegotiated or, in the worst case scenario, denounced by the EU, invoking *rebus sic stantibus*. Needless to say, it may well be natural to expect that such thinking will encounter very strong Turkish resistance. This catastrophe scenario should, by all means, be avoided, not only in the interests of Turkey but perhaps even more so in the interests of the EU itself. In this contribution, it has been made sufficiently clear that, in 1963, the EEC signed a true pre-accession agreement with Turkey. Furthermore, its pre-accession nature has been continuously confirmed at the political level. Not only has Turkey's 'eligibility' for EU membership been incessantly repeated by various EU institutions but, as mentioned, Turkey has also been formally granted candidate State status, has been qualified as 'destined to join the European Union', has been incorporated into the Accession Partnerships created by the EU precisely to prepare candidate States for EU membership, and accession negotiations have been opened. Once this formidable machinery is well established and in motion, then coming up with the argument that Turkey is not a 'European State' and thus does not satisfy the preliminary condition of Article 49 TEU is discourteous and simply not acceptable. Certainly, Turkey must, as any other candidate State, satisfy the political and economic conditions for EU membership. The EU is perfectly entitled to be strict and even to be very meticulous on this: to delay or even refuse accession if Turkey is unable to provide sufficient guarantees for EU membership is not to be excluded. However, rejecting Turkey on the basis of 'insufficient European-ness', after everything that has been done, is close to provocation.

Furthermore, 2005 brought additional difficulties on the road to the opening of accession negotiations not directly linked to the referendums on the Constitutional Treaty. Austria, which in the past had agreed with all the European Council Conclusions on Turkey, including those where Turkey was defined as a candidate State 'destined to join the European Union', now came up with a possible veto on the opening of accession negotiations as planned in October 2005. While enthusiasm in Austria for EU enlargement with Turkey has always been very limited, it soon materialized that this potential veto was part of a political strategy aimed at pushing the opening of accession negotiations with Croatia. Even though, at that time, Croatia was not fully cooperating with the International Criminal Tribunal for the Former Yugoslavia in The Hague, the Council of Ministers decided to open accession negotiations simultaneously with Turkey and Croatia on 3 October 2005; this was enough to avoid an Austrian veto on the opening of accession negotiations with Turkey.

Finally, in the context of EU-Turkey relations, Cyprus is never far away. Cyprus is now a fully-fledged EU Member State and, as any other EU Member State, can partially or completely block the accession process with Turkey. Since the moment of the accession, on 1 May 2004, of the Republic of Cyprus, the application of the *acquis* to the Northern part of the island has been 'suspended' until a solution is found for the Cyprus problem. But the 2004 enlargement created the need for an additional Protocol to the 1963 Agreement with Turkey. This is easy to understand. The 1963 Agreement was a mixed agreement and every enlargement requires an agreement in which the third country takes account of the fact that the EU has enlarged. Applied to EU-Turkey relations, this meant that an additional Protocol to the 1963 Association Agreement was needed, in particular in order to make the rules of the customs union also applicable to the new Member States. One of these States was the Republic of Cyprus, which created a serious political and legal headache since Turkey has recognized the Turkish Republic of Northern Cyprus as an independent State. Only after strong pressure from the EU did Turkey finally sign the Protocol on 29 July 2005 but, since Turkey does not recognize the jurisdiction of the Republic of Cyprus on the Northern part of the island, the Turkish Government issued a unilateral declaration stating that the Republic of Cyprus 'was not the original partnership State established in 1960'.[74] For Turkey, the Greek Cypriot authorities did not represent the Turkish Cypriot people and, for Turkey, 'the signature, ratification and implementation of this Protocol neither amount to any form of recognition of the Republic of Cyprus'. This in turn provoked a counter declaration by the EU insisting that the Turkish unilateral declaration was not a part of the Protocol.[75]

[74] See *Press Statement Regarding the Additional Protocol to Extend the Ankara Agreement to All EU Members* (No 123, Ministry of Foreign Affairs, Republic of Turkey, 29 July 2005).

[75] Press Communiqué Council of 21 September 2005, 1251/05 (Presse 243). For an analysis of this controversy, see S Laulhé Shaelou, *The EU and Cyprus: Principles and Strategies of Full Integration* (Leiden/Boston: Martinus Nijhoff, 2010) 62–8.

While neither the Turkish declaration nor the EU reaction prevented the opening of the accession negotiations on 3 October 2005, the Cyprus Question has seriously affected the course of these negotiations and little progress has since been made. At the time of writing, only 13 chapters of the *acquis,* out of the 35 to be negotiated altogether, have been opened for negotiation and one chapter is provisionally closed.[76] On 11 December 2006, the General Affairs Council of the EU decided not to open a series of chapters for negotiation until Turkey has fulfilled its commitment related to the additional Protocol. These significant unopened chapters cover free movement of goods, the right of establishment and freedom to provide services, financial services, agriculture and rural development, fisheries, transport, customs union, external relations. Moreover, the chapters that are being negotiated will not be closed provisionally. In other words, the EU wants Turkey to 'normalise' its relations with the Republic of Cyprus, which implies that Turkey must open its air and sea ports to planes and vessels from the Republic of Cyprus, something it has so far refused to do. In addition, as a consequence of the non-recognition by the EU and its Member States of the Turkish Republic of Northern Cyprus, Turkish Cypriot ports and airports are not opened to direct trade relations with the EU and only have direct links with Turkey. This is still very much the situation today and there are no signs of a solution of the Cyprus Question. Needless to say, the deadlock in the EU-Turkey accession talks is not helping to create a dynamic environment for enhanced cooperation, including in those areas that are particularly sensitive for the EU. Just to mention one example: the EU is eager to have increased cooperation with Turkey in the area of management of migration flows and to conclude a readmission agreement. Difficult and lengthy negotiations have taken place, which have recently been finalized.[77] However, the linking of this agreement with visa facilitation has so far prevented its signature. Turkey's request for visa-free travel to the EU has met with strong opposition in various EU Member States and may put on hold the conclusion of the readmission agreement. To date, Turkey is the only candidate State for EU accession which has no readmission and visa facilitation agreement with the EU.

D. Conclusion

If, in terms of scope and importance, the political and substantive objectives of the 1963 Association Agreement were singularly far-reaching, the means and instruments to attain them were in many ways insufficient and a lot depended on

[76] The following chapters have been opened: 'Enterprise and Industry', 'Financial Control and Statistics', 'Intellectual Property', 'Company Law', 'Environment', 'Taxation', 'Free Movement of Capital', 'Information Society', 'Media', 'Consumer Protection', 'Transeuropean Networks', 'Food Safety', 'Veterinary' and 'Phytosanitary Policy'. The chapter 'Science and Research' is provisionally closed.

[77] See Conclusion on EU-Turkey Readmission Agreement and related issues, 3071st Justice and Home Affairs Council meeting, 24–25 February 2011.

political goodwill, formally from the Association Council but, in reality, from the EU Member States where the unanimity rule prevailed. This is the main explanation as to why the free movement objectives, except that on trade, have not been successful under the regime of the Association Agreement. In the light of this state of affairs the continued integration-oriented approach adopted by the European Court of Justice when interpreting this Agreement—even when, as mentioned before, certain limits need to be taken into consideration—is all the more striking.

The EU's accession strategy towards Turkey has not been particularly conducive to achieving the free movement goals of the Association Agreement. With the Cyprus Question unsolved and a number of Member States expressing outright opposition to Turkish EU membership, there is little prospect for rapid change: Turkey's EU accession chances appear now further away than ever. And yet its expectations for possible EU accession have a solid legal and political basis: the 1963 Agreement was a genuine pre-accession agreement, it has been interpreted in an integration-oriented manner and political assurances have been provided repeatedly by the European Council, the highest institutional authority of the European Union. This contribution has tried to make this clear. But all of that does not suffice. The biggest danger of a continuous EU rejection of Turkey is that Turkey moves away from Europe. While officially such a move is being denied by the highest authorities in Ankara,[78] there is growing concern also in the EU about the reorientation of Turkey's foreign affairs and particularly its neighbourhood relations. This is not the place to enter into discussion of the ramifications of some of the Turkish foreign policy shifts, but one thing should be clear: the EU cannot eternally continue to pursue an ostrich policy towards Turkey. Turkey has already shown a good deal of patience in its relations with the EU. A crucial question which will probably remain on the table for a considerable time to come is this: is Turkey welcome in the EU if it satisfies the Copenhagen criteria in the way other candidates have complied with them and contributes to finding an acceptable solution to the Cyprus Question? In this context, it is important to recall that the principal reason why the EU is enlarging—almost the dogma of EU enlargement—is that this is a process that contributes to increasing the 'stability and prosperity of the entire European continent'. This motive is, of course, also a valid consideration in relation to Turkey, but the EU's statement that Turkey is 'a candidate State destined to join the European Union' remains loaded with uneasy ambiguity resulting from the challenge to Turkey's 'European-ness'.

This contribution did not intend to examine the political and legal reforms that Turkey has undertaken in the pre-accession context, but that does not mean, of course, that certain aspects of this reform process do not have to be followed closely. While Turkey has committed itself to progressive alignment with EU law and has introduced or has embarked on important legal adaptations—and

[78] See, eg, remarks by Mr Ahmet Davutoglu, Minister of Foreign Affairs, cited in 'Turkey says EU is top priority', *Financial Times*, 9 July 2010.

many of these initiatives have been welcomed by EU institutions—there are nonetheless also a number of worrying signs. Only one or two can be recalled here. For example, while these conclusions are being written, a great number of journalists are detained in Turkish prisons.[79] Many of them are under investigation for alleged coup plans such as 'Ergenekon' or 'Sledgehammer'. They all happen to be critical towards the Government and towards political Islamism. It is not, therefore, astonishing that there is growing apprehension about the state of freedom of the press in Turkey. A recent resolution of the European Parliament expresses serious concern 'about the deterioration in freedom of the press, about certain acts of censorship and about growing self-censorship within the Turkish media'.[80]

A final remark concerns the constitutional referendum of 12 September 2010, through which the Turkish people accepted the constitutional amendments proposed by the Turkish Government. These amendments are seen by the Government as a key step in Turkey's pre-accession reforms and they aim to introduce a series of improvements regarding the protection of fundamental rights and freedoms. But they also include a contentious element on the reorganization of the judiciary, including the Constitutional Court, the High Council for Judges and Public Prosecutors, and Military Justice. The Government was keen to present a 'yes' to the reform package as a 'yes' to the adaptations requested by the EU within the pre-accession context, but political opposition in Turkey, for its part, saw various aspects of the proposed reforms as an unacceptable move to weaken Atatürk's legacy. The opposition's main fear was that the amendments might well constitute a serious threat to judicial independence and to Turkey as a secular State. In an official statement of the EU on the outcome of the referendum,[81] Commissioner Füle welcomed the approval of the constitutional reforms and the continued commitment of Turkish citizens to reforms. However, a lot will depend on the implementing laws that are needed and, in this respect, the Commission's statement urges the Turkish Government 'to show utmost transparency as well as a spirit of dialogue' involving a broad consultation of all political parties, something which had obviously been lacking in the preparation of the referendum.[82] The same holds true regarding the new constitution, which the Prime Minister,

[79] See, eg, *Le Monde*, 24 November 2011, 'Le pouvoir turc accentue ses pressions contre la presse d'opposition' mentioning that about 60 journalists were arrested; see further, on the position of the press in Turkey, *Financial Times*, 23 November 2011, 'Criticism grows over curbs on civil society', and *Financial Times*, 9 March 2011, 'Turkey must halt media intimidation'.

[80] Resolution of 9 March 2011 on Turkey's 2010 progress report, Doc B 7-0156/2011, point 8; see further the Commission's Communication *Enlargement Strategy and Main Challenges 2011–2012*, n 7 above, 6: 'In Turkey, the legal framework does not yet sufficiently safeguard freedom of expression. The high number of legal cases and investigations against journalists and undue pressure on the media raise serious concern'.

[81] Statement by Commissioner Stefan Füle on the result of the referendum in Turkey (Memo/10/402, 13 September 2010).

[82] *Enlargement Strategy and Main Challenges 2010–2011*, n 6 above, 18, sees these constitutional amendments as 'an important step in the right direction'.

Mr Erdogan, pledged to prepare after the elections of 12 June 2011 that brought again a landslide victory for the AKP (which obtained almost 50 per cent of the votes).[83] Adapting Turkey to EU norms and standards should not mean that Turkey needs to give up its secular foundations, which are the cornerstone of the modern Turkish Republic.

[83] However, the AKP parliamentary majority resulting from this election is not large enough to adopt a new constitution without support from other political parties.

17

Reshaping the Human Rights Landscape of the European Union

*Robin CA White**

A. Setting the scene

The foundations of the European Union are economic. The enterprise began with a commitment to the attainment of a common market in goods, and later services. The success of the internal market for the whole enterprise can hardly be overstated. But the objectives of the Union have never been wholly economic. From the earliest days, the broader social and political dimension has been central to the agenda of the Community, and now the Union. That commitment to broader issues is reflected in what is described as the European social model[1] within which the economic policies operate.

The achievement of the economic objectives has led to references to the economic constitution of the Union.[2] Even an economic constitution needs to have regard to certain human rights questions, but social and political cooperation brings these much more to the fore. This contribution is about the evolution of human rights protection within the Community and the Union. The tentacles of European Union law now reach into areas of regulation that the founders of the EEC could scarcely have contemplated. Examples are matters related to marriage, criminal justice, visas and asylum, and the consequences of developing a constitutional concept of citizenship of the Union. The Treaty of Lisbon has, for obvious political reasons, avoided presenting itself as a constitution, but its similarity to the failed Draft Constitution for the European Union and its use in places of constitutional language mean that its significance as a constitutional document cannot be denied.

* Professor of Law, and member of the Centre for European Law and Integration, School of Law, The University of Leicester; robin.white@le.ac.uk.

[1] See, eg, European Commission, *White Paper: European Social Policy—A Way Forward for the Union* COM (1994) 333 final, 27 July 1994.

[2] eg, M Maduro, *We the Court: The European Court of Justice and the European Economic Constitution. A Critical Reading of Article 30 of the EC Treaty* (Oxford: Hart Publishing, 1998); and D Schiek, U Liebert and H Schneider (eds), *European Economic and Social Constitutionalism after the Treaty of Lisbon* (Cambridge: Cambridge University Press, 2011).

This contribution argues that the developments in the Treaty of Lisbon, and in the process of negotiating accession by the Union to the European Convention on Human Rights, represent a deeply significant change in the human rights landscape of the Union. These developments place human rights much more at the heart of the Union. The three constitutional documents—the Treaty on European Union, the Charter of Fundamental Rights of the European Union, and the Treaty on the Functioning of the European Union—to be joined in due course by the European Convention on Human Rights produce a quartet of Treaties that come very close to giving the Union a general competence in this field. This contribution argues that the Union is moving inexorably towards a general human rights competence, and explores the implications of this. It is illogical for a Union with such a broad range of competences to have only a limited competence in the field of human rights. It is also argued that the Member States have little to fear from such a development. The principle of subsidiarity provides a powerful brake on any overzealous legislative proposals from the Union's political organs.

One of the Court's Advocate Generals has recently observed of the Union's human rights competence:

> I shall not waste time or space on a lengthy exegesis of the importance of fundamental rights in the legal order of the European Union. Fundamental rights have been an essential part of the legal order for many years.[3]

Academic commentators have been more sceptical. Andrew Williams has commented that 'despite the consistent pronouncements in favour of human rights we have yet to experience coherence in the EU's institutional activities that could place human rights at the head of any list of value priorities.[4]

Another commentator has described progress on the protection of human rights as piecemeal, adding:

> Although the court has had to accommodate fundamental rights as part of the general principles of law by which Community institutions are bound, the substantive principles at the core of the European legal order remained those related to the project of market-building and regulation. To put this differently, basic rights have entered the European legal order as overriding constitutional norms, but have neither been essential nor foundational to the Community's array of functions.[5]

The thesis in this contribution is that there is scope for viewing the constitutional developments reflected in the revisions put in place by the Treaty of Lisbon, coupled with accession by the Union to the European Convention on Human Rights, as responses to the reservations expressed by Williams and Isiksel. Whereas, in the past, the foundations of the Union's human rights policy have rested on judicial creativity, they now rest on formal documents with deep constitutional significance.

[3] Opinion of AG Sharpston in Joined Cases C-92/09 and C-93/09 *Volker und Markus Schecke GbR and Eifert v Land Hessen* [2011] OJ C 13/6, para 64 (citations omitted).

[4] A Williams, *The Ethos of Europe. Values, Law and Justice in the EU* (Cambridge: Cambridge University Press, 2010) 152.

[5] N Isiksel, 'Fundamental Rights in the EU after *Kadi and Al Barakaat*' (2010) 16:5 *ELJ* 551, 554.

B. From *Nold* to *Kadi*

Judicial creativity in the face of threatened revolts by the constitutional courts of Germany and Italy led to recognition of fundamental rights as general principles of law recognized and respected by the Community legal order. The early case law does not warrant detailed consideration since this part of the story is so well known.[6] But some of the foundational principles developed by the Court are nevertheless worth mentioning. The *Internationale Handelsgesellschaft* case[7] embedded the protection of fundamental rights within the Community legal order, by acknowledging that respect for fundamental rights within that legal order was at least equivalent to the protections afforded by national constitutional orders. In the *Nold* case,[8] the Court acknowledged the importance of respect for fundamental rights within the Community, and regarded the constitutional traditions and the European Convention on Human Rights (ECHR) as the key sources of the identification of these rights. It recognized the protection of property both in the German Constitution and in the European Convention, but nevertheless refused to strike down the contested measure since property rights are not absolute. The *ERT* case[9] extended the earlier case law by providing that the Community institutions would police the activities of the Member States when they were acting within the scope of Community law.

But despite these important case law developments, critics commented that the principles developed were piecemeal and responsive to serendipitous litigation. They were essentially peripheral to attainment of economic objectives in creating the common market.[10] It was also frequently the case that the Court of Justice referred to the protection of fundamental rights, but did not find any breach by the Community. Even the more recent case law displayed uncertainties over whether fundamental rights were more important than the fundamental freedoms in the EC Treaty. Cases such as *Schmidberger*[11] and *Omega Spielhallen*[12] show increasing respect for fundamental rights when they come face-to-face with fundamental freedoms.[13] But on the other hand, cases like *Viking*[14] and *Laval*[15] can be cited

[6] See, in particular, P Alston (ed), *The EU and Human Rights* (Oxford: Oxford University Press, 1999); K Alter, *Establishing the Supremacy of European Law. The Making of an International Rule of Law in Europe* (Oxford: Oxford University Press, 2001); A von Bogdandy, 'The European Union as a Human Rights Organization: Human Rights and the Core of the European Union' (2000) 37:6 *CMLRev* 1307; and S Peers and A Ward (eds), *The EU Charter of Fundamental Rights. Politics, Law and Policy* (Oxford: Hart Publishing, 2004).

[7] Case 11/70 *Internationale Handelsgesellschaft* [1970] ECR 1125.

[8] Case 4/73 *Nold* [1974] ECR 491.

[9] Case C-260/89 *Elliniki Radiophonia Tileorassi* [1991] ECR I-2925.

[10] A von Bogdandy, n 6 above, 1307, 1308.

[11] Case C-112/00 *Schmidberger* [2003] ECR I-5659.

[12] Case C–36/02 *Omega Spielhallen* [2004] ECR I-9609.

[13] See C Sabel and O Gerstenberg, 'Constitutionalising an Overlapping Consensus: the ECJ and the Emergence of a Coordinate Constitutional Order' (2010) 16:5 *ELJ* 511.

[14] Case C-438/05 *Viking* [2007] ECR I-10779.

[15] Case C–341/05 *Laval* [2007] ECR I-11767.

for the reverse proposition: that fundamental freedoms are given priority over fundamental rights.[16] Perhaps the differences in impact of these cases may be explained by the different character of the fundamental rights in issue. In *Schmidberger* and *Omega Spielhallen,* the Court was addressing civil and political rights in the classical sense, whereas in *Viking* and *Laval* economic and social rights were being considered.

It was therefore a major event when the Court of Justice, in the much-contested *Kadi* case,[17] struck down an EU Regulation on the seizure of assets held in connection with terrorist activities, which had been adopted to enable Member States to comply with a resolution of the United Nations requiring the Member States to act. The case is a controversial one on many levels.[18] The contested ground is the extent to which this judgment represents a move towards establishing a constitutional prioritization of fundamental rights per se in the European Union, and a challenge to the proposition that fundamental rights can still be corralled into matters falling within scope of specific provisions of the two European Union Treaties. There is something anomalous about a Union of values only applying those values in certain contexts. However, it would be wrong to look at developments in the case law of the Court of Justice[19] without appreciating developments in the Treaties.

C. The evolution of the Treaties

The judicial creativity of the Court of Justice was needed because the original Treaties were silent on the matter of the protection of fundamental rights—and it might be said also, less than clear on the potential impact of general principles of law, which enabled the Court to fill in gaps in the Treaties. A treaty text on fundamental rights came into being with the introduction by the Treaty of Maastricht of Article 6(1) and (2) of the Treaty on European Union (prior to its amendment by the Treaty of Lisbon). These provisions proclaimed, for the first time, the foundations of the fundamental rights edifice of the Union, as follows:

1. The Union is founded on the principles of liberty, democracy, respect for human rights and fundamental freedoms, the rule of law, principles which are common to the Member States.

[16] See A Hinarejos, '*Laval* and *Viking:* the Right to Collective Action versus EU Fundamental Freedoms' (2008) 8:4 *HRLRev* 714; N Nic Shuibhne, 'Margins of Appreciation: National Values, Fundamental Rights and EC Free Movement Law' (2009) 34:2 *ELRev* 230; and C Semmelmann, 'The European Union's Economic Constitution under the Lisbon Treaty: Soul-Searching Shifts the Focus to Procedure' (2010) 35:4 *ELRev* 516.

[17] Joined Cases C-402/05 P and C-415/05 P *Kadi and Al Barakaat International Foundation* [2008] ECR I-6351, followed in Case T-85/09 *Kadi* Judgment of 30 September 2010, under appeal as Case C-584/10 P.

[18] See N Isiksel, n 5 above, 551.

[19] And to some extent also the General Court.

2. The Union shall respect fundamental rights, as guaranteed by the European Convention for the Protection of Human Rights and Fundamental Freedoms signed in Rome on 4 November 1950 and as they result from the constitutional traditions common to the Member States, as general principles of Community law.

The significance of these provisions is the Treaty basis for the protection of fundamental rights, and their attachment to the values on which the Union is founded. The effect of the restatement in this form of principles initially enunciated by judges, in deciding individual cases coming before them, should not be underestimated. Case law can often reflect the narrow confines of the special features of the disputes coming before courts, which can in turn be distinguished in later cases. Such variations are more difficult to sustain when the statements are included in the foundational Treaties. It should also be noted that the language of Article 6 was not qualified by reference to matters within the scope of the Treaties; though in a treaty system based on conferred powers, it would be a bold argument which suggested that Article 6 is entirely decoupled from the powers conferred on the Union elsewhere in its constitutional documents.

However, despite the commitment to fundamental rights and despite the reference to the European Convention and to the constitutional traditions of the Member States, arguments remained that there was a need for a Union catalogue of rights.[20] The Treaty reference to the ECHR led to renewed calls for the Community to accede to that Convention. But such a proposal was killed off when the Court of Justice ruled, in Opinion 2/94,[21] that the Community lacked competence to accede to the ECHR. The response to calls for a catalogue of Union fundamental rights was the adoption of the non-binding Charter of Fundamental Rights of the European Union at the Nice Council in December 2000.[22] The response of the Court of Justice was predictably to see the Charter as a further source of inspiration for identifying general principles of law on fundamental rights.[23]

This brings us to the changes to the Treaties put in place from 1 December 2009 by the Treaty of Lisbon. Articles 2, 6 and 7 are the key articles. Article 2 provides:

The Union is founded on the values of respect for human dignity, freedom, democracy, equality, the rule of law and respect for human rights, including the rights of persons belonging to minorities. These values are common to the Member States in a society in

[20] K Lenaerts, 'Fundamental Rights to be Included in a Community Catalogue' (1991) 16:5 *ELRev* 367.

[21] Opinion 2/94 *Opinion of the Court of 28 March 1996 on accession by the Community to the European Convention for the Protection of Human Rights and Fundamental Freedoms* [1996] ECR I-1759.

[22] For detailed discussion of the Charter as proclaimed in December 2000, see S Peers and A Ward (eds), *The EU Charter of Fundamental Rights. Politics, Law and Policy* (Oxford: Hart Publishing, 2004). The Charter was arguably legally binding on the political institutions that signed it.

[23] See, eg, C-540/03 *European Parliament v Council* [2006] ECR I-5769, para 38; *Unibet* [2007] ECR I-2271, para 37; and Joined Cases C-322/07 P, C-327/07 P and C-338/07 P *Papierfabrik August Koehler* [2009] ECR I-7191, para 80.

which pluralism, non-discrimination, tolerance, justice, solidarity and equality between men and women prevail.[24]

These values are now much more central to the whole Union enterprise. In terms of location, content and presentation, this is a provision of constitutional significance entirely decoupled from any particular policy of the Union. The text is of overarching significance, using the language of human rights. The provision is also backed by sanctions in the face of gross violations. Article 7 TEU establishes a procedure for suspending a Member State, whose actions present a clear risk of serious breach of the values referred to in Article 2, from certain of the rights deriving from the Treaties. Article 6 TEU restates the commitment to human rights:

1. The Union recognizes the rights, freedoms and principles set out in the Charter of Fundamental Rights of the European Union of 7 December 2000, as adapted at Strasbourg, on 12 December 2007, which shall have the same legal value as the Treaties.
   The provisions of the Charter shall not extend in any way the competences of the Union as defined in the Treaties.
   The rights, freedoms and principles in the Charter shall be interpreted in accordance with the general provisions in Title VII of the Charter governing its interpretation and application and with due regard to the explanations referred to in the Charter, that set out the sources of those provisions.
2. The Union shall accede to the European Convention for the Protection of Human Rights and Fundamental Freedoms. Such accession shall not affect the Union's competences as defined in the Treaties.
3. Fundamental rights, as guaranteed by the European Convention for the Protection of Human Rights and Fundamental Freedoms and as they result from the constitutional traditions common to the Member States, shall constitute general principles of the Union's law.

There are Declarations and Protocols affecting the new developments incorporated in these new provisions. Declaration A.1 concerns the Charter of Fundamental Rights, and Protocol No 30 concerns the application of the Charter of Fundamental Rights to Poland and the United Kingdom.[25] Declaration A.2 and Protocol No 8 concern the requirement for the Union to accede to the European Convention. A number of declarations made by Member States also affect these new provisions.[26]

At first sight, the terms of Article 6 might seem to be a small step forward. It might, after all, be argued that the legally binding Charter does not go much beyond the obligations already to be found in the ECHR, and that accession to the

[24] This is the same wording as former Article 6(1) TEU with a new reference to the protection of minorities.

[25] This Protocol is discussed in more detail below. The Czech Republic is associated with this Protocol, and will become a party to it when the next Accession Treaty is adopted: *The Lisbon Treaty: ratification by the Czech Republic,* House of Commons Standard Note SN/1A/5214, 9 November 2009, para 3.3.

[26] C.53 by the Czech Republic, C.61 by Poland, and C.62 by Poland and the UK.

Convention by the Union is a symbolic gesture showing that the Union takes the protection of human rights seriously. But to view Article 6 in such limited terms would be a mistake. Once the process of negotiating accession to the Convention is completed, there will be a quartet of relevant Treaties: the Treaty on European Union, the Treaty on the Functioning of the European Union, the Charter of Fundamental Rights of the European Union, and the European Convention on Human Rights. The Treaty on European Union sets out the constitutional values that affect everything the Union does, and the Treaty on the Functioning of the European Union confers law-making powers in manifold areas of activity such that it is difficult to identify areas of regulation within the national legal orders which are wholly untouched by the potential for Union legislation. These two Treaties sit alongside a Charter of Fundamental Rights with legal effect, whose compass has been described as the widest of any human rights treaty in the world,[27] and the ECHR, in the case law of the European Court of Human Rights, has shown its ability to address modern concerns through the device of treating its provisions as those of a living instrument moving with the times.[28] The time has now come, therefore, to explore the significance of various features of the landscape of human rights after the entry into force of the Treaty of Lisbon.

D. The Charter of Fundamental Rights

Article 6(1) TEU now provides that the Charter[29] shall have the same legal value as the Treaties, but shall not extend in any way the competences of the Union, and is to be interpreted in accordance with the general provisions in Title VII of the Charter and with due regard to the Explanations which set out the sources of the provisions of the Charter.

Title VII of the Charter seeks to provide reassurance to sceptical Member States, but the drafting lacks clarity, possibly by design.[30] Article 51 provides that the provisions of the Charter are addressed to Member States 'only when they are implementing Union law'. The earlier case law[31] had indicated that Community fundamental rights obligations applied to the Member States when they were acting 'within the scope of Community law'. The Explanations relating to Article 51, referring, among others, to the *ERT* case, say that the Charter is addressed to Member States 'when they act in the context of Community law'. It is unclear whether the intention is to narrow the effect of the *ERT* judgment, or whether there is

[27] D Chalmers, G Davies and G Monti, *European Union Law*, 2nd edn (Cambridge: Cambridge University Press, 2010) 239.

[28] R White and C Ovey, *The European Convention on Human Rights*, 5th edn (Oxford: Oxford University Press, 2010) 73–7.

[29] The Charter as revised appears at [2007] OJ C 303/1, and the Explanations at [2007] OJ C 303/17. The Charter is also reproduced at [2010] OJ C 83/89, where the consolidated texts of the TEU and TFEU may also be found in this issue of the Official Journal.

[30] P Eeckhout, 'The EU Charter of Fundamental Rights and the Federal Question' (2002) 39:5 *CMLRev* 945.

[31] Most specifically, Case C-260/89 *ERT*, n 9 above, paras 42–3.

simply a loose use of language. The Explanations are closer to the language and spirit of the *ERT* judgment, but the language of the Charter can be interpreted as limiting the effect of that judgment. A Commission Communication setting out the strategy for the effective implementation of the Charter refers to it as 'an instrument to enable people to enjoy the rights enshrined within it when they are in a situation governed by Union law'.[32] It would be remarkable if the Court of Justice interpreted the Charter as reducing the fundamental rights protection provided at Union level in a context where, overall, these obligations are beefed up rather than watered down.

Article 52(3) of the Charter provides that, where rights in the Charter correspond to rights guaranteed by the ECHR, 'the meaning and scope of those rights shall be the same as those laid down' by the Convention, although this 'provision shall not prevent Union law providing more extensive protection'. In addition, the Explanations attached to the Charter 'shall be given due regard by the courts of the Union and of the Member States' in interpreting the Charter.[33] It follows that fundamental rights guaranteed by the Union must not fall below the standard required by the ECHR, but may be set at a higher level. Certain provisions of the Charter are said to mirror the provisions of the Convention, while others go beyond the protection afforded by its corresponding provisions.[34]

The Charter is a child of its drafting technique by the Convention, which did not know whether the text it produced would be merely exhortatory or legally binding.[35] But it is not that unusual in referring to rights, freedoms and principles in the context of the material that it covers. When it refers to rights and freedoms, it would appear to be referring to existing defined legal obligations, whereas when it refers to principles, it is referring to those matters that the Charter places on the human rights agenda. Here, implementing measures are needed to give substance to the human rights to be protected. Article 52(5) of the Charter reads:

> The provisions of this Charter which contain principles may be implemented by legislative and executive acts taken by the institutions, bodies, offices and agencies of the Union, and by acts of Member States when they are implementing Union law, in the exercise of their respective powers. They shall be judicially cognisable only in the interpretation of such acts and in ruling on their legality.

[32] Communication from the Commission, *Strategy for the effective implementation of the Charter of Fundamental Rights by the European Union* COM (2010) 573 final, 3. But this document also repeats the language of the Charter in relation to Member States: para 1.3.

[33] Article 52(7) of the Charter. The Explanations, which consist largely of references to the sources of rights, freedoms and principles contained in the Charter, arguably limit the scope of those rights, freedoms and principles.

[34] The Explanations attached to Article 52 of the Charter list 12 provisions where the meaning and scope are said to be the same as the corresponding provisions of the ECHR, and six provisions of the Charter where the meaning and scope are wider than the corresponding ECHR provisions. For a discussion of the significance of the difference in wording between Article 9 of the Charter and Article 12 ECHR by the European Court of Human Rights, see *Schalk and Kopf v Austria* (App 30141/04) Judgment of 24 June 2010.

[35] See G de Búrca, 'The Drafting of the European Charter of Fundamental Rights' (2001) 26 *ELRev* 126.

This arguably makes clear that there are new human rights competences to be found in those matters governed by principles enunciated in the Charter.

The contestation of the Charter by some Member States is reflected in a number of Declarations and Protocols.[36] This contribution will concern itself only with Protocol No 30, which has been presented in some parts of the news media as a British 'opt-out' from the legally binding nature of the Charter. The Preamble indicates that the purpose of the Protocol is to clarify certain aspects of the application of the Charter. Article 1(1) of the Protocol provides that the Charter does not extend the ability of the Court of Justice, or a national court or tribunal in Poland or the United Kingdom, to find that national measures are inconsistent with the fundamental rights, freedoms and principles that the Charter reaffirms. Article 1(2) makes explicit reference to the provisions of Title IV on solidarity[37] and denies any justiciable rights in this area except in relation to situations where the national laws of each of the two States have provided for such rights. Article 2 of the Protocol seeks to interpret the reference to national laws and practices in the text of the Charter as referring to the national laws of each Member State. This would seem to be an attempt to ensure that the Court of Justice does not interpret a Charter provision as generating a binding fundamental right drawn from the common experience of the Member States collectively where such a right is not expressly provided for in the national laws of, respectively, Poland and the United Kingdom.

Protocol No 30 cannot be an opt-out. This much would seem to be perfectly clear from its Preamble. It would be virtually impossible for any Member State to contract out of the values set out in Article 2 TEU; that is what an opt-out from the application of the Charter would amount to, in effect. It would not be tenable to seek to freeze general principles of law at a particular moment in time as the only Union law obligations in the field of fundamental rights. Closer examination of a text which reflects the political compromise that it contains shows that the Protocol is concerned with the further interpretation of Union fundamental rights that might result from the Charter text. Dougan argues persuasively that the 'primary purpose [of the Protocol] is to serve as an effective political response to a serious failure of public discourse'.[38] However, the Protocol and the Member State Declarations are likely to remind the Court of Justice, when called upon to interpret the Charter, quite how contested an instrument it is in some Member States. This may lead to a cautious approach to interpretation rather than an expansive one where the outcome would impact on the fundamental rights obligations of the Member States.[39]

[36] For a narrow view of the significance of the Charter, see D Denman, 'The Charter of Fundamental Rights' (2010) 4 *EHRLR* 349.

[37] Spelling out certain labour rights and social rights.

[38] M Dougan, 'The Treaty of Lisbon 2007: Winning Minds, not Hearts' (2008) 45:3 *CMLRev* 617, 670.

[39] The position taken here is supported by the AG's Opinion and the judgment in Joined Cases C-411/10 and C-493/10 *NS v Secretary of State for the Home Department*, judgment of 21 December 2011, not yet reported. But these remarks must also be set against the long tradition of regarding the ECHR as a 'living instrument' which results in the obligations arising from Convention rights moving

So what has the Court made of a Charter which has the same legal value as the Treaties? Although Article 6 does not express any hierarchy of sources that the Court will use in determining the human rights protected by European Union law, it seems certain that the starting point will be the Charter. After all, this is a comprehensive treaty text on fundamental rights. The Court has shown itself much more ready to refer to the Charter in its legally binding guise than when it had a non-binding status. The joint communication from President Costa of the Court of Human Rights and President Skouris of the Court of Justice of 17 January 2011[40] reported that, since the date of entry into force of the Treaty of Lisbon, the Court of Justice had referred to the Charter on some thirty occasions, and that it had become 'the reference text and the starting point of the CJEU's assessment of the fundamental rights which that legal instrument recognises'.

In some cases, the Court of Justice has referred to the Charter almost in passing as providing further justification of a particular interpretation of a Union act.[41] But in two more dramatic cases, it has annulled part of a Regulation on the basis of the measure's failure to respect rights to private life,[42] and questioned the compatibility of costs rules in the German national legal order with the provisions on a fair trial in Article 45 of the Charter.[43] The underlying message of the cases in which the Charter has been mentioned is to expect the Court to use the provisions of the Charter more and more in elaborating human rights obligations flowing from Union law.

E. Accession to the European Convention on Human Rights

Article 6(2) TEU requires the Union to accede to the ECHR, and Article 59 of the Convention makes provision for accession by the Union.[44] Accession to the ECHR is also the subject of Protocol No 8 and Declaration No 2, which are mutually repetitive. The Protocol and Declaration set out certain requirements relating to Union accession to the Convention:

with the times. It would be surprising if a similar approach were not taken to the interpretation of the Charter of Fundamental Rights over time.

[40] <http://www.echr.coe.int/NR/rdonlyres/02164A4C-0B63-44C3-80C7-FC594EE16297/0/2011 Communication_CEDHCJUE_EN.pdf>.

[41] See, eg, Case C-391/09 *Runevič-Vardyn and Wardyn* [2011] OJ C 194/4; Case C-232/09 *Danosa v LKB Lizings SIA* [2011] OJ C 13/11; and Joined Cases C-57/09 and C-101/09 *Bundesrepublik Deutschland v B and D* [2011] OJ C 13/4.

[42] Joined Cases C-92/09 and C-93/09 *Schecke and Eifert*, n 3 above.

[43] Case C-279/09 *DEB* [2011] OJ C 55/9. On Article 47 of the Charter, see further Joined Cases C-444/09 and C-456/09 *Gavieiro and Torres* [2011] OJ C 55/14; and in Joined Cases C-372/09 and C-373/09 *Josep Peñarroja Fa* [2011] OJ C 139/5.

[44] In *The Study of Technical and Legal Issues of a Possible EC/EU Accession to the European Convention on Human Rights. Report adopted by the Steering Commission for Human Rights (CDDH) at its 53rd meeting 25–28 June 2002,* CDDH(2002)010 Addendum 2, the relative merits of accession through an amending protocol and a separate accession treaty are discussed. See further E Myjer, 'Can the EU Join the ECHR—General Conditions and Practical Arrangements' in I Pernice and others (eds), *The Future of the European Judicial System in a Comparative Perspective* (Baden-Baden: Nomos, 2006) 297.

1. the accession arrangements must make provision for preserving the specific characteristics of the Union and Union law, including (a) the Union's participation in the 'control bodies'[45] of the Convention, and (b) the mechanisms for ensuring that individual applications are correctly addressed to the Member States and/or the Union;
2. the accession arrangements are not to affect the competences of the Union;
3. Member States are to remain free to derogate from Convention rights under Article 15 ECHR.

On the Council of Europe side, Article 17 of Protocol No 14 to the Convention[46] amends Article 59 ECHR by adding a new second paragraph, which simply provides, 'The European Union may accede to this Convention'. There is no significance in the terms of the Treaty on European Union making accession to the European Convention mandatory by its use of the word 'shall', whereas the text of the Convention is permissive by its use of the word 'may'. The Council of Europe amendment is permissive rather than mandatory since a number of significant changes to the structure of the ECHR are required before a non-State party can join that system.[47]

Accession negotiations are well advanced and, at the time of writing[48] a Draft Accession Agreement and a Draft Explanatory Report are nearing adoption.[49] These have been prepared by the informal working group on the accession arrangements established by the Council of Europe's Steering Committee for Human Rights, which has included representatives of the European Commission for this purpose. Initially, accession will be to the Convention and to its first and sixth protocols,[50] but provision will be made for subsequent accession to other protocols. This will avoid initial complications arising from the Union being a party to provisions of the Convention to which some of its Member States are not a party.[51]

[45] The Court of Human Rights and the Committee of Ministers.

[46] Which was signed on 13 May 2004, and entered into force on 1 June 2010.

[47] Explanatory Report to Protocol No 14, paras 101–2. Note also the Report of the Steering Committee for Human Rights (CDDH) entitled 'Study of Technical and Legal Issues of a Possible EC/EU accession to the European Convention on Human Rights', 28 June 2002, DG-II(2002)006.

[48] July 2011. Progress seems to have stalled somewhat as at February 2012; a report was passed to the Committee of Ministers in October 2011 but it contains some unresolved issues for consideration by the Committee itself.

[49] CDDH-UE(2011)16 of 19 July 2011. This includes a Draft Agreement and a Draft Explanatory Report, referred to respectively in this chapter as the 'Draft Accession Agreement' and the 'Draft Explanatory Report'. Once approved by the CDDH, the Draft Accession Agreement will be sent to the Committee of Ministers for approval. Thereafter the Parliamentary Assembly will adopt an opinion on the Draft Accession Agreement, following which the Committee of Ministers will formally adopt it and open it for signature by the Contracting Parties and the European Union. The Accession Agreement will enter into force on the first day of the month following the expiration of a period of three months after the date on which all Contracting Parties and the European Union express their consent to be bound by the Agreement.

[50] Protocol No 6 concerns the abolition of the death penalty in peacetime. It is odd that Protocol No 13 on the abolition of the death penalty in all circumstances has not been included, although the inclusion of either or both is rather odd in the context of including some and excluding other protocols.

[51] Such as, eg, Protocol No 4, to which the UK is not a party. Protocol No 4 concerns freedom of movement and has an impact on matters connected with immigration policy.

A key condition in the making of an application to the Court of Human Rights is the requirement under Article 35(1) ECHR to have exhausted all domestic remedies.[52] Many applications fail on this admissibility ground. In cases involving the European Union, the question arose as to how this requirement might be satisfied. In some cases, the alleged breaches will have been raised before national courts and, unless those courts make a reference to the Court of Justice on the human rights question(s), the Union judiciary may not have had any opportunity to rule on the compatibility of the underlying Union measure with Convention rights. The solution in the Draft Accession Agreement is to be found in Article 3, which also introduces the co-respondent mechanism.[53] Article 3(6) introduces a suspensory procedure under which proceedings before the Court of Human rights will be delayed where the Union is a co-respondent in order to enable the Court of Justice to make an assessment of the compatibility of the Union measure with Convention rights where the Court of Justice has had no prior opportunity to consider the issue.

The co-respondent mechanism deals with those situations where an applicant raises a complaint against a Member State, but not also the European Union, in circumstances where the Member State might argue that it was bound by European Union law to act as it did. An example of such a situation can be provided by recalling the *Bosphorus Airways* case before the Court of Human Rights,[54] and considering how that litigation might have played out if the Union had been a party to the Convention. In *Bosphorus Airways*, the airline brought a complaint against Ireland, which, in seizing their aircraft, had acted in compliance with a Regulation of the European Union. But Ireland claimed that it was obliged to act under the Union Regulation. In such circumstances in the future, it would be likely that lawyers would advise the applicant to make the complaint against both the Member States and the European Union. But, if an applicant does not do this, the provisions of Article 3 of the Draft Accession Agreement enable the European Union to be joined as co-respondent. The complaint against the European Union will be that its legislative measure obliged the Member State to act in a particular way. In other cases, the complaint could be that there is no incompatibility between the Union measure and Convention rights, but that the Member State has acted under that measure in a manner that is incompatible with Convention rights. The introduction of these procedures would seem to signal the end of the presumption of compatibility with human rights standards that the Court of Human Rights

[52] On the requirement, see generally See *Akdivar and others v Turkey* (App 21893/93) 16 September 1996 (1997) 23 EHRR 143; ECHR 1996-IV; and *Demopoulos and others v Turkey* (Apps 46113/99, 3843/02, 13751/02, 13466/03, 10200/04, 14163/04, 19993/04 and 21819/04) 1 March 2010 [GC].

[53] See further below.

[54] *Bosphorus Hava Yollari Turizm ve Itcaret Anonim Şirketi v Ireland* (App 45036/98), 30 June 2005 [GC] (2006) 42 EHRR 1; ECHR 2005-VI. A footnote in the Draft Explanatory Report, n 48 above, para 44, n 19, indicates that only this case, *Matthews v United Kingdom* (App 24833/94) 18 February 1999 [GC] (1999) 28 EHRR 361; ECHR 1999-I, and *Cooperatieve Producentenorganisatie van de Nederlandse Kokkelvisserij UA v The Netherlands* (App 13645/05), Decision of 20 January 2009 would have required the use of the co-respondent mechanism.

ceded to the European Union in the *Bosphorus* case. It would be quite extraordinary if such a presumption survived accession to the Convention. No such accommodation applies to any other Contracting Party to the Convention.

The European Convention on Human Rights also contains multiple references to terms that apply only to States and not to a non-State entity. This has presented a problem in terms of drafting. The solution in the Draft Accession Agreement is not to recast the Convention in more neutral terms, but to deem certain provisions referring to States as referring to cognate interests held by the Union. This is somewhat ungainly, but there is a helpful Appendix to the Draft Explanatory Report, which summarizes all the State-related provisions of the Convention and indicates the possible effects of the access of the European Union on those terms.

There had been discussion about the election of a judge in respect of the European Union and the role of that judge at the Court of Human Rights. The Draft Accession Agreement adopts a simple solution of making provision for a judge in respect of the European Union, who will participate in the work of the Court on equal terms with all the other judges elected in respect of each of the current 47 Contracting Parties to the Convention. Provision is made for a representative of the European Union to participate in the process of election. Provision is also made for the European Union to participate in the work of the Committee of Ministers when it is exercising its function of supervising the enforcement of judgments of the Court of Human Rights under Article 46 ECHR. Finally, the European Union is required to contribute to the costs of the Convention system. Article 8 of the Draft Accession Agreement contains the formula for calculating this contribution.[55]

It is clear that the human rights standards required by the European Union may exceed those set out in the European Convention on Human Rights. In such cases, the Court of Justice will remain the final arbiter of compliance with those higher standards. It will only be where there is an allegation that the level of European Union protection falls below that required by the Convention that adjudication by the European Court of Human Rights will come into play. This will present considerable challenges over time in avoiding contradictions in the case law that determines the content of human rights protection.[56] Of course, under the procedures by which 'domestic remedies' will be exhausted when there is an allegation that European Union law falls below the standard set by the Convention, the Court of Justice will always have an opportunity to put matters right before adjudication and possible condemnation by the Court of Human Rights. That is no different from the position for the 47 State parties to the Convention.

Following completion of the process of accession to the European Convention on Human Rights, the Court of Justice, when called upon to adjudicate on human

[55] The Draft Explanatory Report notes by way of illustration, that, based on the 2011 budget, the European Union would be required to contribute €9.34 million towards the functioning of the Convention system.

[56] See J Callewaert, 'The European Convention on Human Rights and European Union Law: a Long Way to Harmony' (2009) 6 *EHRLR* 768, 776.

rights questions, is likely still to start with the Charter of Fundamental Rights. That might reveal a situation in which the relevant standard in that Charter is the same as that resulting from a corresponding provision of the Convention, or it might be a higher European Union standard. If the Charter standard is the same as the Convention standard, or if the Charter does not apply and the Convention does, then the measure will be compatibile with ECHR rights. It is to be hoped that the Court of Justice's judgments make these distinctions with sufficient clarity that contradictions in the case law of the two courts can be avoided.

F. General principles of law

Article 6(3) TEU retains the classic formulation of general principles of law:

> Fundamental rights, as guaranteed by the European Convention for the Protection of Human Rights and Fundamental Freedoms and as they result from the constitutional traditions common to the Member States, shall constitute general principles of the Union's law.

The retention of these words from the Treaty of Maastricht, which in turn simply borrowed them from the words of the Court of Justice in its case law, indicates that general principles of law remain a source of human rights.[57] There may be occasions where the Court of Justice considers that an underlying value embedded in the constitutional foundations of the European Union requires a particular response to an issue before it, but which is governed by neither the Charter nor the Convention. Here, there may be useful life remaining in general principles of law. Indeed, recent judgments in the sphere of equality have shown that general principles of law retain the capacity to surprise. Though their significance is deeply contested, the Court of Justice, in its *Mangold* and *Kücükdeveci* judgments,[58] provided a further erosion of the prohibition of the horizontal direct effect of Directives in a situation where Directives were merely giving substance to the prohibition of discrimination on grounds of age, which was declared to be a general principle of law.[59] How close are we to a general human rights competence for the European Union?

The statements found at various points in texts forming part of or linked to the Treaty of Lisbon that the changes brought about by that Treaty give rise to no new human rights competences might suggest that the European Union has a very limited competence in this field. That would be an error. The following propositions would seem to be incontrovertible.

[57] In this context still referred to as 'fundamental rights'.

[58] Case C-144/04 *Mangold* [2005] ECR I-9981; and *Kücükdeveci* [2010] ECR I-365.

[59] On the *Mangold* case, see A Dashwood, 'From *Van Duyn* to *Mangold* via *Marshall:* Reducing Direct Effect to Absurdity?' (2006–07) 9 *CYELS* 81; and D Schieck, 'The ECJ Decision in *Mangold*: a Further Twist of Effects of Directives and Constitutional Relevance of Community Equality Legislation' (2006) 35:3 *ILJ* 329.

1. In adopting legislation, the political organs of the European Union must have regard to human rights as spelled out in the case law of the Court of Justice, in the text of the Charter of Fundamental Rights and in the European Convention on Human Rights, in order to ensure the compatibility of the adopted measures with the Union's human rights standards. Any failure to do so could result in the annulment of the offending part of the measure.[60]
2. The Court of Justice has jurisdiction, either in preliminary ruling proceedings or in determining whether a Member State has acted in breach of the Treaties, to determine whether an act of a Member State within the scope of European Union law complies with the Union's human rights standards.
3. The European Union has legislative competence in very many fields.[61] In adopting legislation in those fields where it has such competence, it can legislate on human rights matters. A good example is its legislation in matters of criminal justice, where there is a Directive on the right to interpretation and translation.[62]

The revised text of the Treaty on European Union proclaims its commitment to marking 'a new stage in the process of European integration', and confirms its 'attachment to the principles of liberty, democracy and respect for human rights and fundamental freedoms and of the rule of law'.[63] That attachment is evidenced by the developments chronicled in this contribution. The Charter itself proclaims certain principles and acknowledges that such principles 'may be implemented by legislative and executive acts taken by the institutions, bodies, offices and agencies of the Union, and by acts of Member States when they are implementing Union law, in the exercise of their respective powers'.[64] It is suggested that it is difficult to resist the proposition that the Treaty of Lisbon developments[65] open the European

[60] In Joined Cases C-92/09 and C-93/09, *Schecke and Eifert*, n 3 above, AG Sharpston said, 'I regard it as inconceivable that EU secondary legislation that contravened fundamental rights in general, or the ECHR or the Charter in particular, could be upheld as valid by the Court' (para 64 of the Opinion, citations omitted).

[61] See European Commission, *2010 Report on the Application of the EU Charter of Fundamental Rights* COM (2011) 260 final of 30 March 2011, and *Human Rights and Democracy in the World Report. Report on EU Action July 2008 to December 2009*, available at <http://www.consilium.europa.eu/uedocs/cms_data/docs/pressdata/EN/foraff/114330.pdf>.

[62] Directive 2010/64/EU of 20 October 2010 on the right to interpretation and translation in criminal proceedings [2010] OJ L 280/1, made under Article 82(2)(b) TFEU. This Directive requires transposition in the Member States by 27 October 2013. See further Proposal for a Directive of the European Parliament and of the Council on the right to information in criminal proceedings COM (2009) 392/3.

[63] Preamble, first and fourth paragraphs, TEU.

[64] Article 52(5) of the Charter.

[65] Including, in particular, the collapse of the pillar system, which formerly had the capacity to insulate certain areas of Union activity from established human rights protections. This development may result in a more convincing role for the Fundamental Rights Agency, currently a very marginal player. For an overview of the Agency, and the concerns its establishment raised, see A von Bogdandy and J von Bernstorff, 'The EU Fundamental Rights Agency within the European and International Human Rights Architecture: the Legal Framework and Some Unsettled Issues in a New Field of Administrative Law' (2009) 46:4 *CMLRev* 1035; G Toggenburg, 'The Role of the New EU Fundamental Rights Agency: Debating the "Sex of Angels" or Improving Europe's Human Rights

Union to a whole new human rights exposure. The Union institutions have become accountable for fundamental rights compliance across the whole range of their activities.[66] Fundamental rights questions that were previously excluded from the ambit of matters justiciable before the Court of Justice will become justiciable before both the Court of Justice and the Court of Human Rights.

One consequence of these new areas of exposure, when linked with the areas of competence already enjoyed by the European Union and with the statement on constitutional values in Article 2 TEU, is that the concept of limited competence in the field of human rights looks increasingly anomalous. The European Union demands respect for human rights when its political institutions legislate, from its Member States when they are acting within the scope of the Treaties, and from new applicants for EU membership. It reserves the right to impose sanctions against its Member States under Article 7 TEU where there is a clear risk of a serious breach of the values set out in Article 2 TEU. That clear risk of a serious breach might well arise outside matters within the competence of the Union.

A combination of the ability to sit in judgment on serious breaches of human rights under Article 7 TEU and the sweeping range of rights protected in the Charter of Fundamental Rights, which has the same legal value as the Treaties, means that there is already a form of general human rights competence. Why not now recognize that there cannot be any form of partial competence in the field of human rights? Refusal to do so seems contrary to the notion of respect for human rights as a fundamental constitutional value. The key changes which reshape the human rights landscape are the legal value given to the Charter, the centrality of human rights in the recast Treaty on European Union, the competence to determine serious violations of human rights (however arising) under Article 7 TEU, and the removal of reliance on judicial creativity in the face of litigation for statements of the content of human rights protected by the European Union. The patchwork provision to which Isiksel and Bogdandy critically refer[67] has been replaced with Treaty-based documentation, providing a much stronger foundation for the protection of human rights.

If a general human rights competence is to be recognized, what is to stop the political institutions from going off on a frolic of their own and enacting human rights legislation in entirely new fields? The first response to this is that it is not easy to come up with a real-world example of such legislation. The mechanisms of the legislative process build in a number of safeguards. The Treaty of Lisbon also upgrades the principle of subsidiarity, and a Commission frolic in proposing such legislation that was missed either by the Council or the European Parliament might well fall foul of the procedures spelled out in relation to that principle. The early

Performance?' (2008) 33 *ELRev* 385; and E Howard, 'The European Agency for Fundamental Rights' (2006) 4 *EHRLR* 445. For the latest annual report, and other information about the Agency, see <http://fra.europa.eu> (accessed 15 July 2011).

66 For a valuable analysis, see C Sabel and O Gerstenberg, 'Constitutionalising an overlapping Consensus: the ECJ and the Emergence of a Coordinate Constitutional Order' (2010) 16:5 *ELJ* 511.

67 See text accompanying nn 5 and 6 above.

provisions of the revised Treaty on European Union stress the role of Member States, and Article 5 TEU is explicit that the limits of Union competence are governed by the principle of conferral. This proposition is immediately followed by the requirement that the use of Union competences is governed by the principles of subsidiarity and proportionality. These requirements are reinforced by the detailed Protocol No 2 on their application. Article 8 of the Protocol spells out the jurisdiction of the Court of Justice to review legislative acts on grounds of infringement of the principle of subsidiarity. Subsidiarity and proportionality would operate as very considerable brakes on any overzealous ambition to legislate in the field of human rights, as indeed does the very existence of the Charter, which sets out a current catalogue of rights, freedoms and principles.

G. Concluding remarks

The process of constitution building in the European Community and European Union has never been just about economic matters. The economic or market constitution has always had a human face to it. From early statements about workers being more than a source of labour,[68] to statements about the constitutional significance of citizenship of the Union,[69] individuals have been more than just citizens of one of the Member States. They have occupied a central role in the shaping of the constitution of the European Union. That centrality of individuals, just as much as of businesses, has driven the increasing significance of human rights for the European Union enterprise. But human rights also extend to business entities when matters such as a fair trial and the right to property are brought into play. There is nothing contradictory about an economic constitution that also respects human rights. But it would be wrong to categorize the European Union as offering little more than an economic constitution when it offers much more.

The developments in the Treaty of Lisbon may pave the way for the European Union to accede to other human rights conventions.[70] The contours of the legal landscape of human rights have changed. There has been a shift from a system

[68] See, eg, the remarks of AG Trabucchi in Case 7/75 *Mr and Mrs F* [1975] ECR 679, 697 concerning the need for the Community legal order to correspond to the concept of social justice.

[69] Case C-34/09 *Ruiz Zambrano* [2011] OJ C 130/2, paras 41–2; Case C-103/08 *Gottwald* [2009] ECR I-9117, para 23. See further, among many examples, Case C-209/03 *Bidar* [2005] ECR I-2119, para 31; Case C-403/03 *Schempp* [2005] ECR 6421, para 15; Joined Cases C-482/01 and C-493/01 *Orfanopoulos and Oliveri* [2004] ECR I-5257, para 65; Case C-148/02 *Garcia Avello* [2003] ECR I-11613, para 22; and Case C-184/99 *Grzelczyk* [2001] ECR I-6193, para 31. These words are also used in Directive 2004/38/EC on the right of citizens of the Union and their family members to move and reside freely within the territory of the Member States (cited in this chapter as 'the Citizenship Directive') *corrected version at* [2004] OJ L 229/35, *further corrected at* [2005] OJ L 197/34, Preamble, recital 3, giving them legislative legitimacy.

[70] In January 2011, the European Union ratified the United Nations Convention on the Rights of People with Disabilities, the first international human rights treaty to which the European Union has become a party. This significant event in the human rights history of the Union seems to have passed largely unnoticed but see generally G de Búrca, 'The European Union in the negotiation of the UN Disability Convention' (2010) 35:2 *ELRev* 174.

initially based wholly on judicial creativity to one where the Treaty referred to the protection of human rights but did not fully define those rights, which has now achieved at least adolescence not only in setting down the European Union's values in the sphere of human rights, but in defining in a treaty text the content of the human rights protected by the European Union. The European Union through the developments flowing from the Treaty of Lisbon may now claim to be taking rights seriously.[71]

[71] Echoing words in a journal article that was critical of the expansion of activity in this area through decisions of the Court of Justice motivated by the drive for economic integration; see J Coppel and A O'Neill, 'The European Court of Justice: Taking Rights Seriously?' (1992) 29:3 *CMLRev* 669.

18

Towards a Draft Common Frame of Reference for Public Law?

*Jan H Jans**

A. Introduction

This chapter, dedicated to the memory of Professor John Usher, considers the need for what I would like to refer to as a 'European Administrative Procedure Act'.[1] The reader of this volume will be familiar with the fact that a large part of *substantive* public law in the Member States, such as environmental law, agricultural law, immigration law, transport law and economic law, is of European origin. This substantive law, generally contained in Union Directives, is transposed into national legislation and applied and enforced by national administrative authorities. The Member States are in principle competent to determine (and responsible for determining) the applicable procedures and the way in which they are organized. The starting point as regards application by national administrative authorities of this, by origin European, law is that it is applied on the basis of and under the conditions of national law. In other words, EU law does not in principle concern itself with the manner in which it is applied within national legal orders. This starting point is known in EU law as the principle of procedural autonomy.[2] Procedural autonomy applies 'in principle', but there are exceptions. As an expression of the subsidiarity principle, procedural autonomy implies a degree of variation in the manner in which substantive EU law is applied in the Member States of the European Union. If the EU legislature considers that these differences have become too great in any particular area, it may decide to take legislative action and harmonize national legislation in that area. In such cases, it is not only the

* Faculty of Law, University of Groningen. I would like to thank GJ Harryvan for his assistance in preparing this chapter.

[1] cf also, A Meuwese, Y Schuurmans and W Voermans, 'Towards a European Administrative Procedure Act' (2009) 2:2 *Rev Eur Admin L* 3–35; HC Hofmann, 'Seven Challenges for EU Administrative Law' (2009) 2:2 *Rev Eur Admin L* 37–59.

[2] There is a surfeit of literature on the principle of procedural autonomy. cf JH Jans et al, *Europeanisation of Public Law* (Groningen: Europa Law Publishing, 2007) Ch 2.

substantive law that is harmonized but also the manner in which Member States must apply it. It is against this background that I wish to comment on the need for harmonization in this field of law, what form it should take and which actors should play a leading part. This chapter will focus in particular on evolving issues related to judicial protection and access to justice.

B. Is there a need for general harmonization of national procedural administrative law?

As co-author of *Europeanisation of Public Law*,[3] I have already taken a position in the debate on the desirability of harmonization of national procedural administrative law.[4] My thoughts have not changed essentially in the past few years. In my opinion, it is important to recognize that the influence of EU law on the general rules and principles of national administrative law is of a fundamentally different nature from its influence on the specific areas of law, particularly social and economic law, to which acts of the administration often pertain. European influence on the substantive law in these areas is prompted by the aim of achieving the substantive objectives of the European Union. The doctrines that must be counted as part of administrative law are often no more than instrumental in achieving these aims, an aid to implementing substantive EU law in specific areas. In other words, the impact of Union law on the general part of national administrative law is not prompted primarily by a desire to harmonize, unify or coordinate these general parts 'as such', but is at all times linked to the question as to what extent this is necessary to achieve a certain degree of coordination of substantive law and to guarantee legal protection to those upon whom substantive Union law confers rights. In my opinion, the Union, even in the post-Lisbon era, is not competent to harmonize national administrative law further than necessary to achieve the substantive aims of Union law. After all, the Treaties, not even Articles 197 and/or 352 of the Treaty on the Functioning of the European Union,[5] still do not confer a general competence to harmonize national administrative law rules.

Thus, even in the future, there will continue to be a tension between, on the one hand, the desire to harmonize to some degree topics such as judicial protection and enforcement (in order to ensure uniform application of Union law) and, on the other hand, the importance (from the perspective of national institutional or procedural autonomy) of not impinging unnecessarily upon national legal systems. This does not mean, however, that the EU legislature is not achieving any degree of harmonization at all. It is, but in a fragmented and ad hoc manner.

[3] JH Jans et al, *Europeanisation of Public Law* (Groningen: Europa Law Publishing, 2007).

[4] See in particular ibid Ch 9.

[5] Consolidated version of the Treaty on the Functioning of the European Union [2010] OJ C 83/47.

C. Harmonization by bits and pieces

Another important motive for harmonization is unity of law. Without unity of law, there can be no equality before or predictability of the law. Naturally, this also applies to administrative law. It is not surprising, therefore, that the EU legislature acts where, in its opinion, the divergences in national administrative law are greatest. However, it does not act in a general, but only in a fragmented way. Harmonization of the general topics of national administrative law is, to use a metaphor of Curtin's, harmonization by 'bits and pieces'.[6] This metaphor accurately reflects European legislative practice. There are examples in public procurement law, telecoms law, customs law and environmental law. I will attempt to unfold my thoughts on the nature and desirability of harmonization of general administrative law topics with the aid of an example.

The example concerns Directive 2003/35/EC of the European Parliament and of the Council, providing for public participation in respect of the drawing up of certain plans and programmes relating to the environment and amending with regard to public participation and access to justice Council Directives 85/337/EEC and 96/61/EC.[7] This Directive aims to contribute to the implementation of the obligations arising under the Aarhus Convention (the UN/ECE Convention on Access to Information, Public Participation in Decision-Making and Access to Justice in Environmental Matters), among other things by improving public participation and including provisions on access to justice. One of the measures it amends is the IPPC Directive, Directive 96/61, which includes the following provisions in Article 15a (on 'access to justice'):

Member States shall ensure that, in accordance with the relevant national legal system, members of the public concerned:
(a) having a sufficient interest, or alternatively,
(b) maintaining the impairment of a right, where administrative procedural law of a Member State requires this as a precondition;
have access to a review procedure before a court of law or another independent and impartial body established by law to challenge the substantive or procedural legality of decisions, acts or omissions subject to the public participation provisions of this Directive.

Member States shall determine at what stage the decisions, acts or omissions may be challenged.

[6] D Curtin, 'The Constitutional Structure of the Union: a Europe of Bits and Pieces' (1993) 30:1 *CMLRev* 17.

[7] Directive 2003/35/EC of the European Parliament and of the Council of 26 May 2003 providing for public participation in respect of the drawing up of certain plans and programmes relating to the environment and amending with regard to public participation and access to justice Council Directives 85/337/EEC and 96/61/EC [2003] OJ L 156/17. The amended Directives are Council Directive 85/337/EEC of 27 June 1985 on the assessment of the effects of certain public and private projects on the environment [1985] OJ L 175/40, and Council Directive 96/61/EC of 24 September 1996 concerning integrated pollution prevention and control [1996] OJ L 257/26.

What constitutes a sufficient interest and impairment of a right shall be determined by the Member States, consistently with the objective of giving the public concerned wide access to justice. To this end, the interest of any non-governmental organisation meeting the requirements referred to in Article 2(14) shall be deemed sufficient for the purpose of subparagraph (a) of this Article. Such organisations shall also be deemed to have rights capable of being impaired for the purpose of subparagraph (b) of this Article.

The provisions of this Article shall not exclude the possibility of a preliminary review procedure before an administrative authority and shall not affect the requirement of exhaustion of administrative review procedures prior to recourse to judicial review procedures, where such a requirement exists under national law.

Any such procedure shall be fair, equitable, timely and not prohibitively expensive.

In order to further the effectiveness of the provisions of this Article, Member States shall ensure that practical information is made available to the public on access to administrative and judicial review procedures.

It has emerged from research[8] that there are considerable differences between the Member States of the European Union as regards access to justice with respect to decisions of the administration in the field of environmental law. There are:

- differences in time limits for appeals;
- differences in the admissibility of third parties, in particular the position of environmental groups;
- differences in the duration of proceedings;
- differences in the thoroughness of judicial review;
- differences in costs.

The extract included above from the Aarhus Directive, Directive 2003/35, makes a number of things clear. In the first place, the provision cited illustrates the Union's deference to Member State procedural autonomy, as reflected, for example, in the phrase 'in accordance with the relevant national legal system' at the beginning of the first sentence. Second, it reveals something of the nature of harmonization. The Directive concerns a number of topics that are important from an administrative law point of view:

- access to review before a court of law;
- the concept of interested parties, both in a general sense and in the sense of general interest organizations and possibly even administrative authorities;
- the nature of review by the courts (procedural and substantive legality);
- the relationship between judicial and administrative review procedures;
- final resolution of disputes ('any such procedure shall be . . . timely');
- costs ('any such procedure shall be . . . not prohibitively expensive');

[8] See, eg, N de Sadeleer, G Roller and M Dross (eds), *Access to Justice in Environmental Matters and the Role of NGOs; Empirical Findings and Legal Appraisal* (Groningen: Europa Law Publishing, 2005).

- the provision of information about access to administrative and judicial review procedures (*Rechtsmittelbeleherung*).

In other words, the Directive requires Member States to harmonize their administrative procedural rules in a fair number of not unimportant respects. However, the way it does this differs fundamentally from the way that the national legal orders deal with them.

The Directive does not so much lay down unambiguous, uniform, hard and fast rules, but rather, lays down the ground rules within the limits of which the Member States' procedural autonomy can continue to manifest itself. It sets limits for the law of the Member States and determines, as it were, the bandwidth of their procedural autonomy. The provision on costs ('any such procedure shall be . . . not prohibitively expensive') is illustrative of the way in which the Union concerns itself with national administrative law now and in the future. There is to be no uniform European regulation on costs in administrative procedures; instead, the excesses in some national legal orders will be limited.[9] Or, to put it less crudely: with the Aarhus Directive, the EU legislature has ensured a degree of convergence of national administrative law rules, without wishing to achieve full uniform harmonization. In my view, it thus achieves a healthy balance between, on the one hand, ensuring uniform application of Union law and, on the other, not infringing national legal systems unnecessarily.

D. Harmonization by judicial dialogue and competition

Harmonization 'by bits and pieces' and 'a degree of convergence': is that all there is? In my view, this is not the case. Precisely the open-ended nature of provisions such as those in the Aarhus Directive will ensure a continuous stream of questions in judicial practice about where exactly the European legislature has drawn the line. It is already evident that administrative courts in various countries are confronted with parties arguing that parts of their national procedural law are contrary to the Aarhus provisions. In my estimation, we will in the future regularly come across phenomena that can be viewed as 'judicial dialogue' and 'judicial competition', which will ensure a more far-reaching convergence of national administrative law than would appear to follow at first sight from the written text of the Directive. National courts will refer to one another's decisions, whether in agreement or otherwise.[10] It cannot even be ruled out that a new form of judicial precedent is emerging. Van Harten has coined the phrase 'national European law precedent' for the phenomenon of 'autonomous interpretations of European law by national

[9] cf on costs the Sullivan report, *Ensuring access to environmental justice in England and Wales. Report of the Working Group on Access to Environmental Justice*, May 2008, available at <http://www.wwf.org.uk/filelibrary/pdf/justice_report_08.pdf>.

[10] See on the phenomenon of 'judicial competition' in a broad sense: N Lavranos, *Judicial Competition: Selected Cases in International and European Law* (Groningen: Europa Law Publishing, 2009).

courts that set precedents for future cases in a certain field of law'.[11] Law can no longer only be made within the isolation of national law. In his Maastricht oration, Backes rightly raises the question whether courts should not be required to give reasons if their interpretation of EU law differs from that of courts in other Member States, at least where the foreign courts are courts of last resort.[12]

Provisions such as those of the Aarhus Directive strengthen ties between and produce greater interlacing of national administrative law systems in the Member States. As a result, the discussion about the administrative law topics covered by Aarhus will be 'denationalized' and the participants will no longer be able to confine themselves to a vision that is oriented purely internally towards domestic law. I will try to make it clear what I mean by this by means of several examples.

A Court of Justice decision shows, for example, how the Aarhus Directive connects Dutch administrative procedural law with Swedish law.[13] The case concerned a reference for a preliminary ruling from the Swedish *Högsta domstolen*, which wanted to know whether the Directive permitted national legislation that allowed access to a court of law or other independent and impartial body only to non-governmental environmental organizations with at least 2000 members. At the same time, the question arose whether access to the court could be limited on the ground that the persons concerned had already had the opportunity to express their views during the public participation phase of the decision-making procedure. As regards the latter question, in the key paragraphs 35 and 38 of its judgment, the Court of Justice observed:

> 35 It is also apparent therefrom [Article 10a of Directive 85/337, as amended by Directive 2003/35] that any non governmental organisations which promote environmental protection and meet the conditions which may be required by national law satisfy the criteria, with respect to the public concerned who may bring an appeal, laid down in Article 1(2) of Directive 85/337 read in conjunction with Article 10a . . . participation in an environmental decision-making procedure under the conditions laid down in Articles 2(2) and 6(4) of Directive 85/337 is separate and has a different purpose from a legal review, since the latter may, where appropriate, be directed at a decision adopted at the end of that procedure. *Therefore, participation in the decision-making procedure has no effect on the conditions for access to the review procedure.*[14]

[11] H van Harten, 'National Judicial Autonomy: The Example of National European Law Precedents in the Dutch Case-Law on the Free Movement of Services and the Freedom of Establishment' (2009) 2:2 *Rev Eur Admin L*, 135–53, in particular 139–40.

[12] CW Backes, *Suum Cuique? Enkele opmerkingen over de rechtsmachtverdeling tussen bestuursrechter en burgerlijke rechter* (Den Haag: Boom Juridische uitgevers, 2008) 2.2.

[13] Case C-263/08 *Djurgården-Lilla Värtans Miljöskyddsförening v Stockholms kommun genom dess marknämnd* [2009] ECR I-9967. Compare also the reference for a preliminary ruling from the *Högsta domstolen* on 19 January 2009, Order of the Court of 11 March 2011 in Case C-24/09 *Djurgården-Lilla Värtans Miljöskyddsförening v AB Fortum Värme samägtmedStockholms stad* [2010] ECR I-35, 12.

[14] Case C-263/08 *Djurgården-Lilla*, n 13 above, paras 35 and 38. See further para 48 of the judgment, from which it is clear that access to review procedures may not be limited on the ground that the persons concerned have already been able to express their views in the participatory phase of the decision-making procedure. Emphasis added.

So what does this decision have to do with administrative procedural law in other Member States? At first sight, nothing. But Dutch law contains a provision to the effect that a party may not rely on a breach of a legal rule before a court of law unless this was first raised during the preceding public participation procedure (section 6:13 of the Dutch General Administrative Law Act). And German administrative procedural law (known as *materielle Präklusion*) is comparable to Dutch law in this respect.[15]

In fact, the situation in both Dutch and German law is the reverse of the situation in the Swedish case. As a result of the emphasis on the independent role and function of judicial protection and its separation from the public participation procedure, also in terms of purpose, the question arises as to what extent section 6:13 of the Dutch Act is consistent with the Aarhus Directive. The judgment of the Court of Justice would seem to imply that, as far as access to justice is concerned, it is irrelevant whether or not an organization has taken part in the decision-making procedure.

As regards the '2000-member limit', the Court of Justice ruled that this was also unacceptable. The Court stressed that while it was true that the words 'meet the conditions which may be required by national law' leave it to national legislatures to determine under what conditions environmental organizations may have access to justice, the national rules must both ensure 'wide access to justice' and 'render effective the provisions of Directive 85/337 on judicial remedies', concluding that:

> Accordingly, those national rules must not be liable to nullify Community provisions which provide that parties who have a sufficient interest to challenge a project and those whose rights it impairs, which include environmental protection associations, are to be entitled to bring actions before the competent courts.[16]

It is within the Member State's margin of discretion to require that the environmental organization has as its object the protection of nature and the environment and:

> [I]t is conceivable that the condition that an environmental protection association must have a minimum number of members may be relevant in order to ensure that it does in fact exist and that it is active. However, the number of members required cannot be fixed by national law at such a level that it runs counter to the objectives of Directive 85/337 and in particular the objective of facilitating judicial review of projects which fall within its scope.[17]

Thus, judgment was passed on the 2000-member criterion:

> The Swedish Government, which acknowledges that at present only two associations have at least 2000 members and thereby satisfy the condition laid down in Paragraph 13 of Chapter 16 of the Environment Act, has in fact submitted that local associations could contact one of those two associations and ask them to bring an appeal. However, that

[15] cf M Niedzwicki, *Präklusionsvorschriften des öffentlichen Rechts im Spannungsfeld zwischen Verfahrensbeschleunigung, Einzelfallgerechtigkeit und Rechtsstaatlichkeit* (Berlin: Duncker & Humblot, 2007).

[16] Case C-263/08 *Djurgården-Lilla*, n 13 above, para 45.

[17] ibid para 47.

possibility in itself is not capable of satisfying the requirements of Directive 85/337 as, first, the associations entitled to bring an appeal might not have the same interest in projects of limited size and, second, they would be likely to receive numerous requests of that kind which would have to be dealt with selectively on the basis of criteria which would not be subject to review. Finally, such a system would give rise, by its very nature, to a filtering of appeals directly contrary to the spirit of the directive which, as stated in paragraph 33 of this judgment, is intended to implement the Aarhus Convention.[18]

In this respect, too, there are parallels with Dutch administrative procedural law. Though Dutch law does not have a 2000-member rule, there are other impediments to environmental organizations desiring to bring a matter before the courts. Recent case law of the Dutch Council of State has made it clear that 'litigation-only' NGOs do not have standing.[19] Whether or not this case law is consistent with the Aarhus Directive is not, however, my primary concern in this chapter. My concern is to show that the Directive has created a link between Dutch and Swedish administrative procedural law and that a legal dialogue is emerging concerning the limits that EU law sets when the access of public interest organizations, such as environmental organizations, to the courts is restricted. Good times are indeed coming for comparative administrative law.[20]

This dialogue does not confine itself to the two aspects referred to above (the role of public participation in decision-making in relation to access to justice, and the standing of environmental organizations). In *Janecek*, the Court of Justice concluded that the obligation to draw up air quality action plans had direct effect and that 'natural or legal persons directly concerned by a risk that the limit values or alert thresholds may be exceeded must be in a position to require the competent authorities to draw up an action plan where such a risk exists, if necessary by bringing an action before the competent courts'.[21] Under German administrative procedural law, Mr Janecek, who lived in Munich in an area where the EU air quality standards were regularly exceeded, could not be regarded as an interested party, as an appellant's standing depends not on whether a person is *actually affected* by a decision, but whether *his rights have been breached* by it.[22] The Court of Justice's decision clearly implies that the German administrative court must review Mr Janecek's substantive complaint. Equally clearly, the Court of Justice thus required the German administrative court to apply a wider concept of 'interested party' than is usual in German law. More significant, however, is that the decision will stimulate a fundamental debate about the concept of an interested party. Another issue that the judgment raises is that not only *natural persons* but also *legal persons* that are directly concerned must be put in a position to rely on the Directive before national courts. It seems, therefore, that the Court of Justice really

[18] Case C-263/08 *Djurgården-Lilla*, n 13 above, para 51.

[19] cf HD Tolsma, KJ de Graaf and JH Jans, 'The Rise and Fall of Access to Justice in the Netherlands' (2009) 21:2 *J Env L* 309.

[20] cf also R Caranta, 'Pleading for European Comparative Administrative Law; What is the Place for Comparative Law in Europe?' (2009) 2:2 *Rev Eur Admin L* 155–73.

[21] Case C-237/07 *Janecek v Freistaat Bayern* [2008] ECR I-6221, para 39.

[22] cf N de Sadeleer, G Roller and M Dross (eds), n 8 above, Ch 2, para 4.

has done a thorough job of harmonizing national procedural law, at least as far as Germany is concerned, but possibly also for Austria (and who knows which other countries besides). Elsewhere, I have referred to this manner of harmonization as harmonization 'via the back door'.[23]

Finally, let me give another example, this time from the case law on stating reasons for decisions. In *Mellor*, the simple question before the Court of Justice was whether the reasons for an administrative authority's decision determining that a project was not subject to an environmental impact assessment (EIA) had to be made available to the public.[24] Under English law, reasons only have to be made public where a decision does require an environmental impact assessment and not otherwise.[25] In its decision, the Court seems to be running with the hare and hunting with hounds. It referred to earlier case law and concluded that an administrative authority's decision on whether or not an EIA is required 'must contain or be accompanied by all the information that makes it possible to check that it is based on adequate screening, carried out in accordance with the requirements of Directive 85/337'.[26] Nevertheless, it continued: 'It does not follow, however, from Directive 85/337, or from the case-law of the Court, in particular, ... that a determination not to subject a project to an EIA must, *itself*, contain the reasons for which the competent authority determined that an assessment was unnecessary.'[27]

The duty to state reasons for this kind of 'negative' screening opinion is above all necessary, it emerges from the judgment, in order to protect the interests of third parties. They must be able to satisfy themselves that the administrative authority has acted in accordance with the law, 'if necessary through legal action'.[28] It is interesting that the Court not only refers to 'interested parties' in the generic sense but, in this context, also explicitly refers to 'other national authorities concerned'.[29] In the guise of a judgment about the duty to state reasons, it seems that the Court has also given a judgment, again via the back door, about access to the courts, in this case for national authorities.

Finally, we have to mention a most important recent ruling in the *Trianel* case.[30] This judgment might have a significant impact on key topics of national administrative procedural law. In *Trianel*, a German administrative court referred the question whether environmental organizations should be allowed to argue infringement of rules of law that are intended to protect the legal interests of individuals.

[23] JH Jans, 'Harmonisation of National Procedural Law via the Back Door? Preliminary Comments on the ECJ's Judgment in *Janecek* in a Comparative Context' in M Bulterman et al (eds), *Views of European Law from the Mountain: Liber Amicorum Piet Jan Slot* (Alphen aan den Rijn: Kluwer Law International, 2009) 267–75.

[24] Case C-75/08 *Mellor v Secretary of State for Communities and Local Government* [2009] ECR I-3799.

[25] See commentary by R Macrory in ENDS Report 413 (June 2009) 55–6.

[26] Case C-75/08 *Mellor*, n 24 above, para 55.

[27] ibid para 56 (emphasis added).

[28] ibid para 58.

[29] ibid.

[30] Case C-115/09 *Trianel* [2011] OJ C 204/6.

Clearly, the *Schutznorm* requirement (that an individual who has suffered damage can obtain reparation only if he specifically belongs to the group the rule of law infringed was designed to protect) is at issue here. Granted, the *Umwelt-Rechtsbehelfsgesetz* (Environmental Appeals Act) has improved the position of environmental organizations, but the legislation still limits the possibility of appeals in the sense that such organizations may only argue a violation of legal rules that *Rechte Einzelner begründen* (establish individual rights). According to the ECJ, EU law precludes legislation that does not permit environmental non-governmental organizations to rely before their national courts, in an action contesting a decision authorizing projects likely to have significant effects on the environment, on the infringement of a rule flowing from the environment law of the European Union and intended to protect the environment, on the ground that that rule protects only the interests of the general public and not the interests of individuals.

E. Internal harmonization of administrative law?

Above, I have referred to the fragmented actions of the EU legislature in the administrative law field as harmonization by bits and pieces. I have used the Aarhus Directive as a means of determining more precisely the latitude available to Member States when legislating for legal protection against administrative decisions on the environment. This does not mean, however, that the issue will be approached in the same way, or even in a similar way, in other policy areas that are relevant to administrative law. In a study that I carried out more than 10 years ago together with De Jong, we examined judicial protection clauses in secondary European legislation.[31] We defined judicial protection clauses as provisions in, usually, Directives requiring Member States to take the necessary legislative measures to ensure that rights conferred on individuals in legislation could in fact be enforced by them before a court of law. In particular, we discussed whether there was a need for a degree of internal harmonization of such judicial protection clauses. The study showed that EU legislation could broadly be divided into two categories in this respect. In the first place, there was a large group of Directives containing a fairly broadly worded *standard provision* requiring Member States to guarantee judicial protection. Such a provision covered the following elements:

- reasons must be given for decisions involving rights conferred on interested parties by the Union;
- interested parties must be notified of decisions;
- decisions must refer to a 'remedy'.

It is interesting to note that the standard provision did not generally contain an explicit instruction to Member States to ensure access to justice.

[31] JH Jans and M de Jong, 'Interne harmonisatie van rechtsbeschermingsclausules in het secundaire gemeenschapsrecht' (1999) 2 *Regelmaat* 73.

Second, there was a much smaller group of Directives in which the EU legislature has created a *special*, often more detailed, regime. The Aarhus Directive is an example of this. We noted in 1999 that the EU legislature rarely gave any substantive reasons for such special judicial protection clauses. Nevertheless, we did find that even though the differences were substantial, there was some pattern to be discovered. Further to our findings, we advocated giving more attention to internal harmonization. It is now more than 10 years later and the need for more internal harmonization does not seem to have diminished. This attempt at internal harmonization should not be confined to the issue of administrative law judicial protection, but should also concern other 'general-administrative-law-like' topics.

F. Internal harmonization: yes, but how?

In our 1999 article, we still had thoughts of drafting a number of standard provisions that could be included in a 'legislature directive'. The EU legislature could then refer to this metadirective and so ensure consistency. As an alternative, we suggested including these standard provisions in a kind of 'Guide to drafting EU legislation'. As far as I am concerned, these are still instruments worth discussing. But the most important question remains, of course: what should these standard provisions include and how should they be formed?

On this point, I would like to discuss two processes that could be relevant to drafting standard administrative law provisions. In the first place, the Draft Common Frame of Reference (DCFR), through which administrative lawyers could perhaps learn something from their private law brothers and sisters; second, the Open Method of Coordination (OMC) introduced by the European Council at Lisbon in March 2000.

(1) A Draft Common Frame of Reference for administrative law?

Can administrative lawyers learn from private lawyers? They, after all, have proved able to draw up a large number of definitions, principles and model rules for European private law, the Draft Common Frame of Reference.[32] One of the aims of the DCFR, drawn up by legal scholars, is to serve as a model for possible further activities by the European institutions.

As a starting point for the development of the DCFR, the various resolutions of the European Parliament, adopted from as early as 1989, must be mentioned, in

[32] The DCFR consists of General provisions (Book I), Contracts and other juridical acts (Book II), Obligations and corresponding rights (Book III), Specific contracts (Book IV), Benevolent intervention in another's affairs (Book V), Non-contractual liability (Book VI), Unjustified enrichment (Book VII), Acquisition and loss of ownership of goods (Book VIII), Proprietary security in movable assets (Book IX) and Trusts (Book X). The Outline Edition is available at <http://ec.europa.eu/justice/contract/files/european-private-law_en.pdf>.

which the Parliament has urged harmonization of European private law.[33] In these Resolutions, the European Parliament sought attention for the activities of the Commission on European Contract Law (the Lando Commission), which at the time was already engaged in research into the common principles of European private law. Another important impulse was the European Council at Tampere in October 1999, which spoke out in favour of a study on the need to harmonize Member State legislation in the field of private law. Then, on 11 June 2001, the European Commission published a Communication on European contract law,[34] which formed a first step towards the study promised by the Tampere Council. In the Communication, the European Commission outlined four possible scenarios for EU legislation in the field of contract law, and requested a response to these scenarios from businesses, lawyers, academics and consumers. The scenarios were:

- leaving solution of the problems to the market (ie take no action);
- drawing up Restatements (Principles);
- improving the *acquis*;
- approving a new instrument.

From the many reactions to the Communication, it was clear that, across the board, the option of taking no action was not considered desirable and that the instruments that enjoyed the most support were soft law and further Community legislation.

Then, in 2003, the Commission published an action plan for a more coherent European contract law.[35] This presented the Commission's conclusions further to the Communication of June 2001 and proposed the following measures:

- increasing the coherence of the EC *acquis* in the area of contract law;
- promoting the elaboration of EU-wide general contract terms;
- examining further whether problems in the European contract law area may require non-sector-specific solutions such as an optional instrument.

In 2004, the European Commission published a Communication containing further measures, in which it discussed how the problems identified in the action plan would be solved.[36] The most important measure it mentioned was improving the present and future *acquis*, for which a Common Frame of Reference would have to be prepared. A Draft Common Frame of Reference was to be prepared by a

[33] eg Resolution of European Parliament A2-157/89 [1989] OJ C 158/400 and Resolution of the European Parliament A3-0329/94 [1994] OJ C 205/518.

[34] Communication from the Commission to the Council and the European Parliament on European contract law COM (2001) 398 final. See further the Opinion of the Economic and Social Committee on the Communication from the Commission to the Council and the European Parliament on European contract law COM (2001) 398 final [2002] OJ C 241/1.

[35] Communication from the Commission to the European Parliament and the Council, *A More Coherent European Contract Law: an Action Plan* COM (2003) 68 final.

[36] Communication from the Commission to the European Parliament and the Council, *European Contract Law and the Revision of the Acquis: the Way Forward*, COM (2004) 651 final, 14 et seq.

network set up for the purpose, consisting primarily of academic experts. The Commission would not regard itself as bound by this DCFR, which is also referred to as the Academic Common Frame of Reference, both because of its academic background and to distinguish it from the 'political' CFR, the version drafted by the European Commission on the basis of the DCFR. To ensure the input of stakeholders and to guarantee their commitment, the Commission decided to set up a Network of Member State Experts consisting of public servants from the various EU Member States. At the same time, a network of lawyers from business, courts and other organizations was established (CFR-Net).[37]

Further to this Communication, the Joint Network on European Private Law (the CoPECL Network of Excellence) was established in May 2005.[38] This comprises various universities, institutions and other organizations, including the Study Group on a European Civil Code (chaired by von Bar). The network is funded under the Sixth Framework Programme of the European Community for research and technological development.[39] In December 2007, the network delivered a Draft Common Frame of Reference to the European Commission, and this was presented to the European Parliament in January 2008. In December 2008, the final Academic Common Frame of Reference was presented to the Commission.

The Council and the European Parliament have already discussed the DCFR.[40] In October 2008, under the French Presidency of the European Union, the French Ministry of Justice organized a conference on the theme, 'Which European contract law for the European Union?'[41] In the Communication referred to above,[42] the European Commission outlined the further procedure for adoption of the CFR. It envisaged the following steps:

- the Commission would check whether the DCFR was fit for use;
- the Commission would draft a CFR;
- the European Parliament, the Council and the Member States would be consulted on the Commission's CFR;

[37] See the website of the European Commission on the Common Frame of Reference, <http://www.europarl.europa.eu/meetdocs/2004_2009/documents/dv/p6_ta-prov(2008)0397_/p6_ta-prov(2008)0397_en.pdf>.

[38] This network is usually referred to by the acronym for Common Principles of European Contract Law, 'CoPECL'. These 'principles' form part of the DCFR. The network's website, <http://www.copecl.org> contains detailed information on its activities.

[39] Decision No 1513/2002/EC of the European Parliament and of the Council of 27 June 2002 concerning the sixth framework programme of the European Community for research, technological development and demonstration activities, contributing to the creation of the European Research Area and to innovation (2002 to 2006) [2002] OJ 2002 L232/1.

[40] European Parliament resolution of 3 September 2008 on the common frame of reference for European contract law, P6_TA-PROV(2008)0397 (available at <http://www.europarl.europa.eu>).

[41] See the website of the French presidency, <http://www.ue2008.fr/PFUE/lang/en/accueil/PFUE-10_2008/PFUE-23.10.2008/quel_droit_europeen_des_contrats_pour_l_union_europeenne.html>.

[42] *European Contract Law and the Revision of the Acquis: the Way Forward*, n 36 above, 14 et seq.

- there would be an open consultation in the form of a White Paper, giving stakeholders the opportunity to contribute;
- adoption of the CFR.

The Commission is currently assessing the academic CFR delivered by the CoPECL. It is also engaged in informal consultations with the Council and the European Parliament. It is expected that a 'political' CFR drafted by the Commission will be adopted.[43] Meanwhile, the DCFR is being subjected to extensive discussion throughout the European Union.

In light of the above developments in European private law, it may well be asked to what extent a Common Frame of Reference is a suitable instrument to achieve harmonization of administrative law in Europe. This question was discussed at a conference in Osnabrück in June 2009.[44] From the report of the conference, I gather that the participants expressed the following doubts as regards the possible development of an administrative law CFR. Some, for example, questioned the desirability of codification, given the encroachment on Member States' procedural autonomy that this would entail. Codification would be particularly problematic for Member States such as the United Kingdom and France where national administrative law is not codified. There was also discussion on whether the European Union is actually competent to codify administrative law. Finally, several positive experiences were considered with respect to Member States where administrative law codification has proved successful (Poland and the Netherlands). During the conclusion of the conference it was noted that the legislature alone would not be capable of structuring an administrative law CFR, and it was therefore up to the academic world to devote itself to this task. Establishment of an academic network for European administrative law was advocated as a means to achieve this.

(2) The Open Method of Coordination as a possible method for internal harmonization or codification

The Open Method of Coordination (OMC) was first referred to as such in the Conclusions of the Lisbon European Council in 2000.[45] There, the European Council introduced a new strategic goal: 'to become the most competitive and dynamic knowledge-based economy in the world capable of sustainable economic growth with more and better jobs and greater social cohesion'.[46] This strategy was

[43] Communication from the Commission to the Council, the European Parliament, the European Economic and Social Committee and the Committee of the Regions, *Justice, Freedom and Security in Europe since 2005: an Evaluation of the Hague Programme and Action Plan* SEC (2009) 767 final.

[44] See for the report N Marsch, 'A Common Frame of Reference on European Administrative Procedural Law? Tage des Europäischen Rechts 2009 der Universitäten Münster und Osnabrück' (2009) 124: 22 *Deutsches Verwaltungsblatt* 1430–2.

[45] Conclusions of the Lisbon European Council, 23 and 24 March 2000, available at <http://www.europarl.europa.eu/summits/lis1_en.htm>.

[46] ibid para 5.

to be implemented by using an open method of coordination at all levels. There is now a considerable quantity of literature on this OMC.[47]

The Open Method of Coordination must be seen in the context of the tendency within the EU to make less use of the more traditional hierarchic forms of legislation, such as Regulations and Directives (hard law), and more use of other instruments, referred to by terms such as new governance and soft law.[48] In the background, there is an ongoing discussion in which many refer critically to the use of various forms of new governance.

It is interesting to note that the European Council did not define the terms 'open' or 'coordination'. From the description of the goal of the OMC, it emerges in any event that it is not intended as a means of achieving harmonization, but that Member States can use it to develop their own policies and achieve coordination. The OMC does not provide hard rules that must be implemented in the Member States, but only provides common goals and the means to learn from one another as to how these goals should be achieved. It is thus a means of achieving greater convergence, but allowing a certain degree of divergence.

In the words of the European Council, the Open Method of Coordination serves as a means of spreading best practice and achieving greater convergence towards the main EU goals. The method is designed to help Member States to develop their own policies, and involves four elements:[49]

- fixing guidelines for the Union combined with specific timetables for achieving the goals that they set in the short, medium and long terms;
- establishing, where appropriate, quantitative and qualitative indicators and benchmarks against the best in the world and tailored to the needs of different Member States and sectors as a means of comparing best practice;
- translating these European guidelines into national and regional policies by setting specific targets and adopting measures, taking into account national and regional differences;
- periodic monitoring, evaluation and peer review organised as mutual learning processes.

Although the description of the OMC given above—sticking to the description of the European Council—makes it seem as though there is one particular method, in practice it is more like a cookbook containing various recipes.[50] This means that the various recipes in the OMC cookbook can be adapted by adding a little of this or leaving out a little of that depending on the policy area concerned. The OMC is

[47] See, for an overview, V Hatzopoulos, 'Why the Open Method of Coordination is Bad for You: a Letter to the EU' (2007) 13:3 *ELJ* 309–10.

[48] P Craig and G de Búrca, *EU Law. Text, Cases and Materials* (Oxford: Oxford University Press, 2008) 144. cf also B ter Haar, 'Open Method of Coordination: A New Stepping Stone in the Legal Order of International and European Relations' (2008) 77:3 *NJIL* 244.

[49] Conclusions of the Lisbon European Council, n 45 above, para 37.

[50] F Vandenbrouke, *The EU and social protection: What should the European Convention* propose?, MPIfG Working Paper 02/6, June 2002, available at <http://www.mpifg.de/pu/workpap/wp02-6/wp02-6.html>.

thus a flexible means of attaining greater convergence within the EU in any given policy area. The advantage of this is that the elements that the OMC involves can be tailored to meet the specific policy. According to João Rodrigues, the person regarded as the architect of the OMC, the OMC must be combined with other available methods depending on the problem to be addressed.[51] A disadvantage inherent in this flexibility is that it is more difficult in practice to determine the right method, precisely because there is not just one method.

The Open Method of Coordination is primarily applied in complex, politically sensitive policy areas which involve a great degree of uncertainty as to which solution will achieve the desired results.[52] The OMC has already been applied in a number of policy areas, including the information society, SMEs, economic reform, education, R&D and social inclusion. It is notable that the OMC is applied in various areas where the EU has little or no legislative power. It is for this reason that Senden regards the OMC as a necessary complement to hard European law.[53]

It seems to me that it is worth examining to what extent the OMC can be used to develop best practices in administrative law. Possible topics that lend themselves to benchmarking are, for example, litigation costs, the duration of decision-making procedures, and the role of appeal courts.

G. Conclusion

General codification and harmonization, as a sort of European Administrative Procedure Act, of the national procedural administrative law of the Member States is not to be expected in the short or medium term. This does not mean that harmonization is not occurring. It is, but in a piecemeal way rather than across the board or, as I have referred to it, through harmonization by bits and pieces. These harmonized rules are not intended to serve as ready-made substitutes for national rules but can rather be regarded as ground rules within which national administrative law systems can continue to manifest themselves. It may be expected that these ground rules will prove very suitable for judicial dialogue and judicial competition and that further convergence of administrative law in the EU Member States will take place via this back door.

[51] M João Rodrigues, 'The Open Method of Coordination as a New Governance Tool' in M Telò (ed), *L'evoluzione della governance europea* (Europa/Europe, special issue, Nos 2–3, 2001) 103.

[52] DM Trubek, P Cottrell and M Nance, 'Soft Law', 'Hard Law' and EU Integration' in G de Búrca and J Scott (eds), *Law and New Governance in the EU and the US* (Oxford: Hart Publishing, 2006) 78.

[53] LAJ Senden, *Soft Law in European Community Law* (Oxford: Hart Publishing, 2004) 564.

PART V

ACCESS TO JUSTICE AND JUDICIAL PROTECTION

19

The Lisbon Treaty, the Court of Justice and the Rule of Law

*Francis G Jacobs**

It is a privilege to contribute to a book in memory of John Usher, a fine scholar and a good friend. I knew John for 35 years, having first met him, appropriately, at the Court of Justice in Luxembourg in 1973. I watched him flower, and was happy to be able to recommend him, first to succeed me as the *référendaire* to Advocate General J-P Warner, then to an appointment with Professor John Mitchell at Edinburgh, and later for other university appointments. He was always in demand as a scholar and as a speaker, having a light touch and an occasional dose of irony. Combining much learning with a disarming modesty and a great sense of humour, he was always fun to meet, whether at breakfast in Bruges at the hostel used by the College of Europe, at Leiden with two then very young sons in tow, or at home: he and Jean were fine hosts when I visited Exeter, and I appreciated his cooking skills as well as his intellect. Author of several books, he contributed not one but two titles to the Oxford EU Law Library, on subjects which did not attract all scholars (agricultural law and the law of money), and new editions arrived apparently effortlessly. On many counts, John is greatly missed.

A. The rule of law

An important thread running through the European Treaties and indeed the case law of the Court is undoubtedly respect for the rule of law. Just as this was essential for the establishment and proper functioning of the common market, it is even more essential for the functioning of the European Union, with its far greater impact on the lives of citizens and market participants in the Member States. This is rightly recognized by its inclusion in Article 2 TEU as one of the values on which the Union is founded, which are common to the Member States. In maintaining the rule of law at Union level, the role and functioning of the Court of Justice of the European Union as an institution are of the utmost importance. In this essay,

* Professor of Law and Jean Monnet Professor, King's College London. This chapter was completed in November 2010.

I suggest that the Lisbon Treaty has made a remarkable contribution to the rule of law, illustrated by addressing a number of concrete examples. But we must first consider what is meant by the rule of law. It is clearly a concept of great importance, increasingly and now perhaps almost universally invoked as a fundamental value in the ordering of our society. But what exactly does is mean? My first approach, in an attempt to find an answer to this question, is to seek guidance from political theory—a subject that I taught at Oxford in my first days of university teaching. The rule of law must surely be a topic on which lawyers can learn from political theorists and political philosophers. I am disappointed in my search for an answer. There appear to be three schools of thought on the rule of law, which I shall now outline.[1]

(1) Thin conceptions of the rule of law

Political theorists advancing thin conceptions of the rule of law claim that the rule of law obtains when there are safeguards against arbitrary use of power. Because thin conceptions of the rule of law are concerned merely with preventing the arbitrary use of power, they are sometimes described as negative conceptions of the rule of law.

Thin conceptions of the rule of law ask whether a legal system exhibits certain specified procedural attributes. Only when a legal system exhibits these attributes—when the legal system is *legally healthy*—is there adequate safeguard against the arbitrary use of power. For this reason, thin conceptions of the rule of law are also sometimes described as formal or rule-book conceptions. What may now be regarded as the foundational account of a thin conception of the rule of law comes from Lon Fuller's *The Morality of Law* (1964)—which was indeed a foundational text when I started to try to teach jurisprudence, at the University of Glasgow and at the London School of Economics. Fuller claims that the rule of law obtains when eight principles ('principles of legality') are satisfied.[2] Essentially, laws must be:

1. General
2. Promulgated
3. Prospective
4. Intelligible
5. Consistent
6. Practicable
7. Infrequently changed
8. Reflected by the behaviour of officials

And in Fuller's account, these principles form part of the definition of a legal system. Thus he claims that: 'A total failure in any one of these eight directions does

[1] I am grateful to Neal Carrier, currently Jane Eliza Procter Fellow at Princeton University, for his assistance with this part of the chapter.

[2] L Fuller, *The Morality of Law* (New Haven, Conn.: Yale University Press,1964) 46–91.

not simply result in a bad system of law; it results in something that is not properly called a legal system at all.'[3]

Similar, or even thinner, accounts of the rule of law have been advanced by Professor John Finnis,[4] Professor John Rawls[5] and Professor Joseph Raz.[6] Indeed Rawls claims that the rule of law is merely 'the regular and impartial administration of public rules'.[7] A similar reductionist approach is adopted by Margaret Radin, who claims that any thin conception of the rule of law can be reduced to the following two principles: 'first, there must be rules; second, those rules must be capable of being followed'.[8]

A consequence of thin conceptions of the rule of law is that they are compatible with radical injustice or immorality. This is denied by some (eg Fuller), but is openly accepted by others. Rawls, for example, says that because these precepts guarantee only the impartial and regular administration of rules, whatever these are, they are compatible with injustice.[9]

(2) Thick conceptions of the rule of law

Proponents of thick conceptions of the rule of law say that the rule of law is not compatible with injustice. So for the rule of law to obtain, a legal system cannot merely exhibit some certain specified procedural attributes, it must also in some sense exhibit normative *moral principles* or *principles of justice*. Thick conceptions of the rule of law accept that the rule of law involves legal systems exhibiting certain procedural and formal attributes. But they do not accept that this is the whole story—the rule of law *also* requires that legal systems be moral or just in some substantive sense. As Randall Peerenboom says, because a thin rule of law is consistent with great evil, many scholars and rights activists argue that the rule of law requires 'good laws'. On this view, the rule of law requires laws that are grounded in some normative foundation that transcends the legal system itself. In the past, divine law or natural law provided the foundation; today, the more secular ideology of democracy and human rights may do so. The attempt to remedy the normative shortcomings of thin theories by incorporating particular conceptions of rights and other features of political morality transforms thin conceptions of rule of law into thick ones.[10]

[3] ibid 39.

[4] J Finnis, *Natural Law and Natural Rights* (Oxford: Oxford University Press, 1980).

[5] J Rawls, *A Theory of Justice* (Cambridge, Mass.: Harvard University Press, 1971) 236–9.

[6] J Raz, 'The Rule of Law and its Virtue' in J Raz, *The Authority of Law: Essays on Law and Morality* (Oxford: Oxford University Press, 1979) 214–19.

[7] J Rawls, n 5 above, 206.

[8] M Radin, 'Reconsidering the Rule of Law' (1989) 69:4. *Boston University Law Review* 781–822, 785.

[9] J Rawls, n 5 above, 208.

[10] R Peerenboom, 'Human Rights and the Rule of Law: What's the Relationship?, University of California, Public Law and Legal Theory Research Paper Series, Research Paper No 05–31, 1–152, 20–1, available at <http://ssrn.com/abstract=816024>.

Similarly, according to Ronald Dworkin—widely regarded as the most significant philosopher of law since Herbert Hart—a thick conception of the rule of law assumes that citizens have moral rights and duties with respect to one another, and political rights against the state as a whole. It insists that these moral and political rights be recognized in positive law, so that they may be enforced upon the demand of individual citizens through courts. The rule of law on this conception is the ideal of rule by an accurate public conception of individual rights. It does not distinguish, as the rule-book conception does, between the rule of law and substantive justice; on the contrary it requires, as part of the ideal of law, that the rules in the rule-book capture and enforce moral rights.[11]

(3) Zero conceptions of the rule of law

What is perhaps worse, some political theorists suggest, or at least acknowledge the suggestion, that the concept is meaningless.[12] Professor Jeremy Waldron, noting that the rule of law may be invoked by opposite sides in a debate, recognizes a widespread impression that utterance of those magic words means little more than 'Hooray for our side'.[13] Professor Brian Tamanaha describes the rule of law as 'an exceedingly elusive notion' giving rise to 'a rampant divergence of understandings' and as analogous to the notion of the Good in the sense that 'everyone is for it, but [may] have contrasting convictions about what it is'.[14] Even more devastatingly, Professor Judith Shklar suggests that the term has suffered fatally from ideological abuse: 'It may well have become just another one of those self-congratulatory rhetorical devices that grace the public utterances of Anglo-American politicians. No intellectual effort need therefore be wasted on this bit of ruling class chatter.'[15]

Given this dismal failure to agree on any substantive concept of the rule of law, one might ask whether, rather than looking to political theory for guidance, we (and perhaps political theorists) might derive some benefit from the views of lawyers?

(4) Lawyers' views of the rule of law

Lawyers do not have the luxury of writing off the concept of the rule of law. The reasons for that are outlined, with characteristic clarity, elegance and conviction, by the late Tom Bingham in the opening chapter of his brilliant handbook *The Rule of Law,* published in 2010.[16] But lawyers recognize the same broad dichotomy

[11] R Dworkin, *A Matter of Principle* (New York: Oxford University Press, 1985) 11–12.

[12] See the account by T Bingham, *The Rule of Law* (London: Allen Lane, 2010) 5 et seq.

[13] J Waldron, 'Is the Rule of Law an Essentially Contested Concept (in Florida)?' in R Bellamy (ed), *The Rule of Law and Separation of Powers* (Aldershot: Ashgate, 2005) 119.

[14] B Tamanaha, *On the Rule of Law* (Cambridge: Cambridge University Press, 2004) 3.

[15] J Shklar, 'Political Theory and the Rule of Law' in A Hutchinson and P Monahan (eds), *The Rule of Law: Ideal or Ideology* (Toronto: Carswell, 1987) 1.

[16] See T Bingham, n 12 above.

between thick and thin concepts of the rule of law,[17] and differ markedly in their understanding of it.

The obvious starting point is Albert Venn Dicey, who used the expression 'the rule of law' in his book *An Introduction to the Study of the Law of the Constitution*, published in 1885: his writings seem to be the origin of the expression, even though (a) it is said that the idea itself is much older (but, it may be asked, which idea?) and (b) he used it in what now seem somewhat idiosyncratic senses. Dicey distinguished three senses—which I set out here in a paraphrase, but in language very close to Dicey's own:

1. No man is punishable except for a breach of law established in the ordinary legal manner before the ordinary courts of the land.
2. Every man, whatever his rank or condition, is subject to the ordinary law of the realm and amenable to the jurisdiction of the ordinary tribunals.
3. The general principles of the constitution (such as the right to personal liberty, etc) are the result of judicial decisions determining the rights of private persons in particular cases, whereas in many foreign systems they are general principles of the constitution.

The focus of the first proposition, and in part of the second, is on the criminal law.

Tom Bingham described the core of the existing principle of the rule of law in terms not very far removed from Dicey's formulation, as 'that all persons and authorities within the state, whether public or private, should be bound by and entitled to the benefit of laws publicly made, taking effect (generally) in the future and publicly administered in the courts'.[18] But he went on to formulate eight further principles, which seemed to expand the notion of the rule of law rather substantially. One such proposition is that: 'The law must afford adequate protection of fundamental human rights.'[19] While there should be little controversy about the value of such a principle, there is room for debate as to whether it should be classified as part of the rule of law.

In European law, the term 'rule of law' seems to have a more specific connotation. The preamble to the European Convention on Human Rights refers to 'a common heritage of political traditions, ideals, freedoms and the rule of law' (in French *prééminence du droit*). The European Court of Human Rights relied upon that reference (possibly for the first time) in the *Golder* case,[20] brought against the United Kingdom, in which the Court held that Article 6(1) of the Convention must be regarded as guaranteeing the right of access to court; we shall see later the relevance of this to the reforms of the Lisbon Treaty. The Court stated:

[17] See, eg, J Raz, n 6 above; P Craig, 'Formal and Substantive Conceptions of the Rule of Law: an Analytical Framework' (1997) *Public Law* 467.

[18] T Bingham, n 12 above, 37.

[19] ibid 84.

[20] *Golder*, judgment of 21 February 1975, Series A, No 18, (1975) 1 EHRR 524, para 54.

In civil matters one can scarcely conceive of the rule of law without there being a possibility of access to the courts. . . . The principle whereby a civil claim must be capable of being submitted to a judge ranks as one of the universally recognised fundamental principles of law . . .

In that context, the Court gives the notion of the rule of law a very specific connotation. It is true that, more recently, the Court has declared that 'the rule of law, one of the fundamental principles of a democratic society, is inherent in all the Articles of the Convention'.[21] That seems to go rather far, but it can be understood as emphasizing certain general features of the Convention, for example, that Convention rights must be guaranteed by law, and that limitations on those rights must be, in the terms regularly used in the Convention, 'prescribed by law' or 'in accordance with the law'. In other words, the content of the rights, and any limitations on their exercise, must be laid down and be knowable in advance. That is consistent again with a very specific meaning of the rule of law. The Court's statement cited above should not, I suggest, be understood as meaning that the content and substance of the rights are to be identified with the rule of law. That would surely result in the notion of the rule of law being unduly inflated and would deprive it of any specific value.

The position is similar in the European Union. References to the rule of law and to fundamental rights were introduced into the treaties for the first time through the Maastricht Treaty (in the Treaty on European Union), which entered into force on 1 November 1993.[22] The Member States, in the preamble to that Treaty, confirmed their attachment to 'the principles of liberty, democracy and respect for human rights and fundamental freedoms and of the rule of law'. There is no suggestion in that formulation that respect for human rights forms part of the rule of law, although there are clearly connections between them.

As has not infrequently been the case on fundamental constitutional principles, the ECJ had anticipated the Treaty-making process and had based a key decision on the notion of the rule of law in 1986. Essentially, the issue was whether the Court could review acts of the European Parliament in the absence of treaty provisions conferring that jurisdiction on the Court. The Court held that it could, a central argument being that 'The . . . Community is a Community based on the rule of law, inasmuch as neither its Member States nor its institutions can avoid a review of the question whether the measures adopted by them are in conformity with the basic constitutional charter, the Treaty.'[23] The expression 'a Community based on the rule of law' (in French, *une Communauté de droit*, which recalls *l'Etat de droit*) encapsulates perfectly the idea that the Court expresses by stating that all measures taken by the authorities must be subject to judicial review. And the Maastricht

[21] *Ukraine-Tiumen v Ukraine*, judgment of 22 November 2007, para 49.

[22] The preamble to the Single European Act (an Act which was superseded by the later Treaties) had included references to the principles of 'compliance with the law' and with human rights (*le respect du droit et des droits de l'homme*).

[23] Case 294/83 *Parti écologiste 'Les Verts' v European Parliament* [1986] ECR 1339.

Treaty subsequently saw the force of the principle, expressly providing for review by the Court of measures taken by the European Parliament.

That seems to be an idea of such value that it would be useful to reserve the expression 'the rule of law' for that idea and some closely related ideas. I recognize of course that it is not the traditional nucleus of the term: historically, 'introducing the rule of law' has meant something very different, such as enforcing obedience to the law—and often with no sense that there were any constraints on the exercise of that power. Today, we might refer to that in terms of 'law and order' rather than 'the rule of law'. While of course law and order are of the highest importance, and it is essential that the law should be obeyed and enforced, as a precondition of the very existence of a civilized society, the rule of law today has, I think, at least in Europe, a very different connotation. Essentially, it seems to me, it is no longer about the exercise of power to enforce the law; rather, it is about *the control of power by the law*. After centuries in which the abuse of power led to terrible evils, not least in Europe in the Second World War, the rule of law as now understood in Europe seems to me to embody at its core the idea that all exercise of power should be subject to the law. In particular, it means, on a more concrete but fundamental level, that the decisions of public authorities should be open to effective review by independent courts.[24]

Beyond that central core, the rule of law requires also that both private disputes and criminal proceedings should be subject to due process before independent and impartial courts and tribunals. As for the law itself, it must be reasonably certain and foreseeable. And there must be effective remedies where the rights of individuals, whether in private disputes, in criminal proceedings, or in public law, have been infringed.

How then does the rule of law, so understood, relate to human rights? I would suggest that there is little connection with many rights recognized today as fundamental—for example, the right to family life, freedom of religion, or the right to education. But there is a very close connection with certain other rights, notably with those set out in Article 6(1) of the European Convention on Human Rights, which provides that 'In the determination of his civil rights and obligations or of any criminal charge against him, everyone is entitled to a fair and public hearing within a reasonable time by an independent and impartial tribunal established by law.'[25] Two other rights in the European Convention are especially relevant: Article 7, which requires the foreseeability of the criminal law and embodies the principle

[24] See my Holdsworth lecture, 'The European Union and the Rule of Law' (University of Birmingham, 2007).

[25] It is of interest that Article 6(1) of the Convention addresses *civil rights and obligations* and *a criminal charge*, but does not in terms cover disputes between the individual and the public authorities, today the heartland of the concept of the rule of law. The explanation might be found in the undeveloped state of public law 60 years ago, when the Convention was drafted—especially in England. The European Court of Human Rights has sought to fill that rather large lacuna by treating many public law disputes as involving the determination of civil rights and obligations.

nulla poena sine lege, and Article 13, which guarantees the right to an effective remedy for any violation of the rights set forth in the Convention—including, therefore, the rights guaranteed by Articles 6 and 7.

It is in that light that we may examine the provisions of the Lisbon Treaty on the jurisdiction of the Court of Justice of the European Union. We will take first the substantial new jurisdiction under the former 'third pillar' (now the Area of Freedom, Security and Justice). We consider briefly jurisdiction over the Common Foreign and Security Policy. We then address significant changes in the Court's jurisdiction generally. However, in keeping with the view that the rule of law and human rights are distinct notions, we will not examine here the changes, important as they are, which the Lisbon Treaty makes in relation to the protection of human rights: the obligation for the European Union to accede to the European Convention on Human Rights, and the legal effect given to the EU Charter of Fundamental Rights, which is accorded the same legal status as the Treaties. In conclusion, we consider changes in the system of appointment of members of the EU Courts—changes which can be seen as reinforcing the independence of the judiciary, a central part of the rule of law.

B. The jurisdiction of the Court of Justice in relation to Freedom, Security and Justice

The main changes here follow from the abolition of the 'three-pillar' system introduced by the Maastricht Treaty. Under that system, the jurisdiction of the ECJ remained largely unchanged under the first pillar—the so-called Community pillar. But the new second and third pillars were closer in some respects to the traditional intergovernmental method, and the role of the Community institutions—Parliament, Commission, and Court of Justice—was more limited. Indeed the jurisdiction of the Court of Justice was excluded, with narrow exceptions, under the then second pillar (Common Foreign and Security Policy) and was considerably limited under the then third pillar (Justice and Home Affairs).

The position became more complex under the Amsterdam Treaty. Some matters were transferred from the third pillar to the first (Community) pillar. But they were made subject to variable systems of jurisdiction. Indeed, for the first time, the jurisdiction of the Court depended in some instances on 'opt-ins' by Member States. Meanwhile the remainder of the third pillar continued under the Amsterdam Treaty, but under the new title 'Provisions on police and judicial cooperation in criminal matters'. The resulting patchwork system was widely regarded as opaque, incoherent and generally unsatisfactory.

The Lisbon Treaty is a great improvement in this regard. It does away with the much criticized three-pillar structure, and makes major changes in relation to Justice and Home Affairs—now under the title *Area of Freedom, Security and Justice*; and this leads to substantial extensions in the jurisdiction of the Court.

Subject to certain transitional provisions,[26] the Treaty extends the normal system of jurisdiction to the Area of Freedom, Security and Justice, which is fully integrated into the TFEU. It includes ensuring the absence of internal border controls—although, regrettably, not for all Member States; among those which have excluded themselves is the United Kingdom. The Title comprises the following subjects: policies on border checks, asylum and immigration; judicial cooperation in civil matters; judicial cooperation in criminal matters; and police cooperation.

There are expectations of a substantial body of EU legislation in these areas. The ambitious 'Stockholm Programme' of the Swedish Presidency in the second half of 2009 sought to define the framework for EU police and customs cooperation, rescue services, criminal and civil law cooperation, asylum, migration and visa policy for the period 2010–14. The programme touches on many sensitive areas of policy and is proving highly controversial. It is clear that the Court of Justice will have to tread a careful path in what may prove a legislative and jurisprudential minefield.

Indeed it might be thought that EU law in this area does not require strict uniformity to be imposed by the Court of Justice. Perhaps paradoxically, where the Court is no longer predominantly an economic court but is handling fundamental social issues, there may be a greater need for diversity, or at least what is characterized in Strasbourg as a 'margin of appreciation' for the States. Ideally, in my view, the Court would first consider whether there is truly a need for a single interpretation. Otherwise, the Court might decline to lay down such a ruling. In its jurisdiction to give a preliminary ruling, as distinct from judicial review, the Court is exercising functions that may go far beyond the rule of law. The rule of law could be invoked where the issue was whether the Member State, in implementing EU law, was acting lawfully. And it would be precisely where a ruling was necessary, either to uphold the rule of law, or to secure fundamental rights, that a ruling of the Court of Justice would be appropriate. These preliminary reflections certainly require further consideration. In conclusion, however, the Treaty for the most part extends the jurisdiction of the Court in its entirety to the Area of Freedom, Security and Justice.

C. Jurisdiction over the Common Foreign and Security Policy

In contrast, the Treaty, with very limited exceptions, still excludes the jurisdiction of the Court over the Common Foreign and Security Policy (CFSP).[27] These exceptions are specified in Article 275 TFEU. Under that provision, there are in this area just two aspects within the jurisdiction of the Court. First, the Court is

[26] Under the transitional provisions, the more limited jurisdiction of the Court over measures adopted before the entry into force of the Lisbon Treaty under the former third pillar (Title VI of the former TEU) continues to apply for five years after its entry into force.

[27] Parts of the above section and of the text which follows are based on my chapter 'The Lisbon Treaty and the Court of Justice' in A Biondi, P Eeckhout and S Ripley (eds), *EU Law after Lisbon* (Oxford: Oxford University Press, 2012).

responsible for ensuring that the implementation of the CFSP does not affect the competences of the Union under what were previously 'first-pillar' provisions. This preserves the earlier idea that CFSP acts could not encroach upon the powers conferred on the Community by the EC Treaty. The Court now has jurisdiction to rule on that issue.

Second, the Court has a role in protecting individual rights in the implementation of the CFSP, a role increasingly recognized by the case law and by the Treaties. There have recently been several cases before the General Court and the Court of Justice where, for example, coercive measures against persons alleged to belong to terrorist organizations have been challenged, and one of the key issues has been the availability of judicial remedies. The rule of law requires that even terrorists—or those alleged to be terrorists—are entitled to a degree of judicial protection. The Treaty recognizes this. Where the measures taken by the Council under the CFSP adversely affect individuals or corporations—as the Treaty (Article 275) puts it, 'decisions providing for restrictive measures against natural or legal persons', which are now the subject of a special Title consisting of a single provision, Article 215—the Court (here, in the first place, the General Court) has jurisdiction to review the legality of those decisions.

D. Jurisdiction generally

As regards the jurisdiction of the Courts considered more generally, some of the changes seem of rather limited scope, but collectively they are liable to change the character of the judicial system and perhaps to reflect the changing character of the European Union itself. In formal terms, there are changes in each of the three main types of cases before the Court: enforcement action by the Commission against Member States; judicial review of Union measures; and references for preliminary rulings. All three types of procedure can be considered as aspects of upholding the rule of law: as ensuring that the Member States or the Union authorities, as the case may be, act lawfully. They may be considered in turn.

(1) Enforcement actions by the Commission

The Lisbon Treaty simplifies the procedure for imposition by the Court of pecuniary sanctions on Member States where they fail to comply with an earlier judgment of the Court following infringement proceedings brought by the Commission. The Commission can then bring further proceedings proposing the imposition of a financial penalty. Previously, in such 'follow-on' proceedings, the Commission had to issue a reasoned opinion specifying the points on which the Member State had not complied with the judgment, and had to specify time limits within which the Member State had to take the requisite measures. Now the Commission can take a 'follow-on' case to the Court without the need for those prior steps; the only requirement is that the Commission first gives the Member State the opportunity to submit its observations.

A further significant change simplifies the procedure in cases where the action brought by the Commission against a Member State targets the Member State's failure to notify measures transposing a directive. Here the Commission need not, under the amended provisions, bring a second action before the Court in order to propose a penalty to be imposed by the Court: instead, the Commission may specify in its initial application the penalty which it considers appropriate.

(2) Judicial review of Union measures

Under Article 263 TFEU, which corresponds to the former Article 230 EC, review by the Courts extends to the following categories of measures:

- legislative acts;
- acts of the Council, of the Commission and of the European Central Bank, other than recommendations and opinions;
- acts of the European Parliament and of the European Council intended to produce legal effects vis-à-vis third parties;
- acts of bodies, offices or agencies of the Union intended to produce legal effects vis-à-vis third parties.

The expression 'legislative acts' is new in this context but is defined by Article 289(3) as legal acts adopted by legislative procedure. It appears from Article 289(1) and (2) that those legislative acts are regulations, directives and decisions in the adoption of which the Council and the Parliament take part, so that the head 'legislative acts' covers much the same territory as the corresponding provisions of the previous Treaty—regulations, directives and decisions. Under the previous Treaty, the Courts had jurisdiction over acts of the European Parliament, the Council, the Commission and the European Central Bank. Review now extends also, however, on the one hand, to acts of the *European Council* and, on the other hand, to acts of *bodies, offices or agencies* of the Union.

While challenges to the *European Council* might be expected to be relatively rare, it is symbolically significant that jurisdiction now extends for the first time to the supreme political authority of the Union, which under Article 15(2) TEU now comprises the Heads of State or Government of the Member States together with its President and the President of the Commission. Although the European Council has broad political powers and does not exercise legislative functions, it does have powers to take a remarkably wide range of decisions having legal effect, ranging from the determination of the existence of a serious and persistent breach of the Union's values by a Member State to the decision following an 'emergency brake' on the adoption of a CFSP decision.[28]

[28] For a list of articles in the TEU and the TFEU which enable the European Council to take decisions having legal effects, see J-C Piris, *The Lisbon Treaty: A Legal and Political Analysis* (Cambridge: Cambridge University Press 2010) App 6.

The extension of judicial protection to measures taken by *bodies, offices and agencies* of the Union follows on the protection provided under the Charter of Fundamental Rights. The Charter recognizes that fundamental rights may require protection from all sources of Union action. Accordingly, it provides by Article 51 that 'The provisions of this Charter are addressed to the institutions, bodies, offices and agencies of the Union' (the expression 'bodies, offices and agencies', broadly denoting all authorities of the Union other than the Institutions, is now regularly used: see, for example, Articles 15 and 16 TFEU). Equally, it seems right that judicial protection should extend beyond fundamental rights to all forms of illegality, and that any Union measure intended to produce legal effects vis-à-vis third parties should be open to challenge, regardless of its source. Potentially this could result in a substantial increase in the caseload of the Courts.

It is a striking fact that under the Lisbon Treaty judicial review is available against all authorities of the Union—although not in all circumstances—from the highest to the lowest. This can be seen as a reaffirmation of one important aspect of the rule of law—well expressed by Dr Thomas Fuller in 1733: 'Be you never so high, the Law is above you.'[29] That deals with the question *against* whom, or against what entities, judicial review actions can be brought. Then there is the question *by* whom they can be brought.

(3) Standing before the Court

First, as before, actions may be brought by a Member State, the European Parliament, the Council or the Commission without the need to establish a legal interest in taking proceedings (Article 263(2) TFEU). These are sometimes referred to as 'privileged applicants'. Second, action may also be brought, but only for the purpose of protecting their prerogatives, by others: the Court of Auditors, the European Central Bank and now, under the Lisbon Treaty, by the Committee of the Regions (Article 263(3) TFEU).

Third, there is a significant development in relation to actions by individuals and corporate bodies ('any natural or legal person'). Previously under Article 230 EC Treaty, unless the measure was addressed to him, such an applicant had to satisfy requirements both of 'direct concern' and of 'individual concern'—the latter requirement being strictly interpreted by the Court of Justice. The scope for protection of individuals and companies against *regulatory* acts is increased under the Lisbon Treaty, which maintains the requirements of direct and individual concern in general but for regulatory acts removes the condition that the act should be of *individual* concern to the applicant. That condition has often made it difficult or impossible for individuals and companies to take cases to the Court. In the case of regulatory acts, Article 263(4) TFEU maintains the requirement, more

[29] L Fuller, *Gnomologia: Adagies and Proverbs* (1733), sentence no 943: see T Bingham, n 12 above, Ch 1, fn 8.

appropriate and generally easier to satisfy, that the act is of *direct* concern to the applicant.[30]

The widening of access to the Court for challenges to regulatory acts, removing the requirement of individual concern, follows sustained criticism of the Court's case law on the interpretation of that requirement and the consequential limited standing for individuals. In the *UPA* case[31] in 2002, the Court of Justice declined to change its stance, but the issue became live in the debates under the constitutional convention on the Constitutional Treaty. Although the Court, when maintaining its position in *UPA*, had suggested in its judgment that any change in the law was a matter of treaty amendment, it nevertheless conveyed to the convention its view that no treaty amendment was needed.

The case is perhaps unique in the history of the European Community, in that the Court's view was overridden; previously, treaty amendments on the Court's jurisdiction had frequently endorsed and in effect ratified changes which prefigured in the Court's own case law. This was the case, for example, with actions brought against the European Parliament and with actions brought by the European Parliament. In both cases, the Treaty did not confer jurisdiction on the Court; in both situations, the Court nevertheless asserted jurisdiction and, in both, the Court's solution was subsequently introduced into the Treaty.

It is remarkable also that the Treaty amendment here goes once again in the direction of extending the Courts' jurisdiction. However, the extent of the new jurisdiction is uncertain. The scope of the term 'regulatory acts' is not clear; the term is used nowhere else in the Treaty, and, in contrast to the term 'legislative acts', it is not defined. The reluctance of the authors of the Treaty to define its terms is well known. English law sometimes seems to go to the opposite extreme. The term 'regulatory act' would be likely to be defined if it appeared in an English legislative text. To cite Tom Bingham once again: in his book *The Rule of Law* he gives an entertaining example of the propensity of English law to define: the example is not 'regulatory act' but 'regulation'. The Banking Act 1979 Appeals Procedure (England and Wales) Regulations 1979 provide that: 'Any reference in these regulations to a regulation is a reference to a regulation contained in these regulations.'

While the term 'regulatory act' is not defined with similar precision, or indeed at all, it does seem clear, however, that the term should be given a broad scope, since what is in issue here is no less than the right of access to a court, a right generally recognized today as fundamental. The importance of the right was recognized, as we have seen, in the powerful judgment of the European Court of Human Rights in the *Golder* case in 1975, in which it held that Article 6(1) of the Convention must be understood as guaranteeing the right of access to a court although such a right was not explicitly formulated in that provision; that right is quite simply

[30] The provision also requires that the act does not entail implementing measures; however, if the act does entail implementing measures, it is likely that those measures would themselves be open to challenge.

[31] Case C-50/00 P *UPA v Council and Commission* [2002] ECR I-6677.

central to the rule of law.[32] Indeed the right is recognized by the Court of Justice, for example, and in different forms and different contexts, in such leading cases as *Johnston*[33] and *Kadi*.[34]

Guidance on the meaning of the term 'regulatory act' might be sought in the preparatory work on the Treaty, but such guidance is less appropriate to a constitutional text and can often be misleading, and the Court has in general rightly preferred to interpret the Treaty provisions in the light of their object and purpose. That would plainly necessitate a broad interpretation. In any event, since the Treaty appears to classify acts other than individual measures as legislative or regulatory, the appropriate meaning of 'regulatory act' might seem to be any act that is not a 'legislative' act. That indeed would reflect the legal situation in several Member States, where legislative acts cannot be challenged before the courts directly at the suit of individuals, but secondary measures—delegated legislation and the like—can be so challenged. The position is different, broadly speaking, only in those Member States having a constitutional court (or occasionally the Member State's supreme court rather than a specialized constitutional court) of a kind that does have jurisdiction to review legislation at the suit of an individual; not all constitutional courts, however, have such jurisdiction. It is clear from the scale of criticism of the past case law that this reform will be widely welcomed, at any rate if it is given an appropriately broad application.

(4) References for preliminary rulings

In line with the changes made for direct actions challenging Union measures, the jurisdiction to rule on the validity and interpretation of acts of the institutions (and of the European Central Bank) is extended by Article 267 TFEU (formerly 177, then 234 EC) to cover acts of bodies, offices and agencies of the Union. Since the Court's jurisdiction includes rulings on validity as well as interpretation of the acts in question, the legality of all Union measures adopted under the Treaties can be challenged indirectly by this route, although only where the national court decides to make such a reference. Article 267 also includes a new paragraph affecting, for the first time, the procedure before the Court of Justice on a reference: it provides that where, in the case pending before the national court, a person is in custody, the Court of Justice shall act with the minimum of delay.

E. Appointment of members of the Court

Another important issue affecting the Court, when the Constitutional Treaty was being drawn up and in anticipation of the 2004 enlargement of the Union, was the procedure for appointment of members of the Court. Some of the then members of

32 *Golder*, n 20 above.

33 Case 222/84 *Johnston* [1986] ECR 1651.

34 Case C-402/05 P *Kadi v Council and Commission* [2008] ECR I-6351.

the Court had drawn attention to that issue and had informally expressed their views.[35] That approach apparently encouraged the United Kingdom to raise the issue in the negotiations on the Constitutional Treaty.

The raising of the issue in no way implies dissatisfaction with the *outcomes* of the existing procedures in general, but rather with the principles which should govern judicial appointments, both to ensure that members have the appropriate qualities and to guarantee judicial independence. Before the Lisbon Treaty, the Treaties simply provided that appointments of Judges and Advocates General were to be made by common accord of the governments of the Member States. In practice, the Member States apparently endorsed with little scrutiny each other's nominations. It should be mentioned that some Member States (including the United Kingdom, the Netherlands and Slovenia) had introduced rather more transparent internal procedures for selecting candidates, but the practice of appointment by common accord at EU level had remained unchanged.

The Lisbon Treaty (Article 255 TFEU), following the Constitutional Treaty, makes a radical change in the appointment procedure. It provides for the establishment of a panel to assess candidates for the Court of Justice and for the General Court and to give an opinion on their suitability to perform the duties of Judge and Advocate General. The panel comprises seven persons; they are chosen from among former members of the Court of Justice and the General Court, members of national supreme courts and 'lawyers of recognised competence', one of whom is proposed by the European Parliament. The establishment of the Civil Service Tribunal in 2005 provided a good precedent: a committee of seven, including several former members of the ECJ and the CFI, was set up, and there was a public call for applications for membership of the Tribunal. The Committee produced, from the 243 applications received, a list of the best qualified, taking account of the need for a balanced composition on a broad geographical basis and with respect to the national legal systems represented. The selection made by the Committee was rapidly approved by the Council.

It is of interest that appointments of members under the new procedure refer to the positive opinion of the panel. It should indeed be possible to assume that, if an opinion were not positive, the candidate will not be appointed, and that the Member State will be required to nominate a new candidate. And indeed, at the time of writing (October 2011), it appears that on two recent occasions, a candidate proposed for the General Court has not been given a positive opinion and that, in both cases, the Member State concerned has proposed a new candidate.

(1) Reappointment of existing members

In principle, half the members of the Court of Justice come up for reappointment every three years: 'Every three years there shall be a partial replacement of the Judges and Advocates General'.[36] (But, despite the term 'replacement', the Treaty

[35] With a view to focusing attention on the issue, a high-level conference on the subject was arranged in Brussels in 2003 by the *Institut d'études européennes* under the direction of Professor Jean-Victor Louis.

[36] Article 253(2) TFEU.

adds that 'Retiring Judges and Advocates General may be reappointed'.[37]) The position is similar for the General Court.

Several difficulties arise from the need for renewal after the relatively short six-year term. First, there is a difficulty of principle: not every Member State has recognized what might seem, in the interest of judicial independence, an unwritten constitutional principle: the principle that existing members should automatically be reappointed in the absence of valid reasons relating to those members themselves. Indeed, far from accepting such a principle, one Member State has tended to regard the appointment of a judge for a single term as the norm, and has regularly failed to reappoint the sitting judge. Inevitably the effect of that policy is to weaken the influence of the judge from such a Member State compared with others having greater experience at the Court.

But there is also the risk that a failure to reappoint an existing member, apparently well qualified to be reappointed, might cast doubt on the independence of members of the Court. That has probably not hitherto been a significant issue in practice; but the principle of judicial independence (applying of course to both Judges and Advocates General) is of such fundamental importance that any appearance or risk of a threat should be avoided as far as possible. It is therefore desirable that the new procedures introduced by the Lisbon Treaty will address non-renewal as well as initial appointment.

F. Conclusion

The Lisbon Treaty has made a remarkable body of changes to the judicial system of the European Union in terms of reinforcing the rule of law—understood in a narrower sense of ensuring the availability of judicial review by independent courts of the conduct of public authorities. The above discussion may perhaps also illustrate the usefulness of such a narrower concept, and the disadvantages that might follow from too broad and diluted an understanding of the term 'the rule of law'.

[37] Article 253(4) TFEU.

20

Whose Law is to be Applied under the Rome Regulations?

*Richard Plender**

A. Introduction

Professor John Usher is renowned as a leading exponent of European Union law, whose book, *European Community Law and National Law: the Irreversible Transfer*, expresses in its subtitle his conviction that the surrender of sovereign powers to the European Union by its Member States could neither be arrested nor reversed. To his many friends, John was known as a man of immense humanity and not a little humour. His periods in Nancy and in Luxembourg prepared him well to understand continental systems of law.

The development of the Union's competence in private international law occurred principally after John's death but would not have surprised him. The principal European instrument that shaped Community competence in this area was the Brussels Convention,[1] which promoted the internal market by securing the free movement of judgments in civil and commercial matters; it, in turn, has been superseded by Regulation 44/2001.[2] The Rome Convention,[3] now re-enacted in

* Visiting Professor, University of Groningen; former High Court judge (England and Wales). This contribution is based to large extent on Ch 3 of R Plender and M Wilderspin, *The European Private Law of Obligations*, 3rd edn (London: Sweet & Maxwell, 2009).

[1] Convention on Jurisdiction and the Enforcement of Judgments in Civil and Commercial Matters, Brussels, 27 September 1968, as amended by Conventions on the Accession of the New Member States to that Convention: consolidated text in [1998] OJ C 27/1.

[2] Council Regulation No 44/2001 of 22 December 2000 on jurisdiction and the recognition and enforcement of judgments in civil and commercial matters [2001] OJ L 12/1, corrigenda [2001] OJ L 307/28 (henceforth the Brussels I Regulation). The latest consolidated text may be found at <http://eur-lex.europa.eu/LexUriServ/LexUriServ.do?uri=CONSLEG:2001R0044:20100514:EN:PDF>. As to the most recent amendment, replacing Annexes I–IV, see Commission Regulation 156/2012 [2012] OJ L 50/3. The Commission has proposed replacing Regulation 444/2001, see Proposal for a Regulation of the European Parliament and of the Council on jurisdiction and the recognition and enforcement of judgments in civil and commercial matters COM (2010) 748 final. As to the Agreement between the European Community and the Kingdom of Denmark on jurisdiction and the recognition and enforcement of judgments in civil and commercial matters, see [2005] OJ L 299/62 and Council Decision 2006/325/EC of 27 April 2006 concerning the conclusion of the Agreement between the European Community and the Kingdom of Denmark on jurisdiction and the recognition and enforcement of judgments in civil and commercial matters [2006] OJ L 120/22; the agreement entered into force on 1 July 2007.

[3] Convention on the law applicable to contractual obligations, Rome, 19 June 1980, consolidated version [1998] OJ C 27/24.

two Regulations, built on the basis of the Brussels Convention by establishing common rules to govern the choice of law in disputes of a contractual and of a non-contractual nature. Cross-border contracts and litigation in general are becoming increasingly important, both from the point of view of business—a logical development of the intensification of trade between Member States of the European Union as a result of the proper functioning of the internal market—and from the point of view of consumers, particularly (but, of course, not only) as a result of the growth of transactions over the Internet.[4]

The principal object of both the Rome I[5] and Rome II[6] Regulations is to identify the country whose law is to be applied to a dispute. In order to do this, the Regulations set up rules that designate the applicable legal system. Although those rules indicate relatively specifically what the applicable law is, what actually constitutes an applicable law needs to be specified further. Three needs arise: first, when a rule refers to a party's 'habitual residence',[7] and that party has several residences, it is necessary to specify the party's *relevant* habitual residence; secondly, when a rule designates a certain legal system, it has to be specified whether that designation includes the system's conflicts laws; and, thirdly, when the rule designates the legal system of a State which comprises several jurisdictions having their own laws of contract or of tort, it is necessary to determine which of those jurisdictions is to be regarded as the country whose laws must be applied. This contribution endeavours to shed light on these questions, the resolution of which necessarily affects and supports the effective functioning of cross-border transactions: a fundamental concern of the single market and, indeed, the economic union.

B. The meaning of habitual residence

Article 5 of the Rome Convention assures for a consumer the protection of rules that cannot be derogated from by contract (or, in default of a choice of law, the rules generally) of the country in which he has his 'habitual residence'. That term is not directly defined in the Regulations in respect of consumers; but it appears appropriate to construe it, in common with other expressions in Article 5, as an autonomous concept rather than as an expression to be interpreted in accordance

[4] Indeed in the context of the free movement of goods, the Court of Justice has clearly recognized the importance of Internet transactions, see, eg, Case C-322/01 *Deutsche Apothekerverband eV v 0800 Doc Morris NV et al* [2003] ECR I-14887, para 74; Case C-108/09 *Ker-Optika bt v ÀNTSZ Dél-dunántúli Regionális Intézete* [2011] OJ C 30/2. The gambling cases in the field of freedom to provide services also demonstrate the importance of the Internet (see the contribution of Dutheil de la Rochère in Ch 6 of this book).

[5] Regulation (EC) No 593/2008 of the European Parliament and of the Council of 17 June 2008 on the law applicable to contractual obligations (Rome I) [2008] OJ L 177/6.

[6] Regulation (EC) No 864/2007 of the European Parliament and of the Council of 11 July 2007 on the law applicable to non-contractual obligations (Rome II) [2007] OJ L 199/40.

[7] See Rome I Regulation, n 5 above, Articles 4–7, 10, 12, and Rome II Regulation, n 6 above, Articles 4(2), 5, 10–12.

with the varying laws of the contracting parties. In the case of a natural person, habitual residence denotes the country in which the individual maintains his stable and enduring home, disregarding on the one hand any other country in which he may stay temporarily and, on the other, the individual's domicile (which is his permanent abode), to which he must be taken to intend to return even after a substantial period in which he maintains a stable and enduring home abroad. Habitual residence thus requires only an intention to continue to reside in a particular jurisdiction for a substantial period, whereas domicile connotes (among other things) the absence of an intention to reside elsewhere.[8]

It is appropriate to apply to this expression the definition used in relation to the same words in a different context: the State of a person's habitual residence is 'the State in which the persons concerned habitually reside and where the habitual centre of their interests is to be found'.[9] The person must have the intention to establish the habitual centre of his interests in that jurisdiction for a lasting period.[10] In order to work out that person's intention, the (then) Court of First Instance reasoned in *Anna Herrero Romeu v Commission*[11] that courts should take account of all the factual circumstances which constitute such residence and, in particular, the actual residence of the person. In *Swaddling v Adjudication Officer*,[12] the Court of Justice observed that relevant factual circumstances are a person's family situation, the reasons which have led him to move, the length and continuity of his residence, the fact (where this is the case) that he is in stable employment, and his intention as it appears from all the circumstances.[13] Moreover, it is clear from Article 6(1) of the Rome I Regulation that the reference is to the consumer's habitual residence at the time of the conclusion of the contract.

There is a question as to whether or not the Rome regime requires a consumer to have resided in a jurisdiction for a certain period of time before he can acquire habitual residence in that jurisdiction. In the United Kingdom, the House of Lords affirmed the Court of Appeal's reasoning in *Nessa v Chief Adjudication Officer*[14] that, yes, a person must have resided in a jurisdiction for an appreciable amount of

[8] H Batiffol and P Lagarde, *Droit international privé*, 7th edn (Paris: Librairie générale de droit et de jurisprudence, 1981) Vol I, 385.

[9] Case C-90/97 *Robert Swaddling v Adjudication Officer* [1999] ECR I-1075, 1099 on entitlement to UK income support.

[10] Case T-298/02 *Anna Herrero Romeu v Commission* [2005] ECR II-4599, 4623 (referring to earlier staff cases before it and before the Court of Justice, eg Case C-452/93 P *Magdalena Fernandez v Commission* [1994] ECR I-4295, 4308–9), stating that the place of habitual residence 'is that in which the [Commission] official has established, with the intention that it should be of a lasting character, the permanent or habitual centre of his interests' (ibid).

[11] Case T-298/02 *Anna Herrero Romeu v Commission* [2005] ECR II-04599; IA-295; II-1349.

[12] Case C-90/97 *Robert Swaddling v Adjudication Officer* [1999] ECR I-1075, 1099–100.

[13] In *Swaddling*, the Court noted that Council Regulation (EC) No 1408/71 of 14 June 1971 on the application of social security schemes to employed persons, to self-employed persons and to members of their families moving within the Community [1997] OJ L 28/1 (as amended and updated by Council Regulations 2001/83 [1983] OJ L 230/6, as amended by Council Regulations 1247/92 [1992] OJ L 136/1), Article 1(h) provided that the term 'residence' in that Regulation meant 'habitual residence' and thus had a Community-wide meaning. See Case C-90/97 *Swaddling*, n 12 above, 1099.

[14] *Nessa v Chief Adjudication Officer* [1999] 1 WLR 1937 (HL).

time before he can acquire habitual residence in that jurisdiction.[15] It is, however, uncertain whether this conclusion would withstand scrutiny by the European Court of Justice. That Court, in *Swaddling*, reasoned that actual residence in a jurisdiction for a set period of time should not be a condition to find habitual residence.[16] It was apparently antipathetic to the proposition that a period of residence in a country other than that of an individual's nationality should be necessary to enable him to rely upon the full application of an instrument of European law. Since the context in which the Court of Justice has denied that a requirement of residence for a set period exists is not that of private international law, it is worthwhile considering whether the policy behind choice-of-law rules supports or undermines such a requirement.[17] The connecting factor for consumer contracts is the 'consumer's country of habitual residence' in order that the consumer can use the legal system and law which are most familiar to him. It may be argued that when a consumer moves to a different country, even with the intention to establish his centre of interests there permanently, he is unlikely immediately to be familiar with the local law. Therefore, as this benefit of Article 6 of the Rome I Regulation would not arise immediately, a consumer who moves to a different country should keep the habitual residence of the State from which he moved until he has resided in the different country for a period of time. Conversely, it may be argued that in most cases, litigation will be cheaper for a consumer if it is conducted in a court in the country in which he currently resides (which can be arranged using Articles 15–17 of the Brussels I Regulation), and that court will most efficiently be able to apply its local law. Therefore, if the consumer were to acquire habitual residence in another country as soon as he moves to that country, he could benefit from Article 6 of the Rome I Regulation.[18]

Even so, cases may arise in which it is arguable that the consumer had more than one habitual residence. Whether Article 6 permits the maintenance of more than one habitual residence is unsettled; but it appears desirable to apply in this context the solution adopted by the express wording of the United Nations Convention on Contracts for the International Sale of Goods of 11 April 1980: the law to be applied is that of the place having the closest relationship to the contract and its performance, having regard to the circumstances known to or contemplated by the parties at any time before or at the conclusion of the contract.[19]

[15] This requirement has been followed in all subsequent English cases on 'habitual residence'. See P Stone, 'The Concept of Habitual Residence in Private International Law' (2000) 29 *Anglo-American Law Review* 342, 351 albeit that the length of an 'appreciable time' has varied considerably with context, see P Rogerson, 'Habitual Residence: the New Domicile?' (2000) 49:1 *ICLQ* 86.

[16] Case C-90/97 *Swaddling*, n 12 above, 1100–1.

[17] The Court of Justice in *Swaddling* may have been influenced in its reasoning by the policy that European Union citizens should exercise their right to free movement between Member States, and that this is encouraged when they have access to benefits in those Member States.

[18] In order that parties can establish the law applicable to their contract in advance: see P Rogerson, n 15 above, 101–6.

[19] Vienna, 11 April 1980, Cmnd 8074 (1980) 19 I.L.M. 671, Article 10(a).

C. A branch, agency or other establishment

Article 19(1) of the Rome I Regulation and Article 23(1) of the Rome II Regulation provide that the habitual residence of a company (or other body, corporate or unincorporated) is the place where its central administration is located. The term 'central administration' is not directly defined in the Regulations but it is possible to infer a definition from the doctrine and case law.

An organization may consist of three main parts: a part which is registered under a certain legal system,[20] a part of which controls overall policy and allocation of resources,[21] and a part which transacts business with clients (eg sales or retail outlets). Each of these parts may be located in a different jurisdiction.[22] In order to determine jurisidictional issues, it is convenient to locate a single 'nationality' or 'seat' to a company trading through multiple locations.[23] To achieve this result, two main schools of thought offer competing solutions. Subscribers to the incorporation approach choose the place where a corporation is registered whereas subscribers to the 'real seat' approach choose the place where the organization's central management and control are exercised.[24] European jurisprudence has given an indication of what may constitute an organization's central administration. In *Planzel Luxembourg sàrl v Bundeszentral für Steurn*,[25] the Court of Justice equated a company's business[26] with the place where the essential decisions regarding the management of the company were taken. The Court stated that factors which could identify this place were the location of directors' meetings, the place of determination of general policy, the residence of directors, the place of holding of

[20] eg, under English law, companies are registered in accordance with the Companies Act 2006 (c 46), ss 9 and 31 which registration has the effects set out in ss 14–16 of that Act. Companies are also to allocate a registered office in line with Part 6 of the Act. Charities must be registered in accordance with the Charities Act 2006, s 9.

[21] Generally known in England as the head office, headquarters or (in more modern terms) the executive office.

[22] This is of course possible but not necessary. For examples of cases in which the decision has turned on the location of these three parts of a single business, see Case C-212/97 *Centros Ltd v Ehvervs-og Selskabsstyrelsen* [1999] ECR I-1459 and Case C-208/00 *Überseering BV v Nordic Construction Company Baumanagement GmbH* [2002] ECR I-9919.

[23] S Rameloo, *Corporations in Private International Law* (Oxford: Oxford University Press, 2001); K Bälz and T Baldwin, 'The End of the Real Seat Theory (*Sitztheorie*): The Court of Justice Decision in Überseering of 5 November 2002 and its Impact on German and European Company Law' (2002) 3:12 *German Law Journal*; M Virgós and FJ Garcimartín, *The European Insolvency Regulation: Law and Practice* (The Hague: Kluwer Law International, 2004) paras 46 et seq.

[24] The dictionary definitions of the words 'central' and 'administration' (commonly joined by subscribers to the real seat approach in the term 'central administration') suggest that the seat is to be located at the place of chief management. The French version, *administration centrale*, connotes a similar idea.

[25] Case C-73/06 *Planzel Luxembourg sàrl v Bundeszentral für Steurn* [2007] ECR I-5655. See the Opinion of AG Lenz in Case C-56/96 *VT4 Ltd v Vlaamse Gemeenschap* [1977] ECR I-3143, para 32.

[26] For the purposes of the Thirteenth Council Directive 86/560/EEC of 17 November 1986 on the harmonisation of the laws of the Member States relating to turrnover taxes [1986] OJ L 326/40.

general meetings, and the place where main financial and banking transactions were conducted. When the 'place of business' of a company has to be determined by reference to rules of English law, for example, separate from those of European law, the 'real seat theory' appears to have been influential.[27]

Article 19(2) of the Rome I Regulation and Article 23(1) (second paragraph) of the Rome II Regulation provide for a legal person's branch, agency or other establishment to be treated as the place of its habitual residence. In contractual cases, this will be so when the contract is concluded in the course of the operations of such a body, or where 'under the contract' performance is the responsibility of that body.[28] In the case of non-contractual obligations, this will be so when the event giving rise to the damage occurs, or the damage arises, in the course of such a body's operations.[29]

A branch, agency or other establishment has been defined by the Court of Justice as a body which appears to be permanent, such as an extension of an organization, which has its own management, and which is materially equipped to negotiate business with third parties.[30] Third parties have to be able to transact with the branch, agency or establishment itself, without having to deal directly with the parent body (albeit that parties may know that the two bodies are linked). The way in which two organizations conduct their business relationship and the way in which they present themselves to third parties are key to deciding whether one is a branch, agency or establishment of the other.[31] However, the strict legal relationship between the two organizations is not key.[32] Thus an independent parent company has been held to be an establishment of its subsidiary,[33] and an independent introductions firm has been held to be an establishment of its business partner.[34] On the other hand, a body is not a branch, agency or establishment when it is free from the direction or control of an organization.[35] A body is also not a branch, agency or establishment when it transmits business orders but is not responsible for their completion or execution.[36]

[27] *The Rewia* [1991] 2 Lloyds Rep 325; *Wood and Another v Holden* [2006] 1 WLR 1393; *Royal and Sun Alliance Insurance Co v MK Digital FZE (Cyprus) Ltd* [2006] All ER (Comm) 145; *Ministry of Defence and Support of the Armed Forces for Iran v Faz Aviation (formerly FN Aviation Limited* [2007] ILPr 42 (Comm), [2007] EWHC 1042 (Comm).

[28] Rome I Regulation, n 5 above, Article 19(2).

[29] Rome II Regulation, n 6 above, Article 23(1) para 2.

[30] Case 33/78 *Somafer v Saar Ferngas* [1978] ECR 2183 on the interpretation of Article 5(5) of the Brussels Convention 1968. It was also in this case that the Court of Justice held that the concept of 'branch, agency or other establishment' has to be interpreted independently of national laws having regard to the principles and objectives of the Convention.

[31] Case 218/86 *SAR Schotte v Parfums Rothschild SARL* [1987] ECR 4905, applied in Case 6 O 186/95 *Richard Zellner v Phillip Alexander Securities & Futures Ltd* judgment of 29 April 1996 of the Landgericht Krefeld, reported [1997] ILPr 716.

[32] Case 218/86 *SAR Schotte*, n 31 above.

[33] ibid.

[34] Case 6 O 186/95 *Richard Zellner*, n 31 above.

[35] Case 14/76 *A. De Bloos, SPRL v Société en commandite par actions Buoyer* [1976] ECR 1497.

[36] Case 139/80 *Blanckaert & Willems PVBA v Luise Trost* [1981] ECR 819.

D. Contractual situations under the Rome I Regulation

In contractual cases, responsibility for performance is one of the conditions which have to be fulfilled before a branch, agency or other establishment can be treated as an organization's place of habitual residence. For the purpose of the Article 19(2) of the Rome I Regulation, the meaning of 'under the contract, performance is the responsibility of' may be inferred from cases on Article 4(2) of the Rome Convention.[37] The last part of Article 4(2) states that a party's habitual residence is:

> where *under the terms of the contract the performance is to be effected through a place of business other than the principal place of business,* the country in which that other place of business is situated. (Emphasis added)

It is submitted that there is no difference of meaning between Article 4(2) of the Rome Convention and Article 19(2) of the Rome I Regulation. According to the English Court of Appeal in *Ennstone Building Products Limited*,[38] the last part of Article 4(2) had required an express or implied term of the contract to allocate performance to the other place of business. The fact that performance was *anticipated* to be undertaken by the other place of business was not sufficient to invoke that provision. It is submitted that the words 'under the contract' would lead to the same result under Article 19(2) of the Regulation.[39]

A question arises as to whether performance has to take place in the country where the branch, agency or establishment is actually located.[40] The judgment in *Iranian Continental Shelf Oil Company v IRI International Corporation*[41] suggests that it does not. In that case, the London branch of an American corporation with its central administration in Texas contracted with an Iranian company to supply oil-rig equipment and repair services to it. The court had to decide whether, under Article 4(2) of the Rome Convention, the characteristic performance was to be effected through a place of business (the London branch) other than the principal place of business (the Texas office). The Court of Appeal identified five characteristic obligations of the contract, one of which was to ship the goods into Houston and another of which was to procure a contract of carriage (presumably from Texas to Iran). The court held that because the contract expressed the London branch to

[37] The Rome Convention 1980 on the law applicable to contractual obligations [1980] OJ L 266/1. The French version of Article 4(2) Rome Convention and the French version of Article 19(2) Rome I Regulation are the same.

[38] *Ennstone Building Products Limited v Stanger Limited No 2* [2002] 1 WLR 3059.

[39] See further *Iranian Continental Shelf Oil Company v IRI International Corporation* [2002] CLC 696, CA, [2002] EWCA Civ 1024; and J Hill, 'Choice of Law in Contract under the Rome Convention: The Approach of the UK Courts' (2004) 53:2. *ICLQ* 325, 337–9 III. B. 'Principal Place of Business or Other Place of Business?'

[40] Such a conclusion could be derived from the European case of *Somafer* (Case 33/78 *Somafer v Saar Ferngas* [1978] ECR 2183) on Article 5(5) of the Brussels Convention 1968, in which the Court of Justice said that 'operations of' a branch, agency or other establishment meant, inter alia, contractual undertakings which must be performed in the State where the body is located.

[41] *Iranian Continental Shelf Oil Company v IRI International Corporation*, n 39 above.

be the 'shipper', and because the contract designated that branch to arrange the carriage of goods, under the terms of the contract the London branch was the place of business to effect performance.

The judgment in *Iranian Continental Shelf Oil Company* is not, it is submitted, a strong authority for the proposition that performance need not take place in the country of the establishment. Certainly, in this case a key obligation—the shipping of goods from Texas to Iran—was to be performed if not in, then from, Texas. On the other hand, it was clearly the London branch that had negotiated the contractual terms and made arrangements for their implementation. The Court of Appeal based its judgment on the characteristic obligations undertaken by the London branch, but did not appear to base anything on the fact that the goods were to be carried from elsewhere. Nevertheless, the case implies that under Article 4(2), and thus under Article 19(2), performance may take place in a country other than that where the establishment is located.

The above question may be of little significance in the context of the Rome I Regulation, because Article 19(2) introduces a second ground for treating an establishment's location as an organization's habitual residence, that is, that the contract be concluded in the course of the operations of the branch, agency or other establishment. In the case of *Somafer*,[42] the Court of Justice had stated that the concept of 'operations'[43] covered rights and obligations concerning the management of the establishment (eg its building or employees), contractual undertakings entered into in the name of the parent company which must have been performed in the country where the establishment was established, and non-contractual obligations which arose out of the activities that the establishment had been engaged in at the place where it is established.[44] However, the Court of Justice departed from *Somafer* in the later case of *Lloyd's Register of Shipping v Société Campenon Bernard*,[45] holding that 'operations' could cover obligations performed in a place other than the country where the establishment was located. The Court gave three reasons for this departure: first, that the words of Article 5(5) of the Brussels Convention did not require it to be limited to cases where performance occurs in the country of the establishment; secondly, that to limit 'operations' in such a way would render redundant Article 5(1), which allows parties to be sued in the country of performance anyway; and, thirdly, that there does not have to be a close link between the entity with which a party conducts negotiations and the place where the contract will be performed. In England, the Court of Appeal has held that the principles laid down in *Lloyd's Register of Shipping* are applicable to non-contractual obligations as well as contractual obligations.[46] The law therefore now appears to be that 'operations' covers three things: rights and obligations concerning the management of the branch, agency or other establishment;

[42] Case 33/78 *Somafer v Saar Ferngas* [1978] ECR 2183.

[43] As used within Article 5(5) of the Brussels Convention.

[44] Case 33/78 *Somafer*, n 42 above, para 13.

[45] Case C-439/93 *Lloyd's Register of Shipping v Société Campenon Bernard* [1995] ECR I-961. See further the Opinion of AG Elmer in that case.

[46] *Durbeck GmbH v Den Norske Bank ASA* [2003] EWCA 147.

contractual undertakings entered into in the name of the head organization; and non-contractual obligations arising out of the activities of the branch, agency or other establishment. Of those, the latter two may include undertakings or obligations to be performed in a country other than that where the body is established.

E. Non-contractual situations under the Rome II Regulation

In relation to Article 23 of the Rome II Regulation, when 'the event giving rise to the damage occurs, or the damage arises, in the course of operation of' the branch, agency or other establishment, the habitual residence of an organization will be the location of that entity.[47] Thus, in addition to identifying the relevant operations, a court has to identify the event or damage and whether that occurred or arose in the course of operations. With regard to the latter, it seems that 'occurred' and 'arose' are to be given their natural meanings.[48] It may be inferred from Lord Phillips's judgment in *Durbeck GmbH*[49] that Article 23 requires a nexus, but not a stronger link of causation.[50]

What is less clear is what counts as an event giving rise to damage. For example,[51] imagine that the English branch of a French bank negotiates and concludes a loan agreement with a party for it to purchase a ship, and takes the ship as security. The shipowner defaults on repayments, so the English branch decides to arrest the ship. To give effect to its decision, the English branch contacts the French head office that then arranges and carries out the arrest. The French office arrests the ship while its goods are being delivered in Germany. The recipient of the goods loses his cargo and sues the English branch of the bank. It might be argued that as the recipient has his habitual residence in England, English law is applicable by virtue of Article 4(2) and the second paragraph of Article 23(1) of the Rome II Regulation. Conversely, it could be contended that the second paragraph of Article 23(1) does not apply and that the applicable law under Article 4(1) is German law.

In this scenario, it is the English branch that has taken the decision to arrest, and it is defaults on one of its loans that have made the arrest necessary. However, it is the French office that has actually carried out the arrest. The 'damage' here is the loss of cargo that has happened in Germany. Three possibilities arise as to the application of the second paragraph of Article 23(1). On one view, the relevant 'event giving rise to the damage' is the arrest performed by the French office.[52] Therefore, the body in the course of whose operations the event occurred is the French office. On a second, broader, view, the relevant event giving rise to damage is the decision taken by the English branch. In such case, the body in the course of whose operations the event occurred is the English branch. And on a third view, it may be argued that

[47] Article 23(1) para 2.

[48] *Durbeck*, n 46 above, para 40.

[49] ibid, on the interpretation of Article 5(5) of the Brussels Convention.

[50] ibid.

[51] The following facts have been adapted from the facts of the case *Durbeck*, n 46 above.

[52] Such a view was taken by the High Court in *Durbeck* and not challenged in the Court of Appeal. See ibid para 16.

although the event giving rise to damage is strictly the French arrest, this arrest occurred in the course of the operation of the English branch. This could be because the action was initiated by the English bank, or because it was the English loan that rendered the arrest necessary. In the same way, it could be argued that the damage in Germany actually arose out of the operation of the English branch.

In *Durbeck*, where the arrest took place in Panama with the bank's head office not partaking, Lord Phillips felt able to hold that the dispute arose out of the operation of the English branch of the bank.[53] In the example scenario, a solution is much harder to work out. While it is tempting to relegate its resolution to the findings of fact in individual cases, nevertheless, some general points of law may be made.

The concept of an event which gives rise to damage and the concept of damage itself are separate.[54] For an event to give rise to damage, it may be inferred from the case of *Danmarks Rederiforening*[55] that it is enough for it to be a necessary precondition of the damage.[56] In that case, notice of an industrial action given by one trade union was held to have caused damage that sympathy action of a different trade union had directly inflicted, because the former had been a necessary precondition of the latter. Similarly, in the example case, if the English branch had not decided to take action against the defaults, then the French office's arrest would not have taken place. However, it is submitted that not every event which is a necessary precondition of damage should be able to found habitual residence under the second paragraph of Article 23(1). If this were so, then even the act of the debtor's defaulting could invoke that provision.

Because of this, it is suggested that the phrase 'event giving rise to the damage' should not be given a meaning beyond its natural one. Instead, the focus should be on whether a relevant event 'occurred or . . . arose in the course of operation of' the branch, agency or other establishment. From the case of *Lloyd's Register of Shipping*,[57] we may infer that the purpose of the second paragraph of Article 23(1) is to allow an habitual residence to be the country with which there is 'a specially close connecting factor'.[58] A second purpose of this provision, according to the Commission, is to 'protect the legitimate expectations of the parties'. These objectives suggest that a judge may compare the factors linked with the organization's head office to the factors linked with the branch, agency or other establishment, in order to find a solution.[59] It should also be remembered that, as a result of

[53] *Durbeck*, n 46 above, para 45. Lord Phillips reasoned that the comparison between jurisdictions was to be made between that of the branch, agency or other establishment and that of the principal place of business, not between the former and the jurisdiction where the damage took place.

[54] Case C 21/76 *Handelskwekerij G.J. Bier BV and Another v Mines de potasse d'Alsace S.A.* [1976] ECR 1735.

[55] Case C-18/02 *Danmarks Rederiforening, acting on behalf of DFDS Torline A/S v LO Landsorganisationen i Sverige, acting on behalf of SEKO Sjöfolk Facket för Service och Kommunikation* [2004] ECR I-1417.

[56] ibid paras 29–34.

[57] Case C-439/93 *Lloyd's Register of Shipping v Société Campenon Bernard* [1995] ECR I-961, on the subject of Article 5(5) of the Brussels Convention.

[58] ibid para 21.

[59] As suggested by Lord Phillips in *Durbeck*, n 46 above, para 45.

Lloyd's Register of Shipping, a branch, agency or other establishment can be liable for events taking place outside the country where it is located.[60] As a result, it seems that a judge may look at whether an event, even if performed elsewhere by another party, occurred in the course of operation of the branch, subsidiary or other establishment.

This interpretation accords with the judgment of Lord Phillips in *Durbeck*.[61] Thus in the example case, the fact that the arrest related to a contract made by the English branch, the fact that the arrest was necessitated by defaults on the English branch's loan, the fact that the English branch decided to arrest the ship and the fact that the English branch gave instructions for the arrest all point to the conclusion that the event occurred and the damage arose in the course of operation of that branch.

The concept of 'damage' under the Rome II Regulation excludes indirect damage. Article 4(1) provides:

> Unless otherwise provided for in this Regulation, the law applicable to a non-contractual obligation arising out of a tort/delict shall be the law of the country in which the damage occurs . . . *irrespective of the country or countries in which the indirect consequences of that event occur*. (Emphasis added)

The Court of Justice has held that economic damage suffered in a country where loss-incurring transactions have not taken place[62] and economic damage suffered by parent companies of insolvent victims[63] constitute indirect damage.

F. Habitual residence of individual businesspersons or traders

The habitual residence of an individual businessperson or trader is his principal place of business.[64] In the context of individuals, little case law or commentary exists on this notion, but certain points can be inferred from the Rome Regulations and their legislative history.

First, an individual businessperson or trader's principal place of business is of course to be distinguished from his official registered address. During the legislative process of the Rome II Regulation, the European Commission rejected an amendment suggested by the European Parliament that provided for peripatetic businesspersons to have their habitual residence be their officially registered address.[65] The

[60] Case C-439/93 *Lloyd's Register of Shipping*, n 57 above.

[61] *Durbeck*, n 46 above, para 46.

[62] Case 168/02 *Kronhofer v Maier* [2004] ECR I-6009.

[63] Case C-220/88 *Dumez France SA and Tracoba SARL v Hessissche Landesbank and others* [1990] ECR I-49.

[64] Rome I Regulation, n 5 above, Article 19(2); Rome II Regulation, n 6 above, Article 23(2).

[65] Amendment 49 in the European Parliament's First Report on the proposal for a regulation of the European Parliament and of the Council on the law applicable to non-contractual obligations (Rome II) A6-0211/2005 FINAL. See further, Commission's Amended proposal for a European Parliament and Council Regulation on the law applicable to non-contractual obligations (Rome II) COM (2006) 83 final—COD 2003/0168.

Commission preferred to use 'the actual place where an occupation is exercised rather than an official address which might turn out to be purely fictitious'.[66] Both the Commission and the Council agreed to use the phrase 'principal place of business',[67] and the European Parliament did not subsequently object to this modification.

Having recognized that an individual's 'principal place of business' is not his official registered address, it must be determined whether it is the place where the individual carries out administration and decides on policy, or the place where the individual carries on most of his operations. For example, if a home decorator lives and keeps his financial documents in England, but carries out 70 per cent of his work in Germany and 30 per cent of his work in France, where is his principal place of business? If it were the place where administration took place and policy was made, England, then consistency between the provision on individuals and the provision on legal persons[68] would be achieved. However, if it were the place where the majority of operations took place, Germany, then habitual residence would accord with the place where the businessperson had most contact with third parties.[69]

For the purpose of interpreting 'principal place of business', the Commission's statement[70] may be helpful; it refers to the actual place where the 'occupation is exercised'. However, under English law 'principal place of business' refers to the place from which central management and control are exercised. In light of this discrepancy, American case law may be helpful,[71] as an analogy may be drawn with the 'total activities test' that is used by many American courts.[72] Under that jurisprudence, the principal place of business is likely to be the place of most operations when there is an administrative office in one country and all or a clear majority of operations are carried on in one other country.[73] On the other hand, the principal place of business is more likely to be the place of policy and

[66] Commission's Amended proposal on the law applicable to non-contractual obligations (Rome II), n 65 above, para 3.2.

[67] The Council inserted the term 'principal place of business' into its Common Position (Common position adopted by the Council with a view to the adoption of a Regulation of the European Parliament and of the Council on the law applicable to non-contractual obligations (ROME II) 9751/06) at p 27. The Commission preferred 'what had emerged from the Council' during negotiations. See Commission's Amended proposal on the law applicable to non-contractual obligations (Rome II), n 65 above, para 3.2.

[68] Rome I Regulation, n 5 above, Article 19(1); Rome II Regulation, n 6 above, Article 23(1).

[69] In the contractual field, Article 6 offers some protection to third parties (consumers) contracting with individual businesspersons. However, in the non-contractual field, such protection does not exist.

[70] Commission's Amended proposal on the law applicable to non-contractual obligations (Rome II), n 65 above, para 3.2.

[71] Earlier case law (*Anderson v Southern Bell Tel. & Tel. Co.* 209 F Supp 921 (DC Ga 1962) and *R.G. Barry Corp. v Mushroom Makers Inc.* 612 F 2nd 651, 655 (2nd Cir, 1979)) must now, however, be read in the light of the decision of the US Supreme Court in *Hertz Corp v Melinda Friend, et al* 130 S.Ct. 1181 (2010) adopting a 'nerve centre' test.

[72] R Harnden, 'Corporations: Corporate Citizenship—Principal Place of Business' (1972) 11:3 *Washburn L J* 486, 489 et seq; and LD Saunders, 'Determining a Corporation's Principal Place of Business: A Uniform Approach to Diversity Jurisdiction' (2006) 90:5 *Minn L Rev* 1475, 1481 et seq.

[73] R Harnden, n 72 above, 488; LD Saunders, n 72 above, 1482; and 1 *Moore's Fed Prac* para 0.77 [3-3] (1964).

administration when there are equal amounts of business carried on in several countries.[74] LD Saunders has suggested that courts should look for the place that truly represents an enterprise's principal place of business.[75] It is submitted that this 'true representation' approach is the best one. In relation to individuals, the issue will have to be resolved as a matter of fact.

G. The exclusion of *renvoi*

The penultimate, but important, point is that Article 20 of the Rome I Regulation and Article 24 of the Rome II Regulation exclude *renvoi* in most cases falling within those instruments' scopes. The Rome I Regulation does allow for exceptions by stating 'unless otherwise provided in this Regulation' and the most important exception is Article 7, relating to insurance contracts. In general, however, a legal system's private international law rules are not to be included when that system is designated as an applicable law.

Although recent judicial and academic opinions have supported rather than opposed *renvoi*,[76] the Union institutions have decided that it contravenes legal certainty.[77] In relation to Article 15 of the Rome Convention, the Giuliano-Lagarde Report[78] had stated that, in cases of choice, the parties' selection of law should be upheld, and in cases of no choice, the connecting factor pointing to a law should be upheld. An 'applicable law' will therefore comprise the substantive provisions of the designated legal system, but not its private international law provisions.

H. States with more than one legal system

Finally, Article 22 of the Rome I Regulation and Article 25 of the Rome II Regulation provide that when a State consists of several territories each having its own law of contractual or non-contractual obligations, each territory shall be treated as a separate country. This means that each territory will be subject to the Regulations' choice-of-law rules in the same way as a State would be.[79] When enacting these provisions, the Community had the United Kingdom, Canada, the

[74] R Harnden, n 72 above, 488; LD Saunders, n 72 above, 1482; *Anderson v Southern Bell Tel. & Tel. Co.* 209 F Supp 921 (DC Ga 1962); and *R.G. Barry Corp. v Mushroom Makers Inc.* 612 F 2d 651, 655 (2d Cir 1979).

[75] LD Saunders, n 72 above, 1497 section B.1.

[76] See, inter alia, AV Dicey, JHC Morris and LA Collins, *The Conflict of Laws*, 14th edn (London: Sweet & Maxwell, 2006).

[77] Proposal for a Regulation of the European Parliament and the Council on the law applicable to non-contractual obligations ('ROME II'), COM/2003/0427 final—COD 2003/0168, the part titled 'Article 20—Exclusion of renvoi'.

[78] The Giuliano-Lagarde Report [1980] OJ C 282/1.

[79] Rome I Regulation, n 5 above, Article 22(1); Rome II Regulation, n 6 above, Article 25(1).

United States and Australia in mind.[80] The provisions were inspired by similar ones enacted in some of the Hague Conventions.[81]

Articles 22(2) and 25(2) apply to Member States, especially the United Kingdom, which have several territories capable of being treated as countries. In cases of internal conflict between the territories of one State, that State's legislature or court is not required to apply the private international law rules contained in the Regulations. They may of course opt to do so, in which case (again) each territory is to be treated as a separate country.

A problem of a unique character is presented by Cyprus. The northern part of that island, comprising approximately one-third of the island's surface area, is occupied by a body styling itself as the Turkish Republic of Northern Cyprus (TRNC). The Government of the TRNC exercises its control with the material and military assistance of the Turkish Government, its army and navy. The law actually applied in the north of Cyprus is the law of the TRNC. No state other than Turkey recognizes the TRNC. In *Hesperides Hotels et al v Aegean Turkish Holidays et al*,[82] a unanimous Court of Appeal in London held that although the United Kingdom did not recognize the TRNC *de jure* or *de facto*, the TRNC was capable of making decrees effective in England to affect real property situated in Northern Cyprus. However, the remainder of the island is administered by the Government of Cyprus based in Nicosia. The law applied in this part of the island is Cypriot law, as amended from time to time by the authorities in Nicosia. A significant contribution to the economy of Northern Cyprus is made by expatriates, particularly British nationals who have bought retirement homes there. Among these were Mr and Mrs Orams, who bought a house from the Government of the TRNC and spent some of their capital in effecting works to the property, including the installation of a swimming pool. Their house had previously been sequestered by the Government from one Mr Apostolides, who brought proceedings against Mr and Mrs Orams in a court in Nicosia seeking an injunction directing them to return the house to him having reversed the works that they had carried out. He obtained this order. He then sought to enforce it in the High Court in London.[83] On appeal, the Court of Appeal referred a series of questions to the European Court of Justice which were designed to determine whether an English court was bound to recognize and enforce the judgment of the Nicosian court.[84] Answering that question affirmatively, the Court of Justice relied on Article 1(1) of Protocol 10 to the Act of Accession of the Republic of Cyprus to the European Union,[85] which provides that the *acquis communautaire* shall be applied only in the parts of Cyprus

[80] Proposal for a Regulation of the European Parliament and the Council on the law applicable to non-contractual obligations ('ROME II'), n 77 above, the part titled 'Article 21—States with more than one legal system'.

[81] The Giuliano-Lagarde Report, n 78 above, the part titled 'Article 19, States with more than one legal system.'

[82] [1977] 1 QB 205, [1977] All ER 217. See further *Hesperides Hotels v Muftizade* [1979] AC 508.

[83] See *Orams et al v Apostolides* [2006] EWHC 2266 (QB), [2007] 1 WLR 241.

[84] See Case C-420/07 *Apostolides v Oram* [2009] ECR I-3571, [2011] QB 519. As to this case on return to the Court of Appeal, see [2011] QB 519, 562 et seq (CA).

[85] [2003] OJ L 236/955.

under the effective control of the government based in Nicosia. Counsel for Mr and Mrs Orams did not submit that it would be contrary to English public policy to deprive an English couple of their property acquired in accordance with the judgment in *Hesperides Hotels v Aegean Turkish Holidays*.

I. Conclusion

The issues discussed in this contribution illustrate some of the complexities involved in such a deceptively simple expression as 'habitual residence'. In an internal market which is becoming ever more integrated, and in which cross-border business-to-business and business-to-consumer transactions are ever more everyday occurrences, the Rome Regulations represent significant steps forward in facilitating commercial activities and in bringing significant aspects of private international law between Member States into the mainline framework of European Union legislation. As the European Union continues to develop the internal market into what, for business and for consumers, is increasingly becoming a single marketplace, the developments in the Europeanization of private international law assume major significance. The rethinking of domestic legal concepts and approaches, which is necessary, offers new challenges for lawyers to respond to the dynamics of the marketplace. Fertile ground for more discourse between lawyers and legislators to stay ahead of the game, rather than eternally lagging behind?

Concluding Essay

The Binding of Joseph

Joseph HH Weiler[1]

There is a gentle rhythm to the generational flow in the Genesis saga of our Patriarchs. As the Chosen Son (a choice is always made) ascends, father, with many years still to live, recedes into a relatively uneventful background to emerge at the moment of death and burial by his progeny. So it is with lapidary Abraham as Isaac and the formidable Rebecca come to the fore. So it is when Isaac in his turn fades into the background as Jacob moves to the centre in a life unmatched in trial and challenge. And so it seems when Genesis 36 brings to closure the narrative in which Jacob is protagonist. He settles in Hebron where he and Esau bury their father. Then the curtain raises in Genesis 37 with an Overture which, with remarkable efficacy, will put in place all the salient elements of a narrative which will end decades later with the burial, in his turn, of Jacob by his sons.

And Jacob dwelt in the land of his father's sojournings, in the land of Canaan. These are the generations of Jacob. Joseph, being seventeen years old, was feeding the flock with his brethren; and he was a lad with the sons of Bilhah, and with the sons of Zilpah, his father's wives: and Joseph brought the evil report of them unto their father.

> Now Israel loved Joseph more than all his children, because he was the son of his old age: and he made him a coat of many colours.
>
> Gen. 37:3

The new protagonist is identified as is the sibling rivalry which is essential in a saga which has become an iconographic part of Western civilization, that of 'Joseph and his Brother'.

The stage being set, the story of Joseph begins in earnest with the recounting of his famous dreams, fuelling further the hatred of the brothers and occasioning, too, the ire and subsequent reflection by his father. Then the text tells us:

> And his brethren envied him; but his father kept the matter in his mind.... And Israel said unto Joseph, Do not thy brethren feed the flock in Shechem? Come, and I will send thee

[1] It is my practice if contributing to collections honouring our colleagues to offer a reflection on a biblical text. This bold interpretation is offered with profound respect and affection.

unto them. And he said to him, Here am I. And he said to him, Go, I pray thee, see whether it be well with thy brethren, and well with the flocks; and bring me word again. So he sent him out of the vale of Hebron, and he came to Shechem.

Gen. 37:11–14

Conditioned by the habitual generational rhythm in the Genesis narrative and with attention already turning to Joseph himself it is not surprising that this seemingly innocent passage—in my view singularly important to the narrative of *Jacob*—has drawn less attention than it merits. For most traditional commentators and for many moderns this passage evokes little comment. It is apparently mere transition, a literary device enabling Jacob to bow out as Joseph and his brothers commence their fateful journey.

And yet these innocent looking words conceal drama and anguish and constitute one of the most dramatic and decisive actions in the troubled life of Jacob.

Some lexical difficulties are immediately evident: What matter did Jacob keep in his mind? The matter of the dreams of Joseph? Or the matter of the brothers' envy? Even more striking linguistically, especially in the original Hebrew, is Joseph's response. Here I am—*hinneni*—would be a typical response to a phrase such as: He said to him: Joseph. And he replied: Here I am (*hinneni*). It come less naturally, hardly naturally at all, in the phraseology of the actual text. And still in the realm of text—why the repetitions: 'Do not thy bretheren feed the flock in Shechem? Come and I shall send thee unto them' (Gen. 37:13). And then immediately the same is repeated again (Gen. 37:14).

It is of course the content rather than the lexical choices which poses the more dramatic challenge. Jacob's relationship with his own father, Isaac, whom we are told had a preference for his twin sibling, Esau, was one of affective ambiguity. None is apparent in his relationship to this favourite son, Joseph, to whom is reserved a special love he does not even bother to conceal with the gift of the coat of many colours.

Now Israel loved Joseph more than all his children, because he was the son of his old age: and he made him a coat of many colours.

Gen. 37:3

The commentators grapple with the reason for Jacob's favouritism—after all, was not Benjamin the real son of his old age and was there such an age difference between the birth of Zebulun by Leah and the subsequent birth of Joseph by Rachel to justify the appellation of *ben zekunim*—son of old age? The most intuitive explanation for Jacob's love of Joseph was the transposition to him of the great love of Jacob's life, his deceased wife Rachel—a love that could not so easily attach to his true son of old age, Benjamin, since his birth was the cause of Rachel's death. For me, Jacob sees in Joseph the image of himself as a young man: *'ish tam* and *yoshev ohalim*—an innocent man, dwelling in tents (Gen. 25:27)—compared to his adventurous brothers. He identifies with Joseph and bestows on him the love he never received from his father, Isaac.

And yet, inexplicably and for no discernible good reason, Jacob turns to the son he seemingly and demonstrably loves more than all his other children and sends him into the very jaws of danger and this for no good reason. Rabbi Obadiah ben Jacob Sforno (born in Cesena, Italy in 1475) admits that, 'Truth be told, he could have sent one of his servants'. Indeed, he could have if the true reason of the mission was merely to find out how the brothers were doing.

Joseph is put in harm's way in a double sense. It is hard to imagine in the environs of Jacob a more dangerous place than Shechem—a place which the Talmud characterizes as a place awaiting calamity or *makom muchan lepuranut* (*Sanhedrin* 102a). Rashi explains: 'There the Tribes disgraced themselves, there Dinah was raped, there the House of David split'. Jacob more than anyone else is aware of the danger of Shechem. Genesis 34 is one of those biblical narratives which requires a strong stomach. First we read of the rape of Dinah:

> And Dinah the daughter of Leah, which she bare unto Jacob, went out to see the daughters of the land. And when Shechem the son of Hamor the Hivite, prince of the country, saw her, he took her, and lay with her, and defiled her.
>
> Gen. 34:1–2

He took her, he lay with her, he defiled her. The original Hebrew for 'defile' (*vaye'anneha*) is more nuanced and arguably more brutal. The commentary wonders about the repetition—by laying with her she would already be defiled; why then add an additional verb? A common answer offered is that she was raped and sodomized.

Shechem falls in love with his victim and seeks to marry her and his father beseeches her family. Jacob leaves the negotiations to his other sons.

> And Hamor communed with them, saying, the soul of my son Shechem longeth for your daughter: I pray you give her him to wife. And make ye marriages with us, and give your daughters unto us, and take our daughters unto you. And ye shall dwell with us: and the land shall be before you; dwell and trade ye therein, and get you possessions therein. And Shechem said unto her father and unto her brethren, Let me find grace in your eyes, and what ye shall say unto me I will give. Ask me never so much dowry and gift, and I will give according as ye shall say unto me: but give me the damsel to wife.
>
> Gen. 34:8–12

Dinah's brothers exploit this overture. Once more we can but marvel at the moral honesty of the text—characteristically, it does not try to euphemize questionable behaviour:

> And the sons of Jacob answered Shechem and Hamor his father deceitfully, and said, because he had defiled Dinah their sister: And they said unto them, We cannot do this thing, to give our sister to one that is uncircumcised; for that were a reproach unto us: But in this will we consent unto you: If ye will be as we be, that every male of you be circumcised; Then will we give our daughters unto you, and we will take your daughters to us, and we will dwell with you, and we will become one people.
>
> Gen. 34:13–16

Hamor and Shechem are taken in:

> And Hamor and Shechem his son came unto the gate of their city, and communed with the men of their city, saying, These men are peaceable with us; therefore let them dwell in the land, and trade therein; for the land, behold, it is large enough for them; let us take their daughters to us for wives, and let us give them our daughters. Only herein will the men consent unto us for to dwell with us, to be one people, if every male among us be circumcised, as they are circumcised.
>
> Gen. 34:20–22

The dwellers of Shechem are taken in too. And then:

> And it came to pass on the third day, when they were sore, that two of the sons of Jacob, Simeon and Levi, Dinah's brethren, took each man his sword, and came upon the city boldly, and slew all the males. And they slew Hamor and Shechem his son with the edge of the sword, and took Dinah out of Shechem's house, and went out.
>
> Gen. 34:25–26

Jacob understands the enormity of it all both in moral and functional terms:

> And Jacob said to Simeon and Levi, Ye have troubled me to make me to stink among the inhabitants of the land, among the Canaanites and the Perizzites: and I being few in number, they shall gather themselves together against me, and slay me; and I shall be destroyed, I and my house.
>
> Gen. 34:30

And yet it is to this very place that Jacob sends Joseph. But the danger is not only in the location. The brothers too pose a danger to Joseph. And this, too, Jacob understands so well, for did he himself not have his own personal experience with an envious and, consequently, dangerous brother? The envy and rage of Joseph's brothers is not trivial. In the face of Jacob's blatant favouritism, Joseph's own behaviour is easily to be perceived as meanness—'and Joseph brought the evil report of them unto their father' (Gen. 37:2)—and arrogance as evidenced by his dreams. It is not surprising that:

> And when his brethren saw that their father loved him more than all his brethren, they hated him, and could not speak peaceably unto him.
>
> Gen. 37:4

and shortly after:

> And they hated him yet the more for his dreams, and for his words.
>
> Gen. 37:6

And again:

> And his brethren envied him.
>
> Gen. 37:11

Sending Joseph alone to Shechem would be bad enough. Sending him to his brothers elsewhere, would be no less dangerous. Sending him alone to his brothers at Shechem can only be seen as deliberate double jeopardy. Discomfiting as it may be to the commentators and to us, the text is unflinching: Jacob knowingly and willingly seems to be putting his son in the path of mortal danger.

It is interesting to see how some of the classical commentary deals with this question.

One sure way is to pretend it does not exist: both Rashi and his celebrated grandson, Rashbam, acknowledge the danger that awaits Joseph on his mission, but neither question (as did Sforno) nor offer any exegesis on the reasons for this dangerous mission. Uncharacteristically, Moses Nahamanides (born at Porta, Barcelona, 1194), who often does not shirk discomfiting moral texts uses the same technique—silence. Rabbi David Kimchi (born in Provence, southern France in 1160) confronts the problem differently. Of Joseph's willingness to go, he explains that he was not scared because he was sure that his brothers' fear of his father would protect him. Jacob, he reasons, must have believed the same since: 'had Jacob any hesitation in his heart as to the safety of Joseph, he would not have sent him'. Don Isaac Abarbanel (born in Lisbon in 1437) offers two explanations. The second is close to Kimchi's view. Since Joseph, he explains somewhat disingenuously, had done no harm to his brothers, why would they want to harm him, and why would Jacob even suspect them of such harm? Rabbi Chayim Ben Attar, the celebrated Or Hachayim (born in Morocco in 1696) offers a popular alternative. Following a brief Talmudic cue, he explains that Joseph was not in danger and was not perceived to be in danger because of the doctrine of *Shaliach Mitzvah*—Righteous Messenger—who is protected from danger (which of course raises a delicate question given the fact that Joseph was harmed). The more modern, nineteenth-century, revered commentator, Rabbi Tzvi Yehuda Berlin, the Netziv, combines a bit of both in his approach.

From this brief sampling, the basic structure of most commentary becomes thus clear. Some just move on with no commentary at all. Those commentators who acknowledge the danger, do not contend with the enigmatic and seemingly senseless mission; and those who contend with the mission, find ways of writing away the danger.

I have sympathy with the apologists, who obviously do not want to contemplate the idea that Jacob would willingly have put Joseph in danger's path. But I think I prefer the integrity of Rashi and Nahamanides who basically elect to remain silent or Sforno who 'to tell the truth' admits that there was danger, that the mission did not make sense since, if it was so important, it could have been performed by a servant, but then just leaves the question open.

For it is they who force us to go back to the life of Jacob and search more deeply for other explanations for this dramatic and strange action, explanations consistent with the text, consistent with his life, and for me, consistent with his grandeur.

Let us make two beginnings in this exploration. The first involves a quick revisiting of the textual-lexical rather than narrative difficulties of our text.

Here I am—*hinneni*, says Joseph to Jacob, a somewhat jarring response to the question posed. Clearly the text is giving us a hint. As many traditional commentators note, and as more than hinted at in the title of this very essay, the reader's mind is inevitably directed to those other famous places where this phrase is used:

And it came to pass after these things, that God did [test] Abraham, and said unto him, Abraham. And he said, Here am I (*hinneni*).

Gen. 22:1

And in Exodus:

Now Moses kept the flock of Jethro his father-in-law, the priest of Midian: and he led the flock to the backside of the desert, and came to the mountain of God, unto Horeb. And the angel of the Lord appeared unto him in a flame of fire out of the midst of a bush: and he looked, and, behold, the bush burned with fire, and the bush was not consumed. And Moses said, I will now turn aside, and see this great sight, why the bush is not burnt. And when the Lord saw that he turned aside to see, God called unto him out of the midst of the bush, and said, Moses, Moses. And he said, Here am I (*hinneni*).

Exod. 3:1–4

It is the combination of a slightly ill-fitting expression, filled with gravitas, which suggests that it is a passage of consequence, rather than a transitional passage. Joseph is *called* and he answers in the manner of Abraham and Moses—*hinneni*, a word that evokes mission and even sacrifice. It is as if the text is inviting us to think of these other occasions, notably the *Akeda*—the Binding of Isaac—in Genesis 22.

The text offers us another, less evident, hint in the choice of the response. For it takes us to a signal moment in Jacob's own life when the word *hinneni* signals the start of his deception of his own father, Isaac.

And he came unto his father, and said, My father. And he said, Here am I (*hinneni*). Who art thou, my son? And Jacob said unto his father, I am Esau thy first-born; I have done according as thou badest me: arise, I pray thee, sit and eat of my venison, that thy soul may bless me.

Gen. 27:18–19

How does the evocation of Jacob's deception of his father help in understanding his dangerous mission to Joseph?

Here is the second beginning of our exploration of Jacob's life, a beginning which takes us to his final days. When Jacob descends into Egypt and meets Pharaoh who asks about his years, Jacob responds:

The days of the years of my pilgrimage are a hundred and thirty years: *few and evil have been the days of the years of my life*, and they have not attained unto the days of the years of the life of my fathers in the days of their pilgrimage.

Gen. 47:9 (emphasis added)

There is a slight puzzle in the statement. When these words are uttered Jacob is not on his deathbed. He may have many more years to live. What drives the statement is a deep sense of unworthiness in comparison to his fathers, Isaac and Abraham.

Let us review the highlights and lowlights of the days of the years of Jacob's life.

His struggles begin already in the womb, so much so that the perturbed Rebecca seeks the counsel of God himself, who informs her:

Two nations are in thy womb, And two peoples shall be separated from thy bowels. And the one people shall be stronger than the other people. And the elder shall serve the younger.

Gen. 25:23

Fatefully, she never discloses this directly to Jacob, who is grabbing the heel of his brother—his *'akev*—hence *Ya'akov* (Jacob). Born second, grabbing the heel of his elder, is to mark his childhood and youth. Once again we must admire the unflinching and discomfiting honesty of the text: Isaac prefers Esau, his firstborn. Jacob must find consolation with his mother. There are endless ways, and not one has been eschewed by the commentators to explain away Isaac's preferences. Some are convincing. But all are Isaac-centric. From Jacob's perspective the experience is the same—he is the second born; his father loves him not.

Of the young Jacob it was said that he was an *'ish tam*—usually construed as 'innocent' or 'guileless'. There is a deep irony in this. Jacob is forced to be resourceful, to fend for himself, and guile becomes his principal instrument. Indeed, the root *'akev* (heel) from which his name derives is also 'crooked', Jacob the Crooked. For a pottage of lentils he trades Esau's birthright—a transaction which modern contract law might characterize as unconscionable. It is a deed which he may come to regret and which, importantly, fuels his guilt and dread of his brother. Even more egregiously—egged on by Rebecca (acting unbeknownst to Jacob, to fulfil the revelation she had)—Jacob tricks his blind father to give him the blessing he was planning for Esau.

The cry of Esau is heart-wrenching:

Is not he rightly named Jacob? for he hath supplanted me these two time. He took away my birthright. And, behold, now he hath taken away my blessing. And he said, Hast thou not reserved a blessing for me?

Gen. 27:36

If you wish to discover Jacob's most spectacular feat of guile, read carefully the narrative of understanding with Laban concerning the distribution of the flock and the 'sting' of which Laban deservedly becomes victim (Gen. 30).

Not surprisingly, Esau plots to kill Jacob—something Rebecca informs Jacob. Rebecca intercedes with Isaac and Isaac seems to accept that, indeed, it is Jacob who will become the carrier of the covenant. What was experienced as deception was meant to be. He sends Jacob off to find a wife in the same place that his wife had come from, and on his departure transmits to him the ancestral blessing.

Then Isaac called Jacob and blessed him . . . :
May God Almighty bless you,
And make you fruitful and multiply you,
That you may be an assembly of peoples;
And give you the blessing of Abraham,
To you and your descendants with you,
That you may inherit the land
In which you are a stranger,
Which God gave to Abraham.

Gen. 28:1–4

So now Jacob is on his way (sent, by the way, without fear by his father despite the menace by Esau) and we come to the scene which, in its evocative imagery, has become iconographic: the dream of Jacob's Ladder in which God repeats to him that which he had heard from Isaac, that he, Jacob, will be the bearer of the ancestral covenant:

> Then he dreamed. And behold, a ladder was set up on the earth, and its top reached to heaven; and there the angels of God ascending and descending on it. And, behold, the Lord stood above it and said, I am the Lord, the God of Abraham thy father, and the God of Isaac. The land whereon thou liest, to thee will I give it, and to thy seed. And thy seed shall be as the dust of the earth, and thou shalt spread abroad to the west, and to the east, and to the north, and to the south. And in thee and in thy seed shall all the families of the earth be blessed. And, behold, I am with thee, and will keep thee, in all places whither thou goest, and will bring thee again into this land. For I will not leave thee, until I have done that which I have spoken to thee of.
>
> Gen. 28:12–15

The reaction of Jacob is pregnant with meaning. On the one hand his immediate response is:

> And Jacob awaked out of his sleep, and he said, Surely God is in this place. And I knew it not.
>
> Gen. 28:16

And he consecrates with oil the stone on which he slept. But then, stunningly, we read the following:

> And Jacob vowed a vow, saying, If God will be with me, and will keep me in this way that I go, and will give me bread to eat, and raiment to put on, so that I come again to my father's house in peace, then the Lord will be my God.
>
> Gen. 28:20–21

If? If? If he will help me, then I will make him my God? We can try, as some have, to attenuate the condition by saying that the vow is not to make the Lord his God, but to make that place the house of God. But one way or another, in the wake of Isaac's explicit blessing and God's express commitment not to leave him, we suddenly encounter Jacob the doubter.

This is not asymptomatic. The next time God reveals himself to Jacob is on the eve of his departure from Laban back to his home land with his wives, children and his own large flocks.

> And the Lord said unto Jacob, Return unto the land of thy fathers, and to thy kindred; and I will be with thee.
>
> Gen. 31:3

A divine command, a guarantee of protection. And Jacob? First:

> And Jacob sent and called Rachel and Leah to the field unto his flock,
>
> Gen. 31:4

And then:

> And the angel of God said unto me in the dream, Jacob: and I said, Here am I. . . . I am the God of Bethel, where thou anointedst a pillar, where thou vowedst a vow unto me: now arise, get thee out from this land, and return unto the land of thy kindred.
>
> Gen. 31:11–13

It is only with the encouragement of his wives that he finally makes the move and escapes. On his way home, his past catches up with him. He is to meet Esau. And yet, despite the double promise from God, Jacob takes precautions and splits his camp in two. However, he cannot resist and beseeches God again:

> O God of my father Abraham, and God of my father Isaac, the Lord which saidst unto me, Return unto thy country, and to thy kindred, and I will deal well with thee. I am not worthy of the least of all the loving kindnesses, and of all the truth, which thou hast showed unto thy servant; for with my staff I passed over this Jordan; and now I am become two bands. Deliver me, I pray thee, from the hand of my brother, from the hand of Esau: for I fear him, lest he come and smite me, the mother with the children. And thou saidst, I will surely do thee good, and make thy seed as the sand of the sea, which cannot be numbered for multitude.
>
> Gen. 32:9–12

And then, even after fighting with the angel of God, and prevailing, when the confrontation with Esau arrives, his actions are those of the faithless rather than the faithful.

Jacob the Crooked—one could live with. The text is explicit. Jacob the doubter, maybe—'If God will be with me . . . '. But faithless? This may indeed be going too far. But here we have one key to understanding the persona of Jacob which will serve us well when we shortly return to his dispatch of Joseph to his fate.

What does he doubt? In what or in whom does he not have faith? There is a constant thread through all these passages—it is not God that Jacob doubts, as his faith in God is capacious and expressive. And I think he will have come to develop a great sense of self-reliance too. He is not a *Nebech*. What he doubts profoundly, what he cannot seem to accept, he in whom he has no faith, is himself: himself as the one chosen to be the next link in the covenantal chain, the one in whom, rightly, the blessing bestowed on Abraham, Isaac will now vest. Culture, psychology and theology all combine to create that inner doubt. Culturally, surely the presumptive ancestor would be the firstborn, especially a firstborn who was clearly the one beloved by his father. Jacob knows that a birthright acquired for a pottage of lentils may not be considered legitimate (and he keeps his peace when Leah is almost literally slipped into his bed: 'In our Place . . . '). He is acutely aware of his deception of his father and not less with his father's distress:

> And Isaac was seized with very violent trembling . . .
>
> Gen. 27:33

How can it be he, the second born, the un-beloved, the deceiver, who merits all this? When Isaac sends him on his way and conveys to him the covenantal blessing, Jacob is silent. It cannot really be me, he might be saying in his heart. I have deceived. And when God repeats the promise of protection, Jacob capaciously acknowledges God's majesty, but worries, perhaps, that God, too, is a victim of his deception? Or perhaps his worry is different: and here theology joins culture and psychology. What have I done, Jacob must be asking himself, to merit this. He is aware of the lore of the family. And the difference is striking between him and his illustrious ancestors. They were put to the test. They deserved the blessing. He was neither called upon (and this in his eyes must have been hugely significant) to prove himself in any way as his grandfather and father had been, for in the Binding of Isaac, both Abraham *and* Isaac, were put to the test and prevailed. And there is more. We will note that all his encounters with God are through dreams, angels, messengers. At one moment we thought that God spoke to him directly (to tell him to return) but then it transpires that this too was a revelation in a dream. Consider then, Jacob, who already is racked with doubt because of his birth, his deceptions, and his religiously meritless life compared to his father and grandfather. He will be asking: Is it really meant to be me? Or, perhaps, are these dreams, apparitions, messengers the real thing? How can they be the real thing, if their message is to choose me?

There is much to be learnt by the contrast with Abraham. Abraham was the Knight of Faith; but by considering Jacob we learn something additional about Abraham. The following is emblematic of Abraham:

> Now the Lord said unto Abram, Get thee out of thy country, and from thy kindred, and from thy father's house, unto the land that I will show thee: and I will make of thee a great nation, and I will bless thee, and make thy name great; and thou shalt be a blessing; and I will bless them that bless thee, and curse him that curseth thee: and in thee shall all the families of the earth be blessed. So Abram went, as the Lord had spoken unto him; and Lot went with him: and Abram was seventy and five years old when he departed out of Haran.
>
> Gen. 12:1–4

The Lord speaks to Abraham directly. The effect is dramatic. It is not just great faith in God that Abraham repeatedly shows which, even in that moment of fear and trembling, the commandment of the Binding, his response is immediate: Here I am (*hinneni*) and then, without a word:

> And Abraham rose early in the morning, and saddled his ass, and took two of his young men with him, and Isaac his son.
>
> Gen. 22:3

Not for a minute, through all his travails does Abraham doubt his role, his destiny and his faith in his ability to carry it through.

How different is Jacob. He does not struggle to accept the sovereignty of God but he undergoes a mighty struggle to accept that he is worthy of that which is bestowed on him. Even after he prevails through his night of faith, and is told that his name henceforth will be Israel, he cannot, as we saw, quite accept that destiny. He calls the place of his struggle Peniel, the face of God, since he has seen a divine being face to face; and yet he insists: 'You must bless me'.

I invite you to reread all these difficult passages again with this construction of Jacob in mind.

There is one more passage which merits our attention before we return to Jacob/Israel and Joseph.

With the tragedy of Dinah just behind him, the life of Jacob seems finally to come to some serenity and inner peace. In the chapter just preceding that which ushers in Joseph we read:

And God said unto Jacob, Arise, go up to Bethel, and dwell there: and make there an altar unto God, who appeared unto thee when thou fleddest from the face of Esau thy brother. Then Jacob said unto his household, and to all that were with him, Put away the foreign gods that are among you, and purify yourselves, and change your garments: and let us arise, and go up to Bethel; and I will make there an altar unto God, who answered me in the day of my distress, and was with me in the way which I went.... And God appeared unto Jacob again, when he came from Paddan-aram, and blessed him. And God said unto him, Thy name is Jacob: thy name shall not be called any more Jacob, but Israel shall be thy name: and he called his name Israel. And God said unto him, I am God Almighty: be fruitful and multiply; a nation and a company of nations shall be of thee, and kings shall come out of thy loins; and the land which I gave unto Abraham and Isaac, to thee I will give it, and to thy seed after thee will I give the land.

Gen. 35:1–12

Note the elements of closure: God is speaking directly to Jacob. The vow (the famous If clause) is now discharged whatever reading we gave it—he is called upon to make the altar he promised. But he also instructs his household (!) to put away the foreign gods that were among them. And in this case it would seem that finally Jacob is at peace with himself—that the doubts he may have had about his chosenness seem to be dispelled: 'I will make an altar', he says, 'unto God, who answered me'. And as if to symbolize the transformation God appears and not only renews the covenant, but this time himself, convincingly, renames Jacob as Israel. The old Jacob, tortured with self-doubt, is finally put to rest as Israel, confident and at peace, takes his place.

Not, alas, for Jacob for whom the years of his life were, as we recall, 'few and evil'. For as soon as he moves away from Bethel at peace, it would seem, with God and himself, calamity strikes again.

And they journeyed from Bethel; and there was still some distance to come to Ephrath: and Rachel travailed, and she had hard labour. And it came to pass, when she was in hard labour, that the midwife said unto her, Fear not; thou shalt have this son also. And it came to pass, as her soul was departing (for she died) that she called his name Ben-oni: but his father called him Benjamin. And Rachel died, and was buried in the way to Ephrath (the same is Bethlehem). And Jacob set up a pillar upon her grave: the same is the Pillar of Rachel's grave unto this day.

Gen. 35:16–20

It is not Israel that builds the Pillar, it is the old Jacob, for this calamity was enough to tear asunder his newly found serenity and status.

On my reading it was not just the death of his beloved wife that devastates Israel/Jacob but, possibly two other realizations that dawn on him as he contemplates this latest blow.

Why, why, he must be asking himself, just as my household had renounced all idols and my compact with God was solemnized. And then he must recall another vow, that hapless and reckless vow that anyone who may have stolen Laban's idols would die. And maybe the truth then dawns on him, that it was Rachel who not only deceived her father but deceived him too. And once again Jacob is engulfed not only by sorrow, but by a terrible and nagging doubt, that it was he and his vow that were responsible for the death of Rachel. Engulfed again in the world of deceit, and in trying to understand how his newly found relationship with God could be disrupted so quickly in such cruel manner, he entertains an even deeper doubt, that maybe Rachel never abandoned those idols (we have just read that idols were not uncommon in his household), that maybe she died as a result of that deception too, and in the face of this possible betrayal by his own household his doubts as to his worthiness come back to the fore.

This, many of you will be thinking, is but idle and even irreverent speculation. And, indeed, the hand trembles when committing such to paper. But there are two hints at it from Scripture itself. Jacob does not bury Rachel in the Cave of Machpelah in Hebron (where he buried Leah and where all Patriarchs and Matriarchs were to be buried) even though the distance from her burial is within a day's journey by foot. I have tried to read every single explanation for this omission and found none convincing. Could it be that Jacob did not wish to? And note, too, the singular fact that although the petulant Rachel was Jacob's clear sweetheart and beloved wife, Scripture ultimately preferred the solid and pious Leah. It was from her womb that the house of Judah and David issue. *Mashiach*—Messiah—Son of David, not Son of Joseph!

Be that as it may, it is at this point of the narrative that the saga of Joseph takes over from that of Jacob and we are back where we began: *Lechah ve'eshlachacha*—Come and I will send thee—to Shechem, to your brothers, to danger.

In the light of our exploration of some of the key occurrences in Jacob's life, I want to offer now several possible explanations to this striking deed. I offer none as compelling. Neither are they mutually exclusive—most human actions, and especially human action such as Jacob's, are driven by multiple and complex motives, conscious and subconscious. Please bear this in mind.

There is one explanation which I shall ultimately reject but which so clearly stares us in the face that it must be discussed. Jacob wanted Joseph's death. Imagine that instead of being the living word of God, our story was part of a Greek tragedy. Under this perspective Jacob's actions are obvious. Here is a powerful and prosperous king or chieftain who lords over a household of two wives, two concubines, twelve sons and a daughter. It then transpires that in a dream it is revealed that one of the younger sons, a beloved son, sometime in the long-term future, will depose the father in particularly humiliating circumstances. This of course cannot be tolerated or entertained. Fate has to be thwarted. It would be too crude and unsettling to kill the beloved son with one's own hands. The preferred Greek tragedy way is to take the offender and put him in harm's way. And this is what happens here. The plot seems to succeed—and the father grieves, genuinely, for fate is cruel. And yet, unbeknownst to him, fate cannot be defeated, etc. This tale would be hard to improve upon as Greek tragedy.

I reject it not simply because of my reverence of Jacob/Israel but because such an explanation, though perfectly consistent with the mythological worldview, is so alien to the monotheistic revolution unfolding in the very stories we are examining, a narrative which has a different telos, and is driven by a different set of forces and a different relational dynamic between man and God.

For the second explanation I want to go back to Don Isaac Abarbanel. I said he had two theories, only one of which I outlined and dismissed—the one that said that Jacob had no fear for the life of Joseph since Joseph had not harmed his brethren. I want to outline now Abarbanel's second theory. Jacob says to Joseph (jokingly), 'Your brothers are there and you are here. Why should you be different? Why this special treatment?' Jokingly? I think Abarbanel might be touching on some deep stratum in the soul of Jacob.

Recall:

> And his brethren envied him; and his father kept the matter in mind.
>
> Gen. 37:11

Which 'matter', we asked. Imagine for a minute that it is the brothers' envy that struck Jacob. And as he contemplates this envy, to which until then he was oblivious (it is only when Jacob chides Joseph for his second dream that he begins to see things through the eyes of the brothers), welling up in him are his memories and resentments of his father who loved one of his sons more than the other, and the ruinous envy and calamity that such behaviour wreaked upon him and his brother. Realizing the huge responsibility that his own actions in preferring Joseph may precipitate, he scrambles to try and undo the damage already done. And maybe we can now give some more credibility to the 'no danger' thesis of some of the traditional commentators. Shechem might not be such danger since in Jacob/Israel's last compact with God, just before the Rachel calamity, we read:

> And they journeyed: and a terror of God was upon the cities that were round about them, and they did not pursue after the sons of Jacob.
>
> Gen. 35:5

Maybe that terror would still protect Joseph. And the brothers? Thinking of his past, after all we read in his own saga:

> And Esau hated Jacob because of the blessing wherewith his father blessed him. And Esau said in his heart, The days of mourning for my father are at hand. Then will I slay my brother Jacob.
>
> Gen. 27:41

Well, reasons Jacob, surely they will not dare harm him whilst I am still alive. Even Esau, who had much more to gripe about refrained from that. Indeed, all the more reason to seek reconciliation during his lifetime. And thus:

> Go, I pray thee, see whether it be well with thy brethren . . .

There might be great truth in both limbs of Abarbanel's explanation after all.

I come now to two possible explanations which, each in its own way, seek to relate Jacob's dramatic act in sending Joseph to the face of danger, to the circumstances of his own life and faith.

Recall again:

> And his brethren envied him; but his father kept the matter in his mind.
>
> Gen. 37:11

What then if the matter in his mind was not the envy of the sons—but Joseph's dreams.

If, I explained, this were a Greek tragedy, Jacob would be worried that the dream would come true. Jacob is uncertain whether his house is blessed after all, with the two recent calamities of Dinah and Rachel following one after the other. Let us now recall a further pertinent fact—his eldest son, his heir apparent, Reuben, disgraces himself barely has Jacob laid the earth on Rachel's grave:

> And it came to pass, while Israel dwelt in that land, that Reuben went and lay with Bilhah his father's concubine: and Israel heard of it.
>
> Gen. 35:22

Surely not Reuben is the heir—the carrier of the torch. So the fact that God would have appeared to one of his sons, albeit in a dream and destined him to greatness could, in the eyes of Jacob, be a sign of promise, and hope. In Jacob's circumstance his fear is that the dream would not come true. But what of Joseph? Is Joseph, whom he loves, worthy of the destiny? The one who hangs around the house whilst the others brave danger, may remind Jacob too much of himself as a youth. And what of the *dibbah*—ill report—that he brings (*dibbah*, some of the commentators uncomfortably note, is usually untrue, libel, slander)? So what is the measure of this Joseph? Jacob knows himself to have been plagued by doubt, manifest in hesitation, conditional doubts and all the rest. How can he find out?

> And Israel said unto Joseph, Do not thy brethren feed the flock in Shechem?

Can I add four small words: *ve-yisrael nissah et yosef*—that is, 'and Israel put Joseph to the test'?

Instead of trying to write the danger out of the narrative, on this reading it is the danger which makes the mission significant. Jacob trembles, he hesitates, that is why he asks the question twice. He allows Joseph a way out. And Joseph responds in a manner in which Jacob must have rejoiced because, uncalled for, he uses the same response which the great Abraham used: *hinneni*. He appears to Jacob Abraham-like—never doubting God's promise; never doubting that he is worthy of that promise. Midrash is on our side. It is very skimpy on this passage. It too fears to ask the hard question. But it is less scared than most: 'Said R. Hama b. Hanina: These were the words which Jacob would later recall and his very guts were torn asunder (*meyav mitchtchim*). "You knew that your brothers hated you, and yet you said *hinneni*?"' (*Genesis Rabbah* 84:13).

The devastation of Jacob when the bad news of Joseph's presumed death reached him also makes sense. He mourned him for the rest of his life and failed to be consoled, for, in his eyes, did he not bear some responsibility for this outcome? And no less devastating were Dinah, and Rachel and Reuben, all these calamities did mean what he had feared all along—he was not worthy after all, and the death of Joseph was confirmation of that too.

A variant of this conscious or subconscious explanation for Jacob's act in sending Joseph (and this explanation will, surely be embedded in the subconscious) may be summarized with four slightly different words: *ve-yisrael nissah et yosef*—'And Jacob put Jacob to the test' or, even more audaciously, 'And Israel tested God'. To himself: 'Do I have the courage and faith in the face of this destiny revealed to Joseph, that my father and grandfather had?' Or to God: 'You have turned your face and taken Rachel on the morrow of our renewed compact. Reuben has disgraced me. I, the unworthy, am offering, unasked, my beloved son. I, too, am capable of sacrifice, devotion, I do merit your trust. Of me it should be said that I fear God, that I have not withheld my son from you.'

Of course, we do not know if anything even remotely passed through Jacob's head at that moment. But we should not dismiss entirely this strand from his psyche. The incomprehensibility of his act in sending Joseph into the mouth of danger does not lend itself to simplistic explanations and a trace of this motivation would not be inconsistent with his psychological and religious circumstance.

So far I have insisted on a Jacob-centric rather than Joseph-centric approach to the text. But if we turn briefly to Joseph's perspective, there are some hints that there might be some resonance to one of those explanations, which share the common thread that Jacob willed the dangerous mission.

There has been a great deal of attention to the fact that Joseph waits 22 years and never initiates, as he could have, much earlier contact with his father. There is also much attention given to the fact that when they finally meet, only one cries, and that one is, though the commentators differ, more likely to have been Jacob. Somewhat less attention is given to the obvious coolness, even estrangement which exists between the two once Jacob had settled in Egypt. Could it be excluded that much of the above is driven by a resentful Joseph, who will have had plenty of time in prison to wonder why his father sent him on this dangerous mission and to speculate himself that maybe his father wished to put him in harm's way?

If there is any merit in any of the three theses I have advanced I may be permitted to draw two very tentative conclusions which transcend the immediate narrative.

The first is simply to note how this story too points us to the centrality of sacrifice in the worldview of the religious persona. And it points us, too, to the dangers associated with this institution. This is an issue which has received considerable attention and I do not want to belabour it unnecessarily. The word and world of sacrifice are not of one cloth, of course. There are the ritualistic sacrifices which so easily may descend into hypocrisy and overt idolatry as denounced frequently by the Prophets. Jacob is far from that world. His narrative points to a much purer motive which derives almost ineluctably from the impossible confrontation between man and God. His life foreshadows that of Moses—'humility before God' or *vehatzne'a lechet 'im 'elohecha* (Micah 6:8)—is his hallmark. But even in this purest of contexts the drive to show one's devotion by sacrifice may lead one astray. The line between sanctification of the name of God and desecration of the name of God is at times so thin, as we have learnt from the work of our colleagues, Halbertal and Margalit. There is something sobering in the explicit story of Abraham and the much more nuanced one of Jacob in which it seems that God, except in the most extreme situations, wants the state of mind which is willing to sacrifice all but not the sacrifice itself. Our need to meditate on this tightrope is driven in my view first because the religious persona (incorporating the sacrificial drive) has become so much more central in the public life of our world today—he cannot be explained away with the usual tools of the social sciences.

The second issue returns to my point of departure—the centrality of biblical text in the evolution of our civilization. Although we habitually speak of the Abrahamic religions, it was in fact Jacob who became Israel and in whom and to whom the Judeo-Christian tradition is linked in their respective claims. Why Jacob? Why not Isaac or even Abraham himself, as the Knight of Faith. I have already betrayed my sympathies and prejudices—it is right that it be so. In Jacob/Israel even modern man can see his reflection: tormented, struggling, insecure, and seeking the virtue of humility before God.

Index

Note: documents are given in italics; Fig after Page numbers indicates a diagram; n indicates footnotes.

The manufacturer's authorised representative in the EU for product safety is Oxford University Press España S.A. of El Parque Empresarial San Fernando de Henares, Avenida de Castilla, 2 - 28830 Madrid (www.oup.es/en or product.safety@oup.com). OUP España S.A. also acts as importer into Spain of products made by the manufacturer.
Printed and bound by CPI Group (UK) Ltd, Croydon, CR0 4YY
14/09/2026
02216305-0017